17267108

REF
HN90
R3
A11
M84x
1970
V.3

# FROM RADICAL LEFT TO EXTREME RIGHT

Second edition, revised and enlarged

A bibliography of current periodicals of protest, controversy, advocacy, or dissent, with dispassionate content-summaries to guide librarians and other educators

Volume 3

by

Theodore Jurgen Spahn

and

Janet Peterson Spahn

**The Scarecrow Press, Inc.**
**Metuchen, N.J. 1976**

1151678

**Library of Congress Cataloging in Publication Data** (Revised)

Muller, Robert H
From radical left to extreme right.

Vol. 2 by T J. Spahn, J. M. Spahn, and R. H. Muller; v. 3 by T. J. Spahn and J. P. Spahn.
Volume 3 has imprint: Metuchen, N. J., Scarecrow Press.
Includes bibliographical references.
1. United States--Politics and government--Periodicals--Bibliography. 2. Right and left (Political science)--Periodicals--Bibliography. 3. Radicalism--United States--Periodicals--Bibliography.
Z7165.U5M82 016.3224'4'0973 79-126558
ISBN 0-87506-011-1 (v. 1)

**Copyright © 1975 by Theodore Jurgen Spahn and Janet Peterson Spahn**

**Manufactured in the United States of America**

## TABLE OF CONTENTS

# PREFACE

> ... the relatively low costs of publication, which would not have been possible without the offset press, encouraged ego-tripping malcontents like me to do our strident "thing." --- Trey Ellison, Publisher
> Honky Times

It is hard to think of a "cause" that does not have at least one periodical to further it. As the quotation from Mr. Ellison suggests, this is due in large part to the technique of photo-offset lithography. Using a carbon-ribbon typewriter and sheets of dry transfer cold type, anyone with moderate skill at pasting-up can prepare camera-ready copy. This means that the serials bibliographer need never be idle.

When we started working with Dr. Robert H. Muller in the late 1960s, we thought of polemical periodicals as a more-or-less static field: one that could, with sufficient industry, be mastered and charted and described. How naive! It has been clear to us for some time that, no matter how hard we run, we shall not succeed even in staying in the same place.

Number of periodicals covered.--In this volume, 474 periodicals are covered in signed reviews and an additional 176 in unsigned entries. The titles and addresses of many hundreds of others are listed in the Title Index. The signed reviews in this volume need no explanation: they resemble those in our earlier volumes. The unsigned entries (always prepared by JMS or TJS) are a new feature. They are usually shorter than the signed ones and are sometimes based on information supplied by the periodical, not on our inspection of sample copies. (Some of the periodicals treated in this way may receive full-length, signed reviews in a later volume.)

Linguistic scope.--Almost all of the periodicals reviewed in this volume are wholly or partly in English. A few are wholly or partly in Eskimo, French, German, Italian, Norwegian, Spanish, or Swedish.

Geographical scope.--Most of the periodicals reviewed in this volume are published in the United States. At least 85 come from Canada (every province and territory except Prince Edward Island) and several from other parts of the Americas (Jamaica, Puerto Rico, Uruguay). More than 40 come from Eire, the United Kingdom, and the continent of Europe. There are eight from Asia and the Pacific. The few that come from the Middle East (Israel and Lebanon) can be supplemented with a number of pro-Arab and pro-Israeli periodicals published elsewhere. The 13 African periodicals can be supplemented with the publications of exiles (especially in London) supporting "liberation struggles" in South Africa, South West Africa, Rhodesia, and Portugal's colonies. (Our Geographical Index shows exactly where the periodicals come from.)

Our classification.--Our placing of a periodical into one chapter or another is not meant to express some sort of definitive taxonomic judgment. We have separate chapters only for the reader's convenience, and we know that many periodicals could fit equally well into two or more of them.

New or different chapters.--Five chapters are new: Radical Professional, Labor & Unions, Comics, Conservation & Ecology, and Prisons. One has been given a new name: Feminist (instead of Women's Liberation). Four that appeared in the previous volume have been omitted this time: Rock Culture, Anarchist, Sexual Freedom, and Humanism.

Directory information.--Our method of presenting this is explained in the prefaces to Volume One (p. vii) and Volume Two (p. vii). All page sizes are given except 8 1/2" x 11"--so, if no size is given, it can be assumed to be that.

Defunct periodicals.--Although a large majority of the periodicals covered here were alive when we reviewed them, we have not hesitated to include a number of interesting ones that we knew had died within the last few years.

Citations.--It would add considerably to the size of this book, the difficulty of reading the text, and the cost of composition if we gave exact citations for every quotation. We did so for one review in Volume Two of this edition, to show what it would look like (and to show that our every quotation is documented): The Pyongyang Times, pp. 563-69.

Reviewer's opinion.--We have tried to keep judgments out of the reviews. Occasionally, when a reviewer wanted to express an opinion about a periodical, we placed that opinion at the end of the review, and labeled it "Reviewer's Opinion" or "Reviewer's Judgment." We may do this more often in future volumes.

Indexing of this volume.--There are three indexes: a Geographical Index; a Title Index; and an Index of Editors, Publishers, and Opinions. The first and third are confined to periodicals reviewed in this volume; the Title Index is cumulative, and includes the titles of all periodicals reviewed or mentioned in any of the three volumes of this edition. (It also includes the titles and addresses of hundreds of periodicals to which we have written without receiving a response.)

For fuller information on our procedures, see the prefaces and introductions to the first two volumes of this edition.

## CONTRIBUTORS

| | |
|---|---|
| JA | Judy Allen, M. A. L. S. |
| SA | Sarah Anderson, M. A. L. S. |
| SLA | Susan Appelt |
| JMA | Jeanne Armstrong, M. A. L. S. |
| DB | Dianne Blagburn |
| EC | Elizabeth Clausen, M. A. L. S. |
| CT | Claudia Tilton Cook, M. A. L. S. |
| BC | Barbara Cox, M. A. L. S. |
| SMA | Sr. M. Adela Eiken, C. C. V. I., M. A. L. S. |
| JMG | Janet M. Garvey, M. A. [English], M. A. L. S. |
| MG | Maureen Gorman |
| CH | Carol Hamilton, M. A. L. S. |
| MEH | Sr. M. Esther Hanley, I. B. V. M., M. A. L. S., Ph. D. [Latin] |
| JYH | Julia Hansen, M. A. L. S. |
| MH | Margarette Hills, M. A. L. S. |
| JEH | John Hollister |
| SK | Suzy Kaplan |
| BK | Barbara Keeley, M. A. [Spanish], M. A. L. S. |
| NK | Nancy Klinka, M. A. L. S. |
| PMK | Patricia Kneip, M. A. L. S. |
| KL | Kineret Lichtenstein, M. A. L. S. |
| MM | Mary McKenney, M. A. L. S. |
| JM | Joan Munson, M. A. L. S., Ph. D. [Psychology] |
| SN | Sandra Naiman, M. A. [English], M. A. L. S. |
| MN | Marjorie Nixon, M. A. L. S. |
| WP | Wendy Phillips, M. A. L. S. |
| CP | Cynthia Poppen, M. A. [English] |
| AS | Anne Scruton, M. A. L. S. |
| WJS | William John Simpson, M. A. L. S., J. D. |
| GKS | Gertrude K. Spahn, M. A. L. S. |
| JMS | Janet Peterson Spahn, M. A. L. S. |
| TJS | Theodore Jurgen Spahn, M. A. [History], M. A. L. S. |
| JS | Joanne Spector, M. A. [Psychology], M. A. L. S. |
| IT | Irene Tysall, M. A. L. S. |
| JW | Jane Witek, M. A. L. S. |

# Chapter 1

## RADICAL LEFT

... my despicable and beloved homeland.
--- Genie Plamondon, Minister of
International Affairs,
White Panther Party

The two Youth International Party papers, TAP and Yipster Times, are perhaps the most radical of the group reviewed here. Yippees (who have been relatively quiet in recent years) espouse revolution, refer to themselves as "outlaws," urge their members to live off the "fat cats," and take childish delight in "ripping off" the telephone and power companies. For more details, we suggest that you read their publications, which are enormously entertaining.

Rising Up Angry, White Lightning, and A Single Spark are community-action papers that urge people to form political power blocks, medical and legal aid clinics, and day-care centers. They expose corruption and urge people to take power into their own hands from the politicians and big businessmen.

The Red Tide might have gone into the Underground chapter, except that it seemed more revolutionary than the two other high school periodicals we placed there. The New Prairie Primer (University Activists' Coalition, University of Northern Iowa) and The Varsity are college papers, the latter being the official student newspaper of the University of Toronto. (This is unusual for a radical paper.)

Toronto's The Last Post is aimed at the unorganized left and working people, as is the more rural Wisconsin Patriot, which aims to build a political party based on a worker-farmer-student alliance.

Periodicals with a more-or-less single interest or purpose are: Outside the Net (proposing educational innovations that would make traditional educationists blanch); The Defender (put out by an organization that defends individuals against political and racist repression); Tenants' Newsletter (we have another tenant periodical in the Labor & Unions chapter); The Rap (directed at dissatisfied VISTA volunteers); Two... Three... Many (put out by American volunteers who have returned from service abroad, it exposes imperialism and supports liberation struggles here and abroad); and Common Sense [Washington] (People's Bicentennial Commission, an alternative to the official American Revolution Bicentennial Commission). *

Four press services supply news and articles to underground, alternative, radical, and student periodicals: Liberation News Service and New York News Service are in this chapter; College Press Service and FPS--The Youth Liberation News Service (for high school papers) are in the Underground chapter. Poems of the People (now vanished without a trace) was a free service that distributed poems, stories, and reviews to the "underground/alternate culture/movement press."

Sun is apparently a forerunner of Sundance and the Ann Arbor Sun. Sun was published by a group of rock music enthusiasts in Detroit. The group moved to Ann Arbor and became the White Panthers, then the Rainbow People's Party. Its interests became increasingly political as American involvement in Vietnam deepened. Disillusionment with America, and the love-hate relationship brought about by the war, are well expressed in the phrase by Genie Plamondon quoted at the head of this introduction.

Some of the periodicals in this chapter might equally well have been placed in the Liberal, Underground, or Marxist-Socialist Left chapters. For a fuller discussion of the radical press, see our earlier volumes.

--Janet & Theodore Spahn

*The PBC can't be too radical, or conservative columnist James J. Kilpatrick wouldn't have said (in his syndicated column): "While it may seem sorely out of character, let me put in a plug for the [PBC].... To judge from the literature they are sending out, they are a lot closer to the true Spirit of '76 than the promoters, politicians, and public relations men in charge of the [ARBC].... Some of their stuff makes sense, as when they inveigh against the excessive power of the great corporations...." Although Kilpatrick disapproved of some PBC materials--notably those on students' rights --he added: "Even so ... [their] publications breathe with fire and purpose and sincerity." Column of 4 July 1973, quoted in Common Sense [Washington], 1 (July 1973):1.

## AMPO: Japan-Asia Quarterly Review

Muto Ichiyo [et al.], Ed.
Box 5250
Tokyo International, Japan
Quarterly; $6 (institutions $15)
Started: Summer 1969
Circulation: 2,000
Format: 64-68 pages (7" x 10", offset)

Issues examined: Mar., Summer, Autumn 1973; Winter 1974
Back issues: Bound volume (Nos. 7/8 [1970]-No. 15 [1972]) available from publisher for $15.

This internationally-distributed periodical provides analysis and commentary on "economics, politics, culture, and pollution." Until the Winter 1974 issue the sub-title had been "A Report on the Japanese People's Movements." The new sub-title is a result of editorial changes which have enlarged the scope of the publication. The Summer 1973 issue explains that

> four years ago ... AMPO was launched to bring news of the Japanese People's Movements against the Vietnam War to the world. Since that time the magazine has been transformed from a magazine about anti-war activities into a forum for analysis and discussion of the rapidly expanding Japanese domestic economy and overseas empire. It has become an indispensable tool for patriotic struggles throughout Southeast Asia and Africa, as well as for scholars and others concerned with the developments in Japan and throughout Asia.

In addition, a Pacific-Asia Resources Center has been established, with the goal of "improving and extending the coverage and analysis of AMPO, and building an organization in Japan able to bring together scholars and activists--Japanese, Asian, and Westerners--for broad-ranging studies of capitalism and imperialism." The Center will conduct research, distribute information on imperialism, maintain a news service and library, and publish a bulletin on its holdings.

The periodical's widened coverage is reflected in articles on the Japanese labor movement; women's liberation; pollution, food additives, and the indiscriminate use of drugs developed by pharmaceutical companies; racism; imperialism; South Korea ("Pak Chung Hee *vs.* the People"); the Marcos dictatorship in the Philippines; and political prisoners in South Vietnam. There is also commentary on current Japanese culture.

The articles are often written by academics or scientists. For example, a Tokyo University professor warns that the ultra-rightist Asian Parliamentary Union is attempting to strengthen ties with "reactionary Asian regimes" and hasten "Japan's expansion into Asia." The editor of a Thai journal warns that, despite the success of a recent student uprising in his country, "the old bases of power and various kinds of corruption remain." (His journal has opposed Japanese economic penetration of Thailand.) In "Why Japanese Ham Won't Rot," a Japanese scientist warns of the peril of food additives.

Staff members, who describe themselves as "movement-oriented intellectuals," also contribute articles. In one lengthy analysis, the Communist Party of Japan (third-largest party in the nation) is accused of having achieved its advance "at the cost of its revolutionary principles and by deliberate embrace of bourgeois politics." Another staff article deals with the effects of the oil crisis upon the Japanese economy, and describes the Arab nations as striving "to assert legitimate sovereignty over their natural resources" in order to use them "as a weapon in the struggle against Israeli aggression and its American supporters." The U.S. is accused of moving "aggressively to shore up the supremacy of U.S. multi-national interests over the entire structure of world finance, trade, and investment by deliberately weakening its major capitalist 'allies,' Europe and Japan." (JMS)

Reviewer's opinion:
An interesting and valuable publication, AMPO offers material not found elsewhere, as well as an insight into left-wing forces in Japan.

Feedback:
Editor suggested some minor corrections which were incorporated into the text.

ANN ARBOR SUN: Community News Service

| | |
|---|---|
| Rainbow People's Party | Format: 16-page tabloid |
| 1510 Hill St. | Issues examined: 23 July, 21 Aug., 4 Sept. 1971; 11 May 1972 |
| Ann Arbor, Mich. 48104 | |
| Weekly | |
| Started: 30 Apr. 1971 | Indexing: Alternative Press Index |
| Circulation: 5,000 | |

The issue of 4 September 1971 carried this description

of the Rainbow People's Party and its goals:

> The primary aspect that identifies the people of the Rainbow Colony is culture. Our music, language, dress, literature, art, our world outlook, our rejection of imperialist ... culture, our communal life style--these are the things that identify us as 'a People,' a new post-western, post-industrial, post-Euro-American, Rainbow Culture....
>
> We identify with the rainbow because ... we are red, black, brown, we are yellow and white. The Rainbow Culture itself is made up of elements and traditions that we've learned from other cultures of the world. Our music has its roots in black beautiful magic music, many styles of our dress and living patterns come from native American red culture. Two of our strongest medicines, marijuana and peyote, come from brown and red culture. We've learned of brown rice and other natural foods from the far-out yellow people. From Euro-American white culture we've taken technology. Our political leaders are [Karl] Marx, Crazy Horse, Mao [Tse-tung], Huey P. Newton [Black Panther], [Emiliano] Zapata, [V. I.] Lenin, Kim Il Sung [N. Korea], Bobby Seale [Chicago 'conspiracy' trial], [Kwame] Nkrumah [Ghana], Fidel [Castro], Sitting Bull, Ho Chi Minh, [Ernesto] Che [Guevara].
>
> We are a colony because we are controlled and exploited.... Our raw materials and natural resources are stolen from us by the imperialist's octopus class, the ruling class of Amerika. We share in none of the benefits of our own energy, our own production. These things are done by the same imperialists who exploit and control the people of Puerto Rico, Vietnam, South Korea, the Middle East, and Africa.
>
> ...
>
> The most blatant example of domestic imperialism and exploitation of our colony is the music industry. The musicians/people make the music, they are the workers who produce our natural resource, but the imperialist class control the means of production, i.e., the record companies, studios, pressing plants, printing plants for album covers, and distribution....
>
> ... Our need is ... institutions that are created by us and ... controlled by us. We need food, so we create and control the Ann Arbor food co-op.

> [The editors of this book used to buy their food there, when they lived in Ann Arbor.] We need information, so we create the underground press. We need education, so we create the children's community school. [And so on.]
>
> ...
>
> The over-all difference between People's institutions and pig institutions is that the people themselves rise up and create the institutions.

The Rainbow People's Party was formerly the White Panther Party. The Sun covers the Party's activities, programs, "institutions," and political strategies. (The Party backed George McGovern for President in 1972; has put up candidates for the city council; and has circulated a petition seeking to amend the Michigan Constitution and make the use of marijuana legal.) The Sun also contains sections on rock 'n' roll; "Community-Police Relations"; "Tribal Council News" (a sort of governing-and-communications network for the Party); a calendar of events; and a column by John Sinclair [White Panther leader who served several years in prison on marijuana charges].

In 1972, the Party was preparing to move its headquarters. We wrote to them in June 1974, but received no reply. Inasmuch as our letter was not returned by the Post Office, we assume that it reached the Party through the Hill Street address. (JMS)

## BLÄTTER DES IZ3W

Informationszentrum Dritte Welt
Postfach 5328
D-78 Freiburg, Federal Republic of Germany
10 issues a year; DM 18
Started: Nov. 1970

Circulation: 4,000
Format: 72 pages (8 1/4" x 11 1/2")
Issue examined: Jan. 1974
Indexing: separate annual index
Some back issues available from publisher

News of poor countries throughout the world. Contains articles on topics such as foreign laborers in West Germany; the guerrilla war in Angola; and malnutrition in Ethiopia, and the need for land reform there. Anti-imperialist, anti-colonialist, and anti-capitalist.

Feedback:

"Aims to inform Third World working groups about

recent developments in the Third World. News, analysis and models of action. Special interest: theories of underdevelopment and development projects."

## COMMON SENSE

Box 29
Bloomington, Ind. 47401
Irregular (usually monthly); free
Started: 1972
Circulation: 5,000-7,000

Format: 16-page tabloid (offset)
Issues examined: Dec. 1973; Jan., Feb., Apr. 1974
Microform version in Indiana University Library

Common Sense is concerned primarily with student affairs and issues at Indiana University. Although it does cover national and international issues--often by pointing out Richard Nixon's [Feedback: "the system's"] faults--the focus of feature articles and editorials is on local problems in Bloomington and in the university. The school administration is [Feedback: "taken to task for"--the rest of the sentence up to "fee hikes" was deleted] often attacked as responsible for whatever problem besets the "people": fee hikes, rezoning of lake property to allow for a housing development, or firing of nonunion clerical workers.

Besides news, Common Sense often includes book reviews and poems submitted by readers or reprinted from published works. (The books reviewed are usually about revolution or oppression.) Occasional pieces of fiction appear, usually with topical significance, such as "The Death of a T.A. by Fritz Kafka, Featuring K and the Cockroach," in which the grading system specifically--and ultimately the establishment-- lead a conscientious, kindhearted teaching assistant to an untimely demise.

There is an unusually large amount of advertising for this type of paper, and that is probably why Common Sense can be distributed free. (SA)

Feedback:

The editor made several changes (which we have indicated above, in brackets). Apparently irritated beyond endurance, she then stopped revising, and wrote: "Your 'descriptive' language is not objective. I wish to have the review of Common Sense completely removed from your volume...."

## COMMON SENSE

People's Bicentennial Commission
1346 Connecticut Ave., N.W.
Washington, D.C. 20036
Bi-monthly; $10 (includes a kit of materials on how to organize a PBC in your community)
Format: 8- to 16-page tabloid
Issues examined: May to July 1973

Common Sense is a publication of the People's Bicentennial Commission, the alternative to the official American Revolution Bicentennial Commission.

> The People's Bicentennial Commission is a non-profit group of non-sectarian people. We want to put the American Revolution back to work, and we think the time to do that is now. We're helping to plan a people's campaign for the Bicentennial. A grass roots movement that can focus all our energies into a force for decisive change in the 1970's.

Though Common Sense carries articles on the Revolution of 1776 (e.g., "Who Was the Real Tom Paine?" and "Workers in the Revolution"), the main focus of the paper is on the relation of Revolutionary principles to the events of today, and the deterioration and distortion of these principles at the hands of "corporate wealth" and "a deadening bureaucracy." Articles on this theme in the issues examined include: "July 4th: Army Seizes Declaration of Independence" (the arrest of GIs in Japan for distributing copies of the Declaration); "The Usurpation of Power" (how "Presidents have time and again usurped power through deceit and manipulation"); "ITT: Serving the People" (the power of this corporation in national and international affairs); and "A Tory by Any Name" (accusing the Nixon administration of adopting the anti-democratic attitudes of the Tories of the 18th century).

Regular features include "Tory Social Notes," describing in short items how the corporate and social elite are trying "to convince us that nothing very radical happened back then [i.e., during the Revolution]"; and "The Committee of Correspondence," letters from local branches of PBC describing their efforts for the Bicentennial. (SLA)

Feedback:
Editor expressed no disapproval.

## COMMUNITY

Friendship House
21 E. Van Buren
Chicago, Ill. 60605
Quarterly; $2
Started: 1941 as the Catholic Interracialist

Circulation: 1,500
Format: 28 pages (offset)
Issues examined: Winter 1973; Spring & Summer 1974
Back issues available from: publisher

Community, "a magazine of inter-cultural interests and non-violent action," takes an anti-imperialist, anti-racist, anti-sexist, and anti-war stance. Friendship House is an activist Catholic community organization. Working with the poor and minority groups, it sponsors programs and projects. (Thomas Merton, to which the Winter issue was dedicated, was connected with the New York Friendship House in Harlem before he became a Trappist monk.)

The organization also publishes a bulletin (folded leaflet) called Friendship House Notes. Calendar of activities and events, notices, etc.

## THE DEFENDER

United Defense against Repression
326 W. 3rd St. (Room 318)
Los Angeles, Calif. 90013
Bi-monthly; $3.50
Started: Sept. 1972

Circulation: 600
Format: 4-6 pages (8 1/4" x 11" or 11 1/4" x 17 1/2")
Issues examined: Dec. 1972; Apr. 1973

The bi-lingual Defender is published by United Defense against Repression (formerly, Provisional Committee for a United Defense Organization) and is affiliated with the National Alliance against Racist and Political Repression. The April 1973 issue carries the new organization's statement of principles, decided upon at the founding conference (February 1973) attended by 300 persons from 41 cities in southern California, representing unions, racial and ethnic minorities, and students and professionals. According to the Statement of Principles, "We defend the democratic and constitutional rights of all persons and organizations victimized as a result of struggles for peace, freedom, and economic security --or singled out for attack as a result of racist ... or political repression." The organization helps the activist or victim of repression (who is usually poor, and a member of a minority group) by forming defense committees; arranging public meetings; engaging in mass public education; and providing legal defense. The organization also publishes educational material; stages cultural events; works with like-minded groups; maintains a counseling service on immigration, naturalization, and military conscription; operates a bail fund; and seeks "to wipe from the statute books repressive legislation undermining the Bill of Rights, and to enact progressive legislation, seeking to extend the democratic rights of the people, particularly in the fields of arrest, trial, and imprisonment."

The April 1973 issue contains short articles on cases or causes with which the movement is involved. "Firestone Sheriffs Terrorize Compton" describes the brutal beating by police of three members of a Chicano family. "Mass Meeting for Mongo" concerns an officer of the Young Workers' Liberation League (a Marxist group), framed by police and accused of peddling narcotics, because he refused to be a spy for them. "Amnesty for McNeil" is about another member of YWLL, on trial for refusing to be conscripted into the army. "Indeterminate Sentence--Instrument of Repression" and "Psycho-Surgery?" attack two abuses that plague prisoners. A feature, "National Roundup," takes brief note of cases in other parts of the country.

The organization has supported such persons as Angela Davis, Bobby Seale, and Daniel Ellsberg. (JMS)

## THE LAST POST

430 King St. West (#101)
Toronto 135, Ont., Canada
Eight issues a year; $5 (institutions $7)
Started: Dec. 1969
Circulation: 15-20,000
Format: 52 pages (offset)
Issues examined: Jan., Mar., May, July 1973
Indexing: Alternative Press Index
Back issues available from publisher
Microform version available from Xerox University Microfilms.

In a letter to readers (July 1973), the editors state the purpose and viewpoint of the magazine:

> From the beginning the theory of the Last Post was simple--no more internecine wrangling on the left, no more theoretical journals in the wilderness talking to themselves. A strong newsmagazine must be created to reach the unorganized, the working man and woman. In short the only way to fight control

of the media by business was to build solid organs of information from the left.

In a similar letter in the March 1973 issue the editors state that they are concerned with offering "readers a radical and muckraking approach to the news, an approach seldom found in the dull, conformist columns of the commercial press."

The Last Post focuses on Canadian news, and on world news as it affects Canada. Regular features are "The Month," "Last Pssst," book reviews, and letters to the editor. "The Month" consists of articles on current topics, giving the radical interpretation of the news. It has covered such Canadian topics as changes in the government ("The new cabinet: a rightward shift"), immigration policies ("The open back door slams shut") and the possibility of holding the Olympics in Canada ("Quebec: What's a billion dollars?"). "The Month" also has covered topics in world news in articles such as "Watergate: They Shoot Lame Ducks, Don't They?", "Vietnam: When finished, recycle this war," and "Chile: Strike of the bosses."

Included in "The Month," in between the articles, are clippings from other magazines and newspapers, sent in by readers. In the March 1973 issue, readers "are invited to submit absurd, fatuous, overwritten or otherwise noteworthy items culled from the daily and periodical press." Readers send in headlines such as "Cannibalism Gets Qualified Approval," or "Christmas Day Still Dec. 25." Other contributions include entertaining advertisements and short news stories.

"The Last Pssst" section consists of "verifiable bits of gossip" also sent in by readers. Politicians, businessmen, entertainers, writers, and athletes all are featured in this section. The type of gossip varies from the price of drinks at the New Democratic Party's convention to a description of the opening of the National Capital Equestrian Centre.

Special features present the leftist viewpoint in unexpected forms. The July 1973 issue contains a crossword puzzle with clues such as "Epitaph of loud corporate behaviour," "This Kissinger charter should be dumped in it," and "Up to something fishy, a typical Liberal has misshapen large fin." The March 1973 issue includes a board game called "Hear! Hear! (The One & Only, Altogether Unique Game of Parliamentary Pitfalls!)." The game is designed to instruct new members of Parliament in ways of rising to the top.

The Last Post also contains very pointed cartoons. The July 1973 issue includes a series of pictures and captions under the title "A Few Tips on Becoming a Member of the Committee for an Impotent Canada." Among the suggestions are these: "Be somewhat decisive. Drive a meteor. Eat spaghetti with a hockey stick. Drink Niagara port out of a moccasin." An article about the Watergate conspiracy trial includes a cartoon with three drawings of Nixon and the caption "Will the real bugger please stand up?"

The Last Post supports neither the Liberals nor the New Democratic Party. Liberalism is seen as a "mixture of pseudohumanitarianism and business selfinterest." In the January 1973 issue an article points out that "The Tories' differences with the Liberals are expressed more in style and emphasis than in actual policy." The New Democratic Party is criticized for compromising with the liberals. In the January 1973 issue one article states,

> Our NDP governments are like Schultz's Snoopy pretending he is a polar bear. He becomes a puppy again at the sight of the first snowball thrown his way.

In the same issue an article offers a favorable view of the Parti Quebecois, but expresses some pessimism as to the future success of the party.

The Last Post opposes U.S. involvement in Canada, especially in connection with the war in Indochina. The United States is accused of trying to control Canadian resources to serve its own purposes. Specifically in regard to the war, The Last Post feels that the U.S. is acting as a kind of "big brother," preventing Canada from taking a position of neutrality. (CT)

Feedback:

"The summary looks fine to us."

LIBERATED GUARDIAN

Monthly; institutions $15
Dates: Apr. 1970 - Feb. 1973
Format: 8- to 16-page tabloid
Issues examined: May, Aug., Sept. 1972
Indexing: Alternative Press Index

Liberated Guardian is the end product of a protest by Guardian staff members that that 20-year-old radical weekly was "elitist" and "old left." The dissident staff split off and began publishing its own paper. Emphasis in Liberated Guardian is on anti-war and anti-imperialist activities, the prison movement, liberation struggles in the Third World and elsewhere (e.g., Ireland), and political trials, protests, and demonstrations in this country.

The most extensively reported issue is the war in Vietnam--documents from both anti-war groups and the Vietnamese themselves; reports on anti-war activities, including those of Vietnam Veterans Against the War; news and analysis of the actual fighting as well as the political meaning and impact of the war. This coverage is tied into articles about U.S. imperialism in other parts of the world and repression at home. "Let Me Make One Thing Perfectly Clear: Chase Manhattan Has a Friend in the White House" is part of a longer report by the North American Congress on Latin America (NACLA) on the power structure behind the U.S. election process. Nixon's connections with organized crime and the "masters of monopoly capitalism" (the "Rockefeller group") are examined in detail.

Articles support various guerrilla movements throughout the world, such as the Tupamaros (Uruguay), the Irish Republican Army, and the Palestinians. After the killings of Israeli athletes at the 1972 Olympics the staff commented that "There is moral outrage at the deaths in Munich and not a word about the Palestinian refugees and the Arab victims of Israeli attacks."

> We feel a sense of tragedy about Munich; we feel a pain and sorrow that people are killed in war, no matter what war and no matter what side. But we feel as well the tragedy of the Israeli genocide against the Palestinian people, a tragedy that kills not 20 people but 2 million, and a culture thousands of years old, or tries to. The tragedy is that Jews in Israel have run from persecution and genocide only to perpetrate persecution and genocide, and instill in former friends the hatred from which they have run.

Also greatly emphasized are the prison movement and the trials of political prisoners. Several ongoing trials are covered at least briefly in every issue. Individual and collective communications from prisoners (such as the Green Haven prisoners' "Petition to the Peace Movement"--"compared to the United States government, we are as innocent as babies") are published frequently. One issue has a special "prison supplement" analyzing the state of the prison movement one year after Attica.

> We have been learning that in many ways maximum security is being locked up in jail and minimum security is being locked up in school or in a job you don't like but need to survive; that in fact the very communities in which third world and very poor white people live are 'minimum security prisons' which as yet do not have bars or fences, but where the control of racist, brutal police power is clear. We have been learning that it's the same people, the Rockefellers, Reagans, Oswalds, etc., who are in charge inside the walls and out; the same people who give the orders and pass out the campaign buttons; the same people who control all our lives.

An interview with a member of the Attica Survivors Committee, poetry from prisoners, reports on the cases of Ruchell Magee and Curtis Brown, and an article on the use of "psychosurgery" (lobotomy) on homosexual prisoners complete the supplement.

Articles on community struggles include "West Side 'Urban Renewal': Poor Pushed Out" and "The Battle for Community-Controlled Health Care" (in a Chinese-American community). A regular feature ("Cracks in the Empire") prints items that point toward a victory for the movement. (MM)

Feedback:

"Thank you! Your summary was excellent...." The editor said that Liberated Guardian suspended publication with the February 1973 issue (v. 3, no. 8). (It had been published by Hard Rain, Inc., 149 Hester Street, N.Y., N.Y. 10002.) It has been superseded by New York City Star.

## LIBERATION NEWS SERVICE

160 Claremont Ave.
N.Y., N.Y. 10027
Semi-weekly; undergrounds $240; colleges $360; commercial publications $500
Started: 1967
Circulation: 500

Format: 10-14 pages of copy; 1-4 pages of photos, line graphics (offset)
Issues examined: 6, 13, 17 Oct. 1973
Microform version available from Bell & Howell

This is a collective that supplies information to "the underground and college press, radio stations, libraries, and many organizations in the United States and throughout the world." Each issue includes long news stories, reviews, shorts, and a few pages of graphics.

Correspondents from all over the world write articles on a variety of subjects: "the Indochina War, and the anti-war movement, U.S. military and economic involvement throughout the world, repression, ecology, the women's movement, Third World and working-class struggles in this country and abroad, youth culture, gay liberation." As can be seen from this list, LNS expresses the viewpoint of the radical left.

In the September 1972 issue of More, Nat Hentoff admits that LNS's viewpoint is radical, but adds that the publication is now

> more professional. They are still devoted advocacy journalists. ('We are interested in making people who read LNS material anti-capitalist, anti-imperialist, anti-racist, anti-sexist; and further look toward places like Cuba and China for ideas and lessons about how to shape a new society.') But they are not dishonest journalists. ('We believe in accuracy, we do not believe in lying--which in the end cannot be to our advantage.')

Most of the articles are comprehensive and analytical. Representative titles include: "Getting the Presidential Shaft: Agnew Cops a Plea, Resigns"; "A New Kind of Dehumanization and Terror: Behavior Modification in Prisons"; and "Consumer Group Charges Dangerous Levels of Lead Found in Evaporated Milk; FDA Rejects Evidence."

The graphics section includes photographs and line drawings designed to accompany the articles and present additional comment on the news. One packet included these line graphics:

> Worker at machine that fills boss's pockets with money, over background of want ads;
> Faceless worker makes 'smile' faces;
> 'Bum' points out that he paid as much in taxes as Nixon in '71;
> U.S. imperialist stuffs body in his pipe;
> Nixon (smiling) and Agnew wave, as Spiro's head floats away.

(CT)

Feedback:

"The review was fine."

## NEW CANADA

| | |
|---|---|
| Box 6106, Station "A" | Started: 1969 |
| Toronto 1, Ontario | Circulation: Refused to divulge |
| Canada | Format: 12-page tabloid |
| Monthly; $2 | Issue examined: Feb./Mar. 1973 |

New Canada, "The Anti-Imperialist Newspaper," focuses on U.S. involvement in many areas of Canadian society. It protests the domination of the Canadian labor movement by U.S. unions ("Canadian unions for Canadian workers!"); the dominance of U.S. corporations and cartels in Canadian agriculture and industry ("Bar foreign ownership of land!"); Canadian foreign policy toward Vietnam ("an extension of the U.S. State Department!"); and particularly the overrunning of Canadian universities by American professors ("85% Canadian quota!").

It looks toward a united front of workers, farmers, students, and all patriotic Canadians to fight against the imposition of colonial status on Canada by the "Imperialist United States." (KL)

Feedback:

The editor suggested several minor changes in wording, and we incorporated them into the review.

## THE NEW PRAIRIE PRIMER

| | |
|---|---|
| Semi-monthly during regular academic year, monthly during summer sessions, except for holidays and examination periods; $4 for 20 issues | Started: 1 Oct. 1969<br>Circulation: 1,500-2,000<br>Format: 16-page tabloid (offset)<br>Issues examined: 4 & 15 Oct., 15 Dec. 1969; 9 Feb. 1970 |

This is a radical publication of the University Activists' Coalition at the University of Northern Iowa. It is mainly concerned with topics of interest to students. The sample issues dealt with Vietnam, the draft, and women's liberation. The paper defines its goal as "to make the student conscious of himself as the rational and humane shaper of his and others' future." (IT)

The Primer is illustrated with the cartoons of Ron Cobb, whose work often appears in underground papers. Articles are sometimes accompanied by lists of books (or films) for further reading (or viewing), or by full-length reviews of pertinent books. An issue devoted to the Vietnam War carried articles on conscientious objectors and on emigrating to avoid conscription, and included a three-page list of Iowa GIs killed in the war. Articles in other issues expressed support for Cesar Chavez and the United Farm Workers; and criticized policemen's dislike and harassment of long-haired "freaks." (TJS)

Feedback:

Mail returned (1974): "Out of business." Address had been: 401 1/2 Main St., Cedar Falls, Iowa 50613.

NEW YORK CITY STAR

149 Hester St.
N.Y., N.Y. 10002
Monthly (bi-weekly soon); $5
Started: May 1973
Circulation: 5,500
Format: 16- to 24-page tabloid (offset)
Issues examined: May-July 1973
Back issues available from: publisher

The City Star called our attention to an editorial ("Collective Comment") in the first issue. It explained the aims of the paper, and discussed the backgrounds of those who produce it:

> At this point we are all young people from middle- and lower-middle class backgrounds. We are now workers or unemployed workers, with full- and part-time jobs. We work on the City Star in our spare time and do not pay ourselves....
>
> Many of us are attempting to live together with a number of people--sharing expenses and problems--trying to build new, alternative relationships that have to go hand-in-hand with the new, alternative institutions people are working for and creating.
>
> We have been active in various liberation struggles in this country.... Most of us ... have had experience with "progressive" media such as Midnight Special, Liberation News Service, and the Liberated Guardian--in many ways the progenitor of the City Star.
>
> We are white people, and of course the racial make-up of the City Star staff will be reflected in the paper. Nevertheless, we will include extensive coverage of news from non-white communities in this city as well as the struggles of our Third-World

> brothers and sisters around the globe.... Only three out of our eleven-person collective are women--a situation that's got to change.
>
> We do not share any particular political 'line'--in fact, there are divergent political views and lifestyles reflected within the paper.... However, we are united by our desire to see a new New York city paper grow and by certain fundamental beliefs:
>
> -That people of this city have the right to live decent, meaningful lives ... [and] not to be oppressed or confined because of race, sex, age, nationality, sexual persuasion, or the social class they were born into.
>
> That as things are now, we are being robbed every day; not so much by the brothers and sisters 'on the block' whose backs are <u>really</u> up against the wall, but by the handful of wealthy men who travel by limousine and live in well-protected, well-maintained homes--while we're sweating on the subways, triple-locking our doors, and swatting roaches.
>
> -That we're being robbed, and our life energy drained, by a social system that divides people and sets us against each other.
>
> ...
>
> ... The 'system' is stacked against an independent progressive press. Advertisers will not flock to support a paper that openly opposes big business interests. We cannot and do not want to rely on these people.

The editorial goes on to ask help in putting the paper together and expresses the hope that it "will express the needs, viewpoint, and struggles of working, poor, and oppressed people in this city--all of whom we see as excluded from representation in the mass media." People "are taking matters into their own hands" and "We are working to gain control over schools, day-care centers, hospitals, prisons, and other institutions that affect our lives." The <u>City Star</u> hopes to "speed along the process of radical change that is surely coming" by "not only covering the news from many communities, but by showing existing alternatives and the struggles to build them."

Articles in the <u>City Star</u> reflect the above philosophy. We shall review this paper in more detail in Volume Four.

## NEW YORK NEWS SERVICE

Deanne Stillman & Rex Weiner, Co-Editors
204 W. 10th St.
N.Y., N.Y. 10014
Bi-weekly; $5 (institutions $48)
Started: Aug. 1973
Circulation: over 150
Format: 9-10 pages (8 1/2" x 14", stapled)
Issues examined: 18 Sept., 10 Oct. 1973
Microform version available from: Bell & Howell

This is a "packet of news features and shorts serving over 150 underground and alternative newspapers and radio stations around the world." Each issue consists of "Bits" (news anecdotes), short news items, several longer articles, and a page of graphics.

The articles are generally anti-establishment, anti-war, anti-capitalist, anti-police, and anti-discrimination. Examples: "Judge Orders Government Expose Anti-Left Tricks!"; "The Guru: 'Follow Me and I Will Make Ye Graspers at Straws'" (a put-down of the Divine Light mania); "Mad Doctors Meet Victims" (groups seeking rights for mental patients invade a psychiatrists' convention and pose the question: who's crazy?); and "I Got the Steal This Woodstock Nation Cocaine Blues News."

In addition to commenting on the news, the _News Service_ recommends sources of information, announces meetings, and solicits contributions. (CT)

_Feedback:_

Editor expressed no disapproval.

## OUTSIDE THE NET: A Magazine in Radical Education

Box 184
Lansing, Mich. 48901
Irregular; $2 for 4 issues
Started: 1970
Circulation: 2,500
Format: 32-40 pages (offset)
Issues examined: Spring 2, No. 6, and an undated issue
Indexing: _Alternative Press Index_
Back issues from No. 2 available from publisher

As a magazine created for and by those who desire a radical alternative to America's system of education, _Outside the Net_

> Analyzes schools and media and their relationships to society....

Explores alternative educational life styles....
Reviews educational-related media....
Publishes ... articles, photos, poetry, essays, drawings, cartoons, letters, trivia....
Serves as a link to other Movement media to spread information ... about liberating educational ideas....

One lead article puts forth the views of the Human Rights Party, a Michigan organization which believes that today's public schools serve the interests of only the rich, oppress the poor by reinforcing class differences, discriminate against minorities, and perpetuate sexism. A thirteen-point declaration of student rights calls for "democratically elected student courts and trial by peers" and "freedom of assembly to form or join political organizations and unions and to strike." This group also believes that all education should be free, supported by a steeply graduated income tax on personal income and business profits.

Some contributors object to compulsory education. A statement from an SDS Education Collective in Ann Arbor calls it involuntary servitude. Because they are convinced that the chief lessons learned in schools are submission to authority and the ability to follow tight schedules and compete for grades and recognition, they call for "creative ways of attacking the entire structure of American education from top to bottom." Hal Bennett (in "Gurus Are a Dime a Dozen") contends that conflict and disorder are good materials to work with, so "fighting should be accepted in all schools as a legitimate part of the curriculum." He views "reading, riting and rithmetic" as "the easiest things in the world to teach and to learn. So much so that they should be virtually ignored as legitimate parts of the curriculum of schools." The important thing to teach children is "how to put it all together for themselves."

Colleges, too, are found wanting. One author praises Governor Ronald Reagan for cutting the finances of his state's higher education system, and says that "higher education these days, both in public and private colleges, is so disgusting that the best thing to do is cripple it." Another article praises free universities which "continue to give support to everyone without payment or price."

"Resources" is a feature which gives a bibliography of groups and media working for educational change. Reviews of significant media are often quite long, and the layout of the magazine is attractive and varied. No paid advertising, foundation or government grants are accepted, and both contributions and subscriptions are solicited.

If we are to continue as an alternative to the mindless empiricism of Area Journal, to the Midwest anti-intellectualism of Phi Delta Kappa[n], and to the vacuous liberalism of Saturday Review, Harvard Education Review, and American television, we need your help.

(EC)

Feedback:

Editor expressed no disapproval.

## POEMS OF THE PEOPLE

Monthly; $5 Issues examined: Nos. 4-6
Format: 24 pages (mimeo., (1970)
stapled)

This "is a free press service for the underground/alternate culture/movement press. All the people are invited to submit poems, stories, and reviews...." It is published for the purpose of collecting and distributing works to other underground periodicals.

Although the works included cover a wide range of topics, and each represents the ideas of a particular author, they have many attitudes in common. All of the contributors are in some way connected with the alternate culture, the movement. In general, they are members of the radical left and oppose war, capitalism, imperialism, and the establishment.

Some of the poems deal with specific current events, such as the war in Indochina and the Kent State Massacre. Representative titles: "Uncle Sammy Sucks or My Cuntry Tis of Thee"; "War Pictures"; and "Chicago Protest Consolation Blues."

Morgan Gibson writes:

Bombs have stolen our thunder
paled our lightning
ruined our rain.
Storms no longer terrify.
We laugh when disasters are merely
natural and switch the channel
for massacres.

Prudence Juris expresses herself this way:

He/She sent: A GENUINE GHETTO RAT
to His/Her favorite Pres/C-Man/

Rep/Senator
today
And waxed: AT&T-PUBLIC ENEMY #1
on the 10,000th telephone booth in
town

Another type of expression is found in prose pieces. Walter Lowenfels writes that peace is "respect for the rights of others--peace is the avant-garde manifesto of three billion people." In "Politics Is Poetry," the same author says:

> We can show people by what we do that socialism is a singing thing; that it doesn't make robots of people. On the contrary: it is the capitalist system that turns people into mechanical objects, robs them of personality, of humanity, makes them slaves to bread and to bread alone, takes away the song of life, and gives them a jingle for a brand of deodorant.

The creative artists who contribute to Poems of the People are men and women dissatisfied with American society, who have chosen to make their voices heard through their works. (CT)

Feedback:
Mail returned 1973: "Addressee unknown." Address had been: Box 324, Mt. Pleasant, Mich. 48858.

THE RAP

Monthly; $10
Circulation: 1,300
Started: Apr. 1969
Format: 10-pages (mimeo., stapled)
Issue Examined: June 1970

The Rap, a newsletter directed at dissatisfied VISTA volunteers, endorses a strong central organization, the National VISTA Alliance, and a program of action. It believes that "Now is the time for VISTA Volunteers to take in hand the self-determination we daily preach to poor communities and hurl it at VISTA administration, OEO, and the Federal Government. We must speak and be heard in order to save our projects and the anti-poverty movement."

Articles stress that VISTA volunteers cannot sit idle while "the anti-poverty program is emasculated" and the very existence of VISTA is threatened. The issue examined included the following: a discussion of whether VISTA allowances are tax-exempt; a reprint from The New Republic about Nixon's failure to appoint Richard Blumenthal, a young, liberal, independent Democrat, to be VISTA Director; statements from two VISTA conferences; and a report from the Committee of Returned Volunteers condemning the Peace Corps and calling for its abolition. A few pages are devoted to short items of interest: coming events, projects needing volunteers and support, related publications.

While The Rap was originally printed for VISTA volunteers as an alternative to official OEO-VISTA publications, its subject matter would be of interest to others concerned about social change and action. (JW)

Feedback:

Mail returned 1973, marked "Addressee unknown." Address had been: 3050 Brighton 14th Street (c/o Arnie Korotkin), Brooklyn, N.Y. 11235.

THE RED TIDE: High School Community Information Service

Box 64402
Los Angeles, Calif. 90064
Monthly; $5 (students $3)
Started: Nov. 1971
Circulation: 3,000-5,000
Format: 12-page tabloid (offset)

Issues examined: Mar., Summer, Nov. 1973
Microform version of the women's articles at International Women's History Archives, Berkeley

The Red Tide is put out by high school students in an effort to educate young people about the evils of contemporary society, particularly the evils of the capitalist establishment as seen in their school governments and national governments. Besides performing an informational service, the editors hope to rouse their readers to anger and action. The heading at the top of each issue suggests the tone of their enthusiasm:

> It came--flooding the schools, crushing everything that stood in its way, leaving in its wake a trail of destruction, havoc, rebellion. It razed classrooms; flinging textbooks to the winds, screaming out of turn, leaving foul stains on the desks, ripping the flags from their very poles. It caught scores of students, sweeping them onward on its headlong course, trapping them in the whirpool [sic] of its frenzy. Administrators reeled chocking [sic] on its noxious reek,

> as it tore their offices asunder. Cut slips, tardy slips, suspension notices, bad conduct notices, report cards--all were swept away in its churning midst. It was THE RED TIDE.

The articles cover topics of national interest as well as local student interest. The writers of the articles on such issues as Wounded Knee, the Irish Republican Army, the Chilean coup that toppled Salvador Allende's government, and the Mideast struggle, are careful to provide a sketch of the historical background of the situation and to spell out the implications of the present situation for the oppressed and the oppressors. A long series on black history explored the institution of slavery in an economic context, pointing out its role in the early development of capitalism. Student issues of concern include the tracking system and freedom of expression in the schools--in textbook censorship, in distribution of materials at school, and in choices of speakers for school programs. The earnestness of the writers and the urgency of the issues they are writing about might explain the high incidence of misspelled words and grammatical mistakes found in the articles. (SA)

Feedback:

The editor suggested changing our opening sentences to read:

> The Red Tide is put out by high school students in an effort to educate young people about the evils of capitalist society, particularly the schools. It puts forward--as an alternative--a society in which wealth and power would be democratically controlled by those who produce it. Besides performing an informational service, the editors hope to rouse their readers to anger action [sic], and to take part in day-to-day struggles.

The spokesman suggested deleting the last sentence of the review, "as I though[t] that it sounded kind of conde[s]cending."

RISING UP ANGRY

Box 3746, Merchandise Mart
Chicago, Ill. 60654
Tri-weekly; $5 (institutions $10; free to GIs and prisoners)

Started: Fall 1969
Circulation: 10,000
Format: 16- to 20-page tabloid (offset)
Issues examined: 30 June,

21 July, 11 Aug. 1974
Back issues available from: publisher

Microform version available from: Xerox University Microfilms

Rising Up Angry is published by the organization of the same name. Though the ultimate goal of RUA is a people's revolution, the current thrust--as seen in the coverage of local events--is the control of arbitrary government and corporate power: "Victory at Stewart Warner" (about the rehiring of discharged workers at a local factory); "Brighton Park Citizens Petition Police" (concerning the charge of "whitewash" in the killing of a youth by a policeman); and "Principal Promises Women Equality" (on the sexist treatment of female students at a Chicago high school). RUA is also involved in "north and south side legal clinics; free health center; military counseling and organizing; over 2000 free subscriptions to GIs and prisoners across the country and around the world; support for the United Farm Workers; women's organizing; etc., etc."

RUA is especially active and vocal in attempting to decrease the violence between street gangs [Feedback: "We do this, but it isn't our main focus of work--2-3 years ago it was."]: "Our position is that the basis for unity shouldn't be white clubs against Puerto Rican clubs. We feel poor and working people of all races must unite to take control of the government." RUA is also against drug abuse (seeing it as a government tool for control of the people) and has carried articles on the symptoms and effects of various drugs.

Events of national and international significance are also covered in the paper. In the sample issues, there were articles on: the plight of the Navajo Indians; a famine in the Sahel; racism in the U.S. armed forces; the high cost and shortages of food; rebellion in Portuguese African colonies; and the crimes of Richard M. Nixon ("Jail to the Chief!").

Regular features include letters, cartoons, ads and reprints from other radical publications, and the "People's Grapevine" (short notices on local events, hassles with the police, and other news items). (SLA)

Feedback:
Editor expressed no disapproval.

A SINGLE SPARK

October 4th Organization
Box 14745
Philadelphia, Pa. 19134

Quarterly; $2 ($10 libraries)
Started: July 1973 (Emergency News Bulletin was a single

issue, preceding this publication.)
Circulation: 5,000

Format: 12-page tabloid (offset)
Issues examined: Summer & Fall 1973

Named after a "people's" rebellion against Philadelphia merchants and businessmen in 1779, the O4O (October 4th Organization) is a revolutionary community organization. It sponsors a Legal Program, an Information and Education Project ("to keep people informed of the people's struggles against imperialist aggressors throughout the world"), and a Jobs Project (to help people find jobs, and to assist workers with problems connected with their jobs). This newsletter keeps its readers informed of these programs and related activities and movements in the community. A regular feature ("From the Shop Floor") exposes inequities and unfair practices of local businesses and industries. Readers are reminded of such general themes as women's struggles and government corruption, but the primary purpose of the newsletter is to keep its readers aware of local problems and activities, such as strikes, health facilities, bail funds, and city politics. A firm stand is taken against the use of hard drugs in articles about their illegal use, in warnings about doctors' prescriptions, and in the policy of the Legal Program which refuses legal aid to anyone convicted on drug charges who is unwilling to participate in a withdrawal program. No aid is given to those convicted of selling drugs, for they are "pushers and enemies of the people." The section of the paper entitled "Neighborhood News" highlights activities of the various neighborhood groups and includes many pictures of the "sisters and brothers" at work and play.

Despite their revolutionary rhetoric (e.g., "A single spark can start a prairie fire"), the articles seem geared less to rousing anger than to informing people of how they can help themselves in the face of an unjust bureaucratic system in which the poor always lose. For example, in one issue, after the various problems that beset a poor person (especially a poor black female) seeking medical care are enumerated, a plan for a community health program is described in detail. A free community "health fair" was planned as a first step in the right direction. (SA)

SUN

Gary Grimshaw & John Sinclair, Eds.

Format: 12-page tabloid
Issues examined: Nos. 1-3, 5.

(Nos. 2 & 3 published in or after April 1967; no. 5 dated 1 March 1968 and entitled Warren-Forest Sun.)

Filled with psychedelic art work. Devoted largely to rock music and marijuana. Occasional poems. The Sun was published "as a community service for the people of Detroit" by Trans-Love Energies Unlimited, 4863 John Lodge, Detroit, Mich. 48201.

Vietnam War. An article entitled "Draft" attacked the war and military conscription.

Religion. An inspirational article ("The New Satori") was enthusiastic but incoherent.

Dope. As one issue explained, the Sun was devoted to (1) rock-and-roll; (2) dope; and (3) fucking in the streets. (Each of these was dwelt upon at some length.) A regular feature ("Dope-o-Scene") carried news of marijuana arrests, police harassment, and undercover police agents (narcs). An article ("Speed Freak") warned against amphetamine addiction; another ("Bananas") gave a recipe for preparing and smoking part of the banana plant.

High school undergrounds. Several issues contained sympathetic reports on dissident papers at various schools in the Detroit area in the late 1960s: Aesthetic (Berkeley High); The Daily Planet (Cooley); Diva, "the nation's first teen-age 8-page tabloid underground newspaper," to be edited by Dick Schloss; Elevator (Mumford; perhaps never published); Kulchur (Grosse Pointe High; at least three issues published); Southhampton International Times [SHIT] (Cass Tech; "has recently changed its name to Yellow"); and The Truth (Cooley).

A five-sheet unpaginated (8 1/2" x 11") group of news releases (White Panther News Service, June 1969) was entitled Sun and published by Trans-Love Energies, now located at 1510 Hill St., Ann Arbor, Mich. 48104. The news releases complain of harassment by Ann Arbor and Washtenaw County police. (Editors JMS and TJS, who lived in Ann Arbor in the late 1960s, recall the ill-feeling between police and dissidents; it occasionally erupted into scuffling and street-fighting, but was usually confined to police attempts to insult, intimidate, and embarrass long-hairs, potheads, and anti-war protestors.) (TJS)

SUNDANCE: White Panther Information Service

Started: 4 July 1970
Format: 32-page tabloid
Issue examined: 4 July 1970

Clenched fists. Smiling Ann Arbor radicals. Vietcong flag.

Marijuana and narcotics. A marijuana plant appears at the paper's masthead. There are several photos of Panther officers puffing on reefers. (The Party's chairman, John Sinclair, spent a number of months in prison on marijuana charges.) The article "Junk Sucks Life" condemns heroin and other narcotics, but criticizes the government for persecuting pot-smokers.

Heroes. Various writers quote, with approval, Mao Tse-tung; Kim Il Sung (premier of North Korea); Yippie Abbie Hoffman; and various Black Panthers.

Amerika. An article by the Party's Minister of Culture calls our schools "concentration camps" and in other ways evinces a low opinion of this nation's culture: "honko Amerika," "bullshit Amerika," "pig Amerika," "the pig system," and "the plastic heart of phoney Amerika."

Poetry. In "Pontiac's Speech to the White Man" Americans of European descent are referred to as "weak, pale-faced, rum-drinking cowards." An untitled poem which refers to Melvin Laird (former Secretary of Defense) as "a vampire" suggests that the president of Dow Chemical Co. be forced to perform an obscene act with an armadillo. (The Midland, Mich., company was often the target of ineffectual anti-war protests because it manufactured napalm.)

North Vietnam. Genie Plamondon, the Party's Minister of International Affairs, visited North Vietnam during the war with other "young American freekrevolutionaries": "I immediately fell in love with EVERYbody I met or came in contact with. It's so incredible. It's a whole country of people in love...." She felt sad to leave North Vietnam and return "to the belly of the beast, Babylon, the struggle, my despicable and beloved homeland." (Emphasis added.) Other phrases used in her article: "The great spirit of Ho Chi Minh," "U.S. imperialists and their puppets," a "fucking monster" (referring to Nixon's government), "here in the belly of the beast, in AmeriKKKa," and "the 'United' States is such a farce and its government are fools, assholes, blind in the cosmos...."

Another article consists of an interview with Genie's husband, Pun Plamondon, Minister of Defense (and co-founder) of the Party. Pun was underground at the time--and on the FBI's Ten Most Wanted list. His answers to questions are couched in Basic Dirty English sprinkled with simple-minded left-wing clichés. He expresses admiration for Malcolm X, Fidel Castro, Huey Newton and other Black Panthers; and utters a "beautiful quote from Mao."

Israel. "Palestine Will Win" is an interview with an Arab terrorist who says that Israeli soldiers are "not fighting for a real cause" but are "serving imperialism," serving the U.S.

The paper, doubtless defunct and probably a predecessor of the Ann Arbor Sun (reviewed in this chapter) was published at 1520 Hill St., Ann Arbor, Mich. 48104. The pilot issue's format was attractive and resembled that of some of the better-produced underground papers of the 1960s. (TJS)

TAP

Technological American Party
152 W. 42nd St. (Room 504)
N.Y., N.Y. 10036
10 issues a year; $2

Started: May 1971
Format: 4 pages (offset)
Issues examined: Aug./Sept., Oct., Nov. 1973

TAP (formerly Youth International Party Line or YIPL) is for "phone phreaks" who strive to get free service from the Bell Company. Recently, the newsletter broadened its scope to include technical information on how to defraud the gas and electric companies as well. (Those who try to do so are "power phreaks.") Justification: "The Electric and Gas companies are huge monopolies who have the nerve to sell us the Sun's energy. They have free reign over the rates they charge, the quality of the smoke we're forced to breathe, and the oceans and lakes they conveniently dump their wastes into."

The sample issues contained information and diagrams on connecting illicit extensions on telephones, building an "Answeroo" (a device for answering the phone before it rings), and turning back or shunting meters so as to lighten your power bill. Information upon which articles are based comes from readers. Their letters are reprinted and several were signed "H. Gordon Liddy"! (Liddy was associated with the Watergate break-in in the early 1970s.)

The August 1973 issue describes the Second International Phreak Convention, attended by several hundred people and a few telephone company spies ("agent types"). Eight half-hour videotapes on many phases of phone phreaking, power heisting, and using slugs were shown on video monitors around the room. These alternated with workshops: One on answering equipment, hold buttons, and the like; another on Con Ed, "boxes" of all colors, credit card calls, and "reforming" the phone company. ("Boxes" are clever gadgets used by phone phreaks.)

TAP offers a correspondence course on Basic Electrical Concepts (women, especially, are encouraged to take this course to overcome their built-in fear of electricity) and reprints of past articles on such topics as "Receiving Long Distance Calls Free."

Say the editors: "We print information on technology that is unpublished by all other sources. We do not advocate illegal activities that are described in the newsletter. We don't suggest you refrain from them either. In other words--to each ... [his] own."

TAP also supports a fund to defend Abbie Hoffman, ex-Yippie, against charges of possessing cocaine. (JMS)

Feedback:

"We did not set up the defense fund. It would be more accurate to say that TAP advocates supporting the 'Abbie Hoffman & friends defense fund'."

TENANTS' NEWSLETTER

Cambridge Tenants Organizing Committee
595 Massachusetts Ave.
Cambridge, Mass. 02139
Monthly; $3
Started: June 1970
Circulation: 10,000

Format: 16 pages (offset); recently changed to 16-page tabloid
Issues examined: July, Oct.-Dec. 1973
Back issues from June 1971 available from publisher

Published by the Cambridge Tenants' Organizing Committee, this periodical has evolved from an internal CTOC publication to a radical newsletter that emphasizes local housing matters: tenant union news, evictions, urban renewal, and rent controls. It also covers news of other worker organizations, provides a perspective on Cambridge politics and elections, and discusses broad economic issues such as income distribution and inflation. Stressed is the necessity for a movement "toward the unity of the whole working class around an anticapitalist program."

Recent issues have included "Health Inspectors & Landlords--Your Home Is Their Castle"; "Urban Renewal: No Room for Cheap Housing"; and "As the Property Tax Base Declines, City Workers Face New Battles."

In addition to publishing the Newsletter, CTOC distributes leaflets, pamphlets, and booklets. (JM)

Feedback:

The periodical now has articles in Spanish and Portuguese, as well as English. "We expect to begin Greek translations within a few months.... We index the Newsletter in our office by file card: the index will be available to friendly researchers. We find your description quite adequate otherwise."

TWO ... THREE ... MANY

Quarterly; $5
Dates: Winter 1970 - ?
Issues examined: Winter 1970 through Summer 1971
Indexing: Alternative Press Index

This periodical's title is based on a remark by Che Guevara: "How close we could look into a bright future should two, three, many Vietnams flourish throughout the world...." It was published by the Committee of Returned Volunteers, an

> organization of people who have served as volunteers in countries of the Third World. While overseas, we learned first-hand that our own government was time and again aligned with the forces of reaction, repression, and exploitation of the many by the few, and that our presence was intrically [sic] linked with these forces. As returned volunteers, we have come together to study, expose, and organize against United States imperialism and to build support for liberation struggles at home and around the world.

Articles investigated the effects of U.S. imperialism in all areas of the Third World, indicting the Peace Corps (along with government, business, the military, and the university) for exploitation of Third World people.

One issue dealt with cultural imperialism, defined as

> all the values, attitudes, and behavior patterns which facilitate domination by the imperial power. In the case of the United States, it is a culture of racism, ethnocentrism, materialism, consumerism, individualism, and male supremacy.

"The Case Against the Peace Corps" said that the role of Peace Corps volunteers in cultural imperialism was manifested partly in their "blatant, obvious ways of imposing their

North American values, tastes, and way of life on the host country people." "The Case Against the Imperialist Media" explained that

> The mass media of a colonized country ... are the tools of the colonizer.... In the context of Cultural Imperialism, the mass media impose rationales and values on the colonized majority. They aid and abet reactionary ideas, racism, militarism, and anti-communism.

"The Case Against the University" charged that "education ... is a powerful and effective means" used by the United States "to establish direct economic, political, and military control" of developing nations. The university has two roles as cultural imperialist: (1) It is a socializing agent, carefully training all its students "to think in <u>politically</u> <u>neutral</u> terms." (2) It makes sure that students are "tied in" to U.S. technology: "... over-specialization often makes it difficult for a new Ph.D. to return home. What options has he but to work for U.S.- or European-controlled ... enterprise? His technological training is in a foreign language, the vocabulary often non-existent in his own language, the need for his specialty [in his own country] equally non-existent." "The Case Against Cultural Exchange Programs" criticized these "superficially harmless, even magnanimous," institutions, "many of which receive funding directly from the U.S. government":

> Third World students who come to the United States become fluent in American English and otherwise learn the skills, mechanical and social, so desirable for 'nationals' employed in middle-management positions by American firms abroad. The programs are also designed to display the dazzle of a capitalist consumer-oriented society and to accustom the student to the comfortable middle-class life style of his American [host] 'family.'

Another issue was devoted to analytic and background pieces on Indochina. One article exposed the real reasons for our government's anti-communist stance:

> From Greece in 1947 through South Vietnam in 1971 the United States has actively supported dozens of the most brutal dictatorships who were willing to maintain a market economy, an Open Door to American capital, and a pro-American foreign policy.

> In this light, the term 'Free World' begins to make more and more sense, not as referring to the political freedom of oppressed peoples, but rather to the unrestricted economic freedom of large U. S. corporations to roam the world for raw materials, cheap labor, and continuously increasing markets....

The same issue contained articles on the growing student movement in South Vietnam; a review of a novel about people in a Mekong Delta village who resist a massive attack by Ngo Dinh Diem's troops; and several documents issued by Vietnamese and Laotian communist groups. Profiles of National Liberation Front leaders, and several other articles about Laos and Cambodia, complete the issue.

Each issue contains a bibliography of works on the subjects covered and an extensive list of CRV publications.

(MM)

Feedback:

"The summary is accurate. However, neither the CRV nor the magazine exists any longer. Limited copies of back issues are available from the New World Resource Center, 2546 N. Halsted, Chicago, Ill. 60614." The periodical's address had been: Committee of Returned Volunteers, 840 W. Oakdale Ave., Chicago, Ill. 60637.

## THE VARSITY

| | |
|---|---|
| 91 St. George Street | Circulation: 21,720 |
| Toronto 181, Ontario | Format: 12- to 24-page |
| Canada | tabloid |
| 3 times a week (Sept.-Mar.); $14 | Issues examined: 7 Feb., 23 Feb., 9 Mar., 21 Mar. 1973 |
| Started: 1880 | |

Although it is an official student newspaper (published by the Students' Administrative Council), The Varsity of the University of Toronto is unlike most such papers in the United States or Canada in being an explicitly "progressive, left-wing newspaper." To quote from its 1972-73 editorial policy:

> Neither a disinterested observer nor an indifferent critic, The Varsity strives to offer its readers an honest view of the world around them, ferreting out unknown facts and exposing connections between apparently unrelated events. Clearly aligning itself

> with the alternate press, The Varsity rejects the supportive role the professional press plays for the dominant socio-economic system, providing instead alternate coverage of educational, economic, and political developments.

The issues examined bear out this description. In its news pages The Varsity covers (and uncovers) departmental politics; budget problems; suspensions, firings, and tenure of teachers; political actions of students and campus workers, such as boycotts, strikes, rallies, demonstrations, sit-ins, and union activities; and some national, regional, and community news as well. Many articles report on speeches, conferences, lectures, and luncheon talks by national or university figures, who give their views on pollution laws, land-banking, computers, Chinese mathematics, nationalism, abortion, bankers' influence on the economy, and other subjects.

In a special center section, essays by staff members (or reprinted from The Chevron, a Canadian alternative paper) center on political and educational problems. Some discuss general issues, such as the women's movement, violence in films, or censorship. Others criticize university or national trends, as in "Diverting Our Northern Waters: Canada's Sellout as a Nation"; "Rampant Mediocrity: A U of T Hallmark" (the university is seen "involved in the pursuit of Acadamerica"); and "Who Owns 'Canadian' Sports?" Another article traces the history of dissent at the University of Toronto in "U of T's Changing Attitudes: Dissent Becomes More Assertive." Also in this section are record, play, art, and movie reviews, as well as at least one two-page book review/essay in each issue.

The last two pages of The Varsity are sports pages, but even they are part of the paper's "alternative" coverage. One article on a "radical sports ethic" compares the traditional Lombardi-type ethic (winning is everything) and the more recent counter-culture ethic (cooperation and process are the important things) and proposes a new ethic that combines intense competition with a humanistic concern for the players.

In one issue, this quotation appears on the masthead:

> If the consciousness of the masses is not yet awakened and we attack nonetheless, then that is recklessness. If we stubbornly push the masses into something that they do not want, the inevitable result will be disaster.
>
> -- Mao Tse-Tung

(MM)

Feedback:

"... I found your summary to be most accurate."

## WHITE LIGHTNING

109 E. 184th St.
Bronx, N.Y. 10468
Monthly; $5 (institutions $10)
Started: Nov. 1971
Circulation: 10,000
Format: 16-page tabloid (offset)
Issues examined: Apr., May, Nov. 1973
Back issues available from publisher

The expressed purpose of White Lightning is to "mobilize people to seize control of their lives." It is "dedicated to a second American revolution to give power to the people ... all poor and working people: black, Puerto Rican, and white." It is sold on the street in the north and east Bronx, in "workplaces, hangouts, and high schools."

The editor believes that if a newspaper is to be a voice of the people, it "should be like people's lives: colorful, creative, and expressing many feelings of anger and happiness. It should also be easy to read." The paper encourages people in communities to work together on community problems that affect everyone who lives there. Drug abuse, housing, day care, schools, and high food prices are areas of special concern.

Titles of feature-length articles show strong anti-establishment opinion: "There's No Justice in America!" "Bell Tel, Go to Hell!" "The Sick Relationship Between the AMA and Large Drug Companies," "Nixon's Economy: The Rich Get Richer and the Poor Get Poorer."

Regular features speak to an audience of students and the working poor. "People's Grapevine" and "Unity in the Community" are collections of short write-ups of current events covering local school and community problems. The back page is devoted to "White Lightning Comix," a graphic commentary upon a national problem such as inflation or crooked elections. The paper emphasizes the idea that "capitalism is the source of people's problems ... only a revolution putting us poor and working people in power can fulfill our needs."

(JS)

## WISCONSIN PATRIOT

Wisconsin Alliance
2140 Atwood Ave.
Madison, Wis. 53704
Monthly; $3 (institutions $5)

Started: Dec. 1971
Circulation: 3,000
Format: 12- to 24-page tabloid
Issues examined: Apr. & Dec. 1973; Feb. 1974
Back issues available from publisher
Microform version available from: Xerox University Microfilms

This is the organ of

> a group seeking to build a working people's political party in Wisconsin on the basis of a worker-farmer-student alliance.... To build working people's power we run local and statewide election candidates on working class political programs. We also work actively in support of trade unions, non-capitalist co-ops, and farm organizations. We support the struggles of non-white people, political prisoners, welfare, health care, women's liberation, and the anti-war movement. We have branches in Madison, Milwaukee, Green Bay, Appleton-Menasha.

Most of the articles contain news on state and local struggles: "Packerland on Strike," "Wisconsin UFW Boycott," "Viet Vets On the March"; and other state and local issues: "Racism in the Milwaukee Schools," "Energy Crisis Hits Wisconsin."

National and international news is also carried in articles such as "Women in China" and "The Story of Wounded Knee." Out-of-state strikes, boycotts, etc., are also supported. "We recognize that Wisconsin is only one state among many.... We express our solidarity with working people everywhere who seek as we do to throw off the yoke of U.S. monopoly rule." (SLA)

Feedback:
Editor expressed satisfaction with the review.

## YIP-INFORM

Youth International Party News Service
1404 M St., NW
Washington, D.C.
Semi-monthly; donations

Started: 5 Jan. 1975
Format: 3 pages (mimeo., stapled)
Issue examined: 5 Jan. 1975

This newsletter "is a project of Washington YIP coming

out of the Spokane and D.C. conferences. We hope to come out every 2 weeks or so, filling a noticible [sic] gap between issues of Yipster Times [reviewed in this chapter]."

Contains news of Yipster activities and groups throughout the country.

## YIPSTER TIMES

Youth International Party News Service
Box 392, Canal St. Station
N.Y., N.Y. 10013
Irregular; 25¢ an issue

Format: 16-page tabloid (offset)
Issues examined: v. 1, nos. 7-9 (1973); Mar. 1975

Some of the philosophy behind the Yipster Times is expressed in an "Open Letter to Yippies, Zippies, and Yipsters":

> We hope that YIP will grow and grow and become more and more together to provide a third political force in the world, aside from 'communism' versus 'capitalism'.... We will be ready to go into the streets at any time to change history as needed. We will be constantly living our lives as outlaws to the 'system,' constantly living off the fat cats and driving them insane.

News stories in the Yipster Times seldom resemble those in the Establishment press. One story carefully linked Nixon and his Watergate "plumbers" to the assassination of John F. Kennedy. Much of the newspaper's content instructs readers in ways to "rip off" the Establishment. A "Phone Phreaks Tactical Manual" describes ways of cheating the telephone company. Plans for "smoke-ins" and for sabotaging McDonald's (hamburger chain) are given, as well as ways in which one can "Eat the Rich," i.e., steal from major food companies. Tips are given on resisting FBI inquiries; creating long-lasting and memorable graffitti (scratching on blackboards leaves a durable message); and panhandling ("you're gonna have to be better than hot dog vendors, other panhandlers, and Jesus freaks. Just be the most outrageous act going and you will have easy sailing.").

News of Yippie activities, key personalities, and the "movement" in general is spread through the pages. YIP chapters--26 of them--in the U.S. and Canada are listed in v. 1, no. 8. Feedback from enthusiastic readers fills a few pages in each issue, in the form of letters to the editor.

One "anxious young radical" describes his plan to form a tribe of Yippies: "Can you imagine that--a group of 16-year-old children--posing as a youth Bible-study group and then smoking dope during a Methodist sermon--or bombarding military installations with skyrockets and firecrackers!" And this from an 18-year-old spreading revolution: "Don't get down on Trotsky. He was quite alright.... If Lev were here today, he'd be a Yippie." (SA)

A number of persons and organizations have incurred the dislike of YIP, and Yipster Times criticizes them or suggests ways to harass them.

Jerry Rubin and Abbie Hoffman.--Both were defendants in the "Chicago Seven" trial. One issue reprints an article by Paul Krassner (of The Realist) speculating that Rubin may have acted as a police agent provocateur. An article on Hoffman mentions his arrest on a charge of selling cocaine, and points out "that YIP has not had anything to do with these two clowns since 1968."

Telephones.--One issue prints a list of the telephone credit card numbers of such organizations as AT&T, ITT, Coca Cola, and the Jewish Defense League, and suggests that readers place long-distance calls and try to have them charged to these credit cards. The same issue suggests making crank calls to the home of William F. Buckley, Jr. (of the National Review).

Marijuana.--YIP is opposed to laws forbidding its use, feels sympathy for those busted for smoking or possessing it, and dislikes the narcs and other police agents who try to catch pot-users.

Guru Maharaj Ji.--An article reprinted from New York News Service manifests extreme dislike of this plump teenage religious leader. He and his followers are "fascist bastards" and "nauseating thieves and charlatans." They "are a uniformly self-righteous and infantile lot, the gurunoids, pissing in their pants in doglike ecstasy every time his image is invoked...." The guru himself is called a "smirking little wog," a "fat greasy son of a bitch," and a "self-annointed little bag of Holy Cowshit." ("Wog," an acronym for "wily Oriental gentleman," has long been a derogatory racial epithet, and its use in left-wing periodicals is unexpected.)

Richard M. Nixon.--This American politician is a perennial object of loathing. His name is sometimes spelt with a swastika substituted for the "x." His followers are "Nixonoids." He is sometimes referred to as "Adolf Nixswine" or "Adolf Nixscum." (Earl Butz is identified as "Nixscum's Secretary of Agriculture.") The cover of v. 1, no. 8, consists of a large cartoon drawing of Nixon and his former

Vice-President, Spiro T. Agnew, being assassinated by a modern-day Mister Hyde whose T-shirt bears the inscription, "STP--Stop the Pig--Serve the People." (TJS)

Addendum:

The March 1975 issue contains several articles on Vice-President Nelson Rockefeller. "Rocky Takes Over," a satirical fantasy, describes Rockefeller becoming president after ousting Gerald Ford. "Rocky and the CIA" denounces any investigation of the CIA by a Rockefeller-headed commission as a coverup and a fraud. A cartoon pictures Ford as a moronic ventriloquist's dummy, operated by Rockefeller. Other articles tell how to cheat the telephone company (the 1975 Credit Card Code is given) and how to go about "vandalizing your high school." "School Stoppers Textbook" tells how to sabotage your school by filling door locks with epoxy glue, pasting obscenities on pull-down maps or movie screens, freeing animals in biology class, stealing dishes and silver from the cafeteria, digging bomb craters on the front lawn (to protest the craters in Vietnam), creating food riots, starting fires in waste baskets, and mixing up or stealing file cards from the office. Why? Because "The public schools are slowly killing every kid in them, stifling their creativity and individuality.... [C]ompulsory education and grades destroy the natural curiousity [sic] so many children feel."

Skillful graphics and cartoons. Centerfold and front and back pages in bold colors. (JMS)

## Chapter 2

# MARXIST-SOCIALIST LEFT

> Let the ruling classes tremble at a Communist revolution. The proletarians have nothing to lose but their chains. They have a world to win. ---Class Struggle

> ... it is wrong to reject any tactic in principle. A tactic is correct or incorrect depending on whether or not it advances the cause of the proletariat.... ---Revolution

This section of the Left is notable for its factionalism and continual ideological wrangling. Such epithets as "revisionist," "degenerate lackey," "petty bourgeois," "opportunist," and "decadent" are hurled back and forth among the factions. Class Struggle (Trotskyist) lambastes the Spartacist League (also Trotskyist) and the Socialist Workers' Party; Revolution criticizes the "revisionist" Communist Party USA and the (Trotskyist) Socialist Workers' Party; and the Young Socialist (which says that it is the only socialist student monthly on Canadian campuses) has differences of opinion with Revolutionary Marxists and the Young Communist League.

Communism. --Communist periodicals, unlike those covered in our Radical Left and Underground chapters, have always been against the use of drugs. The Anti-Fascist Commentator sees the narcotics problem as a capitalist plot to drug the masses into submission. Some communist publications, such as American Student, criticize rock music, communes, and Eastern religions as diversions encouraged by capitalist bosses in order to keep American youths somnolent and reduce them to the status of "degenerate lackeys, incapable of carrying out a revolution." (Some Radical Left periodicals also criticize Eastern mysticism, making the youthful Guru Maharaj Ji a figure of fun.) The views of the Communist Party of Canada are put forward by Canadian Tribune and People's Canada Daily News.

Socialism. --Socialist publications reviewed here include Fulcrum, Labor Challenge, and Socialist Press Bulletin (all

Canadian); Third World (Fabian Society) and Socialist Education Bulletin (both London, U.K.); Socialist Viewpoint (Auckland, N.Z.); Internationales freies Wort (Austria); Socialist Revolution (theoretical); Young Socialist; Workers' Power (unions should be revolutionary); and the publications of the "Official" Irish Republican Movement (The United Irishman, Eolas, Rosc Catha, and The Irish People). The goal of these Irish periodicals is to unite workers and small farmers, overthrow British imperialist rule in Northern Ireland, and create an independent Irish Socialist Republic by unifying the island. On the other side, the anti-Catholic Comment (British & Irish Communist Organisation) supports the Protestant view and wants Northern Ireland to remain under British control.

Marxism.--Periodicals that refer to themselves as Marxist or Marxist-Leninist are the Anti-Fascist Commentator; Cinéaste, a journal concerned with revolutionary cinema (cinéma engagé); Utopia (culture and Marxism); Radical America ("independent Marxist"), which analyzes the history and current condition of the working class in Europe and America; the New York Young Worker (Young Worker Liberation League); and the Toronto Young Worker, affiliated with the Young Communist League. (Perhaps there is some connection between the last two.) Il Lavoratore (Canadian Party of Labour) describes itself as a "Revolutionary Communist Newspaper." Another Canadian communist periodical, Northern Neighbors ("The Magazine of Socialism in Action"), depicts the desirable features of life in the Soviet Union. Pakistan Forum, published in Canada, criticizes the Pakistani government; it appears to be Marxist, and frequently quotes Joseph Stalin.

Trotskyism.--Nine Trotskyist periodicals are Class Struggle; Labor Action and Old Mole (both Canadian); Workers' League Bulletin (N.Y.); and the Spartacist League's Revolutionary Communist Youth Newsletter, Revolutionary Marxist Caucus Newsletter, Workers' Vanguard, Young Spartacus, and Young Socialist (N.Y.).

Maoism.--The Maoist American Student criticizes intellectuals for being out of touch with the masses, and accuses this country's decadent educational system of preparing students for roles as "petty-bourgeois oppressors." Getting Together, produced by young Asian-Americans, is meant to jolt the conservatism of San Francisco's Chinese community; although it is not Maoist, it admires Chinese socialism. Three periodicals that embrace both Marxism-Leninism and Maoism are Revolution (aimed at the labor movement), The Call (October League), and Literature & Ideology. The last-named refers to itself as "the only literary journal in North America and Britain that consciously and consistently applies

Marxism-Leninism-Mao Tse-tung thought to carry on the class struggle." The Second Page, originally a feminist periodical, now attacks the women's movement.

Other continents.--The U.S.-China People's Friendship Association (six Midwest groups) may not be communist, but we have included its Newsletter in this chapter because it deals with Chinese socialism. Korea Focus (American-Korean Friendship and Information Center) wants the U.S. to stop meddling in that divided country. MERIP Reports is pro-Arab. (Other pro-Arab periodicals can be found in our Racial & Ethnic Pride chapter.)

Libertarianism and socialism.--We had heretofore considered these two philosophies to be mutually exclusive, but two groups represented in this chapter call themselves "libertarian socialists." Our Generation, which grew out of the anti-war movement of the early 1960s, is put out by a Canadian group. Solidarity Newsletter, which advocates the establishment of workers' councils but opposes Marxism-Leninism, is American. (Perhaps these groups are connected.)

Independent.--Two revolutionary periodicals not aligned with any faction are The Virginia Weekly and The New Voice ("Voice of the Working Class"). The former, produced by an independent group of workers, students, and unemployed persons from several Virginia communities, favors a revolution that will create a state in which the workers hold power. The New Voice also speaks of setting up a workers' state. The scholarly Journal of Contemporary Asia (Stockholm) hopes for social change on that continent.

Students for a Democratic Society.--The National Caucus of SDS Labor Committees, one of several warring SDS factions, published a theoretical journal called The Campaigner (now defunct). This faction thought of itself as revolutionary and socialist, so we have put its periodical in this chapter (rather than in the Radical Left chapter, where other SDS periodicals have gone).

Africa.--This chapter contains brief notices on two periodicals devoted to Africa: African Red Family (London) and Afrika Kämpft (Berlin). We examined them at the Africana library of Northwestern University (Evanston, Illinois), and hope to give them full-length reviews in our next volume. (Other periodicals on Africa--especially on "national liberation movements"--can be found in our Civil Rights chapter.)

--Janet Spahn

AFRICAN RED FAMILY

Remi K. & Ben Mohan, Eds.
Hamibantu Publications
c/o 107 Pevensey Rd.
London E7 OAH, U.K.
$2

Started: Oct. 1972
Format: 64-88 pages (5 1/2" x 8 1/2")
Issues examined: v. 1, no. 1 (Oct. /Dec. 1972) & nos. 3/4

A statement in the pilot issue of this Marxist-Leninist periodical explained that it is "a self-supporting and wholly African journal."

Feedback:
"The journal is primarily directed to the African intellectuals, at home and abroad. It welcomes non-Marxist but objective literary contributions, criticism, and suggestions."

AFRIKA KÄMPFT: Bulletin des Solidaritätskomitees zur Unterstützung der Völker Afrikas im Kampf gegen Rassismus, Kolonialismus, Neokolonialismus, und Imperialismus

Afrika Komitee, c/o
Ernest A. Kraft
Handjerystr. 24
1 Berlin 41, Federal Republic of Germany

Bi-monthly; 1 DM. an issue
Format: 32 pages (8 1/4" x 11 3/4")
Issues examined: June 1972-Dec. 1973

As its sub-title explains, this German-language periodical is the organ of a group that supports the African people in their struggle against racism, colonialism, and imperialism.

AMERICAN STUDENT

American Student Movement (Anti-Imperialist)
Box 6004
Cleveland, Ohio 44101

10¢ an issue
Format: 8-page tabloid
Issue examined: Feb. 1970 (No. 2)

The editors of this Maoist publication criticize "intellectuals" for tending to be out of touch with the masses and their needs. They consider the U.S. educational system to be decadent: its universities prepare students for roles as petty-bourgeois oppressors. Students should be allied with workers, and a strong pro-communist student movement should be built up. Unfortunately, American youth, although potentially a strong ally of the working class, is kept in a somnolent state by the bosses: imperialists and profiteers encourage young people to channel their energy and frustration into such diversions as rock music, communes, and eastern religions. They are thus reduced to the condition of degenerate lackeys, incapable of carrying out a revolution. (It is interesting to note that right-wing groups see rock music as a left-wing plot to corrupt our youth. See above, pp. 814, 826, 827). Modern art and music are based on sensation: they tickle the nerve-endings, but offer no understanding. Here are some of the many things the American Student despises:

Trotskyists: opportunists.

Agnew, Spiro T.: fascist.

Hayakawa, S. I.: fascist.

Maharishi Mahesh Yogi: mystical faker; degenerate fascist; feudalist; racist.

New Left leaders: hacks, opportunists. (Ever since the Free Speech Movement, the University of California at Berkeley has been a center of political muck and misleadership.)

Anarchism and pacifism: too detached from reality and struggle; consequently, pro-fascist (i.e., serving the exploiting class).

Imperialism: "Death to U.S. Imperialism and Soviet Social Imperialism!"

Haile Selassie: the Ethiopian emperor is a fascist dictator, whose thugs murder student activists. U.S. reactionaries harass Ethiopian students attending American universities.

Other opinions expressed in the sample issue:

1. In Quebec, what is needed is not a separate, French-only Quebec, but a united front of all workers (English and French), with other minorities and progressive petty bourgeoises, to drive out foreign (especially U.S.) influence, and extirpate fascism. McGill University (Montreal) is a center of U.S. imperialism and Anglo-Canadian colonialism in Canada. American Student naturally opposes the widespread U.S. ownership of Canadian industry.
2. A revolutionary party, if organized around a single issue, will eventually fall apart. If it is to last, its actions should instead be based upon a comprehensive analysis of society.
3. There is no "overpopulation" on this planet. If the

present unsatisfactory social order is altered by revolution, the problems now attributed to "overpopulation" will vanish. (TJS)

ANTI-FASCIST COMMENTATOR: A Marxist Analysis of Issues and Events

Linda Bergen, Ed.
Box 57, Baychester Station
Bronx, N.Y. 10469
Bi-monthly; $2
Started: March 1973
Circulation: 1,000

Format: 4-6 pages (offset)
Issues examined: March, May, July, Sept./Oct. 1973
Back issues available from publisher

In the view of the Commentator's editors, "In the last few years, things have begun to take a very ominous turn in the U.S., and most especially since the re-election of Nixon." As the U.S. position has weakened abroad, "the U.S. has become less and less able to afford a liberal policy at home." Nixon

> has launched an all-out attack on the people.... The hardest hit, of course, are the black people and others on the 'bottom' .... Nixon is mounting a whole campaign of racist demagogy making black people the scapegoat for the ills of this society, aimed at inflating the hatred of many whites toward blacks and deflecting this hatred from its proper target--Nixon and the big monopolies.... The leadership of the movement against the fascist danger ... can only be accomplished by Marxists actively educating and organizing the working people.... [In the original, "black" was always capitalized, but "white" never was.]

These are the topics developed in other issues of the Commentator. Attempts to promote racial conflict are seen in the plots of television and movie dramas. Nixon is accused of building up his defense establishment and desiring fascism so that he can wage an imperialist war. The drug problem is also laid at his door, with some additional blame for Nelson Rockefeller and others. ("We must recognize that it is a relatively small group of monopoly businesses and their representatives in government, such as Nixon, who are to blame for this drug epidemic.") Their purpose is to drug the masses into submission and to use addicts, especially

Negroes and Latins, as scapegoats for all of society's problems.

Liberals are criticized for their selfishness and lack of dedication. Although they attack Nixon for Watergate and the erosion of civil liberties, they do not go far enough and their motives are impure: "They regard Nixon and the forces behind him as a threat to peaceful and democratic capitalism. Their radical pretensions go no further than a desire to return to 'normalcy' and 'business as usual'." "The truth is that the people need democracy even more than the liberals. ... it is the people who come under the main attack.... They will have to fight the big banks and corporations that are exploiting and oppressing them. They must also fight against the capitalist system...."

Whatever subjects the Anti-Fascist Commentator deals with (POWs in Vietnam, the war in Cambodia, cuts in the budget for social services) it views in the light of the struggle of working-class people against Nixon, monopoly capitalists, and misguided liberals who are deliberately pitting the races against one another in order to distract attention from their real policy of imperialist aggression and protection of the "criminal activities of the large monopoly businesses."

(BK)

THE BAY AREA WORKER

Box 7154
Oakland, Calif. 94601
Monthly; $2.50
Started: 1972
Circulation: 2,000

Format: 20-page tabloid
Issues examined: Dec. 1974; Feb. & May 1975
Back issues available from publisher

The paper consists of a 14-page English-language section and a six-page Spanish-language one ("Obrero del Area de la Bahia"). A statement on the second page of each issue sets forth the periodical's aims:

> The Bay Area Worker reports the issues and struggles of our class: the working class. We stand solidly with all working people against the serious attacks on our livelihoods by the employing class and their lying politicians. And we are fighting back. Our class is the force that can lead all the people to defeat these monopolists.
>
> Our staff, men and women of all races, live in the Bay Area. We are workers, employed and unemployed, welfare people and students. Some of us

> belong to the Revolutionary Union, a national communist organization.
>
> We feel that the struggles of Black, Chicano, Asian, Puerto Rican, Native American and other peoples and their fight against discrimination is crucial to all workers. We also support the people of Indochina and all oppressed nations fighting for independence. The spirit and unity of these struggles are a model for all.

The paper was formed in 1972 as the result of a merger of Salt of the Earth (San Jose), Wildcat (San Francisco), and People Get Ready (East Bay). Some of the concerns expressed in the sample issues are listed below.

Middle East. The paper supports Palestinian "resistance" to Israel. Moshe Dayan, former Israeli minister of defense, is an "enemy of the people."

Imperialism throughout the world is attacked. Examples: U.S. imperialism; British imperialism (in Northern Ireland); Portuguese colonialism. There is support for liberation struggles everywhere (e.g., Eritrea) and respect for the role of women in such struggles.

Labor. There are many reports on abused working people; labor struggles; unfair bosses. May Day celebrations are reported on sympathetically.

Population control is opposed: the problem is capitalism, not overpopulation.

Police brutality is attacked. There is sympathy for a Vietnam veteran framed by "the courts and cops, and the capitalist class they're flunkies for." (TJS)

THE CALL/EL CLARIN: Political Newspaper of the October League

M. Klonsky, Ed.
Box 2278
Bell Gardens, Calif. 90201
Monthly; $5 (institutions $15)
Started: Oct. 1972

Circulation: 15,000
Format: 24-page tabloid (offset)
Issues examined: June, Nov., Dec. 1973

Although The Call serves

> mainly as a newspaper directed at the working class, it is also designed to carry the news and editorials that will help forge a broad united front against imperialism, [a front] made up not only of workers but

> of all those who oppose the U.S. government's policies of discrimination, foreign aggression, and fascist repression. The paper includes a Spanish-language supplement.

The October League and the Georgia Communist League united in May 1972 to build a "new Communist Party in the U.S." and "a united, fighting working class-movement ... with a final goal of ridding this world forever of capitalism and with it exploitation and racism."

This Marxist-Leninist-Maoist tabloid is sharply anti-Russian, and such articles as "Australian Communist Leader Assails Soviet Imperialism" and "Superpowers Impose Mid-East Settlement" condemn Soviet imperialism and the "revisionism" evident in the USSR's military and economic control of eastern Europe, and in its pro-Zionist role in the Middle East (attempting to control Egypt politically, imposing [together with the U.S.] an unacceptable cease-fire favoring Israel, and supplying manpower to Israel by allowing Russian Jews to emigrate).

An editorial in the December issue denounces the Communist Party USA which

> has consistently put forth the lie that socialism can come to the U.S. through the election of 'good leaders' and 'within the framework of the constitution'.... The CPUSA has launched a vicious campaign of slander at the entire anti-imperialist movement and especially at the forces of Marxism-Leninism-Mao Tse-tung thought, who stand as the main alternative to their corrupt, revisionist leadership. A day does not pass, when these 'peaceful' revolutionaries do not openly attack this movement as well as the People's Republic of China, which stands at the center of the world revolutionary movement today.

It also attacks the newly-formed Communist League, "an isolated group of proven splitters and ultra 'leftists' who have attacked everything healthy and developing within the revolutionary movement":

> Within the ranks of the anti-revisionist forces, there are 'left' opportunists who are trying to provide a cover for the revisionists.... From the 'left' they attack Marxism-Leninism-Mao Tse-tung thought and all that it stands for.... [T]hese super-revolutionaries are doing everything possible to isolate the movement and spread disunity and splits.

> Their forces are exemplified by the Communist League ... [which] has based its call for a new party on its 'new' theories of Marxism, which go against all fundamental principles of scientific socialism and therefore are bound to fail.

Articles about China are friendly and admiring and the December issue reprints a commemorative speech by Mao Tse-tung on the Canadian doctor, Norman Bethune, who practiced medicine in China.

News articles deal with labor ("[President Leonard] Woodcock Leads U[nited] A[uto] W[orkers] Sell-out," "Harlan County Miners Fight for Union Rights," and "Los Angeles Rally Kicks-Off Grape Boycott"), or expose discrimination ("Caucus Protests Racist UAW Firing," "Valley College Students Fight Discrimination," and "Boston Papers Fan Racist Hysteria") and police brutality toward minority groups ("Latino Community Fights Police Attacks," and "Cops Kill 10-Year-Old [black child], People Demand Justice in N. Y."--"Police murders and brutality in the black community are part of a systematic program by the police to terrorize black people. This program is backed up by the laws, the government officials, and the judges. Police terrorism is what Nixon had in mind when he speaks of 'law and order'.").

The Call supports women's rights and encourages women to enter the labor market because "more women in production will bring militancy and a higher level of unity to the working class struggle."

Prison conditions are condemned in such articles as "Angola [a prison in Louisiana] Four Expose Prison Conditions" and "Story of Walpole Prison; NPRA Leads Fight for Prisoners' Rights." "Martin Sostre Jailed--Black Activist Threatened with Medical Experiments" and "Psychological Warfare Used on Women Prisoners" show concern over the use of psychiatry and psychosurgery in controlling what authorities consider to be undesirable behavior.

Other articles and editorials condemn Zionism, the Greek military regime, the overthrow (encouraged by the U.S.) of Dr. Salvador Allende's elected Marxist government in Chile, and the Indo-China war, and urge the impeachment of Nixon.

Regular features include three sections of short news items: "On the Line ('A summary of workers' struggles around the country')"; "Taking Up the Call," which proclaims that "Countries want independence, Nations want liberation, People want revolution" and contains such world news as "Massive Bangkok Demonstrations" and "Liberation Forces Win Victories in New Indo-China Fighting"; and "People in Struggle," which covers such items as "Second Battle of Wounded Knee Ends" (on the American Indian movement) and "Political Prisoners Pack Saigon Jails."

The Call also contained a few long articles ("Palestine: A Nation Fights for Its Freedom" [a history of the Arab struggle against Zionism] and "Decline of U.S. Imperialism" [in several parts]); occasional movie reviews; and interviews with such figures as Cesar Chavez, head of the United Farm Workers. Illustrated with photographs. (JMS)

Reviewer's opinion:

Professionally-handled, this tabloid appears to have funds behind it.

Feedback:

The editor thanked us and added that the publication is not "anti-Russian" as was said in the second paragraph of the review, but "is sharply against the present Soviet leadership and Soviet revisionism of Marxism."

## THE CAMPAIGNER

Bi-monthly; $4 for 12 issues
Started: Feb. 1968
Circulation: 2,000
Format: 72-84 pages (5 1/2" x 8 1/2", offset)
Issues examined: June, Sept./Oct. 1969; Jan./Feb. 1970
Indexing: Alternative Press Index

The Campaigner, published by the National Caucus of SDS Labor Committees, provides a forum for political and philosophical analysis of the tactics and ideology of the group. As revolutionary socialists, members of the group are devotedly anti-capitalist, but dispute and castigate the ideology and tactics of other SDS factions and organizations of the Left, such as liberals, the Communist party, the Socialist Workers' Party, black revolutionists, anarchists, and other New Left groups.

Each issue contains from 3 to 5 editorials and articles. Editorials are written and voted upon by committees in several geographic areas in the U.S. and represent the views of the group. Signed articles represent only the views of their authors, and generally present ideological concepts or describe social conditions in the U.S. and other countries.

In 1974, mail addressed to The Campaigner at Box 49, Washington Bridge Station, N.Y., N.Y. 10033, was forwarded to Box 295, Cathedral Station, N.Y., N.Y. 10025; there it was marked "Addressee unknown" and "Not box holder at Cathedral Station," and returned to us. (KL)

## CANADIAN TRIBUNE

924 King St. West
Toronto 150, Ont., Canada
Weekly; $5
Format: 12-page tabloid (offset)
Issue examined: 14 Mar. 1973

Communist Party of Canada newspaper, although it doesn't say so explicitly. Carries news and commentary and official statements of the party.

## CINÉASTE

Quarterly; $3
Format: 36-52 pages (offset)
Issues examined: Summer & Fall 1970; Spring 1971; Winter 1971/72
Indexing: Alternative Press Index

*Cinéaste* is a film journal committed to Marxist politics and *cinéma engagé*. Its articles, interviews, and film and book reviews all reflect this political interest, combining ideology and esthetics.

In the issues examined, the predominant theme of *Cinéaste* is expressed in a series of five articles by Yves de Laurot of the film group Cinéma Engagé. In this series de Laurot combines details about the methods and techniques of his filmmakers with an explanation of

> ... why it is inevitable that engaged cinema--and only engaged cinema--is genuinely revolutionary, both in subject and style, in content and form.
>
> We stress the term *genuinely revolutionary* to distinguish it from the films today, abundantly in supply, that have only revolutionary *pretensions*. We must distinguish between these films, which are *on* or *about* revolution--historical reconstructions, political newsreels, radical underground movies, films that generally make claims to being socially committed--and films that *are* revolution. In making this distinction, we will at the same time recall some of the principles on which engaged cinema is based.

The crucial element of engaged cinema, then, is that "revolutionary cinema films the invisible. Unlike impotent documentaries, newsreels or cinéma vérité, revolutionary cinema does not film what has happened; IT FILMS SO THAT IT MAY HAPPEN! It doesn't follow reality, it forges reality."

In other articles, the problems of making changes in and through film schools are analyzed in "The Film School and Political Action," and cultural aspects of film are discussed in "Film and Cultural Pluralism" and "The Culture Industry." In every issue are interviews with European, Third World, and North American revolutionary filmmakers, such as Jean-Louis Bertucelli (director of "Ramparts of Clay") and Miguel Littin (on film in Allende's Chile). Film and book reviews are also an important part of the journal.

In 1974, mail addressed to Gary Crowdus, Editor, 144 Bleecker St., N.Y., N.Y. 10012 was returned, marked "Moved, not forwardable." (MM)

CLARIDAD: El Periódico de la Independencia

Ramón Arbona, Ed.
30 E. 20th St.
N.Y., N.Y. 10003
Originally bi-weekly, said to be daily now
Format: issue of 25 Nov. 1973 distributed from N.Y. is a 52-page tabloid; Puerto Rican edition of 13 Mar. 1973 is a 16-page tabloid; both offset
Issues examined: see "Format"

Claridad (sponsored by the Socialist Party of Puerto Rico) supports independence and criticizes the present Puerto Rican government and the U.S. The Spanish-language issue of March carried this address: Toscania 1153, Urbanización Villa Capri, Rio Piedras, Puerto Rico. The 25 November issue had 6 pages in English which carried news--of labor struggles, tenant demonstrations, and student protests--and political commentary of interest to the Puerto Rican community in New York. The 46-page Spanish section, divided into several supplements, was concerned with Puerto Rico and bore the Rio Piedras address.

CLASS STRUGGLE

Class Struggle League
Box F
Park Forest, Ill. 60466
Monthly; $1
Started: Jan. 1973
Format: 16-page tabloid
Issues examined: Sept.-Nov. 1973
Back issues available from publisher

In a box on the back page of each issue, Class Struggle sums up its philosophy:

> The Communists disdain to conceal their views and aims. They openly declare that their ends can be attained only by the forcible overthrow of all existing social conditions. Let the ruling classes tremble at a Communist revolution. The proletarians have nothing to lose but their chains. They have a world to win. WORKING MEN OF ALL COUNTRIES UNITE.

Specifically, the Class Struggle League espouses a Trotskyist philosophy:

> ... the traditional Trotskyist approach ... is the view of approaching a working class not yet ready to adopt a program calling for the dictatorship of the proletariat and the total expropriation of the capitalist class with a program that will lead them to conclude that only the total expropriation of the capitalist class will answer their needs.... The Class Struggle League is fighting for such a party....

There is much factionalism among Communist groups, and in several articles Class Struggle accuses the Spartacist League (another Trotskyite group) of "absolute and utter hypocrisy," and concludes that "Such falseness and tinselhood as practiced by the SL serve only sectarian and bureaucratic needs, not the needs of the working class." In an exchange of letters between the two groups (signed "Comradely" and "Fraternally") the Spartacist League accuses the CSL of "hypocrisy" and of having an "opportunist conception." The Socialist Workers' Party also comes in for its share of criticism as a "pitiful pretender to Trotskyism."

Each month the publication educates its readers in revolutionary theory by presenting a section ("The Revolutionary Heritage") which reprints writings of Trotsky, Engels, and other revolutionary leaders.

The September 1973 issue gives the League's "Revolutionary Program for Unions":

> Jobs for All--A Sliding Scale of Wages and Hours
> Organize the Unorganized and the Unemployed
> Nationalize Industry Under Workers' Control
> Independence of the Trade Unions from the State
> Trade Union Democracy

Against Imperialist War--For International Working Class Solidarity
Against All Forms of Racial, National, and Sexual Oppression--Equal Opportunities for All, Equal Pay for Equal Work
For a Labor Party to Organize the Struggles of the Proletariat
For a Worker's Republic

Because of its interest in the working man, Class Struggle often publishes articles dealing with unions and strikes. The October 1973 issue carries an article on a strike against Sears, Roebuck & Co., and another on a walkout of rubber workers at Goodrich plants. The publication criticizes the large unions, and the editors accuse Leonard Woodcock of the United Auto Workers of "misleadership." In the view of Class Struggle, unions which do not follow the CSL program are doomed to failure; union bosses' interests are not the same as the workers' and the latter must unite to struggle for their own needs. Among the points of CSL's program are a thirty-hour work week at forty hours' pay and no cooperation with government wage boards.

The newspaper also publishes articles dealing with class struggle throughout the world. The editors have expressed views on Canada's New Democratic Party, the Middle East conflict, and the late Dr. Salvador Allende's Chilean government whose failure they interpret thus:

> Allende's refusal to arm the workers, his reliance on 'left' elements in the army, and his refusal to smash the middle class sabotage of the economy all contributed to the debacle. When his usefulness was at an end, when he was losing his ability to control the workers, he was removed.
>
> What was needed in Chile, what was needed in Spain in 1936, in France in 1934 and 1968, and what will be needed here, is a revolutionary Trotskyist party which will smash the capitalist state and all its military apparatus as the fundamental prerequisite to the building of socialism.

Class Struggle criticizes the Soviet Union and claims it is ruled by "a parasitical class." A two-part article deals with the question of whether the Soviet Union is a capitalist state or a workers' state and determines that it is in a state of transition. "What is required is the revolutionary overthrow of the Stalinist bureaucracy and not the abolition of some mythical monster called 'state capitalism'."

Everything is viewed in terms of class struggle, and all solutions to problems are linked with that ideology. For example, the problems of American education are laid at the doorstep of capitalism:

> What is supposed to be the product of the city teacher's labor--a person educated to 'a twelfth grade level'--is needed in large but limited numbers in capitalist society.... It is simply not good business sense to train people beyond the level at which they can produce profits for the bosses.

The solution is for teachers to unite with workers in the construction of a classless society.

The energy crisis will also be eliminated in the workers' state advocated by Class Struggle:

> The question of how gas is to be distributed in a workers' state is partly academic, though, because we will immediately proceed to develop a mode of transportation utilizing electric or steam power, whichever proves to be most [sc. more] feasible. This elementary and rational course of action is, of course, almost impossible under capitalism, where all scientific research and production is conditioned upon its private profitability to only a few powerful tycoons.

In a rare discussion of domestic politics, Class Struggle suggests that we not only impeach Nixon, but overthrow "the entire oppressive system of capitalism with a workers' revolution." (BK)

## COMMENT

John Minahane, Ed.
British & Irish Communist Organisation
26 Essex Quay
Dublin 8, Ireland
Fortnightly; $2.35

Started: 10 Aug. 1969
Circulation: 5,000
Format: 6 pages (9" x 14", offset)
Issues examined: v. 2, nos. 10, 13 (Dec. 1973), 14 (Jan. 1974)

Comment is "for the working class, the class that holds the future in its hands." The editor writes that

> The magazine is produced by the Dublin branch of the British & Irish Communist Organisation and therefore the primary editorial policy is to reflect the thinking of the organisation, in a propagandist form, particularly on current affairs in the Irish Republic. Its most distinctive feature is that (unlike all other left-wing papers in Ireland) it condemns the current military and propaganda campaign for a United Ireland, as being an undemocratic negation of the expressed wishes of the Ulster Protestant community for continued union with Britain. Furthermore, it advocates that Irish workers should seek a controlling voice in the economy, on a national level and on a plant level, and maintains that this 'workers' control' should be seen as a transitional step towards socialism.

Unlike the Official IRA (Irish Republican Army--Sinn Fein Party) and the Provisional IRA, Comment devotes much space to attacking the reactionary, conservative, and undemocratic influence of the Catholic Church, and its positions on abortion, divorce, welfare, homosexuality, censorship, and education. The church is "a cancer on Irish democracy" and "Only the Irish working class can destroy the social power of the clergy by the effective use of its mass strength, and thus bring Ireland really and truly into the 20th century." Southern Ireland is described as "a society with an undeveloped public opinion, a powerful Catholic church with a reactionary influence on education and social legislation, a tradition of aggressive Republicanism [that wants Northern Ireland to join the Republic of Ireland] which continually attracts dissatisfied minds, and little tradition of social consciousness--let alone socialism."

Issue #10 was especially called to our attention by the editor because it is devoted to criticism of the Labour Party, one of the major parties and a political force of great importance to Irish socialists. Comment condemns the Labour Party for being "scared of class struggle. Its leaders do not even claim it to be a working class party"; for its "dishonest and cowardly" attitude towards the power of the Catholic Church; and for betraying the working classes by not living up to election promises (specifically, for not implementing a new housing policy, for not legalizing divorce, and for not nationalizing banks and building societies).

Comment also condemns both the Provisional IRA (especially because of its violent tactics) and the Official IRA (Sinn Fein Party) for their goal of a united Ireland, their criticism of the British and their failure to criticize the

Catholic Church; and describes the IRA as being "an enemy of democracy." The publication also criticizes Sinn Fein for not having a clear socialist position and welcomes the Sunningdale Agreement as "another nail in the coffin of anti-partitionism which has been the cause of division and consequent political ineffectiveness in the Irish working class for a century." Irish Republicanism is dead and "The setting up of a power-sharing government composed of Unionists and SDLP [Social-Democratic and Labour Party] has dealt the fatal blow to the basic foundations of Catholic Nationalism."

The articles in Comment are short, and discuss current affairs. (JMS)

Reviewer's opinion:

Articles in Comment are relatively free of the jargon found in some communist periodicals.

Feedback:

"Your draft review of our magazine Comment is on the whole accurate." The editor goes on to add some clarifying information concerning the second to the last paragraph beginning "Comment also condemns the Provisional IRA (especially for its violent tactics)..." "It would be truer to say: (especially because of the anti-civilian nature of its bombing campaign). The tactics of the Official IRA, in its active periods, have been equally violent, and we are not pacifists, though in this instance we would condemn any use of violence because of the undemocratic nature of the objective for which violence is used. Also, we would not condemn anybody just for 'criticism of the British'; the Officials and Provisionals have a hostility to Britain which is purely nationalist, always narrow and bigoted, and sometimes racialist. This we consistently oppose....

"As regards our estimation of the Sunningdale Agreement, in December 1973, we (the British & Irish Communist Organisation) underestimated the tenacity of the anti-partitionists. The SDLP continued to manoevre in the old lines within the Executive, attempting to use the Council of Ireland provision of the Agreement as a stepping stone to a United Ireland, and as a result the Executive was brought down by the general strike of the Protestant workers in May 1974, which we supported. All that has happened since, however, goes to confirm our long-term conclusion, that the attempt to gain a United Ireland by force or diplomatic wile is doomed to failure. There are two nations in Ireland; and the Ulster Protestant nation, which has fought for 100 years to avoid being incorporated into an all-Ireland Republic, dominated by the

Catholic Church, is today more determined and effective than ever, in resisting Republican aggression.

"It should be pointed out that an important function of Comment is to publicize the B&ICO's theoretical journals, The Irish Communist and The Communist and pamphlets. Since our formation in 1965, we have held that the main task facing communists at this period is to bring some theoretical clarity into the communist movement. This has become necessary because of the revisionist takeover in the Soviet Union after the death of Stalin, and the incompetence, muddleheadedness, and latterly, outright nationalism, of the Communist Party of China. To this end, we have published numerous pamphlets and articles on the economics of the new system in Russia and Eastern Europe, the Stalin era, the European Economic Community, the prospects of transition to socialism in Britain, etc. A full literature list may be obtained from the Secretary, British and Irish Communist Organisation."

EOLAS: International Newsletter of the Irish Republican Movement

30 Gardiner Place
Dublin 1, Ireland
Monthly; $5
Circulation: 2,000

Format: 12 pages (7" x 10")
Issues examined: Jan.-June 1974

Eolas "is suitable for anyone who wishes to know more about the situation in Ireland." (For an explanation of the movement's goals and socialist political philosophy see reviews of its other periodicals in this chapter: United Irishman, Rosc Catha, and The Irish People.) The content arrangement varies but in general the publication carries short news articles, longer news essays, and sometimes long discussions or analyses on such topics as "The Imperialist Situation in Europe." The entire March 1974 issue is devoted to "British Government Violations of Human Rights in N. Ireland: A Study of an Attempted Military Solution to a Political Problem."

In the April 1974 issue, "Will Ireland's Oil Belong to the People of Ireland or Will the Irish People Be Paupers in Oil Rich Ireland!" expresses the fear that

> As the experts bring in confirmation of the tremendous oil deposits near the Continental Shelf, get-rich-quick speculators tumble over each other in their eagerness to grab the booty.... Applicant companies

> are either blatantly foreign multi-nationals or the same but masquerading under a coy veneer of Irish surnames.

Such articles as "Bombing Their Way to Oblivion" and "IRA Assails Provisional Aims" condemn the provisional wing of the IRA for its violence. According to Tomas McGiolla, president of Sinn Fein Party (Official IRA),

> It has destroyed every progressive political move, it has divided and confused workers, it has released uncontrollable forces of sectarian hatred and above all it has led to the death and maiming of innocent civilians.

An editorial complains that Ireland is under foreign domination--politically, economically and culturally. "The entire economic sub-structure has been thoroughly penetrated by Anglo-American Imperialism and multi-national corporations." In Northern Ireland, British control is even more evident: "18,000 troops on the streets, daily arrests, and constant harassment of the people." The north is also rent by religious sectarian fighting deliberately fostered by Britain to keep the Unionist Party (union with Britain) in power. Present British policy is to keep the working classes divided and to unite the middle classes in the new Assembly at Stormont. The editorial goes on to say that the aims of the Republican movement are to unite the Protestant and Catholic working classes, to mount a campaign against repression through such organizations as the Northern Ireland Civil Rights Association, and to continue the rent and rate [tax] strikes.

Other articles contained in the sample issues were: "Villagers Angry at Army Raid"; "The Problems of Northern Workers"; "British Tortured Belfast Boys of 13, Claims Psychologist"; "Irish Priests Call on Government to Accept Refugees From Chile"; "At the End of One Year Inside Long Kesh" (concentration camp); and "Sinn Fein Picket at Cork Cottage to Prevent Couple's Eviction."

Eolas also describes conferences, congresses, and programs that the movement participates in. Some illustrations and photographs. (JMS)

Feedback:

"We find it suitable for your suggested directory."

## FULCRUM

Socialist Party of Canada
Box 4280, Station A
Victoria, B. C., Canada
V8X 3X8
Quarterly; $2 for 12 issues

Started: 1968
Format: 12-16 pages (offset)
Issues examined: Mar./Apr. 1972 and v. 6, no. 4 (1973)
Back issues available from publisher

In keeping with its goal of spreading the "Marxian understanding of capitalism among the working class, on the Marxian premise that a majority of the class must be conscious of its existence as a separate class in society with interests opposed to those of the other class," the Socialist Party of Canada publishes and distributes a great amount of information, in the form of leaflets and reprints from other countries' Socialist journals, as well as Fulcrum. The SPC is allied with companion parties from Great Britain, the United States, Austria, Australia, Ireland, and New Zealand, which also publish regular journals.

Fulcrum's main thrust is clarifying Socialist principles. One issue contains a report on recent evidence that many diseases can be blamed on the emotional stresses engendered by the capitalist system, an analysis of The German Ideology by Marx and Engels, a comment on the necessity of lying in politics, another comment on how deception and dishonesty are practiced in social affairs, and a brief critique of the idea of currency reform. Another issue is almost completely devoted to a clarification of the differences between the SPC and the Socialist Labor Party of Canada: the former is characterized as revolutionary, the latter as reformist. The "Declaration of Principles," printed on the back of every piece of literature published by the Companion Parties of Socialism, elaborates on their objective ("The establishment of a system of society based upon the common ownership and democratic control of the means and instruments for producing and distributing wealth by and in the interest of society as a whole") and lists eight basic principles which workers are called upon to support so that an end "may be brought to the system which deprives them of the fruits of their labor, and ... poverty may give place to comfort, privilege to equality, and slavery to freedom." (CP)

(See our review of Socialist Viewpoint for an enumeration of these "Principles." Other "Companion" socialist publications reviewed in this and previous volumes are Socialist Review, The Socialist Standard, and The Western Socialist.)

Feedback:

We are not a leftist organization. We are Marxist. [The SPC 'is the only political organization in this country whose objective harmonizes with that of Marx, that is the ending of the capital vs. wage-labor relationship, world wide.'] Leftists support capitalism (under all sorts of Socialistic sounding names), that is, they support the continued existence of the wage-labor capital relationship (or class ownership of the means of life, privately or through the state, or a mixture of the two). The left-right spectrum, from extreme to extreme, has very little to distinguish each organization from each other, once one has waded through the confusing terminology each uses.

The space you have allocated for your review of Fulcrum is not large enough for an adequate description of our ideas, but the review is accurate aside from the changing of one word.... [That word has been changed.]

## GETTING TOGETHER

| | |
|---|---|
| Gordon Chang, Ed. | Format: 16-page tabloid (offset) |
| 850 Kearny St. | Issues examined: 5 & 18 Oct., 2 Nov. 1973 |
| San Francisco, Calif. 94126 | Indexing: Alternative Press Index |
| Semi-monthly; $3.50 ($5 to institutions) | |
| Started: Jan. or May 1970 | |
| Circulation: 1,500 | |

Published in San Francisco, Getting Together is intended for that city's Chinese community. It is not, however, a typical local newspaper full of engagement pictures, news of social events, and real estate ads. Stressing anti-imperialism and socialism, it deals with the problems of Chinese in San Francisco and with events of interest in China, the Philippines, and other Third World nations.

Front-page headlines in the sample issues deal with Asian-Americans fighting a discrimination case against California Blue Shield; Chinese seamstresses fired for protesting unfair treatment by their employer; and the celebration of the anniversary of the founding of the People's Republic of China (1 October 1949). The paper criticizes conservative elements in the Chinese community which attempted to limit the celebration (and which support the Nationalist regime on Taiwan).

Much favorable publicity is given to the quality of life

in China today. An article describing workers' participation in the management of a Chinese steel mill states that the mill's output has increased greatly under this system. A member of a delegation of California teachers visiting China comments on the vast improvements she noted in education and living standards.

Local events of interest to a Marxist, revolutionary point of view are covered thoroughly. "San Francisco's Chinatown, as the largest in North America, is one of the last bastions of support for Chiang's fading regime." Another article points out hardships suffered by illegal Chinese immigrants under a new policy of the U.S. Immigration and Naturalization Service. On the same page a Chinese politician is called "nothing but a yellow face moved around from committee to committee to try to make it seem the city is doing something for the Chinese."

On the international scene, Getting Together accuses the Thieu regime in South Vietnam of holding "over 200,000 political prisoners.... Once inside a Saigon jail, the prisoner is subjected to brutal and inhuman treatment." The United States, which gives financial aid to South Vietnam, is accused of thereby supporting such activities. "U.S. corporations are the ones who are constructing the new prisons equipped with tiger cages [a torture device]."

Getting Together's support for the Arab position in the Middle East is evidenced by such statements as: "the conflict in the Middle East is completely the result of imperialist policies of aggression. From its very beginning Zionism has conducted crimes against the Palestinian people." It supports the People's Republic of China: "We must also convince the U.S. government that the present government of China is the sole legitimate government of China and that the U.S. should not hinder normalization by meddling in Taiwan which is an internal affair of China."

To underscore the paper's involvement in the affairs of the Chinese community, about half of it is written in Chinese.

(BK)

Feedback:

Editor expressed no disapproval.

## INTERNATIONALES FREIES WORT

| | |
|---|---|
| Bund Demokratischer Sozialisten | Quarterly; S 20 |
| Wienerbergstr. 16 | Format: 4-page tabloid |
| Vienna 12, Austria | Issue examined: Dec. 1972 |

The BDS is one of a group of associated socialist parties. Other members of the group whose periodicals are reviewed in this chapter:

Socialist Party of Canada: Fulcrum.
Socialist Party of Great Britain: Socialist Education Bulletin and Socialist Standard.
Socialist Group of Jamaica: Socialist Review.
Socialist Party of New Zealand: Socialist Viewpoint.

For a statement of the principles of the BDS and its fellow-parties, see our review of Socialist Viewpoint.

In the sample issue, the socialist tendency to perceive conflict in terms of class struggle is exemplified in an article on Northern Ireland. It makes these points: truly religious differences are not at the bottom of the civil strife; no one is really fighting about Papal Infallibility or veneration of the Blessed Virgin. The dominant Protestant class is merely using religion to rally lower-class Protestants against the Catholic minority, thus keeping the working class split.

Book reviews. Letters to the editor. (TJS)

THE IRISH COMMUNIST: A Theoretical Journal of the British and Irish Communist Organisation

Brendan Clifford, Ed.
10 Athol St.
Belfast, Northern Ireland
BT124GX
Monthly; £2.00 (airmail)
Started: 1965
Circulation: 1,000

Format: 25 pages (8" x 10", offset, stapled)
Issues examined: Dec. 1973; Jan. & Feb. 1974
Back issues available from publisher

Marxist-Leninist. Supports "the development of Worker's Control in industry at plant level and at national level ... [as] an essential prelude to the transition to Socialism." [For IC's political views on Northern Ireland see Comment reviewed in this chapter.] Usually contains an editorial and three or four essays.

Other periodicals of the organization: The Communist (British monthly journal); Comment (reviewed); Workers' Weekly (bulletin from Belfast); and Problems of Communism (British quarterly theoretical journal).

THE IRISH PEOPLE

c/o 30 Gardiner Place
Dublin 1, Ireland

Weekly; $20 (quarterly subscriptions accepted)

Started: May 1973 Format: 8-page tabloid (offset)
Circulation: 10,000 Issue examined: 25 Jan. 1974

The Irish People is published by the Official Irish Republican Movement. (For an explanation of the movement's goals and socialist political philosophy see reviews of its other periodicals in this chapter: United Irishman, Rosc Catha, and Eolas.) In the issue examined, an editorial explains why England still wants to control Ireland even after 800 years of wars and strife:

> England still looks upon Ireland as a source of cheap labour and cheap food, and also as a ready-made market for her mass-produced goods.
>
> Like France and West Germany, England rents lower-class workers from abroad (France from Algeria; Germany from Italy, Greece and Turkey; England from Ireland), as all three countries cannot produce their own lower working classes. And, mark you, they rent workers, rather than buy them--if the worker breaks down they can always send him back.
>
> Thus it is still imperative for England to control this labour-source and its concomitant consumer-market. Hence the trade pacts, the links with sterling, the tentacles of English finance that grip so greedily through banks, chain-stores, office block builders, and finance companies. Old Mother England rules us still--by cheque-book rather than by sword. But the control is just as stringent and complete--and entirely in England's interest.

The paper carries news on labor and unions, Irish politics and politicians, Republican movement policies and programs, the ill-treatment of political prisoners, evictions of poor people and squatters from their homes; and exposes corruption in government and business. "The Farmer and the Ministry" discusses the plight of the small farmer who is gradually being forced off his land by an unsympathetic government which favors large agricultural units. "The Mildew in Fenian Street" describes bad housing conditions which may lead to more demonstrations. A section called "Societies and Their Abuses Examined" complains about spiraling home loan interest rates.

The Irish People also contains a half-page Gaelic section, a satirical section with spoofs on the news, advertising, and photographs and cartoons. (JMS)

Feedback:
Editor expressed no disapproval.

## JOURNAL OF CONTEMPORARY ASIA

Box 49010
Stockholm 49, Sweden
Quarterly; $11 (libraries $15)
Started: 1970
Circulation: 2,500
Format: 120-140 pages (6" x 9", offset)
Issues examined: No. 4 in 1973; No. 1 in 1974

The Journal is concerned with "social change in contemporary Asia," and has published articles on Asian political, social, and economic problems. It is "firmly committed to solidarity with the aspiration of the peoples of Asia," but "remains an independent publication with no collective attachment to any state, party, or personality."

Examples of articles: "Backward Capitalism, Primitive Accumulation and Modes of Production" (Marxist); "Formalistic Marxism and Ecology without Classes"; "Culture and Revolution in Vietnam"; "Thailand: The Demise of a Traditional Society"; "Neo-Marxism and Underdevelopment--A Sociological Phantasy"; "Polarity and Equality in the Chinese Peoples' Communes"; and "With the Survivors of the Prisons of Saigon."

The articles are scholarly and documented. The Journal also contains book reviews (some quite long) and a "Book Notes" section (short annotations). A documentary section ("rare documents emanating from various revolutionary movements in Asia") contains such material as letters and statements of governments, politicians, and international conferences. (JMS)

## KOREA FOCUS

American-Korean Friendship and Information Center
160 Fifth Ave. (Suite 809)
N.Y., N.Y. 10010
Published "periodically"; $5 for 4 issues
Started: Oct. 1971
Circulation: 3,500
Format: 64 pages (7" x 10")
Issues examined: Jan./Feb., Sept. 1973

Korea Focus attempts to "educate, inform, and influence U.S. public opinion in the interest of peace, detente, and the lessening of tension in East Asia to force our government to get out of South Korea and leave Korea to the Koreans." Printed on slick paper, enlivened by good-quality photographs, illustrations, and cartoons, the magazine contains articles (mainly by members of the Center), poems, book reviews, letters from readers, and a section called "Koreascope" (brief items about various happenings such as the defeat of a House bill that would limit travel to the Democratic People's Republic of Korea, the recognition of the DPRK by Denmark, Iceland, and Norway, and the discovery at the Korean University library at Seoul of a book believed to be 150 years older than the Gutenberg Bible).

Descriptions of the Park Chung Hee government of South Korea emphasize its censorship and use of martial law: "South Korea is a police state government that depends on the support and approval of the United States government for its existence." Extreme poverty, class struggles, and the vicious suppression of laborers and students are linked to the capitalistic involvement of South Korea with the U.S. The back cover of one issue shows "Wanted" photos of the Watergate criminals (all marked "Apprehended" except Nixon), and several articles connect the U.S. political scene at home with imperialist advances elsewhere ("From Korea to Cambodia, U.S. foreign policy has been dominated by 'Watergates'"). Another article considers the plight of Korean A-bomb victims living in Japan. Readers are exhorted to do whatever they can to further the cause of Korean unification and freedom. (CP)

Feedback:

Editor expressed no disapproval.

LABOR ACTION

113 Boston Ave.
Toronto, Ont., Canada
10 issues a year; $2
Started: Feb. 1970
Circulation: 400
Format: 8 pages (offset); changed in 1973 from 8-page tabloid
Issues examined: May, June, Sept. 1973
Back issues on file at National Library (Ottawa)

Labor Action focuses on the plight of the worker, not only in Canada but throughout the world. It is the voice of the English-Canadian affiliate of the Organising Committee for the Reconstruction of the Fourth International. As Trotskyites, its spokesmen "stand against the Stalinists and the liquidationists for the political independence of the working class from the bourgeoisie, its parties and its state." According to the editors, most of the readers are "advanced workers and social militants."

Much of the news in Labor Action is about local labor disputes and strikes and Canadian politics--particularly the New Democratic Party, the political party through which most readers of this paper must work. International news is covered if it pertains to workers' struggles. For instance, an article on Watergate concludes by viewing the scandal as offering an opportunity to form a strong third party in the United States:

> The bankruptcy of the two-party system now becomes a topic of conversation among working people. In light of the deepening corruption surrounding the Watergate affair, the struggle for the creation of a labor party in the U.S. can take on new strength.

A regular feature ("A Page from Our History") describes and analyzes important labor strikes in Canada's past, such as the 1946 Hamilton Steel Strike and the 1919 Winnipeg General Strike. Some theoretical material (usually excerpts from Trotsky's speeches) is included, but--as of the autumn of 1973--plans were being made to publish Labor Action as a magazine with more such theoretical matter, in order to broaden the periodical's circulation base and to increase its impact "on the tactical level, in the class struggle." (SA)

## LABOR CHALLENGE

Box 5595, Station A
Toronto, Ontario, Canada
Bi-weekly; $4
Started: Feb. 1970
Circulation: 5,000

Format: 12-page tabloid (offset)
Issues examined: 8 & 22 Oct., 5 & 19 Nov. 1973

This socialist newspaper supports the struggles of the oppressed working class throughout the world. In international affairs, it deplores Canada's recognition of the Chilean military junta which overthrew the elected Marxist government of Dr. Salvador Allende. It also deplores Canadian aid to Israel, which it views as the aggressor in the Middle East wars. It calls upon its readers for non-militant action:

> Everything possible must be done to mobilize the largest possible forces to protest the atrocities being

> committed by the imperialist-backed military junta. Demonstrations, protest rallies, teach-ins, etc., must be immediately launched. There is no time to be lost!...
>
> Emergency actions--teach-ins, rallies, picket lines, and demonstrations--should now be launched to mobilize opposition to any and all forms of imperialist intervention in the Mideast war.

Many of the news reports are informative as well as hortatory. Background history is given along with analyses and interpretations of current situations. The New Democratic Party (Canada's "labor" party) is followed closely and supported, as are the activities of the Ligue Socialiste Ouvrière. In keeping with its role as a forum for the oppressed, Labor Challenge also covers Quebec politics, and supports the Quebecois' desire for independence. (SA)

## IL LAVORATORE

Box 1151, Adelaide Station
Toronto 210, Ont., Canada
Every 3 weeks; $3 ($7 for institutions)
Started: Jan. 1973

Format: 12-page tabloid (offset)
Issues examined: 15 Dec. 1973; 5 Jan. 1974

Il Lavoratore, L'Ouvrier, and The Worker are the names of "The Revolutionary Communist Newspaper" published by the Canadian Party of Labour. Half of the paper is written in English; the other half is divided into French and Italian sections. The aim of the paper is to "build the revolutionary communist movement in Canada," to "expose all those who would lead us away from class war; just as the Canadian Party of Labour will organize against them. We will listen and learn from the people, and we will speak clearly, for 'A blunt knife draws no blood'." The articles are written in simple, direct language, with the central points reiterated throughout. The three sections of the paper are not mere translations of each other. Although some stories do appear in all three languages, the subjects covered in each section are often different. The focus is on Canadian workers, but international news is also reported and analyzed. In one issue the English pages reported on local strikes and labor disputes, while articles in the French and Italian sections focused on the Mid-East crisis, placing the responsibility for the clash on the rivalry among the imperialist nations. Both

Zionism and the Palestinian movement were attacked as nationalist movements impeding the success of an international workers' revolution. In another issue appeared reports in French and Italian on the 1973 riots in Greece and the Chilean coup that overthrew Salvador Allende's government. The English section featured articles on the energy crisis, an abortive attempt at a rebellion in India, and the lower-class "genocide" inherent in family planning programs of the Canadian government. Letters from workers appear in the different sections but are not translated into the other languages. (SA)

## LITERATURE & IDEOLOGY

Box 6225
Providence, R.I. 02906
Distributor for North America outside the U.S.:
National Publications Centre
Box 727, Adelaide Station
Toronto 1, Ont., Canada
Quarterly; $3
Started: Spring 1969
Circulation: 4,000 in North America; circulation of edition printed in Ireland for the British Isles not given
Format: 100 pages (6" x 9", offset)
Issues examined: 2 issues in 1970 (Nos. 6 & 7); 1 issue in 1971 (No. 8)
Indexing: On back cover of each issue, table of contents of all previous issues; Alternative Press Index

"Literature & Ideology is sponsored by the Necessity for Change Institute of Ideological Studies, Dublin and Montreal, as part of the worldwide struggle against imperialism. It is the only literary journal in North America and the British Isles that consciously and consistently applies Marxism-Leninism-Mao Tse-tung Thought to carry on the class struggle...." "This publication does not intend to provide opportunities for exercising self-interest or self-cultivation"; nonetheless, "The views expressed in these articles do not necessarily represent those of the ... Institute...."

The articles are signed, and the periodical has drawn on numerous contributors; but the prose style varies little. The epithets "fascist," "bourgeois," and "anti-people" recur often. Most of the writers believe that Marxism-Leninism-Maoism is a unitary body of thought; that it is the only valid thought; and that its content is already well known to the readers, who need not be briefed on its nuances. In the issues reviewed, the articles depreciate a considerable range of literary and graphic artists whose work seems irreconcilable with the present-day Maoist world view. Revolutionaries are sympathetically treated only if they adhere, explicitly or implicitly, to Maoism, and practice what is taken to be Maoist self-abnegation. Armand Barotti writes against a "Fascist Ideology of the Self: [Norman] Mailer, [Jerry] Rubin, and [Abbie] Hoffman," remarking that these men and other "stars of 'The Movement' will shine as long as there [are] national television and mass media owned by monopoly capital." "Eldridge Cleaver the Counter-Revolutionary" is the title selected by Mary Ellen Brooks for her essay on a man whom she calls a "misleader" of the Black Panther Party. In his treatment of "The Politics of Black Modernism," James Riche develops the idea that the work of the black intelligentsia in the United States is merely "reactionary modernism in blackface." (WJS)

Feedback:

"We have studied the summary which was based on information in L&I #8 and the preceding ones. Since many things have changed ... much of your information is out-dated. We suggest that you ... let us prepare a new one. A new draft can be mailed to you the day we hear from you." We accepted L&I's offer, and invited its editors to send us a new draft. They never did.

MERIP REPORTS

Middle East Research and Information Project
Box 3122
Washington, D. C. 20010
Monthly; $16 ($12 non-profit institutions; $25 other institutions)

Started: May 1971
Circulation: 1,500-2,000
Format: 28 pages (offset)
Issues examined: Nos. 17, 19, 21 undated (probably 1973)
Some back issues available from publisher

MERIP was founded in 1970 by seven persons who had had experience in the anti-war movement. Each issue of Reports "presents facts and analysis about aspects of the political economy of the Middle East, the United States role in the area, and the national and class struggles of the people there ..." The Reports have "an independent socialist perspective." Recent issues have covered "U.S. strategy behind its arms policy, Israeli colonization of the West Bank ... and the role of Middle East oil in the current 'energy crisis'."

In addition to a major article, every Reports has several pages on recent developments related to the

> area that have been overlooked or misinterpreted by the American Press. This section frequently includes translations from European and Middle Eastern sources. Each issue also contains a review of one or more recent books or articles dealing with the Middle East.

MERIP feels that there should be "widespread discussion of United States political, military and economic activities in the Middle East." It sees that "Middle Eastern movements for political and economic self-determination" are hindered by "the forces of Western domination and exploitation."

In October 1973 Pakistan Forum (see review in this chapter) merged with MERIP Reports.

## THE NEW VOICE

Box 16140
Sacramento, Calif. 95816
Bi-weekly; $2.60 (multiple user $20)

Started: 27 Sept. 1971
Format: 4 pages (legal size)
Issues examined: 8 Oct., 5 Nov., 10 Dec. 1973

"Voice of the Working Class," the sub-title of The New Voice, gives some indication of the paper's editorial slant, though the publication contains no editorials per se. Most of the articles denounce capitalism. There are frequent references to the imperialism practiced by the Soviet Union as well as by the United States and other countries. A characteristic statement occurred at the end of a front-page article, taking issue with a claim made by Earl Butz "that the average U.S. consumer spends only 16% of his spendable income on food." Having presented arguments against this claim, the article concludes:

> Mr. Butz's use of statistics is typical of the Agriculture Department. It is a department of the state, which is a tool of business rule. The only way to get the truth out of the government is to smash this state and set up workers' state power. But then the statistics will tell a story about a different kind of society.

This paragraph seems to convey the tenor of most of the articles in The New Voice. (Butz was Secretary of Agriculture in the Nixon cabinet.)

The regular feature, "On the Labor Front," which

constitutes about one-fourth of each issue, consists mainly of news articles dealing with strikes in various industries. Occasionally there are articles describing substandard working conditions and other injustices to workers. (SMA)

Feedback:
"Since the summary is a distorted, anti-working class, sarcastic editorial, we cannot accept it. Perhaps some work can be saved on all sides by your simply excerpting the description we publish in the newspaper (identified as such, if you like)." That description reads: "The New Voice is a bimonthly newspaper of political discussion and labor news, reports on the anti-war movement and anti-imperialist liberation struggles, and analysis of life and culture under capitalism."

NORTHERN NEIGHBORS: The Magazine of Socialism in Action

Box 1000
Gravenhurst, Ontario POC-1GO Canada
11 issues a year; $2 for 10 issues
Started: Dec. 1954
Circulation: 12,000

Format: 28 pages (8" x 11", offset)
Issues examined: July/Aug., Sept., Oct. 1973
Microform version available from Xerox University Microfilms

The "northern neighbors" are Canada and the Soviet Union, and this magazine, formerly known as News-Facts, is "Canada's Authoritative Independent Magazine Reporting the U.S.S.R." The articles are short, few extending beyond a page, and most of them describe in a simple, factual style the latest achievements and advances of Soviet society, particularly in science and medicine. As one reader put it in a letter: "N.N. explains many complicated problems to me in an easy-to-understand way. Everything from weather to revolution to health and space ... [is] made understandable to ordinary workers." Socialism, especially as it applies to medical and educational fields, is seen as a remedy for most of capitalism's ills. Other aspects of Soviet life at which the magazine looks are agriculture, historical scholarship, and political dissent. (Such dissenters as Solzhenitsyn and Sakharov are severely criticized: "Capitalism must understand that Socialism will endure and advance when Solzhenitsyn and Sakharov are only a faint stench in the sewer of human history.")

Some of the Soviet medical discoveries described in these pages are the use of beehive glue as a cure for many ailments (from removing corns to treating chronic respiratory diseases); the physical dangers of abortion; and the merits of atomic radiation in healing the ill (Soviet people bathe in and drink radioactive waters, and inhale atomic air). Photographic essays show readers such aspects of Soviet life and culture as a ballet school, horses and troika racing, and schoolchildren.

A few persons connected with the editorial and production ends of Northern Neighbors are named, but none of the articles or photographs are attributed to individuals. For instance, an "exclusive N. N. interview" (on trade deals between the U.S.S.R. and capitalist nations) identified those interviewed only as "economists of [the] U.S.S.R. State Planning Committee."

(SA)

Feedback:
Editor expressed no disapproval.

## OLD MOLE

| | |
|---|---|
| c/o PECU, Sid Smith Hall (Rm 2034), 100 St. George St. | $2.50 for 6 issues |
| | Started: Spring 1971 |
| | Format: 12-page tabloid |
| Toronto, Ont., Canada | Issue examined: Mar. 1973 |

Old Mole was begun by a group of independent revolutionaries at the University of Toronto. They were "dissatisfied with the politics of the organized revolutionary currents" and felt that "The collapse of the New Left and the student movement, generally, in North America, put the question of a revolutionary workers' party on the historical agenda." Why rely on workers to make revolution? "As imperialism decays, [and] revolutions, wars, counter-revolutions, and bloody chaos characterize the social make-up of the entire world," the proletariat

> becomes the only force with the necessary discipline, cohesion, and relation to the productive apparatus to institute a [desirable] world order.... But the working class must develop the necessary consciousness. ...
>
> The instrument ... crucial to the successful completion of this task is a world proletarian party, organized along democratic-centrist lines ... [and working] for the victory of the socialist revolution.

What could serve as the basis for such a party? The Fourth International, founded in 1938 and based on the ideas of Lenin and Trotsky. It has recently been strengthened by "a new generation of revolutionary militants," and is today in the vanguard of the struggle for world revolution and the victory of the proletariat. Old Mole "proudly declares its support for, and adherence to, the program of the Fourth International," for this can serve as the basis for building a revolutionary party.

As might be expected of a Trotskyist publication, Old Mole opposes the "reactionary Soviet bureaucracy." The periodical is illustrated.

## OUR GENERATION

3934 rue St-Urbain
Montreal 131, P.Q., Canada
Quarterly; $5 (institutions $10)
Started: 1961
Circulation: 3,000
Format: 100 pages (7 1/4" x 9 1/4", letterpress)
Issues examined: Fall 1972; Winter & Spring 1973
Indexing: Alternative Press Index
Back issues available from publisher
Microform version available from Xerox University Microfilms

Our Generation is a journal which grew out of the anti-war and anti-bomb movements of the early 1960's.

> The journal attempts from a libertarian socialist perspective to be of service to people who want to persue [sic] an inter-related range of social questions. The editorial collective seeks to encourage research and social analysis in the areas of critical social theory, the development of the respective social and national liberation movements in Quebec and Canada, and a radical analysis of industrial societies in general.

As libertarian socialists the publishers believe that

> The idea that socialism only means the nationalisation of the means of production and planning--and that its essential aim is an increase in production and consumption, albeit on a more egalitarian basis--must be denounced.... The essential content of socialism is the restitution to people of the control over their

own life ... and the union of the culture and the life of the people.

The articles in the journal are lengthy (often 20 pages or more) and most are extensively footnoted. Though most of the statistics, examples, and programs cited are Canadian, the theoretical discussions are also applicable to the United States (as an advanced capitalist nation).

In articles such as "The Story of the Auto Pact: From Colony to Hinterland" and "The National Question in Canada," anti-United States attitudes are expressed. However, the left is warned not to let anti-Americanism be used by socialism's enemies: "We must not let our desire to break American control distract us from the more fundamental project of breaking the existing social order."

This breaking of the existing order is explored in articles such as "The Fiscal Crisis of the State and the Revolt of the Public Employee," where government workers at all levels are urged, through union with their respective clients (social workers: welfare recipients, teachers: students and parents, etc.), to force radical change on the government and the corporate sector.

But the intention of the state to fight to keep the status quo is seen in "The Flowers of Power: A Critique of OFY and LIP Programmes," an article on two government programs designed to reduce unemployment among the young. The author says that the programs are "a response to social instability," designed to keep society undisrupted and to mask the basic cause of unemployment (the operation of business for profit only).

Other articles in the issues examined included: "Towards a Decentralized Commonwealth," "The Driving Force of Imperialism Today," "Colonialism at Home and Abroad," and "The Modern Industrial State: Liberator or Exploiter?" (SLA)

Feedback:

"It's a fine summary."

PAKISTAN FORUM: An Independent Magazine for Pakistanis in U.S.A. and Canada

Monthly; $7
Dates: Oct. 1970 through Sept. 1973
Circulation: 1,000
Format: 12-48 pages (usually 16), offset (saddle-stapled; based on carbon ribbon typewriter composition, and reduced slightly in size)

Issues examined: May-Sept. 1973

Back issues available from MERIP Reports

Dr. Feroz Ahmed, editor and publisher of Pakistan Forum, states that the periodical's editorial policy is

> To present analyses of the social structure, political events, and foreign policies of Pakistan and other Third World countries, with a view to provide a clear perspective to those engaged in the national liberation struggle.
>
> It is addressed primarily to the activists of the people's democratic movement in Pakistan, where thousands read it directly or by way of reprinting of its articles, and secondarily to the Third World struggles, and to the overseas Pakistanis.

Pakistan Forum contains information on the Middle East and Asia, as well as on Pakistan. Because it is addressed to Pakistanis, the average American reader without a knowledge of Pakistani politics, geography, and society may at first be confused. However, most of the articles are clearly presented, and a non-Pakistani who persists will learn much about the Middle East and Pakistan.

As the periodical is in part intended for U.S. Pakistanis, there is an interest in U.S. activity in Pakistan. The comment is largely negative and the U.S. is seen as imperialistic. There is criticism of its actions at the time when East Pakistan seceded to form the new state of Bangladesh:

> In other words, for at least two months in advance the Nixon government knew that Pakistan, since 1955 an ally and client, signatory of a mutual defense treaty with the U.S. and member of Seato and Cento alliances, was to fight a war for its survival. Yet it did nothing worthy of note to prevent the outbreak of hostilities, or to help the invaded ally....

Although there is no statement of Marxist views on the masthead, a Marxist orientation is apparent in Pakistan Forum. Nowhere, however, was there a wholehearted endorsement of communism as practiced in the U.S.S.R. or China, or an outright call for revolution--although the present government of Pakistan came in for considerable criticism. Joseph Stalin is quoted extensively. Phrases such as "class conflict" are used. "The current transition from capitalism to socialism" is called "the single most important facet of our own epoch." Tribalism is called "a contentless ideology which worked as an opiate on the masses." There is talk of the "dialectic" of an "anti-imperialist" struggle. The author of an article on the Baluchi national movement expresses concern that

> a nationalism that defines itself in this era on racial or tribal terms and whose only ground is the ethno-linguistic genesis, half imagined and half real, will necessarily detach itself from the working class movement as a whole and slide into a collision of two reactionary forces.

Many of the articles are accompanied by footnotes which document the statements made. Sources used in an article on Saudi Arabia include the Christian Science Monitor, The New York Times, U.S. News and World Report, and the London Economist. An article discussing the buildup of U.S. forces in the Mediterranean and Indian Ocean cites such sources as the Congressional Record, Armed Forces Journal, and Adm. Elmo R. Zumwalt.

Pakistan Forum has ceased publication and urges its readers to turn to MERIP Reports (reviewed in this chapter) for the type of article previously found in its pages. Its address was: Box 1198, Sault Ste. Marie, Ontario, Canada. (BK)

Reviewer's opinion:

The style used in most of the articles is clear and the arguments are set forth in a logical manner.

PEOPLE'S CANADA DAILY NEWS: National Daily Working Class Newspaper

Hardial S. Bains, Ed.
Norman Bethune Institute
National Publications Centre
Box 727, Adelaide Station
Toronto 210, Ont., Canada

Daily; 15¢ a copy ($4 monthly; $44 yearly)
Format: 4-page tabloid (offset)
Issue examined: 5 Mar. 1973

A publication connected with the Communist Party of Canada. "The main motive behind producing the newspaper is to serve the working and oppressed people in their revolutionary struggles." "Anyone who is part of the oppressed people and the working class and who cannot afford to pay the full subscription rate, but has sentiment to receive the paper, can obtain it at the cost the individual can afford to pay or can even obtain it free of charge."

## THE PROGRESSIVE SCIENTIST

c/o Academic Activities Committee, McGill Student Centre
3480 McTavish St.
Montreal 112, P.Q., Canada

Bi-monthly; $2
Format: 30 pages (offset)
Issue examined: Sept. 1972
Indexing: Alternative Press Index

"The [Progressive Scientist] Study Group is dedicated to the cause of opposing unscientific and fascistic concepts and theories in the sciences and the use of these ideas by the ruling circles of U.S. monopoly capitalism against the interests of the people of the world. We firmly uphold the scientific world outlook, and strive to 'Seek truth from facts to serve the people'." TPS is published by the Study Group in conjunction with the Norman Bethune Institute of Ideological Studies. The periodical has a Marxist-Leninist-Maoist orientation and shows admiration for the achievements of the People's Republic of China (the Soviet Union was never mentioned), quoting the writings of Bethune (a Canadian doctor who practiced in China) and Chairman Mao Tse-tung.

"Zero Population Growth: A Programme for Fascism" puts forward the Study Group's belief that world overpopulation is only a "myth" or "lie" propagated by capitalists as a way of explaining "the sufferings of humanity." "Free abortion and availability of birth control information" are "elementary democratic rights," but capitalist "compulsory sterilization programmes" (said to be put forward by such groups as ZPG and the American Association of Planned Parenthood Physicians, "in operation in numerous Third World countries and amongst the minorities in the USA") are a capitalist-fascist plot.

The status and prospects of American society are described:

> The U.S. monopoly capitalist ruling class is fast heading towards collapse. Internally, the United States has degenerated into a fascist state where not a day passes without incidents of violent repression ... by the state, where the National Guard is called out to brutally suppress almost any demonstration, where the rights of the black and other national minority people have been totally abolished and their existence reduced to subhuman levels, and where active ideological propaganda for fascism is carried out day and night.

A review of The Limits of Growth (Donella H. Meadows et al.; N.Y.: Universe Books, 1972) condemns the authors and their conclusions:

> The Progressive Scientist Study Group has decided ... to combat and expose the 'pseudo-scientists' and 'experts' who are promoted in the universities in North America. It is significant that today when the revolutionary forces throughout the world are becoming stronger and are preparing to wage a fierce struggle against all the evil forces which have held back the growth and development of human society ... we see Meadows and his group peddling their bankrupt ideas, in the vain hope that the masses of people are suddenly going to realize that the main problem in the world is the number of people, instead of the exploiting classes who live off the blood and sweat of the toiling people of this world.... It is not intellectual shortsightedness or intellectual error which Meadows and his group are committing. These people are paid to do it by the monopoly capitalist class and their conclusions are bound to be those which serve the interests of that class.

Other articles in the sample issue were concerned with medicine (including acupuncture) in China; chemical warfare in Vietnam; and the influence--if any--of race on intelligence. A four-page section ("News Briefs") contained reprints of four articles from Peking Review, and an excerpt from China Reconstructs having to do with ecology and anti-pollution measures in China. (JMS)

## THE PROLETARIAN CORRESPONDENCE

Takeshi Yasuda, Publ.
Dotoh Sha Publishing Office
Shiraishi Bldg., 11-2,
Ikebukuro-2, Toshima
Tokyo, Japan 171
Quarterly; $2
Started: Apr. 1971

Format: 40 pages (7" x 10", mimeo., side-stapled)
Issues examined: Nov. 1972; Feb. & Sept. 1973
Back issues Nos. 1-7 available from publisher

The editorial policy of this organ of the Workers' Communist Committee is, in the words of the publisher, to

> represent the common interests of the worker's class

> through the world and contribute to every revolutionary movement of oppressed peoples. Its aim is to promote the proletarian internationalism concerning the struggle by workers and people for seizing political power in each country, and the worldwide emancipation of them.

In consequence, the WCC has many enemies on the right as well as on the left, and TPC attacks them vigorously. (Motto: "Workers of All Countries, Unite!")

France. The leading members of the French Communist Party (PCF) are "infected" with "petti-bourgeois [sic] pacifism."

Soviet Union. Its policy of peaceful co-existence and détente is counter-revolutionary.

Japan. The Japanese government is imperialist. The Japanese Communist Party is criticized for having abandoned the goals of world revolution and dictatorship of the proletariat, and for protecting bourgeois parliamentarianism.

South Korea. "Pak's gang" (i.e., the regime of dictator Pak Jung Hi) is criticized because it sent "big troops to Vietnam [to aid the Pentagon forces, and] slaughtered many Vietnamese people."

Vietnam. The South should be liberated, and the country unified. The South is governed by dictator Thieu and his clique of reactionary oppressors. Sample of language: "The Thieu gang howls...."

Near East. The periodical is sympathetic toward the Palestine Liberation Organization, and hostile toward Israel. (The word "Israel" is sometimes placed within quotation marks, as though to suggest that the nation's existence or legitimacy is in doubt.) TPC reports (with apparent approval) on the opinions and activities of various pro-Arab groups in Japan. One of these, the Support Center for Palestinian People, is described as having praised the kidnapping and murder of Israeli athletes (by Arab terrorists) at the Munich Olympics, and having blamed the West German and Israeli governments for the deaths.

Labor. The AFL-CIO is given as an example of a deplorable right-wing, anti-communist trend in the world labor movement. (TJS)

Reviewer's Opinion:

The English of TPC is not idiomatic. Many words are misspelt. The printing is bad: faint and smudged, with set-off and show-through. Bad writing, bad printing, and pervasive cant make the articles unpleasant to read and hard to understand. Examples of cant: "revisionism," "social-chauvinism," "comprador bourgeoisie," "counter-revolutionary," "robbery war" (i.e., World War II), and "first imperialist world war."

Feedback:

The editor suggested deleting the paragraph on France and the section on the Israeli athletes. He added a comment about the United States: "U.S. government is imperialist, and the primary enemy of workers and oppressed people in the world."

## RADICAL AMERICA

James O'Brien, Co-Ed.
5 Upland Rd.
Cambridge, Mass. 02140
Bi-monthly; $5
Started: 1967
Circulation: 4,000
Format: 120 pages (5 1/2" x 8 1/2", offset)
Issues examined: Mar. & Nov. 1973; May 1974
Annual self-index; Alternative Press Index
Back issues available from publisher
Microform version available from Xerox University Microfilms

Radical America is

> an independent Marxist journal with ... [detailed] analyses of the history and current condition of the working class in North America and Europe, shop-floor and community organizing, history and politics of women's liberation, contemporary socialist theory and practice, and popular culture.

Most issues of the journal are devoted to a single topic. One, for example, had as its theme "Working Class Struggles in Italy." The articles in that issue (some of them translated from Italian journals and books) dealt with the fight for "workers' autonomy," a revolutionary rather than a reformist concept. Some of the articles were: "Italy, 1973: Workers' Struggles in the Capitalist Crisis," "Organizing for Workers' Power," and "Against the State As Boss."

In another issue, the theme was "Workers and the Control of Production," showing through examples in France and the United States that it is possible for workers to gain control of their factories and to manage them efficiently. The main feature of this issue was a symposium on a book called

Strike! The True History of Mass Insurgence in America from 1877 to the Present by Jeremy Brecher. The debate in the articles is whether or not unions and radical organizations have a role to play in this mass insurgency of the workers.

Other issues of Radical America have dealt with the women's movement, black labor, radical history, changes in the class struggle, and the Quebec general strike.

The journal also carries ads for its own pamphlets and reprints and for other radical publications. (SLA)

Feedback:

"It's fine."

REVOLUTION

Revolutionary Union
Box 3486, Merchandise Mart
Chicago, Ill. 60654
Monthly; $3 (institutions $12)
Started: Feb. 1973

Format: 20-page tabloid (offset)
Issues examined: Sept. & Nov. 1973; Feb. & Mar. 1974
Self-indexing at end of each vol.

Revolution is published by an American communist organization to provide "analysis and commentary of major events and struggles of the working class and oppressed peoples of the U.S. and the world, from the view point of Marxism-Leninism-Mao tsetung thought." It is a tough-minded paper that accepts no compromise, brooks no error, and often takes issue with People's World and Daily World, organs of the revisionist Communist Party, USA, as well as with the Trotskyite Socialist Workers' Party's The Militant [see Feedback]. In discussing the kidnapping of Patricia Hearst, an action deplored by some communist and socialist leaders, Revolution's view is that "it is wrong to reject any tactic *in principle*. A tactic is correct or incorrect depending on whether or not it advances the cause of the proletariat and flows from and is linked with the mass struggle" [see Feedback].

The paper speaks principally to a working class audience and some articles are in Spanish. [Feedback: "but we also have among our readers many students, teachers, intellectuals.... [I]t is essential for almost all the American people to be united in one front against the capitalists.... [W]e also have articles dealing with the struggles of students and other sections of the people"] Long, detailed articles give prominent coverage to strikes, demonstrations, wildcat walkouts, and shutdowns by industrial labor unions, farm-worker unions, the unemployed, and prison groups. Terms of union negotiations are covered in detail as well as examples of poor safety conditions, speedups, racist harassment, and lay offs. The headlines set the militant tone: "Throw the Bum Out! Organize to Fight," "Poor People Unite, Rack Rulers, Killer Cops," "New Jersey Postal Workers Walk Out, Battle Police," "Auto Struggle Boils, Woodcock Babbles" [Leonard Woodcock, head of United Auto Workers' union].

Other articles are written to educate readers in Marxism. "How Socialism Wipes Out Exploitation" defines and describes capitalism and exploitation and explains the communist position that "only socialism can eliminate the anarchy, destruction, and misery caused by the capitalist system" by letting the workers decide "how to use all the value they have created."

A principal theme is that "revolutionary intellectuals must bring the theory of Marxism to the working class and combine it with the workers' practical struggles." To promote understanding of this objective, a series of articles dealing with the role of the Communist Party, USA, describes both the early contributions and the later serious political errors made during World War II under Earl Browder. The meaning of important events in the past--such as the Lawrence Textile Strike of 1912, the Spanish Civil War, and the leadership of Malcolm X--is interpreted. Typical pictures show Communist demonstrations in the 1930s and the International Brigade that fought in the Spanish Civil War.

Quotations from Mao, Stalin, Marx, Engels and Lenin are used as examples of correct Marxism, in contrast to the revisionism of "the so-called Communist Party, following in the mud behind the traitors in the Soviet Union beginning with Khrushchev, [which] has fully degenerated into bootlickers of the capitalist class."

The purpose of the Revolutionary Union is clearly stated in a front-page article: "Our aim is to build the mass struggle of the working class and all oppressed people against the imperialist system, with the final aim of over-throwing it and establishing the rule of the working class to build socialism and advance society toward communism." (JS)

Feedback:

"On the whole, we think the review is accurate and fair. One problem you must have, certainly, is trying to get a full picture of a newspaper based on just a few issues. Considering that limitation, we feel what you say is very good in giving a prospective subscriber a general overview.

On the other hand, we think the limitation leads to some problems which we hope can be overcome." The textual changes that Revolution's editor suggested have been incorporated into the review, or noted in the text and explained below by quoting directly from his response.

> We appreciate being called a 'tough-minded paper,' but we aren't sure of what you mean by going on to say that the paper 'accepts no compromise, brooks no error.' It is true, certainly, that we believe in very sharp political struggle with organizations and individuals representing different viewpoints, and on questions of principle there can be no compromise. However, on tactical questions, on questions involving day to day struggle, we of course accept compromise, in the sense of recognizing that it's not possible always to win everything you struggle for in the short term (for example, in a strike, it sometimes is necessary to accept less in the way of a settlement than what is desired). We feel that the 'accepts no compromise, brooks no error,' phrase makes us dogmatic, when in fact we don't think we are.
>
> Another problem is what you say about our editorial on the Hearst affair. The quote, of course, is correct, but taken out of context it can be misleading. We certainly did have differences with other groups who put forward, in our opinion, a very one-sided appraisal of the Hearst kidnapping and the aftermath. However, taking the quote out of context can inadvertently lead the reader to think that we supported the kidnapping, which we did not. Our point was that while no tactic would be rejected in principle, no tactic is any good that doesn't help to advance the people's struggle, and we conclude that isolated acts such as the Hearst kidnapping, while understandable because of people's anger and frustration, are nevertheless not helpful.

## REVOLUTIONARY COMMUNIST YOUTH NEWSLETTER

Bi-monthly; 50¢ an issue
Dates: Oct. 1971 - Aug. 1973
Format: 8-page tabloid (offset)
Issues examined: May & July 1973

The Revolutionary Communist Youth Newsletter (formerly

Revolutionary Marxist Caucus Newsletter) has been superseded by Young Spartacus (see review in this chapter). All three publications emanate from Revolutionary Communist Youth (the youth division of the Spartacist League), which seeks "to build a revolutionary socialist youth organization which can intervene in all social struggles armed with a working-class program, based on the politics of Marx, Lenin and Trotsky." (See also reviews of the League's Spartacist, Spartacist-West, and Workers' Vanguard in this and previous volumes.)

Examples of longer articles in the Newsletter are: "Lessons of the French Student Struggles--Down with the Bourgeois Army"; "Maoists Betray Filipino Struggles"; "Budget Cuts Hit Campuses--Only Workers Can Smash Phase III! [of wage and price controls]"; and "Stalinists, Nationalists Seek to Exclude Communists."

A one-page Editorial Notes section consists of short articles on labor struggles or on SL/RCY's disputes with other progressive student groups. An article in that section, "Lettuce Boycott: SDS Tail-Ends UFWOC," points out the errors of Cesar Chavez, head of the United Farm Workers of California: "The policies of the Chavez leadership are class-collaborationist, national-chauvinist, and racist. Against the Chavez betrayals, revolutionaries must point to the need for a UFW strike and secondary boycott."

"Lessons from History," an historical-theoretical article in the May issue, covers the "Founding Conference of the 4th International." In each issue an RCY directory lists chapters throughout the country, and an RCY Events section lists forums and classes.

This quotation from a lead article, "Condemn CP-Cop Alliance and Labor Committee Holliganism," illustrates the vigilance with which RCYN looks out for doctrinal errors:

> Two tendencies developed out of the disintegrating New Left: right-wing Maoism, exemplified by the Revolutionary Union, the October League, and the Attica Brigade; and the 'pure rage' of the frenzied petty bourgeoisie, best exemplified by the National Caucus of Labor Committees. Both tendencies preserve the worst characteristics of the old New Left: anti-communism in their day-to-day work, gangsterism against their opponents on the left, veneration of the lumpenproletariat.
>
> As faithful apologists for Chinese Menshevik Realpolitik, the anti-communism of the American Maoists takes the form of the 'anti-social-imperialist united front.' The front, which extends from Albania to the

White House, has managed to include both the capitalists and their labor lieutenants in the workers' movement, while conspicuously excluding Leninists. The anti-communism of the NCLC is mediated by their habitual national parochialism and has recently been aimed primarily at the CPUSA.

The address of the RCY Newsletter was Box 454, Cooper Station, N.Y., N.Y. 10003. (JMS)

Reviewer's Opinion:
Some articles (e.g., "Lessons from History," mentioned above) are beyond this reviewer's comprehension. A great part of the paper is devoted to bitter ideological and tactical disputes which lead to constant condemnation of other communist and leftist organizations. The factionalism (in, e.g., "Condemn CP-Cop Alliance," quoted above) can be quite complicated.

## REVOLUTIONARY MARXIST CAUCUS NEWSLETTER

Dates: Feb. 1970-July 1971
Format: 14 pages (8 1/2" x 14", mimeo., stapled)
Issue examined: Dec. 1970

This Newsletter was superseded by the tabloid Revolutionary Communist Youth Newsletter, which was in turn superseded by Young Spartacus. (See reviews in this volume.) These are all publications of Revolutionary Communist Youth, the youth section of the Spartacist League. (See also reviews of the League's publications, Spartacist, Spartacist-West and Workers' Vanguard in this and previous volumes.) The editor had been Mark Tisham, Box 454, Cooper Sta., N.Y., N.Y. 10003.

## ROSC CATHA

Clann na hEireann
318 Lillie Rd.
London SW6, United Kingdom
Bi-monthly; $5
Started: Oct. 1972
Circulation: 6,000

Format: 8-page tabloid (offset)
Issue examined: Jan./Feb. 1974
Back issues available from publisher

Rosc Catha is published by the British branch of the Official Irish Republican Movement. (For an explanation of the movement's goals and socialist political philosophy see reviews of its other periodicals in this chapter: United Irishman, Eolas, and The Irish People.)

The issue examined bitterly attacked the SDLP (Social-Democratic Labour Party) for its part in the Sunningdale Agreement and condemned the Provisional IRA for the useless violence and destruction it has brought to Northern Ireland:

> Victory is no longer a word that is much used in Provisional circles and the quicker they realize that present tactics are only giving the SDLP more breathing space the better it will be for all of us. The SDLP power base among the people can be eroded but this will only come about by rebuilding a mass movement of the people on issues that affect them at this time.
>
> The SDLP have repeatedly broken their promises: on Internment; on the rent and rates strike and the reform of the RUC [police force in northern Ireland]. The recent SDLP conference voted to call off the rent and rates strike even though the Internment camps are more crowded than before.

Other topics covered by the paper were bad prison conditions and ill treatment of political prisoners; police and British Army brutality; labor strikes, disputes and demonstrations; Irish politics and politicians; and programs and political candidates of the Republican movement.

The paper also contained "Readers' Comments" and a half-page section in Gaelic. (JMS)

Feedback:

"The paper is also trying to deal to an increasing extent with the situation of the Irish in Britain (jobs, housing, etc.) and with the attitude of the Irish government to Irish emigrants particularly in relation to the cost of air and boat fares and traveling conditions to Ireland."

THE SECOND PAGE

| | |
|---|---|
| Box 14145 | Format: 12-page tabloid |
| San Francisco, Calif. 94114 | Issues examined: Nov. 1971; |
| $2 for 6 months | Apr./May 1972 |

Although The Second Page is not affiliated with any particular socialist group, it appears to be Marxist-Leninist-

Maoist. The November 1971 issue contains quotations from Lenin and The Chinese Red Army. The paper, originally launched as The Women's Page by a group of women involved in the feminist movement, now operates with a male and female staff and eschews feminist organizations and newspapers as "tools of greedy opportunistic individuals" who, "while claiming to be concerned with the conditions of all women's lives, are actually mainly concerned with establishing groups in which they can maintain private power.... [T]hey don't give a damn about change." One issue contains an interview with four women suing the Bank of America. The paper ridicules their contention that they are seeking "equal opportunity and equal pay for women," accuses them of being only out for themselves (and ignoring the plight of less-educated women at the Bank), and calls them "classy strivers" and a "gruesome foursome." (Frank language is a feature of TSP. Nelson Rockefeller, for example, is called "a raging Fascist.") Elsewhere in the same issue, it is explained that the women's liberation movement "is in fact only concerned with improving the lot of a small number of classy ('exceptional') women...."

The Communist Party, USA, is strongly criticized. By opposing wildcat strikes, suppressing militant workers, and working hand-in-glove with the bosses (government, business management, and the AFL-CIO), the CPUSA "has been blocking real change in this country for the last 50 years." It is also elitist and "classy," and despises the pleasures and concerns of many Americans. "Treating people with classy contempt," it affects to believe that "most anything that large numbers of Americans do or enjoy doing is bad, 'middle class'." For example, it sneers at camping in campers as "unnatural and bad," but approves of "natural folksy picnics" by Party members "on the grounds of some rich lefty's estate" as "fine."

An article in the November issue pointing out the errors of "left-opportunists" criticizes such figures as the Marxist philosopher (arrogant, a phony, a fake, fond of "abstract jibberish" [sic], and given to "boring simpering monologues"); the "entrepreneur" (e.g., one who gave funds to Ramparts); the "movement lawyer" who "makes his reputation and money off other people's misfortunes" (William Kunstler is "one of these pigs"); the "super-moral humanitarian," such as Joan Baez and her (former) husband, David Harris (both are "prissy moralists," and his writings are "incoherent dribble"); and feminists, liberals, and revolutionary activists. It is these groups, and "not police departments or armies," who have suppressed the revolutionary forces in this country.

The April/May issue contains a number of articles on labor--specifically, on persons in jobs that involve drudgery and lack glamor (e.g., clerical and blue-collar jobs). One article points out that the American labor movement has had "zero" effect on redistributing wealth and giving workers the just reward of their labors. How can workers take over the big corporations, which play such a powerful and important part in our society? Perhaps the clerical workers could play a leading role here: although they are underpaid, these workers (usually women) are the "crucial sector" of the corporate work force as they perform "the internal daily transactions of the firm.... the real work of corporate management." In the armed forces, the corresponding group is the non-commissioned officers or "lifers."

The GI movement (represented by GI coffeehouses, and by the servicemen's papers reviewed in our earlier volumes) is criticized bitterly. TSP says that it is in the hands of persons who secretly "hate" GIs. These persons especially hate--quite unfairly--the "lifers" referred to in the preceding paragraph. (TJS)

## SOCIALIST EDUCATION BULLETIN

Socialist Party of Great Britain, Education Committee
52 Clapham High St.
London, S.W. 4 7UN, England
Format: 12 pages (8 1/4" x 11 3/4", mimeo., stapled)
Issue examined: Sept. 1973

The sample copy was sent to us by the Socialist Party of Canada, Box 237, Victoria, B. C., Canada, which probably distributes the periodical. It contained a long essay, "Some Notes on Man's Social Nature and the Capitalist Role of Bolshevism."

## SOCIALIST PRESS BULLETIN

Box 123, Adelaide Station
Toronto, Ont., Canada
M5C 2J1
Monthly; free
Started: Feb. 1956
Circulation: 500
Format: 8 pages (mimeo., stapled)
Issues examined: Oct.-Dec. 1973
Microform version available from Micromedia Limited, Box 34, Station S, Toronto M5M 4L6

Official organ of the Socialist Labor Party of Canada,

the Bulletin contains one or two articles in each issue, frequent editorials taken from the writings of Daniel De Leon (American Marxist and formulator of the Socialist Industrial Union program), and reports of the Party's activities. The articles provide a Marxist-De Leonist analysis of such topics as strikes, inflation, poverty, labor movement strategy and tactics, and De Leon's contribution to Socialist science. Capitalism is seen as the cause of current economic and social problems. Most of the articles end with an exhortation to the working class to unite to establish a new social order, the "non-political, classless, Socialist Industrial Commonwealth, which will enthrone the humanity-redeeming principles of social ownership and democratic control of the industries and services, production for human need, and the retention by all workers of the full social value of their abundant product." (CP)

Feedback:

"Although your content-summary appeared adequate as a whole, we have made some minor changes, and we would like to have our edited version published." This was done.

## SOCIALIST REVIEW

Socialist Group of Jamaica
Box 35
Kingston 14, Jamaica

Format: 8 pages (8 1/2" x 12 3/4", mimeo., stapled)
Issue examined: No. 7, 1972

The last page of the publication contains a list of seven socialist parties which "adhere to the same Socialist Principles." For an enumeration of these Principles see the review of Socialist Viewpoint in this chapter. Other "companion" socialist publications reviewed in this and previous volumes are The Socialist Standard, Fulcrum, The Western Socialist, Internationales freies Wort, and Socialist Education Bulletin.

## SOCIALIST REVOLUTION

Agenda Publishing Co.
396 Sanchez St.
San Francisco, Calif. 94114
Bi-monthly; $7
Format: 128-208 pages

Issues examined: Mar., July, Sept. 1972
Indexing: Alternative Press Index

Socialist Revolution brings a socialist analysis to

discussions about education, the economy, corporations, the family, the left movements, prisons, the international political and economic scene, and other subjects important to the socialist movement in this country. The journal has neither an exclusively "old left" nor "new left" nor "sectarian" approach, but analyzes and criticizes leftist policies and practices from a broad-based socialist point of view.

An introduction to each issue describes the articles to follow, capsulizing their important points and sometimes pointing out limitations in scope. Some articles are followed by a several-page "comment" or "reply" from the collective that publishes the journal, criticizing or answering points in the article.

The bulk of one issue is concerned with "Education and Corporate Capitalism." "Education and the Corporate Order" and "Education and the Rise of the Corporate State" offer history and analyses of education in twentieth-century United States as it developed in response to industrialization and large-scale corporate capitalism. The origins of vocational guidance and extra-curricular activities are examined particularly closely. In "The Bay Area Radical Teachers' Organizing Committee" members of that organization explain its programs and strategy "toward a movement in the schools." Positing a relationship between corporations and education, the authors explain:

> As part of job preparation, students are taught to think of work as unpleasant and to accept deferred, extrinsic rewards for sticking with it. They are readied for the regimentation and stratification that they will find in the corporations that will provide most of them with jobs. The world of the schools is organized to reflect the world of the corporations and its values.

In addition there are three personal narratives of teachers who worked in a rigid public school, a non-political free school, and a political free school.

Another issue contains "a history of the twentieth-century American left" and an article on "China and the Left," which "examines the dual character of Chinese foreign policy and explores the meaning to the left of the contradiction between China's role as a great power and as a part of the world revolutionary movement." "The Trap of Domesticity" analyzes the stultifying aspects of the family:

> What makes the family so devastating is not that a

> combination of people live in one unit, but the social meaning of that living arrangement: an isolated support system, domesticity, sex roles, competitive individualism.

One of the collective's comments following this article:

> Our main criticism is that the article treats the ideology of the family without relating this ideology to an analysis of the family as a historically specific structure within advanced capitalism.

"Trends of the Working Class" is a statistical description of the working class which "stresses the continuing importance of 'blue collar' workers."

Another issue includes articles on "The International Monetary Crisis"; a socialist perspective on "what is positive and liberating in modern art"; "Miami, McGovern, and the Movement"; and the first of a two-part review of Gramsci's Prison Notebooks. (MM)

Feedback:
"Fine."

SOCIALIST STANDARD: Official Journal of the Socialist Party of Great Britain and The World Socialist Party of Ireland

52 Clapham High Street
London SW4, United Kingdom
Monthly; 80p.

Format: 16 pages
Issues examined: Nov. 1972; May & Oct. 1973

This is a party paper with a lively, irreverent style. On a British report on pornography: "The Longford Report is the dirtiest book in town, throwing and smearing mud in all directions." On unemployment: "The first thing to note about unemployment is that it is a working class problem." On the American elections: "During Nixon's term capitalism has been faced with the customary economic problems which, in the customary way, he has promised to control with some 'fine tuning' of the economy. In a nation of car owners, this phrase is easily understood and accepted."

The Standard decries censorship of all kinds, including the "blatant and crushing" variety practiced in Russia. It chides the Maoists in Great Britain for their opposition to the Tory government's Industrial Relations Act, arguing that

"Those who control the means of production in China have used unions as a means of raising production and thereby increasing the amount of surplus value available for reinvestment." Of the native African governments that call themselves socialist, the Standard says: "In this the coloured governments differ from the white rulers.... But one thing is common to all the dozens of countries ... from Cairo to the Cape: there is not a solitary foot of ground where a single vestige of freedom exists."

In addition to surveying the political scene around the world, the Standard comments on Wilhelm Reich, women's liberation, lonelyhearts columns, and prison conditions. Party meetings and lectures are announced, and there is a directory of offices and officers throughout Great Britain.

For an enumeration of the party's principles, see our review of Socialist Viewpoint elsewhere in this chapter. Other "companion" socialist publications adhering to these principles are Fulcrum, Socialist Review, and Western Socialist. (All have been reviewed in this or previous volumes.) (SN)

## SOCIALIST VIEWPOINT

Socialist Party of New Zealand
Box 1929
Auckland, New Zealand
Bi-monthly; $1
Started: Aug. 1971
Circulation: 600

Format: 12 pages (8 1/4" x 10 1/4", mimeo., stapled)
Issues examined: Sept. 1973 - Mar. 1974
Indexing: in the journal
Back issues available from publisher

Here are the long-range goals of this official party journal:

> The establishment of a system of society or social system based on the world wide ownership of the means and instruments for producing and distributing wealth by all the people. This will mean the abolition of money, buying and selling, wages, salaries, and all the paraphernalia necessary under private or state ownership of wealth production and distribution. Our activities are mainly educational and political.

The publication consists mainly of signed theoretical articles on such topics as: "What Is Patriotism?"; "Capitalism and Violence Are Inseparable"; "Keynes's Theories Proven

Wrong"; "The Assassination of Art" ("The Un-American Activities Committee could not destroy Charles Chaplin or Arthur Miller, nor could the Soviets destroy Solzhenitsyn; but artists with less recognition, ahead of their time and people, are frequently destroyed in the power struggles of the world"); and "The Russian Illusion" ("As a substitute for socialist education, the Communist Party and their allies offer us fanciful pictures of the care-free existence of the Russian workers in an alleged paradise, created by the Russian dictators").

Some issues print letters disputing articles published in previous issues. The first page of each issue contains a Directory of Socialist branches in New Zealand, and lists of Socialist journals and pamphlets, as well as of bookstores selling Socialist literature. The last page carries a Declaration of Principles which makes these points: Present-day society is marred by antagonism ("class struggle") between (1) those who own (land, factories, railways, etc.) but don't produce, and (2) the working-people who produce goods but don't own their workplaces. The means of production and distribution should be owned jointly by all. Workers will have to bring about their own emancipation, and their party must fight all parties that don't support this goal. Finally, the machinery of government exists to conserve the power of the capitalist class, so the working class must win control of that machinery [feedback: "by democratic means"].

(Other "companion" socialist publications reviewed in this and previous volumes are Fulcrum, Socialist Review, The Socialist Standard, and The Western Socialist.) (JMS)

Feedback:

"We are more than satisfied with the way in which you have written up the SVP and ... are quite happy for this to be printed." The editor suggested some minor textual changes which were incorporated into the review.

## SOLIDARITY NEWSLETTER

Philadelphia Solidarity<br>Box 13011<br>Philadelphia, Pa. 19101<br>Irregular; 15¢ each<br>Started: Jan. 1972<br>Circulation: 350 (press run 1000-1500)

Format: 4- to 8-page tabloid (11" x 17", offset)<br>Issues examined: 3/4, 6, 7/8 (1973-1974?)<br>Back issues available from publisher

Solidarity Newsletter, published in Philadelphia,

represents a "revolutionary libertarian socialist viewpoint," advocates the establishment of workers' councils, and opposes Marxism-Leninism. Reviews of current literature, mainly Socialist but also more general (e.g., Skinner's Beyond Freedom and Dignity and The Limits of Growth) reflect this orientation. Articles on the student movement, the future socialist organization of workers, the new mysticism, and developments in international socialist countries also follow a counter-revolutionary line [see Feedback]; early concepts of Workers' Councils are branded as obsolete, leaders of the New Left are criticized for becoming mystics, and Angela Davis is severely trounced for supporting the Soviet government's repression of Czechoslovakian political prisoners.

The women's movement gets excellent coverage. One reporter investigated socialist governments around the world to see how women fare; many promises of child care, free abortions, and equal pay have not materialized. "Diary of a Male Housewife" delineates movingly the trials and emotional turmoils (familiar to any housewife) of a man who stayed home for a year with a child while his wife worked. In a large "Letters" section, correspondents argue and pass on information. Cartoons, line drawings, lists of literature for sale, a "Partial Directory of Like-Minded Folks," and a 7-item statement of "Where We Stand" are regular features.

(CP)

Feedback:

As far as indexing goes we'd like to be under both socialist and anarchist--we believe we bridge that 'gap.'

'also follow a counter revolutionary line' We're not sure how your reviewer, in an otherwise fine review, came up with this phrase. We, along with the rest of the anti-Leninist left (anarchists, council-communists, and libertarian socialists, etc.), hold the Leninist left to be counter-revolutionary, as in the past (Russia 1917, Spain 1936, Hungary 1956) they have always been opposed to the spontaneous revolutionary actions of the masses. We would not call ourselves counter-revolutionary from any point of view I can think of.

As a librarian, I appreciate what you're doing--it seems to be a successful reference tool, so keep it up!

THE SPOKESMAN

Bertrand Russell Peace Foundation
Bertrand Russell House,
Gamble St., Forest Rd. West
Nottingham NG7 4ET,
United Kingdom
Semi-annual; $6
Started: 1970

Circulation: 2,000
Format: 124 pages (5 3/4" x 8 1/2", offset)
Issues examined: June 1972; Aug. 1973
Back issues available from publisher

Each issue contains four or five scholarly studies on "imperialism" and "third world struggles for social justice"; book reviews; and the London Bulletin (formerly a separate publication). The Bulletin covers the Foundation's international activities, such as the well-known International War Crimes Tribunal, which exposed atrocities committed against the Vietnamese people by the United States government. The Foundation has also attempted to draw world attention to repression in Brazil, Greece, and Czechoslovakia.

Essays in the August issue dealt with such topics as "colonial India's experience as an object of imperial control and its relationship to the later development of independent Indian capitalism"; the economic and military impact of Holland, Britain, the United States, and Japan on Southeast Asia against a background of revolutionary liberation struggles; and a survey of 150 years of the Monroe Doctrine--"a study in the power, rhetoric, and policy options servicing Washington's continuing hegemony in Latin America." (JMS)

Feedback:
"This is fine. Thanks."

THIRD WORLD: Socialism and Development

Fabian Society
11 Dartmouth St.
London SWIH 9BN, United Kingdom
Monthly (not Aug.); $8.50
Started: Sept. 1972

Circulation: 4,500
Format: 16 pages (offset)
Issues examined: Oct.-Dec. 1973
Back issues available from publisher

Third World ("A forum for the problems of developing peoples") "represents not the collective view of the Society, but only the views of the individuals who write for it."

## THE UNITED IRISHMAN

30 Gardiner Pl.
Dublin 1, Ireland
Monthly; $6
Started: 1948
Circulation: 70,000

Format: 12-page tabloid (offset)
Issues examined: Feb. & Dec. 1973; Jan. 1974

The United Irishman is the organ of the Official Irish Republican Movement, composed of the Sinn Fein party and the IRA (Irish Republican Army). (The "officials" are not to be confused with the Provisional IRA, which split off several years ago and has been participating in the violence in Northern Ireland.) The Official Irish Republican Movement is socialist, and its goals are to unite the workers and small farmers, overthrow British imperial rule in Ireland, and create an independent Irish Socialist Republic.

> We oppose all foreign financiers, speculators, monopolists, landlords, and their native collaborators. We place the rights of the common man before the right of property. We claim the ownership of the wealth of Ireland for the people of Ireland.

Although The United Irishman sharply attacks the main political parties in Eire and Northern Ireland--the Labour Party; Fianna Fail (a southern party with labor ties); Fine Gael (southern liberal party); the Social-Democratic and Labor Party (mostly Catholic); the Unionists; the Conservatives; and the Loyalists (militant right-wing Protestants)--it blames Britain for promoting the violence between Protestants and Catholics.

> Sectarian murder is the most vicious weapon in the hands of the British Army. Vicious not only because it divides worker from worker, but because it fills the community with fear and the hatred that is born of fear.
>
> Carefully gauging the effects of their actions, the officers of the British Army sent their men in mufti into Catholic and Protestant areas of the Six [Northern] Counties with the intention of murdering workers and producing an effect which, they know, will lead to the murder of others.
>
> The pattern is clear. The killing is deliberate, cold-blooded, planned, and calculated to create the impression on Catholics that their attackers

are Loyalists, on Protestants that they are being murdered by Republicans.

The paper urges Catholic and Protestant workers to unite and turn on the common enemy--Britain.

Many articles ("What Is Happening in Our Jails?"; "1,000 Political Prisoners North and South--It Is Only Us Who Can Secure Their Release") describe the bad conditions of the prisons, and the inhumane treatment of the political prisoners. Lists of IRA prisoners are printed, and readers are asked to write to them and to help their families.

Other topics covered are: labor disputes; unions; low wages and bad working conditions; the plight of pensioners; critical housing shortages; raids and atrocities carried out by the police and the British Army; and the activities and programs of the IRA. The paper condemns the Sunningdale Agreement (arrived at by the British government and the coalition governments of Eire and Northern Ireland) because it ends all chances of unifying the island and does nothing to improve the condition of the working class. It will instead cause capitalism and British imperialism to flourish at the expense of the Irish people. The paper also condemns the giving of Ireland "to the moguls of the Common Market," and the exploitation of cheap Irish labor by foreign capitalists who operate businesses and industries in Ireland, and are exempt from taxes for the first 15 years. The paper supports revolutionary movements in other parts of the world.

Although it condemns the traditional views of the Catholic Church in Ireland, The United Irishman does not--as do other Marxist publications--condemn religion utterly. "The Church in Revolution" praises two young missionary priests--now part of the Irish worker-priest movement--who returned recently from South America, where they had rejected the Church's traditional role.

The republican movement encourages the revival of Irish traditional music, and the use of the Gaelic language, so The United Irishman's page-numbers are in Gaelic, and there is a special one-page Gaelic section.

An obituary section eulogizes heroes of the Republican and old Fenian movements.

Elsewhere in this chapter, see our reviews of other Official Irish Republican Movement periodicals: Eolas, The Irish People, and Rosc Catha. (JMS)

U. S. -China People's Friendship Association NEWSLETTER

407 S. Dearborn St. (Suite 1085)
Chicago, Ill. 60605

Bi-monthly
Format: 6 pages (offset)
Issue examined: Jan. 1974

The purpose of the Association, which embraces six midwest groups, is to promote friendship and understanding between the peoples of the two nations.

The sample issue contained a short article, "Chinese Impressions of the U. S. A." (excerpts from an article in China Reconstructs by one of a group of 26 Chinese journalists who visited the U. S.), balanced by a long review--containing many descriptive quotations--of Women and Child Care in China, by Ruth Sidel. The Newsletter also carried news of the Association's activities, photographs of Chinese workers and peasants, and a list of Chinese periodicals to which one may subscribe through the Association. (JMS)

UTOPIA

Dedalo, Publ.
Casella Postale 362
Bari 70100, Italy
Monthly; 3,000 Lire
Started: Jan. 1971
Circulation: 8,000

Format: 32 pages (21. 5 x 28 cm, offset)
Issues examined: none sent
Indexing: in journal
Back issues available from publisher

Subjects: culture and Marxism.

THE VIRGINIA WEEKLY

Monthly; $4 (free to GIs and prisoners; $12 to state agencies)
Dates: 1967-1972
Circulation: 10,000
Format: 16-page tabloid (offset)

Issues examined: Apr., May/June, Sept. 1972
Back issues available from publisher, Box 7002, Norfolk, Va. 23509
Microform version available from U. of Va. Library (possibly)

The Virginia Weekly was published

> by an independent group of workers, students, and unemployed people from several Virginia communities.

> We have joined together to publish a newspaper that will provide an alternative to the biases and interests of the established commercial press.
>
> We believe that there must be a revolution in the United States, a revolution that will take control of the government away from the capitalist class and create a state in which the working class holds power.

The great struggle of the world was seen to be that between the rich and the poor, the capitalist and the worker. The publication was committed to fight racism, sexism, anti-communism and national chauvinism, seen as the tools used by capitalists to divide the people so that they fight among themselves.

One lead article concerned Thomas Wansley, a Lynchburg Negro convicted of raping a white woman. The writer believed he was railroaded into prison by the racist city power structure and called attention to a petition being circulated urging his pardon. Another laid the blame for the flooding of Buffalo Creek in West Virginia on the Pittston Coal Company which blocked the stream with a slag heap that gave way. In the May/June 1972 issue, Nixon's Peace Plan was called a "monstrous escalation of the war."

Other articles were a government report on lack of sanitation in the food industry, a protest against poor conditions in Virginia prisons, and a description of the American tax system as a fraud which "reinforces rather than equalizes the power of wealth in America." Though both Nixon and McGovern were said to represent the capitalist, the latter was endorsed because he offered some advantages to the workers. There were news of union activity and strikes; information on abortion; and articles on oppression and injustice in other states and countries.

A feature, "Voices of Revolution," gave long excerpts from speeches or writings of men such as Ho Chi Minh and Lenin. The paper contained numerous cartoons and photographs. There were no advertisements.

<u>The Virginia Weekly</u>'s address was: Box 336-X, Newcomb Hall Station, Charlottesville, Va. 22901. (EC)

Workers' League BULLETIN

| | |
|---|---|
| 135 W. 14th St. | Started: 1965 |
| New York, N.Y. 10011 | Format: 20-page tabloid |
| Weekly; $4 | Issue examined: 21 May 1973 |

This "weekly organ of the Workers' League," published by Labor Publications, presents news and opinions of the militant labor movement. It is strongly anti-capitalist, anti-Stalinist, and anti-"middle-class radical." It reports on the Trotskyist Young Socialist Alliance ("Young Socialists Plan Rallies To Build National Conference"); problems of militant trade unionism in other countries ("masses of British workers ... in action ... against treacherous leaders"); militant activities within American unionism; and the lack of militant activity by some union leaders ("[Harry] Bridges Won't Fight for Political Alternatives"; "[Leonard] Woodcock Voice of Compromise"). (The two officials mentioned are the presidents of, respectively, the International Longshoremen's and Warehousemen's Union, and the United Auto Workers.) Separate pages, edited by correspondents in different parts of the country, carry news of unions on the East Coast, the West Coast, and in the Midwest. In the sample issue, a film review stressed the role of the cinema as an apologist for capitalism. (KL)

WORKERS' POWER

International Socialist Publishing Company
14131 Woodward Ave.
Highland Park, Mich. 48203
Bi-weekly; $3.50
Started: Jan. 1967
Circulation: 3,000
Format: 16-page tabloid (web-offset)

Issues examined: 2 & 16 Nov., 7 Dec. 1973
Indexing: Alternative Press Index
Back issues available from publisher
Microform version available from Xerox University Microfilms

Workers' Power is a revolutionary newspaper:

> We stand for socialism: the collective ownership and democratic control of the economy and the state by the working class. We stand in opposition to all forms of class society, both capitalist and bureaucratic 'Communist,' and in solidarity with the struggles of all exploited and oppressed people.

Capitalism is a divisive system, controlled by a small minority, that has outlived its time. Built into it are the problems of war, urban decay, racial conflict, pollution, and the deterioration of working and living conditions for the majority.

Efforts on behalf of workers' power must be made on

both economic and political levels. "The struggle of the working people will be deadlocked until the ranks of labor build a workers' party and carry the struggle into the political arena." The liberation of all minorities--Negroes, Chicanos, women and homosexuals--is in the interest of the whole working class. "Though their independent organization is needed, ... we strive to unite these struggles in a common fight to end human exploitation and oppression." This struggle is world-wide, for the working class has direct rule nowhere on earth.

The three lead articles in the sample issues all concerned Richard Nixon: "Nixon's Watergate Rats Leave the Sinking Ship"; "Nixon's New 'Candor': More Destroyed Tapes"; and "Nixon's Regime Tottering." There were editorial demands for his resignation, and criticism of his foreign policy.

Many articles reported on union activities. One called for political efforts inside unions to build a revolutionary workers' movement. Although workers' needs are not met by today's unions, "the attempt to build new revolutionary unions ... is utopian because it dodges the real political problem: winning the workers from their present leaders to a class struggle perspective."

Each issue contains an editorial, an "International Report," letters from readers, and news of the IS fund drive. Often there are reviews of books and films. The paper contains numerous photographs and drawings. The raised fist, symbolizing the revolutionary struggle, is found heading many articles. (EC)

Feedback:

The editor made these two comments:

1. "News of the IS fund drive is printed only during the two months that the drive is in progress. Normally, we carry news of IS meetings, activities, or publications."
2. "We are not for Nixon's resignation, but rather for his being thrown out. But--rather than simply replacing him with [Gerald R.] Ford or the Democrats--we call for the union movement to build an independent political party of the working class to oppose the policies of both capitalist parties."

WORKERS' VANGUARD

| | |
|---|---|
| Spartacist League | Bi-weekly; $3 |
| Box 1377, GPO | Started: Sept. 1971 |
| N.Y., N.Y. 10001 | Circulation: 9,000 |

Format: 12- to 16-page tabloid
Issue examined: July 1973

Back issues available from publisher

This Marxist journal replaces the League's Spartacist. (See our reviews of Spartacist and Spartacist-West in previous volumes, and Revolutionary Communist Youth Newsletter in this chapter.)

Articles in the sample issue dealt with (among other topics) the proposed Equal Rights Amendment to the U.S. Constitution (the League supports it; the Communist Party and the [Maoist] October League do not); attempts to reach a détente between the U.S. and U.S.S.R. ("In the epoch of decaying capitalism, a lasting democratic peace between the imperialist powers is impossible"); the struggle against Peronism in Argentina; labor struggles; and the Spartacist League's activities.

There has been friction between the League and the (Maoist) Revolutionary Union (Bay Area Worker). Workers' Vanguard reports that its salesmen were attacked (outside a California auto plant) by BAW salesmen:

> These violent tactics are simply a manifestation of the frustration resulting from this organization's [Revolutionary Union's] inability to politically defend its betrayals, especially its trade union policies. The RU's present strategy is to seek the absorption of its members into the local [union] bureaucracies by uncritically supporting the local leadership, thus cooperating in their sellouts of the membership. Workers' Vanguard's exposure of the nature of these betrayals has become so threatening to the RU that it attempts to keep auto workers from reading our paper.

(JMS; TJS)

YOUNG SOCIALIST: Official Monthly Paper of the Young Socialists

Labor Publications
135 W. 14th St.
N.Y., N.Y. 10011
Monthly; 15¢ a copy

Started: Apr. 1973
Format: 12-page tabloid (offset)
Issue examined: May 1973

The sample issue of Young Socialist tells us that the first issue of "the only Trotskyist youth paper in the United

States" was "a smashing success," selling out its press run of 10,000 copies in two weeks with Los Angeles and Chicago leading the sales. "The sale of the YS in its very first issue has been larger than that of the revisionists with their phony Young Socialist." (See our review of this rival Trotskyist paper [also out of New York] of the Young Socialist Alliance, pages 83-84.)

Young Socialist, which has a Latino-black orientation, is aimed at students although it has some labor articles. Two pages of the sample issue were devoted to "Heroes of the Russian Revolution." "Young Socialists Take on Watts" discussed the background of the area and told of launching a Young Socialists' branch there. "Sectarianism and the Spartacist League" criticized that Trotskyist group and the "revisionist" Socialist Workers' Party. In "British YS Salutes Publication of Young Socialist," the Soviet government is criticized and the aims of Young Socialist laid out:

> The strength of the Trotskyist movement has been based on the unshakable confidence in the ability of the working class to destroy capitalism and establish a socialist system provided it is given the correct revolutionary leadership. It is also our task to provide that leadership in this revolutionary situation now. That is why we see in ... the Young Socialist not just a monthly newspaper but the expression of a determined movement to fight for Marxist principles. This today means an uncompromising battle against counterrevolutionary Stalinism. Internationally the Stalinist bureaucracy has moved completely over to the defense of imperialism. Its policy of peaceful co-existence can only lead to catastrophic defeats for the working class in every capitalist country.

Examples of articles: "Hartford Youth Prepare [YS] May Conference"; "YS Slate Fights Budget Cuts" (at Pennsylvania State University); "A Return to Child Labor (criticizes Sec. of Labor Peter Brennan's bill to raise the minimum wage only if it excludes young workers); and "Police Terror" (at a Dayton, Ohio, high school, students are harassed by police because of racial disturbances).

The paper includes an international section with articles on or letters from YS groups in other countries. (JMS)

## YOUNG SOCIALIST

Linda Meissenheimer, Ed.
Box 517, Station A
Toronto, Ontario, Canada
10 issues per year; $2
Started: 1970

Circulation: 5,000
Format: 12-page tabloid (offset)
Issues examined: Sept., Oct., Nov./Dec. 1973

The Young Socialist, "only socialist student monthly on campuses and high schools across the country," states its philosophy:

> Young Socialist takes sides. We're with the oppressed, the exploited, the jailed and the down-trodden right around the world. We're proud of that, and we're proud of our record. We don't hide behind 'objectivity' to lie about the struggles of students, women, workers, the Québecois and the native people.
>
> When the bourgeois press attacks or ignores their struggles, Young Socialist is there to provide accurate coverage and a socialist analysis for the student movement across the country.

Young Socialist, Labor Challenge and the French-language Libération constitute the Socialist press in Canada with emphasis on the "socialist alternative to war, sexism, pollution, and repression." Young Socialist covers radical issues and what to do about them. Students' interests--cutbacks in education, rising costs for students, rights of the Québecois, and women students' rights, especially abortion laws and child care centers--are given special attention. Current news such as Quebec elections and the mid-east conflict are analyzed in the light of socialist thinking, and differences with the Young Communist League and the Revolutionary Marxist Group are explained.

The tone of the paper is serious socialist philosophy with a careful selection of news pictures and cartoons. Regular features include a book or movie review, an editorial ("As We See It"), and a column ("From the Back Row") which is a collection of brief news stories about political ironies and extravagances of the rich and powerful around the world. Typical feature articles--"Women and the Chinese Revolution," "Struggles of the Student Movement," "What Happened and Why: Lessons of the Coup in Chile"--are written with an historical background and a socialist interpretation.

Young Socialist advocates that students "try to link their

struggles with those of the working class," but also that "students can and do make important gains even by themselves and they can at times act as a detonator to set other broader social forces into motion." (JS)

YOUNG SPARTACUS

Libby Schaeffer, Ed.
Revolutionary Communist Youth, Spartacist League
Box 454, Cooper Station
N.Y., N.Y. 10003
Bi-monthly; $1
Started: Sept. 1973
Circulation: 9,000

Format: 8-12 pages (11" x 17", offset)
Issues examined: none sent
Back issues available from publisher
Microform version available from Xerox University Microfilms

Young Spartacus supersedes Revolutionary Marxist Caucus Newsletter and Revolutionary Communist Youth Newsletter (see reviews in this chapter).

The editor sent this information: "We seek to build a revolutionary socialist youth organization which can intervene in all social struggles armed with a working-class program, based on the politics of Marx, Lenin, and Trotsky." (See also reviews of the League's Spartacist, Spartacist-West, and Workers' Vanguard in this and previous volumes.)

THE YOUNG WORKER

Judy Edelman, Ed.
156 Fifth Ave. (Rm. 720)
N.Y., N.Y. 10010
Monthly or bi-monthly; $2.50
Started: July 1970
Circulation: 8,000

Format: 8-page tabloid (offset)
Issues examined: July, Sept., Nov. 1973
Some back issues available from publisher

This newspaper is published by the Young Worker Liberation League, the U.S. affiliate of the World Federation of Democratic Youth. The League is "a Marxist-Leninist youth organization of young workers, students (both high school and college), and unemployed youth--black, Chicano, Puerto Rican, Native American and white." The editor describes the goals of the League and its publication:

> We are involved in struggle for a better life for youth. We struggle against racism, male supremacy,

> anti-communism and all other ideas which keep people divided. We seek to unite all sectors of youth in a broad youth front to struggle for our common needs. We are opposed to the capitalist system, with its exploitation of man by man; we work toward socialism in the United States because we believe it is a better system for organizing society--a system free of exploitation, unemployment, and racism. We seek to help unite the working class,... oppressed peoples, and youth toward these ends.
>
> The pages of our publication present current news and analysis of the struggles of youth in the U.S. and abroad.

Some of the means encouraged by Young Worker to implement those goals are high school and college student unions, active support of the United Farmworkers' Union boycott of lettuce, grapes, and Gallo wines, and of the freedom movement for Puerto Rico. A typical article, "Support the Auto Workers," describes the problems faced by the rank-and-file auto worker and the negotiations being carried out by the United Auto Workers' Union for new contracts with the manufacturers.

There is variety in the regular features--poetry, reviews of jazz records, movies and books, and a "Calendar of Events in Struggle Against Racist and Political Repression" that lists dates of meetings, demonstrations and jury trials. One or two articles are presented in Spanish as well as English in adjoining columns. "Young Worker in Action" includes brief descriptions of members who are taking part in demonstrations, boycotts, and elections across the country. (JS)

Feedback:

Editor suggested some minor textual changes which have been incorporated in the review. "Other than these changes we think the review is fine, and appreciate your truly non-biased, non-anti-Communist approach to left literature."

YOUNG WORKER

| | |
|---|---|
| Dan Hammond, Ed. | Monthly; $1 |
| 24 Cecil St. | Format: 8-page tabloid |
| Toronto, 2 B, Ontario, Canada | Issues examined: Nos. 1 & 2 (1973) |

Young Worker is a Marxist newspaper written for

Canadian youth in the job market. It gives close consideration to the problems of unemployment and unemployment insurance, working conditions, and job opportunities. (Affiliated with the Young Communist League, Young Worker supersedes Young Communist.)

Two editorial columns ("As We See It" and "Marxism in Life") explain Young Worker's policy. Signed articles are included that do not necessarily agree with that policy.

Readers are urged to boycott goods from apartheid South Africa and to support self determination of the Vietnamese, the Palestinians, and the French-speaking people of Quebec. Young Worker objects to Canadian involvement in United Nations peacekeeping, and to U.S. policy in Vietnam and Israel.

Articles cover youth participation in international events: the USSR 50th anniversary celebration, the World Meeting of Working Youth in Moscow, and the 10th World Festival of Youth and Students in Berlin. A representative article, "Internationalism in Action: A School for Cuba's Children," describes the work of an international Brigade of some eighty-five young people who gathered in Cuba to build a school and to demonstrate "the spirit of proletarian internationalism" in the "continuing struggle against imperialism."

Pictures and full-page advertisements from the Young Communist League are a prominent part of the newspaper and state the theme of the editorial content:

> Fight for your future! Peace! Jobs! This slogan unites young people across Canada into a fighting organization--The Young Communist League! The YCL has a program which says a defiant NO to unemployment, dead-end jobs that offer no future, war, and U.S. domination of our very lives.
>
> We say NO to the policy of national oppression used to split and divide and breed animosity between the people of our two nations.
>
> We say NO to the government in Ottawa which uses drugs, racism, police brutality to beat our generation into the mould of quiet obedience.
>
> We fight for the future of Canadian youth--we fight for the future of Canada!

(JS)

## Chapter 3

## RADICAL PROFESSIONAL

> Like its big brother the military, education is used to repress people.... ---Edcentric

> We see the dehumanization and alienation of people as part of a social order of exploitation, racism, sexism, and war.... [Our] purpose is not merely to understand this system: it is to change it.
> ---Science for the People

> Some members of URPE ... consider that traditional economics ... may be a distinct social evil....
> ---Union for Radical Political Economics

A recent phenomenon is the appearance of critical and dissenting periodicals put out by idealistic young academics, scientists, and other professional people who question not only the methods and goals (or absence of goals) of their professions, but also the assumptions or theories upon which these disciplines are based. They disparage what they see as the materialistic, self-serving outlook of their elders, and they often want to change the capitalist nature of American society. (We first noted these periodicals in the introduction to the Radical Left chapter of our 1972 volume.)

Science for the People (Scientists and Engineers for Social and Political Action) sees the institutions of our present society as dehumanizing and based upon "exploitation, racism, sexism, and war." Spark (Committee for Social Responsibility in Engineering) complains of "misguided national priorities" and of a weapons technology that "spells ultimate disaster for mankind." It challenges the present orientation of engineering and seeks ways in which engineering skills can be used to solve the "growing ills of our society." Edcentric wants to change not only the educational system (which it feels represses people and keeps them from "defining their own lives and freedoms") but the "whole of society" as well. Specific educational reforms it encourages are open admissions policies, free universities, and an end to discrimination against women. Something Else for Teachers is less radical: it wants only to improve the existing educational system which--it complains--is not meeting the needs of the children.

In the field of medicine, Health/PAC Bulletin (put out by a private educational organization) exposes the inequities of the present health care system and urges the creation of a new one that will deliver good care "based on keeping you well," paid for by "progressive taxation," and "locally governed by health workers and consumers." Notes on Health Politics (Health Professionals for Political Action) also wants fundamental changes in the health care system, and the creation of equitable health insurance which meets consumers' needs. Health Law Newsletter reports on legal activities concerning the health problems of the poor. Issues in Radical Therapy is a forum for psychiatrists, psychologists, therapists, social workers, and others who are working for radical change by--among other things--"exposing and stopping the oppressive misuse of psychiatry by the psychiatric establishment" and by redefining mental health and psychology's role in society.

Some periodicals advance a socialist or Marxist position. Librarians for Social Change (an English periodical which publishes things "that most other British librarianship journals wouldn't touch with a barge pole") carries a lead article that advocates giving libraries back to the people (after the revolution) by turning their control over to residents of the community and to library workers (shelvers and pages?), and by demystifying the classification system so that people without professional training can run things. (The demystification of psychiatry was called for by The Radical Therapist, p. 529 above.) Contributors to No More Teacher's Dirty Looks (Bay Area Radical Teachers' Organizing Collective) try to express (through their teaching, as well as through their relations with students, colleagues, and students' parents) a revolutionary socialist viewpoint. Hotch Pot (published by a collective of workers in human service jobs and activists in the Social Welfare Workers' Movement) presents articles covering social workers' activities in the U.S., and advocates "some kind of democratic [socialist] control and ownership of the wealth and means of production" as "necessary for democracy."

In American librarianship, two activist publications are Synergy (Bay Area Reference Center, San Francisco Public

Library) and its successor, Booklegger Magazine. They cover the alternative/counter culture and its publications, and offer ideas for "revitalizing the library profession and making libraries more accessible and responsive to people."

--Janet Spahn

BOOKLEGGER MAGAZINE

72 Ord St.
San Francisco, Calif. 94114
Bi-monthly; $8
Started: Nov. 1973
Circulation: 2,000
Format: 48-60 pages (7" x 10")

Issues examined: Nov. 1973; May 1974
Indexing: Library Literature
Back issues available from publisher

Booklegger is "published by/for Library Workers" and is the independent successor (i.e., Celeste West is still an editor) of the federally-funded Synergy. It is a journal of alternatives: alternative (small press) publications, most of which are not reviewed elsewhere in the standard library and publishing industry press ("The Great Unreviewed ... For the Great Unwashed"); and alternative ideas, especially for revitalizing librarianship and making libraries more accessible and responsive to more people.

Booklegger consists of articles on plans, projects, and ideas ("On Building People's Libraries"), and bibliographic articles on subjects not covered sufficiently in most libraries (alternative sewage methods--"gettin' your shit together"; decriminalizing prostitution--"yr ass is yr own"; alternative schools; radical therapy; "body books"; divorce; the library free press) as well as several half-page reviews of small press publications (pamphlets, books, periodicals, records).

Regular columns are "Captain Video," about new developments in cable TV and its use in and by libraries; "Kids and Libraries"; and "Grapevine," an annotated listing of new publications. Lots of graphics, too.

A double issue (No. 3/4) has the theme, "On Democratizing Library Management." It includes articles on how the San Francisco Public Library librarians' union was organized; how library students organized a prison library service; how to organize a university library; and a bibliography on worker self-management. Celeste West introduces the issue in "Working Loose":

Libraries belong to the community and to the people

> who labor in them. This Land is Our Land. So why are workers in these supposedly humanistic places so alienated from their jobs? Because we don't control what services we produce, or for whom. 'The Administration,' an out-of-touch minority, with no distinctive skills or education (in San Francisco, no experience is even required), makes the ultimate decisions.... Every human being has the need and right to fulfillment and true participation at work, whether [in an] institution or factory.

In "Union Women," Joan Dillon enumerates the facts about women workers and discusses the difficulty of securing equal job rights for women, even through unions:

> As president of my union ... I deal with all the handicaps inflicted by a history of women's oppression. I have heard women refuse to join our union because their husbands, active union members themselves, forbid it. Women do not assume leadership in the union because of holding two jobs, one as full-time homemaker, the other with the city. I still fight that old, underlying fear that women workers deprive men of jobs. To keep workers in line, the bosses have always called up the spectre of an 'out' group ready to seize jobs: women, blacks, immigrants, third world peoples.

(MM)

Feedback:

Celeste West replied: "We love it." (The review has since been shortened.)

EDCENTRIC

Center for Educational Reform
Box 1802
Eugene, Ore. 97401
6 issues a year; $6 (institutions $10)
Started: 1967 (new format Jan. 1970)
Circulation: 3,500
Format: 8 pages (offset)
Issues examined: Feb.-Apr. 1970
Indexing: Alternative Press Index

Edcentric carries a two- or three-page middle section ("Movement") listing programs, conferences, newsletters, and current protest actions on the university level around the country. Most of the rest of the journal consists of lists of relevant publications, reports of student strikes and conferences, and feedback from the Center's mobile office (a "Big Red Bus" which travels throughout America helping student groups and finding out what's happening).

In the few articles, and in the monthly "Opinion from the Center," the editors' revolutionary base becomes clear. They see colleges and universities as a symptom of the *malaise* of American society: "Like its big brother the *military*, education is used to repress people and keep them from defining their own lives and freedoms." The responsibility of educational reformers is to change the whole society, not just to improve conditions at a few universities. Working for open admissions policies and an end to the discrimination against women, and establishing free universities that will produce people who know what they want to learn and why, rather than deadened Ph. D. candidates, are courses of action recommended by *Edcentric*. (CP)

Feedback:

The editor submitted a re-worded review, several sentences of which merit quoting. '*Edcentric* is a radical magazine which critically examines both the conventional schooling system and the movement for educational change." "The *Edcentric* collective sees traditional schools and universities as an integral part of the *malaise* of American society." "... the responsibility of those engaged in educational change is to transform stultifying social attitudes and institutions into healthy facilitators of human growth."

## ELYSIUM JOURNAL OF THE SENSES

Elysium Institute
5436 Fernwood Ave.
Los Angeles, Calif. 90027
Quarterly; $2
Started: 1968

Circulation: 20,000
Format: 24- to 48-page tabloid (offset)
Issues examined: Apr., July, Oct. 1973

The Institute's "Credo" praises the "essential wholesomeness" of

> the human body and all of its functions. Exposure to sun, water, air, and to nature is a helpful and basic factor in building and maintaining healthy attitudes of mind in the development of a strong body. Human sexuality is part and parcel of our living and no separation or division is possible without denying our ... [humanity].

Elysium Fields, a country estate ..., offers sensitivity and awareness workshops, on a clothing-optional basis....

Elysium In-Town Centre ... is open to the public on a clothed basis.... Experienced professionals offer group activity in the form of workshops, seminars, encounters, participation drop-ins, and idea exchanges, in addition to occasional informal social events.

The Elysium Journal of the Senses ... is dedicated to broadening public recognition of the naturalness and rightness of the human body and its functions, and to reportage of events related to this objective.

Examples of articles: "The Biorhythm Theory and the Human Condition"; "The Tyranny of Manliness" (reporting on a marathon session that tried to help men break the "he-man" image); "Non-Verbal Communication, Berber Style"; and "Sexuality in a Zero-Growth Society." One issue carried a pictorial report on the British Broadcasting Corporation's filming of a nude encounter group at the Institute.

HEALTH LAW NEWSLETTER

Ruth Galanter, Ed.
10995 LeConte Ave. (Rm. 640)
Los Angeles, Calif. 90024
Monthly; free
Started: May 1971
Circulation: 3,000

Format: 4 pages (offset)
Issues examined: Nov. 1973-Jan. 1974
Indexing: in every 12th issue
Some back issues available from publisher

This "reports legal activity in health problems of the poor." It is "designed to explain legal cases and developments, mostly work done by the National Health Law Program (Office of Economic Opportunity-funded Legal Services Back-Up Center), for health workers and consumers and the general public."

Topics covered include Medicaid ("Medicaid 'Spend Down'"); Medicare ("Medicare Financial Liability"); rights of patient-workers in mental institutions ("Patient-Workers' Rights"); and the national blood policy of the Department of Health, Education, and Welfare ("Blood").

From time to time there is a listing of publications available (sometimes free) from the National Health Law Program at the University of California. (MH)

Feedback:

"Your summary looks fine."

HEALTH/PAC BULLETIN

Health Policy Advisory Center
17 Murray St.
N.Y., N.Y. 10007
Bi-monthly; $7 (students $5; institutions $15)
Started: July 1968
Circulation: 5,000
Format: 16 pages (7" x 11", offset)

Issues examined: May, Sept., Oct. 1973
Indexing: in Dec. issue, and in Alternative Press Index
Back issues available from publisher
Microform version available from Univ. of Michigan Microfilm Center

This is the publication of a non-profit, non-governmental research and education organization.

> Since its beginning in 1968, Health/PAC's purpose has been to expose the inequities of the health system and monitor new developments in health reform. ... Together we are working for the creation of a new health system--a system that [1] delivers free high-quality health care paid for by progressive taxation, [2] is based on keeping you well, not on making profits from making you sick, [and 3] is locally governed by health workers and consumers.

The cover story of each issue is an editorial rather than a hard news story. Editorial policy is plainly marked as such so that the reader is not misled. Each issue is built around a theme. First, the Bulletin expresses its editorial opinions on the topic; then it explores various aspects of the subject in the articles that follow. The Bulletin does not call for revolution. It asks for reform, for change, and does so largely by indicating points at which the present system is failing. Throughout all its issues is a concern with the quality of the health care provided to the poor.

As an indication of Health/PAC's concern for the underprivileged, one whole issue is devoted to health care in prisons. It points out that this care is inadequate, and cites delays in providing needed hospitalization, the punitive attitude of the guards, and the low quality of most of those who offer health services to prisoners. On the other side of the coin, it describes the problems of providing care to inmates. "The plain fact is that many prisoners besiege the health section of the prisons with minor complaints. If nothing else, this breaks the deadly tedium of 24-hour-a-day cell life."

An editorial dealing with cutbacks in federal spending for health programs states that money is not the answer. "The real issue is who controls the health system and to what ends." An article in the same issue, "Federal Health Cutbacks," cites many instances of cutbacks and is quite specific about programs and dollar amounts. (According to the extensive bibliography at the end of the article, the figures were taken from the 1974 U.S. Budget, published by the Government Printing Office.)

Almost every issue deals with situations on the east coast, centering in the New York area, with a few articles from the west coast, usually dealing with health in the San Francisco area. This may be explained by the fact that Health/PAC's offices are located in those two cities. (BK)

Reviewer's opinion:

On the whole, a straightforward, well-written, business-like magazine which argues its case for changes in health care delivery openly and persuasively.

Feedback:

"In general, we are pleased with the tone and content. However, I would like to point out a few difficulties. Checking through the last 12 issues I find 16 major stories, 4 of which ... [deal] primarily with NYC. The rest deal with either West Coast or national health matters. It should, of course, be noted that even a 'local' story may have national import. For example, a story on prepaid group practice may use ... examples in California, but what it says will generally be found true of this form of practice elsewhere in the country. I can assure you that the focus of future Bulletins will not be predominantly NYC." "... over-all a good summary of the Bulletin. If the rest of your book is up to this standard, it should be a very worthwhile contribution."

HOTCH POT

"probably monthly" Format: 12-page tabloid
Started: 1970 Issue examined: May 1970

Hotch Pot was published by a political collective of 12 workers in human service jobs and activists in the Social Welfare Workers' Movement who believed that "human service workers have a strategic role and crucial interest in the struggle to make life meaningful in society." The workers held that groups--politically self-conscious human collectives --must be the foundation stones of democratic change. A political movement for democratic changes, they felt, was necessary in America. Hotch Pot workers believed

> that we need radical ideas and commitment because we will discover from working together to get meaningful political changes, that private 'capitalistic' control and ownership of the economic control of our nation's wealth prevents those changes. We think that some kind of democratic control and ownership of the wealth and means of production is necessary for democracy and that radicals and other 'progressives' should keep exchanging ideas to discover what that socialist form should and could be in America.

Unsigned articles covering social workers' activities throughout the U.S.--e.g., the activities of the National Conference on Social Welfare; the Alliance of Black Social Work Students of the U. of Pennsylvania; the Washington, D.C., D of D (Defense of Dissent); and the Black and Puerto Rican Health Workers in New York City--were included in the issue reviewed. Hotch Pot saw itself as giving all social workers support through "communication, the exchange of ideas, and cooperation in regional and national events." (JMG)

A draft of this review mailed to Hotch Pot was returned by the Post Office marked "Moved, Not Forwardable." The address had been Box 2492, Cleveland, Ohio 44112.

## ISSUES IN RADICAL THERAPY

IRT Collective
Box 23544
Oakland, Calif. 94623
Quarterly; $4 ($10 to institutions)
Started: Jan. 1973
Circulation: 4,000

Format: 36-page tabloid
Issues examined: Autumn & Summer 1973
Indexing: Alternative Press Index
Microform version in Women's History Archives

Issues in Radical Therapy is a forum for dialogue and exchange of information among people in the radical therapy movement. (For a definition of "radical therapy" and for the "Radical Psychiatry Manifesto," see our review of The Radical Therapist, p. 528, above; and also p. 945.)

> We are in the process of exposing and stopping the oppressive misuse of psychiatry by the psychiatric establishment. We have created space for dialogues between people who want to demystify the relationship between political oppression and psychiatric disturbance. We are a vehicle for exchange of practical experience and theory about how to be psychiatrists for each other.

The periodical says that it prints articles that grow out of doing radical therapy, articles on oppression in the "psychiatric industry," and articles about political repression and its relationship to psychiatric disturbances. Examples of articles:

1. "Fat Liberation," by a fat therapist working with a fat liberation group. Fat people are an oppressed minority needing liberation. They are discriminated against in employment as well as socially. Fatness is not a problem and loss of weight should not be a goal of fat therapy; instead, the approach should be fat pride and fat power. [Feedback: The last four words are "too rhetorical."]
2. "Cooperation," by Claude Steiner, who started Radical Psychiatry at Berkeley and was once a student of Eric Berne's. White North Americans are indoctrinated with the concepts of "individualism" and "competitiveness" and told that such traits will lead to happiness and success.

> This mystification, which has as its main purpose to shape us into pliable workers easily exploited by a ruling class, is not only not the way to achieve happiness, but it is in fact the most specifically successful manner in which to destroy and liquidate our human potential for harmony with ourselves, harmony with each other, and harmony with nature.

3. "In Behalf of Bisexuality": A bisexual woman-feminist radical psychiatrist gives reasons for loving both men and women:

> Bisexuality inclines a person away from monogamy. . . . I believe that fighting monogamy is a very important revolutionary act, that monogamy is the kingpin of the nuclear family which reinforces our inability to function effectively and succeed in groups. If we are able to love only one person in a deep and meaningful way, we are seriously hindered from developing a collectivized socialist movement in this country.

4. In "Straight Men Are in Drag," a homosexual who passed as straight for many years makes the point that straight men fear close relationships with other men.
5. "Teaching Psychology to High School 'Misfits'" is by a woman who taught "educationally handicapped" high school students using the concepts of radical psychiatry and transactional analysis. Psychology courses and therapy sessions offered in many schools are not being taught to promote changes in the system. They are, instead, means by which teachers and administrators can control students by persuading them that "coping" and "adjustment" are desirable.

> Grown-ups too often usurp youth's power and rights. Therapy and psychology coupled with abused teacher-power can become even more clever ways for abusive grown-ups to oppress the young.... a good teacher will use her knowledge of therapy to give the power of self-direction and self-knowledge back to the students and prove that we are all basically good and fine.

One issue contained chilling articles on the abuses of psychosurgery. Other features of IRT: letters to the editor (some from prisoners undergoing enforced psychiatric therapy and psychosurgery); a few poems ("I Made Love to Myself Last Nite"); and well-executed drawings and cartoons. In layout and appearance, IRT resembles The New York Review of Books.

Rick De Golia, a member of the collective that issues IRT, is a radical psychiatrist who helped to organize the first Radical Psychiatry Conference and was elected in 1972 to Berkeley's local poverty program on the Black Panther slate. (JMS)

Feedback:
"Over-all quite good."

## THE JOURNAL OF CAMPUS-FREE COLLEGE

466 Commonwealth Ave.
Boston, Mass. 02215
Monthly; $2
Started: May 1971

Circulation: 3,500
Format: 8 pages (offset)
Issue examined: Nov. 1973
Back issues available from publisher

The Journal carries announcements and describes the activities of a "continent-wide, non-residential college now available to students in 175 towns and cities in North America." Anyone may enroll. Students may work toward a degree or not, as they please. They are guided in their studies by one of several hundred advisors who "help them [to] plan a college curriculum, design specific learning projects, and gain access to local teachers, courses, programs, and other learning opportunities."

"CFC is affiliated with a number of educational and professional organizations" that "give students access to instruction, apprenticeships, and other learning." A catalog and further information may be obtained from the Boston office.

## LIBRARIANS FOR SOCIAL CHANGE

John Noyce
Flat 2, 83 Montpelier Rd.
Brighton, Sussex, England
3 a year; $6
Started: Oct. 1972
Circulation: 400
Format: 30 pages (8 1/4" x 11 3/4", offset)

Issue examined: Winter 1973
Indexing: LISA
Back issues available from publisher
Microform version available from Harvester Press, Sussex, England

The journal of Librarians for Social Change (LfSC) features articles that have a "radical approach to librarianship and information work." It publishes ideas that "most other British librarianship journals wouldn't touch with a barge pole." LfSC does not set policy for its members; it "is a vehicle for those of differing views." The common bond among LfSC members "is a desire to change the existing library situation and to relate libraries more to the world around us."

In the issue examined, the lead article was entitled "Libraries after the Revolution," written by a London librarian. The author states that, at present, some libraries act "solely to increase profits, maintain governments in power, further mystify knowledge and maintain the present system in general. Even public libraries maintain the status quo in a variety of subtle ways." However, after the socialist revolution, the people, in the form of the residents of the community and the workers in the library, will control the libraries and operate them to their own advantage. In order for people without professional training to run them, "the libraries must become much easier for everyone to understand and operate." As an example of this, "classification systems must be simplified and completely rethought to bring them in-line to prevailing social realities and not try to conform to WASP 19th century values and ancient Greek philosophical systems." The author urges librarians to become involved in revolutionary activity both in and out of the library.

Another article, "Queer Reading," advocates that librarians accept the new homosexual literature and stop "that quaint little habit you have of classifying our kind of love in the shelf headed 'sexual deviation'." The author would like to see homosexual works "proudly displayed in an extensive gay studies section."

A short notice in LfSC reports on the activities of the Children's Literature Collective, a feminist group composed of teachers and librarians who examine and analyze various fields of literature for children. They would like to begin writing non-sexist children's books themselves.

Other features include letters to the editor, book reviews, and a continuing series of articles on left-wing libraries in England. (SLA)

Feedback:

"Okay, except (1) the lead article in No. 4 ["Libraries after the Revolution"] is one person's view. Others don't entirely agree. (2) The Feminist group is very important and do[es] one issue a year of the journal. (3) Censorship in libraries is another important theme in the journal. (4) LfSC publishes mainly short articles. The longer ones are issued as pamphlets by Smoothie Publications (same address). Nice to get a review which gets the feel of the journal!!"

Articles that have appeared in other issues include "Libraries in North Vietnam," "Journals of British Pacifism," "Mentally Handicapped and the Library," "Women in Japanese Libraries," "Guide to Sources of Info on Women's Rights in Britain," and "Sexism in Children's Books: A Bibliography."

## NO MORE TEACHER'S DIRTY LOOKS

Bay Area Radical Teachers' Organizing Collective
388 Sanchez St.
San Francisco, Calif. 94114
Three issues a year; $3 (libraries $6)
Started: 1961
Circulation: 600

Format: variable: 38-42 pages (7" x 10"); or 20-page tabloid
Issues examined: 1972; Spring & Summer 1973
Back issues available from publisher

The teacher-editors discuss their philosophy:

> The goal we set for ourselves ... is to express through our teaching and our relations with our students, their parents, and other teachers, our socialist politics. It is to make our lives and our work an expression of the values of a new socialist movement and a basis for that movement.... For now ... remember that we are socialists, that we want a revolution, and that in some way each article is about how we can make that socialist revolution happen.

Not all articles express a revolutionary point of view; some deal only with educational problems. For example, an article may present a number of innovative math games and examine one teacher's method of presenting this subject. [Feedback: "... the sentence that reads, 'Not all articles express a revolutionary point of view' and gives as an example the math games article is inaccurate. All of our articles are political in that they deal with ways of changing curriculum, methods, and social relations in the classroom within a political context. For example, the math article was selected because it proposed a way of teaching which instead of pitting students against each other encouraged them to work together. We see this as political because it attacks the intense competitiveness that children learn in school.... we see methods and games [as being] as important as content, and are trying to redefine both in a political way."]

Other articles treat subjects from a revolutionary socialist viewpoint. Topics discussed are bussing to achieve integration, sexism in the schools, and discrimination against women. Articles dealing with purely local (San Francisco) issues are rare: the focus is on education in general.

Two issues criticize Jonathan Kozol and other male "super teachers":

> There is no account in their work of how sexism, racism, or authoritarianism make teaching difficult, or how the connections between the problems of the schools and the problems of the society create problems in the classrooms that even the most brilliant teacher in the world couldn't solve.

In another issue an article critical of Kozol's Free Schools complains that "he does not recognize middle-class oppression. He persists in seeing the counter-culture and free school movement as a symbol of privilege, rather than a response to a deepening crisis in people's lives." The concentration on Kozol and the hostility expressed seemed almost personal. [Feedback: "We do have intense personal/political feelings about Kozol and the super-teachers, and see nothing wrong with that. As women, we see much that is called personal as political...."]

A special issue introducing the kinds of materials available at the new BARTOC Educational Resources Center gives samples of children's writings intended to be used to teach reading to other children, misspellings and all. [Feedback: "Delete 'misspellings and all.' It takes away from the main point ... that children show a greater interest in learning how to read when they are presented with materials that interest them--particularly materials that are written by them and their ... peers."] The Center offers material on black history; labor history; and the Spanish-speaking American movement, La Raza, with reviews of books on the movement. Selections from books and papers on the women's movement are also reprinted. They deal with women on welfare; defend the lesbian; and discuss sex-role stereotypes, and aspects of women's history. This issue (Summer 1973) is particularly attractive, with bold type and bright pictures and drawings. All of the issues contain black-and-white drawings which add a cheerful note to the periodical.

Teachers of similar political persuasions will find NMTDL to their taste. (BK)

Feedback:

"There are most definitely some changes we would like to make...." (These changes have been indicated in the text.) "The rest of the review seems fine."

## NOTES ON HEALTH POLITICS

| | |
|---|---|
| David Blumenthal, Ed. | Started: Oct. 1972 |
| Health Professionals for Political Action | Circulation: 2,500 |
| Box 386, Kenmore Station | Format: 4 pages (offset) |
| Boston, Mass. 02215 | Issues examined: none sent |
| Monthly; "no price" | Back issues available from publisher |

The following information was received from the editor:

> The newsletter ... expresses the commitment of our membership of young health workers to fundamental

change in the health care system.... [It] carries commentary and analysis on current health issues with a special focus on problems relevant to national health insurance. HPPA's primary goal is ... the creation of a comprehensive, equitable health insurance system which is responsive to consumer needs.

## ST. LOUIS JOURNALISM REVIEW

FOCUS/Midwest Publishing Co.
Box 3086
St. Louis, Mo. 63130
Bi-monthly; $6
Started: 1970
Circulation: 6,500
Format: 16-page tabloid (offset)
Issues examined: Oct. 1973; Jan. & June 1974
Indexing: Alternative Press Index
Back issues available from publisher

As a "critique of journalism by working journalists," the St. Louis Journalism Review "reports on news media" in the St. Louis area and "evaluates their performance." The Review also makes its columns available to "lay critics of the press, particularly to those who have been denied access to the regular media or whose stories have been distorted."

One major concern, expressed in several articles, is "media concentration" or "cross-ownership" in the St. Louis area. "Strike Shows Close Post-Globe Ties" discloses that the St. Louis Post has a profit-sharing agreement with the St. Louis Globe that deterred the Globe from publishing during the Teamsters' strike against the Post. In addition, the publisher of the Post owns KSD-TV and KSD-AM while the owner of the Globe owns KTVI (TV). Several articles report on the Justice Department's efforts to challenge license renewals of KSD-AM, KSD-TV, and KTVI because of this cross-ownership.

The news programs of St. Louis television stations are often subject to criticism. "Broadcast Media Con St. Louis Readers with 'Expanded News' Pitch" exposes the failure of local television and radio stations to provide the promised "expanded news" coverage during the 1973 St. Louis newspaper strike. "New Faces--Same Old KMOX-TV" concludes that KMOX's revamped news format stresses the "style and appearance of its reporters rather than content."

Occasionally coverage of individual news items is criticized, as in "Take Your Pick: Sloppy Reporting or Police Coverup." This article speculates on the reasons for the omission of certain details about a police auto chase from a Post article.

Newspaper Guild grievances against the Post were aired in two successive issues. "Post Holding Back on Wages Despite Governmental Ruling" emphasizes that Post employees were denied wage increases stipulated in their contract despite a favorable Cost of Living Council ruling.

The Review is concerned about racism and sexism in news media coverage and hiring practice. "Bill Fields Speaks Out on St. Louis Television" describes racist and sexist practices on such shows as KMOX's "liberal 'At Your Service' programs" which have never had a "full-time black host" or "any women (or hostesses) or orientals or anyone except white middle-class oriented males."

A "Letters and Comments" section appears frequently, and "Major personnel changes in the St. Louis news media" are listed as a regular feature. The Review is apparently a successor to FOCUS/Midwest, which we reviewed on pp. 157-58. (JMA)

## SCIENCE FOR THE PEOPLE

9 Walden St.
Jamaica Plain, Mass. 02130
Bi-monthly; $12 (free to prisoners)
Started: June 1970
Circulation: 3,000
Format: 40 pages (offset)
Issues examined: Jan., May, July 1974
Indexing: in v. 5, no. 5; also Alternative Press Index
Back issues available from publisher
Microform version available from Xerox University Microfilms

This is the journal of Scientists and Engineers for Social and Political Action.

> We are scientists, engineers, students, teachers, technicians, and many others brought together by the common experience of frustration in our attempts to be socially productive human beings. We see the dehumanization and alienation of people as part of a social order of exploitation, racism, sexism, and war.... [Our] purpose is not merely to understand this system: it is to change it.

SftP is "produced by editorial collectives, consisting of 5-8 different people for each issue." The collective sees "the production of an issue ... as a creative political act in which the collective solicits, organizes, and edits material to produce a work of political art and propaganda."

Each issue focuses on one or two topics, but includes articles on other problems. (Many of the articles have extensive footnotes.) For example, one issue concentrated on health care and its inadequacies and inequalities, in articles such as "Midwest Workers Fight for Health and Safety," "Polyvinyl Chloride Causes Cancer" (on an ingredient of plastic products), and "How To Look at Your Plant: Worker's Guide to Health and Safety."

A series of articles in another issue explored the question of birth control in underdeveloped countries. Differing viewpoints were presented on whether birth control (including abortion and sterilization) is another aspect of imperialism or a necessity if these countries are to advance socially and economically.

Another issue presented papers on the use of psychosurgery and behavior modification, especially in prisons and mental hospitals: "Genocide of the Mind"; "Violence Center: Psychotechnology for Repression," criticizing a UCLA project aimed at altering undesirable behavior; "Prisoners' Verdict: The Prisons Are the Crime"; and "Now Kids...," about the use of drugs to control hyperactive children.

Other topics covered in the sample issues: the energy crisis and its manipulation by the oil industry; "the imperialist uses of ecology"; the Philippines seen as the next Vietnam; and "The Struggle against Army Math," about the trial of the person who bombed the Army Math Building at the University of Wisconsin (killing one student) and the continuing fight by radical scientists to shut down the building.

Regular features include letters; "News Notes"; "items of interest and humor," often poking fun at bureaucratic idiocy or repression; "Science for the People Activities"; notes on projects and struggles in need of support; and a Science Teaching Column. The journal also carries ads for other radical publications. (SLA)

Feedback:

"We thought that your summary was fair and unbiased, also informative and ... interesting to others." "Previous issues have focused on Technology and the Third World (July 1973); ... Science Teaching (Sept. 1972); and The IQ Controversy (March 1974)."

## SOMETHING ELSE FOR TEACHERS

5334 S. Kimbark (Apt. 3)
Chicago, Ill. 60615
Monthly
Started: May 1969

Format: 21 pages (mimeo., side-stapled)
Issue examined: May 1969

Something Else for Teachers is written by and for teachers in the Chicago area. In the first issue, the editor writes:

"We are frustrated teachers, frustrated because the educational system in the city of Chicago is not meeting the needs of the children of Chicago, frustrated because conditions make it almost impossible for us to teach. The problems are familiar and ever-present--huge class sizes, excessive paper work, irrelevant or unobtainable teaching materials, infrequent substitutes, insufficient preparation time, *ad infinitum*.

"We have no simple solutions for the problems that we face every day. We do know that we cannot solve our problems in isolation....

"As concerned teachers we want to know what our colleagues are doing all across the city. And we want to know what they are thinking ... we can only profit from listening to each other's ideas.

"This magazine is intended to be a free forum in which teachers may communicate their ideas, and a source of school news from all sections of Chicago. It will also contain items of interest to teachers that do not necessarily pertain directly to school problems.... We hope that the exposure and discussion of educational alternatives will help teachers generate direction and thrust for needed change."

The first issue contains articles expressing the teachers' opinions on strikes; the Chicago Teacher's Union; discriminatory certification; poor union leadership; and apathetic, politically-oriented, authoritarian administrations. Teachers are asked to participate actively in the improvement of teaching and learning conditions. One article advises: "Let's not continue in the role which has been thrust upon us by design --that of being passive, non-participating puppets in the school system.... Let's stop grumbling and start action. Let's use the few tools we have to fight for the right and the opportunity to teach." Another teacher, writing about decreased state funding, felt that "intense public pressure" was necessary to obtain needed allocations, and urged her colleagues to "Raise hell about this scandalous neglect."

The issue also contains a book review, and an interview

with Negro student leaders. Requests are made for future contributions of articles, cartoons, letters, news, book reviews, opinions, and ideas. (PMK)

SPARK

Committee for Social Responsibility in Engineering
475 Riverside Drive
N.Y., N.Y. 10027
Semi-annual; $10
Started: Spring 1971
Circulation: 3,000

Format: 32 pages (8" x 10", offset)
Issues examined: Fall 1972; Spring & Fall 1973
Back issues available from publisher

The first page of each edition of Spark contains the publishing organization's statement of purpose:

> Engineers face today increasing unemployment and job insecurity, conditions that stem from misguided national priorities. Thousands of engineers feel that their engineering talents are misused in both civilian and military projects, and believe that the constant development of weapons technology spells ultimate disaster for mankind. The COMMITTEE FOR SOCIAL RESPONSIBILITY IN ENGINEERING seeks to challenge the present orientation of engineering and to explore ways in which engineering skills can be used to solve the obvious and growing ills of our society. It is essential that we end unemployment and pollution and provide adequate medical care, housing, education, transportation and communication systems for all people.
>
> We invite you to explore these matters with us.

Readers are encouraged to submit news items and articles; letters to the staff are also published. Titles suggesting the range of subject matter include: "Responsibility to Women; Women in Engineering," "Occupational Safety and Health," "Movement in Appalachia," "Hazardous Hospital Devices," "Bonds Buy Bombs," and "Is Your Corporation Helping to Generate Another Vietnam?" Most of these articles were submitted by readers; unsigned articles are written by staff members.

Films and slide/tape presentations (most of them antiwar) produced by CSRE and other groups are frequently reviewed in Spark, and sometimes book reviews are included. (SMA)

SYNERGY

Celeste West, Ed.
Bi-monthly; free to libraries
Dates: 1967 - Jan. 1974
Circulation: 2,250 (and waiting list of the same number)

Format: 44-48 pages (offset)
Issues examined: Nos. 36-38 (1972)
Indexing: Alternative Press Index; also self-indexed, 1967-71

Self-described as "a shot of brash ADVOCACY JOURNALISM with CON III BIBLIOGS and reviews of the ALTERNATIVE PRESS," Synergy is "for media-massaged librarians." This freewheeling, richly-illustrated publication of BARC staff members covers all aspects of the counter/alternative/radical culture, and explores ways for young-at-heart professionals to extend and improve library services and get involved in their communities.

A typical issue covers subjects from lesbianism to natural childbirth to cable TV* in the form of two or more bibliographic essays; several shorter bibliographies; several half- to full-page reviews (usually of privately- or movement-printed books, pamphlets, and periodicals). Usually there is a general article on some aspect of librarianship, such as using photography to reach kids, or on a special or unconventional library, such as the Meiklejohn Civil Liberties Library; and a report on the latest underground comics or government documents. Several issues have been devoted to a single topic: gay liberation, libraries, women, the family, right-wing publications, to name a few. "Somebody Asked Us" is a special feature of unanswered questions received by the BARC staff. (MM)

*to VD, war tax, homeopathy, welfare, arts and crafts, cookbooks, alpha waves, backpacking, cheap living, children's liberation, men's liberation, divorce reform, adobe, feminism, bikes, drugs, campaign politics, community research, elderly people, prisons, massage, computers, education, pollution, technology, and biological transmutation.

Feedback:

"What a smashing review! 1,000 blossoms of gratitude! Howsome ever, probably you should know our time is running out. The State Library Lady says publication must cease this year. (Jan. 1974 R.I.P.) We fought like hell. Should be two or three more issues. When I finish the current one (No. 41), am leaving to begin a collective venture:

Booklegger Magazine [reviewed elsewhere in this chapter], built to begin where Synergy left off."

The address of Synergy had been: Bay Area Reference Center, San Francisco Public Library, Civic Center, San Francisco, Calif. 94102.

## TELOS

c/o Sociology Dept., Washington University
St. Louis, Mo. 63130
Quarterly; $8
Started: 1968
Circulation: 2,000
Format: 180 pages (6" x 9", offset)

Issues examined: none sent
Indexing: in journal
Back issues available from publisher
Microform version available from Xerox University Microfilms

"Telos tries to offer its readers a wide assortment of articles dealing with radical approaches in politics, philosophy, art and literary criticism, and social theory. Our review section in each issue provides ... review essays of what we consider to be important new contributions to leftist scholarship. All unsolicited papers are read by several editors, but potential contributors should be forewarned that this reading requires a considerable amount of time."

## URPE NEWSLETTER and THE REVIEW OF RADICAL POLITICAL ECONOMICS

Union for Radical Political Economics
Office of Organizational Services
Michigan Union
Ann Arbor, Mich. 48104
Quarterly; $20 for both publications (libraries $30)
Started: 1969
Circulation: 2,000
Format: Newsl. 40 pages. Review 120-160 pages (7 3/4" x 10 1/2"). Both offset.

Issues examined: Newsl. June 1974. Review Winter 1972, Spring, 1973, Spring 1974.
Indexing: Review 1969-71 issues in Winter 1972; 1972 issues in Spring 1973; also Alternative Press Index
Back issues available from publisher
Microform version available from Xerox University Microfilms

According to a brochure sent by URPE, the organization (formed in September 1968)

> brings together people who see the need for a drastic re-examination of the role of the economist in our society. URPE was created at a time when the Vietnam War, the black rebellion, the urban crisis, and an increasing alienation from the style of life in the United States had made manifest the limits of American capitalism. URPE members are attempting to use their economics training to better understand these events and the processes which brought them about. Of increasing importance, URPE is helping to develop the framework for alternative forms of society and the strategies for achieving them....
>
> Common dissatisfactions with the economics taught and practiced in this country led to the formation of URPE as an organization. For some of us, although the tools of formal economics appear to have their uses, the basic questions of neoclassical economics appear wrong. They take for given in their parameters the very institutions of society and the attitudes imposed on the individual by society which we are challenging.... Some members of URPE ... consider that traditional economics ... may be a distinct social evil, in that it trains students to avoid the larger questions relating to capitalist institutions and modes of decision making, and inhibits the challenging of these institutions and their operations.

In the Spring 1973 issue of the Review, the editorial board said that it solicited "articles which contribute to the development of an egalitarian, anti-capitalist movement that will struggle for the revolutionary transformation of American society."

> Although our stance is self-consciously 'radical,' we do not define this term in any narrow, dogmatic, or sectarian way. Articles need not adhere to any particular 'line.'

This was somewhat modified a year later, when the board decided to "attempt to shift the selection criteria so as to obtain materials which constitute more direct contributions toward the development of Marxian economics." (In the board's discussions, "There was virtually no dissention to the view that there is no real alternative to Marxism as a science for analysing contemporary human society.") It was also decided that the Review should not be limited to strictly economic subjects, but should enlarge its coverage without becoming too general.

Each issue--which contains five or six documented essays--is built around a theme, such as "Dependency and Foreign Domination in the Third World." The Winter 1972 issue initiated a book review section: "We want to publish analytical book reviews, and they can be as long as an article." A new section ("Theoretical Notes and Comments") is to be added to encourage briefer contributions from members, and to further theoretical debate.

URPE Newsletter is reviewed on pp. 532-33, above.

Criticizing the establishment can be dangerous. Soma Golden, in "Radical Economists Under Fire," writes that members of URPE "have begun to feel like an endangered species on some American campuses." The New York Times, 2 February 1975, sec. 3, p. 1.

## Chapter 4

# LABOR & UNIONS

> The big businessmen use everything they can to keep us down. They run the governments, the courts, and the police....
>
> ---The StethOtruth

> We've got two fights on our hands. One against the employers to win what is rightfully ours and the other against do-nothing union officials who would rather switch than fight.
>
> ---The Fifth Wheel

This is a new chapter: in our earlier volumes such periodicals were classified as Liberal or Miscellaneous. Some of the journals reviewed here do not follow "official" union lines and are often critical of union bosses and policies.

The Marxist Economic Notes publishes studies of social, political, and economic problems that affect labor. Journal du FRAP (put out by a workers' party in Montreal) and Steth-Otruth (health workers) are socialist. New Unity wants a workers' party, as does Wisconsin Patriot (in the Radical Left chapter), published by a worker-farmer-student organization. The Christian socialist Guide offers an alternative to the capitalist-socialist dilemma: a philosophy of labor stressing the dignity of the worker and the satisfaction that jobs ought to offer.

Other periodicals that seem liberal--even radical--in comparison with the usual union fare are The Fifth Wheel (truck drivers criticizing corrupt Teamster leadership); Employee Press (non-academic university workers opposing war, racism, and sexism, and demanding a share in decision-making); Tenant (looking toward eventual tenant control of all housing)*; and the anti-racist United Labor Action.

American Teacher and Changing Education are published by the American Federation of Teachers. Viewpoint represents the AFL-CIO's Industrial Union Department. The English Industrial Unionist is a "Wobbly" periodical. Labor in

Perspective (Zaïre) deals with the labor movement in Africa, and Perjuangan reports on trade unions in Singapore.

--Janet Spahn

*There are hundreds of tenant newsletters, according to Ruth Rejnis, "In Newsletters, the Talk Is of Security and Dogs," The New York Times, 19 January 1975, sec. 8, pp. 1, 8. She names a few of them, discusses typical concerns of the genre, and lists several organizations from which samples (and advice on how-to-edit one) are available.

AMERICAN TEACHER: Democracy in Education, Education for Democracy

American Federation of Teachers /AFL-CIO
1012 14th St., N.W.
Washington, D.C. 20005
Ten issues a year; $7 (with Changing Education)
Started: 1916
Circulation: 450,000

Format: 32-page tabloid (offset)
Issues examined: Nov. & Dec. 1973; Jan. 1974
Back issues available from publisher
Microform version available from Xerox University Microfilms

Editor David Elsila says: "We publish articles by and for classroom teachers on such topics as teacher unionism, racism in education, academic freedom, education and the economy, and other such questions of current concern."

Page after page in American Teacher brings news of the present state of negotiations and teachers' strikes: "New York Strikers Win Pact"; "Fines, Jail Sentences Hit Two N.Y. Districts"; "Strike Makes History in California"; and "College Strikers Defend Tenure."

Teacher evaluation and accountability, two sensitive issues in current teacher-school board relations, are discussed in various articles: "Teacher Evaluation: Trick or Treat?"; "Evaluating Teachers: The Search for the Perfect System"; "One Family [of teachers] Views the 'Accountability' Smokescreen"; and "Detroit Shelves 'Accountability' Plan."

The struggle for teachers' rights is reported: "AFT Backs Maternity-Leave Cases Before Supreme Court"; "AFT Asks Affirmative Action on Female College Employment"; and "Federation to Appeal Dismissal Linked to College-Union Activism." AFT support is detailed in numerous stories: "Fired Teacher Sues for $1 Million" (about the union's contributions to the defense of 11 teachers) and "Wisconsin Professor Wins Free-Speech Case, $6,000." The rights of women teachers are not forgotten: "AFT Delegates Push ERA," and "What Nixon Has Not Done for Women."

The struggles of other unions in the AFL/CIO are sympathetically reported. "The People vs. Willie Farah" describes a film released by the Amalgamated Clothing Workers of America, supporting a long strike by Farah workers. "Union Teachers Help Launch Latin-American Labor Council" relates how "Four AFT members, attending both as delegates and observers, participated in the founding conference of the Labor Council for Latin-American Advancement...."

"AFT Legislative Boxscore" reports regularly on pending legislation, to guide teachers in writing to Senators and Representatives. Each issue has one long article on a topic such as "Lifting the Curtain on Labor," "The Elementary School of the Future," or "How Teacher Unions Work."

If American Teacher focuses on the necessity for organized action as the way to fulfill the teachers' desires for decent living and working standards and for the rights all citizens should enjoy, Changing Education looks at the children in the schools--with their teachers and administrators--and asks what can and should be done to help them. If the first considers teachers as workers, the second considers them as professionals.

Each issue of Changing Education is organized around a theme: "Education for Global Survival"; "Inequality: Responding to Jencks" (on Christopher Jencks's Inequality: A Reassessment of the Effect of Family and Schooling in America); or "The Hidden History of Educational Administration." Ethnic education and intergroup tensions, children learning about war, dropouts and jobs, and intelligence tests for bilingual pupils are discussed. The problems of school administrators and the demand of the teaching staff for a voice in curriculum development are analyzed. "Of Prostitution and Abortion" considers the role of the school counselor, and "How Schools Can Fight the VD Menace" suggests actions that should be taken. (GKS)

Feedback:

Editor expressed no disapproval.

CHANGING EDUCATION

David Elsila, Ed.
American Federation of Teachers/AFL-CIO
1012 14th St. N.W.
Washington, D.C. 20005
Quarterly
Started: 1966
Circulation: 425,000

Format: 42-44 pages (offset)
Issues examined: Spring, Summer, Fall 1973
Indexing: Current Index to Journals in Education
Back issues available from publisher
Microform version available from Xerox University Microfilms

For review, see American Teacher, earlier in this chapter.

## ECONOMIC NOTES

Labor Research Association
80 E. 11th St.
N.Y., N.Y. 10003
Monthly; $3
Started: 1931
Circulation: 2,000
Format: 8 pages (offset)
Issues examined: Oct.-Dec. 1973
Annual index available from publisher
Some back issues available from publisher

The LRA was founded in 1927 "to conduct investigations and studies of social, economic and political questions in the interest of the labor and progressive movement." Its bulletin's Marxist orientation is shown in such articles as "U.S. Backed Fascists in Chile" and "Rush for Cheap Labor." The October issue advertises a pamphlet by Karl Marx, ("A Workers' Inquiry") as an "antidote" to the "tendency in some quarters to flee from the hard thinking of Marxian economics." An article in the December issue ("Confusing Forecasts") analyzes the possibility of recession and increased unemployment and predicts that the attempt to increase capital spending will fail. In the same issue, "U.S. Backed Fascists in Chile" discusses the "prospects for U.S. imperialists under the fascist military junta" and the "decision of the junta to return nationalized properties to their former, mainly U.S. capitalist, 'owners.'"

Recurrent concerns include welfare, multinational corporations, weapons contracts, and U.S. foreign investment, as well as over-all economic problems. The first article in every issue is an overview of contemporary economic conditions, emphasizing inflation, unemployment, and recession. Economic Notes "digests and analyzes main economic trends" by using ample statistics and quotations from the Wall Street Journal, Business Week, and similar publications. These quotations are interspersed with interpretive remarks aimed at illustrating the unpleasant implications of these economic trends. (JMA)

Feedback:

"Your summary of the contents of Economic Notes is adequate. It gives a good idea of our views and we'll be glad to see the final product."

## EMPLOYEE PRESS

2490 Channing Way (Rm. 207)
Berkeley, Calif. 94704
Monthly
Started: July 1967
Circulation: 3,000
Format: 8-page tabloid (offset)
Issues examined: Oct.-Dec. 1973
Back issues available from publisher
Microform version available from Bell & Howell to Oct. 1971; International Women's History Archive Oct. 1971 to June 1973

Employee Press is the newspaper of Local 1695, American Federation of State, County, and Municipal Employees, AFL-CIO. This local represents non-academic employees and academically employed students at the University of California at Berkeley. Policies of Local 1695 and its paper are "for the right of workers to decent salaries, working conditions, and control over their lives on the job." [Feedback: "The local has also taken strong positions against racism, sexism, U.S. involvement in Indo-China, and on other political issues."] The editorial staff, which varies from issue to issue, includes a considerable number of women.

Each issue contains articles on the local's activities, such as wage issues and grievance cases, some of which involve racial discrimination by supervisors. Local 1695 took up the cudgels for a black woman denied a merit increase because of her supervisor's racial hostility, and condemned the "racist behavior which is deceitfully supported by the general UC administration." The purpose of such articles is to publicize union activities, especially wage gains won by the union, and thus encourage employees to join and support the union. Occasionally, pro-union cartoons are also used for this purpose.

Cartoons from the mass press are used frequently to criticize the federal administration's policies. Examples are Mauldin's cartoon on the oil "conspiracy" and Oliphant's on "Dr. Butz's Starving Man's Diet." (Earl Butz was Secretary of Agriculture under Nixon and Ford.) Several articles urge boycotts in support of striking unions, for example, "Help Chicana Strikers--Don't Buy Farah Pants." Regular features include a monthly calendar of union events; an article on new union members and why they joined; a list of committee heads; and "AFSCME's 10 Basic Demands." In addition to coverage of the local's activities, articles discuss a factory occupation in France, the coup that overthrew the elected Marxist government of Dr. Salvador Allende in Chile, the welfare system, and the formation of a union at Stanford University.

"AFSCME's 10 Basic Demands" give an indication of the union's political orientation. Demands for "employer-paid, parent- and staff-controlled child care" and for "involvement of employees in ... decision-making which affects their on-the-job lives" exceed traditional trade unionism. Despite its radicalism, the paper's reporting avoids polemical and rhetorical excesses. (JMA)

Feedback:

Editor expressed no disapproval and suggested several minor textual changes which have been incorporated into the review.

THE FIFTH WHEEL: A Bay Area Rank and File Monthly

Box 23902
Oakland, Calif. 94623
Format: 4- to 8-page tabloid

Issues examined: Feb., July, Oct., Dec. 1973

The Fifth Wheel provides news and comments concerning events of interest to truck drivers, particularly to those in the Oakland area. Interviews with union officials are sometimes featured, but editorials are slanted toward the viewpoint of "rank and file" union membership. More frequently, interviews take the form of public opinion polls, covering such issues as the fuel crisis and whether women drivers should be allowed in the union. These present the reactions of truck drivers from various locals, often accompanied by photographs of the drivers whose opinions were solicited.

Criticism of union leadership appears in many articles. The following brief quotations are typical examples: "Teamsters all over California are beginning to speak out against the attempt of 'our leadership' to destroy the United Farm Workers Union (UFW)." "Large-scale corruption among top Teamster officials is in the news again." "Many Teamsters and other workers across America were heartened by the victory of Miners for Democracy over the Boyle machine in the United Mine Workers' Union." "When will IBT president Fitzsimmons get off the golf links and call a special nation-wide rank-and-file conference to formulate plans for a national Teamster-A&P union contract?"

On the other hand, editorial comment is also directed against the disenchantment with unions which might result from these quarrels with leadership. Articles frequently urge the importance of organized efforts to protect workers' rights. The editorial policy was capsulized in a congratulatory statement on the first issue of a "rival" rank and file publication:

> We'd like to see rank and file papers in other locals too.... We've got two fights on our hands. One against the employers to win what is rightfully ours and the other against do-nothing union officials who would rather switch than fight. We can count on the Nor-Cal Teamster for gossip about which B.A. took a ride on the Goodyear blimp. But for serious discussion of the issues confronting the union, rank and file papers are a must.

(SMA)

THE GUIDE

Christian Labour Association of Canada
Edward Vanderkloet, Ed.
100 Rexdale Blvd.
Rexdale 603, Ontario, Canada
10 issues a year; $5
Started: 1952

Circulation: 9,000
Format: 16-24 pages (8" x 11", offset)
Issues examined: July, Labour Day, & Oct. 1973
Back issues available from publisher

The Guide promotes "a Christian social movement, and Christian social economic action as a meaningful alternative to the current capitalist-socialist dilemma." It is the official publication of "a government-certified Christian trade movement in Canada, especially in the provinces of Ontario, British Columbia, and Alberta. CLAC is not affiliated with any church denomination."

In many ways, the viewpoint of the editorial staff is not what one might expect from organized labor (more benefits, more money, shorter hours). Instead, The Guide is more concerned with the value of the work done, with greater dignity for the worker, and with making the job more interesting on a level much deeper than that implied by the popular phrase, "job enrichment." Naturally, it is also concerned with labor issues, such as a recent Canadian railway strike, or elections to determine whether CLAC or another union will represent workers in a particular plant. Although The Guide takes a radical stance in expressing anti-capitalist opinions, and pushing for representation of workers on company boards of directors, it leans toward the conservative in its views on women. "We cannot accept the world's standards and encourage women to abandon their homes for jobs they only think will be satisfying." (Emphasis added.) The Guide's viewpoint is its own and a reader cannot assume that because it holds one opinion on a certain subject, he can predict its views on others.

The Guide is of interest to anyone looking for an expression of a Christian socialist philosophy of labor, but it is, by its own intent, primarily an organ of CLAC and of greatest interest to its members--as demonstrated by the reports from various local chapters included in each issue. However, the uniqueness of its philosophy and its handling of issues of general interest (such as religion's relation to labor, and urban development viewed as part of God's plan) may interest non-members of CLAC. (BK)

## HUELGA

United Farm Workers
3419 Michigan Ave.
Detroit, Mich. 48216

Format: 6 pages (legal size, mimeo., stapled)
Issue examined: Mar. 1972

Covers the activities, strategies, boycotts, and politics of the United Farm Workers' Organizing Committee. Huelga was formerly called Detroit Newsletter - UFWOC.

## ILO INFORMATION

International Labor Office
1750 New York Ave., N.W.
Washington, D.C. 20006
Quarterly or bi-monthly; free
Started: Aug. 1973
Circulation: 10,000

Format: 8 pages (9 1/4" x 12 1/4", offset)
Issues examined: Aug. & Nov. 1973
Back issues available from publisher

ILO Information superseded Panorama (often called ILO Panorama) in February 1971. In August 1973, the ILO's Public Information Branch began publishing a separate edition of ILO Information for the U.S. This edition "will contain articles of particular interest to American government officials, employers, workers, and others who maintain an interest in ILO activities." The International Labor Organization (of which the International Labor Office is the secretariat) was founded in 1919 and became associated with the United Nations in 1946. One of ILO's functions is to "help improve the social and economic well-being of working-people everywhere by building up a code of international labor standards."

The August 1973 issue reports on new labor standards adopted at the annual ILO conference in the areas of child labor, cargo-handling in docks, and paid educational leave. The newsletter is especially concerned with Third World problems. In the November 1973 issue, sample titles are "Jobless Millions in the Swollen Cities of the Third World" and "Typhoon Damage and Job Creation in the Philippines." Articles advocate "labor-intensive techniques" as a partial solution to unemployment in the Third World. "Labor-intensive work, where economically feasible, is recommended by the ILO's World Employment Program as a step to be considered by developing countries in the fight against unemployment." While most articles focus on labor issues, related problems (such as poverty and drug addiction) are also explored.

(JMA)

Feedback:

"The summary looks o.k."

## INDUSTRIAL UNIONIST

c/o 116 Chadderton Way,
Oldham
Lancashire, United Kingdom
"As necessary"; $5 for 6 issues, airmail
Started: Oct. 1973
Circulation: 6,000

Format: 52 pages (6" x 8 3/4", offset); new format 16-32 pages (8" x 12")
Issues examined: No. 1 undated (Oct. 1973) under title Workers' Opposition; No. 2 undated (in 1974)

The first issue of Workers' Opposition is a blend of fiction and theoretical articles. An explanation of the journal's purpose appears on the title page:

> Workers' Opposition will endeavor to expound the principles of workers' self-management and apply them to modern life, the problems of the worker in particular and the oppressed in general. It is our policy to encourage, stimulate, and promote all efforts in this direction.
>
> It is our understanding that the best-organized

> expression of how workers' self-management of society might be accomplished is to be found in the application of the principles and tactics of the Industrial Workers of the World (IWW). Therefore, although this magazine is not an official publication of the IWW, we, as individual members of Metal and Machinery Workers' Industrial Union 440 and Furniture Workers' Industrial Union 420 of the IWW, intend to further understanding of Industrial Unionism through this magazine.
>
> The columns of the magazine are always open to discussion on relevant issues. Unsolicited manuscripts welcomed.

A boxed slogan on the last page says "Labor needs the weight of the One Big Union to cope with the boss. Join the IWW." This movement is opposed to communism in any form. (For a fuller explanation of this radical anarchist workers' movement see our review of <u>Industrial Worker</u> on page 122.)

<u>Feedback:</u>

Since this review was written the periodical has moved from Chicago to Britain, changed its format and name, and now proclaims itself the "official publication of the General Organizing Committee of the Industrial Workers of the World in Britain." An editor informs us "We put forth the ideas of the IWW as the vehicle with which workers can achieve a self-managed society and abolition of the wage system." A four-hour day, "production for use and not for profit" and "a new social order based on the scientific administration of industry" is also advocated. Democracy is stressed and union leaders are to be elected for one year and can serve only three successive terms.

The second issue ("It's taken a year to bring [it] out ... because we have ... been breaking entirely new ground. We've had to rapidly build up knowledge of the industrial action of the last few years and try to contact rank and file militants who understand what has been taking place.... This ... issue ... reflects this") deals with the basic programs and philosophy of the I.W.W. which we hope to review further in Volume IV.

JOURNAL DU FRAP

Monthly; $5 Circulation: 3,000
Dates: Oct. 1972-1974

Format: 8-page tabloid (offset)	Issues examined: Sept.-Nov. 1973

Journal du FRAP, formerly Liaison, is a French publication of Le Front d'Action Politique, a political organization of workers in Montreal. Their motto (translated)--The liberation of workers will be the work of the workers themselves--represents the view of this organization that workers in Canada, particularly in Quebec, are oppressed and must band together to win their rights. Most of the articles in the issues reviewed are concerned with the 1973 elections and the necessity of unity at the polls to defeat the existing liberal, but anti-worker, government. Although specific grievances vary with the specific strikes the basic demands which are voiced in the pages of this paper are common to all workers: the right to unionize and to strike, the outlawing of scabs, and the publication of company records. Factory workers are not the only workers whose protests reach Journal du FRAP; the reader learns that teachers face the same enemy and have the same problems as their fellow workers: job insecurity, difficulties of unionizing, the outlawing of strikes. And as for all workers, only a united front can lead to victory.

Any international news which is reported is noted for its implications for Canadian workers; the Chilean coup carried an important lesson to workers throughout the world: any compromise or coalition between the working class and the bourgeoisie will end in disaster for the workers.

Although Journal du FRAP is a French-language periodical, and is published in Montreal, it does not touch upon the issue of Quebec separatism. (SA)

Feedback:

"Le Journal du FRAP is no more published. Militants who were members of the Front d'Action Politique, which has been dissolved, are now grouped in le Groupe Socialiste des Travailleurs du Quebec (GSTQ)" which "publishes monthly Tribune Ouvrière" (a 4-page tabloid) from the same address: International Socialist Press, 3960 Saint-Denis, Montreal H2W 2M2, P.Q., Canada. Publication began November 1974.

LABOR IN PERSPECTIVE: A Review of Recent Events of Interest to Trade Unions

African-American Consultative Committee	Panafrican Trade Union Information Center

Box 1788
Kinshasa
Zaïre
New York address (for American subscriptions):
AALC - ID
New York APO 09662

Monthly; free
Started: Aug. 1970
Circulation: 350
Format: 25 pages (mimeo., stapled)
Issues examined: Mar.-May 1974

This periodical is intended to be

> a means to circulate news about developments in the African labor movement, and a vehicle to disseminate news of events in economic and other related fields that would be of interest to African trade union leaders.

It is published in separate English- and French-language editions.

NEW UNITY

Box 891
Springfield, Mass. 01101
Monthly; donation
Started: Aug. 1971
Circulation: 5,000
Format: 8-page tabloid (offset)

Issues examined: Mar., Oct., Dec. 1973
Back issues available from publisher
Microform version available from Xerox University Microfilms

New Unity is published by a diverse and independent group of workers dedicated to government "from the bottom up," which they feel will result when workers gain control of capital, tools, resources, and the power to make decisions. They favor an attack on big business; the formation of [Feedback: "democratic"] unions; and the organization of a political party for the working class.

Readers are urged to send in whatever they think should be printed: job and union news, complaints, opinions, questions, and ideas. The paper will print "Songs, cartoons, poems, drawings, photos, etc. Research into issues and institutions and rulers. Your thoughts on solving this or that problem." A discussion of conditions in Chile begins:

> U.S. ROLE. FASCISTS KILL A POPULAR, ELECTED, SOCIALIST GOVERNMENT.
> THE U.S. RULERS have been fostering the conditions

> for a coup in Chile for a long time. Almost as soon as Allende was elected in 1970 the U.S. Big Business interests put up economic roadblocks to Allende's reforms.

Each issue brings news of recent or current strikes. "Runaways Threaten Job Security" details multi-national corporations' actual and threatened moves of their plants to overseas locations where wages are lower. Articles and cartoons describe the history of the labor movement with stories about individuals and events. (GKS)

Feedback:
Editor suggested a few textual changes which have been incorporated into the review.

PERJUANGAN

V. R. Balakrishna, Ed.
Trade Union House, Shenton Way
Singapore 1
Monthly; $2.50
Started: 1964
Circulation: 20,000

Format: 16 pages (10" x 14", offset), plus special supplements to cover important events
Issues examined: Oct. & Dec. 1973; Mar. 1974
Back issues available from publisher

Perjuangan (a Malay word meaning "struggle") is the official publication of the National Trades Union Congress of Singapore. The largest part of the Perjuangan is given over to union news. The October 1973 issue contained several articles dealing with the Seventh World Congress of the International Federation of Petroleum and Chemical Workers, held in Singapore. There were messages to the delegates from international and local union officials, pictures of these leaders, news of the Congress, and an article on the Singapore petroleum industry. In the same issue, another item details various cooperative undertakings of the NTUC in Singapore. As an outgrowth of its belief that "organised labour in a developing society can and must play a more meaningful role along with the private sector and the public sector with a view to contributing more positively in the process of the overall national development both material and social," the NTUC has established a number of cooperatives. Among them are an insurance cooperative, a dental care cooperative, and a cooperative supermarket. The December issue carries articles on various union struggles and victories. "Report on Labour" includes news on industrial accidents, workman's compensation awards, factory safety inspections, and wage settlements.

In addition to union news, Perjuangan carries items on other subjects, such as Singapore's tree-planting program; the British Parliamentary System; and the food value of rice.

There are reminders that Perjuangan originates in Singapore. For example, the remarks of the NTUC Secretary General quoted in the October issue include references to Third World Nations:

> 'The right to work' and 'the right to organise' and all the other sacred cows of trade unions in the developed countries are the RESULT and not the CAUSE of economic growth and progress.
>
> And yet, as far as the Third World nations are concerned, it is generally assumed in the developed countries that these sacred cows can exist and thrive without even the grass, i.e., economic development to feed them.

A reprint of a speech on "Multinationals and the Third World" by Devan Nair, the Secretary General, reflected the concerns of the NTUC and suggested international regulation of such companies and the end of "protectionism." Nair was opposed to a bill then before the U.S. Congress, fearing that it would have "catastrophic consequences" for the Third World. That this bill was supported by the AFL-CIO illustrates that while the NTUC is strongly affiliated with international unionism and with other unions throughout the world, there are nevertheless times when the interests of unionism in Singapore are not the same as those in other parts of the world. Nor, as the article continues, are our views as to what constitute the most serious current problems identical, for

> the most alarming fact of the modern world is not 'Watergate,' which may be a personal tragedy for certain people; it is not even the 'Middle East crisis.' The most urgent fact of the modern world is the ever-widening gap, development gap, technological gap, income gap between the developed minority of mankind and the developing majority of mankind.

The lead article in the March issue illustrates that NTUC unions have problems caused by the fact that many of the corporations doing business in Singapore have their headquarters in other parts of the world. The article, which deals with released time for employees to attend union-run courses, reflects this problem in these words:

> Here we come up against the second misconception, one born of the class consciousness developed in many employers as a result of the experiences in their countries of origin, thousands of miles away from our shores.
>
> This class feeling makes the employer always suspicious of anything organised by trade unions. He feels that trade union affairs must, by definition, always be aimed against the employer, and this must include trade union education.

The same article also reflects another quality which appears again and again in Perjuangan: pride in Singapore and in the union movement there. "Here, in the past 15 years, we have established the most successful modern society in South-east Asia, and one of the two great success stories of economic development in Asia."

The political orientation of Perjuangan is a largely middle-of-the-road one that American trade union officials would agree with. An article on foreign aid points out that the United States has been far more generous than Russia in helping the underdeveloped countries of the world. Another, on the difficulties of inflation, suggests ways in which the union member may stretch his money by more careful buying--a far from radical approach to an economic problem.

The impression given by Perjuangan is of a successful, prosperous union movement. There are pictures of smiling, well-dressed union leaders at banquets and meetings. Even the ads for cognac, stout, hair tonic, banks, and trucking firms indicate that the advertisers believe the readers are prosperous enough to use their products or services.

Although an occasional phrase (such as "Probably 20 cents' worth of ikan bilis will give as much nutrition as a much publicised brand of chicken essence") reminds the reader that Perjuangan deals with life in Singapore, most of the time its articles are much the same as one would find in union journals published in other parts of the world, reflecting concern for the worker and narrating the various activities and successes of the union. (BK)

Feedback:

"We are of the view that your summary is a fair

portrayal, and have, therefore, no remarks or corrections to make.... Would you mind if we publish this review in Perjuangan in order to give an idea to our Singapore workers what others think of their national journal?"

THE STETHOTRUTH

4-6 issues a year; $2
Dates: Dec. 1971-1974
Circulation: 3,000
Format: 12- to 16-page tabloid (offset)
Issues examined: Dec. 1972; Aug. & Oct. 1973
Back issues available from publisher

Published by the Tri-County Workers and the Tri-County Health Workers, this periodical arose out of a union struggle at a Detroit hospital:

> As a result of that struggle we became aware ... that this society is run for 'profits not for people.' The StethOtruth [motto: "People, Not Profits"] ... is a part of a growing movement of men and women who want to build up the unity and power of working people.
>
> ... as working people we produce all the wealth for this society. Without our labor, there would be nothing. But most of this wealth and power are taken from us by a small clique of businessmen (2% of the population). They use what we have created to control our lives for their own benefit.
>
> The big businessmen use everything they can to keep us down. They run the governments, the courts, and the police (including the FBI and CIA), from the smallest communities to Washington. The mass media ... all repeat the lies they must make us believe. They get richer, while here and overseas the workers get poorer. Their power increases at the expense of our civil rights.

The "StethOtruth Platform" goes on to say that blacks, Chicanos, Indians, and women are at the bottom of the heap, and that working people must unite "to make all the decisions about how our labor is used. We have the ability to run the whole society so that each person does what he can and gets what he needs. And since we built it we should be running it!"

The paper advocates that workers form food co-ops,

medical clinics, legal clinics, day-care centers, etc., and demands (among other things) the complete overhauling of the educational system and the health care system. StethOtruth, which seems to be aimed at a black audience, has a socialist orientation. The sample issues contained several articles on health care in China and Cuba.

The address was Box 166, Hamtramck, Mich. 48212.

(JMS)

Feedback:

"The Tri-County Workers and Tri-County Health Workers recently dissolved and no longer exists.... The summary appears to be an accurate appraisal of the paper."

TENANT

| | |
|---|---|
| Helen Watt & John Crawford, Co-Editors | Format: 8-page tabloid (offset) |
| 24 W. 30th St. | Issues examined: Oct.-Dec. 1973 |
| N.Y., N.Y. 10001 | Back issues available from publisher |
| Monthly; $2.50 | |
| Started: 1970 | |
| Circulation: 6,000 | |

Tenant is a publication of the Metropolitan Council on Housing (Met Council). This non-profit volunteer organization is the largest tenant group in New York City and the only city-wide union of tenants. Founded in 1959, it includes neighborhood councils, block associations, community groups, and housing committees of labor unions.

The publication covers news of interest to tenants, and focuses on legislative action and rent strikes. Each issue contains signed reports of tenant activities on the west and east sides, Brooklyn, Harlem, and the Bronx. Many stories are accompanied by photos. There is a bulletin board featuring Met Council tenant activities in these areas. The lead story appears in Spanish and English. Cartoons, drawings, letters from individual tenants, announcements of housing workshops or classes, and editorials also appear. Since Met Council is financed by memberships, contributions, and fund raising activities, readers are apprised of budget status and frequently urged to contribute. One of the issues examined contained a review of a pamphlet entitled Life Without Landlords, and another printed a theatrical review.

An article in the November issue ("Housing and Hanky-Banky") reprinted portions of Jack Newfield's series in The Village Voice exposing the influence of banking and real estate interests on the New York state legislature.

The centerfold of the December issue was devoted to the revised Tenant's Bill of Rights, drawn up at the second annual Met Council Legislative Conference. This was to be taken to the state capitol for lobbying efforts. Issues included in the statement were "mandatory, REAL state-wide rent control, the return of housing home rule to New York City, the repeal of MBR [maximum base rent], the repeal of vacancy decontrol, and the rollback of rents to June 1970, as essential demands."

The goals of Met Council are presented in a brochure entitled Tenants: You Are Not Alone:

> Met Council's immediate goals are tenant rights and decent integrated housing at rents people can afford. Our ultimate goal is for all housing to be in the public domain under tenant control built with direct allocation of government funds. We feel that housing is a human right and that the narrow property interests of banking and real estate concerns must give way to human rights.

(JA)

Feedback:

"O.K. with us."

## UNITED LABOR ACTION

Kenny Lapides, Ed.
Center for United Labor Action
167 W. 21st St.
N.Y., N.Y. 10011
Monthly; $1

Started: Sept. 1971
Circulation: 10,000
Format: 4- to 8-page tabloid (offset)
Issues examined: Dec. 1973; Jan. 1974

"Our policy is to support the struggles of working people, esp. the more oppressed sections, i.e. the black, Latin, women, & unorganized. We aim to raise the political level of workers, to fight white racism wherever it is found--in the labor movement, among the corporations or in the gov't. We report on the activities of our organization, the Center for United Labor Action, as part of our fight to defend the interests of all labor, whether they be economic, political, or social."

This motto appears on the masthead: "An injury to one is an injury to all." Illustrated with photographs and a few political cartoons.

## VIEWPOINT

Industrial Union Dept., AFL-CIO
815 16th St., N.W.
Washington, D.C. 20006
Quarterly; $2

Started: Spring 1971
Circulation: 35,000
Format: 28 pages (offset)
Issues examined: Spring 1971 - Second Quarter 1973

"It is our policy to select one subject and dig into it as deeply as we can within the confines of our space limitations." Some of the topics treated in past issues have been "Imports vs. Jobs" ("We are exporting jobs, capital, and technology--importing products we should be making"); "the national economy and the role of our unions in winning decent pay scales for our members"; "The Lopsided Tax Structure"; "Inflation and Wages"; the United Nations ("Labor must give it full support"); and "Open the Road to the Ballot Box!" (critical of the American political system in which the rich can buy ambassadorships, and only 55% of the eligible citizens vote).

I. W. Abel (President of IUD), who often writes the editorials, described Viewpoint's purposes in the maiden issue: It was to be

> a new forum for ideas and discussion of labor's valid interests.... Since labor's interests are wide-ranging, our subject matter will be designed to cover many facets of American society, as they affect our lives at work, in our communities and nation, and at home.

Contributors have included two U.S. Senators, our Ambassador to the U.N., and the U.N.'s Secretary-General.

Viewpoint is an illustrated, professionally-produced magazine. It supersedes Agenda. (JMS)

Feedback:

"... your summary of Viewpoint ... strikes me as both correct and adequate and entirely proper for inclusion in your [book]...."

## WILDCAT

Box 8264
San Diego, Calif. 92102
Monthly; $3
Started: Apr. 1972

Circulation: 6,000
Format: 12- to 16-page tabloid (offset)
Issues examined: Nov. 1973;

Jan. & Mar. 1974 from publisher
Some back issues available

This "tool of working and poor people" is published by an independent group of rank-and-file workers from many occupations (laborers, assemblers, seamstresses, clerks, machinists, telephone operators, and welders, working in union and non-union shops) and students. "Some of us are communists who feel that the only permanent solution to our problems will be socialism." The paper is distributed around the country "by friends inside and outside the plants."

Wildcat offers news of union locals in the San Diego area (support for rank-and-file members, as opposed to sometimes-corrupt officers); labor strikes and struggles; boycotts throughout the country; and individual case histories of abused workers. The paper, concerned that workers have healthful and safe working conditions, has been running articles on that subject.

Racism and sexism are strongly condemned. "White people are taught to think that people of color are inferior to them." These values are harmful and are "used to keep us from seeing our common class interest and to keep us divided so we can't fight back."

The paper called for the impeachment of Richard Nixon and criticized the "rightist" and hawkish voting record of Gerald Ford when he was a Congressman. In "Food Prices Soar, Corporations Clean Up" the paper blames some grain dealers, meat processors, corporate farmers (but not small independent ones who are being driven out of business), and rich men (such as Sen. James Eastland and actor John Wayne) who own a lot of farm land and collect from the government for letting it lie idle. "Gigantic Oil Ripoff" alleges that the multi-national corporations that control the oil industry--and not the Arab countries and their boycott--were responsible for rising oil costs.

Some news of foreign countries appears: "Miners, Peasants Revolt in Bolivia" against military dictator Hugo Banzer; and "Miners Force Vote in England." The paper condemns South Vietnam's (former) dictator Thieu for imprisoning his political opponents, and alleges that Israel "attacked" Egypt and Syria in 1967.

Part of each issue is in Spanish. (This section is entitled Obrero Rebelde.) Some--but not all--of the articles in this part are translations of those appearing in the English-language part.

Illustrated with cartoons and photographs. (TJS)

## Chapter 5

## UNDERGROUND

> The underground press incorporates all the new ideas about dirty words, sex, drugs, civil liberties, war, imperialism, and ecology.... The underground may appear crude and amateurish, but there is one level on which it far surpasses its bloated rivals: an honest effort to bring truth to the people.
>
> ---Both Sides Now

Underground papers seem to have a shorter life span than any other publications we cover--except perhaps for servicemen's papers. At least seven of the tabloids reviewed in this chapter are already defunct. Some papers, such as The Eugene Augur and The Rag, have managed to survive since the 1960s and build up sizeable circulations, but this is exceptional.[1] The underground paper is being replaced by a new type of alternative or community-activist paper, less concerned with drugs or dropping out.

High school underground papers are particularly ephemeral. Usually published by four or five precocious, independent students, they fold when the editors graduate. DSS Free Press,[2] New Improved Tide, and The Wurd are examples of the high school underground,[3] which also has its own press service: FPS--Youth Liberation News Service, dedicated to helping young people "learn the concrete skills to fight against their oppression." College Press Service, Liberation News Service and New York News Service, all reviewed in this volume, supply material for the adult underground/alternative and college papers.

Often underground papers spring up near college campuses and are involved not only with student concerns but with community problems and politics as well. Fishcheer, Free for All, and Weather Report are such student community papers. The Daily Rag, Freedom Reader, and Patriot also stress community action, food co-ops, free schools, clinics, day care centers, and counter-cultural activities.

Among the other periodicals reviewed are Rama Pipien,

which bills itself as an international digest of alternative and underground press materials; Collage, which calls itself a visual newspaper consisting of 70% graphics; Storrs Weekly, which tried to be an alternative newspaper for students at the University of Connecticut; and Honky Times, which tried for six months to shake the complacency of San Antonio.

For a fuller discussion of the underground press, see our earlier volumes--or the many articles and books that have been written on the youth culture.[4] --Janet Spahn

[1]Other long-lasting papers reviewed in our earlier volumes are Berkeley Barb, The Fifth Estate, Georgia Straight, Los Angeles Free Press, North Carolina Anvil, Other Scenes, Second City, and Village Voice.

[2]The review of DSS Free Press is based largely on a letter from the former publisher, and gives a picture of the difficulties encountered by such papers.

[3]Another example, The Red Tide, is in our Radical Left chapter.

[4]An unusual type of paper is described in Joann S. Lublin's "Underground Papers in Corporations Tell It Like It Is--Or Perhaps Like It Isn't," The Wall Street Journal, 3 November 1971, p. 8. These sub-rosa papers blast "company policies and executives with a mixture of fact, satire, exaggeration, and--occasionally--libel." Those mentioned by Lublin are AT&T Express (Pacific Telephone & Telegraph Co.); Black Light (INA Corp.); Brookhaven Free Press (Brookhaven National Laboratory); GE Resistor (General Electric Co.; 1969-70); Met Lifer (Metropolitan Life Insurance Co.; early 1970- ); and Stranded Oiler (Standard Oil Co. of California; June 1970- ).

## LA BARBA [The Barb]

Clancy, Ed. [Luis Morales Velázquez]
Num. 238 Bda. Carmen
Salinas, Puerto Rico 00751
Monthly; $2

Started: 4 Nov. 1969
Circulation: 2,800
Format: 8 pages (legal size, mimeo. or offset, stapled)
Issues examined: Feb.-Apr. 1970

La Barba is the only Puerto Rican underground rock music paper we know of. (See also our review of Claridad, a Puerto Rican radical or underground newspaper.) The editor says: "our format is really poor, but underground is underground, to be poor [is] to be in the underground." The paper is, of course, in Spanish.

The editor sent this information [reproduced without alteration]:

> La Barba is based in bring the knowledge of whats going on in Puerto Rico's youth. Mostly rock and roll music news, comments, knowledgement and help to the bands, groups and tribes. Sometimes we published on radicals comments, because we feel the cause of the movement and the culture. But our 90% of policies & editorial develope are and were the rock culture. We really likes to cover on everything. For example on the cause of the maryjuana legalization. We help the organization for pot legalization writting and publishing classified ads regarding to help them. Also we give, promote and advertise records and rock groups, who involved on the cause of the maryjuana legalization. We give musicians classified ads, opurtunity and we look for contracts on them. Our main theme were, 'Help Youre Brother, that will Make You Powerful'; We belive in the movement and we try, and are on everything. We think rock music give you all. When youre in rock youre in revolution. Music is revolutionary. When youre in rock, youre in sex; youre in, cause youre in love; Music gives power to everything. Our paper is based in help, not in be rich; we need the money to continue publishing, but not to live of it. We want everybody to get into the cause, not to get into money. That are what La Barba try to do; to be the people, to be the cause; to be the music; to be the feel; LA BARBA IS THE FEELING, IS THE CAUSE, IS THE MUSIC, IS THE WORLD OF THE MOVEMENT.

The paper reports on rock festivals and concerts; reviews record albums, rock and folk groups (most of which seem to be American or English), and folk singers (e.g. Bob Dylan, Joni Mitchel); and reviews local musicians and groups appearing in night spots and bars. Underground figures such as Abbie Hoffman, Dave Dellinger, "Rennard Davies," and "Tom Hayde," are often mentioned and much admired. Abbie Hoffman's book, Woodstock Nation, is reviewed, as are some underground films. The April 1970 issue carried several revolutionary poems. The paper has a classified section and carries a few advertisements for stores such as Playboy's Box--"beautiful clothes for beautiful people." (JMS)

Feedback:
"All the reviews are fine."

BOTH SIDES NOW

Free People
1232 Laura St.
Jacksonville, Fla. 32206
Irregular; $2 for 10 issues
Started: Nov. 1969
Circulation: 4,000-5,000
Format: 20-page tabloid (offset)
Issues examined: Aug. 1971; 1972; Aug. 1973
Back issues available from publisher
Microform version available from Bell & Howell

"The underground press incorporates all the new ideas about dirty words, sex, drugs, civil liberties, war, imperialism, and ecology.... The underground may appear crude and amateurish, but there is one level on which it far surpasses its bloated rivals: an honest effort to bring truth to the people." The truth that Both Sides Now attempts to present to its readers is the guilt of the American establishment in such matters as Vietnam, Watergate, and pollution. It is seldom the news headlining the establishment's papers, and usually the "news" is used as a starting point for an attack on the system. One issue in 1971 (before Watergate) focused on Richard Nixon's morality, and examined the implications of the Pentagon Papers' revelations, public response to the Lt. Calley (war crimes) trial and conviction (the nation showed itself insensitive to its own war crimes), and the oil profits made in Southeast Asia--all of these things pointing to "a rottenness of the American soul that has been building all through this iniquitous war [Vietnam]." An imaginative study of the economics of the heroin "industry" revealed that--just like war--heroin addiction provides a lot of jobs and contributes significantly to our Gross National Product. Jobs are created for policemen, druggists, architects for rehabilitation centers that never get built, social workers, counselors, reformed-junkie lecturers, psychiatrists, writers of books and articles, psychologists, and so on.

Besides news and feature articles, there are pages of poetry, cartoons, reviews of the arts, and interviews. The staff urges its readers to contribute cultural materials. Swami Sivananda's Astrological Forecast "should give you the necessary inspiration, instruction, and provocation to go out and commit an obscene act. Obscenity is the first and last line of defense for the liberated." [Feedback: "A new feature, 'Alternatives in Religion,' explores the current spiritual explosion in quest of a relevant contemporary faith."]

Both Sides Now is published by The Free People, a non-profit educational and information group. The Free People see themselves as "conservative in trying to preserve the original vision of our country as a land of the free, and radical in demanding basic social and economic changes to bring about true justice and equality." "We reflect a Movement orientation in a tradition that is non-violent and American."

(SA)

Feedback:

The paper sent a number of suggested textual changes, and we have incorporated some of them into the review. It added some remarks on its mission:

> Some people thought that with the Indochina cease-fire there would be no need for an alternative press, but since then we have found out that the same Establishment which gave us the war also brought us Watergate, the 'energy crisis,' nuclear (and other) pollution, inflation, and--a continued war in Indochina.
>
> We feel that an alternative press is needed NOW MORE THAN EVER to let people know that there is an alternative to the Establishment way of seeing and doing things. It is a response to the big-business-controlled mass media which feed us only the information they want us to consume. The system--through its institutions of the family, churches, schools, and mass media--keeps trying to tell us, 'This is the way things will be because this is the way they are.' Our kind of publication says [that] things don't have to be the way they are because there might be an alternative and better way. Furthermore, things aren't always the way we are told they are, because we have been lied to.

BUGLE AMERICAN

Subdued Publications
2779 N. Bremen St.
Milwaukee, Wis. 53212
Weekly; $6.50
Started: 1970
Circulation: 12,000

Format: 56 pages (offset)
Issues examined: 1 & 29 Nov., 5 Dec. 1973
Back issues available from publisher

Although this does not have a tabloid format, its content resembles that of Underground newspapers: comics, satire, criticism of the Establishment, unusual graphics, and photographs. Short exposés on politics, the war machine, and the energy crisis. News of rock music, women's liberation, ecology, and community-based service groups. Calendar of events. Classified advertisements. Member of Alternative Press Syndicate, Zodiac, Pacific, and Liberation News Services. (JMS)

Feedback:

"We are an alternative newspaper.... We regularly publish special issues: Photo, Planting, Music, Community Resource Handbook, etc."

Due to the fact that "The offices of the Bugle were firebombed by arsonists a few weeks ago and completely destroyed," the editor enclosed a temporary address (11 March 1975): Box 2318, Milwaukee, 53212.

COLLAGE: Scrapbook of the 70s

| | |
|---|---|
| John Wilcock | Started: May 1970 |
| 204 W. 10th St. | Circulation: 5,000 |
| N.Y., N.Y. 10014 | Format: 16-page tabloid |
| Eventually weekly; $1 for next three issues | Issues examined: v. 1, no. 1 (undated), no. 2 (July 1970) |

According to its first issue, Collage is meant "to stimulate creativity: it is a picture paper created by its readers." It is a visual newspaper, 70% of which consists of graphics (including collages, photos, comic strips, and calligraphy). Its two main themes: sex and social injustice.

In an interview, Paul Krassner of The Realist describes himself: "The evolution of me from that privileged little kid [a six-year-old violinist at Carnegie Hall] to a long-haired dope-taking anarchist who wants to overthrow the system ... is what's taking me so long." In "Watch Out for Criminals" the various ways "criminal freeloaders" have developed of "thieving from unsuspecting corporations" are detailed. An astrology column tells how to "bring off the transformation of society, to make America a truly representative republic." It suggests breaking the back of a ruthless, inhuman economic system: stop paying taxes, and change all insane laws.

Other articles in the sample issues: "The Dope Column" (instructions in using the chillum, a pipe used mainly for hashish); "Building a Dome Home" (how to build a 39-foot 4-room house for $2,800); and "Under Shelley's Poet's Tree" (a column of world art news). (DB)

## COLLEGE PRESS SERVICE

1764 Gilpin St.
Denver, Colo. 80218
Semi-weekly; $90 to $185 for member papers depending on frequency; libraries $50 for nine months (academic year)
Started: 1962
Circulation: 400 newspapers
Format: 8 pages (legal size, offset)

Issues examined: 10 & 27 Apr., 4 & 15 May 1974
Self-indexing 3 times a year; and Alternative Press Index
Some back issues available from publisher
Microform version available from Xerox University Microfilms

An editor member of the collective sent this information about College Press Service:

> CPS is a non-profit corporation run as a task- and decision-sharing collective of four men and three women who receive subsistence pay. Collective members are usually former college editors who stay with CPS for no more than two years. This keeps the collective in touch with student opinions and lifestyles; it also allows CPS to serve as a professional training ground for young journalists. Since College Press Service is produced specifically for use in college papers, our first duty is toward our member publications. In that sense we strive for news coverage that is primarily college-related, but about one-third alternative news coverage--both written in an objective style. We receive no outside funding and have no ideological strings attached, although collective members maintain their own strongly-held views and interests which determine the kinds of stories they cover. So there is 'movement' coverage (e.g., anarchists, the alternative press, blacks, women, gays, anti-military groups), but as it relates to college students and in the objective, factual style our member papers demand. In addition to the twice-weekly releases, CPS also operates the Center for the Rights of Campus Journalists to fill the need for censorship and harassment counseling of college papers. Starting in the fall of 1974, the center will publish a censorship newsletter every two months that will be sent to all CPS members and not-for-publication subscribers.

CPS says it's the oldest and largest student press organization serving campus media, and its news releases go out to nearly 400 campus editors across the country. "Written by former college editors specifically for the college press, our members find CPS copy line-for-line more usable than the traditional news and wire services."

News stories cover government activity and programs affecting higher education and students, events and activities on individual campuses, conferences and activities of national student and educational groups, trends in education and educational change, movements for social change and reform, and surveys of student lifestyle and opinion.

CPS feels it has one of the most extensive resource-gathering mechanisms in the field, for it receives more than 400 college and university papers and has an exchange with other higher education publications such as The Chronicle of Higher Education and Higher Education Daily. In addition it maintains a network of stringers and contacts at campuses across the nation.

> CPS's Center for the Rights of Campus Journalists (CRCJ) has been used as a resource by the CBS Evening News and is the authorized campus representative of the Reporters' Committee for the Freedom of the Press. CRCJ maintains the most up-to-date files on college paper censorship cases in existence and publishes a bi-monthly newsletter that CPS members receive in addition to the twice-weekly news-releases.

Examples of articles in the issues examined were: "Kent State Student Killed by Narc in Drug Bust"; "Documents Reveal American Automakers Aided Nazi War Effort"; "FBI Illegally Wire Tapped, But Wounded Knee Trial Goes On"; "Distrust of Government is Main U.S. Problem, Students Say"; "Nixon Declined Use of Tape Unscrambling Agencies"; "Former Student Wins False Arrest Settlement"; "New York Student Newspapers Threatened with Fund Cut"; and "Oregon Woman Enrolls in Men's Phys. Ed. Course."

Underground, alternative, and college papers are sometimes summarized or quoted as to their editorial views, as when the article, "SLA: Henchmen or Revolutionaries," discusses three views taken by left-wing papers of the kidnapping of Patricia Hearst.

The news releases also contain two pages of editorial cartoons and graphic art. (JMS)

Feedback:
Editor expressed no disapproval and suggested two minor textual changes which were incorporated into the review.

DSS FREE PRESS: Downsview Free Press

Irregular; 11 issues in 3 years; 10¢ an issue
Started: Dec. 1969
Circulation: 100-500
Format: 6-10 pages (offset, stapled)

Issues examined: Dec. 1970; Feb.-May, Sept. 1971; May 1972
Back issues available from publisher by Xerox at cost

We print the following letter from a former DSS editor because it's an interesting account of the history and demise of a high school underground paper, typical because such high school papers usually die when the editors graduate.

> The first issue proclaimed revolution and advocated anarchy. It was very 'Radical' and ... gave quite a shock to the school administration. The effect reached to the top echelons of the school board. Technically fair in quality, most of the articles were only reprints from other newspapers. The paper sold for ten cents and was a modest success.
>
> The second issue came out three months later. The contents were improved, the printing and layout quality was much better, the staff and contributions increased, and the Free Press had won the first round against the school administration. The paper was not sold but given away for donations to get around an obscure Board of Education rule that unauthorised materials cannot be sold on school property. So far, so good.
>
> The third issue (promised for April) came out in November. A noticeable change could be seen in the editorial contents at this time. The editor ... was now school president and some of the Free Press staff were in the council executive. This led to a reduction of the shooting-off-at-the-mouth radical hate literature and an increase of relevant timely, hard-hitting serious articles that raised the literary level of the paper to ... [one] never seen at Downsview S.S. before. In fact the publication of the third issue took the Free Press two issues further than any other previous school paper.

> The fourth issue continued quite the same, only now there was some competition from another school newspaper. This was the 'official and legal' administration-approved paper. Now it was an all-out battle between the two factions. The Free Press went back to being openly sold for ten cents. (The third issue was an outright giveaway as a last and successful attempt to boost readership). A life-or-death situation developed. The Free Press was in a rather secure position, but the slightest relaxation of editorial policies or standards of quality could ring the death knell.

The special election issue of May 1972 was

> where the Free Press came to its untimely end. In June 1972 the remaining few Free Press staffers graduated from Downsview and went their separate ways. Our demise was not publicly announced because there was no paper to announce it in. The little blurb about returning in September at the bottom of the last page of the Election issue was there only to give the school administration something to worry about over the summertime.
>
> The D.S.S. Free Press is still remembered by those who knew it, and became rather infamous in its own way. In fact when we received your letter we were astounded to think that our little high school newspaper actually got beyond the city limits. We are really terribly flattered about the whole affair and deeply thank you for contacting us.

The editor also sent this information:

> The editorial policies of the DSSFP are much the same as a lot of other school newspapers. That is, to be a platform for student reform. To show the students and some teachers what the administration is up to and how to change it. To entertain and to help individuals communicate. Freedom of speech (press) was most important to us at all times. We stressed anti-censorship views strongly, giving contributors the security of having their true thoughts and feelings given to the masses in their original way.

The Free Press contained short amusing articles and satires

generally critical of: the student council; the school administration; certain rules, such as the "archaic system of attendance" whereby the students "regardless of age, must degrade themselves by getting notes from home signed by 'Mummy and Daddy' on occasions of absence"; the rival official school paper, of which it made great fun; and the purposes of education in general.

> The school system is, after all, nothing more than a 'boot-camp' for business and industry, and standardization requires that marks exist as an index revealing an effort-intelligence product, paramountly useful in relegating the peasants to their appropriate niches. Those who complain that marks mean nothing are right.

The paper also contained humorous drawings, photographs, and cartoons, some drawn by students, and some by such professionals as Jules Feiffer and Ron Cobb.

The address is: L. Scott Crowe, Publisher, Box 723, Downsview, Ont., Canada M3M 3A9. (JMS)

Feedback:

> Although I hadn't expected you to use my little dissertation this way, on the whole it's very well put together. I noted a few little corrections [incorporated into the review] and I would like, if possible, to give credit where credit is due--to Steven G. Ellams, founder of the Free Press, without whom all that came to pass would not have been possible and all the people who worked for and read and supported the Downsview Secondary School Free Press; thanx.

THE DAILY RAG: A Community Newspaper

Box 21026
Washington, D. C. 20009
Bi-weekly; $6 (free to prisoners and GIs)
Started: Oct. 1972

Circulation: 20,000
Format: 16-page tabloid (offset)
Issues examined: 9 Feb., 6 Apr., 4 May 1973

This alternative newspaper's primary coverage is of community groups such as theater, movement and women's groups, food co-ops, free schools, and radio stations. It publishes information sources, such as where to get health services or how to find your landlord; reviews of plays, books, and poems; and coverage of political and counter-cultural activities in the D. C. area. It also covers such national issues as the meat boycott, amnesty, abortion legislation, and Watergate.

Most of the paper consists of news articles; there were no essays or lengthy analyses of institutions or events in the issues examined. In one issue two controversial stories about internal conflict within a food co-op and a job co-op were prefaced by an editorial on the kind of journalism The Rag would like to publish:

> We decided to print the stories because we concluded that the most important thing The Rag can do to foster a sense of community around our alternative institutions is to publish as much information as possible about them all.... We do not pretend to be totally objective--rather we proclaim an intense interest in fostering a sense of our alternative community. Precisely because our bias is out front, our reporting will have more impact.

(MM)

Feedback:

The editor proposed several minor changes in the wording of our first paragraph. "The rest of your description seems fine to us."

THE EUGENE AUGUR

454 Willamette St.
Eugene, Ore. 97401
Bi-weekly; $5
Started: Oct. 1969
Circulation: 10,000
Format: 24-page tabloid (offset)
Issues examined: 14 Sept., 5 & 26 Oct. 1973
Indexing: Alternative Press Index
Back issues available from publisher
Microform version available from Xerox University Microfilms

"The Augur features world news unavailable to Associated Press members, utilizing news sources unaffiliated with the American printing establishment. We are also a showcase for information concerning emerging technologies and lifestyles in the Northwest and around the world," states a member of the collective which owns and staffs the newspaper.

World news is obtained through Liberation News Service,

Tricontinental News Service, Zodiac News Service, Pacific News Service, and New York News Service. News articles are written in an objective, journalistic style, and some are signed. Topics included: the coup in Chile and the involvement of the United States; Watergate; the United Farm Workers' Union; the oil crisis; nuclear plants; new drug laws; and a welfare forced-work plan.

Representative local events or issues covered: concern for an expanded methadon program; demonstrations to free prisoners; cannery accidents; food inspection; an "Impeach Nixon" rally; a Women's Clinic; freeway construction; and an interview with Jane Fonda about North Vietnam prison conditions.

Additional articles presented opinions on national and local issues by Augur staff members. Several columns were included in each issue. "Drug Report" presented a drug analysis project report from the Drug Information Center, as well as a feature article on a specific drug in each issue. "Community News" included short articles about local events, notices, and comments from organizations. "Community Guide" listed local organizations to contact for specific information such as Anti-war, Education, Food, Gay, Health, Housing, Legal, Media, Third World, and Women. "Auguries," a calendar of events, also listed a few free classified advertisements. The back page of each issue contained cartoon strips. Book reviews and poetry were occasionally included.

(NK)

## EXPRESS

Weekly; $9
Started: 28 Sept. 1972
Circulation: 30,000
Format: 20- to 28-page tabloid (offset)
Issues examined: 8 & 15 Nov., 6 Dec. 1973
Some back issues available from publisher
Microform version available from Bell & Howell

Andrew Kowal, publisher of this Long Island student (SUNY) weekly, says that it will print "Anything of interest to the local alternative-type community reader. We stress left-of-center advocacy journalism, while constantly trying to maintain a high humor level."

A regular feature, "Expressions," presents editorial comment on material in the current issue as well as on news items from other sources. A discussion of unexplained aspects of John Kennedy's assassination ends: "With the public mood one of truth-seeking, the Watergate investigations might stretch back further than anyone expected. A man as ruthless in his weilding [sic] of power as Richard Nixon shouldn't be expected to have been any less ruthless in gaining that power."

There are discussions of noise pollution, a nearby planetarium, and gay sex--as well as regular articles by Ralph Nader and Jack Anderson. One interesting report, "Crabs Scratched," illustrated by a picture of a 2 1/4" x 3 1/2" louse, assured readers that rumors of "a crab lice epidemic" in University housing were grossly exaggerated and that the infirmary had "no more cases ... than [in] any other year."

The periodical carries ads for rock concerts, research papers, and confidential, legal abortions. Personals range from "Need meaning to your life? Jesus Christ is the answer" to "Dear Matt K: I think your [sic] the cutest guy on campus and I love your ass. Love, your secret admirer." Comics, poetry, short stories, and an occasional recipe add variety to the publication.

Address of the publication was Express, Andrew Kowal, Publ., 113 Broadway, Hicksville, N.Y. 11801. (GKS)

Feedback:

Mail was returned marked "Moved--left no address" after being forwarded from the above address to Express Enterprises, 18 Soundview Rd., Huntington, N.Y. 11743.

FPS: The Youth Liberation News Service

2007 Washtenaw Ave.
Ann Arbor, Mich. 48104
Monthly; $5 for kids ($8 for adults; $12 for institutions)
Started: Sept. 1970
Circulation: 600
Format: 24 pages (offset)
Issues examined: Sept. & Nov. 1973; Jan. 1974
Back issues available from publisher
Microform version available from Bell and Howell

FPS is a news service for high school and junior high school underground and independent newspapers. By publishing both practical and theoretical journalism, the staff attempts to "help young people to learn the concrete skills to fight against their oppression. The areas of concentration are schools, and to a lesser extent, family relationships and juvenile prisons."

A summary of the contents introduces each issue. Regular features include "Letters," "Youth News," "More

News," and "Resources." Drawings and cartoons submitted by readers as well as slogans are interspersed throughout the periodical. These graphics emphasize the publication's liberal [Feedback: "radical"] position.

The News sections reprint summaries of items concerning young people. Examples of these reports are the announcement of a District of Columbia court decision granting that the right of privacy which entitles women to abortion, cannot be arbitrarily denied to juveniles; or the report by a clinical psychologist that some 70,000 to 80,000 young people will attempt suicide within the next year.

In the issues examined, the Resource section included a list of non-sexist feminist publishers, announcement of a pamphlet entitled Women in the Middle East--the Continuing Struggle published by Women's Middle East Study Collective, Box 134, W. Newton, Mass. 02156 for 50¢, and a review of two manuals available from Youth Liberation, Student and Youth Organizing and How to Start a High School Underground.

The September 1973 issue announces a new feature, "FPS Information Exchange." This "will be a place where any young person(s) who are trying to organize and educate others can share strategies and thoughts."

There are several three-page articles in each issue. One of the interesting feature stories concerned a student account of the restrictive atmosphere of a supposedly progressive alternative public high school. "How to Start a High School Group," an explanation of "why and how people in school can get together to better understand and try to change their situation," was covered in another issue.

FPS prints articles "about the liberation of other oppressed groups in this country and the world." An article concerning U.S. involvement in Chile points to the interference of U.S. corporations in Latin American governments. A report on the status of the war in Indochina concludes with this observation: "The U.S./Vietnamese war is a turning point in world history. The American Empire is fundamentally undermined. Weak and oppressed people all over the world now understand that they can defeat the most powerful enemy if they are willing to unite and struggle with total dedication." (JA)

Feedback:

"Looks fine...."

## FISHCHEER

Semi-monthly
Started: Jan. 1970
Circulation: 3,000
Format: 8-12 pages (offset)
Issues examined: none sent

We received the following information from Conni Yates, former editor:

> We were basically a community-oriented paper. Our staff was 75% university students. We attacked city policies, environmental issues with a small degree of success. We also tried to feed different viewpoints about national/international events to the community.

"We also published Grit City News, but both are now dead." The address of Fishcheer was: Box 1583, Pensacola, Fla. 32597.

## FREE FOR ALL

Box 962
Madison, Wis. 53701
Tri-weekly; $4 (institutions $12)
Started: Mar. 1973
Circulation: 8-10,000
Format: 16- to 20-page tabloid (offset)
Issues examined: 19 May, 19 Nov., 10 Dec. 1973
Indexing: Alternative Press Centre
Back issues available from publisher

Free For All is interested primarily in exposing "the capitalist monster to our readers ... bluntly with articles or columns on Nixon or the energy fraud, or more subtly, through a writing style which gets our point across." Such a writing style includes deliberate misspellings and a wide variety of names for the former president of the U$: Nixswine, lying slimebag, King Richard, and his successor Gerald Edsel. A regular feature, "On the Road to Fascism," reports on the latest developments in the latest president's government. The "Wong Truth Conspiracy" is a compilation of interesting and bizarre short items from various underground news services and newspapers, as well as rewritten items from the straight press and other sources. National and international news is reported but most news is at a local level, bringing readers up to date on labor disputes, boycotts, or, in the case of one informative article, the opposition to nuclear power plants in Wisconsin. Local campus activities and demonstrations are of course publicized frequently.

But the most interesting features of this paper are the less conventional services it renders to its readers. Articles have appeared giving tips on hopping freight trains and detailed instructions on how to build a telephone extension, including, for the conscience-stricken, ten reasons why the "fone" company should be ripped off (e.g., "because they're rich; because phones should be a free service; because ITT supports fascism here and the world over"). Recipes and articles on nutrition appear regularly, and in one issue "Farmer Rodecake's Shop" listed several drugs currently in town, giving prices and quality. We learned, for example, that "rotten" cocaine was going for $60-65 for one gram and really pure yellow acid was selling for 75¢ to a dollar "but you need 2 hits." [Feedback: "We would prefer the dope part to be cut, since we voted to discontinue the dope column."] (SA)

Feedback:

"It would be nice if you could work in something to the effect that we are an independent paper, not allied to any leftist group, particularly the more doctrinaire socialist organizations. We are not afraid to attack any other leftist group, if the criticism is constructive. Since about February or March [1974], the paper has taken on more of an anarchist perspective on things, reminding readers that a socialist society based on totalitarianism is not necessarily in the interests of the people.

"In general, I was impressed with your review: I thought it captured our spirit pretty well."

## FREEDOM READER

Monthly; $3 for 15 issues
Started: June 1971
Circulation: 12,000

Format: 24-page tabloid
Issues examined: Dec. 1971; Jan., Mar., Apr. 1972

Freedom Reader is the local underground paper of Flint, Michigan, and a paper of the youth culture in general. The most frequently discussed subject is drugs (it supports the abolition of marijuana laws but is opposed to the use of heroin and the way it serves capitalism). However, articles and news items touch on all aspects of the youth and counter culture, such as the free clinic movement (and other health issues), the war in Southeast Asia, the freedom (now won) of John Sinclair (founder of the White Panther Party), and the oppression of black and poor people and of women.

The paper emphasizes the importance of young people's voting, in local as well as national elections, and its reporters have interviewed some members of the Flint City Council and published the platform of the Human Rights Party of Ann Arbor. "Shop Raps" is a regular feature in which union members discuss the demands and progress of labor in their workplaces. The "Bust Page" covers news of drug busts and advice on how to avoid them. These are two general statements of the philosophy of Freedom Reader:

> We, the people, are the new breed. To survive we mobilize. We mobilize not to kill for a revolution, but to survive after a peaceful inner revolution. We have learned from past wars, revolutions, holocosts [sic], and so forth, why we fight. The reason (for those who don't know): Racism, facism [sic], oppression, and poverty, due to the oppression and the lack of cooperation from people who have not yet realized that you are their brother.
>
> Man has to find his place on earth, he has to live in harmony with nature and the Universe. Man has to learn to care, to take the time to understand each other, to make the effort to change what is wrong. We have to learn to care for ourselves as well as each other. Poisons in food, filth in the air, scum in the waters, people starving while others make millions and control the government. War expanding, H-bombs stand ready, napalm burning, as Nixon's war machine keeps turning. Bodies burning, as minds are turning inward, American ego. Why do we have to be the number one nation, when there isn't supposed to be a number one nation at all. America teaches her children that they must be a success, it teaches 'kiss that man's ass while you step on that person.' American ego in every man, to compete, to be better than another man is wrong. If we don't learn to live together, if we don't let love rule our lives, there ain't gon'na be no one living at all.

Several articles are reprinted from other publications. Poetry and graphics are regularly featured. (MM)

Feedback:

Mail returned (1974): "Box closed, no order." Address had been: Box 1337, Flint, Mich. 48501.

THE GAR

Box 4793
Austin, Tex. 78765
Monthly; $3
Started: Sept. 1971

Circulation: 3,500
Format: 24-page tabloid (offset)
Issue examined: Dec. 1971

The sample issue was sympathetic toward, and carried news of, the struggles of Chicanos and women. It also carried news of a group ("The Dirty Thirty") of liberal members of the Texas legislature; and an article on communications media, discussing the rise of the underground press, the death of such picture magazines as Look and the Saturday Evening Post, and the "centralizing" effect of radio and television.

Other features: poems; recipes; short fiction; photographs and other illustrations; several comic strips; articles on rock music; and advertisements for health food stores, head shops, candles, book stores, and other Texas periodicals. (TJS)

Feedback:

> We try to present a good sampling of the creative activity of our area (Texas and the southwest): writing, art, photography. Special subjects of interest are urban trends and city problems, ecology, education, media, and reviews from a regional angle, of books, records and local music.

GUERILLA

201 Queen St. East
Toronto, Ontario, Canada
Bi-weekly; $10 for 52 issues
Format: 12-page tabloid (offset)

Issue examined: 24 Mar. 1973
Indexing: Alternative Press Index

"This paper does not receive provincial government advertising. This ... [discriminatory] practice towards us by a government which had 3 large scandals ... makes us proud.... the significance of Corruption in high places will not be lost on us. Though we fear the Mafia whether in its legal or illegal forms, we will in future present the facts of the provincial government record--both public and private--whenever and wherever we can. Guerilla invites information about the provincial government and its officials. The pork barrel and the old ... connections in this province have got to go. What we fear to print we will at least know for ourselves. Contact must not be made over our phone lines. Better to try the federal government mail system."

The paper is concerned with municipal corruption, labor, ecology and pollution, minorities, and prison conditions. It carries theater, film, and record reviews. Illustrated with photographs and cartoons. (JMS)

HONKY TIMES

Monthly; $5
Dates: June-Fall 1972
(seven issues)
Circulation: 5,000
Format: 20-page tabloid
(offset)
Issue examined: Fall 1972
Microform version available from Bell & Howell

The last issue of Honky Times appeared in the fall of 1972, after six months of publication had failed to win enough support in the San Antonio area. The publisher writes that his major editorial policy was "Fuck the capitalistic system." [See Feedback.]

The final issue deplored the re-election of Nixon; defined Republicans as "the rich, the selfish, the complacent ... who get to fiddle while America burns: the Machiavellians"; advised "this shitty city that many of San Antonio's most highly respected icons are naked as jaybirds"; applauded American women who "are plotting their ascendency" while their men "sit Sundays stupefied before the tube, watching giants assault one another"; asked "Why aren't longhairs ever on juries?"; and warned that the dangers of nuclear power plants are being glossed over.

There were reviews of rock records, numerous cartoons (one making fun of Nixon and Billy Graham as hawks), and two pages of poetry. Ads told where to buy natural food, records, incense, black-lights, wigs, leather goods, water beds, stereo systems, cycles, original jewelry, books, and "A" or "B" term papers (from $2 a page up).

The staff's farewell statement was: "In parting, we say to all who have tried to help Honky Times, 'Thank you.' To all you motherfuckers who have been gutting us, we say, 'Fuck off.'"

Address was: Trey Ellison, Publ., Box 12277, San Antonio, Tex. 78212. Current address is 340 Jones St. (Rm. 2591), San Francisco, Calif. 94102. (GKS)

Feedback:

The editor sent us an interesting letter, part of which is quoted below:

> Now that I see the paper is to be a subject of serious scholarship, I regret--and retract--my petulant reply to your earlier question form, that my major editorial policy was 'fuck the capitalist system.' While my policy was far left, it was not the 'smash the state' brand of leftist commentary that has been fashionable for 'underground' publications. In all seven issues, citizens of San Antonio were urged to take a closer look at the activities of political, social, and economic leaders, to view the propaganda of the kept media with a more critical eye.
>
> The first 6 issues were less bombastic than the 7th, where I pulled out all the stops--and tried to say 'fuck' a lot. It had been a hell of a job trying to keep the thing solvent with advertising revenue alone, and I was burned out.
>
> If you'll change the 2nd sentence, the comments, as written, are fair and unbiased. I would only add that the graphics that held the paper together were important too. My contribution to the publication was writing about politics and selling the ads.... The artwork of [Jim] Harter, and the people he supervised in the layout and design of _HT_, is hard for me to define. It just seemed to fit the tone of what I wanted to say.
>
> I am very interested in your work, having followed with some interest the tribulations of the 'underground press' for several years. It seems to me that the relatively low costs of publication, which would not have been possible without the offset press, encouraged ego-tripping malcontents like me to do our strident 'thing.' Anybody who chooses to alienate ... [himself] from the dominant culture and hustle the fringes of the hip can do it. And an odd bunch of characters have done and are still doing it.
>
> As an example, the experience I had with a ... [certain paper] may be of interest to you.
>
> ... last spring, I wrote a short article on ... [such-and-such a topic, and the publisher of that paper] ran it. I showed him back issues of _Honky_

Times and offered to sell ads for his paper. This was just after the Hearst kidnapping, and paranoia, always bubbling in the 'underground,' boiled over. [He] ... somehow got the idea that I was an FBI agent trying to infiltrate his staff to get the goods on the SLA--so he ran me off. (I haven't seen him since--but I still read his paper which is a pretty good one.) The whole matter really upset me for about a month--but I've decided it is all part of the game.

NEW IMPROVED TIDE

Monthly; free
Dates: mid-1967 through June 1973
Circulation: 1,500
Format: 10-14 pages (8" x 12", offset)
Issues examined: June & Nov. 1971; Jan. 1972

New Improved Tide was an "underground" paper originated in 1967 by students of John Marshall High School in Los Angeles. According to the last editor, Tony Safford, the paper's chief purpose was "to foster freedom of speech and thought." He stated that the paper had served as an open forum "to maintain stimulating dialogue between appropriate authorities on various conflicts, interests, etc."

The paper was generously illustrated. Each issue included cartoons dealing with topics of interest to students and usually employing characters from well-known comic strips. Some issues relied heavily on articles reprinted from other sources. Contributions by John Marshall students treated of such varied topics as the Vietnam War, prison reform, "free schools," venereal disease, and the juvenile court system. The political stance of most of the writers was very much left of center. Typical titles included "New Death Machines in Vietnam," "Beating the Lottery, or Slicking Sam's Selective Service System," "Prison Torture" (describing treatment of Vietnamese prisoners captured by American and Saigon troops), and "To the World Working Class." The latter article ended with the slogans: "All power to the people! Workers of all countries unite!"

Each issue included some poetry written by the students, much of it dealing with political issues or students' rights. There were also reports on interviews with school officials, in which such matters as dress codes, suspension, racism and the "underground" press were discussed.

One article listed ten suggestions intended to help

students avoid arrest for possession or sale of drugs. Among the warnings included was the following paragraph:

> There is a club sponsored by the LAPD [Los Angeles Police Department] called the 75-25 club. Its members get $75 a month plus 25¢ a head for every name and arrest of people like you. We have narks on campus. Students like us. They listen, they inform. Beware. Its your neck and mine. Recently a guy got 7 years for possession of 4 kilos.

The address of New Improved Tide had been: 3880 Franklin Ave., Los Angeles, Calif. 90027. (SMA)

Feedback:

"I cannot help but be a little disappointed as to your summary of the New Improved Tide. You fail to understand that the NIT was an open forum structured paper and, therefore, opinions expressed in articles were not necessarily the views of the editor. This is stated quite explicitely [sic] in the Staff Box. NIT brought forth issues otherwise unmentionable through official, established channels. What do you gain by quoting an article ('The latter article ended with the slogans: "All power to the people! Workers of all countries unite!"') if the views of the author are not necessarily representative of the paper? The purpose of the paper becomes distorted when these views are taken out of context. The NIT was an open forum paper with no other editorial policy than that defined by the terms 'open forum.' I cannot permit your summary to be considered as being an accurate representation of the New Improved Tide."

## NORTHWEST PASSAGE

Box 105, So. Bellingham Sta.
Bellingham, Wash. 98225
Fortnightly; $6
Started: Mar. 1969
Circulation: 4,000
Format: 32-page tabloid (offset)
Issues examined: Mar., Apr., June, July 1974
Indexing: Alternative Press Index
Back issues available from publisher

"We are a totally volunteer, anarcho-communalist, antisexist journal which tries to voice the ideas and opinions of the alternative community of Western Washington [Seattle and Bellingham area]. We edit submissions for unconscious (and conscious) sexism and any language deemed offensive to a large portion of our audience."

The issues examined contained news, commentary, and articles on community groups and affairs, ecology, pollution, Indian and Chicano struggles, art, films, wild food, gardening, nature lore, Aikido, a gay prisoners' organization, impeachment, Bessie Smith, Attica, oil, and Third World women; and stories, poetry, interviews, and letters.

Imaginatively illustrated with photographs and graphics. (JMS)

Feedback:

The editor expressed no disapproval.

PATRIOT

Sunshine Publications
Box 687
Kalamazoo, Mich. 49005
$4 ($8 to gov't institutions; free to POWs)

Format: 24-page tabloid (offset)
Issue examined: 7 Dec. [1971] (No. 29)

"The Patriot is a community newspaper which educates people of [sic] the class nature of this capitalist system and how peoples in this country and other countries are liberating themselves from this type of system and building a free world which is fit to live and grow [in]." The following paragraphs illustrate some of the paper's concerns:

Local politics. An article on anti-student zoning ordinances in Kalamazoo complains that "The City Commission has appointed itself God."

Students. Their rights are supported, and contempt is expressed for such things as absurd dress codes (e.g., requiring high school girls to wear brassieres).

Women's liberation. A case history (reprinted from Women: A Journal of Liberation) concerns a woman abused by her husband and unable to obtain any protection from the authorities.

Vietnam war. The U.S. role is opposed, and Nixon's "troop withdrawals are [called] a ruse."

U.S. plutocracy. "... the only thing that registers in the minds of the people who run this country is the cash register."

Right-wing groups. An article on philosophies of history makes fun of the "Conspiratorial Conception of History" held by "nutty candy manufacturer Robert Welsh [i.e., Welch]," founder of the "fascist" John Birch Society.

Features. Calendar of events; free classified ads; news of counseling services, rock concerts, food co-ops, recycling stations; cartoons; poems; letters to the editor; and useful phone numbers (e.g., draft counseling; birth control). "The Zoo" is a section of brief news notes opposing racism and the U.S. establishment (e.g., "Nixon Aids Fascist Portugal"). (Some of these items are from Liberation News Service.)

(TJS)

THE RAG

2330 Guadalupe
Austin, Tex. 78705
Weekly; $8 ($12 institutions; free to prisoners)
Started: 1966
Circulation: 5,000
Format: 16- to 30-page tabloid (offset)
Issues examined: 26 Mar., 14 May, 1 & 15 Oct. 1973
Back issues available from publisher
Microform version available from Xerox University Microfilms

The Rag sent the following information:

> We have no editor or any established positions, but we have general policies set by a concensus [sic] of the collective. In general we are against capitalism and all of its manifestations, racism, sexism, and any other system of economics ... or human relationship which exploits and oppresses people and destroys the environment. We are for socialism, with differing definitions of what this means, but we are all for a society based on cooperation rather than competition, and for a society which seeks to live with its environment rather than waging constant war against it.

The Rag is an unusual underground paper, in that it has been around since 1966. (See original review in Vol. I.) "Rag Triumphant," in one issue, describes the legal battle that the Regents of the University of Texas here waged since 1969 to keep the newspaper from being sold on campus. The American Civil Liberties Union took on the case, which eventually went all the way to the U.S. Supreme Court. The matter was resolved in favor of The Rag, because the "Regent's Rules were [declared] unconstitutional in restricting speech and associational activities protected by the First Amendment."

The Rag is partly a community paper (each issue carries a "City Council Report"), although it also covers national and international news. Recent topics covered by the paper have been Chile and the overthrow of the elected Marxist government of Dr. Salvador Allende, with the--alleged--aid of the U.S. Central Intelligence Agency; Watergate; the feminist movement; the use of electro-psychological and neuro-physiological techniques on prisoners; Guru Maharaj Ji (wasn't impressed); and pollution and ecology and the dangers of nuclear power.

The Rag is less actively revolutionary than it was in 1968 when our first review was written, and devotes less space to talking about marijuana. The content seems more serious. (JMS)

Feedback:

"This looks good."

RAMA PIPIEN

Charles A. Raisch, Ed.
1380 Howard St.
San Francisco, Calif. 94103
Bi-monthly; $7 (institutions $10)

Started: Feb. 1970
Circulation: 10,000
Format: 60 pages (offset)
Issues examined: Brochure sent, no sample issues

The following information was taken from the brochure:

> Rama Pipien, the Peoplesmedia Digest, is an international digest of alternative and underground press material--presented bi-monthly in a permanent journal format. Rama offers people's liberation coverage; natural living; earthworks; technology; movie, music, and book reviews; columns; poetry; and contemporary graphics. The popular investigative essay and other new forms of experimental journalism fill each issue. We are a group of writers and artists working to offer personal, social, cultural, and political analysis from a root-change humanist and nonviolent perspective. We believe in truth, love, beauty, community, technology, and ourselves.

The magazine has had such contributors as Ramsey Clark, Jane Fonda, Jules Feiffer, John and Yoko Ono Lennon, Huey Newton, Jerry Rubin, and John Sinclair.

THE SOUTHERN VOICE: Alternative Views on the News

Mike Condray, Ed.
3402 Caroline
Houston, Tex. 77004
Semi-monthly; $5
Started: Nov. 1973

Circulation: 5,000
Format: 20- to 24-page tabloid (offset)
Issues examined: 2 Aug. & 24 Sept. 1974

The editor sees his paper as "a vehicle for writers/photographers/artists who are (and we feel quite justifiably) frustrated by establishment" newspapers. It "pushes no ideology" and "strives to be an informative alternative news/entertainment" periodical.

STORRS WEEKLY

Weekly; free
Dates: 24 Oct. 1972 - 8 May 1973
Circulation: 5,000

Format: 4- to 16-page tabloid (offset)
Issues examined: Oct. 1972 - Apr. 1973

One of the editors sent this information:

> The Storrs Weekly has ceased publication (8 May 1973).... There is no steady alternative newspaper at the Univ. of Conn. The Storrs Street Fish Gazette published one edition: a group of community individuals feeling responsible towards the education that comes about from ... [detailed] reporting, and subjective reporting. Contact is a regular campus paper put out by the Afro-American Center. Forward Motion printed one issue: a group called the Coalition who are dedicated to combining forces in presenting important, neglected campus issues to the administration and community.

A three-member staff put together the paper, which was originally called Storrs Weekly Reader, "and after a change of name became the Storrs Weekly--after an interesting lawsuit by a large corporation with a similarly-named paper." The Weekly acted as an alternative to the student-funded campus paper, and attempted "to educate students to issues involving them." This education included information and opinions on national, state, and university topics.

The Weekly supported George McGovern, gay liberation, and the feminist movement, and carried articles against chemical warfare, the Alaska pipe line, capital punishment, and the lowering of emission standards for automobiles. An editorial chid the governor for supporting capital punishment ("legal murder") while calling abortion "murder." Other articles dealt with student issues and politics, such as: certain student fees it felt unfair; bad and expensive housing; high food costs; and the highly inflammable issue of whether --in the interests of free speech--Arthur Jensen, whose genetic theories suggest that Negroes are inferior, should be allowed to speak on campus.

The Weekly also carried poetry, recipes, a few ads, cartoons, and drawings. Its address was: Box U167, Inner College Trailer, Storrs, Conn. 06268. (JMS)

TAKE OVER

Box 706
Madison, Wis. 53701
Bi-weekly; $8 (institutions $15)
Started: Oct. 1971
Circulation: 5,000
Format: 16-24 pages (offset)

Issues examined: none sent
Indexing: Alternative Press Index
Back issues available from publisher
Microform version available from Bell & Howell

The following information was supplied by one of the editors:

> No explicit political line. Pragmatic anarchist? Cultural revolutionary libertarian socialist? New Left. Material ranging from gossip column to poetry to County Board politicking to how-to-do-it articles for outlaws to generalized fucking with our readers' minds ('You can't believe everything you read in the papers.') We are still into confrontation politics--among other kinds--now more than ever. We like juicy sensationalist exposés and scandals (assassination cover-ups, Nixon & the Mafia, local ruling-class scandals). Other papers like to reprint our layouts. Madison Kaleidoscope started June 1969; internal strife led to a split into two successor papers, T. O. [Take Over] and King Street Trolley, which appeared alternate weeks. Trolley faded away summer 1972.

## WEATHER REPORT

Box 1221
San Marcos, Tex. 78666
Bi-monthly; $2.50 for 15 issues
Started: 5 Oct. 1970

Circulation: 1,500-2,500
Format: 12- to 16-page tabloid (offset)
Issues examined: Sept. 1972; Apr. & June 1973

The editor writes that this is a completely free press that prints what contributors say, whether or not the staff agrees, and thus "Editorial policies depend upon the individual writer...."

Weather Report is primarily concerned with the problems of town and gown: San Marcos, Texas, and Southwest Texas State University. A double-page ad addresses students: "Maybe they gave you the right to vote because they thought you'd never use it. Prove them wrong, register and vote." A headline reads: "Students Provide Upset in City Council Races."

News articles tell about a university professor believed fired because he exercised his right of free speech, and a co-ed fired by a restaurant because she dated a Negro. "Fuck Bell" gives detailed instructions on how to "cut your phone bill by 100% merely by utilizing Amerika's credit card consciousness."

There are a number of stories of police harassment and brutality, and the firing of a campus policeman is applauded because he "had gained the reputation as a 'Super Cop' among local police agencies, and as a super-pain-in-the-ass with students...." Consumers are warned about "Those damn' black downers," mysterious pills being peddled in the area which "will deactivate a consumer for at least two days --sometimes three."

An article rejoices that "Governor Briscoe, bless his little fascist heart, signed the majority rights bill passed by the legislature," so that students from 18 to 20 can buy beer and liquor, enter into contracts, and "serve on juries and limit some of the outrages that juries stacked with older people have been able to perpetuate."

Weather Report belongs to the Underground Press Syndicate.
(GKS)

## THE WURD

25¢ an issue
Dates: Mar.-May 1969

Circulation: 1,000
Format: No. 1, 19 pages

(legal size); No. 2, 18 pages
Issues examined: Mar. & May 1969 (only issues published)

Photocopies of back issues available from editor

Contributors to this high school publication were concerned with deficiencies in the Canadian educational system and in their particular schools. One writer complained that students were urged to contribute to a school paper, but were censured if their opinions conflicted with those of the editors. Another believed that students who criticized the system were watched closely by the powers that be.

A contributor deplored white suppression and exploitation of the Indians and Eskimos and warned that the importance of their heritage must be recognized. American intervention in Vietnam and the complicity of the Canadian government in that war were roundly condemned in two articles.

The editor found a lack of personal freedom in the schools with their buzzers, dress codes, restricted hair lengths, and limited smoking areas. The issues contained reviews of films, records, and books; and poems by the editor and others.

Address was: Barbara Bekerman, Ed., 113 Longwood Dr., Waterloo, Ont., Canada. (GKS)

# Chapter 6

## COMICS

> The average American defecates more than FOUR TONS of fecal material in his lifetime! A city of one million could quickly fill an area the size of Lake Eerie. This remarkable feat was accomplished by Cleveland, Ohio, in 1966!
>
> ---"Kitchen's Amazing Facts," in _Mom's Homemade Comics_

Nothing is sacred to the underground comic book: motherhood, God, womanhood, the American middle class, politicians, intellectuals, policemen, marriage, sex, the political-military-industrial establishment, the American flag, patriotism, and the war in Vietnam are ruthlessly satirized. On the other side of the coin, hippies, the drug culture, feminists, revolutionaries, lesbians, motor cycle freaks, and Hare Krishna devotees are also made fun of.

Artwork ranges from bad to good, from mildly erotic to incredibly vulgar, and from representational to extremely fanciful. (The illustrations of _Illuminations_ are especially exotic: as in Hieronymus Bosch paintings, many things are going on at once.) Some of this comic book illustration has found its way as pop art into reputable galleries.

The quality varies in the comics examined--some are clever satires while others are merely vulgar and tedious. A sociologist might say that the anti-heroes found in the underground comic are a reaction against the good, clean superheroes of the comic book of yesteryear and all of the patriotism, hypocrisy, and unreality contained therein. Some of the editors say their purpose is social criticism (see feedback on _Bijou Funnies_). The male editor of _Amazon Comics_ informed us, perhaps with tongue in cheek, that one of its major themes is the relation of women to war-making. The female editors of _Pandora's Box_ and _Tits & Clits Comix_ (first prize for vulgarity) say their purpose is "humorous, iconoclastic feminism." _Abortion Eve_ attempts to make abortion information available to women. The purpose of some of these comics, we suspect, is merely erotic entertainment.

The comic books that we've reviewed in this chapter are but a small sampling of what's available. --Janet Spahn

ABORTION EVE

Chin Lyvely & Joyce Sutton, Publs.
Nanny Goat Productions
Box 845
Laguna Beach, Calif. 92652
One-time publication (not a periodical); 50¢
Date: 1973
Format: 32 pages ( 6 7/8" x 9 5/8")
Still available from publishers

Co-publisher Lyvely states: "It was our desire to make general abortion information available to women of all incomes. We are strongly in favor of women's rights and strongly opposed to any institution ... [that] suppresses them." The work "could not have been written without creative contact with women's groups, free clinics, schools, young people, referral agencies, hospitals, and doctors."

The inside front cover asks, rhetorically, whether some people are more likely than others to suffer from unwanted pregnancy, and answers:

> ... not one General of the Army, Admiral of the Navy, or even a lowly helicopter pilot has ever contracted this malignant plague. Bank presidents, nuclear physicists, pipe fitters, and sanitary engineers are also statistically 'clean.'
>
> You may well ask who, then, is it that suffers the most? For some strange reason typists do, as well as nurses, secretaries, welfare mothers, and sopranos.... Extensive analysis shows the one common denominator ... is: THEY ARE ALL FEMALE!

The text shows a number of women (of different races, ages, and backgrounds) visiting a (female) counselor, working out their problems (religious or ethical scruples, fear of pain, static from husbands, or whatever), and undergoing and recovering from the operation. Why should women undergo it? Childbirth is messy, painful, and unpleasant, and lets them in for "two years of slave labor and 16 years of responsibility.... You never have a moment's freedom." (TJS)

## AMAZON COMICS

Rip Off Press
Box 14158
San Francisco, Calif. 94114
One-time publication (not a periodical); 50¢
Date: 1972
Format: 24 pages (7 1/4" x 10")
Still available from publisher

Scene.--The siege of Troy. A group of Amazons, led by Queen Penthesilia, fights on the side of the Trojans.

Action.--As they fight the Greeks, there is great mayhem:

kicks in the groin
spears & swords & arrows through bodies
biting of genitals
attempted rape
cutting off of a penis
grabbing of breasts
gouging

The last four pages (and the inside back cover) show pedantic male professors discussing the Iliad, and portray them as male chauvinists. In a seminar, their female students object to their sexist utterances, and a dispute--almost as bloody as that in the Trojan War depicted earlier--breaks out.

A "vice-president/shipping clerk" of Rip Off Press describes the purpose of Amazon Comics as "having a good time and trying to pass it on." (TJS)

Feedback:

The review of Amazon Comics seems rather superficial, consisting in the main of descriptions of violent action and lacking mention of major themes such as the relationship of women to war-making.

Amazon Comics is enjoying strong popularity among feminists.

There is one error of fact in the review: I thought I was being asked the purpose of Rip Off Press; you have quoted me as describing the purpose of Amazon Comics which I would not presume to do.

Sincerely,
Don Baumgart (vice president/shipping clerk)

BIJOU FUNNIES

Jay Lynch, Pres.
Bijou Publishing Empire
Box 3506, Merchandise
Mart Station
Chicago, Ill. 60654
"There are 8 issues. Bijou is published when we see fit; 75¢ per issue; $1 for Bijou 8, which I recommend you read for its editorial on censorship."
Format: 32 pages (6 1/2" x 8 1/2")
Issues examined: #2 & #3 (1969)

Drugs.--The sample issues contain examples of taking LSD, amyl nitrate, and uppers and downers; and of pushing heroin.

Activities.--The characters are engaged in--among other things--coprophagia, masturbation, rape, and heterosexual intercourse.

Characters.--These include weird creatures, and many voluptuous females.

Criticism.--A state governor (with swastikas in his eyes) wonders whether "Spiro Agnew still wears leather underwear." Policemen are brutal, and beat people. In the second issue, three "wierdos" [sic] urinate on a policeman, and are promptly shot dead by him. (TJS)

Feedback:

Mr. Lynch replied:

> I am very glad you want to present, in your words, 'a fair and unbiased portrayal' of Bijou Funnies in your directory of periodicals. I suggest you begin your task by washing your mind out with soap.
>
> Your summary fails to include the fact that Bijou is a satire magazine aimed at adults. It also fails to include anything other than references to sex, excretion, and drugs. Why no references to the following material included in the issues you reviewed: 1950's nostalgia; detective fiction; the press; daytime television; Norman Mailer; robots; divorce; physical education; Samuel Clemens; Charlie Chaplin; bad living conditions among Chinese in mid-50's America; advertising; American popular music of the 1940's; farm life; intolerance; hypocracy [sic], and thousands of other things.
>
> We assume our readers--adults--are mature enough to be able to read a satirical piece in which sex, like other aspects of life, might play a part,

without the reader dwelling upon this area to an unwholesome degree.

Mr. Spahn, I would hate to see someone with your perspective review Shakespeare, Voltaire, or the Bible. It is true that ... [characters engaged in masturbation, rape, and heterosexual intercourse can be found in] almost every great work. Yet most of us are intelligent enough to perceive a writer's message as going a little deeper than masturbation, rape, and heterosexual intercourse.

Artwork from Bijou Funnies has been shown in the Louvre in Paris, the Huntington-Hartford in New York, the Phoenix in Berkeley, the Corchran [sic] in Washington, D. C., and in many other prestigious galleries....

Most of the drug references you mention are from ... a comic strip by Jim Osborne in Bijou #2, which is without a doubt an anti-drug strip. I shudder to think of your interpretation of such a simple Bible story as, for example, Sodom and Gomorrah--not that I'm comparing Bijou to the Bible, but it seems that you lack the ability to see the point of a lesson in clean living.

Other drug references in Bijou are not pro-drug per se. Drugs were included in the early issues as they were part of the so-called youth culture of that time, which these stories satirize.

Bijou Funnies has been coming out since 1968. There are over one million Bijous in circulation, including foreign editions. Bijou has been distributed in England, France, Belgium, Sweden, Denmark, Holland, Finland, and Australia, and has received favorable reviews in books, art journals, magazines, and newspapers in these countries as well as in the United States.

I'm enclosing an extensive bibliography of U. S. and foreign books and periodicals which have found a little more to say about Bijou Funnies than you did. Perhaps you will even take the time to learn what reviewers for The New York Times, the Chicago Sun Times, the Chicago Daily News, and the National Observer had to say about Bijou.

You have overlooked possibly the most important aspect of Bijou's existence, which is that it was one of the first three comic books to defy the Good Comics Code.

Before the Code was established in 1955, over

> fifty per cent of the comic books published were read by adults. Code censorship and manipulation led to the destruction of half the comic book industry--thanks to the other half of the comic book industry, which profited by the demise of its competitors. Thus the code rendered the comic book a medium for children only. Because of the ice-breaking effect of Bijou and Zap, by 1972 there were more non-Code titles than Code titles available.
>
> I am very glad to hear that you are more than willing to include my remarks in your summary, and I will look forward to seeing them there. However, I would appreciate your care in printing all my remarks verbatim.

We regret that we do not have the space to reproduce Mr. Lynch's bibliography (or the time to verify all of the items in it, some of which are from Dutch, French, and Swiss magazines).

## GIRL FIGHT COMICS

| | |
|---|---|
| The Print Mint | Format: 32-pages (6 3/4" x 9 3/4", or 7" x 9 1/2") |
| 830 Folger Ave. | |
| Berkeley, Calif. 94710 | Issues examined: Nos. 1 & 2 (1972, 1974) |
| 50¢ an issue | |

Women are the strong and virtuous characters in GFC. Two female detectives foil villains. A team of female archaeologists makes an interesting find. Female guerrillas march through the streets.

Amazons and female astronauts figure in both of the sample issues. An astronaut discovers a planet inhabited by male chauvinists--and outsmarts them. Lesbian astronauts defeat male space-pirates. In "Space Dykes," astronauts from different galaxies submerge their rivalry and join to fight the common enemy: men.

A tribe of Amazons is discovered in a South American rain forest. Their queen visits the U.S., and feminists show her the ills of American society: crime, vice, and sexism. Sickened, she returns to her jungle. In another story, South American lackeys of the Central Intelligence Agency try to crush a popular revolutionary movement. An African chief's daughter foils a plot by warmongering American capitalists.

In a continuing series ("Fantasy"), women turn on their

oppressors: whores beat their pimps; and country wives, "sick of baking bread and having babies on the kitchen table," leave their lazy men and "split for the big city." (Cf. Illuminations, in which groupies assault rock musicians.)

The sexual content: restrained Lesbian lovemaking; attempted heterosexual rape.

In one issue, artist Trina Robbins draws and describes herself. She says she's a feminist who likes to wear pink satin and draw beautiful women. (TJS)

GOTHIC BLIMP WORKS

c/o East Village Other
116 St. Mark's Place
N.Y., N.Y. 10009
Monthly; $6

Started: 1969
Format: 24-page tabloid (offset)
Issues examined: nos. 5-7 [1969]

Gothic Blimp Works pushes love, peace, nudity, unrestrained sexual experimentation, and drug experiences. Its liberated philosophy is strikingly at odds with the violence, degradation of women, and grotesque imagery of many of the comic strips. Some science fiction stories are drawn in a style not so much "far out" as incomprehensible; most of the drawings are highly detailed, bizarre representations of human beings (and some animals, and some combinations) in sexual or violent confrontations. Political content is limited to some jokes about paying taxes for marijuana, inclusion of some well-known political figures in the action, and some references to the draft. The artists' styles vary, although the women they draw all have the standard Body, and all of the comics are somehow reminiscent of R. Crumb's (one of the contributors). Unless those who give only their first initials are women, all of the artists are men. (CP)

Feedback:

Mail returned 1974: "Moved, left no address." Remailed to 105 2nd Ave., N.Y., N.Y. 10003: no response.

HIGH-FLYIN' FUNNIES & STORIES

Print Mint
830 Folger Ave.
Berkeley, Calif. 94710
50¢ an issue

Date: 1970
Format: 32 pages (6 3/4" x 9 3/4")

The main character is a revolutionary alligator who exhorts us to "Screw the system: do it now & tell all your friends." He meets a sorcerer and a talking ostrich, and has other adventures. Butts of the humor are super-patriots (singing "Gawd Bless Amerikaaa"); Dow Chemical (makers of napalm during the Vietnam War); the police (a pig-snouted cop hassles young people who want to dance and make music in a public park); American politicians, spouting about law-'n'-order; and Richard M. Nixon. (TJS)

ILLUMINATIONS

The Print Mint
830 Folger Ave.
Berkeley, Calif. 94710
50¢ an issue

Format: 32 pages (6 3/4" x 9 3/4")
Issue examined: 1971(?)

Contributions by a number of artists. Imaginative (psychedelic) art work.

In the main story, a little boy floats away from earth in an ascension balloon; finds spiritual enlightenment in some celestial sphere; returns to his earthly parents after 20 years, transfigured; shows them how to seek enlightenment; and so on. A peaceful story, only mildly erotic in comparison with shorter strips in the same issue.

A sampling of the one-page strips: criticism of canned music (Muzak); depiction of a motorcycle gang's sordid party; a sadistic nightmare by S. Clay Wilson; "Funny Nazis," making fun of National Socialists as sadistic murderers; and groupies assaulting the rock musicians who have exploited them. (This last strip is by Trina Robbins, artist of Girl Fight Comics.) (TJS)

MANHUNT

Print Mint (publisher)
830 Folger Ave.
Berkeley, Calif 94710
Terry Richards, Ed.
Box 6331
San Francisco, Calif. 94104

50¢ an issue
Format: 40 pages (6 3/4" x 9 3/4")
Issue examined: July 1973

Contributions by a number of artists. At least seven of the stories are about unsatisfactory marriages or love affairs. (One involves a heterosexual transvestite.) Parodies

## PANDORA'S BOX

Chin Lyvely & Joyce Sutton, Publs.
Nanny Goat Productions
Box 845
Laguna Beach, Calif. 92652
50¢
Started: 1973 (succeeds Tits & Clits Comix)

Circulation: 20,000
Format: 32 pages (6 3/4" x 9 3/4")
Issue examined: No. 1 (1973)
Copies available from publisher

These comics relate the adventures of the Peters Sisters: Glinda (frizzy-haired, thin as a rail), Wanda (obese), and Fonda (well-constructed--see review of Tits & Clits Comix).

Glinda sleeps with a diseased long-hair. Wanda is engaged to a frizzy-haired vegetarian drummer. When she moves in with him, he and his friends soon start treating her as a drudge. When his cat pees on her toy panda, it's the last straw. She leaves him. In another episode "politically sophisticated" Glinda steals food from a supermarket, and she and her sisters feast on wine and crabmeat.

The sisters meet an attractive girl who tells them she is a lesbian: "... men never did much for me except leave me with a lot of fantasies and gobs of lethal" seminal fluid. They are intrigued.

In the centerfold, Fonda enjoys the attentions of three male friends. In another episode, she visits a massage parlor, in which three attractive young men send her into carnal ecstasy.

In "The American Dream," a suburban housewife, exploited by everyone (husband, small children, former lover), wearies of life and commits suicide by telling one of her children to "pull the little lever"--the trigger of a revolver pointed at her.

The co-publishers do all of the drawing and writing, and are--as far as they know--"the first women to publish comics in this country." Their comics, meant to be examples of "humorous, iconoclastic feminism," center on relations between men and women, have a high erotic content, and avoid taking political positions (on war, police, marijuana, or whatever). (TJS)

Feedback:

Editor Sutton replied: "Your review is fine.... Tits & Clits was published 8/72. Pandora's Box would have been Tits & Clits number 2, but we got scared by recent obscenity rulings in the fall of 1973 and decided to make the title more unimpressive. We narrowly missed being arrested for 'publishing obscene material' in Orange County, California, in Dec., 1973, and have been working to improve our image and remain radical in spite of ourselves and political pressures. Lyn [Chevli, whose pseudonym is Chin Lyvely] and I will publish again as Tits & Clits, very possibly in 1975. We have many stories ready and all we need is the time to do them. We may publish from an area more able to accept our material (such as San Francisco) because where we live sex is still a very politically explosive topic."

## SAN FRANCISCO COMIC BOOK

Gary Arlington, Mng. Ed.
3339 23rd St.
San Francisco, Calif. 94110
Bi-monthly; 50¢ an issue
Started: Jan. 1970

Format: 32 pages (6 1/2" x 9 1/2" or 6 3/4" x 9 3/4")
Issues examined: Jan. & Mar. 1970

Among the characters in the first two issues of SFCB are: pot-smokers harassed by policemen with pig-snouts; wierd imaginary creatures; an hermaphrodite; a robot; and a geek (who bites off the heads of live chickens).

Actions depicted include: heterosexual intercourse and cunnilingus; homosexual fellatio; masturbation of various types; rape; sexual mutilation; and the injection of narcotics by a hypodermic needle.

There is satire of the Hare Krishna movement, and of America's political-military-industrial Establishment.

Violence: people are shot full of holes; pecked to death and eaten by roosters; stomped; slain by tigers; knocked on the head; thrown into a river and drowned; and have their brains blown out and their penises lopped off.

Women are usually sex-objects: occasionally, they are sadistic Amazons who compel or entice men to couple with them; more often, they are the victims of sexual assault.

(TJS)

## SNARF

Kitchen Sink Enterprises
Box 5699
Milwaukee, Wis. 53211
65¢ an issue

Format: 32 pages (6 3/4" x 9 3/4")
Issues examined: Nos. 2 (Aug. 1972) & 5 (Mar. 1974)

## TALES FROM THE OZONE

The Print Mint
830 Folger
Berkeley, Calif. 94710

Format: 32 pages (6 3/4" x 9 3/4")
Issue examined: No. 2 (1970)

The content of the sample issue was partly political, partly fantastic.

Among the stories were these plots: a naive girl is raped by her boy friend and his pals; a bloodthirsty cop stabs a "hippie chick" to death; a modern Dr. Frankenstein drinks his own abominable concoction and loses his face; and a patricidal severed head prays for more blood to drink, so that it may gain the strength to kill its father. "Sour Fat Folk" shows copulation of the obese middle-aged, and a convention of child-molesters. Donald Duck is exploited by a lecherous genie. A wolf, escaped from Disneyland, peddles smut in Mexico.

George McShitski, "All-American Chomp," is a square suburban homeowner. We first see him (short haircut, button-down collar, horn-rimmed glasses) in front of an American flag whose stars have been replaced with swastikas. Suddenly, "filthy perverted dope-fiend teenagers" in the nearby park start playing "loud filthy perverted music" and shouting obscenities over a microphone. George is outraged. (The same flag is seen in another piece, in which a harmless man is arrested by the Amerikan secret police.)

A Negro private third-class in Vietnam is always given the most dangerous assignments. One day, as he is on lookout duty far ahead of his company, swarms of the enemy attack him. For a while--until he succumbs--he holds them off by bashing them with his only weapon: an American flag on a pole. "He gave his life for his buddies, for freedom, and for the defense of America!"

In an untitled piece, marijuana starts growing everywhere, to the dismay of beer-drinking squares and rednecks. The Pentagon drops napalm on "this disgusting commie menace," with an unforeseen result: as thousands of acres of the weed burn, a cloud of smoke blankets the country and everyone--even cops--becomes stoned. (Marijuana figures in several other stories, and the back cover of the issue pleads for its legalization.)

(TJS)

## TALES OF TOAD

Print Mint
830 Folger Ave.
Berkeley, Calif. 94710
50¢ an issue

Format: 32 pages (6 3/4" x 9 3/4")

Issue examined: No. 1 (1970)

The adventures of a lecherous toad are garnished with masturbation, voyeurism, and "mooning." A three-page section on "World Records" has nothing to do with the toad, and is an amusing take-off on such works as the Guinness Book of Records. In it, we learn about the largest rectal suppository; the greatest number of obscene telephone calls placed by one person; and the most repulsive animal, which resembles Richard M. Nixon: "the tongue and lower teeth seem to float in a wet, circular motion." (TJS)

Reviewer's opinion:
The toad's adventures are pointless and boring.

TITS & CLITS COMIX

Lyn Chevli & Joyce Sutton, Publs.
Nanny Goat Productions
Box 845
Laguna Beach, Calif. 92651
50¢ a copy
Started: 1972; 2nd ed. in preparation

Circulation: 40,000
Format: 32 pages (7" x 9 3/4")
Issue examined: No. 2 [?] (1972)
Back issues available from publisher

The goal of T&C is "humorous, iconoclastic feminism." The main character in the sample issue is a droopy-breasted thirtyish ingénue with hairy underarms, Mary Multipary. When her period comes unexpectedly and she hasn't the money to buy enough sanitary napkins, she tries various substitutes. The most satisfying is a distinctively-shaped piece of sponge rubber. She decides to let her (female) friends in on this "thigh-quivering experience," and invites them over for a party. They sit around a table cutting out tampons and drinking "Abzug Beer"--apparently named after a Congresswoman from New York City.

In another episode ("The End of the World"), Mary finds herself alone on the earth with Lastman, who suggests to her that they re-propagate the human species. Mary spurns him because she's already had enough kids--and besides, his membrum virile is too small. Insulted and infuriated, he rapes her, and--after an appropriate lapse of time--Mary gives birth to 15 libidinous infants, who soon leave her to "start a commune."

In "The First Day of Spring," Mary is out walking in the woods and fields when she feels the urge to pee. She squats and urinates, and her urine undergoes a surprising (and erotic) metamorphosis.

The other character in T&C is Fonda Peters, a libidinous and comely sensualist. (See review of Pandora's Box.) In one episode ("With a Little Help from a Friend"), she is about to copulate with Harry when she realizes that she has no contraceptive devices at hand. She phones a (female) friend and asks for advice. The phone conversation is interminable, and frustrated Harry is driven to seek solitary relief.

In another episode ("Vaginal Drip"), Fonda suffers from an embarrassing complaint. When her gynecologist (Dr. Quimfeel) is unable, despite much probing ("jam, shove"), to prescribe a cure, she calls up Mary Multipary, who advises her to try a yogurt douche. This works, and in the final panel Fonda is entertaining five men at once. (TJS)

Feedback:

See Feedback for Pandora's Box.

## YELLOW DOG COMICS

830 Folger Ave.
Berkeley, Calif. 94710
Quarterly; 50¢ a copy
Started: June 1968

Circulation: 20-30,000
Format: 32-48 pages (6" x 9", offset)
Issues examined: #13/14, #17 (1969)

Strange characters romp through the pages of Yellow Dog Comics: Garbageman almost saves "Big City" from total inundation by garbage; Captain Guts stands guard against the "dark and sinister forces of the world communist conspiracy," only to be mindblasted by Wyatt Wing-head, the super acid freak; super breasts from Mars invade the earth; Binky Brown suffers the pains of puberty. A satiric comment on the Altamont rock festival and comics by R. Crumb and Jayzey Lynch are also featured. The emphasis is on a fairly simple story line and scatological humor; although some of the drawings are hard to figure out, most are straightforward. (CP)

Feedback:

"O.K."

## Chapter 7

## LIBERTARIAN

> Collectivism brought nothing to any nation but bombs, chains, and mounds of corpses.
> ---The Torch

> Warning: Governmental Power May Be Hazardous To Your Freedom. ---The Torch

Libertarians are a diverse group whose most famous spokesperson is Ayn Rand. In general, they follow a conservative line on welfare, social security, private enterprise, and dislike of socialism and governmental interference; and a liberal line on the Vietnam War, censorship and pornography, military conscription, and the legalization of marijuana. Freedom is an all-important concept for libertarians.

--Janet Spahn

### THE ATLANTIS NEWS

| | |
|---|---|
| Warren K. Stevens, Ed. | Started: Sept. 1968 |
| RD 5, Box 22A | Circulation: 200 |
| Saugerties, N.Y. 12477 | Format: 2 sheets (offset) |
| Semi-monthly; $4.50 | Issue examined: 1 May 1970 |

Operation Atlantis, a program for those pessimistic about the chances for liberty in the U.S., and proposing the formation of a new sovereign nation, has purchased a "permanent staging area," the Sawyerkill Motel near Saugerties. Other activities such as selling silver (Decas) from the Bank of Atlantis, making plans to establish an independent nation on a seamount between Jamaica and Nicaragua, and holding meetings of the Mises Circle (attended occasionally by Ayn Rand and Professor von Mises) are described in The Atlantis News. The lead article in the sample issue discusses the failure of Freeport (Grand Bahama Island) to become a suitable place for a branch plant or office: capitalist entrepreneurs from Canada, Great Britain, and the U.S. have taken over, and the local politicians are now concentrating on getting control of the new prosperity.

The philosophy put forward in The Atlantis News is similar to that of Ayn Rand. Advertisements invite readers to visit Atlantis I (the Sawyerkill Motel) for Freedom Forums every Sunday afternoon, and urge them to invest in "an inflation-proof vehicle which pays 3% dividends in silver." Operation Atlantis will even buy, store, and sell your silver for you. (CP)

Feedback:

"We discontinued publication over a year ago [i.e., in 1972] and do not intend to resume until our offshore base is established. We would prefer you did not publish any reference to our program, as we are trying to maintain minimum exposure during these critical months."

## THE AYN RAND LETTER

201 E. 34th St.
N.Y., N.Y. 10016

Format: 4 pages (offset)
Issue examined: 3 Jan. 1972

The issue examined contained a philosophical essay by Ayn Rand addressing the question, "What can one person do?" (to change the world). She warned against joining the "wrong" ideological groups or movements: groups or movements with vague, ill-defined, or even contradictory political goals. Examples of such groups are the Conservative Party, which she accuses of subordinating reason to faith, and substituting theocracy for capitalism; and the "libertarian hippies," whom she accuses of subordinating reason to whims, and replacing capitalism with anarchism. It is foolish to forsake one's philosophical principles and join such groups merely for the sake of "doing something" or carrying out "some superficial political action which is bound to fail."

A section entitled the "Objectivist Calendar" listed events and activities of interest to readers. (JMS)

## BOOKS FOR LIBERTARIANS

422 First St., S.E.
Washington, D.C. 20003
Monthly; $6
Started: July 1972

Circulation: 11,000
Format: 8 pages (offset)
Issues examined: Oct.-Dec. 1973

This book review service is "directed to a libertarian audience, and so should be of material interest to this group." Each issue offers detailed reviews of recordings and books (both fiction and non-fiction). A number of the books reviewed stress the rights and personal freedom of the individual, the strengths of capitalism, and the dangers of government controls. As long as they are deemed to be of interest to libertarians, the books may be in any field: history, philosophy, science, economics, psychology, or education. (MN)

Feedback:
"Looks fine!"

DEFIANCE

Dates: Sept. 1971 (ceased by or before Feb. 1972) Issue examined: Sept. 1971
Format: 8-page tabloid (offset)

Articles are almost all taken from Liberation News Service or from underground newspapers. (Among the subjects of the reprinted articles: marijuana; federal subsidies to farmers for not growing crops; a lynching in Arizona; U.S. support of the Moroccan dictatorship; childbirth and women's right to control their own bodies; and hopping freights without falling under the wheels or being arrested.)

An editorial in the initial issue explains that "This paper is the language of yet another movement trying to save mankind from destroying himself [i.e., itself]." It continues, in a libertarian vein:

> our rights are usurped in institutions set up by the state, such as taxation, building ordinances, government schools, etc. The state seizes control of more of our lives every day.

Other features: a few sketches; several quotations (Bakunin, Thoreau, Dostoevsky); and advertisements for Ann Arbor businesses. (TJS)

Feedback:
> We haven't put out Defiance for a while, & don't plan to do so in the near future. So please don't put the paper in your directory. We wouldn't want people to think we stopped doing the paper because it was too difficult, too much work, we changed our

> ideas, we couldn't get others to work on it, etc. It stopped for personal reasons. We did the paper right after our freshman year at U. of M. We've since decided to do much more studying of political philosophy before we put out a paper on a steady basis.

Defiance had been published in Ann Arbor, Mich., and edited by Karen Haas and Ron Rossi.

LIBERTARIAN OPTION: Freedom or Tyranny

Marshall Bruce Evoy, Ed.
Libertarian Enterprises of Canada
Box 603, Sta. "F"
Toronto, Ont., Canada
M4Y 2L8
Bi-monthly; $6.50
Started: Jan. 1973

Circulation: 1,000
Format: 24 pages (offset)
Issues examined: May/June & Sept./Oct. 1974; Jan./Feb. & Mar./Apr. 1975
Back issues available from publisher

The editor informs us:

> We have been up until now objectivist-oriented, and pro-Libertarian Party (both Canada and USA). We have just adopted a new policy in order to reach a larger public. The new policy will cut out "Randian rhetoric" and almost all references to the LP except in one column titled "On the Barricades." We are pro-civil liberties and pro-economic freedom. Although so-called anarcho-capitalists write for Option, the editorial policy is definitely pro-limited government and pro-free enterprise. We oppose all tyrannies from extreme left Communism through all shades of pink Socialism to extreme right Fascism. The change in editorial policy by no means implies a change of principle. The Editor is the founder of the LP of Canada, and is currently the secretary of the Ontario LP.... [He] upholds the statement of principles of both the American and the Canadian LP. However, Option is not a mouthpiece for the LP and is free to criticize it whenever the Editor so chooses. Option is a totally independent magazine upholding individual rights and liberty in both the civil and economic spheres.

Some issues were entitled Option.

THE NEW BANNER: The World's Only Consistent Journal

W. Robert Black, Publ.
Box 1972
Columbia, S.C. 29202
Fortnightly; $9 for 20 issues
Started: 4 Feb. 1972
Circulation: 3,000-10,000
Format: 8-page tabloid (offset)
Issue examined: a triple issue: 4 & 18 Mar., 1 Apr. 1973
Back issues available from publisher

The publisher informed us that the paper had "temporarily ceased publication due to arrest and indictment of myself and three members of the editorial staff--arising out of philosophical and political views expressed in The New Banner." For his publication's editorial policies, he referred us to a Declaration of Principles which made these points: (1) Human affairs should be guided by reason; (2) Man should live for himself. Altruism is wrong, as is "coercive collectivism"; (3) Laissez-faire capitalism is the only good socio-economic system.

The paper stresses anarchist libertarianism and is against (among other things) the income tax.

RAMPART COLLEGE NEWSLETTER

Box 11407
Santa Ana, Calif. 92711
Bi-monthly; free
Started: Jan. 1964 in Larkspur, Colo., with a different format
Format: 4 pages (offset)
Issues examined: 15 Sept. 1968; Mar. & June 1974

The old Rampart College Newsletter, out of Larkspur, Colo., ceased publication on 15 September 1968, when the college was relocated in Santa Ana, Calif., at the end of that year. Its purpose was "to report events at Rampart College; and to offer brief insights into applications of the freedom philosophy by those associated with the college as teachers and students." The present newsletter does not have the professional appearance of its predecessor and does not use photographs in its format. It reports the activities--courses, workshops, seminars, discussion groups--of Rampart College and gives news of conferences, projects, and former students' activities in promoting libertarianism. The newsletter also devotes a page or two to philosophical and political discussion.

> Often we are asked for the 'libertarian' answer or view toward an issue, as if there were a party line; a single response which all libertarians would make to a given question. But the character of libertarian thought precludes such a narrow approach. The main distinction we apply, whether to individual actions or social systems, is whether they are voluntary or coercive in nature. Once it is established that libertarian answers are always voluntary in approach, the direction becomes clear. A variety of viewpoints and solutions can be expressed.

Libertarian books and periodicals are listed in the newsletter and a book service is offered whereby individuals can order from the college.

The Rampart Journal of Individualist Thought was reviewed in the first edition of From Radical Left to Extreme Right, p. 141, and a fuller discussion of the group's philosophy can be found there. The Journal ceased publication with the Winter 1968 issue. The founder and president emeritus, Robert LeFevre, now publishes a newsletter, LeFevre's Journal.

This group leans more toward anarchism than do some of the other libertarian groups, and its March 1974 issue notes the upcoming "first continental anarchist congress."

(JMS)

Feedback:

"Just fine--and thanks!"

## THE TORCH

| | |
|---|---|
| Jeffrey Rogers Hummel, Ed. | Circulation: 600 |
| Box 574, Grove City College | Format: 5 pages (mimeo.) |
| Grove City, Pa. 16127 | Issues examined: Special Issue ("The Best of Volume I") and Dec. 1969 |
| Monthly; $1.50 | |
| Started: Oct. 1968 | |

This anti-collectivist paper is published by the Grove City College Conservative Club. Each issue consists of a couple of fairly long articles analyzing current events. Articles in "The Best of Volume I" anthology included "The War in Vietnam"; "Individual Rights vs. Public Welfare"; "Race Pride"; and "Fluoridation: Compulsory Mass Medication." One of the articles clearly expresses the anti-collectivist viewpoint:

> Collectivism brought nothing to any nation but bombs, chains, and mounds of corpses. The premise of individualism brought the United States into being and transformed poor boys into millionaires, log cabins into skyscrapers, and this nation into the hope of the world. Now widespread acceptance of the collectivist premise is changing the dream into a nightmare. The only hope is to choose again the premise that a man belongs to himself alone.

Contributors believe strongly that each person should be free to make his own decisions and to take the responsibility for those decisions. Any kind of government intervention that makes decisions for people destroys initiative and restricts individual freedom. One article suggests that all Congressmen, bureaucrats, and interest groups "be compelled to wear on their foreheads this statement: 'Warning: Governmental Power May Be Hazardous To Your Freedom.'" Libertarians believe that governmental power not only limits an individual's freedom, but also allows him to become lazy. In "Hymn to the Welfare State," an anonymous writer describes the attitude that may result from such government programs as social security and public welfare:

> The Government is my shepherd,
> Therefore I need not work.
> It alloweth me to lie down on a good job.
> It leadeth me beside still factories;
> It destroyeth my initiative,
> It leadeth me in the path of a parasite
> for politic's sake.
> Yea, though I walk through the valley of
> laziness and deficit-spending,
> I will fear no evil, for the Government
> is with me.
> It prepareth an economic Utopia for me,
> by appropriating the earnings of my
> own grandchildren.
> It filleth my head with false security;
> My inefficiency runneth over.
> Surely the Government should care for
> me all the days of my life!!
> And I shall dwell in a fool's paradise
> for ever.

(CT)

## Chapter 8

## UTOPIAN

> What we are most into is living in touch with this region of land we inhabit....
>
> ---The British Columbia Access Catalogue

The Utopian chapter is considerably larger than that in our last volume. There seems to be a growing movement among young people (and the middle-aged as well) toward alternative lifestyles: getting back to the land and leading a less mechanized existence. Even doctors and 65-year-olds are dropping out, according to Black Bart Brigade, which dedicated its first issue to "middle-aged, middle-class Americans." Communes (and periodicals devoted to them) are constantly springing up--and folding--as more and more people try to escape from the "rat race" of life within the Establishment.

If you want practical advice on how to homestead or start a commune, where to find land, how to put up buildings, keep goats, store vegetables, make soap, or use chicken manure to generate electricity, you can find it in such periodicals as Black Bart Brigade, British Columbia Access Catalog, Ozark Access Catalog, Communities, and Lifestyle! They will also help you to locate persons of a like mind.

For those who want to change their lives, but not drastically, North Country Anvil offers ways to achieve economic independence. It stresses the need for collective action in mutual aid projects, cooperatives, and political action groups. For persons interested in building "loving communities," Communication has practical ideas and contacts with others (through its membership directory). --Janet Spahn

### ALTERNATIVE FEATURES SERVICE

Bi-weekly; $125 and up (sliding scale)    Started: June 1971
Circulation: 180

Format: 24-page tabloid (offset)
Issues examined: none sent
Back issues available from publisher

The following information received from the publication: "Ceased publication for now. Left of center. Interested in material on alternative life styles; investigative political and social reporting." The address was Box 2250, Berkeley, Calif. 94702.

BLACK BART BRIGADE: The Outlaw Mag

Irv Thomas, Ed.
Box 48
Canyon, Calif. 94516
Twice a year, with interim newsletters; donation (recommend $5 individual, $10 institution; "I make sure that people get 4 issues for their donation, and am moving toward a % of income as donation")
Started: Nov. 1971
Circulation: 500
Format: 48 pages (7" x 10", offset)
Issues examined: nos. 1, 5, and 6
Indexing: Alternative Press Index
Recent back issues (and microform version) available from publisher

Irv Thomas, who has edited Black Bart Brigade since November 1971, says in Issue No. 5 that the magazine reflects the changes in his own consciousness as he has struggled through the aftermath to his decision to drop out of the System. The first issue is dedicated to the notion of personal revolution, a radical change in lifestyle, and directed primarily to middle-aged, middle-class Americans. Black Bart was chosen as a patron saint because of a poem he left behind on one of his Wells Fargo stagecoach robberies: "I've labored long and hard for bread, / For honor and for riches, / But on my corns too long you've tred, / You fine-haired SONS OF BITCHES!" Black Bart is an appropriate ideal outlaw for other reasons. A 45-year-old gentlemanly business failure when he became a stagecoach bandit, he never had a horse, he robbed only the express box and the mails, never the passengers, and he eluded the Wells Fargo private police for eight years.

Most of the articles in the first issue are enthusiastic reports of successful beginnings of projects by people who confront the dominant society by creating alternatives. Communes in Oregon, a community renovation of an old warehouse in San Francisco, and the New Vocations Project which helped people find employment are among the undertakings described. Personal testimony on dropping out is given by a California doctor and a 65-year-old Minnesotan who envisions a return to tribal living as a sensible rebellion against game-playing.

Articles in later issues seem more sober in their assessments of where personal revolution among middle-aged people has taken them. Irv Thomas writes a continuing philosophy section which details many of the questions and difficulties he has struggled with (including his decision to keep the magazine circulation small by not advertising nationally), and describes, in Issue No. 5, his brief, disappointing experience with communal living. A middle-aged woman's hitchhiking trip from California to New York; a family's decision to leave a plush government job for part-time employment, a garden, good schools, and fresh air in Vermont; a report of the beginnings of community action in Akron, Ohio; a description of Total Loss Farm, a fairly stable, four-year-old commune in Vermont by one of its founders who left at one point but eventually returned; several specific, detailed accounts of experiments in organizing reasonable and non-exploitative economies; and explanations by people who choose to work within the system in a revolutionary way of how they maintain their integrity appear along with cartoons, a few poems, and the regular feature "The Outlaw Trail," short reviews of books, magazines, and happenings. Black Bart is published by the Canyon Collective, the group that puts out WorkForce, formerly Vocations for Social Change [Feedback: "Incorrect! The Canyon Collective (VSC) was our original sponsor and inspiration, but we have functioned independently since Issue #3 (mid-1972)"] and the format is similar.

(CP)

Feedback:

"This is a beautiful writeup, and I think your whole concept and execution of it is a very fine thing--the project itself, I mean."

## THE BRITISH COLUMBIA ACCESS CATALOGUE

David Crocker
Box 65688, Station F
Vancouver 12, B. C., Canada
Annual; $5 ($6 outside Canada; institutions $10)
Started: Spring 1971

Circulation: 7,000-10,000
Format: 144 pages (offset)
Issue examined: No. 3
Self-indexed
Some back issues available from publisher

Cartoons, photographs, poems, recipes, and line drawings enliven the pages of British Columbia Access, a catalogue of sources in that Canadian province. Articles, letters, book reviews, and reports of alternative projects are organized loosely into subjects which blend into each other. An informative factual report on the availability of public land for homesteading begins Catalog #3; placer-mining, living in the Yukon, and tips on building shelters suitable for low budgets and cold weather follow. There are articles on growing vegetables (including one on hydroponics, soilless gardens), nutrition, hallucinogenic mushrooms, food co-ops, massage, and bicycles. One section features simple toys and games for children; another is devoted to Women's issues ("Her-story"). Government grants for special projects, self-help agencies, and many resources all over Canada are listed. The experiences of catching a swarm of bees and running a VW bus on liquid propane are shared, along with detailed directions on rescuing birds from oil slicks.

The tone of the magazine is anti-U.S., anti-corporations, very much pro-back-to-the-land and do-it-yourself. Evidently many people shared in putting the articles together; the editors practice anarchy, calling Access a state of mind and eschewing any regular or predetermined publication deadlines. What they've tried to do is establish a communication network "... where people from all over B.C. can plug in and share their knowledge, spirit, ideas; an information exchange." They add, "This goal or main objective is sometimes lost in the immediate goal, publishing the next issue. We get caught up in format, what to publish here or there, and personal trips, and forget the network we are trying to build. And it is hard to carry on conversation when the pauses are six months long." The layout is lively and fanciful; the information seems solidly useful, based for the most part on hard experience. (CP)

Feedback:

Mr. Crocker replied:

> Thanks for the effort of reviewing our publication. In general, very good. But we must say that a Canadian periodical is necessarily going to be outside the context of American political classifications and subject to misinterpretation--which is precisely what has happened with your reviewers.
>
> Either delete the review entirely, or make these changes: 'The tone of the magazine is anti-U.S., anti-corporation'--delete this phrase. In Canadian

eyes we are as orthodox as crumpets or the Boy Scout Handbook. We are not anti-U.S. per se, or anti-corporations. This statement is fuel for the ghosts of Sen. Joe McCarthy and his ilk--it used to be called 'the big smear.' Again, simply a juxtaposition of different cultures. What we do object to is having our beaches despoiled by oil slick. But the American constitution and your form of government are quite okay and we would never willingly wish to see our neighbours harmed. We hope you can see that difference, and hope you will make these changes as it will avoid unpleasantness.

In your country, the consumption of certain species of wild mushrooms is not allowed by your authorities. These mushrooms are represented in our flora by several local varieties, and gathering them is a common practice not frowned upon. However, as we would not wish to promote prohibited behavior, the issue of our magazine containing this information will not be sold outside Canada. Please delete the reference to 'hallucinogenic mushrooms' as it will save us having to answer a lot of crank letters.

A final note: we (the bunch of us who put the catalogues together) just do it for fun. It's not a business with us. Practising anarchy? Perhaps, again in the context of the simple act of printing a book. What we are most into is living in touch with this region of land we inhabit (if I may presume to speak for the whole). As you sit in Chicago, living your life there, I prepare to travel up to the mountains, and clear streams, and bear and deer, to work my beehives. [It is not clear whom Mr. Crocker envisions as sitting and living in Chicago. The reviewer (CP), member of a commune, lives in an old farmhouse and tends an organic garden. The editors (TJS & JMS) also tend such a garden (although less successfully), and can see--almost in their back yard--deer, beavers, raccoons, and pheasants. All stay as far as possible from Chicago.]

Please don't try to judge the 'tone' of our little efforts. And remember you can't graft your politics onto our Canadian context and hope to have your observations viable. It's a different world, y'see. And some things just aren't to be taken seriously. Least of all the B. C. Access Catalogue.

COMMUNICATION: A Monthly Journal of Well-Being

Frank Potter, Coordinator
Box 887
San Anselmo, Calif. 94960
Ten issues a year; $2 a copy for non-members; free to members
Started: Jan. 1972
Circulation: 500
Format: 16 pages (Xeroxed from typescript; 3-hole punched)
Issues examined: Oct. 1973 - Jan. 1974
Back issues available from publisher

Communication is a publication "with practical ideas for building community, case studies, newsletter reporting happenings and experiences of members" of Well Being. This non-profit organization, coordinated by an Episcopal priest, is a "mutual support system of persons who care for each other, and who share insights about building free and loving communities in a future shock world." Among the services offered to members are consultation, personal correspondence (through exchange of cassette tapes with coordinator), clearinghouse of information in community building field, religious liberation workshops, and research results.

The monthly publication is written in an informal style. Most articles are by the Reverend Frank Potter, coordinator of Well Being. Some issues revolve around a theme. The November 1973 issue is devoted to a report on communities in the Washington area over a three year period from 1970 to 1973. Articles in other issues carry titles such as "Our Extended Family" by Barbara Potter, "The Feminine Priestly Symbol and the Meaning of God," excerpts from a paper by Urban T. Holmes edited with comments by Barbara Potter, and "Toward Religious Liberation; the Non-Rational Element and Human Community," by Frank Potter. An introduction and editorial open each issue.

The December issue is a membership directory listing names, addresses, telephone numbers of 310 members. Brief biographical sketches, such as the following, are included: "A beautiful woman, much into liberation, working in college administration and on her own personal growth. Divorced from _____ who was a Lutheran minister. We love both deeply."

(JA)

Feedback:

"We think this is great. You've done a good job!"

## COMMUNITIES

Community Publications Co-operative
Box 426
Louisa, Va. 23093
Bi-monthly; $6 ($10 to institutions)
Started: Dec. 1972
Circulation: 4,000

Format: 64 pages (offset)
Issues examined: Dec. 1972; Feb. & Apr. 1973
Indexing: Alternative Press Index
Back issues available from publisher

Communities is published by a working collective of members from six communal groups. "The magazine is designed to be an inter-community communications tool as well as to be a source of information for others interested in the communal movement." It is a merging of several previous publications including Communitas, Communitarian, Alternatives Newsmagazine and Modern Utopian.

Issue one contains a commune directory and lists names and addresses of communal groups. The directory may briefly suggest the aims and makeup of various groups. Diverse information such as religious affiliation or special interests may be noted. Other factors such as drug counseling or racial makeup of group may be offered. Frequently schools or means of community support are listed.

Articles vary in length and are normally written by members of the communes. Sample issues contain an article on the selection of members for a commune with a succinct recommendation not to accept "sloths, boors, crazy people, or too many dependents." The author, whose style is pleasantly informal, also suggests practical methods for insuring group agreement and lists particularly helpful work skills. Another article, which suggests that it could be the forerunner of a regular column, deals with the development of an activist law project and its search for priorities. Also included in these issues is an excerpt from a conversation with Roger McAfee, the California farmer who put his dairy farm up as bail for Angela Davis. This article explores McAfee's background and beliefs.

Several regular columns are offered in Communities. "Resources" lists available catalogs or other marketing tools. "Reach" is a section which puts groups or individuals into contact with one another, and "Grapevine" offers news about other communes. "Community Market" is "a catalog of goods and services produced by communes, collectives and co-operative groups in North America. It is designed ... to help such groups support themselves and grow." Books are reviewed both briefly and extensively.

This little magazine is handsome in appearance. Articles are enlivened with sketches and photographs. Exchange ads are accepted from other communes. The book review digest is sometimes in the form of a separate pamphlet. [Feedback: "The last sentence of your review is not correct. The only pamphlet that we put out is a brochure of community-related books which we offer for sale."] (MN)

Feedback:

"Thank you for sending us a copy of your review before publication. It looked very good. One thing that would be helpful to us would be if you mentioned that an updated version of the Commune Directory is available in Issue No. 7.... This is probably the most accurate directory ever produced. We did a telephone follow-up just before printing. (There are still a few mistakes, of course, but no list is perfect.)"

COUNTRY SENSES

Box 465
Woodbury, Conn. 06798
Monthly; $3
Started: Jan. 1969

Circulation: 7,000
Format: 22-30 pages (offset)
Issues examined: Sept. & Dec. 1969; Mar. 1970

Country Senses is described as a non-political "free-form publication on a beauty trip, whose purpose is to help 'Get it together,' to facilitate an alliance between man and nature, man and the cosmos." A central theme is used for each issue, so that "the magazine becomes a part of a whole or flow," through the use of free-form poetry, short essays, and photos and other illustrations.

The December 1969 issue contains a list of names and addresses of Underground Press Syndicate members in the U.S., Canada, Europe, and the G.I. Press, as well as listings of COSMIC, the Overground Press (Celestially Oriented and Aspirational).

Imaginatively illustrated with graphics, photographs and cartoons, the publication also carries ads for straight items or services such as banks, insurance companies, and restaurants. (KL)

## LIFESTYLE!

Bi-monthly; $6
Dates: 1972-73
Format: 128 pages (offset)

Issue examined: Apr. 1973
Indexing: Alternative Press Index

This is "A magazine of alternatives" with an ecological orientation. Many of the articles oppose the excesses of technology and provide philosophy, information, experiences, and the how-to-do-it of alternative life-styles, recycling, and survival tactics in an anti-establishment milieu. First-hand accounts are emphasized: do-it-yourself guides to various modes of living (communes, co-ops, homesteading); working (farming, foraging, natural food businesses and bakeries, used bookstores); traveling (campers, bikes, hiking); education; and eating (cheap and nutritionally sound recipes).

In an extensive "Contact" column, those interested in communes, homesteading, or crafts seek others of a similar bent. (KL)

Feedback:

"Great!" The magazine is now defunct. Its address was: 49 W. Main St., Madison, Ohio 44057.

## NATURAL LIFE STYLES

Gordon & Breach, Science Publishers
1 Park Ave. S.
N.Y., N.Y. 10016
Bi-monthly; $9
Started: Mar. 1971

Circulation: 10,000
Format: 80 pages (9" x 12", offset)
Issues examined: v. 2, no. 1, and two undated issues (probably 1973)

"NLS is a guide to organic living for city dwellers as well as homesteaders. We care about thoroughness, originality, and style. A gourmet approach to natural foods, we hope NLS will be a continuing cookbook." The issues examined dealt with such subjects as childbirth at home, herbal astringents, building houses of stone or earth, Japanese communes, an organic food-buying cooperative, cheap land, crafts, mushrooms, gardening, wood stoves, and baking bread. NLS also contains recipes, book reviews, and a children's section. (JMS)

Reviewer's opinion:

A beautifully-illustrated, delightful, and informative publication!

Feedback:

The publication informed us that NLS is no longer being published as a periodical, but as a book series.

NORTH COUNTRY ANVIL

Jack Miller, Ed. & Publ.
Box 37
Millville, Minn. 55957
$4.50
Started: June 1972
Format: 80 pages
Issues examined: none sent

Indexing: Alternative Press Index
Back issues available from publisher
Microform version available from Xerox University Microfilms

The publisher sent this information:

> We are trying to provide, for the Upper Midwest region in particular, a source of information that emphasizes the need for people to break out of the confines of mass society and to free themselves to live more human lives and to help others to do so. We stress both the need for individual action (such as finding ways to achieve economic independence--build your own house, get a job that allows you to speak and act freely, etc.) and collective action (mutual aid projects like cooperatives, political-action projects such as support for [American Indian] Wounded Knee defendants and the United Farmworkers; forming union rank-and-file movements; etc.).
>
> We publish a lot of material that tries to provide people with a base of ideas on which to build a strong, new, decentralized, libertarian, radical-revolutionary movement that will grow directly from people's daily lives--including especially their working lives--and lead to direct action for creating a better society, and not to a new oppression dominated by revolutionary bosses or any other kind of bosses.

OZARK ACCESS CATALOG

Edd Jeffords, Ed.
Box 506
Eureka Springs, Ark. 72632
Quarterly; $5 (libraries $6)
Started: Nov. 1972

Circulation: 1,200 subscribers; 30,000 copies sold
Format: 32-page tabloid (offset)
Issues examined: Apr. & July

1973; and undated nos. 3 & 4 | Back issues available from publisher
Indexing: at end of no. 4

Ozark Access Center functions as a clearinghouse for regional information on the Ozark Mountains of Oklahoma, Missouri, Arkansas, and Kansas. The Ozark Access Catalog is a reader-based publication of the Center. The content is a "reflection of its readers, a crossfeed of shared information designed to make life in the Ozarks a little more comfortable, stimulating, and ecologically sound." The emphasis of the Catalog is on "alternative methods, survival information, and doing more with less."

The issue of January 1973 carries a lead article introducing the Ozark region with maps, photographs, and descriptions of major population centers and vacation areas. There is a two-page listing of publications, colleges, libraries, and radio and television stations of the area. Later issues update this list of media as well as adding directories of social services and craftspeople. Some of the other articles in the first issue deal with solar heating, native crafts, and windmills.

The second and third issues of Ozark Access Catalog cover the geology and waterways of the Ozarks. Information on land availability, bluegrass music, tools, fish farming, organic gardening, farm animals, shelters, herbal remedies, and recipes is usually included. Several pages are devoted to letters from readers.

Most articles are accompanied by a list of sources for further information (both printed and personal). Many of the publications listed are free. The Center will supply any book cited by mail for list price plus 25¢ handling.

A feature introduced in Number 3, called "The Molasses Jug," gives such interesting formulas as the following 1890 Cough Syrup recipe:

> Early Day Cough Syrup: Approximately 1 cup chopped onion. 1 to 2 tbsp water. Boil until the onions are tender and add 1 cup sugar (or 2/3 cup honey). Simmer until very thick.

Number 4 contains a subject index as well as a quick reference index arranged under the following topics: The Whole Ozarks, Food, Homesteading, Land, Media, Ecology, Recreation, Shelter, Crops.

In summing up the first year of publication the editors express the hope that they have eased the way for retired persons and young folks who are "seeking control of their own destinies by returning to the land." (JA)

Feedback:

"With the corrections and updates we've added [all of which have been incorporated into the review], the draft is a good statement of what OAC is all about."

## Chapter 9

## CONSERVATION & ECOLOGY

... Man should live on the Earth's income, not its capital. ---Not Man Apart

Audubon, Conservation News, National Parks & Conservation Magazine, and Outdoor America have been around for many years, long before such words as "ecology," "conservation," and "environment" became popular. They deal mainly with wildlife, plant life, and the conservation, ecological, and recreational aspects of our national resources.

Since 1970 a new group of activist periodicals has sprung up, encouraging legislation, social action, and citizen education: Environmental Action, Impact, Environmental Quality, and Not Man Apart deal with wider aspects of the environment. They are concerned with air, water and noise pollution, energy conservation, water management, transportation systems, population growth, preservation of open spaces, wholesome food, and the creation of bicycle paths. They oppose the destruction of the environment by industry, the development of nuclear power plants, strip mining, and the widespread development of oil pipelines and refineries in the north. The Ecologist, an unusual British publication, advocates de-industrialization as the only solution to problems created by the Industrial Revolution, and takes a sociological approach to ecology. Environmental Education will interest teachers and junior and senior high school students; Alternative Sources of Energy will interest those who want to build solar-heated houses, get electric power from the wind, generate methane fuel from garbage, or purchase a composting toilet; and National Fluoridation News will interest those concerned about the chemicals in their drinking water.

--Janet Spahn

### ALTERNATIVE SOURCES OF ENERGY

Route 2, Box 90A
Milaca, Minn. 56353

Quarterly; $5 for 6 issues
Circulation: 3,000

Format: 60 pages (offset)
Issues examined: Oct. 1973; Feb. & May 1974
Indexing: Alternative Press Index
Back issues available from publisher
Microform version available from Xerox University Microfilms

The publication sent this information:

> Alternative Sources of Energy is a newsletter for people concerned with the development of an alternative technology--a technology oriented towards a decentralized society, in harmony with the earth we share. Alternative concepts, both new and old, in energy sources, agriculture, architecture, transportation and communication, are given a widespread communications network.
>
> ASE is dedicated to the free exchange of ideas, to bringing people together in the development of skills, and to encouraging experiments in individual and cooperative management of goods and services.
>
> Readers are encouraged to submit articles and letters. Material will not be edited as to content.
>
> Begun out of a concern over pollution, over our depleted supply of fossil fuels, and over the dangers of nuclear power, Alternative Sources of Energy prints new ideas concerning environmentally sound, alternate technologies, publishes plans and diagrams so readers can begin to convert to ecological, decentralized energy sources, tries to reach all people, not just engineers and scientists. Articles are edited to make complicated ideas clear.

Past issues have dealt with such topics as how to get electric power from the wind, building solar-heated houses, generating methane fuel from garbage, and energy conservation. Recent sample issues contained from 15 to 20 articles of varying length--some only a page and others as long as eight pages with complicated diagrams. Some examples are: "Low Energy Underground House"; "Sail Windmill in India"; "Geothermal Electric Generator"; "The Most Important Thing in the World" (opposed nuclear power--"a particularly deadly fraud"); "The Energy Crisis in Historical Perspective"; and "Insulate With Cardboard."

The publication also reviews books, manuals, and pamphlets dealing with energy and ecology, and describes new commercial gadgets, machinery, and plans. Examples: a Swedish "composting toilet" [also described in Organic

Gardening and Farming, April 1975] and a "Fireplace Heat Exchanger."

Regular features: "Learning Opportunities"--a section that describes conferences, schools, and centers that have to do with ecology, and alternative energy and lifestyles; "Contact's Reports"--contributors report their activities from different areas of the country; "Reader Interest Questionnaire"--readers who want to join ASE's communications network are asked to describe their interests and experience in such fields as solar energy, water power, architecture, and agriculture. The responses are printed so that individuals may contact each other; "People Offering Help"--individuals with their fields of interest are listed according to areas of the country; and "Feedback" from readers.

ASE has also put out a compilation in book form of the first 10 issues of the magazine. Issue #15 (September 1974) will list ASE's lending library materials, as well as the entire "Reader Interest Questionnaire" results. ASE is also preparing pamphlets on Wind Power; Energy for a Small Community; and Wood. (JMS)

Feedback:

"Review is O.K."

ALTERNATIVES: Perspectives on Society and Environment

c/o Trent University, Peterborough
Ontario, Canada
Quarterly; $3 (institutions $5); add 25¢ for U.S.
Started: Summer 1971
Circulation: 1,700
Format: 44 pages (offset)
Issues examined: Winter, Spring, Summer 1973

Indexing in periodical; abstracted by Environment Information ACCESS (New York); Pollution Abstracts (La Jolla); Current Index for Journals in Education (Boulder); Ecolert (Montreal); and Environmental Periodicals (Santa Barbara)

Alternatives is a serious Canadian journal covering "Resources, Pollution, Conservation and Wilderness," put out by faculty and students at Trent University in Ontario. According to its Statement of Purpose, "we must confront the implications" the environmental crisis "has for our economic structures, our political process and institutions, our living habits, and the moral basis of our philosophy and culture. We must pose and offer imaginative and serious ALTERNATIVES." By virtue of its contributors' backgrounds and reputations alone, it can be described as scholarly--most of the writers are professors at major universities in Canada and the United States. The articles are often lengthy, and are usually extensively documented. Regular features include book reviews, many of which include further recommended reading relevant to the subject; editorials which are well documented informative articles in themselves; letters; and an author and book review index which appears in the summer issue. Many of the articles are concerned with Canada in particular--"The Arctic in Perspective," "A Scenario for Nova Scotia's Future," nickel mining and the environmental controversy in the Sudbury area of Ontario, a subject discussed in several articles in different issues of Alternatives. Some of the writers view their subjects on a broader scale; for example, political scientist Mulford Sibley wrote in one issue on "The Relevance of Classical Political Theory for Economy, Technology, and Ecology." [Feedback: "There is also an attempt to include a minimum of 25% non-Canadian material; to date most of this has been American. Future issues will have articles from Sweden, Japan, and the Soviet Union."] Reprints of the more popular articles are available at little cost, as are 7- to 14-page bibliographies (mostly of Canadian books and articles, but including about 2,000 U.S. titles) on a variety of environmental topics. Other non-literary services sponsored by Alternatives are conferences, wilderness trips, and a village project designed to use limited natural resources. (SA)

Feedback:

"I found the summary of our journal excellent and most fair. I have added a phrase and two lines to better clarify the over-all mix of materials we are attempting." [These have been added to the review.]

AUDUBON

950 Third Ave.<br>N.Y., N.Y. 10022<br>Bi-monthly; $13<br>Started: 1900 (as Bird-Lore)<br>Circulation: 280,000

Format: 100-200 pages<br>Issues examined: May-Sept. 1973; Jan., Mar. 1974<br>Indexing: available from editorial office, each year

Audubon, official publication of the National Audubon Society, is particularly noteworthy for its photographic representations of wildlife, many of them full-page and in color. By means of these, the reader can share the visual experience of a wilderness trek through areas ranging from desert to rain forest, from torrid regions to frigid zones, and all the gradations between. Each issue usually contains several illustrated articles on a similar theme, to which the cover photograph is related. One edition, for example, featured undersea photography in "Life in a Cold Ocean." Other articles in the same issue dealt with Cape Hatteras National Seashore, Nantucket Island, a "desert island" in the Gulf of Mexico, and the fishing industry in Maine. A special issue of Audubon was devoted to deserts and arid lands in the western United States; another featured the wildlife of the Galapagos archipelago.

Unusual treatment of less exotic subjects also characterizes the magazine. For example, colorful photographs of insects--some magnified to more than twenty times life-size --were used in one issue to present the "Hidden World of a Pond."

Each issue of Audubon has a special section entitled "The Audubon Cause." In this part, which is termed "The Conservation Newsmagazine Within a Magazine," articles deal with current issues in conservation and ecology, stressing political, legal, economic, and social aspects. (SMA)

Feedback:

Editor expressed no disapproval.

Center for Science in the Public Interest NEWSLETTER

| | |
|---|---|
| 1779 Church St., N. W. | Format: 4-6 pages (offset) |
| Washington, D. C. 20036 | Issues examined: Spring, |
| Quarterly; $5 | Summer, Fall 1973 |
| Started: 1971 | Back issues available from |
| Circulation: 3,000 | publisher |

The Newsletter states that "The Center for Science in the Public Interest is a non-profit, tax-exempt organization which advocates that science and technology be truly responsive to human needs," and--judging by its reports and activities--this goal is being actively pursued. Each issue lists a dozen or more reports (costing from 50¢ to $12) available from the Center: Chemical Additives in Booze; Fluorides and Human Health; Asbestos and You; Science in the Public Interest; and How Sodium Nitrite Can Affect Your Health. A number of articles on the subject of these reports inform the reader of action the Center is taking. For instance, together with the Center for Study of Responsive Law, CSPI is suing the government "to bar all unnecessary uses of nitrites in meat."

The Center wages war against deceptive advertising, mentions manufacturers and their products (Chrysler Corporation, General Mills, Standard Brands), and asks the Federal Trade Commission to take appropriate action against such companies.

A regular feature ("Center Shorts") lists current activities at the Center: complaints to government agencies, participation by staff or supporters in panels, etc.

Although similar in some ways to various consumer publications, the emphasis here is not just on getting the best buy and avoiding defective or dangerous articles but on how and where pressure can be brought to bear on lawmakers and government bureaus in order to change things. (GKS)

Feedback:

The directors of the Center approved the draft.

CONSERVATION NEWS

National Wildlife Federation
1412 16th St. NW
Washington, D.C. 20036
Semi-monthly; free on request
Started: 1937
Circulation: 50,000

Format: 16 pages (6" x 9", offset)
Issues examined: none sent
Back issues available from publisher

The editor sent the following information: "CN is devoted to issues of general conservation/environmental interest--serious [and detailed] ... treatments combined with human interest features and humor. Covers anything of wide interest in natural resources and outdoor areas--energy, wilderness, water, air, wildlife, etc. Uses b & w photos and visuals."

THE ECOLOGIST

Edward Goldsmith, Publ.
73 Molesworth St., Wadebridge
Cornwall, PL27 7DS
United Kingdom
Monthly; $12

Started: July 1970
Circulation: 10,000
Format: 40 pages
Issues examined: Nov., Dec. 1973; Jan. 1974

The Ecologist is a British publication which advocates de-industrialization as the only workable method of solving problems created by the Industrial Revolution. Feature articles cover a wide range of topics related to sociological aspects of ecology. Representative titles include: "The Urban Crisis," "Parenthood--Right or Privilege?" "Technology & Violence" and "Does Building Houses Increase Homelessness?" The ecology of health has been investigated in a number of articles advertised as available in back issues of the journal, including "The Diseases of Civilisation: the declining health of urban man," "Should We Forbid Smoking?" and "The Delaney Amendment: a defence of the US law that prohibits the use of food additives suspected of being carcinogenic." Articles dealing with the cultural impact of modern institutions include "Musical Imperialism" and "Education: What For?" The former describes the degeneration of musical life in non-industrial societies after the introduction of capitalistic production methods. The latter depicts modern education as a destructive social force which not only has failed to banish illiteracy, but has caused the breakdown of traditional cultures. The following quotation from this article is representative of The Ecologist's editorial viewpoint:

> One cannot socialise people when there is no society for them to be socialised into. One must first re-create a society. To do this, one must re-establish those conditions within which the family and community can once more become self-regulating units of behaviour. This basically means deindustrialising society, for with economic growth, the tendency can only be in the opposite direction, as every one of its institutions conspires to bring about their disintegration.

The longer articles are usually documented; bibliographic footnotes are provided. Regular features of the journal include editorials, book reviews, letters to the editor, and "Friends of the Earth," which reports on the activities of the FOE organization. (SMA)

## ENVIRONMENTAL ACTION

| | |
|---|---|
| Peter Harnik, Ed. | Semi-monthly; $10 |
| 1346 Connecticut Ave. N.W. (Room 731) | Started: Apr. 1970 |
| Washington, D.C. 20036 | Circulation: 8,500 |
| | Format: 16 pages (offset) |

Issues examined: 4 & 18 Aug., 1, 15 & 29 Sept., 13 Oct. 1973

Microform version available from the Library of Congress

Environmental Action is published by a political lobby concerned with the environmental crisis. The stated goal of both the lobby and the periodical "is to protect and preserve the environment through legislation and social action and through citizen education."

Among the lead articles in the issues examined was a two-part series on "Logging in Alaska" which looks at forestry practices in South Tongass National Forest. The articles are critical of both timber companies and the U.S. Forest Service: "The conservationists, who look at Alaska as our last chance to handle wilderness properly, watch the U.S. Forest Service cave in to demands for timber and mineral exploitation on a huge scale." The author deplores the fact that a vast quantity of wood is being cut faster than it can be regrown (a violation of federal law) and that "they are taking it in a manner that precludes any other forest uses for generations or even centuries to come."

Another article comments on the problem of solid waste, and Senate deliberations on the subject. Others discuss the hazards of light-water reactors; the dangers of hard pesticides; billboards; and the trans-Alaska pipeline.

Regular features: "Feedback," the letters to the editor section; "Eco Notes," short articles of interest to environmentalists; "Government Environment," containing news of government action or inaction; and "Business Briefs," giving similar information from the business world. On the back cover of some issues is a breakdown of Congressional voting on important environmental legislation discussed in one of the stories inside.

Environmental Action has an attractive layout, is illustrated with appropriate black and white photographs, and is printed on recycled paper. (EC)

ENVIRONMENTAL EDUCATION

Pollution Probe, University of Toronto
Toronto, Ont., Canada
3 issues a year; $1.50
Started: Feb. 1973

Circulation: 1,000
Format: 16 pages (offset)
Issues examined: Apr. & Sept. 1973

Environmental Education seeks to increase teachers'

awareness of environmental concerns, and to provide teaching aids to stimulate interest in the problem among students. It is likely to find its greatest appeal among involved, active teachers of junior and senior high school students living in urban areas. Each issue is devoted to a single, current topic of environmental concern, such as the energy crisis, transportation systems, or the automobile-dependent society.

The most provocative regular feature of the journal is the "Problem of the Month," an article which expresses an anti-environmentalist point of view or reflects conflicting viewpoints on a topic for the purpose of encouraging classroom debate. Other features include a lead article written by a member of the University's Pollution Probe staff, one or two other brief, informative articles on the same theme, suggestions for related classroom projects and paper topics, lists of available resources, and an annotated column on recent "Books of Interest." Contributions in the form of letters, articles, questions, projects, or studies from both students and teachers are encouraged. (BC)

Feedback:

"... there really is no 'regular feature.'"

ENVIRONMENTAL QUALITY: For Consumer, Ecological and Social Awareness

Monthly; $10
Dates: 1970 through 15 Aug. 1973
Circulation: 125,000
Format: 84 pages
Issue examined: Aug. 1972

Environmental Quality ceased publication after three years of struggling to protect the world environment. The editorial policies of the magazine reflected a primary interest in facts: "we are committed to printing facts on environmental problems when they are known, expert opinion when the facts are under study." Advertisers were chosen selectively according to the companies' environmental concerns and commitments. Twenty per cent of the subscription price was donated by EQ to one of nineteen environmental organizations.

Some of the regular features in the magazine included a Washington report; short news items of interest to the consumer--touching on legislation or products; a column on businesses in the field of ecology; "Vanishpoint"--a series on endangered species of animals; and book reviews. The articles covered a variety of topics, all related to the fight for a better life for plants, animals, and humans. An article on the existence and potentials of sperm banks set forth the facts of what is possible today, but it ended with a series of unanswered questions regarding the possibly negative ramifications of such a reality once perfected and organized. An article on deserts described their formations and exploded the erroneous assumption man has that deserts and desert life are indestructible; on the contrary they are delicate and are being slowly destroyed by uncontrolled development and use. An architect contributed an article on organic burials which allow rather than prohibit the life-death cycle to operate on human beings as it works on other forms of life. Other topics covered have been noise pollution (with highly practical suggestions for the individual's search for peace and quiet); the energy crisis; strip mining; bicycling in New York; and the healthful and the polluting foods we try to digest. Drawings and color photographs made this an attractive magazine as well as an interesting and informative one. (Address was: 10658 Burbank Blvd., North Hollywood, Calif. 91601.) (SA)

Feedback:

Mail returned Oct. 1973: "Out of business."

EQUILIBRIUM

Zero Population Growth
4080 Fabian Way
Palo Alto, Calif. 94303
Quarterly; $3
Started: Jan. 1973

Circulation: 16,000
Format: 40-48 pages (offset)
Issues examined: none sent
Back issues available from publisher

"A quarterly magazine for the person interested in creating a society which is in balance with the world's physical limits."

Friends of Animals REPORT

11 W. 60th St.
N.Y., N.Y. 10023

Format: 32 pages (offset)
Issue examined: Fall 1971

"This volume has been compiled to give you background information to incorporate in your letters of support for our animal protective program, and in otherwise speaking for the animals. One voice--your voice--raised alone can do much to influence others to help protect animals from human harm.

Collectively, we can hope to achieve for animals the objective which we prize so highly for ourselves--freedom--and a ... [healthful] environment in which to exercise it. Working in collaboration with other humane conservation organizations, our voices will be heard in the Congress...."

Examples of articles in the sample issue: "Murder on the Ice the Canadian Way" (slaughter of seals); "The U.S. Secretary of Interior Believes That the Russians Protect the Polar Bear So That American 'Sports-Hunters' Can Have Fun Killing Them"; and "The U.S. Fish and Wildlife Service ... Has Been Indiscriminately Using Chemical 1080 and Other Poisons for Many Years."

## IMPACT

Box 13018
Reno, Nev. 89507
Quarterly; $5
Started: 1973
Circulation: 45,000

Format: 8-page tabloid
Issues examined: Apr., May, Summer, Fall 1973
Back issues available from publisher

Impact, published by a non-profit organization, aims "to inform and arouse citizen participation for solving our local problems: Air pollution, Water pollution, Transportation, Consumer justice, Honesty in politics, Energy, and Open Space preservation." Discussions center on environmental and public interest issues around the Reno area. [Feedback: "Conflict of interest, campaign finance, etc."]

Major community concerns center on zoning and land use ("The Law and Land Use: An Analysis of Zoning Policies"); population growth ("Growth: Just How Far Can We Go?"); water management policies ("Water: From Where?"); and political recourse for environmental aims ("1973 Nevada Legislature: Highly Productive for Environmentalists," a listing of all bills in the Nevada legislature relating to environmental concerns).

Provides a forum for organizations involved in the environmental and consumer movements. Regular contributors include Common Cause ("A Word From Common Cause: Nevada Fails to Enact Meaningful Conflict of Interest Legislation"); the Sierra Club ("Sierra Club Reports"); and the League of Women Voters ("A Word From the League").

A "Public Action Guide" in each issue provides phone numbers and addresses of Reno area Senators, Representatives and Assemblymen who are to be contacted regarding environmental and consumer legislation. (KL)

Feedback:
Editor expressed no disapproval.

## MEDIA ECOLOGY REVIEW

Media Ecology Program of
The New York University
School of Education
733 Shimkin Hall,
Washington Sq.
N. Y., N. Y. 10003
Quarterly; $4
Started: 1971

Circulation: 350
Format: 24 pages
Issues examined: Dec. 1973; Jan. & Feb. 1974
Indexing: Alternative Press Index
Back issues available from publisher

According to a statement in the *Review*, it is meant to be "a forum for research, opinion, and speculation, as well as a directory to other source materials concerned with media and communications."

Contains articles, interviews, original research, an "Articles Abstracts" section of one or two pages, and a "Technology" section (about films, video tapes, and media equipment).

## NATIONAL FLUORIDATION NEWS

Ethel H. Fabian, Ed. & Publ.
Route 1, Box 77
Gravette, Ark. 72736
Quarterly; $2
Started: 1955
Circulation: 12,000

Format: 4-page tabloid (offset based upon letterpress)
Issues examined: Apr. & July 1973
Back issues available from publisher

This is published "in the interest of all organizations and individuals concerned with keeping our drinking water free of chemicals not needed for purification." Its purpose is to crusade against the fluoridation of drinking water for purposes of preventing tooth decay. It does this by printing articles such as a report on research (first published in the *Journal of the American Medical Association*) which indicates that excessive fluoride intake may cause kidney damage or that persons with kidney disease are unable to eliminate fluoride from their bodies.

Another article in the same issue summarizes the proceedings of a conference on fluoride research at Magdalen College, Oxford. Again we find a connection between fluoride and the kidneys.

We also find articles dealing with pollution from fluorine gas (which is not the same as putting minute quantities of fluoride into drinking water); doctors and dentists refuting the value of fluoridating drinking water; and news of anti-fluoridation activity in various communities of the U.S. and abroad. An article entitled "Holland's High Court Declares Fluoridation Illegal" says that the Court "considered the fluoridation of a public water supply to be a medical measure and outside the purpose of the Dutch waterworks law." This illustrates one of the techniques of NFN: if research points to the fact (acknowledged by pro-fluoridation forces) that fluoride is a poison and can be dangerous when taken in sufficient amounts, or that fluoride contamination can cause damage to humans, animals, and crops, NFN prints it. It does not exaggerate the facts, but it does imply that there is a connection between the facts and the crusade against fluoridation. In the article on Holland, for example, the first reaction of the reader is that Holland's High Court has rejected fluoridation because it is harmful, not because medical additives are not covered by the law in question.

Inasmuch as people consume varying amounts of water, it is difficult for them to control their intake of fluoride. Should the reader wish to remove fluoride from his drinking water, the July issue tells where to purchase an appropriate device.

(BK)

Feedback:

"Your summary seems good to me."

NATIONAL PARKS & CONSERVATION MAGAZINE: The Environmental Journal

1701 18th St., N.W.
Washington, D.C. 20009
Monthly; $10
Started: 1919
Circulation: 45,000
Format: 32 pages (offset)
Issues examined: Nov. 1973 - Jan. 1974

Back issues available from publisher
Microform versions available from Bell & Howell (microfiche) and Xerox University Microfilms (microfilm)

The association that sponsors this publication is described in the magazine as follows:

> National Parks & Conservation Association ... is an independent, private, non-profit, public-service organization, educational and scientific in character.

> Its responsibilities relate primarily to protecting the national parks and monuments of America, in which it endeavors to cooperate with the National Park Service while functioning as a constructive critic, and to protecting and restoring the whole environment.

Many articles warn of threats to the environment and to wildlife from various forms of development (e.g., industrial wastes) and exploitation, and suggest alternative ways of doing things. Titles indicative of these topics include: "Civilization and the Animals," "The Big Thicket: A Texas Treasure in Trouble," and "The California Desert: Crisis in a Ravaged Land." One article in each issue is about an endangered species of plant or animal, e.g., "The American Paddlefish: Signs of Distress."

Other articles provide general information about national parks, wildlife, and natural history that could be of interest to hunters, backpackers, campers, and other outdoorsmen and students of nature. Among the articles in this category are "Oysters on Trees" (edible mushrooms), "Running a Desert River," and "Coyotes--In Maine?"

Photographs (mainly black-and-white) accompany all articles. Regular features include "Conservation Docket" (legislation relating to the environment) and "NPCA at Work" (activities of the Association). (SMA)

Feedback:

A number of changes of wording were suggested, and most of them have been incorporated into the review. The editor was disturbed by the thought that _hunters_ might find anything of interest in the magazine.

## NOT MAN APART

Tom Turner, Ed.
529 Commercial St.
San Francisco, Calif. 94111
Monthly; $15 annual dues (includes subscription); $5 non-member subscription

Started: Dec. 1970
Circulation: 20,000
Format: 16-page tabloid
Issues examined: Feb., Mar., May, June, Aug.-Nov. 1972

_Not Man Apart_ is published for Friends of the Earth, the John Muir Institute for Environmental Studies, and the League of Conservation Voters, groups actively involved in exposing worldwide and national ecological and conservation problems. Covers all fronts in the activist conservationists' struggle against the extermination of wildlife and the destruction of the ecosystem by industry, government, or individuals.

Reports and reacts on issues of ecological importance, such as the activities of the National Park Service ("Continuing Battle for Olympic National Park"); the development of nuclear power plants, or "nukes" ("Why Are We Building the Damned Things?"); the struggle to limit the development of oil pipelines and refineries in the north ("Another Pipeline Threatens the Arctic"); and strip mining ("Stripping Comes to Big Sky Country").

Provides detailed reports on politicians and on pending legislation that might affect ecological and conservationist interests.

Regular columns cover environmental news from Alaska, the Pacific Northwest, New England, and "Congress In-Action," as well as European efforts to halt pollution. Each issue contains extensive book reviews and beautiful photographs of wildlife and the natural environment. (KL)

Feedback:

"Your summation of Not Man Apart seems fair and complete.... Our editorial prejudice is to protect wilderness, and urge the creation of a steady-state economy that will not require the use of vast amounts of non-renewable and polluting resources. We ... support the idea that Man should live on the Earth's income, not its capital. NMA is one of FOE's ways of getting out the call for a more rational use of the ecosphere, of calling for a renewed stirring of love for the Earth, and respect for its limits. NMA is also designed to work as a pressure-applier to make government and industry and society as a whole more responsible to the Earth; we often ask for our readers to write their legislators in support of good legislation, and in opposition to bad. NMA was, by the way, called 'The New York Times of the environment' by the now-defunct Clear Creek magazine."

## OUTDOOR AMERICA

1800 N. Kent St., Suite 806
Arlington, Va. 22209
Monthly; $10
Started: 1922
Circulation: 60,000

Format: 12-page tabloid (offset)
Issues examined: Sept., Oct., Dec. 1973
Back issues up to one year old available from publisher

Outdoor America is published by the Izaak Walton

League of America, a "national citizen conservation organization ... working for the wise use and conservation of America's natural resources and for the restoration and maintenance of a high quality environment." The periodical is published to "report what is being said and done in the environmental field and to provide a forum for intelligent exchange between its readers." Executive orders, Congressional legislation, and Supreme Court orders are reviewed and criticized, with regard to their success, inadequacies, and enforcement. In addition, the regulations, programs, and studies that are being conducted on state and national levels are also evaluated. In one article, a law protecting wetlands was said to have "too many loopholes to be truly effective." Outdoor America also presents the opinions and achievements of other conservation clubs and organizations throughout the nation.

Articles describing the beauty, and the ecological and recreational aspects, of the environment are highlighted by photographs. Others expose the despoliation and pollution of natural environments, and here the photographs give proof of the damage. The journal does not hesitate to point out exactly who the despoilers are. For example, poachers, strip miners, real estate developers, and unconcerned citizens are all criticized. One article suggested that "Much of the destruction masquerades under the banner of progress and the rationale is always given that the new construction will serve the public, but the primary motive is profit." Throughout the journal, readers are urged to actively participate in conserving the environment. Specific advice is given on what can be done by groups and by individuals to improve the situation. In one article, game law violators were seen as being "benefitted by an apathetic citizenry." In another, on pollution, the success of national and state legislation and programs was felt to "largely depend upon the effectiveness with which citizens organize for action and press for pollution control."

Regular features include: "Letters"; "IWLA News Notes," reporting activities of the League's own chapter members; "Washington Watch," reviewing governmental activities; and "Urban Scene," which relates projects and other efforts by citizens and communities to plan and improve their own city environments. The following "Editorial Comments" were included in the issues that were examined: "What most people don't realize is that energy conservation is just about the only maneuver that offers any remote possibility of alleviating an impending fuel shortage this winter." "Saturday night gas-guzzling made front page news everywhere. Sensible, mandatory speed limits are but one of the long-range solutions offering real hope." "The high cost of hamburger brought the jacklighters out of the woodwork this past summer, and, as the leaves begin to fall, ill-gotten venison will appear on more tables than at any time since the Depression." Article titles included the following: "Deep-Water Ports: Solution or Environmental Hazard?" "Drive-In Zoos: Blessing or Blasphemy?" "Alternatives to Resource Exploitation." "Open Season on Poachers." (PMK)

Feedback: "It appears to be accurate. Enjoyed the comments on OA."

THE PROVOKER

St. Catharine's
Ontario, Canada
Bi-monthly; $3.50
Started: 1960
Circulation: 220,000

Format: 32 pages (offset)
Issues examined: Sept. & Nov. 1973; Jan. 1974
Some back issues available from publisher

The Provoker, written by John H. Tobe, stresses natural ways to achieve and maintain health. Tobe, who says that he is the "foremost proponent of 'raw food for health' in the world," recommends organic gardening, warns against the use of chemical fertilizers and poisons, and is "opposed to drugs, chemicals, and processing in food and healing."

One regular feature, "Dr. Warmbrand's Corner," discusses various health problems such as cancer and mental depression and warns of the dangers in treatment with radiation and chemotherapy. The writer suggests natural ways of healing and offers case histories or letters from readers. There are articles on consumer education in the field of health, such as "The Pill and Cancer." The editor has no respect for the Food and Drug Administration and believes it is more concerned with safeguarding drug corporations' profits than the public's health. He also derides women's liberation (which he refers to as "women's lib"), for which he sees no need: women are not exploited or oppressed, "so what is it that women want to be liberated from?"

Over 650 books and pamphlets are available through the publisher. They are on subjects related to mental, physical, and spiritual health, and are either annotated or listed according to subject matter. A classified section has ads for castile soap, organic foods, herbal remedies, hearing aids, etc. The reader can find a faith-healer, a secret way to increase luck in gambling, or a health-minded mate. (GKS)

Feedback:

"I think that you made a fairly good appraisal of the publication ... and I thank you for being fair and openminded."

## STRAIGHT CREEK JOURNAL

Stephen Foehr, Ed.
1521 15th St.
Denver, Colo. 80202
Weekly; $7
Started: 10 Feb. 1972

Circulation: 30,000
Format: 20 pages (offset)
Issues examined: none sent
Indexing: Alternative Press Index

The editor sent this information:

> Major editorial policies are humani[s]tic, pro-environmental, leftist politically, open to everything. We do not believe that biggest is greatest. We attempt to make people more aware of the forces acting on the[ir] cultural, social, political, and environmental lives, and how they can influence and change those forces to benefit themselves.

## TOIYABE TRAILS

Ron Guidotti, Ed.
Box 8906
Reno, Nev. 89507
10 issues a year; $2
Started: *ca.* 1955

Circulation: 850
Format: 12- to 16-page tabloid (offset)
Issues examined: Oct. 1973 - Jan. 1974

*Toiyabe Trails* is published by the Toiyabe Chapter (Nevada and Eastern California) of the Sierra Club, a conservation organization founded by John Muir in 1892. Its editorial policy is "to present conservation and environmental issues and information to our readers, so that they will be abreast of the latest in these areas ... so they can take appropriate actions should they so desire." "It is a means of communicating with our geographically-widespread membership." Coverage includes national, regional, local, and some international news. Information is presented by means of reprinting articles drawn from such sources as the Sierra Club *National News Report*, newsletters of Sierra Club chapters, local Nevada newspapers, and scholarly and technical journals. Cartoons and comic strips are also reprinted.

Editorials comment upon issues that might be of interest to environmentalists: "wilderness classification ... does not provide any protection against intrusion by mining activities--including the construction of mill sites and roads to the mine or mill sites--into a national forest area"; "The Making of an Energy Crisis"; and the necessity for "the establishment of comprehensive, realistic, city-wide bicycle pathways" in Nevada to reduce the number of bicycle accidents.

Conservation notes on the national level review court decisions (e.g., a U.S. District Court decision "that has the potential to end clear-cutting on all public forest lands"); the status of bills in Congress ("Senate passes strong strip-mining control bill"); presidential policy ("Nixon endorses timber panel recommendations to boost timber cutting"); activities of Congressional committees; actions of such government agencies as the Interior Department's Bureau of Land Management; and reports on ecology and wilderness conferences. Local conservation notes are oriented toward Nevada and California, with special emphasis on Las Vegas, Reno, and Lake Tahoe.

Regular features include letters to the editor, "Energy Briefs," "Enviro-Tech Briefs" (factual information about technology), and "New Literature" (short reviews of pertinent publications). There are frequent tips on outings, and articles on wildlife (including endangered species). (JM)

Feedback:

"Good review."

## Chapter 10

# LIBERAL

> ... never trust City Hall; government by its nature is deceitful. The reporter must dig out truth from the muck of propaganda and public relations. ---Washington Watch

This chapter is a catch-all for periodicals that don't belong in other chapters with "liberal" interests: Feminist, Utopian, Civil Rights, or Racial & Ethnic Pride. (For a discussion of beliefs, see the Liberal chapters in our earlier volumes.)

Among the periodicals in this chapter are two newsletters (Communiqué and Washington Watch) put out by individuals who wanted to express their outrage over the dishonesty and injustice they saw in all sectors of business and government.

Several periodicals have more-or-less single objectives: Leaflet wants to reform the marijuana laws; Community Schools wants changes in current educational methods and attitudes; and Media Mix contains information on materials it thinks of value to educators.

ACME News (University of Hartford) and Triton College News are student papers. New Times began as a campus paper, but has broadened its coverage and appeal.

The 4th Estate, Toronto Citizen, Oklahoma Observer, Portland Scribe, Chicago Express, and Changes serve a given community, giving local and national news and often covering a wide variety of subjects. Penn House Newsletter is put out by a self-help organization for welfare recipients and low-income families.

The Vermont Freeman (hard to categorize) is an unusual paper with a liberal outlook, some libertarian goals, and a deep interest in ecology and alternative sources of energy. For those who want political action, The Populist stresses the organization of citizens' groups to lobby at the local level for such things as a fair tax system, better health care, and a more equitable distribution of income, wealth, and power in America.

The Catholic Agitator is interested in social action. Metanoia offers philosophical commentary on religious, political, and social issues from a radical Christian point of view. (Post-American is also a radical Christian periodical.) Freedom (Church of Scientology) is interested in current social problems, and Stance (Community of Christ) represents reformist Christianity. --Janet Spahn

ACME NEWS: UH News

Ed Bernstein, Mng. Ed.
200 Bloomfield Ave.
West Hartford, Conn. 06117
Weekly Sept. to May; $6
Started: 1957, as campus newspaper; has had various names, such as Hot Lumps and most recently Acme Newservice
Circulation: 5,000
Format: 32-42 pages (9" x 12", offset); format changed to 20-page tabloid
Issues examined: 7 & 28 Nov., 12 Dec. 1973

The managing editor writes, "We are a campus newspaper [University of Hartford], of a left wing political persuasion, but with our primary responsibility the life on and around this university...." The issues examined support this statement, for there is broad coverage of school activities, problems, expenses, events, courses, faculty changes, etc.

There are also articles on the energy crisis, impeachment, unions and the E. & J. Gallo Winery, and the possibility that Wall Street might be planning to "oust Richard Nixon from office and replace him with a Gerald Ford-Nelson Rockefeller Administration." (This was predicted in December 1973.) Commercial ads and a classified section (free to students) are conventional. (GKS)

Feedback:

Editor informed us that the publication has changed its format and title. He also said he could not take credit for the prediction that Wall Street might be planning to oust Nixon and replace him with Ford and Rockefeller. "If you'll look at the article a little more closely, you'll notice a credit line to another newspaper, the Real Paper out of Boston. (Well, we did have the foresight to reprint it, anyway.) Otherwise, your summary of our paper is accurate."

## ACTION

Citizens' Action Program
2200 N. Lincoln Ave.
Chicago, Ill. 60614
Monthly; $5

Format: 4-page tabloid (offset)
Issue examined: Nov. 1973

A community-action exposé paper.

## AGENOR

John Lambert, Ed.
13 rue Hobbema
1040 Brussels, Belgium
Weekly; $8 (libraries & institutions $16)
Started: 1967
Format: 28 pages (offset)
Issue examined: Dec. 1973

Owned and financed by a European cooperative, Agenor takes a critical look at world news--especially about labor and politics--and concludes that although European governments are rigid and unimaginative, the European left also needs new strategy.

In English, Agenor reports on the women's movement in Europe, European responses to the oil crisis, a secret club of western European employers organized to combat political activism, and neo-fascism in the Mediterranean area. The news is interpreted from a progressive point of view; speaking of the efforts of a citizens' group in Hamburg to stop construction of a new airport, the writer says: "They argue, surely rightly, that the advice given by the 'coastal regions commission' back in 1961 is not a sound basis for such a vast project; in view of the enormous noise problem from giant jets, a site on the coast would be better...." Pollution of the environment, censorship, and ownership of natural resources are ongoing concerns reflected in the book reviews as well as the articles. (SN)

## ALTERNATIVE TO ALIENATION

Box 46, Station M
Toronto, Ont., Canada
M6S 4T2
Bi-monthly; $3 for 12 issues
Started: Mar. 1974

Circulation: 2,000
Format: 20-page tabloid (offset)
Issues examined: Mar.-July 1974

Alternative to Alienation is published by the group (now

expanded) which published the Radical Humanist (only one issue came out). The paper's editorial policy is "to raise our readers' consciousness about their own personal alienation, and to offer an alternative," and it promotes a humanistic philosophy and lifestyle. An editorial explains:

> The horrible reality is that our present environment keeps us divided from our own inner power. We blindly abide by dehumanizing ethics imposed on us from outside ourselves, and we forget our own.... Because of our passive character structures, we cannot conceive of alternatives, let alone create them. At some level, most of us have the tendency to accept, however unconsciously or resentfully, that everything is the way it is and there's nothing we can do about it. But becoming free is possible. If we make the choice, and learn to change our passive characters, we can develop toward the alternative. Alternative to Alienation intends to explore what is blocking our individual and social growth, and what paths we can take in this direction.

The paper is illustrated, and has an attractive layout. Examples of articles: "Sex Under Capitalism"; "How Communes Can Work"; "What Montessori Saw in Children"; "Women's Liberation, Social Change for All"; "Challenging the Work Ethic"; "Wild Food"; and "Care Less Daycare." (JMS)

## CANADIAN FAR EASTERN NEWSLETTER

James G. Endicott, Ed.
232 Wychwood Ave.
Toronto, Ontario, Canada
M6C 2T3
10 issues a year; $2.50
Started: Jan. 1948

Format: 4 pages (8 3/4" x 12 1/2")
Issues examined: Jan. 1949; Apr. 1969; Sept. 1973
Back issues available from publisher

The editor ("born in China, missionary 1925-46, and long visits in China 1952, 1956, 1959, 1973, and 1975") describes his publication as a personal opinion letter for (1) "factual reporting and interpreting revolutionary China"; (2) "commenting on events in Far East"; and (3) "interpreting the peace struggle and the Sino-Soviet dispute," which Endicott "tried to keep in the middle of."

The September 1973 issue discusses documentary evidence that North Korea did not start the war, but was invaded by the South: "before North Korea moved in a military way the South Korean army was well inside the northern borders and had occupied the town of Haeju." "Some day when 'top secret' [Pentagon] papers are revealed, the whole shameful story of how the U.S. government instigated the 1950 Korean War will be revealed."

In much of the Newsletter, Endicott discusses material from many sources. A phrase from a book on Indo-China impresses him: "All anti-communism corrupts; absolute anti-communism corrupts absolutely." He comments:

> Anti-communism is used everywhere as a smoke-screen to cover up oppression. That oppression is for the purpose of refusing justice to the poor, preventing much-needed social change and any taking-away of the political power of plunder from the rich and powerful. It is when we look at the rising tide of the revolution against the old order in the Philippines, Vietnam, Laos, Cambodia, Thailand, Burma, and in many parts of Africa and Latin America that we can see the real meaning of the phrase 'absolute anti-communism corrupts absolutely.'

(JMS)

Feedback:
"O.K."

CATHOLIC AGITATOR

Ammon Hennacy House of Hospitality
605 N. Cummings St.
Los Angeles, Calif. 90033
9 times yearly; 50¢
Started: Jan. 1971

Circulation: 3,000
Format: 4-page tabloid (offset)
Issues examined: none sent
Some back issues available from publisher

The editor described the publication as devoted to "agitation to Christian/personalist/social action."

CHANGES

PEER Collective
Box 27
Simpsonville, Md. 21150
Every 6 weeks; $5 for the lifetime of the paper

Circulation: 6,000 printed
Format: 44-page tabloid (offset); future issues smaller
Issue examined: Spring 1974

> Changes is a way to provide us and ... other community groups with an organizing tool, and to provide you with a source of information that is different ... [from] what you usually get fed by the mass media, the schools, and the government. There is no democracy without free speech and free access to information....
>
> We would like Changes to be a community paper. But we are aiming at several different communities: (1) the Howard County/Columbia community of 120,000 including 6,000 high school students; (2) the people of Washington and Baltimore and in between who want information on alternative lifestyles, sexuality, women's liberation, faggots, and radical politics; (3) our sisters and brothers across the country who are engaged in similar organizing efforts.... Changes is an experiment to see whether a paper like this can be valuable to all of these communities.

The paper asks (1) for volunteers to help put together and distribute the paper, (2) for feedback from readers, and (3) for donations.

> If we can raise the money ($500), Changes No. 4 will be published in the next 4-6 weeks. The content will include a women's section; more on health care and witches; a men's section; a high school section; healthy food; ... electroshock at Taylor Manor Hospital; and local-to-international news. Our feature will be Columbia-corporate fascism, the facade of community government, and taxation without representation.

The Spring 1974 issue contained a "Report on Racism" covering all areas of society--the economy, schools, courts, the prison system, etc.

## THE CHICAGO EXPRESS: The Sea Level Weekly

Weekly; $12 for 50 issues
Dates: 21 June 1972 - July 1974. First three issues (Mar., Apr., May 1972) were entitled Daily Planet

Circulation: 30,000
Format: 12-page tabloid
Issues examined: 14 Feb.-9 May 1973; July 1974

The Chicago Express usually contained two or three

longer articles (sometimes on local problems) with a large portion of the tabloid devoted to criticism and reviews (in the form of regular columns) of record albums, musical groups, new films (on TV and around town), plays and drama groups, art and artists, dance and dance groups, etc. Two other regular columns were "Mondo Cheapo" (where to obtain bargains in just about everything from funerals to taffy apples) and "The News" (short items from everywhere).

The articles were signed, and usually well written. Some examples: "I Was a Teenage Guru" (critical of the escapism indulged in by some Divine Light followers of the youthful Guru Maharaj-Ji); "Rennie, the Guru, and Remembrance of Things Past" (gentle disapproval of Rennie Davis's conversion); "Public TV Arm Wrestles for Survival" (because of government pressure, and a veto of appropriations); "Rock: Grease to Peace" (rock music as a social force and barometer of the times); "Life and Death at Wounded Knee" (supporting Indians' seizure of that town, and exposing Indian grievances and viewpoints not published in the Establishment media--e.g., the Indian council president, who opposed the radical element, was allegedly a puppet of the U.S. government and had a "goon" squad to keep the local Indians terrified and under his control); "Arbus: Through a Lens Darkly" (on the photographic genius of Diane Arbus, the Sylvia Plath of photography); "POWs: Nixon's Venerable Relics Come Home" ("name of the play is manipulating mass emotion"); "But Thieu's Afraid to Let His Go" (two French teachers, held for several years as political prisoners of the Thieu regime in South Vietnam, describe the brutal treatment accorded them and other prisoners); "Well, NOW, What's Happening?" (a woman criticizes a conference of the National Organization for Women as superficial and unrepresentative: too many lesbians, not enough poor or Negro women; in the next issue of the newspaper, a man who had attended the conference defended it). Women were well-represented on the Express, as article writers and in editorial positions.

The paper also contained political cartoons; occasional photographic essays; a calendar of events; and classified and display advertisements. It opposed Richard Nixon's policies, and the Indochina war. As for the Watergate burglary, a satirical article portrayed Nixon asking Chicago's mayor Richard J. Daley for advice on how to cover up the scandal. (JMS)

Feedback:

Editor expressed no disapproval. The address of the paper was: Denise DeClue, Editor, Shoestring Pub. Corp., 3105 N. Sheffield, Chicago, Ill. 60657.

COMMUNIQUÉ

Dates: started in May 1963 under title Information (consisted of a page or two); Communiqué began Sept. 1963 and ended May 1966

Circulation: 100

Format: pages vary up to 25 (8 1/2" x 14", mimeo., stapled)

Issues examined: complete backfile (except Apr. 1964)

The newsletter Communiqué began as a result of one woman's desire to "expose at least some of the hypocrisy and rampant injustice that exists, and, in some manner, to combat these evils." Through the publication she tried to make available:

> documented material on civil liberties, civil rights, the peace movement, nuclear testing, censorship and intellectual freedom, usually not printed in the mass media.

In addition to the news articles, she printed some lighter stories, short poems, and humorous anecdotes.

Each issue began with the quotation from Socrates: "Do not be angry with me if I tell you the truth." The articles were excerpts or full reprints from a variety of journals, including National Guardian, I. F. Stone's Weekly, The Southern Patriot, New America, and The Petal Paper. Views expressed were primarily anti-discrimination and anti-war. Issues often included copies of the Community Peace Calendar, a list of events prepared by the Philadelphia Peace Center. Information was also provided for the reader on recommended books, periodicals, and reports.

Articles in Issue No. 31 included "More C. I. A. Dirty Tricks?" "How We Help the Good People of Vietnam Enrich Their Lives," "The Draft Hits the Negro Hardest," and "Secret Police Tactics in Spying on Travelers."

In the January 1965 issue, the editor of Askance aptly described Communiqué as:

> the kind of publication all too rare today. It is a newsletter in the spirit of the early American press, drawing on the best material published in a wide range of publications.

(CT)

Feedback:

"The review is fine 'as is,' factual and concise." The address of Communiqué was: Ms. Alice Johnson, 10 E. Palmer St., Philadelphia, Pa. 19125.

## COMMUNITY SCHOOLS

Community School Workshop
171 College St.
Toronto, Ontario, Canada
10 issues a year; $5 ($2.50 students; $15 institutions)
Started: Spring 1971
Circulation: 3-4,000

Format: 32 to 64 pages (8" x 11")
Issues examined: Mar., Apr., May/June 1973
Indexing: Alternative Press Index
Back issues available from publisher

The philosophy and flavor of Community Schools are well summarized in this statement by Myra Novogrodsky, an editor:

> We are basically a local education periodical dealing specifically with the public schools in Toronto. But since the main problems standing in the way of [high] quality education in Toronto are similar to the obstacles facing people in most North American cities, the magazine is valuable to people outside of metropolitan Toronto. Issues we have focused on ... include teacher unionism, community control, sexism in the schools, the relationship between business and education, streaming [tracking] in the schools, vocational education, and immigrant education.

Articles in Community Schools champion a Student Bill of Rights, question whether vocational schools teach a marketable craft, and war against censorship of student publications. In a more radical tone, the periodical inquires whether vocational schools are not really a capitalist method of keeping the poor in their place. This theme is repeated in the article, "Our Schools Serve the Ruling Class." Frequent articles describe the struggle and plight of the unjustly-fired teacher, and support teachers organizing to assert their rights. Not all of the articles are contentious, however. One, dealing with sex education, finds both good and bad aspects in the program. Another is largely favorable to a remedial reading program in one of the vocational schools.

While Community Schools is well-written and -edited, and deals with basic issues of interest to all educators, it is nonetheless primarily a publication for those wanting to know more about education in Toronto, and all [see Feedback, item #1] of its articles deal with details of that city's schools. Criticism and praise apply only to particular situations in Toronto. We can infer that if vocational schools in Toronto are ineffectual, vocational schools in other communities may share some of their problems, but we cannot go further than this [see Feedback, item #2]. (BK)

Feedback:

The editor replied:

1. We are local, but even the issues you saw deal with: Cornwall, Quebec, Philadelphia, Peterborough, Sault Ste. Marie, as well as Toronto. I think you should indicate this.

2. This is fair enough. I do think articles like 'Our Schools Serve the Ruling Class' and 'Behind the Budget Cuts' go deeper than you have suggested. I think they're fairly clear about why (e.g.) vocational schools have problems--and why nothing short of real social change will change them.

Thanks.

THE 4TH ESTATE

(offset)

Nick Fillmore, Ed.
1823 Hollis St.
Halifax, N.S., Canada
Weekly; $8
Started: Apr. 1967
Circulation: 22,500
Format: 36-page tabloid

Issues examined: 6, 13, 27 Sept. 1973
Back issues available from publisher
Microform version available from Dalhousie University, Halifax

The 4th Estate, "Nova Scotia's only provincial weekly publication," gives particular attention to such topics as "problems of minorities, slum housing, economic problems of a slow-growth area, preservation of natural environment, Canadian economic and cultural independence." Its basic political approach, according to the editor, is "left of centre."

The contents range widely, from news stories, interviews, and commentaries on Canadian, American, and international affairs by well-known journalists, to a full section on entertainment and a sports page. The editor's statement of policy is confirmed by such articles as those on the controversy over the Quinpool high-rise project in Halifax (with objections raised by the Ecology Action Centre); the position of non-aligned nations and implications for the world oil situation; an interview with Prof. Ian McDougall of Dalhousie Law School on the need for Canadian oil export controls; a projected nuclear power plant to be set up by an American firm on Stoddard Island off the coast of Nova Scotia; and a zoning dispute in the "picturesque fishing village." Topics selected for editorial comment in the issues examined include: container facilities in the port of Halifax, quality of education, regional development, and the preservation of historic buildings in Halifax. The large entertainment section contains news, programs, and criticism on TV, radio, and movies, and articles on concerts, stage presentations, and crafts. A page next to the editorial section is given to letters to the editor, with readers' comments on any matters of concern and interest. (MEH)

Feedback:
Editor expressed no disapproval.

Reviewer's opinion:
Good variety, straightforward reporting, and serious editorial commentary characterize this newspaper.

FREEDOM: The Independent Journal of the Church of Scientology

Church of Scientology of California
5930 Franklin Ave.
Los Angeles, Calif. 90028
Bi-monthly; $2.50 for ten issues
Started: 1971

Circulation: 350,000
Format: 12- to 16-page tabloid (offset)
Issues examined: Sept. & Dec. 1973; Feb. 1974
Back issues available from publisher

Published by the Church of Scientology of California, Freedom does not deal primarily with religious subjects. The masthead explains that "Scientology is an applied religious philosophy which enables able people to become more able by improving their ability to communicate." A box on the front page carries the message, "Liberty--Frankness-Outspokenness. The right of an individual or group to be, to do, to have. Freedom from ... Freedom to ..." In an effort to carry out these ideas, Freedom has selected a limited number of issues with which it deals in detail, thus hoping to effect some improvement in these areas. It concerns itself especially with the American Medical Association, health care, psychiatry, the use of drugs in the treatment of mental patients, the care of the mentally retarded, the Food and Drug Administration, the Internal Revenue Service, the tax rebellion, and the invasion of privacy by the IRS and credit rating bureaus.

In the September 1973 issue, the American Medical Association is criticized for investing some of its retirement funds in pharmaceutical stocks, thus creating a conflict of interest. A few pages further on, the AMA again comes under fire (in "Human Experimentation"):

> The AMA, in general, exists to protect the rights of doctors to practice medicine without any interference from the public or from the patients, and in no way protects the rights of patients or experimental subjects.

Although Freedom is interested in health care in general, and attacks doctors for performing unnecessary surgery, its chief interest is in mental health. "The Creed of the Church of Scientology" states "That the study of the mind and the healing of mentally-caused ills should not be alienated from religion or condoned in non-religious fields." Consequently, Freedom is critical of psychiatry as practiced today. For example, it printed an article by a Professor of Medical Sociology at the University of California which reveals that high doses of phenothiazines (widely used as tranquilizing drugs) may cause patients to develop irreversible neurological effects. The author goes on to criticize the Food and Drug Administration for inaction regarding this drug. In addition to the physical dangers of tranquilizing drugs, Freedom also points out--by publication of letters from a mental patient who received these drugs--that they act to dull and confuse the patient, without enabling him to improve his condition. As might be expected, Freedom is vigorously opposed to psychosurgery.

As part of its crusade to improve the care of the mentally retarded, Freedom printed a series of articles by Joel Freedman, a social worker who called one state school for the mentally retarded "a grim warehouse of human neglect." Another school which he calls "better than average" is still less than adequate, because

> The Department of Mental Hygiene spends too little time and effort on residents of state institutions. Most of the effort seems to be geared toward creating top-salary jobs for grinning bureaucrats and so-called mental health experts who, for the most part, are totally indifferent to the plight of those they are supposed to serve.

In another article which deals with the problem nationwide, Freedman states that

> The mental health establishment has a vested interest in maintaining the status quo and will go to extraordinary lengths to obstruct reforms and to malign those who seek to enact changes. Flagrant perversions of psychiatric power can be illustrated by several occurrences....

As part of its campaign against the Food and Drug Administration, Freedom published a letter from Senator William Proxmire criticizing a proposed FDA regulation that would classify many vitamin and mineral preparations as drugs rather than food supplements. He points out why this would cause a rise in prices for such items without improving their quality.

Another object of Freedom's reform efforts is the Internal Revenue Service. In one issue, it describes what it sees as a growing revolt on the part of taxpayers, many of whom are refusing to pay their taxes and are engaging in long legal battles to establish their right not to pay or to pay considerably less than the IRS claims. Similar articles follow in other issues, including an interview with Congressman David Towell of Nevada, who states that "There are pockets of people all around the country ... getting together to put pressure on the IRS."

The IRS also comes in for criticism because of Freedom's interest in preventing unfair invasion of an individual's privacy. In addition to the IRS, this campaign is aimed against credit bureaus' storing vast amounts of information in their computers. It is also concerned about the data held in various government offices: the Defense Department, the Justice Department, the FBI, the Immigration and Naturalization Service, and many state and local authorities. If this information is false, there is little that most of us can do to correct it. Even if it is true, how readily available should it be? Freedom quotes (former) Senator Sam Ervin expressing his concern over this problem: "For the more the government or any institution knows about us, the more power it has over us."

It can be seen from the collection of topics just discussed that Freedom has chosen some powerful enemies--groups or institutions that most of us are slightly uneasy about to begin with.

Politically, Freedom is not classifiable. It is a reform journal, but not dedicated to reform through a particular political philosophy. It is impossible to identify it as right or left politically. On one hand, it encourages a taxpayers' revolt, apparently harking back to an almost forgotten right-wing (or libertarian) hope of repealing the income tax. On the other, it champions the rights of mental patients in a way that would gladden any ACLU attorney.

The back of the magazine is devoted to lighter subjects, such as discussions of music or art, or reproductions of photographs. The last page of each issue contains an article by L. Ron Hubbard, founder of Scientology. Each of these articles offers inspiration and encouragement to Freedom's readers, and includes a drawing or other picture of Mr. Hubbard. His writing style is more emphatic than that of the editors of Freedom, and is marked by the extensive use of words written in all capital letters. (BK)

Feedback:

"It is a well-written and excellent statement which accurately reflects the nature of the publication as we see it."

THE FRIENDLY AGITATOR

Friends Suburban Project
Box 54
Media, Pa. 19063
Bi-monthly; $2 donation
Started: Oct. 1969
Circulation: 1,500

Format: 10 pages (mimeo., stapled)
Issues examined: Sept. & Nov. 1973
Some back issues available from publisher

The Agitator's purpose has been "to expose Friends and others to new attitudes and ways of thinking on vital social issues...." It attempts

> to speak to the basic and historic concerns of Friends, renewing them, and bringing them up to the here and now of our lives ...: war and peace, banishment to exile of dissenters, discrimination against minorities of other races and creeds, repression of freedom, criminal justice, prisons, capital punishment, Friends' use of their corporate property, to mention a few....

Among the articles in the sample issues were two on "human services" in Delaware County (one on day-care centers, the other on the effect of federal cutbacks in spending); and one supporting general and unconditional amnesty for deserters and draft resisters.

The Agitator often quotes such persons as the Berrigan brothers and the late A. J. Muste. It is said to be received by many prisoners. (JMS)

Feedback:
The editor added that although the publication is concerned with the problems in its own locality, these problems are universal.

THE LEAFLET

Larry Schott, Exec. Ed.
2317 M St., N. W.
Washington, D. C. 20037
Quarterly; $15 (students & military $10)
Started: Nov. 1971
Circulation: 22,000

Format: 6-8 pages (offset)
Issues examined: Mar., May, July, Oct. 1972; Jan., Apr., July 1973; undated v. 2, no. 4/v. 3, no. 1; Apr. 1974
Back issues available from publisher

The Leaflet is published by the National Organization for the Reform of Marijuana Laws,

> a non-profit public interest lobby dedicated to achieving legislative reform of the current marijuana laws, on both the state and federal levels. We do not advocate the use of marijuana. But we know of no medical, legal, or moral justification for sending those to jail who do use it. We believe the present marijuana laws cause more harm to society than the substance they seek to prohibit.

Most of the articles describe, without editorializing, efforts being made to liberalize the laws governing the possession and use of marijuana. In addition, publicity is given to individual legal cases, notably in Texas, where--it is alleged--defendants convicted of the possession of marijuana have been treated more severely than people convicted of murder.

Considerable space is devoted to reporting the findings of commissions assigned to study the non-medical use of drugs. Results of surveys showing the number of Americans who smoke marijuana are also reported.

Sometimes included are short reviews of books and a column ("Potpourri") of news briefs describing ancillary events such as the endorsement by the District of Columbia Medical Society of a resolution calling for "decriminalization of the private use and possession of marijuana," or commenting on the arrest of an Hawaiian car dealer for such deceptive practices as placing marijuana in the cars of recalcitrant customers and then threatening them with arrest. (SN)

Feedback:

Editor expressed no disapproval.

MEDIA MIX: A Newsletter about Film, Print, and Sound in Education

Jeffrey J. Schrank, Ed.
Claretian Publications
221 W. Madison St.
Chicago, Ill. 60606
8 issues a year; $7
Started: Oct. 1969
Circulation: 2,000
Format: 8 pages (offset)
Issues examined: Jan.-Mar. 1970
Self-indexing every four years
Back issues available from publisher

According to the editor, this newsletter "culls information from over fifty media publications and hundreds of books." The publication "concentrates on material which could help to humanize."

Brief announcements of new equipment, paperback publication dates, reviews, and educational programs are entered under the following topics: feature films, 16mm films, television, print, and the popular music scene. (Formerly, every other issue included a topical supplement, e.g., "Media Resource Guide for Inhabitants of a Poisoned Planet" and "Media Resource Guide to War, Peace, and the Draft.")

The newsletter is meant to keep educators and others who work with young people in touch with both underground and overground. (JA)

Feedback:

Editor supplied several corrections which have been incorporated into the review.

METANOIA: An Independent Journal of Radical Lutheranism

Douglas Stange, Ed.
2126 University Ave.
Dubuque, Iowa 52001
Quarterly; $3
Started: 1969
Circulation: under 10,000
Format: variable
Issues examined: none sent
Indexing: Alternative Press Index, Religious Periodicals Index, Guide to Social Science and Religion in Periodical Literature, Index to Select Periodical Literature
Back issues available from publisher
Microform version available from Xerox University Microfilms

The publication sent this information:

> Metanoia ... has endeavored to be an open forum for the discussion of religious, political, and social issues. Among its contributors have been Martin Niemoeller ... [and] Harvey Cox.... Although radical, it does not exclude nor ignore the conservative voice. While professing to work within the Lutheran tradition, its pages are open to authors of any religious or non-religious standing in order to be in free communication with everyone seeking radical repentant change and the promotion of truth, justice, and love.
>
> ...
>
> The catholicity of Lutheranism in our present day has been seriously circumscribed.
>
> The voice of this church, a community born in revolution and reformation, repeats pious platitudes to a world yearning for prophetic leadership. This journal seeks to restore a forum wherein privatism and apathy may be vigorously answered. Moralism is no response to the needs of our world and of our nation and states and cities.
>
> Institutions and structures need more than simple adjustments to render them adequate for present crises, when radical change is required....
>
> Metanoia takes its place in the tradition of the 'little magazine' and will be published ... as long as the need for such a forum remains.

A blurb quotes from the AIMS [American Institute for Marxist Studies] Newsletter, which called Metanoia "a relatively new magazine of consequence in terms of the ongoing Marxist-Christian dialogue...."

NEW INTERNATIONALIST: The People, the Ideas, the Action in the Fight for World Development

P. A. C. Ltd.
74 A High St.
Wallingford, Berks.,
United Kingdom
Monthly; $9
Started: Mar. 1973
Circulation: 20,000
Format: 26 pages (8 1/4" x 11 5/8", offset)
Issues examined: Sept., Oct., Dec. 1973
Back issues available from R. P. S. Ltd., Victoria Hall, Fingal St., London SE10 ORF

U.S. distributor: 419 Boylston St. (Rm. 209)
New World Coalition Boston, Mass. 02116

The New Internationalist is interested in world development, in correcting injustices in our relations with the Third World, and in showing "the rich world" how to succor the underprivileged millions of "the poor world."

Sponsored "by Oxfam and Christian Aid," the periodical has carried interviews with a number of heads of state (e.g., Julius Nyerere of Tanzania). It plans articles on new ideas in education; trade unions in poor countries; and Christianity in the Third World. A regular feature, the "Myth-Exploder," demolishes the viewpoints behind such clichés as "Why Don't They [i.e., poor countries] Help Themselves?"

According to a brochure, articles in past issues have dealt with such problems as "The End of Cheap Food," "The World Health Scandal," and "The Drought in China"; commented on Juan Peron's return to power in Argentina; and presented a profile of Martin Luther King, Jr.

## NEW TIMES

Box J
Tempe, Ariz. 85281
Weekly (not published in summer); $8
Started: May 1970
Circulation: 40,000
Format: 16- to 28-page tabloid (offset)

Issues examined: 24 Apr., 1 & 15 May 1974
Indexing: Alternative Press Index
Back issues available from publisher
Microform version available from Xerox University Microfilms

The editor sent this information: "We try to provide an alternative to the single daily that dominates the state. Although we provide some national news through such services as Liberation News Service, our focus is on happenings within the state government; the environment, Indian affairs, and feminist concerns are a few of the areas we have tried to cultivate. Our prison editor has been awarded two grants by the Fund for Investigative Journalism. Planned outreach to the community at large has spurred us to expand consumer and labor coverage. Entertainment copy still plays a large role."

The New Times, founded as a reaction to the Kent State University killings that followed the U.S. invasion of Cambodia, has gradually changed from a youth-oriented radical newspaper to a community-action newspaper. It gained state-wide recognition when it attacked the dismissal of drunken-driving charges against a U. S. Senator from Arizona. (The New Times article was picked up by radio stations and suburban newspapers in Arizona, and by columnist Jack Anderson.) Other New Times articles that attracted attention were its coverage of a band called the "eagle raiders" (patterned after the Chicago area's "Fox") which attacks corporations in the name of ecology, and its exposé of a county attorney who used perjured testimony.

A New York Times article (3 Feb. 1974) noted that New Times had achieved what was "believed to be the first successful public stock offering by any paper whose origins date back to the press revolution of the late 1960s." Although New Times began as a free-distribution paper on college campuses in Tucson and Phoenix, its readers now include minorities, as well as working-class and professional people, and it receives support from liberal Democrats.

(JMS)

## NORTH STAR

Box 661
Del Mar, Calif. 92014
Bi-weekly; $5
Started: 21 Apr. 1971
Circulation: 12,000

Format: 20-page tabloid (offset)
Issues examined: 15 & 29 Oct., 12 & 26 Nov., 10 Dec. 1973

An alternative newspaper put out by the North Star collective serving San Diego, the North County area, and the University of California. "We will not print copy which is racist, sexist, or imperialist." Illustrated.

## OAS WEEKLY NEWSLETTER

William Velloso, Ed.
General Secretariat
Organization of American States
Washington, D. C. 20006
Weekly; free

Started: 1963
Circulation: 37,000
Format: 4 pages (offset)
Issues examined: none sent
Back issues available from publisher

The editor sent this information:

> News on economic, social, cultural, artistic, scientific, technological, educational, political, moral,

spiritual development and efforts to break down barriers of customs, attitudes, interests, and other [things] that hamper free trade and exchange of goods, people, ideas. Notes on scientific and technological advancement, population control, economic integration, bi-national and multi-national efforts, all kinds of activities that may contribute to enhance quality of life in the developing countries and make the world a more pleasant, equitable, comfortable ... [healthful] place to live. Items on minorities, on unfair discrimination, and attempts at putting aid and other kinds of assistance in the proper perspective from the point of view of the receiving countries, and how sometimes much-touted 'help' is mostly to the donor's benefit.

Former title: Alliance for Progress Weekly Newsletter.

THE OKLAHOMA OBSERVER: A Journal of Commentary

Frosty Troy, Ed.
Box 53371; 116 Madison
Oklahoma City, Okla. 73105
Twice monthly; $10
Started: 1969
Circulation: 4,734
Format: 12-page tabloid (offset)

Issues examined: 10 Nov. - 25 Dec. 1973
Back issues available from publisher
Microform version available from Xerox University Microfilms

The Oklahoma Observer carries articles dealing with social issues in Oklahoma and at the national level. Areas frequently dealt with include civil liberties, drugs, education, women's rights, and politics.

The journal prints a Ralph Nader column, TRB from Washington, letters to the editor, and satirical cartoons in each issue. Other regular features include Observations (a page of half-column comments on personalities and local politics), Observerscope (a page of brief quips directed towards state and national concerns), and Editor's Notebook (an essay on social issues).

The 25 November 1973 issue carried a two-page article by Governor David Hall on penal reform, including recommendations and costs. Another issue featured a debate between Representative Donald Riegle, Jr., of Michigan and John S. Knight, newspaper editor, on the question of President Nixon's impeachment. Articles by Common Cause also appear. There is a minimum of local advertising. (JA)

Feedback:

"Summary is well done."

PENN HOUSE NEWSLETTER

1035 Pennsylvania St.
Lawrence, Kans. 66044
Monthly; $5 donation
Started: Feb. 1971
Circulation: 1,300

Format: 6 pages (legal size)
Issues examined: Nov. 1971; Apr., July, Oct. 1973; Jan.-Apr., June 1974

This publication from Penn House ("a private non-profit self-help organization for welfare recipients and low income families") considers itself "The nitty-grittyest, grass rootsiest, down homeiest thing in Kansas! Run by and for poor people." Members of the organization believe that personal rights are more important than property rights, and that no person in America should lack adequate food, clothing, housing, medical attention, or the opportunity for needed education or training for a job.

The February 1974 issue explains that the Newsletter has a dual purpose: "to carry information to low income families that will help improve their lives on a day-to-day basis, and to notify persons of concern and influence of pressing community problems." There are many articles explaining welfare and social security regulations as well as other government red tape, but those who need more help are invited to visit Penn House, where necessary legal or school counseling can be arranged for. Subscribers are told how Penn House will provide emergency food, clothing, medicine, or transportation (for elderly or disabled to the welfare office or the doctor). People are urged to join the cooperative food-buying club and eat better for less money.

There are many accounts of people who have recently received assistance or who are presently in trouble. The periodical calls for volunteers, money, apartment listings, clothing, furniture, food, and other things that can be distributed to the needy. A section (Special Thanks for Special Folks) honors those who have donated money, equipment, expertise, or labor to help others.

The Newsletter has a friendly, encouraging style and is simply and clearly written so that it could be understood by those with problems in reading or comprehension. (GKS)

Feedback:

We at Penn House will be pleased and proud to have

> our Newsletter included in From Radical Left to Extreme Right. May we brag on ourselves by quoting from your content-summary in a future issue of our Newsletter? We have neither corrections nor additions to your content-summary. You have done an excellent job of capsulating what we are really all about.

## PLAIN TALK

Iberus J. Hacker, Ed.
Multi-Media Project
Uptown Community Organization
1222 W. Wilson Ave.
Chicago, Ill. 60640

Monthly; 10¢ a copy
Format: 8-page tabloid (offset)
Issues examined: Aug. & Sept. 1973

Plain Talk's masthead announces that it is the paper of the Poor People's Union and Rainbow Union. "It is an open forum and your views are welcome." According to a reprint of an article that appeared in the April 1972 issue, the Uptown Community Organization started 15 months ago

> with a few very basic principles. We have not been swayed from those principles by scattered shots from character assassins or by attempts at political blackmail by people in power and people who crave power.
>
> One of our basic principles is that community problems must be solved within the community and that decisions should be made by the people directly affected by those decisions.
>
> Second, we seek to build an all-volunteer self-help group that will be independent of federal, state, or municipal funds and the controls they carry with them. We cannot serve the people of our community while trying to please some Administration bookkeeper.
>
> Third, we intend to remain free to call the shots as we see them without fear or favor. Therefore, we will not dabble in partisan politics, and we will resist the efforts of partisan politicians to dabble us.

The article goes on to say that the UCO is "dedicated to finding ways the poor, the minorities, and the disenfranchised can have an opportunity to speak for themselves," and to serving as "an amplifier for the voice of the people. The

UCO listens and the UCO leads. We believe that through the building of a strong community organization we can involve all the people in solving Uptown's problems."

The activist paper carries news of the community: activities, action groups, projects, social services, and people. It exposes corrupt city officials, slum conditions, and racial prejudice, and fights against the destruction of the community by ill-planned urban renewal projects. "Our principle, and I hope yours, must be: not one more damn' building destroyed for any purpose whatever until construction is started on housing we can afford to live in." It also urged the impeachment of Richard Nixon. Illustrated. (JMS)

THE POPULIST

| | |
|---|---|
| New Populist Action | Started: July 1973 |
| 1921 Pennsylvania Ave., N.W. | Format: 4 pages (offset) |
| Washington, D.C. 20006 | Issue examined: July 1973 |
| Bi-monthly; free to members | |

New Populist Action, an organization headed by Fred R. Harris, former U.S. Senator from Oklahoma, puts out The Populist for the purpose of informing members "about New Populist Action activities, congressional activities, lobbying strategies at the national and local levels, local coalition events, and upcoming NPA events."

In the first issue of The Populist, Harris explains the goals of NPA, which is attempting to "organize coalitions of average citizens to lobby at the local grassroots level for their own self-interest--for a fair tax system, for better health care, for fewer monopolies and more free enterprise, for a truly representative democracy." The organization's first major project, The Tax Action Campaign, has coalitions in over 40 cities and is in "constant communication and consultation with groups such as Common Cause, Ralph Nader's Reform Research Group, Tax Analysts and Advocates, and others."

The tax system is only one of the problems with which the organization plans to deal:

> The real goal of NPA is to organize networks for action on any issue concerning average Americans. By educating, organizing, lobbying, and holding public officials accountable to their constituents, average citizens can translate majority opinion into majority power. And that's what New Populism is all about....

[It] seeks a way to bring about a more equitable distribution of income, wealth and power in America. (JMS)

PORTLAND SCRIBE: Weekly Neighborhood News

215 S.E. 9th Ave.
Portland, Ore. 97214
Weekly; $10
Started: Feb. 1973
Circulation: 4,000

Format: 24-page tabloid
Issues examined: 15 & 22 June, 5 July 1974
Indexing: Alternative Press Index

"The Scribe exists to provide alternative sources of news on local, national, and international events; to be a forum for the left/cultural community; to provide access to information (city survival, calendar) and promote group interaction; and to serve as a focus for community organizing."

Underground format--illustrated with photographs, cartoons, and interesting graphics.

POST-AMERICAN

Institute of Contemporary Thought
(People's Christian Coalition)
Box 132
Deerfield, Ill. 60015
Bi-monthly; $5

Started: Fall 1971
Format: 16-page tabloid
Issues examined: Mar., May, Sept., Nov. 1973
Some back issues available from publisher

A "radical Christian" publication which contains scholarly political and social essays. Excellent graphics.

READER: Chicago's Free Weekly

Robert E. McCamant, Ed.
Box 11101
Chicago, Ill. 60611
Weekly; $6

Format: 16-page tabloid (offset)
Issue examined: 28 Sept. 1973

"Chicago politics, Chicago's Alternative Culture, Chicago Survival, plus guides to cheap dining, media, feminism, the gay scene, and much more."

RICHMOND MERCURY: A Weekly Journal of News and the Arts

John Carr, Ed.
16 E. Main
Richmond, Va. 23219
Weekly; $7
Started: Sept. 1972
Circulation: 7,000
Format: 24-page tabloid (offset)
Issues examined: 26 Sept. & 3-17 Oct. 1973
Back issues available from publisher

The editor sent this information: "We are a journal of news and the arts published in Richmond by young liberals who supported McGovern.... We also run book, sound, 'getting along,' literary, and personal finance supplements. We run one investigative piece an issue and film, drama, concert, rock 'n' roll reviews in the back. We are not 'underground' or 'counter-culture.'"

The paper has an artistic and pleasing format with some excellent graphics.

RIGHT ON

Sharon Gallagher, Ed.
Christian World Liberation Front
Box 4307
Berkeley, Calif. 94704
Monthly; $3 (foreign $5)
Started: July 1969
Circulation: 65,000
Format: 12-page tabloid (offset)
Issues examined: Mar., June, July 1974
Back issues available from publisher

Sophisticated in appearance and tone, and illustrated with photographs and graphics, this radical Christian periodical is circulated on college campuses. Each issue carries one or two interviews with such persons as Paul Krassner (editor of The Realist, reviewed on p. 111), Billy Preston (rock star), or Theodore Rosznak (professor and author of The Making of a Counter-Culture), concerning their work and beliefs. The March issue carries the text of a lecture given at Berkeley on Alexander Solzhenitsyn.

Other regular features are a testimonial by an individual who has changed a troubled life through Christ; a Media Review which stresses books, films, and recordings; "The Androclean Outlook," a gentle column offering Biblical quotations in answer to problems or questions voiced by prominent persons; "The Radical Christian," which recommends books, comments critically upon current events, and prints pertinent quotations from various sources; and letters to the editor.

The subject matter of feature articles varies widely: "Christianity and American Racism"; "Vietnam Today" (criticizes the "vast program of American military aid" that only prolongs the war and discourages President Thieu from negotiating a political settlement with the Communists; and describes the bad living conditions of prisoners kept in South Vietnamese "tiger cages"); "Old Testament Israel as Counter-Culture and Possible Model for Radical Christianity"; and a discussion of Leonard Bernstein's "Mass" as a type of Christian art.

The March issue carries a statement by the staff, saying that although it does not condone the tactics of the Symbionese Liberation Army in kidnapping Patricia Hearst,

> what has happened to Patty is, in large part, due to the sins of the upper class of which the Hearsts are a part. They are part of an unjust establishment which allows some to have millions and others to live on the brink of starvation, and which drives some of its young people to extreme acts in an attempt to redress the imbalance. We are sure to see other events of this kind unless our society changes.

The statement also asks why the Hearsts, practicing Christians, have "not submitted to the Lordship of Christ in their lives in the matter of wealth? Why have they not done what Jesus commands them to do as one of his wealthy would-be followers--that is, give[n] their riches to the poor?"

(MN; JMS)

## THE ROSE HIP

Bi-weekly, later monthly; $3
Dates: Jan.-Sept. 1973
Circulation: 500-1,000
Format: 12- to 16-page tabloid (offset)
Issues examined: 26 May, 21 July, 20 Aug. 1973
Back issues available from publisher

This "represented an effort by a group of concerned citizens, mainly young (20's and 30's), mainly middle class, to expose issues neglected by the 'straight' press and to advocate fair housing ordinances, bikeways, women's rights, cessation of the war in Southeast Asia, etc., as well as to offer exposure to artists and writers."

The address of The Rose Hip was Alternatives, Box 682, Norwich, Conn. 06360.

## SIERRA REVIEW and TOWN CRIER

Richard G. Spencer, Publ.
Box 769
Quincy, Calif. 95971
SR bi-monthly, $6; TC monthly, 25¢ an issue
Dates: SR, Jan. 1971-Apr. 1973; TC, Apr. 1973-present
Circulation: 500-600

Format: SR, 12-page tabloid (offset); TC, 8 pages (8" x 12", letterpress)
Issues examined: SR, Jan.-May 1971; TC, Apr.-Sept. 1973
Back issues available from publisher

The publisher sent this information: "Plumas County, 12,000 pop., has one paper, Feather River Bulletin. The Sierra Review was the initial publishing venture--meant for West Coast distribution. Town Crier is intended to offset the influence of the ultra-conservative F. R. Bulletin." The Sierra Review had contained "news commentary and review."

## STANCE

Community of Christ
Mrs. Valborg Anderson, Ed.
1310 21st St., N.W.
Washington, D.C. 20036
About 8 issues a year; free (donations for postage)
Started: late 1965
Circulation: 450

Format: 24 pages (mimeo., stapled)
Issues examined: 14 issues between Nov. 1970 & Summer 1973
Some back issues available from publisher

The editor supplied this information: "... our editorial policies lean toward radical (root) theology, reform in the institutional church..., pricking the conscience of the king (political), social welfare (hunger, housing, amnesty), and a stance of non-violence. We have supported such things as the grape and lettuce boycotts and impeachment; we have opposed Gulf's African policy, ITT, Honeywell's making anti-personnel bombs. David Earle Anderson writes most of the editorials. Most of the articles, poetry, reviews are written by members of the Community of Christ, an ecumenical fellowship of Christians. Guest writers are identified as such. We manage to stir up a bit of flak occasionally!"

TORONTO CITIZEN: Midtown's Community Newspaper

171 Harbord St.
Toronto 4, Ontario, Canada
Bi-weekly; $5
Started: 1970

Circulation: 8-10,000
Format: 16-page tabloid
Issue examined: 9 Mar. 1973

This worker-oriented newspaper presents news of the central city, stressing citizen participation in town planning through community groups ("Bathurst-St. Clair Citizen Task Force Planned"; "Federation of Ward 5 Groups Founded") and the encouragement of reform candidates for City Hall and the Board of Education. An Arts Section reviews plays and books, and a Citizen Calendar lists cultural, political, and community events in the city. (KL)

Feedback:
Editor expressed no disapproval.

TRITON COLLEGE NEWS

2000 5th Ave.
River Grove, Ill. 60171
Bi-weekly; free
Started: Sept. 1972
Circulation: 2,500
Format: 12-page tabloid
(offset)

Issues examined: Mar., Apr., 9 & 23 Oct., 14 Nov., 4 Dec. 1973
Back issues available from publisher

This independent "student-run newspaper" is written "for and by" students at a community college in a suburb west of Chicago. The editor says that the paper presents the students' views, especially in articles that had been rejected by the official school paper, The Trident.

Almost every issue contains poetry, short fiction, or criticism of the school administration. Political content: calls to impeach Richard M. Nixon; boycott Gulf Oil (accused of maintaining an unholy alliance with Portuguese colonialism in Africa); and boycott non-union lettuce (thus giving support to Cesar Chavez and the United Farm Workers).

Illustrated with drawings and photographs. Carries advertisements. (JMS)

VERMONT FREEMAN

Roger L. Albright, Ed. & Publ.

Hanksville Schoolhouse
Starksboro, Vt. 05487

Semi-monthly; $8.50
Started: Jan. 1969
Circulation: 2,500
Format: 16- to 24-page tabloid (offset)
Issues examined: early Nov., Thanksgiving, early Dec. 1973
Back issues available from publisher
Microform version available from U. of Vermont Library

The Vermont Freeman is "an open journal, concerned with root causes and basic change" as they relate to such concepts as "human dignity, environment, alternatives, political action." In an article, "Options for Americans," the editor expresses the philosophy behind these concepts:

> [A populist movement] would probably interpret 'life, liberty, and the pursuit of happiness' in a more literal way: life meaning a liveable environment and adequate life-sustaining goods and services, including health care, for all; liberty meaning the minimal amount of government meddling consistent with the general good; and the pursuit of happiness meaning opportunity for each to participate in the life of the community in self-fulfilling ways.

This philosophy is reflected in articles dealing mainly with local and state problems in Vermont: "Proposals for Vermont's Power Problems," "Hunger in Vermont," "Issues in Vermont Education," and "A Message from Windsor Prison." Some national stories, especially from Washington, D.C., are also covered.

Editorials from other Vermont newspapers, letters, and cartoons are regular features. (SLA)

WASHINGTON WATCH: A Private Newsletter

3308 South Cedar St. (#11)
Lansing, Mich. 48910
Semi-monthly; $12 ($7.50 to students and the elderly)
Started: 15 Oct. 1971
Circulation: 9,500
Format: 4 pages (offset)
Issues examined: 1 & 15 Nov., 1 Dec. 1973
Back issues available from publisher

Washington Watch developed from letters to the sociologist, David Riesman, from Tristram Coffin, author and political observer. Riesman shared the letters with Erich Fromm and others who thought Coffin's views and observations deserved more readers. After first being distributed to members and friends of Business Executives Move for Vietnam Peace, the publication became an independent, non-profit newsletter. (See our review of BEM News Notes in this Chapter 16.)

It is asserted in the letter's promotional brochure that "government by its nature is deceitful," concealing truth behind a "muck of propaganda and public relations." The publishers believe that their "function is to give the reader the truth behind the news. A major portion of newspaper reporting is simply rewriting press releases--Washington Watch gives the implications and far-ranging results of U.S. political actions."

The style is terse, and there are numerous quotations (information and opinion) from individuals, newspapers and other periodicals. Among the topics discussed in the issues examined: "Impeachment, a Bill of Particulars"; "The Mafia Connection," a report on some of Nixon's finances; "Justice Department," giving reasons why William Saxbe was a poor choice for Attorney-General; and "After Nixon What?", citing important national priorities. These include a restoration of the people's confidence in government, better handling of the fuel shortage, and a halt to inflation. Since "the moral atmosphere is as dirty as the fog that comes out of the polluted Potomac River," we also need "a new sense of public service and a concern for people."

There is also a prediction that Nixon will retire or be impeached after "a series of events: his 'counter attack' fails, the fuel crisis hits heavily, Southeast Asia war flares anew, Congressman Ford is confirmed as Vice-President, Nixon's deals with organized crime come to light, and, possibly, an attempt to use the fuel crisis to grab dictatorial power."

This publication contains only Coffin's commentary on current events. There are no contributed articles or advertisements. It is printed on recycled paper. (EC)

Feedback:

Editor expressed no disapproval.

WHOSE CITY?

Almost monthly; free
Circulation: 3,500
Format: 4 to 8 pages (offset)
Dates: Dec. 1971 - Apr. 1973
Issues examined: none
Some back issues are available from publisher

According to a statement from one of the persons who had been associated with it, this community newsletter had been "oriented towards City of Toronto 'reform' politics," had placed "emphasis on neighborhood involvement in [urban] planning," and had gone in for "investigative reporting." It died for lack of money. Its address had been: Pollution Probe, University of Toronto, Toronto 181, Ontario, Canada.

Feedback:
"O. K."

## Chapter 11

## CIVIL RIGHTS

> ... the history of the Soviet elections can not cite a single instance of a failure of even a most unpopular candidate. Everything and everyone there is elected with a 99.98% margin.... As far as the jurors are concerned, they do not participate in the judicial process at all. It's not by chance that they are called 'stage props'.... The defense attorney knows in advance that he cannot really help the defendant any more than a corpse can be helped by a heating pad.... ---The Samizdat Bulletin

Several kinds of civil rights movements are covered in this chapter. A number of them oppose what they consider to be repressive regimes in one country or another. (Very seldom--for obvious reasons--are their periodicals published in the countries they criticize.) Here is a continent-by-continent outline of periodicals of this type:

Europe.--Greece: PAK Newsletter. (Since our review was written, the military junta has been overthrown.) Northern Ireland: Civil Rights and American Committee for Ulster Justice Newsletter. (The desire to free Northern Ireland from British domination is also expressed in periodicals of the two branches of the Irish Republican Army: the Officials [see our Marxist-Socialist Left chapter] and the Provisionals.) Soviet Union: The Samizdat Bulletin. (See our Anti-Communist chapter for other periodicals opposing communist totalitarianism.)

Middle East.--The Palestinian Fedayin is concerned with discrimination against Palestinians living in Israel and the occupied territories--discrimination in jobs and education. Along with other Arab journals (placed in our Racial & Ethnic Pride chapter) it looks toward the liberation of lands lost to the Israelis.

The Americas.--Libération is in favor of Quebec separatism, and Unidad Latina wants independence for Puerto

Rico. The LAWG Letter covers Latin America as a whole, while Brazilian Information Bulletin reports on repression in one country.

Asia and the Pacific.--Philippines: Silayan. South Vietnam: Thoi-Bao Ga.

Africa.--Ethiopia: Challenge. Rhodesia: Zimbabwe News and Zimbabwe Review. South West Africa: Namibia News and Namibia Today oppose South African rule of this former German colony. Tanzania: Free Zanzibar Voice. South Africa: Afrika Must Unite, Anti-Apartheid News, Azania Combat, Azania News, Dissent, Mayibuye, SASO Newsletter, Sash, Sechaba, Southern Africa, and X-Ray. A number of periodicals support "national liberation" struggles against Portugal's rule in its African colonies: Angola, Cape Verde, and Mozambique: Afrika Must Unite, Angola in Arms, CFM News and Notes, Guerrilheiro, Mozambique Revolution, Nö Pintcha, PAIGC Actualités, Portuguese and Colonial Bulletin, and Southern Africa. (Since our reviews were written, the Portuguese government has moved toward the left and made some gestures toward ending the expensive colonial warfare.)

The remaining periodicals in the chapter cover freedom generally--throughout the world--or one aspect of it (such as intellectual freedom, or the rights of the poor). The Brief is one of the publications of the American Civil Liberties Union. Human Rights News and WDL News attempt to help servicemen, veterans, and the unemployed, while Poverty Law Report tries to provide the poor with legal protection. Freedom to Read Foundation News is published by the American Library Association's Office for Intellectual Freedom. Freedom at Issue assesses the degree of liberty in countries throughout the world.

Various ethnic, racial, social, and sexual groups seek broadened "rights" for their members: feminists, homosexuals, prisoners, Indians and Eskimos, Latinos, Asian- and Afro-Americans, and Appalachian whites. Their periodicals can be found in other chapters of this volume.

--Theodore Spahn

AFRIKA MUST UNITE: An International Journal of Current Afrikan Affairs

Arusha-Konakri Institute, Publ.
Box 17509
Chicago, Ill. 60617
$5

Format: 24 pages (8 1/4" x 10 1/2")
Issues examined: v. 2, nos. 15/17 & 17/18 [sic], 1973

This journal favors national liberation struggles in Africa, and opposes the South African regime and Portuguese colonialism.

American Committee for Ulster Justice NEWSLETTER

353 W. 57th St.
N.Y., N.Y. 10019
Monthly; free
Started: Apr. 1972
Circulation: 800
Format: 4 pages (offset)
Issues examined: Mar., Oct., Nov. 1973
Back issues available from publisher

The purpose of the ACUJ Newsletter is "to educate the American public, especially those Americans of Irish descent, to the basic injustice of the British occupation of Northern Ireland." The October issue says that the Newsletter is being published again after a seven-month absence. "Our problems, a shortage of funds and volunteers ... but we are convinced that some attempt must be made to answer the efforts of the British Information Service to paint the current struggle in Northern Ireland as a 'religious war.'"

The Newsletter contains editorials and political commentary on current affairs and politics in Ireland; a short chronicle of events ("News Summary"); an activities section which mentions books, pamphlets, radio programs on Ireland, and activities of the organization; a "Legal Notes" section which mentions trials, arrests, and legal aid groups in Ireland; and a section of "Financial Notes" (companies, corruption, loans for development, and finances in Ireland).

The Newsletter has covered such topics as the bad conditions in prisons and internment camps, torture of suspects by the British Army, collaboration between the UDA (Ulster Defense Association--a right-wing Protestant terrorist group) and the British Army, discrimination against Catholics in Northern Ireland, and the complexities of Irish politics.

(JMS)

Feedback:
Editor expressed no disapproval.

ANGOLA IN ARMS

Propaganda and Information Dep't (Delegation in Tanzania)
People's Movement for the Liberation of Angola
Box 20793
Dar es Salaam, Tanzania
Bi-monthly; $4

Started: Jan. 1967
Format: early issues: 16-24 pages (8" x 10", mimeo., stapled). Later issues: 8-22 pages (8 1/2" x 13 1/4" or 8 1/2" x 11 1/2", offset)
Issues examined: June 1970; May & Sept. 1971; Jan.-Aug. & Dec. 1972

This journal supports the struggle against "Portuguese colonialism" in Angola.

ANTI-APARTHEID NEWS: Newspaper of the Anti-Apartheid Movement

89 Charlotte St.
London W1P 2DQ, United Kingdom
Monthly; £1 (air mail £3)
Format: 12-page tabloid
Issues examined: Apr. & May 1974

AZANIA COMBAT

The Mission to Europe & The Americas
Pan Africanist Congress of Azania
22a Hillview Gardens
London NW4 2JH, United Kingdom
Format: 12-14 pages (8 1/4" x 11 3/4", mimeo., side-stapled)
Issues examined: 1973, no. 3; 1974, no. 1

Azania Combat (Motto: "Service, Sacrifice, and Suffering") opposes "South African apartheid terrorism...."

AZANIA NEWS: incorporating The Africanist

The Revolutionary Command --PAC
Box 2412
Dar es Salaam, Tanzania
Monthly; $6 (air mail $12)
Format: 20 pages (8" x 13", mimeo., stapled)
Issue examined: Dec. 1973

This Official Organ of the Pan Africanist Congress of Azania "deals in political events, which it analyzes and anticipates. It gives you the news behind the news and tries to explain universal revolutionary concepts in terms of the African Revolution in general and the political situation in Azania in particular."

## BRAZILIAN INFORMATION BULLETIN

American Friends of Brazil
Box 2279, Station A
Berkeley, Calif. 94702
Quarterly; $3 ($5 for institutions)
Started: Feb. 1971
Circulation: 2,000

Format: 20 pages (offset, saddle-stapled)
Issues examined: Jan., June, Fall 1973
Back issues available from publisher

The Brazilian Information Bulletin contains news of political repression in Brazil, a subject that is not covered adequately in other news media. Most of the articles are written in a factual, relatively non-inflammatory style and are extensively documented. Some aspects of this repression that are examined in the Bulletins are the role of foreign governments, particularly the U.S., in supporting the Brazilian military regime; the role of the Catholic Church in opposing the government; and the struggle of the Brazilian people against the repression. The development of a military-industrial complex, supported largely by U.S. resources, is seen as a way in which Brazil is being put in a "position to take over some of the policing operations for the United States in this part of the world ... whether it be suppression of left-leaning governments in Uruguay, Bolivia or Guyana or, as it did in Santo Domingo in 1965, providing troops to share in occupation of Latin American countries."

Opposition of the Catholic Church toward the Brazilian government is shown to be a strong force in several articles of one issue. "If, as it appears, the Church is now on a collision course with the government, there is little doubt who will win in the end. The government may be able to suppress a handful of left-wing 'terrorists,' but the Catholic Church has for nearly 2,000 years thrived on persecution and martyrdom, and always come out on top." Other articles have looked at the plight of the laborer since the abolition of the labor unions; Brazilian involvement in the 1973 Chilean coup; the destructive effects of censorship on the cultural life of the country; and the plight of the Brazilian Indians faced with a government whose first interests lie in land speculation, and which has converted Indian reservations--"unproductive lands"--to cattle ranches and highways.

In addition to the articles are reading lists on related topics, excerpts from relevant speeches or conferences, and reprinted letters. Some of the letters are from political prisoners offering graphic descriptions of the tortures to which they have been subjected. (SA)

Feedback:

Editor enclosed a descriptive brochure, and commented: "This is the way we state our goals--but we think you have done it better."

THE BRIEF

American Civil Liberties Union
6 S. Clark St.
Chicago, Ill. 60603
Bi-monthly

Format: broadsheet (22" x 17", folded to make 3 sections)
Issue examined: Nov. 1972

Published by the Illinois Division of the ACLU, and by the Roger Baldwin Foundation.

CFM NEWS & NOTES

Committee for a Free Mozambique
616 W. 116th St.
N.Y., N.Y. 10027

Contributions requested; postage $3
Format: 4 pages (stapled)
Issue examined: Apr. 1974

"CFM News & Notes has historically covered topics related to the activities of the Mozambique Liberation Front (FRELIMO) in fighting on military and political fronts to attain independence in Mozambique, and to the role of the United States in aiding Portuguese policy in Africa. Articles have included interviews with FRELIMO cadres; analysis of U.S. policy on such topics as the Azores; eyewitness reports on FRELIMO actions. After the Portuguese coup in April 1974, CFM has added a clipping service of articles from the press on rapidly changing developments in Africa. CFM will continue to report on the building of a new Mozambique through a FRELIMO government, independence in June 1975. Also report on projects to raise support (funds, etc.) for FRELIMO."

The description quoted above was supplied by the periodical's editor.

CHALLENGE: A Journal of the World-Wide Union of Ethiopian Students

Banti Tsehayu, Ed.
3811 Clarke St.
Oakland, Calif. 94609

Format: 40 pages (5 1/4" x 8 1/2", offset)

Issue examined: Feb. 1973

An "Editorial Note" says: "The concrete conditions in Ethiopia, viz., the country's semi-colonial and semi-feudal status, necessitate that the struggle for national liberation be based on an anti-imperialist and anti-feudalist line."

CIVIL RIGHTS

Northern Ireland Civil Rights Association
2 Marquis St.
Belfast 1, Northern Ireland
Monthly; £2
Circulation: 4,000

Format: 5 pages (8 1/4" x 11 3/4", offset)
Issues examined: Nov. 1973; Sept. 1974
Back issues available from publisher

The declared purpose of this publication is to "educate people on the necessity for movement and struggle against repression and for civil rights, democracy, and social justice." The journal explains that NICRA was set up because of the lack of democracy in Northern Ireland:

> ... despite five years of campaigning, over 1,000 deaths, tens of thousands of injuries, millions of pounds' worth of damage, intimidation, the misery suffered by large sections of our people, and undeclared martial law, successive British Governments refuse to see the writing on the wall.
>
> They will not concede that there will be no long-term end to violence until normal standards of democracy exist in this area. The whole legal basis for repression in Northern Ireland is the Emergency Provisions Act.... At present a committee ... is examining the Act to see how it can be made more democratic. NICRA has prepared a submission to this committee giving our objections to the Act and demanding that it ... be repealed ... [because it is] the cover for repression, harassment, brutality, and torture.

Civil Rights reports on many instances of civil and physical abuse perpetrated by British soldiers and the Royal Ulster Constabulary (Northern Ireland police described as a paramilitary force).

(See reviews of other Irish periodicals in our Marxist-Socialist Left chapter.)

DISSENT

National Union of South African Students
202 Film Centre,
17 Jameson St.
Cape Town, South Africa
R 3.10 for 10 issues (excluding postage)
Started: Oct. 1972

Circulation: 1,200
Format: 24 pages (7" x 9")
Issues examined: Sept./Oct. [1973?] "Experimental Edition"; Oct./Nov. 1973
Back issues available from publisher

An association of white students reports on repressive acts of the South African regime. Dissent carries theoretical articles, reviews news reports in the South African press, and acts as the Union's mouthpiece. It is also aimed at other leftist groups in South Africa and at overseas readers.

An editor explained that publication is irregular because of financial difficulties:

> You will appreciate that a group like ours who were banned from receiving finances from outside the country and who are committed to radical change within our country, are pretty short of money.... publications are sometimes not top of the priority list for absorbing our funds. For this reason, Dissent appears in a number of different forms and will in future probably appear in a very cheap format.

Feedback:
Has been incorporated into the review.

FEDAYIN: Journal de L'Association Québec-Palestine

Rezeq Faraj, Ed.
1015 Ste. Catherine East
Montreal 132, Quebec, Canada
Monthly (actually, bi-monthly); $12
Started: Mar. 1973

Circulation: 4,000
Format: 16- to 20-page tabloid
Issues examined: Sept. 1973 through Jan. 1974
Back issues available from editor

Fedayin is staffed by Palestinians and Palestinian supporters. It is "anti-imperialist, anti-Zionist and anti-Arab reaction" and "espouses the official line of the Palestinian Liberation Organization." The AQ-P aims to inform the public about Palestinian problems; support and aid Palestinians;

and combat Zionism and anti-Semitism. Fedayin stresses its lack of anti-Semitism by printing such items as a letter and poem from an "anti-Zionist Jew."

Articles emphasize that peace is possible only after the destruction of Zionism and the creation of a democratic state. Israel's Zionism is viewed as racist and expansionist and thus an impediment to peace in the Middle East. Israeli expansionism is demonstrated by maps showing Israel's gradual growth through appropriation of Arab lands since 1948. The recommended alternative to a "Zionist" state is a "democratic, non-sectarian state where Jews, Christians, Muslims and others ... can live without discrimination of race, color and religion...."

Fedayin opposes both the present (1974) cease-fire and the proposed creation of a Palestinian "mini-state." The creation of such a "mini-state" is regarded as an unsatisfactory solution because the West Bank is already overpopulated and cannot accommodate all the refugees. [See "Feedback."]

Israel's alliance with the Western powers, especially the United States, is criticized. According to Fedayin, the U.S. supports Israel because Washington considers it the "most reliable of its police in the Near East." U.S. interest in Middle-East oil and "monopolistic control of the region's economy" are also cited as reasons for its support of Israel. Statistics on "Israel's War Costs" and its receipt of U.S. aid are used to corroborate this thesis.

"Dossier" is a regular feature on the condition of Palestinians in Israel. Job discrimination against Palestinians, inferior Palestinian schools, and expropriation of Palestinian lands are denounced in various "Dossier" articles. Other regular features are editorials, an "Activitées de L'Association Québec-Palestine" section, and WAFA (reports from the Palestine News Agency). WAFA contains news briefs on Fedayin and Israeli army activities. Fedayin regularly includes short articles on pro-Palestinian demonstrations and longer articles on Arab and Palestinian conferences. Although most articles are in French, each issue contains several articles in English. (JMA)

Feedback:

The editor proposed that the preceding sentence be reworded: "The creation of such a 'mini-state' is regarded as an impediment to the realization of the expressed aims of the Palestinian people (i.e., the total liberation of Palestine) and the establishment of a democratic state."

## FREE ZANZIBAR VOICE

A. S. Kharusi, Ed.
The Zanzibar Organization
68 Hudson Rd.
Southsea, Hants., United Kingdom PO5 1HD
Monthly

Started: 1966
Circulation: 600
Format: 10-12 pages (8" x 13", mimeo., stapled)
Issues examined: Feb., Mar., May 1974

Opposes the regime of the Tanzanian president, Julius Nyerere. Reports on political repression in Tanzania and demands "the alleviation of the sufferings of the Tanzanian masses and the abolition of the Tanzania Preventive Detention Act under which thousands of innocent people are rotting in jails."

The main purpose of the organization "is to restore democratic institutions and the rule of law in Tanzania--Zanzibar in particular. The Organization has published various pamphlets on the horrible situation existing in Zanzibar, such as Zanzibar: Africa's First Cuba; Zanzibar Cries for Help; and Letters Smuggled Out of Zanzibar."

## FREEDOM AT ISSUE

20 W. 40th St.
N.Y., N.Y. 10018
Bi-monthly; $5
Started: Apr. 1970
Circulation: 6,000
Format: 24 pages (offset)

Issues examined: Jan., Sept., Nov. 1973
Indexing: in journal (irregular)
Back issues available from publisher

Leonard R. Sussman, executive director, comments that "Specialists in public affairs--human rights, academic integrity, international relations, national security, constitutionalism and related issues--discuss on our pages the impact of current and likely future events on individual freedom."

The September issue considers "the clash of concentrated power" between government and the news media and prints an article by Alexander M. Bickel on this subject, while Oscar Handlin discusses Watergate. Eugene V. Rostow's "Too Much Puritanism" concludes that U.S. domestic and foreign affairs are in better shape than we realize.

The January issue reports on the present level of freedom (civil, political, trends) around the world in both nations and territories, and concludes that the status of human rights is low in two-thirds of the world. [Feedback: "Every

January-February and July-August number updates the Comparative Survey of Freedom."] The article carried a photograph of The Map of Freedom, a 20-foot display at Freedom House in New York. (GKS)

Feedback:
Editor made a minor addition (incorporated into review) and said "O.K. as is."

FREEDOM TO READ FOUNDATION NEWS

Office for Intellectual Freedom
American Library Association
50 E. Huron St.
Chicago, Ill. 60611
Format: 4 pages (offset)
Issue examined: Fall 1973

The Foundation, started in 1969, is "the legal arm of ALA's intellectual freedom program," and has

> supported ... individual librarians in need because of their stand in support of intellectual freedom. It has prepared legal briefs to aid libraries and school systems in combatting censorship attempts. It has undertaken legal action ... to have the California Harmful Matter Statute declared unconstitutional.... The most recent action ... was its petition ... for a rehearing of the U.S. Supreme Court's ominous ... decisions on obscenity.

FTRF News covers the activities of the Foundation.

GUERRILHEIRO

Bulletin of the Committee for Freedom in Mozambique, Angola, and Guiné
Top Floor, 12 Little Newport St.
London W.C.2, United Kingdom
Bi-monthly; 50p (£1 overseas)
Started: 1970
Circulation: 1,550
Format: 12-20 pages (dimensions quite variable)
Issues examined: Jan., Mar., July 1972; Feb., June, Oct. 1973

Reports on political repression in Portugal and its African colonies. Attacks relations between British (and other) capitalists and Portuguese colonialists, and accuses the former of employing slave labor.

Feedback:

"Reports on the progress of the liberation struggle in Portugal's African colonies--the policies of the liberation movements; related developments in Portugal; the role of Britain and the West in collaborating with colonialism and racism in Southern Africa, and the interests of Western imperialism in the area."

HUMAN RIGHTS NEWS; WDL NEWS

Alfred Russel, Exec. Dir.
Workers' Defense League & Fund for Human Rights
150 Fifth Ave. (Rm. 437)
N.Y., N.Y. 10011
5-6 times per year; free
Started: WDL News-1936; Human Rights News-1969
Circulation: 6,000
Format: HRN 4-8 pages (offset, 8 1/2" x 11" or legal size); WDLN 2-4 pages (same sizes)
Issues examined: WDL News-Dec. 1970; Sept. 1972; Nov. & Dec. 1973; Human Rights News-Nov. 1972; May & Sept. 1973
Back issues available from publisher

Human Rights News, published by the Fund for Human Rights, and WDL News, published by the Workers' Defense League, are related publications, both having the same executive director and the same principles. The principles of both newsletters are to "defend the poor and those who suffer discrimination" and to "protect first amendment rights." An allusion to "the memory of Norman Thomas who made 112 East 19th Street a memorable place" suggests that the papers are socialist, perhaps related to the Socialist Party. However, the two groups are self-avowedly non-partisan in their willingness to defend "those who would otherwise be defenseless because of their economic, nationality, color or minority status...."

Both newsletters contain "reports of activities of WDL and FHR," specifically, examples of legal defense provided to servicemen and workers. While Human Rights News reports exclusively on servicemen's cases, WDL News reports cases in the "area of workers' rights, GI rights, and immigration." A sample case involved a Vietnam veteran with psychiatric problems. The army is represented as unconcerned with such problems and "trying to cover up for its lack of true concern, by allotting him [the veteran] time in the psychiatric ward." Each such article includes the issues of the case; legal action taken; results obtained; and occasional comments on political implications of the case. The

September 1972 issue of WDL News was devoted entirely to unemployment insurance--legitimate but disqualified claims and recent benefit cuts. (JMA)

Feedback:

"WDL & FHR, while deriving from a Socialist background, are non-partisan human rights organizations. WDL specializes in helping unemployment insurance claimants; FHR specializes in helping servicemen and veterans. Neither has a political affiliation. WDL News and HR News are newsletters reporting on activities of each organization. Your report seems fair to me.

"P.S.: WDL archives are at Reuther Library of Wayne State University, Detroit, Mich."

LAWG LETTER

Latin American Working Group
Box 6300, Station A
Toronto, Ontario, Canada
Bi-monthly; $3
Started: Jan. 1973

Circulation: 500-700
Format: 16 pages plus 5 page insert (mimeo.)
Issue examined: Mar. 1974
Back issues available from publisher

The sample issue contained this explanation and description:

> The LAWG Letter is the result of the coming together of our recent newsletters on Chile and previous LAWG initiatives to provide current information and analysis on the Latin American Reality. This new format will allow us to continue to give as much coverage on the struggle in Chile while resuming the coverage of other Latin American nations as in the former LAWG Newsletter.
>
> The new format, which we hope to continue, contains news briefs, analysis, calls for action/support, book reviews, and other items relevant to the advancement of the liberation of the peoples of Latin America. Some of the material we have produced ourselves; other items are reprints that would not likely be available to our readership. Both Latins and Canadians are preparing the material for the LAWG Letter, examining the Latin American reality and aspects of Canadian involvement in that reality.
>
> Two items [articles entitled 'Argentina--One Year

Later' and 'Panama'] of analysis ... reflect our concern at this time to highlight the internal contradictions and imperialist influences that these nations are now experiencing. While the article, 'On Their Way,' deals with the acceptance into Canada of political refugees from Chile (and the associated issues and struggles), the following article ['Chile--A Return to Free Enterprise'] deals with the internal economic contradictions within Chile that pose a situation of repression as brutal as that of the tortures, arrests and executions of the last months.

Because the Canadian press, reliant on foreign news sources, virtually ignores the nations of Latin America, or distorts that which it does record, we have included a sizeable section of 'news briefs'--short pieces of information to keep people up-to-date on the changing events in the various countries....

The publication was illustrated with drawings and cartoons.

Feedback:
Editor expressed no disapproval.

LIBÉRATION

Box 641, Succ. N
Montreal, P.Q., Canada
H2X 3M6
Monthly; $3
Started: Apr. 1971

Circulation: 6,000
Format: 12-page tabloid (offset)
Issues examined: Oct. & Nov. 1973 (and Oct. Special issue)

This French-language newspaper supports a variety of causes. In the words of its editor, it is "devoted to encouraging the independent organisation, mobilisation, and struggles of the oppressed masses in the fight for independence of Quebec, socialism, women's liberation, trade-union rights, and working-class internationalism and political action." News of international interest appears regularly: Israeli aggression against the Arabs was deplored, and a parallel was drawn between this aggression and that of the Canadian government against the people of Quebec. The coup in Chile (which overthrew the elected Marxist government of Dr. Salvador Allende) was given extensive coverage. Most of the articles, however, pertain to Canadian affairs--in particular, political struggles in Quebec. Matters of concern to the readers and contributors of Libération were issues at stake in the 1973 elections: complete and immediate independence for Quebec, with French the primary language in schools and workplaces; workers' right to strike; and the legalization of abortion. These points were on the platform of the Ligue Socialiste Ouvrière, the party supported by Libération.

The oppression from which French-speaking Quebecois suffer extends into many areas of their lives. One article illuminated the problems faced by French-speaking prisoners in the Kingston penitentiary. Members of the staff speak only English, and the prisoners may not listen to French-language radio or television stations. Unlike the English prisoners, the French cannot obtain day passes that would permit them to work in Kingston. (SA)

## MAYIBUYE

African National Congress of South Africa
Box 1791
Lusaka, Zambia
Weekly

Started: 1967
Format: 16 pages (8" x 10", mimeo., side-stapled)
Issue examined: 17 June 1968

Mayibuye is the bulletin of the African National Congress of South Africa. The Congress, founded in 1912, is a "broad national liberation movement, a political organization in whose ranks are found men of different philosophical outlooks, social strata and religious beliefs: Catholics, protestants of various denominations, non-believers, communists and capitalists." The policy of the African National Congress (ANC) is one of active, as opposed to passive, non-violence. A bitter rivalry exists between the ANC and the Pan-Africanist Congress (PAC). PAC accused the ANC of being communist-dominated and rejects its policy of cooperating with other racial minorities. At the ANC 1949 Annual National Conference, a program was adopted that called for such "methods of struggle" as strikes, boycotts, civil disobedience and "non-cooperation." Because it is suppressed by the South African government, the ANC has been forced to operate underground, using Zambia and Tanzania as bases.

Great Power Conspiracy, an ANC pamphlet, accuses Britain, France and the United States of having "actively striven to maintain and strengthen white minority rule in Southern Africa" because of extensive foreign investments there. The "neo-Nazi revival of old links between West Germany and South Africa" is also criticized, whereas East Germany is praised for its support of the liberation movement through its Afro-Asian Solidarity Committee.

A Mayibuye article, "Rumblings among the Racists," examines the split within the "ranks of the oppressors," the Verligtes advocating an assertive foreign policy and the Verkamptes being isolationist. An article on the Luangwa Bridge "tragedy" condemns terrorist activity as an enemy tactic used to "turn Zambians against the Freedom Fighters." Another article caustically examines Western social scientists' interest in South Africa's "unique experiment of separate development" by comparing this scientific interest in apartheid to the Nazi's "scientific" interest in conducting experiments on humans. "PAC Splits" criticizes the Pan-Africanist Congress for its inconsistency and its attempt to exploit the Sharpeville massacre. "News from the Front" reports on guerrilla activities of the "ZAPU-ANC forces," and on policies of the opposition armies.

"White supremacy rule," "imperialist aggression," "capitalist greed" and "fascists" are frequently denounced in the bulletin. Articles are characterized by critiques of apartheid supporters and documentation of apartheid's damaging effects on Africans. (JMA)

Feedback:

A. Nzo, Secretary-General of the African National Congress (South Africa), replied:

> We regret to inform you that ... Mayibuye is now defunct primarily because of financial difficulties. We would advise you to review our monthly organ, Sechaba ('Nation'), published since 1967, whose editor is Mr. M. P. Naicker, 49 Rathbone St., London W1A 4NL, United Kingdom.... [See pp. 530-31 of volume II.] In connection with your remarks on the contents of Mayibuye and your interpretation of our policy, we would like to make comments and corrections. In the late 1960s, the ANC policy was not 'one of active, as opposed to passive, non-violence,' as you state. On 16 December 1967 a military wing of the ANC, Umkhonto We Sizwe, was formed and began military operations in Zimbabwe in alliance with our Zapu comrades. The ANC's policy today is that of an all-round preparation for armed confrontation with the enemy. Even the 'bitter rivalry' which --according to your review--exists between the ANC and PAC is an exaggeration. What actually happened is that in 1958 a disgruntled clique broke away from our movement to form the PAC. They differed with the policy of our movement. They did have some

support at the beginning, but today they are not significant at all (at least not inside South Africa). Your contention that the ANC is 'using Zambia and Tanzania as bases' is inaccurate. Our strength and base are the people at home. On the whole we find your review favourable and it is in this spirit that we make these critical remarks.

(See review of Sechaba in this chapter.)

## MOZAMBIQUE REVOLUTION

Department of Information
Mozambique Liberation Front
Box 15274
Dar es Salaam, Tanzania
Bi-monthly?
Format: 24 pages (8 1/2" x 10 1/2")

Issues examined: July & Oct. 1973; Canadian reprints of Jan. & Oct. 1973
reprinted & distributed by:
Liberation Support Movement Information Center
Box 94338
Richmond, B. C., Canada
V6Y 2A8

The July issue contains an editorial which emphasizes "the reasons for the confidence with which FRELIMO [Frente de Libertação de Moçambique] militants and the Mozambique people as a whole are facing this tenth year of armed struggle." The same issue carries a feature article analysing FRELIMO's political, military, and diplomatic achievements of the past year. Other articles cover details of military operations in Mozambique; eye-witness accounts of a massacre; impressions of visits to liberated areas by foreign journalists and film-makers; and youth festivals (in Tunis and East Berlin) in which FRELIMO's youth participated. One article complains that "So long as the ruling Social Democratic Party of Federal Germany does not take an unequivocally clear stand against Portuguese colonialism, FRELIMO will not be able to establish relations of cooperation with it," and another article hails the proclamation of the Republic of Guinea-Bissau, "a further success in our common struggle."
(JMS)

## NAMIBIA NEWS

South West Africa People's Organisation [SWAPO] of Namibia

21/25 Tabernacle St.
London EC2, United Kingdom
Bi-monthly; £2 (airmail £4)

Started: 1968
Circulation: 3,500
Format: 12-16 pages (8" x 11 3/4")
Issues examined: Jan., Sept., Nov. 1973

Namibia News, journal of SWAPO, "calls for South Africa's complete withdrawal from Namibia and an end to South Africa's military occupation of the territory, which is in defiance of UN resolutions and the World Court."

Subscriptions are also available from LSM Information Center, Box 94338, Richmond, British Columbia, Canada.

NAMIBIA TODAY

South West Africa People's Organization [SWAPO] of Namibia
Box 577
Lusaka, Zambia
Format: 20 pages (8 1/2" x 10")
Issue examined: Nov. 1973

This official organ of SWAPO opposes the South African regime and demands a free and independent Namibia (formerly German South West Africa).

NÖ PINTCHA

Partido Africano da Independência da Guiné e Cabo Verde (PAIGC)
Box M365
New Bedford, Mass. 02744
Format: 18-26 pages (mimeo.; side-stapled)
Issues examined: Feb. & Apr. 1974

Opposes Portuguese colonialism.

PAIGC ACTUALITÉS: Bulletin d'Information Edité par la Commission d'Information et Propaganda du Comité Central du Partido Africano da Independência da Guiné e Cabo Verde

Box 298, Conakry, Guinea and Box 2.319, Dakar, Senegal
Monthly
Format: 16 pages (stapled)
Issues examined: No. 51 (Mar. & Special Apr.-Aug. 1973 ed.)

This periodical opposes Portuguese colonialism and reports on "La vie et la lutte en Guinée et Cap Vert." The edited quarterly English translation costs $3 and is issued by the LSM Information Center, Box 94338, Richmond, B.C., Canada V6Y 2A8. (We examined only the translated edition.)

## PAK NEWSLETTER

Panhellenic Liberation Movement
Box 594, Station Q
Toronto 7, Ont., Canada
Monthly; $3
Started: Feb. 1972
Circulation: 2,000

Format: 14-16 pages (offset printing, stapled)
Issues examined: Feb., July, Aug., Nov., Dec. 1973
Back issues available from publisher

PAK Newsletter carries the views of a group which is "dedicated to the overthrow of the Greek dictatorship and the establishment of a democratic, free, independent, and socialist Greece. In a broader context it is part of the anti-imperialist struggle in the world today. We support liberation movements which are part of that struggle."

Andreas Papandreou, ex-economic minister of Greece and son of the late prime minister, George Papandreou, seems to be the most prominent leader in the PAK movement and his words are often quoted in the Newsletter. In the July issue he urged the Greek people not to vote in the junta's referendum, but to invalidate their ballots as an act of defiance. The August issue reprinted an introduction by Papandreou to Prince Norodom Sihanouk's book, My War With the CIA--an introduction that was dropped from the American edition published by Pantheon. In it Papandreou draws parallels between the American imperialist subversion of his country and that of Cambodia:

> The goal in all instances is clear. It is the complete economic, political, cultural, and military subjugation of a country to the interests, economic and military, of U.S. imperialism.... We too in Greece have reached the same conclusion as Prince Sihanouk and the Cambodian people [that armed struggle is the only road to freedom against imperialism]. And for this reason we have forged the Panhellenic Liberation Movement.... [T]he nations that have fallen prey to aggressive American imperialism must coordinate their actions on a global basis.

In the November issue (before the toppling of dictator

Papadopoulos) Papandreou said there exist no possibilities for development toward a democratic government within the framework of the 1968-73 constitution:

> The U.S., after six and a half years of military dictatorship in Greece [the PAK movement looks upon the military regime as an American occupation of Greece], managed to draft a constitution which subjugates the state officially and constitutionally to the Army, which in itself is controlled by them--so that the armed forces and not the people govern. The Army belongs to the U.S. Pentagon and Greece is under 'lawful' occupation. Second, the permanent policing of the political life of Greece by the judicial junta becomes institutionalized. There can be parties and there can be candidates only by the grace of the judicial junta.... elected deputies and even members of the cabinet can be thrown out of office when the judicial junta decides.

Papandreou predicted the imminent collapse of the Papadopoulos regime, and the November and December issues are full of news of the student uprising which began with a memorial service for George Papandreou in Athens and culminated in a fatal confrontation between students and tanks at the Polytechnical School. (The December issue contains a dramatic chronicle of that day's events reprinted from a confiscated Greek newspaper.)

The Newsletter also contains news of Greek political prisoners (one issue carried a list of such prisoners, told where they are being held, and urged people to help them and their families) and accounts of political trials; letters or reports from inside Greece (one such letter described the rigging of elections); and interviews with Greek patriots who have escaped the country. One such patriot is Pericles Korovessis, whose The Method emphasized the American training and techniques of his torturers. Korovessis presented testimony before the Council of Europe which led to Greece's expulsion from that body. In an interview, he describes Greek socialism: "We must be prepared for a new movement of the masses.... The only need now is to work among the mass of people to construct groups prepared to carry out a socialist revolution." Greek socialists "are not so much interested in finding models of revolution elsewhere as developing one of their own.... what we seem to be doing is learning from all these experiences, from Vietnam and Korea and even from the early period of the Soviet Union.... I see

Greek socialism as something quite beautiful.... every idea and tendency is allowed to contend because you are not afraid that you seek what is not correct."

An interesting development in PAK is a women's liberation movement which surfaced early in 1973 at the PAK seminar in Würzburg, Germany, where a document originating from the Women's Section, Central Committee, Friends of PAK was circulated. The Greek woman is fighting not only for a new socialist and democratic Greece but "for a Greece where there will be financial and social equality between men and women. She is fighting for a Greece that will not make it necessary for the village girl to go to the textile mills.... to live alone in the basement, to fulfill first the.... needs of her employer, in order to earn money for a dowry to buy her husband"; and she will stop "being considered an inferior subject necessary only for bed, kitchen, and hanging up the clothes."

Another liberation struggle with which PAK feels solidarity is the nationalist movement in Portuguese Guinea, and the February issue pays tribute to a leader of that movement, Amilcar Cabral, who was assassinated by Portuguese Colonial Army soldiers.

The Newsletter is sparsely illustrated with drawings, cartoons and poorly reproduced photographs from (primarily Greek) newspapers. (JMS)

Feedback:

"We find it an excellent sum-up of the spirit of our journal, as well as its content." The spokeswoman added: "It is possibly the only bulletin on the Left published in North America with European news and analysis."

## PORTUGUESE AND COLONIAL BULLETIN

Quarterly; £1. 50
Dates: Feb. 1961 to Oct. 1974 (65 issues)
Format: 10 pages (8 1/2" x 10 3/4")
Issues examined: Oct. 1973; Jan. & Apr. 1974
Back issues available from publisher

This periodical opposed Portuguese colonialism [Feedback: "and fascism"]. Its address was: K. Shingler, Publ., 10 Fentiman Rd., London S. W. 8, United Kingdom.

Feedback:

"The Bulletin was the regular publication written in

English which ... fully and comprehensively covered political events in Portugal, and to a certain extent in the Portuguese colonies, too, during the period 1961-74: that is, until the overthrow of the fascist regime in Portugal on 25 April 1974."

## POVERTY LAW REPORT

119 S. McDonough St.
Montgomery, Ala. 36101
Quarterly; free
Started: Jan. 1973
Circulation: 48,000
Format: 4-page tabloid
(offset)
Issues examined: Mar. & June 1973; Jan. & Feb. 1974
Indexing: in journal
Back issues available from publisher

Poverty Law Report is published by the Southern Poverty Law Center which was established to provide legal protection for the poor, especially blacks, and to fight laws that discriminate against blacks and poor whites. The purpose of the newsletter is to serve as a "clearing house of news on all aspects of the new civil rights movement." In an editorial, the "new civil rights movement" is defined as "the fight for equal rights for America's poor."

Most articles deal with specific civil rights cases taken on by the Southern Poverty Law Center. One case concerns three black men believed to be unjustly convicted of raping a white woman. Although the article proclaims the innocence of the defendants, its major emphasis is on the injustice of capital punishment. An editorial on the same topic demonstrates the racial and economic discrimination of capital punishment insofar as most of those sentenced to death are blacks, and "all of them poor." Other laws, such as the summary seizure statute, are also criticized for their discrimination against the poor.

The Center is also involved in combatting segregation. One article reports on the hardships experienced by black children who are denied admission to white orphanages and thus sent to reform schools. Other articles describe the Center's efforts to fight discriminatory hiring practices by the State of Alabama and by federal government departments in Alabama.

Occasional articles discuss issues of interest to women. An article on the Frontiero v. Richardson case shows how the Frontiero decision was an important gain in women's rights because it requires that dependency benefits cannot be justified by a "sex-related presumption." An article on the U.S. Supreme Court's abortion decision debates the relevance of the decision for poor women who may still be unable to afford abortions. "Free abortion on demand" is proposed as a solution to the problem of poor women.

Julian Bond, president of the Southern Poverty Law Center, has an editorial column in the paper. He advocates reapportionment and voter education as a means of electing more responsible representatives who will be interested in the problems of the poor. "The Docket," another regular feature, gives the current status of some of the Center's cases. (JMA)

## SASO NEWSLETTER

South African Students' Organisation
86 Beatrice St.
Box 2346
Durban, South Africa

Bi-monthly; 20¢ an issue
Format: 20 pages (7 1/4" x 9 1/2")
Issues examined: Mar., Sept., Nov. 1972

The Newsletter reports on the state of education for black Africans in the Republic of South Africa, whose authorities don't provide adequate facilities. The result is a "looming crisis in black education." The November issue reports on (and has photographs of) harassment of the Newsletter's vendors by the police.

A Black Students' Manifesto printed in each issue makes these points (among others): the white world is "arrogant," and has no business telling blacks how to behave; the black community is oppressed, and should be liberated; its students presently receive a "racist education," but should strive to the best of their ability to serve their community, search for "black truth," and "encourage and promote black literature relevant to our struggle."

## THE SAMIZDAT BULLETIN

Box 6128
San Mateo, Calif. 94403
Monthly; $8
Started: May 1973
Circulation: 164
Format: mimeographed articles (18-24 pages) are stapled separately and collected in a folder
Issues examined: Oct.-Dec. 1973
Back issues available from publisher

"The Samizdat Bulletin contains extracts from the Free

Press in the U. S. S. R. Until today, the publication of these documents in the English language either was not available, or was obtainable only in the form of brief, fragmentary quotations [with the exception of the Chronicle of Current Events]. The aim of our Bulletin is to acquaint the English-speaking reader with the ideas and direct course of free thought in the Soviet Union." The Bulletin is prepared and distributed by private individuals in a limited printing without profit, and its distribution depends on the support of the readers. Open to all Samizdat publications in the republics of the Soviet Union, the editors do not discriminate in their choice of texts, and materials are presented without comments except for a few explanatory notes.

What is "samizdat?" An introductory article (reprinted from the British magazine Encounter) by a Russian Jewish émigré once active in Moscow samizdat and Human Rights circles, explains that the word originally came from a longer word meaning "publishing house for oneself" and is applied to texts produced unofficially which circulate through unofficial channels. A free, uncensored literature. "Today many people 'publish' themselves and others--in typescript, for instance. There are many 'self-publishing houses' but there is only one name for them all--SAMIZDAT. And all output from this SAMIZDAT is also called samizdat." "Readers of samizdat are not exactly spoiled by typographical luxury. Frequently, they have to read barely legible tenth-carbon copies, typed in single spacing, when one or two letters of the typewriter were not articulating into the bargain."

This Russian underground literature consists of fiction; plays; poetry; songs (sometimes on tape); pieces of research and articles; private correspondence; open letters and appeals; accounts (or stenographic records) of trials (and the defendants' final statements), meetings, denunciations, brainwashing sessions, and interrogations; records of compulsory hospitalization and discussions on psychiatry; accounts of arrests and roundups and demonstrations; reportage from prisons, labor camps, and asylums; regular information bulletins such as the Chronicle of Current Events (which records violations of human rights in the USSR and comes out bi-monthly with new samizdat material and gives brief summaries of it in the section "Samizdat News" [see Feedback.]); biographies and "service records" of the executioners and biographies of their victims; official documents; lists of cuts made by the censor in official publications; etc. Some of this samizdat finds its way out of Russia by being passed to foreign tourists and is delivered to certain groups or publishing houses such as Possev in West Germany.

The October 1973 issue, which appeared as six items (some only a page long), contained the alarming article (first published by Possev in longer form), "Who Needs War With China?" It describes the military and psychological preparations that the USSR is making for war with China:

> The Soviet rulers are confident that now is the most favorable moment to eliminate once and for all a truly dangerous and, so far, not too strong enemy. Strictly from a military point of view, setting aside all other considerations, this is true. They are preparing a surprise onslaught while they have the superiority in the field of nuclear weapons.

The December 1973 issue is composed of four items, three of them only a page or two in length. The fourth is a long article, "Soviet Court Procedures as Seen by a Lawyer," which describes the almost total lack of justice under the Soviet judicial system. As for judges, "the history of the Soviet elections can not cite a single instance of a failure of even a most unpopular candidate. Everything and everyone there is elected with a 99.98% margin.... as far as the jurors are concerned, they do not participate in the judicial process at all. It's not by chance that they are called 'stage props'" and "The defense attorney knows in advance that he cannot really help the defendant any more than a corpse can be helped by a heating pad, but he must earn his fee (the services of defense attorneys in the USSR are compensated by the state)...." "It is well known that for an identical misdeed a nonparty member is hauled before the court, whereas a member of the Communist Party ... gets off with a reprimand...." "Although the Soviet press systematically trumpets about the growth of crime rate in capitalist countries, the crime rate in the Soviet Union is probably one of the highest in the world. Crime statistics do not get published."

As an example of the equality of Soviet citizens before the law, the article describes the case of violinist David Oistrakh, Lenin Prize laureate, whose apartment was robbed of valuables estimated at more than half a million rubles. "It should be noted that although the amount of gold and currency owned illegally by Oistrakh was only slightly smaller than that possessed by Rokotov, the latter was executed, whereas no one even thought of prosecuting Oistrakh." Another case is that of the manager of the Sverdlovsk Railway Restaurant, citizen Vorobiev, who was executed by a firing squad. "His only trespass was that for a number of years his restaurant was selling meat pies with a margarine content that was one gram below the prescribed norm. Although no customers had ever complained about the meat pies, Vorobiev was sentenced to death on the grounds that over the period of ten years of his activity he had absconded with 15,000 rubles' worth of margarine belonging to the state."

"In political trials the verdict is rendered essentially at the time of the arrest.... officially, political trials are conducted by senior prosecutors of the district, but actually everything has been prepared, prearranged, and falsified by the officials of the KGB."

Other items that have appeared in the Bulletin are "Copyright in the USSR" (one of the effects of which will be to prevent the publication abroad of nonconformist writers); "An Open Letter in Defense of Academician Sakharov"; "A Letter to the Politburo of the Central Committee of the Communist Party" from a group of Soviet Jews badly treated by the government for attempting to emigrate to Israel; "Effects of Moiseyev's Martyrdom" (reprinted from Cahiers de Samizdat which is published in Belgium), letters received by the family of Ivan Moiseyev, a young man tortured to death for his Christian beliefs, who since has become a Russian samizdat hero; "Adrian Tarasov," biography of a young non-conformist student sentenced to hard labor and never heard from again; and "A. I. Solzhenitsyn--To the Minister of Internal Affairs of the USSR" on the subject of joining his wife and children in Moscow, which he did in spite of being denied permission to do so.

The Bulletin occasionally reprints documents that have appeared in recent publications of the Committee on the Judiciary of the United States Senate. (JMS)

Feedback:

"... very well written." The spokeswoman explained that Chronicle of Current Events first appeared in 1968; was suppressed by the KGB in 1972; and resumed publication after an interval of 18 months.

SASH: The Black Sash Magazine

| | |
|---|---|
| 501 Lestar House, 58 Marshall St., Marshalltown | Format: 34-38 pages (5 1/2" x 8 1/2"; old format 7 1/4" x 9 1/4") |
| Johannesburg, South Africa | Issues examined: Nov. 1972; Feb., May, Nov. 1973; Feb. 1974 |
| Quarterly; R1.60 | |
| Circulation: 2,250 | |

Indexing: in the journal

Back issues available from publisher

The Black Sash is an organization of liberal white South African women who protest the repressive acts of the regime and are "striving for justice and morality in Government." Its periodical reports on "banning" and other such acts, and on the organization's protests. "Particular emphasis is given to the pass laws, the migrant labour system and the work of the Black Sash Advice offices in urban centers of the republic."

Feedback:
Has been incorporated into the review.

SECHABA: Official Organ of the African National Congress, South Africa

49 Rathbone St.
London W1A 4NL, United Kingdom
Monthly; $12 (air mail) to U.S. and Canada
Started: Jan. 1967

Circulation: 25,000
Format: 24 pages (8" x 11 1/2")
Issues examined: Jan.-Apr. 1974

Opposes the South African regime and "racism in general; analyzes the economic and political situation in South Africa. Regularly features events inside South Africa and espouses the non-racial cause of the African National Congress of South Africa."

See our review of the same organization's now-defunct periodical, Mayibuye, elsewhere in this chapter.

Feedback:
Incorporated into the preceding sentences.

SILAYAN

Catherine Tactaquin, Ed.
c/o NCRCLP, Box 26108
San Francisco, Calif. 94126
Monthly; $5

Started: 15 July 1973
Format: 32 pages (offset)
Issue examined: 15 July 1973

Silayan is the official newsmagazine of the National Committee for the Restoration of Civil Liberties in the Philippines. An editorial states the magazine's policies:

> One cannot justify journalistic support for the Manila government with 'objectivity' or the desire to present both sides. We must cull through reports of the government-controlled media there to get at the truth, and not print wholesale blatant distortions.

Further editorial comments state:

> We believe that one day those who keep the Philippines in darkness will be swept away by the irresistible tide of history ... that one day freedom of the press, civil liberties, and democracy will be established in the Philippines.

"The Defection of Consul Baliao" is about a Filipino diplomat who defected from the Philippine Foreign Service because (as he put it in a letter to his superiors) "I cannot in good conscience continue serving your administration which is dedicated to the perpetuation of President Marcos's despotic rule and the continued suppression of our people's civil liberties."

In the article, "Repression in the Philippines," Sen. Alan Cranston (D., Calif.) blasts the martial law regime in the Philippines. (The article is a summary of a speech he delivered on the floor of the U.S. Senate.)

A list of 110 persons blacklisted by the Marcos regime is published. In the opinion of Silayan, "the immediate intent of the blacklisting is to intimidate and silence those who have actively opposed the Marcos dictatorship." "Philippine Constabulary Tortures Woman Activist to Death" details the end of a 21-year-old who had--before the imposition of martial law--been editor of a school newspaper.

Other features of the maiden issue: notes on cultural activities in the Bay Area; a patriotic song (words in Tagalog and English); and cartoons making fun of the Marcos dictatorship. (DB)

## SOUTHERN AFRICA

New York Southern Africa Committee
244 W. 27th St. (5th floor)
N.Y., N.Y. 10001
11 issues a year; $5 (institutions $15)
Format: 36 pages (7 3/4" x 10" or 8" x 10 1/2")
Issues examined: Mar., May, June 1974

This periodical reports on: national liberation struggles,

including the fight against Portuguese colonialism; political repression in South Africa; student unrest; and the relationships between the South African regime and U.S. politicians and capitalists.

Feedback:

"Each issue looks at current events in Namibia, Zimbabwe, South Africa, the former Portuguese territories of Mozambique and Guinea-Bissau, Angola, the United Nations and Southern Africa, [and] activism in the U.S. and internationally. Features include reprints, eyewitness report, political analysis."

THOI-BAO GA

Vietnam Resource Center
76a Pleasant St.
Cambridge, Mass. 02139
Monthly; $5 (institutions $10)

Format: 16 pages (offset)
Issue examined: May/June 1974 (double issue)

This newsletter "draws upon Vietnamese-language sources to present short analytic articles on current aspects of the struggle in Vietnam. Much of what appears in its pages is translated nowhere else." The Center (which has been publishing material since 1968) is staffed by Vietnamese students in the United States whose political feelings are expressed in the following quotation:

> The struggle in Vietnam is far from over, American interference in the country is far from ended, the movement here and now to bring an end to the U.S. role must continue. The aggressive policies of the U.S. government and the Thieu regime have not been significantly decreased since the signing of the Paris agreements, but the U.S. Congress continues to vote aid for Thieu. It is essential that the people of this country, and members of Congress, clearly understand that any and all aid for the Thieu regime is money that will be used to prolong the fighting and increase the sufferings of the Vietnamese people. Until Thieu releases the political prisoners, allows the refugees to return to their homes, and carries out other provisions of the Paris accords, continued U.S. aid for the Thieu dictatorship serves only to encourage him to continue his oppression against the people of Vietnam, and very possibly provoke a full-scale Third Indochina War.

UNIDAD LATINA

Bi-weekly; $6
Dates: Mar. 1971 to 22 Dec. 1973
Circulation: 4,000
Format: 16-page tabloid (offset)
Issues examined: 30 Jan., 17 Mar., 1 July-20 Oct., 27 Oct.-22 Dec. 1973

This bi-lingual periodical began publication as the newspaper of El Comite (The Committee), which calls itself a Leftist National Puerto Rican Movement whose goal is the liberation of Puerto Rico. The "political growth of ... El Comite is closely related to one of the major problems affecting the Puerto Rican people and the poor in general in this society: the lack of decent housing."

Unidad Latina (Latin Unity) reported world and local news in light of "the relationships between rich-poor, oppressor-oppressed, whites and the Third World." Emphasis was largely political, as reflected in such articles as "Watergate --Comments," "Haitian Refugees Persecuted," "Who Rules Puerto Rico?" and "Chile in Crisis." Historical political essays were presented in a series of articles which included "Middle East: Historical Development" and "Development of Class Struggle in Spain."

Articles entitled "Inflation and Cost of Living" and "Copper Mines and Economic Exploitation in Puerto Rico" reflected economic issues, while "Comstock Prison," "Walkout at Ford: Workers Protest Work Conditions," and Indians at "Wounded Knee" concerned issues of human rights.

Unidad Latina ceased publication "temporarily" with a 22 December 1973 Supplement in which El Comite stated: "We arrived at the point in which the discrepancies between methods of work and political positions led to crisis...." The paper's address had been: 577 Columbus Ave., N.Y., N.Y. 10024. (MH)

X-RAY: Current Affairs in Southern Africa

The Africa Bureau
48 Grafton Way
London W.1, United Kingdom
Bi-monthly; free in England; £2 overseas
Started: 1970
Circulation: 4,000
Format: 4 pages (8 1/4" x 11 3/4")
Issues examined: Jan., Mar.-May 1974

The publication covers guerrilla war in Rhodesia;

foreign investments in South Africa; French arms to South Africa; African wages; food shortages; repressive actions of the South African regime, etc. Articles are footnoted (sources often South African newspapers) and filled with figures on, e.g., wages.

Each issue of X-Ray is accompanied by a numbered issue of another serial: either Africa Bureau Fact Sheet (one sheet, 8 1/4" x 11 3/4") or Africa Bureau Document Paper (one sheet, 8 1/4" x 11 3/4").

## ZIMBABWE NEWS

| | |
|---|---|
| Publicity and Information Services | \$6 U.S. and Canada (air mail \$12) |
| Zimbabwe African National Union | Format: 22-26 pages (7 1/2" x 10 1/2") |
| Box 2331 | Issues examined: Feb.-Mar. 1974 |
| Lusaka, Zambia | |

The masthead announces "Forward with the Revolution" and "Let Us Liberate and Rebuild Zimbabwe." (The present name for Zimbabwe is Rhodesia.) Each issue carries this information about the publication:

> Zimbabwe News gives up-to-date and accurate information on the guerrilla struggle in Zimbabwe in particular and Southern Africa in general. A subscription to Zimbabwe News not only covers Zimbabwe News airmailed to you every month, but also special brochures, press releases, policy statements, and war communiques issued from time to time.

The periodical also gives information (time, band, etc.) on "Voice of Revolution" broadcasts.

## ZIMBABWE REVIEW

| | |
|---|---|
| Box 1657 | Format: 10 pages (8 1/4" x 11 3/4", mimeo., stapled) |
| Lusaka, Zambia | Issue examined: 29 June 1974 |
| Quarterly; 5 ngwee an issue | |

This publication is the "Official Organ of the Zimbabwe African People's Union [ZAPU], Rhodesia." It opposes the Rhodesian regime and gives news of other liberation struggles in Africa.

A quarterly Canadian edition (of which we examined two undated 1974 issues) is available for $3 from LSM Information Center, Box 94338, Richmond, B. C., Canada V6Y 2A8. It is 16-26 pages in length.

## Chapter 12

# PRISONS

> We wash our faces in the toilets, there are roaches in the food, and there are homosexual attacks on inmates while the guards look on for sport.... You are robbing us of our humanity, our human rights.
>
> ---*The Freeworld Times*

> We see the prison movement as part of that worldwide fight of people for freedom from imperialist domination....
>
> ---*Midnight Special*

The prison periodical is a recent addition to the political and civil rights scene. Often produced by a combination of ex-prisoners and concerned citizens, it describes the brutality and bad living conditions that obtain in many American prisons, and urges reforms. As *Outmates* expresses it, the existing penal system is "an abettor of recidivism" and "a creator of criminals rather than a deterrent to crime" or "initiator of rehabilitative efforts." The now-defunct *Freeworld Times* offered straight news of prison conditions around the country and contained serious analyses of our penal system and of strategies for change.

These periodicals might have been placed in our Civil Rights chapter, inasmuch as they are concerned with rights: not only the right to humanitarian treatment and hygienic living conditions, but also the right to adequate legal counsel and to rehabilitation through various training programs. Many of the periodicals pay some attention to the legal aspects of the criminal justice system, and the *Prison Law Reporter* is devoted entirely to legal developments in the correctional field.

As might be expected, these periodicals are against capital punishment, long periods of solitary confinement (which they see as mind-destroying), and psychosurgery. There is a tendency on the part of some (such as *Midnight Special*) to view inmates as "political" prisoners and to see the prison movement as part of a "worldwide fight of people for freedom from imperialist domination."

Prisoners' Digest International is the product of a religious movement within prisons: the Church of the New Song, whose members call themselves Eclatarians.

Contributions from prisoners are often a feature of the periodicals: letters (complaining of mistreatment and living conditions), stories, poems, and artwork. The Lunatic Fringe, describing itself as a black humor magazine, consists entirely of such self-expression. --Janet Spahn

## FORTUNE NEWS

David Rothenberg, Ed.
29 E. 22nd St.
N.Y., N.Y. 10010
11 issues a year; $5
Started: Nov. 1967
Circulation: 25,000

Format: 8-page tabloid
Issues examined: Dec. 1973; Jan. & Feb. 1974
Back issues available from publisher

This is published by the Fortune Society, a non-profit organization of ex-convicts and other interested persons. The Society also sponsors a radio program, a course in criminology, and a pen-pal correspondence program involving 4,000 civilians.

Each issue contains letters, essays, poems, and articles with a theme such as freedom, finances, or squaring up (making it on the streets). Most of the articles are contributed by prisoners. Regular features include an editorial page; "Convict News Roundup"; and "Through These Doors Walked. . . ." (photographs and biographical sketches of two ex-convicts who have created a meaningful life on the outside). The back page lists books about crime and prisons which are available by mail from the Society.

The articles are divided between factual accounts and personal reflection. Most of the longer ones are accompanied by photographs. In one issue, several articles expose the circumstances of the death of an inmate at Trenton State Prison. Another issue discusses financial mismanagement by state and federal correctional departments. A particularly interesting article describes a suit brought by a prisoner seeking a ruling that federal prisoners have a right to correction through rehabilitation programs.

The periodical emphasizes the worth of the individual and his value to society. (JA)

Feedback:
Editor expressed no disapproval.

## THE FREEWORLD TIMES

Monthly; $5 ($3 to inmates & students)
Dates: Jan. 1972 - Apr. 1974
Circulation: 600
Format: 12- to 16-page tabloid (offset)
Issues examined: May, Aug.-Sept., Nov.-Dec. 1973
Some back issues available from publisher

The Times is published by the Murton Foundation for Criminal Justice, and by the University of Minnesota. Its object is

> to provide information relative to current conditions in prisons, analysis as to why these conditions exist, and strategies for change. To this end, The Freeworld Times includes straight news, commentary, and theoretical discussions--such as how change comes about. Our editorial policy is to seek out this kind of information from reputable and knowledgable people such as inmates, correctional officials, scholars. We are generally willing to print signed articles provided [the] statements made therein are documented.... We desire a minimum of rhetoric and prefer to let facts speak for themselves.

The Times is composed primarily of straight news stories from around the country on all aspects of the penal system. Most of them make the point that violence is almost a way of life in most American prisons. Examples of articles:

1. "Illinois Inmates Riot" because of inhuman conditions. ("We wash our faces in the toilets, there are roaches in the food, and there are homosexual attacks on inmates while the guards look on for sport.... You are robbing us of our humanity, our human rights.")
2. "Indiana Prison Erupts, Inmates Seek Firing of Warden." (An inmate accused of wounding a fellow prisoner told newsmen that the victim, who was intoxicated with prison-made liquor, assaulted him and another prisoner in the "adjustment center" because no guards were present to stop what was happening. "I am not a violent person until they throw me against the wall.... This is a dog-

eat-dog world in here and we have no protection. If I don't defend myself, I get killed.")

3. "Death Stalks Angola Prison Farm." (The mediaeval conditions in this isolated Louisiana prison--until recently swarming with hundreds of gun-toting inmate "guards" who indiscriminately beat and killed other prisoners--have been improved slightly since the appointment of the first woman in the history of penology to head a state prison system. Over 30 inmates have been killed since 1970, and "Rehabilitation is a mockery at Angola, again due to the remoteness of the prison ... no one wants to travel to Angola; it is buried too far from civilization; it is too close to hell.")
4. "Citizens, Legislature Condemn Ohio Prison." (The inmates assert that, after a guard was killed by a prisoner, other guards treated the prisoners brutally. These assertions are confirmed by a task force appointed by the state's governor.)
5. "Inmate Death Linked to Guard Rackets."
6. "Guard Found with Heroin."
7. "Juveniles Confined Illegally in Pennsylvania."

The newspaper also contains an editorial or two; a book review (of e.g., Jessica Mitford's Kind and Usual Punishment); an obituary column (prisoners who were murdered or committed suicide); letters to the editor (sometimes from prisoners, describing their living conditions); one or two analyses of such topics as "The Death Penalty" (the Times is against it) or "Inmates' Rights and the Psychosurgery Question" (the Times is against such surgery); photographs; and a cartoon.

Some of the articles in The Freeworld Times are reprinted from prison newspapers--such papers are often suppressed by the authorities--or are based on interviews with, or letters from, inmates. One such letter described the mind-destroying effects of long-term solitary confinement. (The writer said that 20% of the inmates in his prison--a federal penitentiary at Marion, Illinois--were in solitary. The Times asked the head warden to comment, but received no reply.) Another prisoner described conditions at Leavenworth: prisoners being disciplined were taken to a dungeon-like place called "63" and placed in "a smelly, nauseating, stripped cell with only cold water, poor heating, and poor plumbing. Lights blare [glare?] for 24 hours.... If any complaint is voiced, the inmate is threatened by a guard.... Then 20 buffoons come running over with crash helmets, night sticks, and metal flashlights.... The '63' building is a place where an inmate can be stomped, beaten, or murdered, unseen by the inmate body.... It is a jail in a jail." (The warden of Leavenworth declined to comment.) (JMS)

Feedback:
A notice dated 17 April 1974 read: "Unfortunately, we have been forced to suspend publication at this time due to a lack of funds." Address had been: Tom Murton, Ed.; Lois O'Brien, Mng. Ed.; 314 Social Science Tower, University of Minnesota, Minneapolis, Minn. 55455.

THE HUNTER

Alex La Fontaine, Ed.
North American Indian League of the Montana State Prison
Box 7
Deer Lodge, Mont. 59722
Monthly; $4.50
Started: 1970
Circulation: 300

Format: 28-35 pages (offset; stapled)
Issues examined: Jan., June, Sept., Oct. 1972; Apr. & July 1973
Back issues available from publisher

This self-help organization "consists of Indian inmates from different tribes.... The aims of NAIL are to help the Indian in various areas, such as school and job plans for parole. We want people out there to know that there are Indians who are helping themselves in Prison until they are eventually released." NAIL is also "concerned with the preservation of the Indian culture and bringing about better understanding of the Indian in our society in general." (The organization has the enthusiastic approval of the warden.)

The Hunter's content is not exclusively local or concerned with prisons, but includes articles on Indian culture, history, and ceremonies; herbal remedies; alcoholism; the Bureau of Indian Affairs (not responsive to Indian needs); Indian organizations and programs; the Indian occupation of Wounded Knee (supports the American Indian Movement and its leaders) and other actions such as the occupation of Alcatraz; Indian legal issues (in regard to land claims, broken treaties, and fishing and hunting rights); legislation and court decisions affecting Indians; poetry; and occasional discussion of books on Indians. Editorials often air Indian grievances. (These are usually not connected with prison. Unlike other prison periodicals, The Hunter contains few complaints about conditions.)

The source for many of the articles is the American Indian Press Association. Some articles are also reprinted from other Indian periodicals. The Hunter is illustrated with drawings and photographs (poorly reproduced). Each cover carries a drawing, and the October 1972 issue was decorated with a handsome silk screen print. (JMS)

## A JOURNAL ON EXPOSING THE DANGERS OF BEHAVIORAL MODIFICATION PROGRAMS AND HUMAN EXPERIMENTATION

United Defense against Repression
326 W. 3rd St. (Rm. 318)
Los Angeles, Calif. 90013
Bi-monthly; $3 for 10 issues

Circulation: 600
Format: 30 pages (stapled)
Issue examined: v. 1, no. 1 (undated)

The maiden issue of this journal, published by United Defense against Repression (see our review of The Defender, elsewhere in this volume), covers a number of points of concern to prisoners. "Behavior Modification through Genetics" warns against the "dangerous" and "racist" theories of Arthur Jensen, Richard Herrnstein, and William Shockley. (The last-named, a Nobel Prize winner in physics, has aroused controversy with his genetic theories, which allege that Negroes are inferior to whites.) "These scientists are representative of a new trend in America.... It is a trend towards a society based on the genetic and behavioral manipulation of Americans, a certain segment now, but all Americans eventually." "Behavior Modification through the Courts" discusses the practice of castrating certain prisoners and compares it with the Nazis' castration of some Jews in concentration camps. "Behavior Modification and Mental Institutions" quotes excerpts from a proposal by the National Council on the Rights of the Mentally Impaired, warning that many persons are improperly committed to institutions. "Behavior Modification and Psychiatry" discusses the practice of prescribing drugs to control "problem" children without first ascertaining whether these children suffer from brain dysfunction. It also criticizes the tendency of certain psychiatrists to act as "agents of social control." ("In 1967, following the Detroit ghetto rebellions, ... two neurosurgeons and a psychiatrist very active in 'studying violence' in Boston wrote a letter suggesting that 'violent slum dwellers' are different from their 'peaceful neighbors' and perhaps if we could better diagnose the many that have some organic brain pathology, we could treat them and thus markedly decrease violence in the ghetto. Presumably, the treatment of choice would be neurosurgery, since this is what these authors have advocated in their other writings.") "'Prisons,' Behavior Modification" discusses a novel proposal: the planting in convicts' brains of electronic equipment, so that they can be controlled after their release from prison.

Some sections of the journal include bibliographies, news clips, and reprints of articles from other sources. The maiden issue's layout and reproduction are poor. (JMS)

THE LUNATIC FRINGE

John H. Coutermash, Ed.
Fringe Press
Box 237
South Salem, N.Y. 10590
Quarterly; $3
Started: Mar. 1970

Circulation: 500-600
Format: 40 pages (5 1/2" x 8 1/2", letterpress and mimeo.)
Issues examined: Autumn & Winter 1972; Spring 1973

The Lunatic Fringe (entitled The Gunman's Gazette in one issue) is a poetry and black-humor magazine for institutionalized men and women. (About half of the contributors and subscribers are in prisons or jails.) The editor claims: "We are an anti-do-gooder and [anti-] bleeding heart publication that believes that 'man' should be allowed to be 'man' (woman, --woman)." He describes those connected with the periodical as being of the "W. C. Fields-Jessie James variety. You know: punch an old woman, kiss a flower." The cover of each issue is illustrated with a design of a skull on a large pair of wings.

Much of the poetry is about the sub-cultures of our society, from drag queens to convicts. Most is highly personal, venting anger at a former lover, doctor, professor, or uncle. Many verses deplore war, unrequited love, and loneliness--but not everything is so sad. Perhaps the editor puts it best:

> Poetry-reading is among the most personal things that one can perform with one's self. Want to (just for a moment) feel what you might feel if society closed that big door on you? Or maybe taste that terror of watching the war machine turn your best friend into a 'red haze'? And on the happy side? ... Long-forgotten memories of 'sunnier days' can spring from the page of the poet. You might find that an evil and ruthless cloud that hangs above will slip silently away leaving a smile upon your lips and a warmth amid your breast.

Several pages of "notes" conclude each issue. These are personal items, often news of a reader's or contributor's release from prison, sometimes news of new poets and newly-published books of poetry. Often the writer of these notes--presumably the editor--will use the space to express his liking for or approval of one of his readers (or poets). One such tribute to a correspondent appeared in the Autumn 1972 issue:

> He spent a week in the slams for draft-dodging by his own admission, so naturally we took an immediate liking to him. Being somewhat of a savage, I can understand, identify with, and interpret the doing of time for draft-dodging for the sake of draft-dodging. I cannot, however, look kindly at these altruists that commit the same 'transgression' and call it a protest. Clyde Collins is a man; the others are simply the color of bananas.

(SA)

Feedback:
"Excellent job."

MIDNIGHT SPECIAL: Prisoners' News

23 Cornelia St.
N.Y., N.Y. 10014
Monthly; $7.50 (free to prisoners)
Started: Sept. 1971
Circulation: 4,000

Format: 24 pages (8 1/4" x 11", offset)
Issues examined: Oct.-Dec. 1973
Back issues available from publisher

This is produced by a collective of ten men and women who have either been in prison, worked in prisons, or been active in prison support groups. In the December 1973 issue, the collective issued a statement of its purposes in publishing the magazine:

> Through our first two years the main function we saw for the paper was to serve as a vehicle for prisoners to communicate their ideas and experiences with one another as a way to overcome the isolation inherent in prisons. We are now beginning to understand that prisons function not just to isolate prisoners from one another, but also from other oppressed and struggling people throughout the world. We see the prison movement as part of that worldwide fight of people for freedom from imperialist domination and particularly as an integral part

> of the third world peoples' liberation struggle within the U.S.... We think the paper could do more to provide more input from the outside, to carry articles about liberation movements in other countries, and about struggles in minimum security - Amerika.

The magazine provides "news of the situation within prisons from the prisoner's point of view," and disseminates "legal information which will be of direct help in securing and expanding prisoner rights." The legal information is in the form of trial briefs, discussions of bills, and descriptions of court cases. Articles identify and explain prisoners' rights. Articles, letters, poetry, and art work from prisoners are printed each month. Often some kind of action is suggested and encouraged. (CT)

## ON ICE

Chicago Connections
Box 469
Chicago, Ill. 60690
Formerly 6-8 issues a year (in future, 5-6 are planned, plus possible supplements); $5
Started: May 1971 (present title since Dec. 1973)

Circulation: 3,000
Format: 4- to 16-page tabloid (offset)
Issues examined: v. 2, no. 3; v. 3, nos. 1 & 2; Feb. 1974
Publisher might furnish photocopies of back issues

On Ice (formerly Chicago Connections Newsletter) "is intended to serve as a channel of information to Illinois prisoners, and from Illinois prisoners to the concerned public." The paper is committed to work to secure rights for prisoners, including

> The right to organize freely around all political, religious, labor, and social issues; The right to adequate medical, legal, educational, and social services by independent professionals of one's own choice; The right to unrestricted two-way communication with the courts, the press, public organizations, and individuals by telephone, mail, or face-to-face meetings; The right to equal protection of the U.S. Constitution from discrimination in disciplinary procedures, wages, and physical conditions; The right to dissent in any peaceful manner; to full access to all files concerning oneself; to unrestricted private visits with one's family and friends.

Articles describe conditions at Menard, Stateville, and Marion; efforts of inmate leaders to organize and resist those conditions; and measures taken to segregate and punish inmate leaders. Although the focus is on prisons and jails in Illinois, news of relevant activities in other states--such as efforts to unionize inmates--is included. Detailed information is given about basic legal procedures and services available to prisoners and their families. Letters and poems from prisoners are also published.

A supplement to one issue discusses the increased use of behavior modification techniques--sensory deprivation, isolation from family and friends, electroshock, and drug conditioning--in American prisons. Signs of a revival of lobotomy as a means of making prisoners tractable are described. The writers take the position that these "1984" techniques are intended primarily to destroy the efficacy of the prisoners "who have participated in work stoppages, prison rebellions, and other protests against the oppression of prison and its conditions." (SN)

Feedback:
Editor expressed no disapproval.

OUTMATES

Box 174
Storrs, Conn. 06268
Bi-monthly; $2
Started: Sept. 1972
Circulation: 400
Format: 12 pages (7" x 8 1/2", offset)
Issues examined: June-Nov. 1973
Back issues available from publisher

Outmates, an organization established at the University of Connecticut, strives to "eradicate outmoded priorities that govern the American Penal System." The organization (made up of students, ex-convicts, and concerned citizens) sees the

> penal system as an abettor of recidivism and as a creator of criminals rather than a deterrent to crime and an initiator of rehabilitative efforts. It also recognizes the alienation of convicts and society in terms of the stereotyped image of the con fostered by the media, the Establishment, and prison administrators. It recognizes the fact that a political awareness prevalent throughout the prison system has sparked the convicts toward a greater effort in

> gaining back their human dignity lost to the dehumanizing machine which the prison system has become. It recognizes the enragement of the convicts and seeks to provide a positive vehicle through which that enragement can be channeled....

Outmates provides prisoners with reading materials, referral services, and information on educational opportunities (through "Prisoners' Yellow Pages").

The organization's newsletter consists largely of articles reprinted from other prison magazines, plus letters and poetry written by prisoners. Other features include classified ads and "writing on the wall" (selected graffiti from prison walls). According to the organization's founder, the magazine's purpose is to present inmate views of prison life and also to present the goals and activities of the organization. (CT)

Feedback:
Editor suggested a minor change in wording, and it has been incorporated into the review.

PRISON LAW REPORTER

David M. Shelton &
Donald S. Chisum, Eds.
1500 Hoge Bldg.
Seattle, Wash. 98104
Monthly; $15 (inmates $5)
Started: Oct. 1971
Circulation: 1,500

Format: 50 pages (offset)
Issues examined: July & Dec. 1973; Jan. 1974
Annual self-index
Back issues available from publisher

This is "a project co-sponsored by the Young Lawyers Section and the Commission on Correctional Facilities and Services of the American Bar Association." Its aim is to report on "strictly legal developments in corrections (jails and prisons)." Articles contain full or edited texts of both judicial and administrative decisions. New legislation and original articles are also included.

The cover story is usually long and engrossing. One concerned a Boston jail of such poor quality that it was named in a suit by its inmates. The suit charged that conditions in the jail constituted cruel and unusual punishment and denial of due process. After a full investigation of charges, a federal judge found in favor of the plaintiffs and condemned the jail.

Other regular sections include a report on U.S. Supreme Court cases; and "Decisions" (full or edited texts of decisions of lower courts). Discipline, pre-trial detention, investigation of prison conditions, denial of rights to ex-convicts, and the rights and treatment of those in non-penal institutions are among the areas covered. "Administrative News" is reported and a bibliography (recent books, hearings, articles, and book reviews pertaining to prison reform) is included.

This periodical's coverage is wide. Through its annual self-index, one can locate cases through subject or case name. (MN)

## PRISONERS' DIGEST INTERNATIONAL

Box 89
Iowa City, Iowa 52240
Monthly; $12
Started: June 1971
Circulation: 9,000

Format: 12- to 16-page tabloid
Issues examined: Jan., Feb., Apr.-June, Aug., Sept. 1973
Indexing: Alternative Press Index

The Digest is published by a collective whose members also work for the Church of the New Song, the National Prison Center, and the National Prisoners' Coalition. It covers news, court decisions, government actions, and conferences of interest to prisoners and those helping them.

Regular features.--"What's Happening" consists of news briefs describing conditions or events in specific prisons. "Law Section" covers in detail some aspect of prisoners' rights. (Representative articles: "Prison Censorship and Freedom of Speech" and "Important Ruling in Due Process in Disciplinary Action." Additional legal information is included in other sections of the periodical.) "Letters" from prisoners describe prison conditions. "Free Exchange" (also from prisoners) consists of brief requests for correspondence, information, supplies, etc. Readers occasionally contribute poems or art work.

In addition to its regular features, the Digest includes articles, cartoons, and news briefs. The articles cover conferences, actions of government, and other current topics ("The Courts and the Prisons: A Crisis of Confrontation"). Most issues contain information on the Church of the New Song, a religious movement within prisons. The movement is based on the Book of Revelation and

> seeks to spiritually validate all of the People--to

> give a new birth of Truth, Peace, and Freedom as promised by our Constitution and the Scriptures.

The editors are Eclatarians (members of the Church of the New Song) and see the Digest as one means of accomplishing the goals of their religion. They state their purpose in publishing the newspaper:

> We are, and urgently hope to remain, into doing what is best for the People, what will most effectively procure their Truth, Peace, and Freedom, and return the Earth to splendor. That may sound ineffective, but it is real. We are not super-human. We are simply Eclatarians who fight forthrightly the good fight--ever upward and onward. We seek no recognition, just positive vibes and constructive assistance.

(CT)

Feedback:
Editor expressed no disapproval.

SCAR'D TIMES

374 Fore St.
Portland, Me. 04111
Quarterly; free (donations accepted/needed)
Started: May 1973
Circulation: 4,000

Format: 16-page tabloid (offset)
Issues examined: May, Sept., Dec. 1973
Back issues available from publisher

"We take turns doing editorials. Policy decisions are collectively decided." This information was sent by a "servant of the people." A blurb in the September 1973 issue says:

> The Scar'd Times is printed monthly by SCAR in conjunction with the New England Prisoners' Association. The paper is printed by a working collective and is reflective of the ideas and actions of SCAR, NEPA, and various prisoners and friends.
>
> In the future we will begin to expand the perspective of the paper to deal with the problems within the communities that perpetuate prisons. We hope, over the coming months to make the transition from a prison ... paper to community ... paper dealing with not only prison problems but other related

problems, e. g., housing, inflation, and health.
We welcome all comments, letters, poems, articles, graphics, etc.

An editorial in the December 1973 issue says the paper has not been put out for three months because of financial difficulties. "It [December] is perhaps our best issue. It deals with struggles and solidarity. We the People. Prisoners, Third World, Women, Low-income people, and workers organizing and fighting for justice. Attica is all of us." [In the early 1970s a bloody prison revolt took place in Attica, N. Y. ]

Southern Committee to Free All Political Prisoners NEWSLETTER

Quarterly; contribution
Dates: Summer 1971 - 1974(?)
Circulation: 500-1,000
Format: 6 pages (mimeo., stapled)
Issues examined: Aug. 1972; Dec. 1973
Back issues available from publisher

The publication notes that it is "Affiliated with the National Alliance against Racist and Political Repression." The August 1972 issue is headed "Angela Davis Southern Committee to Free All Political Prisoners," but the questionnaire returned to us does not use Davis's name. The editor defines the publication's major editorial policies as "Working to free all prisoners who are jailed because of their political activities for peace, justice and freedom; to free those who are placed in jail because they are poor and black or [of] other minority status, rather than because they are 'criminals'...."

The sample issues call for support for "Thomas Wansley, a young black man who has been in prison for 10 years on a phony rape charge, [and] has become a symbol of the way such charges have been used to crush the black liberation movement in the South." One issue contains a petition to free Wansley which the reader can sign and return to the Southern Conference Educational Fund in Louisville, Ky.

Under the heading, "Political Prisoners," the cases of other persons accused and jailed on criminal charges are described, and some addresses are given to which concerned people may write to offer help. An article details the "brutality to blacks" of Sheriff Willis McCall of Lake County, Florida. McCall's record was reviewed in 1959 by the

National Negro Congress in New York, which "sentenced him to death in absentia for his crimes." (GKS)

Feedback:

"I hate to tell you this, but the Newsletter is no longer published. I don't expect it to revive any time soon. The Southern Regional Office, National Committee against Repressive Legislation, is still here." An enclosed flyer explained that that organization "engages in education and political action work to protect free speech and association rights under attack from inquisitorial committees, government surveillance, and repressive laws. Its program includes repeal of 'no-knock' and 'preventive detention' laws, the federal 'anti-riot' law, and the abolition of the House Internal Security Committee (former HUAC) and all other inquisitorial agencies." The address of the Southern Regional Office of NCARL: Box 4235, Memphis, Tenn. 38104. The address of the Newsletter had been: Mike Honey, Ed., Box 4643, Memphis 38104.

## Chapter 13

## FEMINIST

> ... the Equal Rights Amendment is the battle-cry of a resurrected struggle for political justice for women.... You must support the person who supports your legislation, and slay the person who does not, regardless of party.
> ---The Cleveland Feminist

> According to a recent study ... physicians tend to take their male patients' symptoms of illness more seriously than those of their female patients. ---Her-self

> Let your boy know the challenge of tackling a recipe; let your girl know the challenge of tackling another kid. ---Ms.

> We are totally, radically, opposed to a society in which sexuality is destiny.
> ---The New Feminist

> A woman's movement means women loving women, women living and working with women. It means concentrating our energy on getting women together without wasting our time and effort educating men.... ---The Other Woman

> ... married women must adopt the surname of the paterfamilias, just as plantation blacks once did.... ---Women's Rights Law Reporter

The corresponding chapter of our 1972 volume carried a review of the Pussycat League's Adam's Rib. We have nothing like it this time, and none of the periodicals in this chapter can be considered truly conservative (i.e., traditional). They range from the moderate to the militant, from scholarly discussions of what has been, is, and should be, to challenging appeals to smash stereotypes and grab a piece of the action. They are so diverse that there must be one to interest any woman who dares to lift her eyes above her saucer of cream or, for one minute, stop worrying her cat-nip mouse.

Women's Studies and Mother Lode are thoughtful studies of why people and customs are the way they are, while The New Feminist and The Second Wave concentrate on advocating strong measures to stop their being that way. La Luchadora, concerned with the blue-collar working woman, speaks to a different group than On Campus with Women, and--as women in all economic and social classes age--Prime Time guides the older woman toward a more satisfying life, especially in the world of work. Women and art, women and the movies, women and careers, women and the law, women and divorce, women and abortion, women and civil rights, women and male chauvinism, women and labor unions: name your interest and there's a publication devoted to it. If Good Housekeeping and the Ladies' Home Journal leave you cold and you just want a good general magazine without a specific axe to grind or wrong to right, there is always Ms., the liberated woman's answer to the slicks which have been journalism's traditional offerings to the Queen of the Kitchen and Boudoir.

In addition to those publications addressed to a particular group or supporting a specific cause, there are many for strictly local consumption, which cover news and events interesting to the women of a particular area. They attempt to appeal to women of many kinds and persuasions, to act as a bridge between the moderate and radical camps, and to provide forums where women may try their wings among friends, accustom themselves to expressing their ideas and feelings publicly at a local level, and--perhaps--get ready to speak out in a state or national arena.

Although they are as diverse as the women who read them, all of these periodicals express a deep dissatisfaction with the sexual status quo and share the conviction that women must come together, talk together, stand together, and work together if things are to be different.

The study of these periodicals leaves the reader with the impression that the yeast is surely fermenting and "The times they are a-changin'."

--Gertrude Spahn

## OUTLINE OF WOMEN'S PERIODICALS

### General--Primarily Local--Reportorial--Mixed Bag

Amazon (Milwaukee). Radical feminist.

Broadsheet (New Zealand). Strictly local. Conservative to radical.

The Cleveland Feminist. Attempts to appeal to women of moderate views without compromising publisher's beliefs.

Coming Out. Oberlin College.

Distaff (New Orleans). News, local events. Displays the work of female artists.

Feminist Newsletter (Chapel Hill). News, announcements, articles for local women.

Her-self (Ann Arbor). Local news coverage but also medical investigation and research reports of interest to women. Covers local and national women's movement.

Joyous Struggle (Albuquerque). Women's Center, University of New Mexico. Local events.

New Directions for Women in New Jersey (Dover). State and federal legislation. Inequities in education.

On Our Way (Edmonton). Local news for women. Reports on oppression of women, and on steps being taken toward change.

The Other Woman (Toronto). Varied approach to liberation. Diversity of articles, including some quite radical.

Pandora (Seattle). News about women, and forum for women of the state.

Secret Storm. Published by the Chicago Women's Liberation Union, and aimed at women in high schools and junior colleges.

The Texan Woman (Austin). State news. Forum for the state's women.

US (Tampa). Forum. Promotes understanding and cooperation between conservatives and radicals.

Voice of Women (Canada) periodicals:

The BC Voice (British Columbia). Activist, multi-purpose.
Bulletin National Newsletter. The national periodical. Outgrowth of the peace movement. Freedom, ecology, civil rights, etc.
Ontario Newsletter.

What She Wants (Cleveland Heights). Attempts to offer something to all kinds and persuasions of women.

Whole Woman (Madison). Published by a collective, it gives considerable coverage to national topics and events.

Woman. Berkeley campus, University of California. Purely local.

Women. Berkshire County, Massachusetts.

Women in Struggle (Winneconne). Covers Wisconsin.

Women's Place Newsletter (St. John's). Covers Newfoundland.

Women's Voice of Greater Hartford. Local newsletter about liberation and feminism.

## General: Politics, Economics, Sex, Beauty, Fashion--Broad Range, Moderate, Aimed at Literate Women

Ms. Produced by, and aimed at, women. Competition for the traditional women's-magazine market.

New Woman. For professional and career women.

## Women in Specific Groups

Country Women. The rewards, problems, skills involved in turning away from urban life to embrace life closer to the land.

La Luchadora. Liberation of Puerto Rican and poor, blue-collar working women.

On Campus with Women. Women as students and employees of higher education.

Prime Time. Conditions and problems of older women, especially as workers. Volunteer work is not the only way of keeping from brooding on past full life, present loneliness and uselessness.

Triple Jeopardy. Women of the Third World: Asians, Africans, black Americans. Considers women's struggle as one of many related struggles.

Women and Jobs; Unions

The Alert [Washington]. Professional women.

Change. "A Working Woman's Newspaper." Pro-union.

Chicago Women in Publishing News.

The Executive Woman.

La Luchadora. (See "Women in Specific Groups," above.)

Union WAGE (Women's Alliance to Gain Equality). Problems of women workers on the job and at home. Importance of unions for women in order to improve pay, conditions, benefits.

Windsor Woman. Aimed at working women.

Call for Reform--Call for Action--Let's Get Moving

Aurora. Attempts to be a forum for a broad range of feminist philosophy. Actually, more of a liberal viewpoint and an appeal to implement feminism.

NOW periodicals:

KNOW News Service (Pittsburgh).
Majority Report. Encourages women to speak out and work for reform. "The NOW York Woman Section" is a regular feature.
NOW! (Berkeley).
NOW! (Los Angeles).
NOW Newsletter (Princeton).
The San Joaquin NOW Newsletter.
The Vocal Majority (Washington, D. C.).

The New Feminist. Radical. The whole society must change. Get rid of the idea that "sexuality is destiny."

Saskatoon Women's Liberation Newsletter. Re-shape society. Destroy relationships based upon power.

The Second Wave. For all women who want a strong push toward change.

Speakout. Urges women toward journalistic expression, and provides a vehicle.

The Spokeswoman. General newsletter for women. Covers conferences, seminars, organizations, events, demonstrations aimed at liberating women.

Womankind. Radical. Attacks sexism and the oppression of women. Calls for change and gives advice on ways to bring it about.

Woman's World. Radical feminists: Redstockings. Interested in power. Hostile toward men.

Women: A Journal of Liberation. Effect revolutionary change in society; free women from subjection in school, church, family.

## Thoughtful, Scholarly, Questioning, Research Approach

Black Maria. Where is the women's movement going? A periodical in which women can express themselves.

Canadian Newsletter of Research on Women. Scholarly report on current research, events, organizations, publications. No editorial comment.

Feminist Studies. Sociological, historical. Academic contributors.

Libera. Published by feminists at the University of California (Berkeley).

Mother Lode. Published by a women's commune. Self-examination and thoughtful analysis of what is and what might be.

Notes. Annual anthology of radical articles on feminism.

Off Our Backs. A national journal covering a number of aspects of the women's movement.

Plexus. Problems of working women. Ecology. Rape.

Velvet Glove. Literary and political articles.

Women Speaking. British. Sociological, historical. Interested in the role of women in the (Christian) church.

Women's Studies. Interdisciplinary journal for scholarly analysis of women's place in society.

Women's Studies Newsletter. Feminist study programs in schools. Published by The Feminist Press, whose activities are reported in News/Notes.

Women's Work and Women's Studies. An annual bibliography. (Barnard College.)

Specific Goals--Axe to Grind--Crusade

Women and the Arts; Literature; Cinema

The Feminist Art Journal. Spotlight on women as artists. History and present accomplishments. Looks into exploitation and discrimination.

Moving Out. Literature and the arts.

The Sportswoman. Recreational arts.

WIA. Newsletter for the organization, Women in the Arts.

Women & Film. Studies the ways in which women are portrayed in movies.

Women and Civil & Legal Rights

Alert [Middletown]. Reports on Connecticut and federal legislation. Supports Equal Rights Amendment, abortion rights.

The New Broom. Massachusetts and federal legislation.

Feminist Alliance against Rape Newsletter. Legal aspects. Practical advice.

Pro Se. By and for women law students. (Northeastern University Law School.)

The Woman Activist. Virginia and federal legislation.

Women's Rights Law Reporter. Keeps lawyers up-to-date on litigation affecting women. A clearinghouse for information. (Rutgers University Law School.)

Women and Male Chauvinism

Berkeley Men's Center Newsletter. Men striving to free themselves from sex-role stereotypes.

Brother. By and for men, it encourages readers to view themselves and women objectively; to examine present attitudes and understand them in relation to past conditioning; and to free themselves from stereotyped images and opinions.

Women and Divorce

ADAM & EVE Newsletter. Opposes sexist practices and decisions in divorce, custody, alimony. Originally for men, now for women also.

Women and Their Bodies

The Monthly Extract. Insistence upon women's right to manage their own bodies.

WONAAC Newsletter. Women's right to control reproductive function through contraception and abortion.

--Gertrude Spahn

## ADAM & EVE NEWSLETTER

Louis J. Filczer, Publ.
343 S. Dearborn
Chicago, Ill. 60604
Irregular; free to members (50¢ an issue to others)

Started: 1970
Circulation: 3,000
Format: 4-6 pages (mimeo.)
Issues examined: Nos. 101-3, 106

The Newsletter reports on news of interest to the American Divorce Association for Men, a "Chicago-based non-profit, non-sectarian, educational organization devoted to the interests and welfare of men's rights, equality, and their children." The name of the organization was changed after a few years to include women--ADAM & EVE (American Divorce Association for Men and Women). Most of the articles examine the legal difficulties facing men in divorce cases: obtaining custody of the children, high alimony payments, prejudiced divorce lawyers and judges. News of legislative bills and landmark divorce cases is given, and the activities of the organization are publicized. In one issue practical suggestions were made to aid a man in his private investigation of his wife's activities, as he sought factual proof for the divorce litigation. Among such hints were: "When tailing, never use your own vehicle. When tailing or on stake-out, if you are in your own car, wear a disguise. Have a camera with flash attachment, tape recorder, and a set of binoculars handy at all times." In another issue photographs and descriptions of a man's daughter and ex-wife were printed in an effort to find the eight-year-old daughter who had been in his custody when the mother kidnapped her during a weekend visitation.

Although much of the material in the newsletters is directed toward "winning" divorce cases, one of the sharpest criticisms levelled at divorce lawyers by the organization is that they make no attempt at reconciling parties; serving their own financial interest, they often work actively against any such possibility. ADAM would rather see more in the way of family preservation. Ultimately, it sees as its greatest problem the "Hocus Pocus, Mumbo Jumbo, legal system." The only effective solution will be "to get rid of the lawyers and lawyer judges!!!! Throw away the legal books and procedural processes and run our civilization according to practical comprehensible rules that the ordinary man can understand."

(SA)

Feedback:

Publisher expressed no disapproval.

ALERT: Women's Legislative Review

| | |
|---|---|
| Nancy Ferguson Fernandez, Ed. | Started: Nov. 1972 |
| Box 437 | Circulation: 13,000 |
| Middletown, Conn. 06457 | Format: 4-6 pages (offset) |
| Monthly; $4 | Issues examined: Oct. 1973 - Jan. 1974 |

*Alert* is a non-partisan information sheet, inspired by the defeat of the Equal Rights Amendment and the passage of a restrictive anti-abortion law in the Connecticut Legislature during 1971-72. A group of feminists saw the need for a newsletter to inform Connecticut women of state and national legislation that would affect them. *Alert*'s Editorial Board takes a political stand on women's rights legislation with the approval of the advisory board. However, the aim of the newsletter is to offer a "sounding board to members of various women's groups, and to individual women."

Each issue centers around a theme such as "Working Mothers," "Women and Sports," or "Legislative Priorities--1974." Short articles summarize court decisions and call attention to the activities of commissions and conferences dealing with the month's theme. A fifty- to seventy-five word book review is included. Forthcoming publications, new organizations, and classes concerned with the women's movement are announced. An active job referral service is provided through ads in the "Job Development Section." Alert also operates a speakers' bureau.

Alert was named winner in the category, Communicating For and About Women's Rights, in the 1973 "Communicating for a Better Tomorrow" National Awards Program of Women in Communications. (JA)

Feedback:

"Since our last communication, Alert has changed its format to a tabloid-size newspaper.... The rest of the summary is still accurate; I should add that Alert is on file at the International Women's History Archives, Berkeley, California...." (These files are now at Northwestern University Library.)

## THE ALERT

Federation of Organizations for Professional Women
1346 Connecticut Ave. N.W. (Rm. 1122)
Washington, D.C. 20036
Quarterly; institutions $25
Started: Fall 1973

Circulation: 1,500
Format: 8 pages (offset); Summer 1974 issue is 4-page tabloid
Issues examined: Fall 1973; Spring & Summer 1974

The purpose of the Federation is "to unify and coordinate efforts of many and diverse [women's] organizations." "We try to publish articles and information of interest to our membership which is varied and diverse, but consists mainly of professional women. Hence our interest in Affirmative Action, legislation, and activities such as International Women's year. We are also interested in ERA and the activities of our membership." The Summer issue contains a list of 46 affiliates, mostly academic and scientific organizations.

## AMAZON

Amazon Collective/Women's Coalition
2211 E. Kenwood
Milwaukee, Wis. 53211
Monthly; $3 (institutions $10)
Started: 1972
Circulation: 500
Format: 20-page tabloid (offset)
Issues examined: Oct. 1973 through Jan. 1974
Back issues on file at Northwestern University Library

Amazon presents "a radical feminist viewpoint" and deals almost exclusively with news of the women's movement in the Milwaukee area. Among the articles appearing in the issues examined were a series of interviews with Milwaukee feminists, a summary of the workshops held during Women's Week at the University of Wisconsin-Milwaukee, and a report on prison visitation regulations by the Prisoner Solidarity Committee Organized by Women. The articles appear to be a combination of ones which encourage the reader to examine and evaluate her image and life-style, and others which offer practical advice in dealing with problems encountered by women in such areas as employment, credit, divorce, and abortion. The magazine's tone is activist; a slight anti-male stance is present.

Regular features include reviews of books, films, and records. Items reviewed are always written by, and are usually intended for, women. Original poetry, short fiction, and graphics lend visual interest to each issue. "Letters to Amazon" and a small number of classified ads also form a part of each issue. (CH)

Feedback:
Editor expressed no disapproval.

## AURORA: Prism of Feminism

24 DeBaun Ave.
Suffern, N.Y. 10901
Quarterly; $4 (institutions $6)
Started: June 1971
Circulation: 2,000
Format: 40 pages (offset)
Issue examined: No. 3 (1972)
Back issues on file at Northwestern University Library
Microform version available from Bell & Howell

"This journal attempts to be a prism of feminism, a place where women's ideas--conservative or radical, thoughtful or light--may come together to be expressed in their own way." Despite this opening statement found in the magazine, there is little expression of conservative ideas, and according to the editors, more emphasis is placed on "how to implement feminism" than on studying the ideology of the movement. Some short fiction is published in the magazine along with articles on such topics as women in prison, women in universities, and the difficulties of travelling alone as a female. Most of the articles are written from the author's personal experiences; in some cases extensive outside work has been done to corroborate the author's ideas, as in an article exploring myths of feminine evil.

Two particularly unique features of this magazine were added to the format in 1972: "A Common Woman's Whole Earth Catalogue" which lists sources of "information, supplies, tools and other catalogues that may make our lives easier and more efficient"; and a "Merry Mechanix Manual," a self-help section which provides basic information on fixing things, a job ordinarily left to men. In the issue examined, very explicit and understandable instructions were given for taking basic care of one's car, wiring a light, fixing a toilet and faucet, and even for giving oneself a medical examination. (SA)

Feedback:

Editor expressed no disapproval.

## THE BC VOICE

BC Voice of Women
Mrs. T. D. Birmingham, Ed.
Box 235
Nanaimo, British Columbia, Canada

Bi-monthly; $1
Format: 10 pages (mimeo., stapled)
Issues examined: Feb., Apr., Oct. 1973

The BC Voice, a newsletter published by an activist women's group in Canada, is multi-purpose in content and concerns itself with "war, pollution, over-population, and poverty." It also sees itself as dedicated to "the liberation of all humans (but especially women) from demeaning roles."

Contents include reprints from other periodicals. One article suggests caution as a response by the peace groups to the cease fire in Viet Nam. The war is labeled as tragic, criminal, and unnecessary. A second story deals with reactions to the extraction of Canadian oil for U.S. consumption. "It will fuel American industry, American bombers, American space rockets, and the dollars will go into the pockets of Wall Street giants."

Brief commentary embraces such diverse subjects as a suggested study of Indian Land Rights, release of political prisoners held by the Thieu regime, VOW representation at a World Congress of Peace Forces in Moscow, and recycling. One unique feature is a listing of commercial products to be boycotted, indicating that their purchase will lead to the support of "racist repression" and "colonial wars."

Regular features include letters to the editor and news items of interest from the members. Books and articles are reviewed for the newsletter. "Hi Lights from Minutes" indicates group activities, while "Calendar of Events" documents upcoming events. (MN)

Berkeley Men's Center NEWSLETTER

2700 Bancroft Way
Berkeley, Calif. 94704
Irregular; free
Started: 1970

Circulation: 150-250
Format: 2-4 pages (mimeo.)
Issues examined: none sent

One of the members of the Berkeley Men's Center sent the following information:

> We are a collective of men struggling to free ourselves from sex-role stereotypes and to define ourselves in positive, non-chauvinistic ways. We have been going since 1970 and at this location since 1971 and include men of all sexual orientations. We distribute material on men's struggles and gayness. We help in the formation of men's consciousness-raising groups in the Bay area and answer mail which we receive from all over the country and abroad. We have a Monday evening drop-in rap at 8 p.m. and telephone information service. Projects include anti-sexist actions, television and radio programs, bake sales, and men's work-playshops every few months with child care.

Included with the information we received was a copy of the Berkeley Men's Center Manifesto which begins:

> We, as men, want to take back our full humanity. We no longer want to strain and compete to live up to an impossible oppressive masculine image--strong, silent, cool, handsome, unemotional, successful, master of women, leader of men, wealthy, brilliant,

> athletic, and 'heavy.' We no longer want to feel the need to perform sexually, socially, or in any way to live up to an imposed male role, from a traditional American society or a 'counterculture.'

A member of the Center told us that the Newsletter publishes "articles furthering understanding of new sex roles (esp. male) and ideas which clarify and deepen the relationship between sexual and social experience."

BLACK MARIA

815 W. Wrightwood Ave.
Chicago, Ill. 60614
Quarterly; $4.50
Format: 60 pages (6" x 9", offset)
Issue examined: Spring 1974
Back issues available from publisher

An editorial described the publication this way:

> It's been close to a year since an issue of Black Maria has come out. In that time, the original collective has disbanded and a new one has taken its place. We're still smaller than we'd like to be, but new women keep joining and we find ourselves steadily growing.
>
> We've changed the format slightly.... We've also published two articles about working women (secretaries) that we hope are the beginnings of a series of articles about the directions the women's movement is going in, both nationally and internationally....
>
> As we put together this issue, we were very conscious of continuing the tradition Black Maria has of giving women a place to express their personal selves, their social selves, and their political selves. We want to continue to explore the lives of women, to contribute to and support a movement that is central to all of our lives, and to reach out to all the women who have yet to speak.

Besides several articles, the sample issue contained a "Books Received" section (long annotations of five books), stories, and poetry.

BROADSHEET: The Feminist Magazine

Auckland Women's Liberation
48 St. Andrews Rd.
Epsom, Auckland 3, New Zealand
Ten issues a year; $4 N. Z.
Started: July 1972
Circulation: 2,000

Format: 19 pages (8" x 13 1/4", offset); new format: 40 pages (8" x 11", offset)
Issues examined: Aug., Oct., Nov. 1973; Feb. 1974
Back issues available from publisher

Broadsheet "tries to coordinate all the feminist groups in New Zealand." It has an "open editorial policy," and ideas expressed range from conservative to radical. Only local material is encouraged, and reprints from other sources are seldom used.

Regular features include book reviews, letters to the editor, cartoon strips, notes on feminist groups in other countries, and "Broadsheet Report," which informs readers of the meetings and activities of the New Zealand feminist organizations.

"Kicking against the Pricks" is another regular feature. It reports on sexist court decisions, newspaper articles, bureaucratic decrees, etc., from around the world. For example, a report from an African nation states that women there can be jailed for wearing mini-skirts; and an item from a New Zealand paper states that a woman runner was denied recognition for a record-breaking race because she was in competition with a male athlete.

"Talking to Polynesian Women" is an article on the relation of women's liberation to Maori women. They are faced with similar problems vis-à-vis the movement as are black women in the U. S.: should their commitment be to the advance of their race or to the advance of their sex (since they face discrimination on both counts)? Many Maori women see the movement as a white, middle-class innovation of little relevance to their oppressed situation. Tribal organization is patriarchal, and Maori women seem reluctant to cause further deterioration in their traditional life-style, which has already suffered under white rule.

Another article contained a series of interviews with housewives and concluded that many women who do not work outside the home are subject to mental and drug problems due to isolation and frustration. An interesting comment was provided by a man who stayed home for a year while his wife worked:

> I nibble instead of eating. I have put on weight and

> run to seed. I no longer care about my appearance.... I mope around all day in bedroom slippers and dressing gown, alternating between nicotine and valium.... I ... pour another glass of sweet sherry and do the ironing later.

Division within the movement was shown in articles and letters on abortion and sexuality; but unity was expressed in the report on the women's convention where the delegates had "a tremendous feeling of unity and strength of sisterhood."

Other articles included "Women Grow Old But Men Mature," an excerpt from a Susan Sontag book on the double standard of aging and "Sex Games at the Games," a commentary on the sexist discrimination shown in activities and coverage of the Commonwealth Games. (SLA)

Feedback:

The editor informed us that the magazine is now being distributed through bookstores. The format is enlarged and new features have been added. The publishers are hoping for good sales because "The distributors, who have a monopoly in New Zealand, will only keep distributing it if it is financially worth their while." Since "New Zealand women's magazines are of the cooking and knitting variety, we think it important to provide some alternative publication ... [that sees] things from a more intelligent and critical viewpoint."

Each issue now concentrates on one topic such as "Women and Violence," "Women in the Arts in New Zealand," and "Older Women." "However from time to time we will have an issue of general mixed topics."

BROTHER: A Forum for Men Against Sexism

Box 4387
Berkeley, Calif. 94704
Irregular; $3 (institutions $10)

Started: Apr. 1971
Circulation: 3,500
Format: tabloid
Issue examined: Summer 1972

*Brother*'s subtitle was originally "A Male Liberation Newspaper." It was changed because the phrase "male liberation" confused many into thinking it was the antithesis of Women's Liberation. On the contrary, the staff of *Brother*, as well as the various men's groups that have been formed around the country, support the women's movement and are attempting to rid themselves of the notion of male supremacy and male role conditioning. The usual content of men's consciousness-raising groups is described in "A Men's Group Experience":

> When we began meeting we spent a lot of time talking about our pasts--growing up as men, learning to compete and be masculine, to think and not to feel, to 'succeed' and feel bad if we 'failed,' to treat women as inferior sexual objects, and the host of male roles we've been taught to play. We talked about how we were often out of touch with our feelings or how we simply refused to admit to ourselves that we felt incompetent with women, unable to live up to the images expected of us by parents and society, unable to communicate with other people, lonely and isolated. It was and is extremely hard to admit that we feel left out when we see 'happy' couples together and we are not relating to a woman, or that we feel our own relationship is inadequate and that what we really need is a 'better woman.' We also talked about subjects that still cause us guilt and confusion such as masturbation: we continue to have difficulty talking about homosexuality and our fears about becoming intimate with men.

Some of the articles in Brother are by gay men or deal with homosexuality. Most involve the authors' attempts to understand sexism and to rid themselves of the attitudes and practices of male supremacy, as well as to become closer to themselves and other men. Articles such as "Life in the Military," "How My High School Taught Me To Repress Me," and "Struggling Against Male Chauvinism in Prison" deal with these issues. In addition, "Guidelines for Fathers" explains just what a father must do in order to share fully in child care; "Who's Ripping Off Our Minds" criticizes the attitudes of some psychiatrists toward homosexuality; and "Vietnam: A Feminist Analysis" interprets the United States' "unprecedented sadism" in the Vietnam War as a product of the mentality of rape, "the socialization of male sexual violence."

(MM)

Feedback:

The respondent was "very pleased to read your well-balanced and informative synopsis."

## CANADIAN NEWSLETTER OF RESEARCH ON WOMEN

Margrit Eichler, Co-Editor
Department of Sociology
University of Waterloo
Waterloo, Ont., Canada N2L 3G1

3 issues a year; $6 (institutions $12)
Started: May 1972
Circulation: 500
Format: 60-70 pages (multilith)

Issues examined: Feb., May, Oct. 1973; Feb. & May 1974
Some back issues available from editor

The Assistant Editor, Patricia Carter, explains the purposes of the periodical:

> The Newsletter was established to: (1) establish ... or improve communication among people in Canada who are doing research on women; (2) list on-going research on Canadian women in particular; (3) list selected relevant research on the international scene; and (4) provide for an exchange of ideas on courses about sex-roles or women.
>
> While the Newsletter does include the international work being done in the above four areas, it does not include references to American information, since there are many other very valuable publications which cover that area.

The word "newsletter" is perhaps a bit misleading: this is a scholarly publication. Contents regularly include a list of on-going research on women, abstracts of recent research reports and publications, book reviews, bibliographies, announcements (of meetings, seminars, films), and syllabi for courses in women's studies. In addition, there are frequent status reports (e.g., one from the University of Waterloo, one from Queen's University, and one on federal programs). There is no editorial comment. (SN)

Feedback:
"Great!"

CHANGE: A Working Woman's Newspaper

968 Valencia St.
San Francisco, Calif. 94110
Every six weeks; $2 (institutions $5)
Started: Jan. 1971
Circulation: 4,000
Format: 8-page tabloid

Issues examined: Dec. 1972 - Apr. 1973
Microform version available from Bell & Howell
On file at Northwestern University Library

Change is concerned with political discussion about

topics of importance to working women. The newspaper is written and published by a group of about fifteen women. The majority of the newspapers are distributed free to women outside offices in downtown San Francisco.

Both national and local issues are featured in fairly lengthy articles. Numerous articles are concerned with "the needs for unions and for unions' responsiveness to rank and file especially women's demands."

Local issues predominate, and many articles advocate strong unions which are concerned with women's rights. Subjects include the telephone company layoffs due to automation; Metropolitan Life Insurance Company efforts to thwart unionization; the establishment of a local federal government employees' union; the Bank of America dropping cab fares for women employees; the Shorter Work Week Coalition; and "A Look at Maternity Benefits."

Other local and state concerns featured in articles are disability for pregnant women, state disability insurance benefits, the exploitation of the temporary worker, the municipal transportation system cutbacks in service, and the conditions in women's prisons.

Articles of national concern include "Day Care Slash"; "Phase 3; Wage-Price Squeeze"; "Boycott Farah Pants!"; "Shell No!" which urges a boycott of the Shell Oil Company during a strike; and "... And the War Goes On" in South Vietnam after the Peace Agreement.

There are several columns which appear on a regular basis. "Your Employee Advisor" describes work conditions, salary, etc., of specific local companies. "Books" features reviews of current books of interest to women. "What's Happening" in San Francisco is included in all issues. This column is divided into "Events," "Classes," "Services," "Work Activities" (boycotts, union activities), and "Miscellany." (NK)

## CHICAGO WOMEN IN PUBLISHING NEWS

| | |
|---|---|
| Patricia Lane, Pres. | Started: 1973 |
| Box 11837 | Circulation: 200 |
| Chicago, Ill. 60611 | Format: 4 pages (offset) |
| 10 times yearly with membership of $6 | Issue examined: June 1973 |

Covers activities of the organization, lists job openings, and mentions honors or positions that women have obtained in publishing.

Feedback:

"To present information that can help improve the status of women in publishing work in the Chicago area; serve as a forum and exchange of information."

## THE CLEVELAND FEMINIST

Monthly; $5
Dates: Aug. 1973 through Jan. 1974
Circulation: 2,000
Format: 20-30 pages (5 1/2" x 8 1/2", offset)
Issues examined: Aug., Oct. - Dec. 1973
Back issues available from publisher

Because TCF wanted readers on the periphery of the women's rights movement, as well as the totally committed, it tried to be "inoffensive to the middle-class woman, without being mealy-mouthed or compromising." The coverage was primarily of events in the Cleveland area, but the problems discussed were of concern to women everywhere.

The sample issues contained several articles defending a woman's right to an abortion. Others dealt with self defense, no-fault divorce, the Equal Rights Amendment, consciousness raising, and the future of marriage (not promising).

There was an interview with a woman obstetrician, an article on Jane Fonda, and a reprint of a speech made at a celebration of the fifty-third anniversary of Woman's Suffrage, sponsored by the Cleveland chapter of NOW. The speaker was Josephine Irwin, who for many years has been a champion of the rights of women. She recounted the history of the movement in the U.S. and paid tribute to its leaders. She pointed out that several years after the passage of the Nineteenth Amendment, the struggle for women's rights lost its momentum:

> Sigmund Freud was, beyond doubt, largely responsible for that decadence. It was he who first said, 'Anatomy is destiny'.... To me, the Equal Rights Amendment is the battle-cry of a resurrected struggle for political justice for women.... You must support the person who supports your legislation, and slay the person who does not, regardless of party.

Regular features included editorial comments, book reviews,

letters to the editor, a report on state legislation, and a section of short news items. The periodical was illustrated with photographs and pen-and-ink sketches. Its address was: Fran Mares, Editor, 10206 Clifton Blvd., Cleveland, Ohio 44102. (EC)

COMING OUT: A Women's Newspaper

Irregular; $3
Started: Fall 1972
Circulation: 1,000
Format: 12-16 pages (offset)

Issues examined: Sept. & Nov. 1973; Apr. 1974
Back issues available from publisher

This feminist magazine is written and produced primarily by college women in Oberlin. It is filled with brief news items and one- or two-page articles on topics of interest to women.

Several articles are devoted to discriminatory hiring practices. A number of items call attention to the dangers of certain contraceptive drugs and feminine hygiene products. There is a commentary on the barring of women from intercollegiate sports. A young Lesbian writes of her difficulties in learning to acknowledge herself. Commercial media are criticized sharply for their "image of the liberation of women."

One issue is devoted largely to the need for a Women's Studies Program at Oberlin, to balance the college's curriculum. (The present curriculum is said to be patterned "on the study of ideas, lifestyles, and achievements of those who have been 'successful' by white male standards.")

There are occasional items of national or international news. Photographs and cartoons brighten the issues. Some issues include a directory of groups of interest to women. (MN)

Feedback:

*CO* "has not been published since November of 1974 and it seems that future issues are unlikely to appear. The goals of the paper were never met--to provide a forum for *both* college women and town women and to be an example of a *collective* enterprise with shared and rotating responsibility." Nora Jones, former Editor, Box 44, Oberlin, Ohio 44074.

COUNTRY WOMEN

Box 51
Albion, Calif. 95410

Bi-monthly; $4
Started: Oct. 1972

Circulation: 7,000
Format: 64 pages (offset)
Issues examined: Oct. 1973; Jan. & July 1974
Back issues available from publisher
Microform version available from Bell & Howell

Country Women is written by and for women who live in the country or are considering moving there. It is "devoted half to sharing the personal experiences of women living in the country, and half to exchanging new-found skills."

Most of the women are ex-urbanites who have deliberately rejected the comforts and conveniences of city living in the hope of finding tranquility--and themselves--in the hard physical work of survival in the country: "Living in the country ... is hard because, without those multi distractions of city life, one comes face to face with oneself, one's life, one's choices." Many live in houses built with their own hands, without electricity or running water. Their experiences are told in short articles written by themselves as testament and encouragement to other women seeking to escape a repressive society or a stagnant marriage.

Some of the practical skills needed for living in the country are detailed in articles such as: "Water Systems: Gravity Feed and Centrifugal Pumps," "Better Barns and Gardens," "A Rose by Any Other Name" (building an outhouse), and other pieces on raising bees and chicks, composting and soil preparation, and other practical guides. These articles are intended not only to pass on important information, but also to give self-confidence to urban women newly-arrived in the country.

Other features in the magazine are poems, lessons in self-defense, and advertisements for women who want to live in groups or communes in the country. (SLA)

## DISTAFF: New Orleans Monthly Feminist Forum

Marilyn Nelson, Ed.
Box 2465
New Orleans, La. 70176
Monthly; $3
Started: Jan. 1972
Circulation: 3,000
Format: 12-page tabloid
Issues examined: Sept., Oct., Dec. 1973
Back issues available from publisher

Distaff is "for, by, and about women" in the New Orleans area. Issues deemed of interest have included local political candidates and campaigns, cases of job discrimination against women, Miss America beauty contests, and other symbols of exploitation. The focus is on activities and news in the New Orleans area. Besides serving as a forum for news, the paper regularly contains poetry, photography, and graphics by local female artists, most of whom speak out strongly for the feminist movement. Reviews of the arts are published occasionally.

Each issue contains a guide to women's organizations and their activities and a directory of services of which a reader might have need. The YWCA and League of Women Voters are included along with less-established organizations such as Ananda Marga Yoga and Lesbian Rap Groups. A regular feature ("Over the Pork Barrel") publicizes examples of male chauvinism and insult to females: "Richard M. Nixon, who, in announcing his choice for vice-president ... said, 'after considering all the qualified men and other people'"; and "The Mexican Market on Decatur Street for advertising Fanny Pinchers--89 cents--in its main display window." (SA)

Feedback:

Editor suggested several minor changes, all of which have been incorporated into the review.

THE EXECUTIVE WOMAN: An Exclusive Monthly Newsletter for Women in Business

Sandra Brown, Publ.
747 Third Ave.
N.Y., N.Y. 10017
Ten issues a year; $20
Started: Sept. 1973
Circulation: 1,500

Format: 6 pages (offset)
Issues examined: Dec. 1973; Apr. & May 1974
Back issues available from publisher

"Geared to Professional Women--nationwide circulation." Contains business and financial news and sections on businesses owned by women; women appointed to top positions; "Breakthrough 'Firsts' for Women"; "Opportunities for Businesswomen: Mergers and Acquisitions--Venture Capital"; "Events" that include announcements of workshops, seminars, and conferences for women; and a classified ad section listing jobs available. Sometimes there are annotations of new books by women. (JMS)

Feedback:

Editor expressed no disapproval.

## FEMINIST ALLIANCE AGAINST RAPE NEWSLETTER

Box 21033
Washington, D. C. 20009
Bi-monthly; $5
Started: June 1972 (as Rape Crisis Center Newsletter); Aug. 1974 under present title
Circulation: 800

Format: 14 pages (mimeo., stapled); new format: 12-24 pages (7" x 8 1/2", offset)
Issue examined: undated Aug. 1974 issue
Back issues for current year available from publisher

The Alliance is a coalition of "community-based and feminist-controlled anti-rape projects." Its Newsletter was formerly published by the Washington, D. C., Rape Crisis Center. (Women at that Center helped to set up the Alliance, and "the same individuals who formerly worked to put out the D. C. Center's Newsletter are now publishing the FAAR Newsletter.")

Part of the sample issue consisted of eight pages of National News Notes covering organizations, projects, and legislation dealing with rape. (The Alliance hopes to expand this news coverage.) Other items: an article ("The Rape Trial: Questioning the Witness") instructing women on how to handle a difficult situation; discussion of a bill to "establish a National Center for the Prevention and Control of Rape"; and a list (with some annotations) of new publications of interest to feminists.

FAAR intends to be a clearinghouse for information and referrals, as well as a consulting service (agencies or groups requesting consultants will be referred to participating FAAR members in their vicinity); and it will offer information on setting up anti-rape projects. It hopes to expand its Newsletter to become "a forum for the exchange of ideas." The second issue of the Newsletter will "focus on issues related to incarceration and the penal system." (JMS)

Feedback:

The editor expressed no disapproval.

## THE FEMINIST ART JOURNAL

Cindy Nemser, Ed.
41 Montgomery Place
Brooklyn, N. Y. 11215
Quarterly; $4 (institutions $5)

Started: Apr. 1972
Circulation: 4,000
Format: 24 pages (11 1/2" x 14 3/4", offset)
Issues examined: Apr. &

Fall 1972; Winter 1973 from Xerox University
Microform version available Microfilms

In an editorial in the April issue, the editors state their editorial policies:

> The Feminist Art Journal is here to carry women artists' voices throughout the world. Our aim is to enhance the status of women in all the arts by publishing articles on their past history and on their current history-making activities. With this goal in mind, we will encourage women artists of all persuasions to discuss and illustrate their work. We shall also expose and discredit all personages and institutions which exploit or discriminate against women artists. Since artworld politics vitally concern women in the arts as well as men we also intend to deal with policy-making issues, in criticism, museumology, art education, etc. Here too we will expose and discredit those who prey upon the artist and public and supplement our exposés with programs for change.

The Journal includes "scholarly articles, interviews and profiles about distinguished women artists, plus spirited accounts of the current activities of the women artists' movement." Most of the articles are written to examine in detail the work of women artists, or to expose those who discriminate against them. Representative titles are "Stereotypes and Women Artists," "Are Museums Relevant to Women?" "Male Chauvinist Exposé," "Conspiracy of Silence Against a Feminist Poem," and "If DeKooning Is an Old Master, What Is Georgia O'Keeffe?" Accompanying the articles are reproductions of a variety of works by women artists, and photographs of prominent women artists, recent demonstrations, etc.

The Journal reports on women's status and achievements in all areas of the art world. It is edited by an art critic, and its contributors include poets, painters, sculptors, photographers, film makers, craftswomen, and art historians. Any topic of interest to women artists can find its way into the Journal.

The attitudes of the editors can best be summed up in their own words. In the first issue they wrote: "Women artists, we now have our own place to be our own selves in print. The battle has begun." (CT)

Feedback:

The editor suggested several changes in wording, and they have been incorporated into the review.

## FEMINIST NEWSLETTER

Feminist Newsletter Collective
Box 954
Chapel Hill, N. C. 27514
Bi-weekly; $4
Started: Autumn 1969

Circulation: 400
Format: 10 pages (mimeo., stapled)
Issues examined: 19 Aug., 30 Sept., 28 Oct. 1973

"The Feminist Newsletter prints viewpoints and news of events which are interesting to feminists in the Chapel Hill area. WOMEN, not WOMAN, contribute to the Newsletter, making for a diversity of announcements and articles. These pages serve as a forum for the opinions of our sex and as an opportunity to publish (for the first time in most cases) our thinking and feeling."

Articles appear on such topics as self-defense, women and money, the struggle of women to break into new fields of employment, self-help clinics, consciousness-raising, and celibacy.

Regular features include a calendar of upcoming events, "Free Ads," and "Announcements" (which may have mention of national events in the Women's Liberation movement, or new books--or other resources--on the subject). There are occasional articles on women in the arts, or reviews of a woman-produced album or book. Each issue carries an illustration on the cover. (CH)

Feedback:

"We are very pleased with what you have selected above."

## FEMINIST STUDIES

417 Riverside Dr.
N.Y., N.Y. 10025
Two double issues a year; $8 (institutions $12)
Started: Fall 1972

Circulation: 1,000-1,200
Format: 118 pages (6" x 9", offset)
Issue examined: v. 2, no. 1 (1974)

Feminist Studies is a scholarly journal "founded for the

purpose of encouraging scholarly and other analytic treatments of issues related to the status of women ... providing a forum for feminist analysis, theory, debate, and exchange." In the issue examined (only one was read as all of the back issues were sold out), four lengthy (20- to 30-page) articles appeared along with a book review and several poems. The contributors for this issue teach or have taught at such places as M.I.T., Smith, and Temple University. The articles are written in a serious style and are based on extensive research, usually in connection with the author's field of study. The titles of the articles give a good indication of the type of material contained in this publication: "Fine Arts and Feminism: The Awakening Consciousness"; "Crime and the Respectable Woman: Toward a Pattern of Middle-Class Female Criminality in Nineteenth-Century France and England"; "Nietzsche and Moral Change"; and "Their Sisters' Keepers: An Historical Perspective on Female Correctional Institutions in the United States, 1870-1900." The reading is not, however, dry. The article on female criminals in England and France throws much light on the relationships between the sexes at that time. In case after case evidence proved the guilt of a woman in seducing and occasionally murdering her lover, but the "court refused to believe that a 'pure' young woman could have been behind such a plot.... It shows, too, how the presumed innocence of middle-class women produced a remarkable impunity, despite the demonstration of guilt."

Abstracts of the articles appear in Women Studies Abstracts. (SA)

Feedback:

Editor suggested textual changes which were incorporated into the review and asked that the last quotation in the review be deleted, which we decided not to do.

HER-SELF: Women's News Journal

225 E. Liberty
Ann Arbor, Mich. 48108
Monthly; $5 (businesses & institutions, $10)
Started: Apr. 1972

Circulation: 10,000
Format: 24-page tabloid
Issues examined: Mar.-June 1973; Apr. 1974

This is a "community newspaper" that--like Off Our Backs in Washington, D.C.--has a scope far outside the local concerns of its community. Its speciality is investigative medical reporting and research of interest to women.

According to The New Women's Survival Catalog, articles first appearing in Her-self have led to hearings by the Food and Drug Administration. Her-self also publishes material on all aspects of the national and local women's movement, such as women's history, working women's problems, child care, prisoners, and sports.

The April 1974 special health issue has articles on "How Confidential Are Your Medical Records?"; "Can Being Hospitalized Kill You?" (problems of faulty devices, from testimony before a Congressional Subcommittee on Medical Device Legislation); "What Your Doctor Doesn't Know About Sex" (about "sexual propagandizing and misinformation within America's medical community"); and "DES: Gynecology or Genocide?" New research is reported in "Maternal Alcoholism and Fetal Damage"; "New Biopsy Technique for Breast Cancer"; an article on the dangers of an intra-uterine device; "Placydil for Pregnant Women?"; and "Birth Control Pills and Liver Tumors." In "Men Get Cured ... Women Get Drugged," the author discusses the common practice of physicians' prescribing mood-altering drugs for women:

> According to a recent study by Dr. Linda Fidell, psychologist at California State University at Northridge, physicians tend to take their male patients' symptoms of illness more seriously than those of their female patients. She also found that doctors tend to stereotype women as hypochondriacs.

Her-self has no editorials. "We will print any article having to do with the women's movement in the broadest possible terms." (MM)

## JOYOUS STRUGGLE

Women's Center<br>University of New Mexico<br>1824 Las Lomas<br>Albuquerque, N.M. 87131<br>Monthly; free

Circulation: 2,500<br>Format: 7 pages (legal size)<br>Issues examined: Nov. 1973; undated 1974 issue

This newsletter is concerned with "activities of the Center, campus, and community." Its staff is paid by the University.

Information is given about workshops for women; forthcoming events; available jobs; a rape crisis center; and groups in need of financial aid.

Topics explored in longer columns include women's employment rights in Albuquerque; the outlook for women in sports; the results of a gynecology questionnaire; and reactions to a women's self-help clinic.

One article reports on the organization of a black feminist movement, and describes its statement of purpose. In a story reprinted from a local newspaper, a black woman rejects the white liberation movement: "Black women must realize and never forget that white women helped create some factors of oppression against blacks."

Poetry appears throughout the newsletter, and there is an open letter from a young mother complaining about the sacrifices she is called upon to make for her children. (MN)

Reviewer's opinion:
Although Joyous Struggle lacks organization and professional polish, it contains a variety of information for local women students.

Feedback:
Editor expressed no disapproval.

KNOW NEWS SERVICE

Box 86031
Pittsburgh, Pa. 15221
Irregular; $6 ($10 institutions and overseas)
Started: 17 Aug. 1970
Circulation: 1,500
Format: 10-16 pages (offset, stapled)
Issues examined: 15 July, Sept., Oct./Nov. 1972; Jan., June 1973

This bulletin is published by KNOW, Inc., a non-profit corporation founded by Pittsburgh National Organization for Women (NOW) members who believe that you "can't have a revolution without a press." Main objectives are: (1) to disseminate literature concerning the women's movement to women and men at a cost they can afford; (2) to construct an information network to be used to propagate social change; and (3) to be successful enough as a business enterprise to pay people, especially women, for their work in the women's movement.

Each issue focuses on one of the above objectives. Most articles are reprints from diverse sources and encompass a variety of feminist issues. An example is "The Return of Lobotomies" in which women are the predominant victims. This article originally appeared in The Washington

Post. "Abortion: 'Is This Really 1971?'" is from The Drummer, and "Women's Lib, Pro and Con: The Compleat Argument" is from The Greensburg Accent. Original articles include "Reporters You Can Trust," a list compiled by Know, Inc., which is regularly updated.

Reprints of letters concerning women's rights, such as appeals for support for legislative action, support against job discrimination in specific cases, and suggestions to publishers about sexism in children's books frequently appear.

Information is also given about conferences, classes, job openings, and legislative action. In addition, feminist journals, books, pamphlets, posters, and materials available from KNOW, as well as other feminist groups and publishers, are listed.

One issue of the bulletin is almost entirely devoted to "Women in the Curriculum," a project on the Status and Education of Women sponsored by the Association of American Colleges. This paper describes the establishment of a Women's Studies program and includes a bibliography of resources for planning such a course. (NK)

Feedback:

Editor expressed no disapproval.

## LIBERA

Eshleman Hall (Room 516),
University of California
Berkeley, Calif. 94720
3 issues a year; $3
Started: Winter 1972

Circulation: 1,500-2,500
Format: 60 pages (10" x 8", offset)
Issues examined: Winter and Summer 1972

Libera, named after the feminine form of the Latin word for "free," is a women's journal from the University of California at Berkeley. The first two issues provide a large sampling of poetry and graphics, two short stories, two film reviews, and several general articles.

"Women's Liberation in the Media: Feminists or Female Hitlers?" is an answer to a columnist in the San Francisco Chronicle who had castigated "Germaine Greer and her 'more strident colleagues.'" The author comments on the columnist's

> misconceptions concerning the nature and scope of the 'cause,' the relationship between the cause and such protests as Greer's, the meaning of 'equality

> for women,' and the real obstacles to women's having or attaining equality with men....

"How to Degrade, Demean and Distort in Less than 25 Steps" consists of satirical advice to the media in dealing with "the image of women today and of the Women's Movement," such as:

> When referring to professional women, do not neglect to add the prefix 'lady,' 'woman,' or 'female' (i.e., lady lawyer, woman doctor, female engineer). This is unnecessary for women in service occupations, for here such usage would be redundant (i.e., lady librarian, woman nurse, female secretary).

"The Liberation of Clio" discusses the sexism inherent in most historians' outlooks and the necessity to study Women's History without the traditional male prejudices. The author discusses the social conditioning evident in many books about women written by men and recommends other books that take women seriously and "successfully integrate women into the broader context of American social movements."

Other articles include two opposing views in "The Germaine Greer Controversy"; "A Feminist Look at the Abortion Campaign"; and "Body and Soul," the text of two letters written to "flippant, cavalier, inhuman" gynecologists by dissatisfied patients. (MM)

Feedback:

The respondent supplied additional information on Libera's background and objectives:

> The magazine is a feminist journal; it serves as a forum for divergent views, rather than representing only one approach to feminism.
>
> Libera, a collective of about 30 women, originated in the summer of 1971. It is funded by the Associated Students of the University of California. None of us had ever been involved in putting out a magazine from start to finish; eventually, after much experimentation, a structure emerged. We formed nonhierarchical committees to select poetry, articles, fiction, reviews, and graphics, with everyone doing what she could to help with the general busywork. The first issue took seven months to put out, the second only two. Because we are an open collective, we welcome new members at any time....

On a political level, Libera deals with the contemporary woman as she joins with others in an effort to change her condition. Emotionally, it explores the root level of our feelings, beyond the ambitions and purposes women have traditionally been conditioned to embrace. One of our objectives is to provide a medium for the new woman to present herself without inhibition or affectation. By illuminating not only woman's political and intellectual achievements, but also her fantasies, dreams, art, the dark side of her face, we come to know more her depths, and redefine ourselves.

We of the staff work individually and collectively. Each of us contributes a unique attitude and approach toward a single objective.

## LA LUCHADORA

| | |
|---|---|
| Women's Union | Started: 1971 |
| Box 274 | Format: 8-page tabloid |
| Bronx, N.Y. 10451 | Issue examined: June 1971 |
| 10¢/issue | |

La Luchadora, feminine for "the fighter," is a product of the Women's Union, "an organization made up of Third World Sisters, primarily Puerto Rican, dedicated to the liberation of Puerto Rico and women." The publication is aimed at the poor, blue-collar woman who is oppressed both by society and by the men of her class.

Articles, written in both Spanish and English, discuss the exploitation of the housewife by advertising media, the unfair treatment of women workers, "machismo," and welfare regulations, in an attempt to bring an awareness of their exploitation to the Third World woman. Much more than awareness, however, is requested; the goal of La Luchadora may best be stated as the arousing of the Third World woman "to have a role in the struggle. We must begin to do things outside the home. Join the struggle side by side with our men. We must take part in the fight to end the murder of our Nation." (CH)

Feedback:

Mail returned marked "Address unknown" and "Not Bronx, N.Y. 10451 boxes."

## MS.

Subscription Department
123 Garden St.
Marion, Ohio 43302
Monthly; $10
Started: Spring 1972

Circulation: 350,000
Format: 128 pages (offset)
Issues examined: Spring & Sept. 1972; Dec. 1974-May 1975

Unlike most women's movement periodicals, Ms. is marketed through the mass media, contains standard big-name advertising, and seems designed to reach those who normally read traditional women's magazines. Yet it is different from the latter in its overall feminist tone and the degree to which women not only write and edit its contents but control (publish) it as well.

The following is a brief summary of some of the major subjects covered in the issues examined.

Commentary on the arts/literature/language. "Real Novels About Real Women" is a discussion of the novels of Margaret Drabble, an English feminist. "The Rise and Fall of a Fellini Poster" describes the campaign of some women in Cannes to spraypaint a poster advertising a Fellini movie --showing a nude woman on her hands and knees, with three breasts. A poster carried by one of the women read, "Women are people, not dirty jokes."

"Reconsidering Sylvia Plath" is an extensive survey and discussion of the late writer's works and their feminist (and non-feminist) overtones. "Desexing the English Language" suggests the alternative of "tey," "ter," and "tem" for the generally used "he," "his," and "him" when the subject could be male or female.

Poetry and fiction. One or two short stories and a few poems appear in each issue. One story is usually for children, and all are apparently meant to be free of the sex roles and assumptions encountered in most fiction. Yet one story focuses on the relationship between a boy and his father, with little attention given to the mother's situation.

Long poems published have included Eve Merriam's "A Conversation Against Death" and Sylvia Plath's "Three Women: A Play for Three Voices."

Biology/health/sexuality. In this category, articles have dealt with male biology ("Men's Cycles"); birth control ("Whatever Happened to the Male Pill"); abortion; weight control; and the "sexual revolution" ("The Sexual Revolution Wasn't Our War").

Lesbianism is the subject of "The Return of the Amazon Mother," about the social stigma of lesbian motherhood ("an affront to paternity and a denial of the assumed necessity of the male in any family structure").

> Lesbian motherhood as a phrase means I'm going to have my child and my sex too. My sex meaning both sex *per se* and my own sex--a double transgression. Behind the taboo and sickness theories of lesbianism is the acknowledged but unspoken challenge: a lesbian's prime commitment to another woman.

"Can Women Love Women" is an interview excerpted from *Notes from the Third Year* with two women who had recently begun a lesbian relationship with each other. The only other mention of homosexuality in the issues examined is an article which quotes a psychiatrist on "the assumption ... that superficial masculine and feminine identities and activities [i.e., rigid sex roles] will prevent sexual confusion." "Boys become homosexual," he says, "because of disturbed family relationships, not because their parents allowed them to do so-called feminine things."

*Psychology.* The article just quoted is "Down with Sexist Upbringing," which discusses the "cultural brainwashing techniques" devised to teach children sex roles. The author advises readers to "Let your boy know the challenge of tackling a recipe; let your girl know the challenge of tackling another kid." At the end of the article is a selected bibliography of non-sexist children's books.

"Why Women Fear Success" explains the psychological and social mechanisms that make women unselfconfident and prone to failure.

*Women's history.* "So You Think You Know Women's History" is a quiz on significant contributions by women in history. "The Woman Who Ran for President in 1872" is a profile of Victoria C. Woodhull, who "had she been a man ... would almost certainly have made a more decisive mark in history."

*Feminist social issues and politics.* In this category are such articles as "The Black Family and Feminism"; "Child Care Centers: Who, How, and Where"; "Welfare is a Women's Issue"; "Heaven Won't Protect the Working Girl" (details of sex discrimination); and "The Beauty Queen Who Wouldn't" (exposé of the Miss U.S.A. contest). "Rating the Candidates" and "The Year of the Women Candidates" view the national political scene from a feminist perspective.

*Other social issues.* "Daniel Ellsberg Talks About Women and War" suggests that if women "were less afraid of losing the approval of men," there would be no more secretaries in the Pentagon. In "A Black Guide for White Folks," two black women advise whites on the social amenities between the races. Kate Millett has a two-part article "On Angela Davis."

Regular features. Ms. on the Arts; Manners for Humans; Populist Mechanics (e.g., "The Bike-Buyer's Handbook"); Men (e.g., "How Does It Feel to be the Husband of ...?"); Woman's Body, Woman's Mind; Notes from Abroad (e.g., "What Frenchwomen Are Up To"); Lost Women (women's history); No Comment (examples of sexism from the mass media, etc.); and Stories for Free Children.

Between publication of the first and third issues there was apparently a controversy over the advertising in Ms. The first issue abounds with such ads as "Women: Stand up for your right to sit down at dinner time" (electric food warmer); "It lets me be me" (haircolor); "The Death of the Dead-end Secretary," offering free stickers reading, "Free the Secretary" (word processing systems); "If you'll read this first, you won't have to buy it just for its looks" (hi-fi system); "Guys dig flabby girls. Guys blindly in love" (figure salon); as well as ads for perfume, furs, and (more than any other single product) liquor. Readers' comments on the advertising were solicited and several published in the "letters" column. The third issue contains very little advertising of any kind.

Additional features of Ms. are classified ads, a list of movement publications, and addresses of "Where to Get Help." (MM)

Feedback:

Editor expressed no disapproval.

Addendum:

Recent issues examined contained articles on such topics as the mysterious death of a nuclear plant worker, Karen Silkwood, who was about to turn evidence over to The New York Times concerning safety irregularities; the improved status of Cuban women under the present revolutionary government; women in Congress; the distorted image of American women in movies and the dearth of women directors and screen writers; sex roles in other cultures (some societies are controlled by women); female imagery in art (a discussion by several women artists from around the country on whether female art is different from male); women who bring their babies to work (includes a Ms. staffer and an Illinois state representative); day care programs; breast cancer; the controversy surrounding newly-ordained Episcopal women priests; whether women can match men in physical strength and endurance (there's now only a 10% difference or less between Olympic speed records of men and women); a woman alcoholic; and historical articles on famous women such as Mary Shelley and Gisele Freund (photographer). Each issue contains a sizeable section, "Ms Gazette," which gives "News from All Over" on a variety of topics. (JMS)

MAJORITY REPORT

74 Grove St.
N.Y., N.Y. 10014
Monthly; $3 ($5 to libraries)
Started: 10 May 1971
Circulation: 20,000
Format: 20-page tabloid (offset)

Issues examined: Apr.-June 1973
Back issues on file at Northwestern University Library
Microform version available from Bell & Howell

This newspaper is controlled and produced in a democratic manner by a twelve-woman group of advocacy journalists. It is dedicated to providing women with a medium to help them in their efforts to improve their status. "Women's liberation is taken seriously, and feminist trends and events are covered without prejudice to any one group." The periodical has no political ideology, partly because the views of the staff are diverse, and partly because they believe that "the women's movement is more subversive than any mere political philosophy." The staff offers no endorsements, writes no editorials, and includes no poetry or fiction in the paper. "All [news] stories are read to the group for a democratic vote. Outside articles all are heard."

In the sample issues, one lead article took the position that Martha Mitchell and Mrs. E. Howard Hunt were the real victims of Watergate; another deplored the defeat of a gay civil rights bill by the New York City Council; in a third, Ti-Grace Atkinson sharply criticized Betty Friedan.

Among the regular features are letters from readers; columns ("Molly Muckenraker" and "Hot Flashes") containing short items of interest; and "The NOW York Woman Section," a newsletter for local members of the National Organization for Women and supplement to Majority Report. There are also reviews of books and movies, and a calendar of the month's events. The paper has an attractive layout and carries advertisements. A page of photographs in each issue shows women from different places and circumstances of life, e.g., "Women in Prison," "Women of the River" (Brazil), and "Women of Wounded Knee."

Majority Report's secondary purpose is

> to provide a way for women to learn firsthand the full operation of a newspaper.... We set our own type, design our layout, take and develop news photos, sell display ads and drive a truck to the distributors. That probably sounds dull, but to women it means a whole new attitude toward ourselves.

(EC)

THE MONTHLY EXTRACT: An Irregular Periodical

Lolly & Jeanne Hirsch, Eds.
Box 3488, Ridgeway Station
Stamford, Conn. 06905
Irregular (approx. bi-monthly); $3.50
Started: Aug. 1972
Circulation: 2,000

Format: 12 pages (7" x 8 1/2", offset)
Issues examined: Mar. & May 1973
Microform version available from Bell & Howell

The Monthly Extract is "a communications network for the Feminist Gynecological Self Help Clinics of America." Each issue states that "The purpose of this Newsletter is to fire the Revolution by which women will rightfully reclaim our own bodies." It is published by a mother-daughter team whose attitude can best be described in their own words: "OUR PUBLISHING EFFORTS ARE THE RESULT OF OVERWHELMING NEED FOR AMERICAN WOMEN to get control of our bodies back from patriarchal, unconcerned medical, legal, and religious professions." In addition to publishing this newsletter, the Hirsches have written a booklet, The Witch's Os, on the Self Help Clinic concept, and have given frequent lectures to women's organizations along the east coast.

Each issue consists of "a brief 'editorial' about some current concern of Self Help," and a large section for communications between women on their health. Also included are announcements of conferences, recommended literature, and requests for information. (CT)

Feedback:
Editors expressed no disapproval.

MOTHER LODE

Irregular; $5 for all six issues published

Dates: Jan. 1971 to Spring 1973

Circulation: 5,000
Format: Broadsheet (17 1/2" x 22 1/2") or 8- to 12-page tabloid
Issues examined: Jan., Apr., Summer 1971; Spring & Summer 1972; Spring 1973
On file at Northwestern University Library

Mother Lode, published by the Mother Lode Collective (a women's commune), was started by five members of the collective. Many other women in the feminist movement also worked on various issues. The commune has now broken up and ceased publishing Mother Lode.

Much of the material in Mother Lode was auto-biographical, that is, by women examining themselves, their roles in society, their relationships with men, parents, and children, so as to share their knowledge and experiences with other women. "Why I Want a Wife" (by a woman who works, takes care of children, house, husband and just about everything that happens to come up so husband can go to school), which has been reprinted in many women's publications, appeared in the first issue. The second issue published experiences of women in prison. "We interviewed women who had been in prison [prostitutes, juveniles] and used the written accounts of political prisoners such as Angela Davis, read unpublished prison accounts, and did a lot of investigation into our own lives in order to understand the parallels between these women and ourselves."

The third issue ("It's All in the Family") concerned itself with relations between parents and children, reprinting and analyzing some advisory letters received by daughters from their fathers.

> When one of us received a series of letters from her father, we at first saw them as an isolated personal attack, but as we read them over we began to see that the letters expressed very well the power relationships that operate in families. The other letters and articles in this issue were included for the same reason.

The 1972 Spring issue ("Medical Treatment of Women") encouraged women to become familiar with their own anatomy through self examination of their breasts and cervix (diagrams and step-by-step instructions included in the issue) and to be less intimidated by their male doctors. Other articles dealt with vaginal infections, abortion methods, birth control, "Surgical Mistreatment of Women" (such as unnecessary hysterectomies and radical mastectomies) and women's health collectives. The issue also contained some letters from women about medical experiences. One woman (who almost died because of the arrogance and insensitivity of her male doctors) told how during a sterilization operation her intestine was perforated and when she later complained of terrible pain a doctor insisted she was merely suffering from "psychosomatic" manifestations of "guilt feelings" about being sterilized.

The Summer 1972 issue was devoted to Lesbian Mothers and explored their legal (in California not one custody case has been won by an admitted lesbian) and personal problems (such as rejection by other lesbians who do not have children).

> Lesbianism is a tremendous threat to male supremacy and to the nuclear family and to most institutions of our present system. But lesbian mothers are even more of a threat because we are transferring our values to at least part of the next generation.... They [the children] see women not as slaves to men but as independent human beings. They see our love relationships outside the sexual role stereotypes, and they are encouraged to explore their own possibilities for relationships with other human beings on the basis of who they are rather than on the basis of gender.

Layout and artwork (pen and pencil drawings) were excellent. Mother Lode's address was: Box 40213, San Francisco, Calif. 94140. (JMS)

Feedback:

Sandy Boucher, a member of the collective, told us that it still exists (and can be reached at the above address), although it is no longer publishing Mother Lode.

MOVING OUT

169 Mackenzie Hall
Wayne State University
Detroit, Mich. 48202
Semi-annual; $1
Started: Mar. 1971

Circulation: 3,000
Format: 100-116 pages (8" x 11", offset)
Issues examined: v. 1, nos. 1 & 2 (1971); v. 2, no. 1 (1972)

Moving Out is a feminist literary and arts journal of varied content, with the feel of an anthology: political articles, practical articles, personal narratives, poems, stories, and graphics. Most contributors are from the Detroit area, and some have been published previously.

In the most recent issue examined, articles deal with sex roles, housewives, medical treatment, the "male Left," how to change a tire, women's radio, prison life, a women's liberation interpretation of Genesis, and male chauvinist language. (MM)

Feedback:

"To update your summary: Moving Out has become increasingly literary, with emphasis on literary criticism, plus poetry, fiction, and drama. We also have become more of an 'arts' journal, including prints and drawings by reputable women artists, articles on art, and interviews with artists. Also, more than half of our contributors are from outside the Detroit area [and many are] recognized writers."

NOW!

| | |
|---|---|
| National Organization for Women, East Bay Chapter | Started: Jan. 1969 |
| Peggy Hora, Ed. | Circulation: 350 |
| Box 7024 | Format: 8-12 pages (mimeo.) |
| Berkeley, Calif. 94707 | Issues examined: May, July-Sept. 1973 |
| Monthly; $4 | |

NOW! presents positive images of women, uncovers instances of sex discrimination, and reports on activities of NOW. Two regular features are "Lee's Legislative Line-Up," covering legislative action of concern to feminists, and a list of job openings for women.

The magazine is not concerned with merely informing women; it is designed to also call them to action. Women are urged to be active members of NOW, to act against exploitation of women in advertising, to boycott products, to write to their members of Congress in support of abortion, to attend training workshops, etc.

NOW! is a source of information on women's history, abortion and self-help clinics, and rape crisis counseling services. Included in each issue is a calendar of NOW events in Berkeley and a list of names and phone numbers of resource people in the organization. (CT)

Feedback:

Editor supplied several minor corrections, which have been incorporated into the review.

## NOW!

National Organization for Women, Los Angeles Chapter
743 S. Grandview St.
Los Angeles, Calif. 90057
Monthly; $6 (libraries $10)

Started: Jan. 1967
Circulation: 1,000
Format: 6-8 pages (offset)
Issues examined: Jan. & June 1971; June 1974

This periodical's main purpose is to publicize activities of this NOW chapter and to encourage women and men to participate. In its continued belief in the possibility of reform and the efficacy of the legal system, NOW differs from the radical women's movement. When the radical left was demanding that Angela Davis be freed, NOW called instead for a fair trial.

NOW! concentrates on traditional methods of gaining equality, especially legislative action and control of the media. In the June 1971 issue, an article reviews several California bills relating to women and urges readers to write their legislators. The same issue has a short article urging women to write advertisers about sexist ads. In the January 1971 issue, a special section devoted to committee activities describes the work of a few L.A. Chapter committees--Women's Image, Legislative Action, Public Relations-Press, and Media Report and Political Action. This same issue reviews a book and a play, both feminist, and contains two feminist poems. There are also some feminist want ads.

Besides Chapter meetings, activities publicized in the newsletter include seminars, lectures and rap sessions on various aspects of feminism. Each issue has several short articles on events of interest to feminists. Longer articles explore such problems as sex bias in the media. A regular feature is a calendar of NOW chapter activities. (JMA)

Feedback:
Editor supplied several minor corrections, which have been incorporated into the review.

## NOW NEWSLETTER

Central New Jersey Chapter
National Organization for Women
Box 2163
Princeton, N.J. 08540

Monthly; $3.50
Circulation: 250
Format: 8-20 pages (mimeo., stapled)
Issues examined: Mar.-May

1971
Back issues on file at Northwestern University Library

Microform version available from Bell & Howell

This feminist newsletter contains notes on Chapter activities and information on topics ranging from abortion to sexism in children's literature. Federal and state legislation concerning women's rights is discussed. Guides to combatting misguided legislative action are given, including demonstrations and writing to legislators. (Sample letters are provided.)

Sex-role stereotyping is ridiculed by including quotations from newspapers and magazines. (They are well chosen, pertinent, and often amusing.) Books and magazine articles related to women's liberation are reviewed. (The newsletter formerly included an annotated booklist.) (IT)

Feedback:

The editor suggested several minor changes, all of which have been incorporated into the review.

THE NEW BROOM: A Legislative Newsletter for Massachusetts Women

Laura Rasmussen & Suzanne Wells Sabath, Eds.
Box 341, Prudential Center Station
Boston, Mass. 02199

Monthly; $6
Started: Oct. 1970
Format: 4 pages (offset)
Issues examined: Oct.-Dec. 1970; Jan., Mar.-July 1971

An independent newsletter, The New Broom informs Massachusetts women of their legal rights, and of current state and federal legislation affecting them.

Each issue deals with one topic, such as "Sex discrimination in politics," "Equal employment," and "Women and health." Suggestions for action are included, and a guide to further reading is provided. (IT)

Reviewer's opinion:

The topics are not new, but the suggested solutions are sane and professional, and the tone is restrained. The New Broom could serve as a useful guide to women interested in publicizing women's rights and legislation in their own states.

## NEW DIRECTIONS FOR WOMEN

Box 27
Dover, N.J. 07801
Quarterly; $3
Started: Jan. 1972
Circulation: 50,000
Format: 12- to 16-page tabloid (offset)

Issues examined: Autumn 1973; Winter & Summer 1974
Indexing: Completely cross-referenced index available for 1972-1974 issues

New Directions for Women (formerly ... in New Jersey) provides comprehensive coverage of news and issues relating to the women's movement, particularly in New Jersey. Exploitation of women in the public school system receives much attention in these pages--the textbooks used, the disparity between girls' and boys' athletic programs, and the predominance of men in administrative positions are a few of the issues the writers examine. News of conferences and organizations working toward equality for women receives extensive coverage, as does state and national legislation affecting women. Most of the writing is straightforward, factual, and noninflammatory.

Besides news, the paper contains features and columns. The book reviews in each issue include recommendations of children's books and new feminist periodicals. Occasionally records and films for schools are reviewed. The adult books which are reviewed or recommended are related, naturally, to women. Television programs are reviewed for their good and bad portrayals of women, and articles appear on women poets, writers, architects, and artists. A legal column answers questions such as how to keep one's maiden name or how to establish credit. The "Male Bag" focuses on the liberation of men (a conference of the Task Force on the Masculine Mystique of the National Organization for Women was covered in one issue).

Through their news and articles the women behind this paper aim at raising other women's (and men's) consciousness of problems facing them. A list of suggestions of "consciousness razors" (reprinted from a publication of the Feminist Press) included: "At 11 p.m. on the nineteenth day of every month think about what you've done all day. Next consider what you might have done that day if you had been a man (woman). By January 1 figure out what to do about this."

(SA)

Feedback:

Editor suggested some minor textual changes which were incorporated into the review.

## THE NEW FEMINIST

Joan Johnson, Ed.
Box 597, Station A
Toronto 116, Ont., Canada
Quarterly; $3

Started: Nov. 1969
Format: 18-26 pages (offset or Gestetner, stapled)
Issues examined: Mar. & May 1970

This periodical came out of the radical feminist organization, New Feminists, founded in April 1969. Its goal is the total liberation of women, that is, the elimination of sex roles. An editorial states:

> The total society is based on discrimination of sex roles, and the total society must be changed. Any act ... that changes the unequal power balance between men and women has necessarily political consequences. We are totally, radically, opposed to a society in which sexuality is destiny.

Val Perkins, speaking for The New Feminist, describes its content and purpose: "We have poetry, movie reviews, book reviews, etc. This paper is a forum where women can write in to express their views and experiences. We follow no set format--just what seems to be good at the time we publish." The author of an article on "Social and Sex Roles" feels that

> the ideal situation would be one in which all ascribed roles are eliminated (with one partial exception being the ascribed role based on age). That is, where the important decisions in a person's life are not made for him or her on the basis of his or her sex, race, religion, social class background, or ethnic group.... The existence of ascribed roles of any sort is unnecessary and essentially restrictive, discriminatory, and nondemocratic....

Both of the sample issues listed coming events of interest, including conferences; reported the formation of New Feminist groups; carried notices of like-minded periodicals; and contained letters to the editor. (DB)

## NEW WOMAN

Box 24202
Fort Lauderdale, Fla. 33307

Bi-monthly; $7.50
Format: 112 pages (offset)

Issues examined: Oct. 1971;
June-July 1972

New Woman, which has been variously subtitled "First Magazine for the Thinking Woman" and "New Lifestyles for the Involved Woman," combines traditional women's magazine format and advertising, Cosmopolitan-type attitudes toward sexual freedom, and a moderate political stance on equal status for women. Aimed largely at female executives and other career women, its philosophy is illustrated on the cover of the October 1971 issue: beneath caricatures of a frizzy-haired woman making a fist ("I hate men, marriage, motherhood!") and a frowsy matron ("Woman's place is in the home") is a photograph of a cover girl and the caption, "Between these two extremes stands the New Woman."

"The only magazine dedicated to the elevation of the status and image of the thinking woman" devotes monthly space to these departments: "New Life Plan for the Frustrated Housewife" ("case histories of how some housewives like you got back into the world--and how you can do it too"); "Know Your Rights" (legal advice); "Non-Sexist Child Rearing"; "Things Your Husband/Lover Never Told You About Sex"; "Financial Advisor" ("Insider's advice for women who sincerely want to get rich on Wall Street"); "Divorce Dilemma" (parallels women's magazines' "Can this marriage be saved?" except that it is subtitled, "Should this marriage be saved?"); and astrological interpretations by Sydney Omarr.

Although many articles concern themselves with the political and social advancement of women, several are based on fashion or beauty spreads. "The Rise and Fall of the American Bust" follows a 14-page fashion/jewelry/cosmetics advertisement for several companies. The prose content of "Confessions of a Short Woman" is exceeded by the full-page fashion displays ("Fashions for You if You're 5'2") and smaller advertising inserts in the copy. "Amour in the Tub" suggests how to make bathing with a lover particularly agreeable; brand names and prices of various bath salts, crystals, and perfumes are quoted in the text.

In other articles, "The Big Phallic Fallacy" asserts that "The primary criterion for the successful lover is not phallic immensity, but a considerate and knowledgeable coital attitude." "Flaws Are Chic" reassures the reader that "being different" is "what being a New Woman is all about--searching out one's own identity, exploring one's own individuality, believing in one's abilities, discovering who or what one is or might be and daring to be that person." "Cooking with Spirits," although subtitled (and billed on the cover as)

"Couples Who Share the Chores," concerns itself with the first but not the second, except in photo captions. "Sex and the New Woman" argues that anger between lovers or marriage partners should be expressed so that it does not become destructive to the relationship.

Articles on women's status include "Alimony for Men--Yes or No?" (The answer comes from a New York attorney: "The man's first responsibility in this society is to create the conditions which permit women to be equal. Until then, he does not have the right to alimony.") Others are "What Makes Jewish Women So Darn Smart" (ten variables from tradition to their status in the family as "prizes"); "The New Woman in New China," a reprint from China! Inside the People's Republic by the Committee of Concerned Asian Scholars; an interview with "President Nixon's New Woman: Barbara Franklin"; "The Fertility Pill" ("Will You Love it in December as You Did in May"); and "New Woman's Guide to Abortion in 50 States." (MM)

NOTES

Box AA, Old Chelsea Station
N.Y., N.Y. 10011
Annual; $1.50
Started: 1969

Format: 144 pages (7 1/2" x 10 1/2", offset)
Issue examined: Notes from the Third Year

Notes is a "yearly collection of radical feminist writing," of which Notes from the Third Year: Women's Liberation is the third volume. Articles are solicited from all parts of the women's movement, and the result is an anthology that includes new as well as reprinted, well-known articles written during the year.

Notes from the Third Year is divided into five parts: "Liberating History"; "Women's Experience"; "Theory and Analysis"; "Building a Movement"; and "The Arts." The last page contains a selected bibliography of feminist literature. The following is a brief commentary on each of the chapters under their respective headings.

Liberating History. "The First Feminists" is a "brief discussion of the ... feminist movement in America in the 19th and early 20th centuries." This section also includes an account of "The Trial of Susan B. Anthony."

Women's Experience. "Getting Angry" urges the recognition by women of their rage ("a woman in our society is denied the forthright expression of her healthy anger"). "Woman in the Middle" discusses the plight of the forty- to fifty-five-year-old woman who is "at the point in her life when her aging parents are becoming increasingly dependent and her children, past eighteen, should be increasingly independent, but are not."

> If she is to save herself, the woman in the middle must learn to reject the myths regarding her family ties and responsibilities. She must no longer accept as natural her designated role as servant to all. She must question and challenge the privilege that excludes men from responsibilities and involvement with other human beings. She must reject the passivity of husbands, fathers, and brothers who sit by while wives, daughters, and sisters struggle alone with the devastating hardships involved in caring for the dependent.

"Black Feminism" dispels some of the myths about black women, such as the belief that for her the black struggle must supersede all else ("In the business world sex is more of a barrier than race") and the myth that "matriarchy" is what destroys the black family.

> It is the pressures of poverty and slum life that grind down the black family and destroy the role of the male as father-protector. It is these pressures, not black women, that make the confidence man the ghetto hero.

"Loving Another Woman" is an interview conducted by Anne Koedt (author of "Myth of the Vaginal Orgasm") with "a woman who talked about her love relationship with another woman. Both these women had previously had only heterosexual relationships...."

"A Feminist Look at Children's Books," reprinted from School Library Journal, discusses sexism in children's literature and some prototypes of books that encourage the passivity and inferiority of girls. Some of the recommended books from the bibliography, Little Miss Muffet Fights Back, are discussed for their positive images.

"Speaking Out on Prostitution" is a paper presented at a New York State Legislature hearing on "Prostitution as a Victimless Crime." The speaker, Susan Brownmiller, asserts that "Prostitution is a crime, gentlemen, but it is not victimless. There is a victim, and that is the woman." She goes on to discuss myths about prostitution, such as the belief that the prostitute is a "free participant in her act," by citing research findings and her own experience.

> I have no trouble identifying with either the call girl or the street hustler, and I can explain why in one sentence: I've been working to support myself in the city for fifteen years, and I've had more offers to sell my body for money than I have had to be an executive.

"Men and Violence" is the transcript of a consciousness-raising session taped for a radio station in New York City. The participants relate personal experiences they've had with harassment from men on the street and in social situations.

Theory and Analysis. "The Building of the Gilded Cage" describes the "agents of social control" that keep women in their place and relates the history of and present legal status of women. "Independence from the Sexual Revolution" discusses the oppression of women under the banner of "sexual liberation." "Marriage" also discusses the legal status of women, but as it relates to the institution of marriage. The author contends that "marriage is a form of slavery" and outlines the various legal drawbacks for women in marriage. ("The marriage contract is the only important legal contract in which the terms are not listed.")

"ADC: Marriage to the State" is about another kind of marriage--Aid to Dependent Children, "a substitute MAN." The author discusses the role of "women's work" in this society and dispels the myths about welfare women. ("... the majority of women receiving ADC are white.... If a woman has a large family [two or more children], she will most likely not be able to support her family on a woman's wage rate.")

"Slavery or Labor of Love" discusses housework and "woman's primary oppression as unpaid domestic," and the necessity to fight women's unequal status in the home as well as in the paid labor force. "Prostitution" covers the oppression of women not only in that profession but in the related institutions of marriage and motherhood and argues against the legalization of prostitution ("because it is the ultimate in degradation for women and legally sanctions this kind of abuse of women by men").

"The Spiritual Dimension of Women's Liberation" details the history and effects of "institutional religion's role in the oppression of women" and puts forth the belief that the women's movement "is a spiritual movement because it aims at humanization of women and therefore of the species." "Rape: An Act of Terror" shows that rape is "an effective political device," that the purpose of terror in the oppression of women is to "ensure ... the acceptance by women of the inevitability of male domination." "The most important aspect of terrorism is its indiscriminateness with respect to members of the terrorized class. There are no actions or forms of behavior sufficient to avoid its danger."

"The Woman Identified Woman" by Radicalesbians asks, "What is a lesbian? A lesbian is the rage of all women condensed to the point of explosion." The authors discuss the difference between the social treatment of lesbians and male homosexuals, the ways that the label "lesbian" holds women in line, the importance to the women's movement that lesbianism be dealt with, and the meaning of the term "woman identified woman." As for the difference between lesbians and heterosexual women:

> a lesbian is not considered a 'real woman.' And yet, in popular thinking, there is really only one essential difference between a lesbian and other women: that of sexual orientation--which is to say, when you strip off all the packaging, you must finally realize that the essence of being a 'woman' is to get fucked by men.

Another article on gay women, "Lesbianism and Feminism," talks about lesbian-baiting, the relationship between lesbianism and feminism, the belief by some lesbians that gay women are the "radical feminist vanguard," the gay movement as a civil rights movement, and the necessity to struggle not only for lesbians, but for all women.

"A Woman's Place Is in the Oven" is an overview of the image of women in some recent movies, and in the culture in general.

Building a Movement. "Free Space" discusses some of the group processes involved in a women's consciousness-raising group.

> the small group is especially suited to freeing women to affirm their own view of reality and to think independently of male-supremacist values. It is a space where women can come to understand not only the ways this society works to keep women oppressed but ways to overcome that oppression psychologically and socially. It is Free Space.

"Consciousness Raising: A Dead End?" is a brief article asking what happens after consciousness-raising. "The Selling of a Feminist," reprinted from The Nation, reviews Germaine Greer's The Female Eunuch and criticizes it for not being a feminist book at all:

> Yes, Germaine Greer says all the right things about the economics of sexism. Yes, she is extraordinarily observant about some of the physiological results of our sexual conventions. Her chapters on female anatomy are brilliant. Where she falls down is in her inveterate dislike of women, her idiotic exhortations to revolution and nonviolence alike, and her passionate identification with all things male.
> ...
> ... if Germaine Greer didn't exist, Norman Mailer would have had to invent her.

"The Fourth World Manifesto" criticizes the attempts of some to "turn the independent feminist movement into simply another adjunct to the anti-war and anti-imperialist movements --with the same male-dominated perspective which those movements have." The article goes on to discuss the women's movement as it relates to the New Left, female and male culture, and the colonization of women.

The Arts. "The Independent Female (or, A Man Has His Pride)" is a play written, directed, and designed by women in the San Francisco Mime Troupe. "Women's Private Writings: Anaïs Nin" is one of a series of radio talks on women's diaries and letters. "Women Writers and the Female Experience" discusses several well-known women writers and their treatment by male critics. (MM)

Feedback:

"It's fine."

## NUEVA ACCIÓN FEMENINA

Ofelia Machado Bonet, Ed.
Rambla Republica de Perú
815 (Apt. 1101)
Montevideo, Uruguay
Frequency varied: monthly, bi-monthly, quarterly

Dates: 15 July 1968-Apr. 1972
Format: 6- to 8-page tabloid
Issues examined: Sept. 1968; Mar. & Nov. 1969; Aug. & Nov. 1970; May 1971 through Apr. 1972

This "independent periodical," now defunct, campaigned for women's rights and sought a larger share for women in the political process. It was edited by Professor Machado Bonet, Uruguayan representative on a United Nations commission on the legal and social status of women.

The sample issues contained historical articles on feminism; excerpts of articles from foreign periodicals; reports on feminist meetings (conferences, seminars) around the world; articles exposing discrimination against women in various countries; a list of pertinent publications received; and a look at the status of women in other countries (e.g., France and West Germany).

Regular features of NAF: a continuing "who's who" of Uruguayan women ("La Mujer Uruguaya: Quien Es Quien"); brief "Noticias" of women accomplishing things around the world (becoming cabinet ministers; serving on United Nations commissions); and "Discriminaciones," examining the membership of various private and governmental boards and committees in Uruguay, and giving the numbers of men and women serving on such bodies. (Example: Delegation to the Tenth Regional Conference of the United Nations Food and Agriculture Organization. Men: 4. Women: 0.)

In accordance with its non-violent principles, NAF reprobated the 1968 invasion of Czechoslovakia by the Warsaw Pact countries. (TJS)

OFF OUR BACKS: A Women's News Journal

1346 Connecticut Ave., N.W., Room 1013
Washington, D.C. 20036
Monthly; $5 (institutions, $15)
Circulation: 20,000

Format: tabloid
Issues examined: Summer 1971; Apr. & July 1972
Indexing: Alternative Press Index

Off Our Backs is a national journal that covers--through reportage of events, investigation of the condition of women, and personal experiences of women as relayed in prose, poetry, and artwork--the essential aspects of the women's movement in this country. The prevailing intentions and politics of most contributors are summed up in this excerpt from "Sisters Inside--Sisters Outside," an article in a special "Women in Prison" issue:

> the women's movement must relate to women in prison as one part of women's oppression. Our responsibility is developing this material and political support for our sisters while changing the consciousness of women in and out of our movement to understand race, class and lesbian oppression. Our major task now is building a movement which speaks to the needs of more than young middle-class women, a broad-based movement working for revolutionary change in economic and political power.

Several issues have been devoted to a single topic or have contained supplements on various subjects. One such supplement ("On Women and Health," Summer 1971) is meant to fill in the gaps left by inadequate information about women's health. It explains the basic facts about female anatomy (especially the sexual organs) and discusses some common health concerns of women. The writers explain why it is heavily weighted in the direction of women's sexual-reproductive health:

> Most of our contact with the health system, therefore most of our health experience, has to do with gynecological check-ups and prenatal care. We have been particularly humiliated and misinformed about our sexuality, about menstruation, about pregnancy and childbirth, about menopause.

All these subjects are covered in the supplement, and there are also sections on "herbal medicine" and nutrition; a "supermarket survival guide"; excerpts from an article about medicine in China; and an article on population control ("Ruling class interests developed the ideas and sponsored the growth of population control").

Most of the contributors to the April 1972 "Women in Prison" issue, referred to above, are prisoners and former prisoners from different institutions. Articles discuss our "Criminal 'Justice' System," the conditions in Eastern U.S. jails as experienced by a young woman, pregnancy in prison, a sit-in, "Love [between women] in Prison," political prisoners, some famous women prisoners in history, and conditions in various institutions. The articles are usually written from personal experience, as are two pages of prison poetry. An ex-addict discusses a drug rehabilitation program she left to form a political organization "currently exposing the dangers of methadone maintenance programs, doing political education about drug dependency of any kind, and working to build a people's movement to rid ... communities of drugs and pushers." The issue provides a prison bibliography and the names and addresses of some prison support groups.

Other issues have criticized the Institute for Policy Studies and investigated the working conditions of women at the Library of Congress, "Children's Privacy and Compulsory Schooling," and all other concerns of the women's movement, such as day care, rape, lesbianism, sex roles, and marriage. Regular features include "Bringing It All Back Home" (news of women and organizations in the Washington metropolitan area); "Droppings" (brief news notes, addresses of new groups and publications, and other tidbits compiled by "Chicken Lady"); "Culture Vulture" (literature, music, the arts); "Survival" (car mechanics, etc.); and "Struggle" (demonstrations, projects, successful actions). (MM)

Feedback:

> We liked your review of us and were amazed at your kindness in overlooking our myriad faults.
>
> If it's relevant to your review format you might want to know that we have the largest circulation of any women's newspaper and are, so far, the longest-lived women's paper. We were cited by Time, Newsweek, and the Christian Science Monitor for our terrific sense of humor.... We also printed a 'Mr. April' centerfold two years before Cosmopolitan.

ON CAMPUS WITH WOMEN

Project on the Status & Education of Women
1818 R Street, N. W.
Washington, D. C. 20009
Erratic: 3-4 issues a year
Started: Fall 1971

Circulation: 5,000
Format: 10-16 pages (offset)
Issues examined: none sent
Back issues available from publisher

The publication sent this information: "On Campus with Women capsulizes developments in the higher education community that affect the status of women: new curriculum, new counseling techniques; new research; legal developments that affect women as employees and students."

ON OUR WAY

D. V. Russell, Ed.
Box 4508
Edmonton, Alberta, Canada
Monthly; $3
Started: Aug. 1972
Circulation: 1,500

Format: 16-page tabloid
Issues examined: Feb., Mar., Sept./Oct. 1973
Back issues available from publisher

Some of the issues of On Our Way are devoted to a particular theme, such as "Women in the Media" or "Native Women's Rights." Each issue contains an editorial; announcements of Edmonton events of interest to women; reviews of books, movies, or television (in regards to their treatment of women); original poetry; letters from readers; and--sometimes--a "fix-it" column, with instructions for fixing or repairing household items.

Historical sketches of women prominent in history appear in each issue, e.g., Nellie McClung, a pioneer feminist and political leader (1873-1951) who spoke out for women's rights.

Of major concern is informing readers of the oppression of women in social, political, and economic areas, and of what is being done to counteract that oppression. The issue devoted to "Native Women's Rights," for example, describes the Supreme Court case of Jeanette Lavell, an Indian woman, who--as a result of marrying a white man--lost her "treaty status and accompanying rights and privileges." Her comment: "My fight is about the right of Indian women to decide for themselves about their status. Indian men have that right; Indian women want it too."

The article "Women's Overnight Shelter" is an account of one kind of help available to a segment of female society in need of it. Edmonton Women's Shelter is "a place where women may come for rest, companionship and help; a place which endeavors to provide the basic needs for food, shelter and clothing, but which does not infringe on the individual's right to refuse rehabilitation."

On Our Way comments on the female putdown in the current written and spoken word in its issue devoted to "Women in the Media." The lead article ("Romance Mags") points up how the romance magazines depict working-class women as sexual objects in "stories that encourage a spirit of passivity, a frustration towards attempting change, and a bitter acceptance of what exists, regardless of how bad it is."

Another article ("A Little Bit of Soap") states:

> There are definite stereotypes portrayed in the story content of the soap operas. All of the men tend to be either doctors, lawyers, or highly talented businessmen. Women, on the other hand, are seen as housewives, secretaries, governesses, nurses, or non-working wealthy women who, having nothing better to do with their time, serve as manipulators, competing with and putting down other women.

News of abortion laws, maternity leaves, pension plans, unemployment insurance, and women in the armed forces is also covered.

The editorial staff requests readers to send in "suggestions, comments, criticisms, articles, cartoons, illustrations, poetry." (MH)

Feedback:
"O.K."

THE OTHER WOMAN

Box 928, Station Q
Toronto 7, Ont., Canada
Bi-monthly; $2 (institutions $10)
Started: May 1972
Circulation: 3,000
Format: 20- to 24-page tabloid
Issue examined: Mar. 1973
Back issues available from publisher

The Other Woman is put out by volunteers in Toronto and depends solely on contributions for its printing and circulation costs. Letters to the editor, announcements of activities, book reviews, poetry and other forms of creative writing appear along with longer articles of interest to the women's liberation movement in Canada and abroad. In the issue examined articles covered the dilemma of immigrant women, the role of women in South Africa's liberation movement (reprinted from an African paper), women's liberation in Santo Domingo, and the relationship of Canada to the United States compared to that of a dependent woman to her man. A few articles examined the role of women in Canada's early history, and a photographic essay looked at six Canadian women.

Regarding editorial policy one of the editors writes: "I don't feel that it is our concern as a newspaper to be putting forth position papers.... We are not a 'party' with a 'line.' We are a lot of individuals working collectively to try to help women to share with each other what we have." A few of the writers declare their radicalism in no uncertain terms: "As for myself, and for other Dykes who loathe Man and Man's Woman (both seek to destroy us) I want to reiterate: we are here, a decided threat to the Straight, Sexist world, and to any other form of Sexism, be it Straight or Gay. Sexism is the banal tie-in with males that provides them with so much satisfaction.... I want to repeat that Dykes are organizing: this being the only group of females who are [a] threat to the male structure, and who can create agony within." In an article condemning the concept of "human liberation" as a cop-out, the author writes:

> A woman's movement means women loving women, women living and working with women. It means concentrating our energy on getting women together without wasting time and effort educating men....

> A woman's movement means letting go of the precious little we have scraped together through our relationships with men in order to struggle to create a whole new social order....
>
> (SA)

Feedback:

Editor expressed no disapproval.

PANDORA: A Washington Women's News Journal

Box 94
Seattle, Wash. 98105
Monthly; $6
Started: Oct. 1970
Circulation: 4,000

Format: 16-page tabloid (offset)
Issues examined: 12 & 26 June, 12 July 1973
Back issues available from publisher

The purpose of Pandora is to "provide a forum for women across Washington to communicate with one another, and to give fair and accurate coverage on issues and events concerning women." It provides a calendar of statewide activities, organizational meetings, special exhibits, caucuses, and demonstrations for its readers. It publishes articles about such topics as the older woman, teenagers and juvenile court ("Problems with Parents Force Teens into Court"), rape, child care, women and religion, psychology, contraception, job discrimination, sexuality, marriage and divorce, minority women, women in sports ("Sports at U.W.: Equal but Separate"), and sex stereotyping ("Group Urges End to Sex Role Stereotyping in Schools"). Pandora also contains opinions about, and analysis of, the women's movement ("[Betty] Friedan Unresponsive to Movement") and book and movie reviews with a feminist viewpoint. As an independent newspaper "open to many different opinions," Pandora provides opportunities for reader participation in its "Letters to Pandora" column. Pandora also publishes poetry, short stories, and drawings contributed by its readers. According to the editors, the name Pandora was chosen because "like so many myths and misunderstandings about women throughout history, Pandora was a victim.... The name Pandora was selected because our goal is to report the truth about women of the past and present." (JYH)

Feedback:

"... this listing with the noted corrections is accurate." (All corrections suggested by the editor have been incorporated into the review.)

## PLEXUS

Box 3119
Berkeley, Calif. 94703
Monthly; $5
Started: Mar. 1974
Circulation: 3,000

Format: 16-page tabloid (offset)
Issues examined: Mar.-July 1974

"Plexus is a living network, an interwoven arrangement of parts, created to be a part of the living systems of activity, experience, and energy of Bay Area women. Our function is to be a source of information, a sharing of ideas, an open conversation, and the seed of something new." In this paper news about women is reported and analyzed: strikes and working conditions of nurses, female factory workers, typists, and midwives; sex discrimination settlements; political struggles; and the ever-present problem of rape. In addition to news, the pages are filled by cartoons, book reviews, much poetry, and feature articles about and by women. One unusual feature of the paper is a regular section ("Earth") which deals with the destruction of the natural world by the technological civilization (i.e., men) which has also oppressed and exploited women. "Men have similar ways of talking of things in nature, oppressed peoples, and women. 'You see one redwood you seen 'em all.' 'They all look alike.' and 'In the dark they're all the same.'" It is the duty of women to preserve our natural world, according to Plexus, and this section provides suggestions and encouragement toward this goal.

In a letter describing the paper's ideology, a staff writer explains:

> ... it seemed that Plexus didn't have a definite identity. The Paraclete [another San Francisco women's paper] was a Radical Feminist forum, with a clear definition of what radical feminism was about. Plexus was ideologically open, a motley group of diverse individuals with no particular roles, but with a strong communicative ability together.... We are emphasizing positive energy and new alternatives whenever possible. We believe that women can forge ahead, singing, and do things we have never done before, along with things we haven't done for a long time.

(SA)

Feedback:
Editor expressed no disapproval but wanted several lines deleted, which we saw no reason to do.

## PRIME TIME

232 E. 6th St. (Apt. 5C)
N.Y., N.Y. 10003
Monthly; $5
Started: Sept. 1971
Circulation: 2,000
Format: 14 pages (offset)

Issues examined: Mar., Apr./May, June 1973
On file: Northwestern University Library
Reprints of major articles available from publisher

"Prime Time is an independent feminist monthly for the liberation of women in the prime of life. We believe that every period of a woman's life should be a prime time--a time of growth and fulfillment--whether she is in her 30s, 40s, 60s, or 90s. We deplore all the forces in this society that hold us back. We are staunchly opposed to sexism, ageism, and racism." Such is the philosophy behind this periodical which examines the special problems and difficulties of older women, particularly with reference to their position in the working world. In one article volunteer work is shown as the only "acceptable" work for an older woman "with time on her hands." She is encouraged by others to volunteer in order to "drive away thoughts ... combat loneliness ... seek enrichment." On the other hand such activity is virtually unheard of for older men. Other areas explored are Social Security benefits for housewives (a NOW proposal), the frustrations of older women pursuing higher education, and the women's movement in general (considered in an article boldly titled "Of Women, Money, and the International Revolutionary Potential of Housewives"). Usually there is only one full-length article in each issue; occasionally this may be a long book review. Letters--responding to previous articles or just relating personal experiences and thoughts--occupy several pages. Classified ads, announcements of speakers, job opportunities, cooperative women's organizations, and OWL activities make up another major portion of an issue. Many of the notices are from the New York City area, but a significant number of them are from other parts of the country. The editor states that Prime Time aims to be a "national, and eventually an international, forum for older women." Reprints of Prime Time articles are available for a small fee due to the large number of requests for them.

(SA)

## PRO SE: National Law Women's Newsletter

Lin Horwitz, Ed.
c/o Northeastern University
Law School
400 Huntington Ave.
Boston, Mass. 02115

4 times a year; $5 (law students $3; libraries $25)
Started: Dec. 1971
Circulation: 2,500
Format: 8 pages (offset)
Issues examined: Oct. 1972; Nov. 1973; Mar. & Sept. 1974
Back issues available from editor

The purposes of Pro Se are "to maintain communication and sisterhood among women at law schools around the country and to give coverage to events and projects which concern law women's struggles for equality and humanity." The staff is "entirely volunteer and mostly women law students contribute articles."

Extensive coverage is given to conferences and symposia on women and the law. Pro Se's October 1972 issue reported on the Association of American Law Schools' symposium on Law School Curriculum and the Legal Rights of Women. Issues considered at this symposium included the need for courses on women and the law; property law's disabling effects on married women; and the "corroboration requirement, which is peculiar to rape in most states."

"For Consenting Adults Only," Julian Bond's letter on involuntary sterilization, was reprinted in the March 1974 issue. Bond describes two cases of forced sterilization. One was the case of two teenagers sterilized after the FDA had banned the experimental birth control drug they were being given. In Bond's words, "Little did the Relfs know they had been human guinea pigs for experimental drugs."

The November 1973 issue contains interviews with mothers in law school contrasting their hardships with the beneficial effects of their experience on family relationships. Another article debates the pros and cons of the three possible part-time legal careers: "practicing alone, possible from one's home; teaching in a law school; or working in a sizable firm."

The September 1974 issue is mainly devoted to rape and includes an article by a woman attorney analyzing general rape laws and specific California provisions; a summary of rape myths and research by a former director of a rape counseling center; and coverage of the Massachusetts State Conference on Rape. Also in this issue is a discussion ("Too Dangerous for Cattle--OK for Women") of the legal aspects of the DES-cancer controversy. DES, a synthetic estrogen (also used in cattle feed and recently banned by the FDA), is administered to women in danger of miscarrying and it is the daughters (exposed to DES while in the womb) of these women who have developed cancer.

Discrimination against women by the laws, law schools

and the legal profession and efforts to combat that discrimination are frequent concerns of Pro Se. Letters to the editor, lists of contacts at law schools around the country, and recommended pamphlets, articles, and books (short reviews) are regular features. (JA)

Feedback:

The editor offered some corrections and additions which were incorporated into the review and added: "Thank you for the consideration. Your work looks to be the most helpful kind of bibliography."

THE SAN JOAQUIN NOW NEWSLETTER

Carol Benson, Ed.
NOW San Joaquin Chapter
Box 4073
Stockton, Calif. 95204
Monthly; $4
Started: Nov. 1971
Circulation: 100-150

Format: 22 pages (ditto, stapled)
Issues examined: 3 undated 1974 issues
Some back issues available from publisher

The editor informs us that she and a friend started a county chapter of NOW and that the Newsletter

> began simply as a 'letter' to keep NOW members informed of local NOW activities; evolved into that plus a kind of review of news about the feminist movement around the U.S. and around the world. Only hard and fast editorial philosophy is to try to provide as much news about feminist activities as can be crammed into space allotted. Thus no space (unfortunately) for graphics or illustrations. Contributions of 500 words or less from feminist writers are invited (payment in copies only). It's strictly a low-low budget operation. Everything--from writing, typing, running off on ditto machine, addressing, and mailing--is done by editor. Unfortunately the Newsletter must be published on ditto machine and thus product is not aesthetic and sometimes not even terribly clear.... All this is necessitated by a desire to provide [as much] ... content [as possible] and still keep cost within reason. Newsletter is paid for through membership dues to NOW and newsletter subscriptions--no ads.

## SASKATOON WOMEN'S LIBERATION NEWSLETTER

Saskatoon Women's Centre
#4 - 124A Second Ave. N.
Saskatoon, Saskatchewan, Canada
Monthly or bi-monthly; $3 Canada; $4 USA (institutions $10)
Started: Sept. 1970
Circulation: 800
Format: 20 pages (mimeo., stapled)

Issues examined: Apr. 1973; Feb.-June 1974
Photocopies of the first 15 issues are available from the publisher for $12. (These issues are: Sept. 1970; Feb., Apr., Nov. 1972; Jan., Apr., June, July, Oct., Dec. 1973; Feb.-June 1974.)

A member of the publishing "collective" sent this information:

> Obviously our approach[es] to issues are different from those of NOW (as a facet of the [feminist] movement) or of the Canadian Status of Women.... At this very minute I am putting together the most up-to-date list of the feminist movement centres and groups and periodicals and services in Canada. I expect to run this off (as well as publish it in the [feminist] Calendar--explained elsewhere) and mail it out ... as soon as possible.

The Calendar referred to above was described to us in a letter from a member of the Women's Calendar Collective:

> The Women's Calendar Collective began in May of 1973, funded by a Government Grant. The calendar was patterned after the American Liberated Woman's Appointment Calendar but used solely Canadian content and adopted the philosophy of dealing with positive items and achievements by women.

An editorial in the April 1974 issue explains the movement's goals:

> The goal of Women's Liberation is to end the oppression of women. Women are oppressed by male chauvinism and by capitalism. Women are the most exploited section of the work force. All our efforts must be directed to end this oppression rather than simply cope with it.
>
> The Women's Movement is in danger of being

> co-opted unless it adopts an overall perspective which directs women's consciousness of their oppression towards a strategy to end that oppression. The 'single issue campaign' such as child care, abortion law repeal, and self-help is susceptible to co-optation by government. Isolated demands can become diluted government programs that do not alter the status and role of women. For example, day care is being made more accessible to poor women, but the Saskatchewan government still maintains that women's place is in the home caring for children.

These goals can best be met by a radical reshaping of society, as the <u>Newsletter</u>'s editorial policy points out:

> 1. We must continue and encourage a theoretical discussion of historical reasons for what we are today.
>
> 2. We see women's oppression as an integral part of this society, but confronting masculine and feminine goals cannot be done in <u>isolation</u>. In other words, we steer clear of taking a fragmented view of our oppression and attempts to change it in isolation from the rest of society. Society functions as a whole; therefore, parts cannot fundamentally change --the whole society must change.
>
> 3. We seek to destroy power relationships, not usurp power. This leads us to work towards a socialistic society where women and men have control of (not power over) the means of production. The present goal of industry is to create profit, not to meet the needs of people. Women in positions of power can be as oppressive as men. Therefore, all our actions must encompass a striving towards this goal.
>
> 4. It is necessary that women work together and concentrate their energies in developing an analysis and strategy that will destroy sexism. <u>Present socialist analysis does not ensure this.</u> Only as women together can we create the base, make accessible the information, direct our energy, and develop the skills necessary to break down ... oppression.

In addition to covering the activities and strategy of the parent organization, the <u>Newsletter</u> gives news of legislation affecting women, and of clinics, courses, other groups, women's projects such as "Women and Film," counselling services, and workshops. It also carries some historical articles, short stories, and essays. (JMS)

THE SECOND WAVE: A Magazine of the New Feminism

Female Liberation
Box 344, Cambridge "A"
Cambridge, Mass. 02139
Quarterly; $3
Started: Spring 1971
Circulation: 5,000
Format: 48 pages (offset)

Issues examined: v. 1, no. 1; v. 2, no. 1 (1972)
Indexing: Alternative Press Index
Microform version available from Bell & Howell

Every issue of The Second Wave carries on its title page this quotation from Kate Millett (author of Sexual Politics):

> It may be that a second wave of sexual revolution might at last accomplish its aim of freeing half the race from its immemorial subordination and in the process bring us all a great deal closer to humanity.

Its title also refers to the present women's movement as "the second wave of feminists in an ongoing struggle," the first being the nineteenth-century suffragist movement.

Female Liberation, the organization that publishes The Second Wave,

> encompasses all aspects of the feminist struggle, including education, consciousness-raising activities, and action around such basic demands of the movement as childcare, abortion, and equal pay. No woman is excluded from Female Liberation who is interested in the development of a strong, autonomous women's movement capable of bringing about change on every level.

The Second Wave covers a wide variety of issues. "Nixon Child Care Plan a Disaster" criticizes the proposal as "intended to get the poor off welfare rolls and to enlarge the lowest echelon of the labor force." ("All adult welfare recipients must register for work and accept any job or their funds will be cut off.") "The Case for Studied Ugliness" explains that

> In dressing contrary to social standards we are ...

> not only refusing to fritter away our time, energy, and money noncreatively supporting a coterie of male fashion pimps who have created a false and humiliating image of femaleness, we are actively discrediting that image; we are asserting our human dignity and our right to control our lives.

From "Women's Liberation and Nationalism":

> It should be our position as Third World women that the struggle against racism must be waged simultaneously with the struggle for women's liberation, and only a strong independent women's movement can insure that this will come about.

Other articles in the issues examined include: "In Defense of Angela [Davis]"; "Lesbians in the Women's Liberation Movement"; "Making the Trip: Women and Prisons"; "Faculty Wife"; "Psychosurgery: The 'Final Solution' to the 'Woman problem'?"; "A Look at Love Comics"; and "Help Wanted: Domestic" (about household workers and the National Committee on Household Employment).

Poetry, book reviews, and film reviews appear regularly. (MM)

Feedback:

Editor expressed no disapproval. A later communication from the editor informed us that Female Liberation Newsletter, also published by Female Liberation, has ceased publication. The Second Wave thinks of itself as a radical feminist publication which emphasizes works by and about women, and "as a forum for feminist thought."

SECRET STORM

| | |
|---|---|
| Chicago Women's Liberation Union | Format: 4-page tabloid (offset) |
| 2748 N. Lincoln Ave. | Issues examined: 2 undated |
| Chicago, Ill. 60614 | 1974 issues |
| Bi-monthly | |

CWLU has organized and sponsored such groups and activities (in the Chicago area) as Pregnancy Testing; Legal Clinic; Health Evaluation and Referral Service (HERS); Liberation School ("offers classes in many interesting areas from introductory readings in women's liberation and our bodies our selves to auto mechanics, silk screening, self defense, the history of the women's movement"); Direct Action for Rights in Employment (DARE), which "can help you file a sex-discrimination charge or organize with women where you work"; Prison Project ("gives classes in women's prisons and works with women prisoners and women out on work release"); and Rape Crisis Line ("counsels women who have been raped.... They will go with you to the hospital and the police, and they have been instrumental in getting more women on the police assigned to rape cases").

Secret Storm carries short articles written in a simple style. Examples are "Growing up Female"; "Horner Park Puts Women in Their 'Place'" (captain of a women's softball team was beaten by a member of a male team who refused to relinquish the playing field for which the women's team had a permit); and "Birth Control: Helpful Hints for the Long Hot Summer Ahead."

The paper contains letters to the editor and is illustrated with photographs and small drawings. (JMS)

Feedback:

"Good review. Secret Storm is geared for high school- and junior college-aged women."

SPEAKOUT

Box 6165
Albany, N.Y. 12206
11 issues a year; $3.50 (institutions $5)
Started: Jan. 1972

Circulation: 1,000
Format: 18-28 pages (mimeo., stapled)
Issues examined: Apr., May, July 1973

Speakout is "dedicated to the women's movement and to encouraging women in all phases of journalistic endeavor. It attempts to give women who desire to speakout an opportunity to do so." Each issue centers on a specific topic. Some topics examined are motherhood, marriage, international sisterhood, employment, and women in business.

The journal carries a calendar of local events as well as job listings, announcements, and a column of letters to the editor entitled "Speak-Up." Speakout appears to be particularly conscious of the role of organized women as a political movement, and gives thorough and specific coverage to legislation and legislators, both local and national, affecting the women's movement.

Speakout limits its editorial staff to women, but will

accept articles written by men. [Feedback: "Lately we've been printing short stories and poetry, as many women in our area are turning to writing fiction, to express who they are and how they feel."] (JYH)

Feedback:

Christine Root, one of the editors of Speakout (and a librarian), replied: "I wish you 'energy' rather than 'peace,' as it certainly takes a lot for any publishing venture on the alternate side of the press world.... We are all amateurs in journalism and publishing. We ... look forward to future contacts with COSMEP and its members."

THE SPOKESWOMAN: An Independent Monthly Newsletter of Women's News

5464 South Shore Dr.<br>
Chicago, Ill. 60615<br>
Monthly; $7 (institutions $12)

Started: 1971<br>
Format: 12 pages<br>
Issues examined: Jan.-Apr. 1972

The Spokeswoman reports national news about women. In an easy-to-follow format the text is printed in two columns, with headings indicating the content of each item. The main emphasis--sex discrimination--and the tone are similar to those of the National Organization for Women. Some of the main headings used are Welfare, Employment, Education, Business, Law and Order, Women's Studies, and Unions.

In addition to news items of general interest to feminists, The Spokeswoman offers a great deal of factual and bibliographic support, giving addresses, names of organizations, details on planned demonstrations or other actions, particulars of relevant publications which will give further information. On the last two pages of every issue are a list of conferences and organizations, and a section on "media" with addresses and descriptions of new periodicals, books, films, articles, and other publications.

Although much of its attraction is to middle-class women interested in equal pay for equal work, job advancement, etc., The Spokeswoman does report on news of interest to gay, black, Chicana, and welfare women. Although it does not generally publish literature or lengthy articles, it did in one issue reprint the short satire, "The Psychoanalysis of Edward the Dyke." (MM)

Feedback:

The editor pointed out that The Spokeswoman also contains "a monthly help-wanted advertising section which lists professional openings with major companies and educational institutions. These are openings rarely made known to women."

## THE SPORTSWOMAN

Marlene Jensen, Ed. and Publ.
Jensen-Fane Publications
Box 2611
Culver City, Calif. 90230
Bi-monthly; $4.50
Started: Mar. 1973
Circulation: 15,000

Format: 56 pages (offset)
Issues examined: May & July 1974
Back issues available from publisher (ask for list)
Microform version available from Xerox University Microfilms

A slick, professionally-done magazine on women in sports.

## THE TEXAN WOMAN

Frieda L. Werden, Ed.
Box 1267
Austin, Tex. 78767
7 issues a year; $3.50 (institutions $5)
Started: June 1973

Circulation: 10,000
Format: 32 pages (offset)
Issues examined: Aug. 1973; Apr. 1974
Back issues available from publisher

The Texan Woman seeks:

> to provide a forum for the voices of Texas women.... One purpose is to circulate information among and about Texas feminists--to announce the existence of groups and activities, link individuals struggling for change, report success or failure of tactics in the fights for equality, fair play, and role restructuring.... Another purpose is to be a showplace for women's culture.... Also, the Texan Woman wishes to keep Texas women apprised of those more traditional activities ... that are of interest to us as women.

Each issue contains poetry, short stories, articles, photographs, and book reviews by women and a few "token men." Also in each issue are several articles and announcements about meetings and conventions, legislation, jobs, and finances. A regular feature is a list of names, addresses, and announcements; the latest issue available says that "Listings attempts to serve as a limited clearinghouse for the exchange of information of interest to women." Included in Listings are names and addresses of organizations, feminist publications, opportunities for expression, and "CLOUT: Employment/Discrimination/Careers." (MG)

Feedback:
Editor expressed no disapproval.

TRIPLE JEOPARDY: Racism, Imperialism, Sexism

Third World Women's Alliance
346 W. 20th St.
N.Y., N.Y. 10011
Bi-monthly; $3.50 (institutions $8)

Started: 1971
Circulation: 5,000
Format: tabloid
Issue examined: Apr. 1972

Triple Jeopardy sees the three interlocking causes of oppression of Third World people (Asians, Africans, black Americans, etc.) to be racism, sexism, and imperialism. Although it is a feminist paper, it puts more emphasis on related struggles and less on specifically female problems.

The sample issue covered most major areas of the Third World, reporting on sexism within the Chicano movement; the political similarities between the Vietnam War and the Korean War; the role of women in the Korean Workers' Party; "the life and death of Doris Torresola," a Puerto Rican nationalist; U.S. imperialism in Colombia; the death of a Mexican guerrilla; a Vietnamese student occupation of the Vietnamese consulate in New York; and the U.S. Information Agency's world-wide version of the Angela Davis case. Two or three items championed unknown political prisoners, reporting the names and addresses of several. Other articles relating more specifically to women included "Feminine Stink Mystique," the politics of feminine hygiene sprays; "Painless Childbirth" (the Lamaze Method); and one black woman's experiences working in a toy factory. An editorial urged women to combat their own passivity rather than male chauvinism only; and two apparently regular features discussed "common infections of the vaginal area" ("Health") and what to do for a person who ingests too much heroin ("Skills"). (MM)

Feedback:

Editor expressed no disapproval.

US [UNITED SISTERS]: A Florida Feminist Monthly

Ginger Daire-Reber, Ed.
4213 West Bay Ave.
Tampa, Fla. 33616
Monthly; $7
Started: Mar. 1973

Circulation: 500
Format: 24-pages (offset)
Issues examined: Mar., Nov., Dec. 1973; Jan. 1974

The idea for US (which grew out of the Tampa Women's Liberation newsletter, Birthright) originated at the January 1973 Florida Radical Feminist Conference in Tampa.

> One of the goals of this conference was to establish an effective means of communication between the many grassroots feminist organizations that were forming state-wide.... The magazine has incorporated both the newsworthy achievements and the artistic and literary endeavors of feminists both state- and nation-wide. Going one step further, US hopes to bridge the gap that seems to exist between conservative and radical feminists by its promoting the celebration of and a better understanding for all aspects of feminists' lives and life-styles.
>
> Owned and operated entirely by women, US encourages and supports feminist interests. In the past, US has published The Candidate's Handbook: Florida Edition (by Mary C. Dunetz) for the Florida Women's Political Caucus, as well as the program for the first Florida Conference of the National Organization for Women. Currently, US is sponsoring an established feminist artist in her production of holiday greeting cards, provides copyright services for feminist songwriters, is preparing a directory of Florida feminists, provides low-cost typesetting services to other feminist publications, and will eventually establish a Feminist Foundation to fund feminist-oriented endeavors.

The magazine consists of several short articles; one or two book reviews; poetry; sometimes a short story; letters to the editor; a "Women's Directory of Businesses and Services"; and news of the organization's activities, other feminist groups, conferences, workshops, court decisions and legislation concerning women. Regular features: "Raising Our Consciousness" has covered such subjects as male and female stereotyping, discrimination against women in the job market, and women's fears that if they appear too intelligent and competent they will be undesirable to men; "A Feminist Looks at Insurance" advises women; and "Recycling Our Money--An Economic Revolution" discusses the group's plans to invest money in goods and services that are manufactured or run by women, such as day care, handicrafts, and literary works.

Examples of articles: "Support Your Local Needlewomen" (on an ancient and little-appreciated art); "Women and Money" (wives are dependent on their husbands' money and have little to say about spending it); "Women and Religion" (in many societies and religions--Catholicism for one--women have been looked upon as unclean [because of menstrual periods] temptresses); and "Rape Rap" which describes a rape panel organized by Women Against Rape.

US is illustrated by simple ink drawings done in a realistic style. It carries some advertising. (JMS)

Feedback:

Editor expressed no disapproval.

UNION WAGE

2137 Oregon St.
Berkeley, Calif. 94705
Bi-monthly; $2 (institutions $5)
Started: 1 May 1971
Circulation: 4,000
Format: 8- to 12-page tabloid (offset)
Issues examined: Jan.-May 1973
On file at Northwestern University Library
Microform version available from Bell & Howell

Union WAGE (Union Women's Alliance to Gain Equality) is an organization working for equal rights, equal pay, and equal opportunities for women workers. The purpose and goals expressed in each issue of the paper acknowledge the double burden of working women: discrimination against them as women and as workers, at the job and at home. The paper focuses on issues related to women at work and in their unions. Among the organization's stated goals are: "affirmative action programs, unionizing women workers, activizing women unionists, raising contract demands like maternity benefits, child care, state protective laws for all workers, Labor Equal Rights Amendment, $3 an hour, 35-hour or less workweek with double pay for overtime." Union WAGE articles cover these issues in the form of news reports, as opinions, or as features on aspects of the "movement." "Labor Heroines" is a particularly interesting feature in each issue, in which a woman labor leader from the past is examined in a brief history and commemoration. Such salutes have been made to Mary Harris Jones (Mother Jones), Agnes Nestor, and Rose Schneiderman--all active around the turn of the century. Many of the articles are about specific companies, and are written by angry female workers employed in them. (Such articles usually expose poor working conditions or unfair pay.) Strikes are advertised, as are other efforts toward organizing women. Short news items--usually of national interest--are included. (SA)

Feedback:
Editor expressed no disapproval.

VELVET GLOVE

Box 188
Livermore, Calif. 94550
$5

Issues examined: May & Dec. 1971

Velvet Glove, whose motto is "Free Women Writing Freely," began as a literary journal for women but has expanded to include political articles as well. One of the issues examined is a special issue on "Woman as Writer." Articles include "Discrimination in Publishing; Perils of Priscilla," by an author who faced resistance from male publishers; and "Women and War," which urges women to build peace

> as consumers in changing the direction of the economy, as citizens in changing the direction of government, and most important, as women in changing the social attitudes that nurture the warrior virtues.

The other sample issue includes "The Polemic of an Ex-Shit-Worker," by a woman who worked for Rolling Stone, the rock magazine, and encountered the same sexism that one finds in more traditional establishments; and "Feminism Raped by Male-Power Politics," about a takeover within the ranks of San Francisco N.O.W. Both issues include short stories and poetry; the serialization of Moll Maguire, Avenging Female Angel (meant for publication in April 1972); two letters from the "Alphabet of Extinction," every letter being a living creature made extinct by man; and "Forgotten Women of His Story [History]." (MM)

## THE VOCAL MAJORITY

Davida Daemon, Ed.
1713 Hobart St., N.W.
Washington, D.C. 20009
Monthly; $5 (institutions $15)
Circulation: 700-800
Format: 20 pages (offset)

Issues examined: Apr., July, Aug. 1974
Back issues on file at Northwestern University Library
Microform version available from Bell & Howell

This is a digest of news and articles of interest to members of the Washington NOW chapter, as well as to other women in the area. It "is meant to serve as an open forum" for the concerns and activities of the members. Regular features include summaries of the board meeting and business meeting, ads and notices of interest to women (such as free breast examinations), and information on sister chapters. Statements and position papers from local chapters and the national organization are also presented.

This chapter of NOW attempts through local action to put into effect the aims of the national group. For example, the Control of Our Bodies Task Force reported on the results of a questionnaire sent to 63 obstetrician-gynecologists in the D.C. area. The purpose of the questionnaire was to ascertain the doctors' attitudes toward birth control and abortion and toward welfare patients and single women seeking their services. Most of the doctors did not reply. The names of those doctors were listed, with the question, "Is one of them yours?" This article and others advocate the right of women "to plan their reproductive lives" without government interference.

The problems of female prisoners, rape victims, and female students are also of concern to the chapter. An article entitled "Too Much Black and Blue" reports on the problems of battered wives: "Beneath the rhetoric about equality between men and women lies a simple truth: they can beat us up. As a rule, men are stronger than women, bigger, heavier...." Society offers little in the way of protection for wives beaten by their husbands. The writer of the article found that police and courts in the D.C. area place a low priority on wife-beating cases.

Another local activity in which the chapter is involved is city elections. The task forces prepare statements "proposing solutions to problems crucial to D.C. women, such as childcare, education, and employment discrimination" which they attempt to get candidates to endorse. They also plan to "translate the position papers into specific city government programs."

Other activities noted in The Vocal Majority include fund-raising projects, and meetings and publications of allied groups. (SLA)

Feedback:

"Sounds good." The editor suggested some minor textual changes which were incorporated into the article.

Voice of Women/La Voix des Femmes BULLETIN NATIONAL NEWSLETTER and ONTARIO NEWSLETTER

1554 Yonge St. (Rm. 4)
Toronto, Ontario, Canada M4T 1Z7
BNN quarterly; ON monthly; $5 each
Started: BNN 1960

Circulation: BNN 3-4,000; ON 500
Format: BNN 8-page tabloid (offset); ON 4 pages (legal size)
Issues examined: BNN Sept. 1973; ON Nov. 1973

The Bulletin National Newsletter is published for national members of the Voice of Women, an outgrowth of the peace movement now involved primarily in the women's rights movement, and composed of regional groups in various parts of Canada. Each such group publishes a monthly mimeographed newsletter (e.g., Ontario Newsletter) from which items of interest may be included in the Bulletin National Newsletter. Short articles from other sources (periodicals, letters, newspapers, reports) are also excerpted in BNN.

Voice of Women is concerned with such issues as dictatorship (opposition to the Chilean military junta which overthrew Dr. Salvador Allende's elected Marxist government; and to the military junta which ruled Greece until July 1974, and imprisoned and tortured its opponents); political prisoners (approves of Amnesty International); ecology (opposition to nuclear power); civil rights (support for women's demand for political power); colonialism (opposition to Portuguese rule in Angola); and totalitarian nations divided into leftist and rightist halves (preference for North over South Vietnam).

The quarterly BNN is printed with various type faces and in appearance somewhat resembles underground newspapers. Readers' attention is sometimes called to items in which they might be interested (books, films, periodicals) by lists.

The regional ON provides information on meetings and other events on the local level, as well as short items of political interest. (KL; TJS)

## WIA

Women in the Arts
Cynthia Navaretta, Ed.
435 Broome St.
N.Y., N.Y. 10013
Monthly (except Aug.); free
Started: June 1973

Circulation: 600
Format: 4 pages (offset)
Issues examined: Dec. 1973-June 1974
Back issues available from publisher

"To date, newsletter has functioned as a source of information only for its membership, concentrating on activities and events of interest in the art world such as jobs and opportunities, exhibition space, exhibition listings, and summary of meetings with the emphasis on reportage. Under discussion is a change in format and editorial policy to include feature articles, editorials, and letters."

## WONAAC NEWSLETTER

150 Fifth Ave.
N.Y., N.Y. 10011
Quarterly (approx.); $3
Started: July 1971
Circulation: 6,000

Format: 8-16 pages (offset)
Issues examined: Jan. & Oct. 1972; Feb. 1973
Some back issues available from publisher

WONAAC Newsletter is the publication of the Women's National Abortion Action Coalition, an organization pledged to further the right of women to control their own reproductive lives. The group supports legalized abortion and unrestricted distribution of information on contraception, and it opposes forced sterilization. The newsletter reports each month on international, national, and local events--many of them sponsored by WONAAC--which are designed to demonstrate the need for abortion reform. Progress and setbacks of the movement are described. One issue, for example, was largely devoted to an analysis of the 1973 Supreme Court ruling on abortion. Reports on conditions in several states were used to indicate the need for continued action to insure the rights granted by the court. Brief articles monitor the activities of anti-abortion groups. New York Times articles and editorials on the abortion reform movement are frequently reprinted.

Articles in the issues examined also included "position papers" submitted by groups and individuals, brief discussions of such topics as gay women and abortion reform, "A Child's Right to Be Wanted," and proposed action programs for the movement. (AS)

Feedback:
"The summary ... seems fine to us."

WHAT SHE WANTS

Box 18072
Cleveland Heights, Ohio 44118
Monthly; $3
Started: May 1973

Circulation: 2,000
Format: 12-page tabloid (offset)
Issues examined: Apr., June, July 1974

> The great question that has never been answered, and which I have not yet been able to answer despite my thirty years of research into the feminine soul, is: 'What does a woman want?'
> --S. Freud

The quotation above poses the question to which What She Wants addresses itself. Said to be Cleveland's only women's newspaper, it is put out by a collective of 10-15 women whose politics are "distinctly left." A staff member states that the paper is "an attempt to communicate with women of the Cleveland area on current issues, activities, and projects, and the personal accounts of individuals within the women's liberation movement." The emphasis is on community awareness, although there is also an attempt to inform readers of national and international news. What She Wants celebrates female culture--art, literature, and life.

Each issue runs about 12 pages and is liberally sprinkled with illustrations. Regular features include a poetry page which prints unsolicited poems; a "Find It Faster" column of important phone numbers; and "What's Happening," a page of short blurbs on local goings-on of interest. Occasional reviews of movies (Ingmar Bergman's Cries and Whispers) or books (Ellen Frankfort's Vaginal Politics) focus on subjects relating to women.

Major articles touch upon a variety of topics: "Gay Women's News--Lesbian-Feminist Conference"; "Sexism and the Catholic Church"; "8,000 Remember Kent" (a rally commemorating four Kent State University students shot dead by national guardsmen in May 1970, after Richard Nixon's invasion of Cambodia); and "Men and Marriage" (concerning freedom of choice and alternate forms of marriage). One can also find humorous articles which switch the usual male/female roles: "8 Ways to Remain Woman and Husband" is directed--tongue-in-cheek--toward the male, with advice on sex, birth control, physical appearance, and the like; and "Let Me Call You Sweetheart" describes a parody of the Miss America contest, staged to make money for a People's Free Clinic.

The aim and performance of the paper are summed up in "Letter to You, Our Supporters" (July 1974):

> We have tried to develop each issue so that there is something for every woman who reads it: something for women who work in or outside their homes, something for students, something for gay women, something for straight women, something for everyone. We don't always reach this goal, but we try.

Our questionnaire had been sent originally to Rantings, c/o Nancy Wood, 11205 Euclid Ave., Cleveland, Ohio 44106. It was returned, filled out by What She Wants, with the explanation that Rantings "Merged its newsletter functions into our newspaper format in September 1973, after four or five issues." (SK)

Feedback:

"We like it."

Reviewer's judgment:

An extremely readable and interesting paper. Terrific illustrations.

## WHOLE WOMAN

1628 Winnebago St.
Madison, Wis. 53704
Monthly; $4.50 (institutions $7)
Started: Sept. 1972
Circulation: 1,500

Format: 16-page tabloid (offset)
Issues examined: Mar., Apr., June 1973
Back issues on file at Northwestern University Library

Whole Woman is put out by a small collective of women. Most of the news stories cover events in the Madison area, but many of the articles relate to women's liberation anywhere in the country. Each issue contains a directory of women's organizations and community services in Madison, and announcements of local events and activities of interest to the movement. Often a full-length article will cover a local organization or activity in depth: a free counseling service for women run by women on the university campus was examined, and a young woman who campaigned as a lesbian for a seat on the Madison Board of Education was interviewed. Also included in most issues are poems and drawings and photographs by women. In a column called "Herstory" the past is reexamined with an eye on women. (For example, in one issue the reader is informed that the idea of a cotton gin was originally conceived by a woman, not by Eli Whitney. Calamity Jane and the various misleading--i.e., sexist--portrayals and biographies of her are examined in another issue.)

Articles of current national and international interest have covered topics as diverse as the dangers of weather-control research (much of which is done in Wisconsin) and women's liberation in France. (In the former article, the author frequently emphasized the seriousness of her message in a rather comic way by warning the reader that the following paragraphs should be read only if the blood pressure is normal, and tension is low.)

Articles directed more specifically toward women's issues have covered Lesbianism; rape; and the degradation of the child-bearing experience by modern technology and male-chauvinist obstetricians. Suggested reading lists are often appended to the longer and more substantial articles.

The staff of Whole Woman is as much interested in the process of putting the paper together, as in the final product. The presence of the writers themselves is apparent in the interview format used for many of the articles, and in such personal touches as were seen in the article on weather-control. (SA)

Feedback:

"O.K."

## WINDSOR WOMAN

Irregular; $2 Issues examined: none sent
Format: 4-8 pages

The publication, which was put out by a women's newspaper collective, sent this information: "Windsor Woman is, I am sorry to report, defunct. It was aimed at working women & was pro-abortion, did a feature on rape, and was into many issues concerning women. It supported the start of Women's Place."

The address was 1309 University Ave. W., Windsor, Ont., Canada.

WOMAN

| | |
|---|---|
| 201 Sproul Hall, University of Calif. | Circulation: 1,000 |
| Berkeley, Calif. 94720 | Format: 12 pages (7" x 8 1/2", offset) |
| Monthly | Issues examined: Jan., Feb., Apr.-June 1974 |
| Started: June 1972 | |

"Newsletter intended for campus events and as an inter-departmental communication paper. We make no pretense of being a literary newsletter." The publication's purpose is "to serve as an informational newsletter helping to prevent overlapping of effort and function between the many different women's groups serving the Berkeley campus."

THE WOMAN ACTIVIST: An Action Bulletin for Women's Rights

| | |
|---|---|
| 2310 Barbour Rd. | Circulation: 600 |
| Falls Church, Va. 22043 | Format: 8 pages (offset) |
| Monthly; $5 (institutions $10) | Issues examined: Feb.-May 1973 |
| Started: Jan. 1971 | |

_The Woman Activist_, "a monthly action bulletin for women's rights to provide current information and calls to act 'from the Courthouse to the White House'," is edited by Flora Crater, the first feminist to run for state-wide office (Lieutenant Governor) in Virginia history. (She received almost 100,000 votes.) The bulletin regularly features news, information, and lists of new national and state legislation affecting women (e.g., abortion, divorce, health, the Equal Rights Amendment), excerpts from speeches in the _Congressional Record_, and news and statements of feminist organizations such as the National Organization for Women and the National Women's Political Caucus. Each issue includes brief articles on such things as the Nixon administration's budget cuts to social services ("Man the Life Boats. Women and Children Last"), and a chronology of U.S. Congressional action on the ERA. "Actions for the Month" are recommended tasks that will help further women's rights. The issues examined contain running commentary on the progress of the editor's campaign for Lieutenant Governor. (MM)

Feedback:
Editor expressed no disapproval.

WOMANKIND

Chicago Women's Liberation Union
852 W. Belmont
Chicago, Ill. 60657
Monthly; $4 ($12 if you are an institution; free if you are in an institution)

Started: Sept. 1971
Format: 16-page tabloid (offset)
Issues examined: Dec. 1972; Mar.-Apr. 1973
Back issues available from publisher

Womankind is the official organ of a radical organization whose "primary purpose is to attack sexism--that's the systematic oppression of women for the benefit of the people in power." The organization has "aimed at changing the lives of all women and building a new society in which all people will have the opportunity to develop their full potential." While recognizing that blacks, Latins and the poor are also oppressed, the paper emphasizes woman's plight in society. In addition to articulating the philosophy of the organization, each issue describes briefly the Union's various programs: a Liberation School, Health Care, Legal Program, Rape Project, Job Discrimination, Art and Music, and Spreading the Word. Notices and a calendar of activities related to women's liberation in the Chicago area are given. Such activities include study groups on rape and abortion, legal aid, films, and music. Relevant boycotts are advertised. Longer articles cover such subjects in greater detail. A series of articles about venereal disease was reprinted from the VD Handbook. The material on the disease and its treatment was highly factual, although the final word was an attack on the inadequate health care system in our society. News of national interest is covered, consistently written from the viewpoint of the exploited. Articles have appeared on the Indians at Wounded Knee, woman's role in China, and Nixon's 1972 election victory. Often a full page article appears on food and soaring prices, sometimes with suggestions on coping with poor products and high prices. Occasionally a book will be reviewed if it is of particular interest for the field of liberation. (SA)

## WOMAN'S WORLD

Bi-monthly; $2
Dates: 15 Apr. 1971-1972
Circulation: 3,000

Format 12- to 24-page tabloid
Issue examined: July 1971

Woman's World was a radical feminist paper that challenged much of the contemporary literature of the women's movement. Members of the staff were interested less in proving that they had nothing against men, than in being truthful about their hostility and explaining why they felt it was justified. [Feedback: "The staff is less interested in proving that they have nothing against men than in developing a truthful analysis and explaining why they feel it is justified."]

> We are tired of all the phony claims of political idealism--of humanitarianism, democracy, communism, Christianity, etc.--which only cover up the self-interests of the groups or individuals behind them. Women, especially, have been kept in bondage in the name of these ideals for too long. After all, that is what 'serving others' has been all about for us ... serving. We have been 'loving our enemy,' too, for thousands of years--officially, anyway--and where has it gotten either ourselves or our sex? Anything women have been able to get has come through plotting and struggling for every little inch, every little gain, not through 'loving' either one man or mankind. [Feedback: The respondent suggested deleting the last five words in the preceding sentence: 'Since you're quoting this out of context, we feel the accompanying changes in this text correct for distortion of our true meaning.' She also suggested deleting the first sentence of the following quotation.]
>
> We are not interested in ideals at this point. We are interested in REALITY. We are also interested in POWER, power for ourselves, and--because our circumstances, love it or not, are inextricably linked with those of the rest of our sex--we must go all out for power for women, the power which male supremacists have denied all of us for so long.

In "Male Psychology: A Myth to Keep Women in Their Place," Carol Hanisch argues against the "sex role" theory of women's oppression:

> And so we are not 'taught' or 'conditioned' to do what we do. In men/women relationships, women do what we do to survive, to get what we need and what we want and deserve, and to avoid being punished. Men do what they do because they get some benefits out of it ... [or] to avoid being harassed by other <u>men</u> for breaking the male code.

A special "Men's Page" in the sample issue questions the motives of "men's liberation" and the men who belong to the National Organization for Women on an equal-power basis. [In the following sentence, Feedback suggested deleting the portions that appear within square brackets.] Other articles deal with Youth Against War and Fascism (YAWF) women--["agents of male supremacy"]--who attacked a feminist forum; women who are suing the Catholic Church; [and a protest against furriers in New York City].

Woman's World uses the Redstockings' slogan, "THIS TIME WE ARE GOING ALL THE WAY!" (MM)

Feedback:

"We have discontinued Woman's World, but the back issues are available for a sum of $2.00. We will soon be announcing publication of a new journal, an annual called The Redstockings Journal: Feminist Revolution." For back issues, write to Woman's World, Box 1284, Stuyvesant Station, N.Y., N.Y. 10009.

WOMEN: A Berkshire Feminist News Journal

Box 685
Lenox, Mass. 01201
Every 6 weeks; $3 (8 issues)
Started: Feb. 1972
Circulation: 700
Format: 32 pages (offset)

Issues examined: 7 issues between 9 Dec. 1973 and 15 Sept. 1974
Some back issues available from publisher

"Women includes news of local (Berkshire County, Massachusetts), state, and national women's news, 'thoughty' articles (commentaries, opinions, ideas), reviews, women's culture, sports, religion, and cartoons. We welcome articles, photos, graphics, and poetry from women."

## WOMEN: A JOURNAL OF LIBERATION

3028 Greenmount Ave.
Baltimore, Md. 21218
Quarterly; $4 (institutions $10)
Started: Fall 1969
Circulation: 20,000
Format: 64-72 pages (offset)
Issues examined: Vol. 3, Nos. 2-4
Back issues available from publisher
Microform version available from Bell & Howell; Xerox University Microfilms

Women: A Journal of Liberation attempts to fulfill "two purposes: to introduce women to our movement, and to further dialogue among women who are working for revolutionary change in our society."

Each issue is built around a theme. For example, the issue on "Building a New Culture" contained articles on the use of the media (music, theater, film) by women to form a new culture stressing "self-identity and collectivity," and articles on anthropology and language showing the dominant place of the male in our culture.

Another issue, "Women Locked Up," reviewed the condition of women in prisons, mental hospitals, and old-age homes; but also explored the more subtle forms of imprisonment for women: schools, religion, family. Especially, male domination of the mental health field and the resulting degradation of the female is attacked:

> ... the normal woman, who totally accepts the narrow, rigid limits suggested for her personality, is passive, inferior, irrational, anxious, and possibly frigid--in other words, sick by definition. The normal male, on the other hand, is strong, independent, rational, etc.--in other words, the normal person, healthy by definition. Dr. Chesler calls this phenomenon the 'masculine standard of mental health' in which women are 'psychiatrically impaired'--whether they accept or reject the female role--simply because they are women.

The "International Women" issue contained articles on the condition of women in Cuba, Spain, Ireland, Japan, and China. In addition, Third World women living in the United States discussed the role of the women's movement in their lives. Describing the Mexican-American woman's role, one Chicana stated:

> Man is the superior being in her life.... She has no

> dignity, no rights, and no voice.... Chicano women's liberation will only come about when she frees herself from the domination of the Chicano male.

But a black woman presented a different view:

> At this ... time many Third World women do not feel that sexism is of primary importance. We are struggling as a people within our own Movements and cannot afford a division between men and women.

This is the dilemma which has faced the women's movement since it moved out of the white, middle-class sphere: is sex, race, or class identification the primary determinant of action?

> Out of this sense of need [to challenge all existing institutions that exploit both women and men] we on the Journal staff and many other women across the country have formed socialist-feminist groups. We are attempting to place our analysis of women's oppression within a broader political framework....

The issues examined also contained poetry, letters, film reviews, and reprints from other feminist publications. (SLA)

WOMEN & FILM

Siew-Hwa Beh and Saunie Salyer, Co-editors
Box 4501
Berkeley, Calif. 94704
Tri-annually; $3 (institutions $5.50)

Started: Jan. 1972
Circulation: 2,000
Format: 80 pages (offset)
Issue examined: Jan. 1972

"Our goal is to create a People's Cinema where human beings are portrayed as human beings and not servile caricatures." With this purpose in mind, Women & Film features articles on the problems of sexism in films, such as "A One-Sided Story: Women in the Movies" which deplores the sexual stereotypes of women, and "Hawks' Women: Don't You Think I Could Know a Girl?" which is concerned with Howard Hawks' superficial treatment of women in the films he has directed. Other articles pertain to how media have shaped cultural influences.

Films by Bergman, Goddard, and Kate Millett are

reviewed, as well as the Chinese dance drama Red Detachment of Women. The San Francisco Film Festival is discussed, and examples of male chauvinism are cited.

The following statement summarizes the philosophy of the magazine: "We are non-professionals who dare put a magazine together because there is a real need for an arena for debate and presentation of views especially from a feminist-marxist-anarchist direction." The marxist-anarchist viewpoints were not emphasized in the issue reviewed, but the feminist viewpoint was presented in numerous articles.

(NK)

Feedback:

The editors supplied a ready-made blurb (one full page, single-spaced) and said: "Please use this rather than the one you have." We chose not to.

## WOMEN IN STRUGGLE

J. C. Taylor, Ed.
Box 324
Winneconne, Wis. 54986
Bi-monthly; free to Wisconsin women

Started: Oct. 1970
Circulation: under 500
Format: 8 pages (offset)
Issues examined: Nov. 1972; Jan. & Mar. 1973

Women in Struggle is published for the purpose of advancing the cause of women. In the words of the editor, the "aim of the publication is to present information and comment on feminist issues briefly in a sharp style." Since the magazine is a Wisconsin publication, sent free to women in that state, events in Wisconsin receive especially thorough coverage.

Each issue begins with a short quotation in which a famous woman comments on the status of women. In the November 1972 issue Abigail Adams is quoted as saying, "Whilst you are proclaiming peace and good will to men ... you insist upon retaining absolute power over wives." The quotations establish the attitude of the magazine, one of constant struggle against male dominance. The general lack of success in the struggle is apparent in the pessimism and sarcasm which pervades the magazine.

Women in Struggle is largely composed of "notes" or short paragraphs on the news. Political Notes, Abortion Notes, Wisconsin Notes, Sports Notes, and Obituaries are some of the fairly regular sections of the magazine. The notes include such information as the success of women in recent elections, the fate of new laws or amendments concerning women, and instances of discrimination against women in areas of employment, athletics, etc. Women in Struggle is also a source of information on women's health clinics, educational opportunities, special conferences, and feminist literature.

In addition to the shorter "notes," each issue contains one or more longer articles. These articles consider in greater detail recent court decisions, elections, etc., that concern women. The January 1973 issue has an article commenting on the Supreme Court's ruling against the Texas and Georgia anti-abortion laws. The March 1973 issue includes an article on Wisconsin's rejection of the Equal Rights Amendment. Some of the longer articles analyze not only the position of women, but also the condition of the United States as a whole. An article on the 1972 election (November 1972 issue), entitled "Recycling the Presidency," expresses disenchantment with both political parties and deplores the fact that the United States seems "hopelessly addicted to war."

In between the more serious articles and news notes are paragraphs pointing out recent comments or articles which downgrade or misrepresent women. They are treated as anecdotes. Comments following the quotations give the feminist reaction. The March 1973 issue includes this paragraph:

> E.R.A.: Washington state on March 22 became the 30th state to ratify the Equal Rights Amendment to the Constitution. Although Washington has passed a state E.R.A., there were several hours of debate; one legislator was quoted as saying he voted for ratification 'because it's like an ingrown toenail: I want to get it out of my hair' (the kind of medical problem that comes from putting one's foot in one's mouth).

Simple cartoons also contribute to the tone of the magazine. The article covering the 1972 election is illustrated with a cartoon bearing the caption "So--the election's over, do I celebrate or just get stoned?" Other typical captions are "From now on--no more Ms. nice guy!" and "I am furious female." (CT)

Feedback:

"The content-summary is more than fair. I can find only two quibbles, both in the second paragraph. For 'sarcasm' I would say 'sardonic humor' ... but this is a matter for your judgment, and I am perhaps reacting to a fashion in words. The masthead quotes were exactly as you describe them on the issues you received, but I like to use bits from contemporary poets ... to set the mood of a season or of the issue; quotes are always by women.

"I really appreciate the careful reading you have given the newsletter."

WOMEN SPEAKING

C. Esther Hodge, Ed.
The Wick, Roundwood Ave., Hutton
Brentwood, Essex, U.K.
Quarterly; $3
Started: 1958
Format: 24 pages (7 1/2" x 9 1/2")
Issues examined: Oct. 1970-Apr. 1971
Back issues available from publisher
Microform version available from Bell & Howell

The articles in Women Speaking consider such issues as discrimination against women in higher education; the prehistoric roots of current attitudes toward women; and the pressures on women to have children even if they don't want to. The ordination of women to the historic orders in the Christian Church is urgently advocated, and news of progress towards this is regularly followed.

Regular features are correspondence from readers; book reviews; a report from the United Nations; and a section ("For the Record") listing achievements of women around the world.

(A statement of the journal's purpose appears on pp. 689-90 of Volume II.) (CP)

Feedback:

The editor suggested a change in wording, and we have incorporated it into the review.

Women's Place NEWSLETTER

4 Prescott St. - Box 5021
St. John's, Newfoundland, Canada
Irregular
Started: July 1972
Circulation: 200
Format: 10 pages (8 1/2" x 11" or legal size, offset)
Issues examined: Feb. & June 1974, and one undated issue entitled Women's Space

This newsletter contains information and articles of

interest to women in Newfoundland. Most of it is devoted to local meetings, demonstrations, and projects of feminist groups there. Examples of these local activities include: "Working Women in Newfoundland," a project to gather "information on working conditions in various occupations, day-care, trade unions, training that is available, and labour laws"; and "Women and Film," a program designed "to make women aware of" and "to offer the opportunity of involvement in" closed circuit television and filming in Newfoundland.

Other local activities promoted are the organization of day care centers and a tenants' association to fight rent increases, and demonstrations in favor of abortion.

Some articles, such as "Are You Getting Good Gynecologic Health Care?" and "Consciousness Raising," do not concern local issues, but are of interest to all feminists.

(SLA)

## WOMEN'S RIGHTS LAW REPORTER

Rutgers Law School,
180 University Ave.
Newark, N.J. 07102
Quarterly; $12 (institutions $24)
Started: July 1971
Circulation: 1,600
Format: 80 pages (offset)

Issues examined: Spring 1972; Fall/Winter 1972/73; and Summer 1973
Indexing: Alternative Press Index
Back issues available from publisher

The Women's Rights Law Reporter describes itself as

> a clearinghouse for women's litigation. It is designed to keep lawyers informed on recent developments in areas of law that affect women as women. Such areas include education, employment, abortion, domestic relations, criminal law, and constitutional law. In order to function effectively as a clearinghouse, WRLR needs help from lawyers and law students. We need information on women's rights cases, including copies of all pleadings, so that we can make them available to other attorneys. We need comments on recent cases, and suggestions for future legal strategies. We need manuscripts and letters. Full communication among persons involved in women's litigation is a prerequisite to winning the struggle for women's rights.

The Spring 1972 issue contained case summaries divided into

such categories as "Divorce and Separation," "Child Custody," "Education," and "Poverty"; a special section on "Abortion Cases in the United States" (a compilation of state and federal cases challenging the constitutionality of abortion laws); a "Legal Bibliography of Recent Articles" on such topics as abortion, adoption, divorce, education, and the proposed equal rights amendment; announcements about women's conferences and symposia, handbooks and pamphlets, counseling centers, employment agencies, etc.; and a case index which lists all cases (about 250) summarized or commented upon in that issue. (Pleadings of certain cases listed may be ordered from the publication.)

That issue also contained two short articles on women's cases which had had historical implications, such as Reed v. Reed, whereby a unanimous court declared unconstitutional an Idaho statute that gave men preference over women in administering deceased persons' estates.

Two issues received after this review was written had much the same content and layout. The Fall/Winter 1972/73 issue contained over 100 case summaries with index and articles on "Married Women's Common Law Right to Their Own Surnames"; and "Downhome: A New Focus On Thirteenth Amendment Slavery" ("married women must adopt the surname of the paterfamilias, just as plantation blacks once did, and the U.S. Supreme Court in 1972 upheld this rule. Yet nowhere have I seen such vestiges legally attacked as badges and incidents of slavery prohibited by the Thirteenth Amendment.").

The Summer 1973 issue contained about 90 case summaries with index; a book review section; and such articles as "The AT&T Settlement" (having to do with discriminatory employment practices of American Telephone and Telegraph Company against women) and "The New York Telephone Settlement: A Study in Contrast" (on the same subject).

The publication is illustrated with reprints of old etchings and woodcuts. (JMS)

WOMEN'S STUDIES: An Interdisciplinary Journal

Gordon and Breach Science Publishers
440 Park Avenue South
N.Y., N.Y. 10016
3 issues a year; $10 (institutions $29)
Started: Spring 1973
Format: 168 pages (6" x 9", offset)
Issue examined: v. 1, no. 1

Women's Studies is an interdisciplinary journal for

scholarly analysis of women's place in society. It is edited by Wendy Martin, Department of English, Queens College, Flushing, N.Y.

> Women's Studies has been founded to provide a forum to discuss and explore the implications of feminism for scholarship and art, to chronicle changing consciousness, and finally to help to create a more equalitarian society.
>
> Women's Studies does not intend to perpetuate a separate culture for women, nor does it intend to isolate women from the academic and artistic communities; rather, the journal is founded on the premise that careful and disciplined research illuminated by a feminist perspective by both women and men can contribute to effective social change.

Articles in its first issue include "The Literature of Impoverishment: The Women Local Colorists in America 1865-1914"; "Sex, Sentiment, and Oliver Wendell Holmes"; "Victorian Feminism and the Nineteenth-Century Novel"; "Centuries of Womanhood: An Evolutionary Perspective on the Feminine Role"; and "Religious Arguments Against Higher Education for Women in England, 1840-1890."

In "A Review of Sexism in American Historical Writing," the authors examine eight male historians' views of the nineteenth-century feminist movement, specifically, how they interpret the feminists' actions by "psychologizing" the women's anger, analyzing their private lives, and using "objectivity" to discredit the movement or its leaders:

> The male point of view is masked in these books when the authors write as if they are members of a third sex, uninvolved in the struggle against male dominance and unaffected by the demands of the feminists that men give up their privileges.

The authors find, in fact, that "Nowhere in these books do we find a sustained investigation of the real social conditions which are the sources of women's problems and rebellion."

(MM)

Feedback:

"This is fine."

## WOMEN'S STUDIES NEWSLETTER and NEWS/NOTES

Tamar Berkowitz, Co-Editor
The Feminist Press
Box 334
Old Westbury, N.Y. 11568
Quarterly; $5 (institutions $10)
Started: Winter 1972
Circulation: 1,200

Format: WSN 16 pages, N/N 8 pages (both offset)
Issues examined: WSN, Spring, Summer, Fall 1973; N/N No. 4
Some back issues available from publisher

Women's Studies Newsletter reports on feminist study programs at the college, secondary, and elementary level. In each issue several organizations report on their activities in signed "Closeup" articles. These range from reports by an elementary teacher concerning sex role discussions in her sixth grade to a description of a course examining the possible sexist assumptions in social work. An enlightening article from Bowling Green State University outlines the technique used in a course, "The Problems and Potential of Women." Women are encouraged to brag, thus exposing the damaging effect of second class status on women's self-esteem.

Special articles in the issues examined were devoted to reports on foundations and rosters. The Fall 1973 issue contains a listing of twenty-six foundations and their past grants for feminist projects. A partial listing of professional groups which have rosters in operation appears in the Spring 1973 issue along with a progress report on a national roster of women and minorities.

The newsletter occasionally contains poetry, short excerpts from books, and signed book reviews. There are lists of new and forthcoming books from The Feminist Press as well as publications of the Clearinghouse itself. Frequently there are bulletins concerning women's groups abroad. Conferences are reported on in news story format.

Regular features include job listings, conferences, news media, publications (including research reports and bibliographies), resources and projects of interest to women's groups. These sections serve as an idea exchange. The Fall 1973 issue institutes briefly annotated listings of significant books for teachers of women's studies at various levels. Descriptions of college and high school courses appear in each issue.

The Feminist Press also publishes News/Notes. This eight-page annual report is free to subscribers of Women's Studies Newsletter. It covers projects and publications of the press. An order blank is included. (JA)

Feedback:

"Fine."

WOMEN'S VOICE OF GREATER HARTFORD

Women's Liberation Center
11 Amity St.
Hartford, Conn. 06106
Monthly; $3
Started: Spring 1972

Circulation: 800
Format: 8-10 pages
Issue examined: Dec. 1973
Back issues available from publisher

This is essentially a newsletter of the Women's Liberation Center, and its major concern is "feminism" and related issues: "Lesbianism, abortion, rape prevention, day care, self-help, feminist history, related political theory, etc."

The sample issue included an article on self-help clinics which "are bringing control of women's medicine back to women"; advice on how and where to obtain an abortion; and one woman's account of an encounter with male chauvinism. Regular features are "Center News and Business," "Notices, Ads, etc." and paid advertisements. (CH)

Feedback:

Editor suggested several minor changes, all of which have been incorporated into the review.

WOMEN'S WORK AND WOMEN'S STUDIES

The Women's Center
Barnard College
N.Y., N.Y. 10027
Subscriptions: KNOW, Inc.
Box 86031
Pittsburgh, Pa. 15221
Annual; 1971 issue: $4.50 looseleaf, $7.50 hardbound; 1972 issue: $5.25 looseleaf, $8.50 hardbound

Started: Oct. 1972
Circulation: 1,000
Format: 162-247 pages (offset)
Issues examined: 1971, 1972

This is an "annual interdisciplinary bibliography listing published and in-progress research on women and on issues of interest to women, as well as unique innovative action projects for women." The editors' interest in both theory and practice led them to include not only standard and movement books, articles, chapters, unpublished papers, and theses, but also groups, services, projects, presses, and other agents of change. Most listings are annotated. The major divisions in the 1971 volume (with some examples of subdivisions) are

Bodies (birth control, pregnancy, health services).
Sex-Role Induction and Stereotyping (vocational rail-roading, stereotyping through the family).
Socio-Psychological Consequences of Sex-Role Induction (marriage and family, "criminal" women).
Socio-Economic Consequences of Sex-Role Induction (labor force, legal/political status).
Changing the Status Quo (child care, education, employment).
History (biography, social history, historiography).
Literature, Arts, Media (images of women, criticism of women writers and artists).

Divisions in the 1972 bibliography are similar. (MM)

Feedback:

Editor expressed no disapproval.

## Chapter 14

## GAY LIBERATION

> We have been fucked over all our lives by a system which is based on the domination of men over women, which defines male as good and female as only as good as the man you are with. ---The Furies

> To be shockingly blunt, it is the male principle in human beings that has brought us historically to the verge of extinction.... ---The Double-F Journal

> We can be as 'liberated' as we want and still get fired from jobs, slandered and ridiculed, harassed by cops, beaten up, discriminated against.... ---The Body Politic

The periodicals reviewed in this chapter range from non-violent liberal to angry, aggressive radical. A "conservative" Gay Liberation periodical would be a contradiction in terms unless it published only one number, advising readers to soft-pedal their life-style in order to avoid publicity and censure--and then took its own advice and dutifully folded. Perhaps "liberal" is not the right adjective for any of these periodicals, for the movement is inherently radical: its members, not content with urging increased understanding and tolerance of different ways of living, demand drastic changes in society's attitude toward, and treatment of, homosexuals. Indeed, the very publication of these periodicals--not to mention their open distribution--would probably be considered a radical act by many, if not most, Americans today.

Agapé and Action is typical of periodicals speaking for those who want an honorable place in a religious community and hope to attain it without violence. The two periodicals devoted to mental health want to help gay people achieve happy and creative lives without changing their sexual orientation. At the other extreme, Fag Rag and The Furies give militant support to revolutionary ideas and actions. Several of the lesbian periodicals express unremitting fury: Cowrie turns thumbs down on the straight world and--at times--condemns all men; Spectre almost scalds the reader, for it is in a constant state of seething rage--mad at men, mad at the older generation, mad at parents--mad, mad, mad!

An interesting strain in the movement is represented by men (Double F Journal) who support the radical feminists and oppose not only the straight male but also the man who tries to be dominant.

The alienation and loneliness of gay life today are evidenced by the space given to lists of bars, clubs, night spots, and motels in which readers can expect to feel welcome and find friends. Their many reviews (of books and entertainments that might interest homosexuals) and advertisements (of a sort not usually printed elsewhere) make these publications useful to a group of people trying to find their way and make a good life in a generally unfriendly and suspicious world.

--G. K. Spahn

AGAPÉ AND ACTION: News Notes for a Revolution of Concern and Service

Committee of Concern for Homosexuals
Box 4089
Berkeley, Calif. 94704
"Usually monthly"; $5

Started: June 1970
Circulation: "small"
Format: 6 to 8 pages (mimeo.)
Issues examined: Oct. 1970; Jan. & Feb. 1971

This is the newsletter and commentary publication of the Committee of Concern for Homosexuals, which is part of the radical Christian coalition, "You Are the Rising Bread." (Other members of the coalition: the Berkeley Free Church, the Society of Priests for a Free Ministry, the Ecumenical Ministry in the Haight-Ashbury, the Pacific Counselling Service, and the Brotherhood of the Love of Christ.) One of the Committee's services is the Gay Switchboard, a "hotline" service through which people can get information on gay liberation in the Berkeley area.

The newsletter contains no regular features, but consists of articles (dealing with Christianity and gay liberation) and letters to the editor (with editorial comments). It also contains news of meetings and of other publications that might interest its readers. The editor says that "It has a heavy gay liberation and radical Christian orientation.... It is also, in effect, the radical-Christian-anarchist-non-violent faction of gay liberation in Berkeley." (JEH)

## AIN'T I A WOMAN

Box 1169
Iowa City, Iowa 52240
Irregular (approx. every 2 months); $5 (institutions $20)
Started: June 1970

Format: 12-page tabloid (offset)
Issues examined: v. 2, nos. 3-7
Indexing: Alternative Press Index

Ain't I a Woman is "published by a collective of 16 [number fluctuates] women functioning as a world-wide conspiracy of Radical Lesbians, and don't you forget it." The paper's primary concerns are the problems of being gay, being working-class, and making a revolution.

> Basically we feel we are working toward a material analysis of this society and its class nature, and to work to destroy the society as it exists--all from within a feminist perspective. We have moved away from a strict feminist analysis to an analysis that includes all oppressed groups.
>
> Because we are gay women we give weight to the issue of lesbianism in our paper, of course. Gayness and class, economic oppression, health concerns, survival tactics for women alone, etc.--all of these concern us too. They are important, immediate problems that involve us all and should be dealt with, because we live in this society and will have to continue to do so for a long time to come.

In a style that is personal, yet analytical, contributors discuss theoretical issues, such as age chauvinism and oppression of children, class and feminism (i.e., the ways in which the two are related), separatism vs. coalition (gay women working with straight women, women working with men), and the politics of being gay. They also discuss immediate problems that many women face, such as being in prison, living with children, and running away from oppressive parents. A great deal of space is given over to practical articles on various health problems and procedures (VD, self-examinations, etc.) and survival tactics such as self-defense and "ripping off capitalist enterprises" (shoplifting). (MM)

Feedback:

"We have been sent numerous drafts like this to be included in various publications, but yours was the best and most sensitive and correct."

AMAZON QUARTERLY: A Lesbian-Feminist Arts Journal

554 Valle Vista
Oakland, Calif. 94610
Quarterly; $4 unwrapped; $5 wrapped, or outside the U.S.; libraries $6
Started: Sept. 1972

Circulation: 3,000
Format: 72 pages (offset)
Issue examined: May 1973
Indexed in Women Studies Abstracts

Amazon Quarterly seeks to present "the best in fiction, visual arts, essays, reviews, poetry, and biographies of little known artists and writers ... who are exploring new directions in their lives." In addition to these departments, there are also a lengthy section of letters to the editor ("Love Letters"), a chatty editorial page ("What's What"), and a briefly annotated list of recent books of interest to AQ readers ("New Ink"). The review article in the sample issue is a critical discourse on a new biography of Virginia Woolf. There is no advertising other than AQ subscription promotion.

The orientation of the journal is both personal and political, presenting the Lesbian-Feminist perspective through a variety of media. Graphic features, which in the sample issue include, among other items, a woodcut ("The Artist and Her Demons") and a disturbing series of photographs, are outstanding for their consistent high quality. The written material is similarly diverse and well-executed.

One of the feature articles in the "Explorations" section of the May 1973 issue is a transcript of the keynote address given by Feminist Robin Morgan at the West Coast Lesbian-Feminist Conference held last April. In her speech Morgan entreats all women to join together in active commitment to "The war outside, between women and male power [which] is getting murderous." A clear distinction is made, however, between the overthrow of traditional male dominance and absolute separatism. Throughout the speech and the journal as a whole there is a pervading appeal for tolerance, for peaceful coexistence, among all the diverse elements in society. Morgan calls for

> a real Feminist Revolution, a proud gynocratic world that runs on the power of women. Not in the male sense of power, but in the sense of a power plant--producing energy. And to each, that longing for, the right to great love, filled in reality, for all women, and children, and men and animals and trees and water and all life. An exquisite diversity in unity.

The second feature article in the sample issue is a long essay on "The Lesbian Love Ethic." Again, though on a more personal level, the author emphasizes the necessity for social unity, tolerance, and the right to love according to one's personal preference: "Here, then," she concludes,

> is a great opportunity for Lesbians--not to utterly reject that larger society which has so shamefully rejected them, but to appropriate its best ideals of honesty and consideration for others in the pursuit of meaningful, though not necessarily permanent and perfect relationships.

(BC)

Feedback:

"This is fine, with the few corrections I've made." (All corrections have been incorporated into the review.)

THE BODY POLITIC: Gay Liberation Journal

Jearld Moldenhauer &
Gerald Hannon
4 Kensington Ave.
Toronto, Ont., Canada
M5T 2J7
Bi-monthly; $2 ($2.25 U.S.)
Started: Nov. 1971

Circulation: 6,000
Format: 24- to 28-page tabloid
Issues examined: July 1972 (by MM); Winter 1973 (by SA)
Indexing: Alternative Press Index

The Body Politic is mostly male-oriented. The July 1972 issue includes poems (by Paul Goodman and others) and a number of articles of analysis or strategy concerning the gay movement. The author of "Of Men and Little Boys" discusses the "sizeable minority of gay men who are primarily interested in sexual relationships with adolescents" and how this kind of sexuality works toward the destruction of the nuclear family.

> The familial power structure is oppressive and stultifying and based on mutual manipulation. The child is one of the possessions of the parents, a eunuchoid doll that is supposed to attain to sexual awareness at 18, gleefully enduring celibacy thereafter until an appropriate marriage has been consummated. Anything which could free the child from this enervating environment is important. Sex is something that does.

In "Oppression Begins at Home" another writer traces

the historical origins and development of "the oppressive character of the nuclear family." "Social Analysis and Gay Lib" is a discussion (based on the writings of Freud and Marcuse) of the repression society enforces, especially against homosexuals, and a comparison of capitalist and communist countries in this regard. A "Community Forum" feature has a member of the gay movement analyzing the drawbacks of the Toronto movement and arguing against the "counter culture" (already liberated) theory.

> We can be as 'liberated' as we want and still get fired from jobs, slandered and ridiculed, harassed by cops, beaten up, discriminated against in myriad ways. Oppression is not just in our heads, it is part of material reality.

"A Court-in' We Will Go" describes what happens in court when one is arrested on homosexual-related charges. A regular feature, "News of the Gay," gives rather extensive coverage of the movement in other cities, such as Saskatoon, Vancouver, Ottawa, Montreal, Buffalo, Miami, and even Copenhagen and West Berlin. In local news, the OHRC (Ontario Human Rights Code--or, "O.nly H.eterosexuals R.eceive C.onsideration") is analyzed, and reactions are studied to Toronto Gay Action's demands for inclusion of sexual orientation in the code. Also included in this issue is a review of Parker Tyler's Screening the Sexes: Homosexuality in the Movies. A regular feature is a gay gossip column by "Twilight Rose."

Items relating to women include "I Remember," a two-part fiction about a young girl's sexual awakening; "Born a Woman," about sex roles; and a cartoon of two girl characters from the "Peanuts" strip holding hands and saying, "Who needs Charlie Brown?" (MM)

In the Winter 1973 issue, an editor reflects upon The Body Politic's role:

> Providing news coverage of the Canadian and International gay movements, publishing the views and theoretical articles of Canadian activists, and encouraging the contributions of gay artists--The Body Politic has filled a media vacuum which itself has been an important element in sustaining gay oppression.... Naturally, we are sympathetic to every attempt to better the social and political situation of

> homosexuals within a society which is both anti-sexual and sexist. At the same time, we uphold the critical function of social analysis as a vital need in our struggle to create a new society.

A few pages are devoted to alerting readers to activities of gay activists. The Community Page is a directory of gay groups throughout Canada. (In the sample issue, 27 organizations are listed.) A detailed map of Toronto's "gay spots" (bars, clubs, baths, restaurants, parks) appears with the warning: "You should be aware that sex in a public place is illegal: go home, or to a private place." News items on gay activities and interests appear on a few pages; an article on the National Gay Election Coalition describes the rising voices of Canadian homosexuals in bringing their issue before the people and the politicians. A book section reviews nine books on homosexuality.

Several other books are reviewed at length in the course of a long article attacking psychiatrists as preservers of the status quo--particularly in reference to the issue of homosexuality.

Art contributions to the Winter 1973 issue include a few pages of explicitly homosexual subject matter, and some original cartoons. There is also a literary portrait of "heteros as just plain bores"--an amusing satirical response to an article about homosexuals which had appeared in a national Canadian magazine. (SA)

Feedback (to MM's review):

"The Body Politic is the only gay paper published in Canada. Your analysis of Issue 5 is quite accurate. It should be pointed out, however, that certain changes have occurred.... In recent (and future) issues we have given (and will give) more space to book reviews and Canadian gay news. As well, recent issues include more contributions by gay women."

THE CHICAGO GAY CRUSADER: The Total Community Newspaper

Box 872
Chicago, Ill. 60690
Monthly; $6 (free to sisters & brothers in prison, mental institutions, reform schools, and the armed forces)
Started: May 1973

Circulation: 3,000
Format: 12- to 20-page tabloid (offset)
Issues examined: June 1973-Feb. 1974
Back issues available from publisher

"We are primarily a paper to improve communication, relations, and unity among the Chicago gay community...."

CHICAGO NITES

3161 N. Cambridge (#204)
Chicago, Ill. 60657
Monthly; free

Format: 20 pages (5 1/2" x 8 1/2")
Issues examined: #1 & #4 (1973)

The first issue carried this information:

> Good evening and welcome to Chicago Nites. We hope you enjoy our first issue. We had fun putting it together for you. We are in the business to entertain you, nothing more. We don't plan to discuss politics or try to unite the gay community. We figure that you'll do that on your own. We'll be available at your favorite bar on the 15th of each month.

The issues examined contained descriptions of bars, restaurants, night spots, shows, etc., and mentioned favorite bartenders and entertainers. There was also a gossip column, book review, theater calendar, and announcements of "gay" doings. (JMS)

COWRIE: Lesbian Feminist

Liza Cowan & Carol Hardin, Co-Editors
359 E. 68th St.
N.Y., N.Y. 10021
Bi-monthly; $5 (institutions $10)
Started: June 1973

Circulation: 600-700
Format: 24 pages (offset)
Issues examined: Oct. & Dec. 1973
Back issues available from publisher

Cowrie, formerly the Newsletter of Community of Women, is an independent project of C.O.W. A quotation explains the magazine's title: "The Kauri (Cowrie) shell is one of the most potent magical or feminine symbols.... Its similarity in color and shape to the female vulva, its origin from fecund waters, filled with the rhythm of the birth organs...."

The magazine consists of a few short articles; stories or personal experiences (love affairs between women, feelings about lesbianism, etc.); poetry; and letters to the editor. [Feedback: "Please add to the list: Lesbian heritage, book and theatre reviews...."] The style is personal, anecdotal, and sometimes vehemently anti-male:

> Well, I'm so fucking angry that I'm going to force you all to acknowledge my Lesbianism and don't bother to reject me, I have already rejected all of you. You who refuse to see things as they really are, you women who insist on defending men even while being fucked-over by them--stay out of my way. Don't try to force me to live your way. I will live my way. I will talk about it and act on it --and if you get in my way I'll blow your fucking brains out!

An editorial (Dec. 1973) explains the magazine's purposes:

> We are anti-heterosexual. We don't intend ever to print anything that even hints at heterosexuality. We work exclusively with women and for women. We sell only in Women's Centers, Women's Bookstores and Gay Bookstores. Cowrie has 36 subscribers at this time, it is sold in 12 bookstores across the country.... This is our second Lesbian issue.... Although we expect to grow to meet the needs of the Lesbian Community, we are not interested in changing to appeal to a broader audience. We are movement women, we are Lesbian separatists and not interested in human being theories, because 'human being' always means men. We make our own rules. The oppressor cannot make the rules and strategies for the revolution.

The same issue has a photograph on the cover of an ancient Greek vase painting of Amazons, and contains an article on "What the Well Dressed Dyke Will Wear--History of Lesbian Clothes, Part One: Amazons."

Cowrie is illustrated with black and white drawings and photographs and carries a few advertisements. (JMS)

Feedback:

The co-editor, Liza Cowan, replied:

> I think that you chose two excerpts that were somewhat identical, that is, they do not represent the variety that we try to present in Cowrie. I would prefer you to print one of the two following excerpts instead of the one which starts, 'Well, I'm so fucking angry....'

1. Someday ... women will have privacy. We'll go to the theatre and watch other women act out our lives and dreams. We'll be able to have dreams.... Amazon is probably an overused word in the movement, but I'd really like to talk to someone with a real Amazon Society on her mind. We could whisper and look behind us and draw pretty pictures and wear costumes and play-like and walk down the street pretending and work hard to make it real. Maybe this is some place beyond anger, perhaps it's in the middle of anger, but someday we're going to have a large group of angry, intimidating, strong, women-loving women who have women stories to tell and women-business to do.

2. See how liberal they are, how accepting! So their world is still intact, untainted by my 'deviant' behaviour. They protect themselves by trying to negate me! By ignoring my Lesbianism they don't have to deal with something that they were never programmed to handle.

DAVID: Entertaining and Informing Gays

Box 5396
Jacksonville, Fla. 32207
Monthly; $9

Format: 80 pages (offset)
Issues examined: June, July, Nov., Dec. 1972

David is not militant. It contains no exhortations to political action and there is very little news of discrimination against homosexuals or of attempts to challenge existing laws or customs.

Regular features. Humor (a page of "Jokth"); poetry ("Verse--From Our Readers"); a pin-up centerfold ("Boy of the Month"); letters to the editor; a directory of gay bars, restaurants, bookstores, cinemas, hotels, and motels; some very brief editorial comments upon Gay Liberation in the news; classified advertisements (sometimes placed by persons seeking companionship); reports on activities in gay bars in Chicago, New York, and other cities (often with photographs of the entertainers, who are frequently impersonating females); and many display advertisements for gay bars (and sometimes gay bookstores) throughout the country. (Several of the sample issues appeared just before the 1972 presidential election, so some of their letters to the editor dealt with the candidates' stands on homosexuality.)

Irregular features. Notes on records, plays, ballets,

books, or movies ("Let's fact it, A Clockwork Orange is the most brilliantly-directed piece of trash ever to happen.... It's pure sickness."); and short fiction (never more than one story in an issue). A very small portion of David is given over to reporting on lesbian activities.

Illustrations. David is full of photographs of muscular young men in various stages of undress--with their genitals always chastely shielded. (TJS)

DIGNITY

755 Boylston St., Room 514
Boston, Mass. 02116
Monthly; $10
Started: 1969
Circulation: 1,500-2,000

Format: 14 pages (offset, stapled)
Issues examined: Oct.-Dec. 1973

Dignity is a publication of the Gay Catholic community. According to Paul Diederich, National President of the organization called Dignity, the newsletter is "concerned with the whole Gay community" and reports progress in all areas, "especially legal, educational, the professions, religious."

The first national Dignity convention stated: "We believe that homophiles can express their sexuality in a manner that is consonant with Christ's teachings. We believe that all sexuality should be exercised in an ethically responsible and unselfish way."

An editorial in the November 1973 issue suggests that "A group such as Dignity could be the middle ground on which the Gay Catholic Community and the clergy meet in a ministry that truly ministers--serves, not a ministry that seeks to dominate, to change culture and life-style for the sake of sexual uniformity."

In addition to editorials, letters, and news items, a column ("The Very Words") reports favorable statements about homosexuality by professional individuals or organizations. Entire addresses by priests and psychiatrists are printed. (For instance, the October 1973 issue carries the report given to the American Psychiatric Association, "Homosexuality and Cultural Value-Systems: Should Homosexuality Be Classified as a Mental Illness?") Each month "Chapter News" lists forthcoming meetings, social events, and masses in Dignity missions in various U.S. cities.

The whole tone of the periodical is religious, and staff writers and contributors are eager to work toward a dignified, active, and close relationship with the Catholic Church.

(GKS)

Feedback:

Editor expressed no disapproval.

THE DOUBLE-F JOURNAL: The Flaming Faggots

Kenneth Pitchford, Ed.
109 Third Ave.
N.Y., N.Y. 10003
"Approximately" quarterly; $2 for 5 issues
Started: Summer 1972
Issue examined: Summer 1972

The "double-F" in this title stands for "Flaming Faggots," a group of "faggot militants" who are leading the new Revolutionary Effeminism movement. (The term faggot comes from the Middle Ages, when homosexual men were tied in bundles and, with bundles of wood [i.e., "faggots"], were burned at the feet of witches sentenced to death by fire.)

The first issue is written almost exclusively by Kenneth Pitchford. In "Faggot Militants: From Sexual Liberation to Revolutionary Effeminism" he discusses this new movement; the switch in terms from gay to faggot ("faggot, the word of choice with which to replace gay and other euphemisms--faggot, a word of pride like black or lesbian became when those groups grew militant about fighting their oppression"); and the differences between Revolutionary Effeminism and Gay Liberation:

> just as Black Liberation emerged to the left of the civil rights movement, and Radical Feminism has emerged to the left of women's liberation, so our movement of faggot militants is beginning to be heard to the left of gay liberation.

Revolutionary Effeminists support the Radical Feminist movement, which sees sexism as the root of all other oppressions:

> we are convinced that faggots will never be free until women are free.... Our task is simply to support, defend, and promote effeminism in all men everywhere by any means necessary. To be shockingly blunt, it is the male principle in human beings that has brought us historically to the verge of extinction; if we are to survive it will be because the female principle, once omnipotent in pre-history, is returned to power so that our warped existence can be set right again after being awry for ten thousand years.

. . .

> . . . only by destroying sexism itself can any of the society's evils (that is, capitalism, racism, etc.) be decisively eradicated once and for all.

Critical of "masculine solidarity," whether it be among straight men or male gay liberationists, Pitchford says that "by excluding women and faggots from all important matters (except as sexual objects or boot-lickers), [this masculine solidarity] can be called homofascism, a heightened form of the prevailing sexist system."

In this issue is reprinted "The Flaming Faggots Manifesto," a poem written by Pitchford in response to discrimination toward gay people by the Venceremos Brigade (cane-cutting brigades of foreign radicals in Cuba).

"Where We Came From and Who We Are" describes the evolution of The Flaming Faggots (originally "a small consciousness-raising group of revolutionary male homosexuals" in New York) and the politics of the Revolutionary Effeminism movement:

> The effeminate in us is both the source of our oppression and the clue to our liberation. Nor is this merely a matter of body-type (a typically straight-male fixation)--effeminacy appears in men as the willingness to cooperate rather than compete, as the preferring of collectivity to individualism, personal solution, or privatism, and as the valuing of what is tender and gentle in men, what is delicate, sweet, lyrical, affectionate, considerate, aesthetic.

Further,

> The dominative straight man and the dominative male homosexual both emphasize ripping off their own needs at the expense of others. Both are one-track-minded, self-preoccupied, goal-oriented toward orgasm or aggrandizement--rather than polymorphous, outgoing, open-ended, process-oriented toward sharing and giving without first striking bargains about 'results.' Both bristle with excitement at the chance for competition, at the evaluation of themselves and others in terms of superficial measurements: who has the biggest muscles, the loudest mouth, the most intimidating manner, the largest penis, the most of this, the greatest that.

(MM)

## DRAG MAGAZINE: The International Transvestite Quarterly

Queens Publications
Box 1271
N.Y., N.Y. 10009
Quarterly; $7 (third class); $10 (first class)
Started: Nov. 1969

Circulation: 10,000
Format: 52 pages (offset)
Issues examined: 4 issues in 1973
Back issues available from publisher

"Drag is published to enlighten the transvestite about himself (historical as well as contemporary). We are trying to instill pride in the individual about his transvestism and help him adjust to his being different by letting him know he is not alone."

A large part of the magazine is devoted to pin-up pictures of drag queens and transvestite performers (some are nude from the waist up and have large breasts) accompanied by comments and gossip. The magazine also contains a news section. Articles: "Hormones Do Make a Difference," "Shakespeare's Boy Actresses," "It's a Girl!" (transsexual operation), "Here Comes the Bride" (drag wedding), and "Queens Liberation Front." A "Getting Together" section carries personal ads. Advertisements are for such things as lingerie and wigs. (JMS)

## ECHO OF SAPPHO

Sisters for Liberation
Box 263
Brooklyn, N.Y. 11217
Bi-monthly; $3

Started: June 1972
Format: tabloid
Issue examined: June 1972

Dedicated "to Sappho, to the Memory of Sappho," this lesbian paper is similar in format to the now-defunct Spectre. The maiden issue is made up largely of scattered thoughts (mostly from Sappho and Edgar Cayce, the clairvoyant), drawings, and short to medium-length news items, personal/reflective statements, facts, statistics, a few poems, one very brief film review, graffiti, real-life experiences, and comparisons of our culture with others in respect to attitudes toward homosexuality. Most of these items pertain to lesbianism or sexism. A few pieces are longer, one of them a number of statements by lesbians about their "coming out" in public; another--by lesbians and non-lesbians--about their views on lesbianism; and a third, a prose portrait of one writer's former lover.

The publishers "will try to show all sides of lesbianism without bias: political/non-political, social/non-social. Our main purpose is to inform." The entire back page of the first issue is composed of thoughts of Edgar Cayce, cures for cancer and the common cold, and observations on the treatment of burns, the healthful effects of castor oil, and chemical additives in orange juice. (MM)

FAG RAG: Gay Male Newspaper

91 River St.
Cambridge, Mass. 02139
Quarterly (irregular); 50¢ an issue (25¢ in Boston)
Started: June 1971
Circulation: 5,000

Format: tabloid
Issue examined: Summer 1972
Indexing: Alternative Press Index

Fag Rag "[lives] within the schisms and chasms of Amerikkkan faggotry." Gay Male Liberation, its publisher,

> is premised on consciousness-raising around sexism towards the goal of sexual liberation for all. It seeks a perspective for revolution based on the unity of all people--i.e., there can be no freedom for gays in a society which enslaves others through male supremacy, racism, or economic exploitation (capitalism).

In explaining its irregularity of publication, the staff says,

> We reject the pig state and all its values of predictability, schedules, 'work,' etc. We'd just as soon be travelling or living marginally on our own than be owned by GM, USMC, GE, UCLA, GD, OSU, USA, etc. 'Freedom's just another word for nothing left to lose.' After destructuring our lives, we are not about to restructure them (at least on a straight line, hierarchy basis) for GLF [Gay Liberation Front], GML [Gay Male Liberation], GAA [Gay Activists' Alliance] or even FAG RAG.

Much of the emphasis of Fag Rag is on the power structure in American society and its reflection in human relationships. In "Hoover Goes Underground," the dangers of a male-dominated society are explored through the example of J. Edgar Hoover. "We'll probably never know for sure if he was a homosexual, but I think we can be pretty sure it's true."

> Hoover was living proof that straight society provides a male supremacist outlet for homosexual men and that such men, if they function within the scheme of male dominance, are an integral part of that straight society. We recognize that such homosexuals may choose such a role out of the need to obtain power that they feel is not really a part of their own selves. But we also realize that to act upon these feelings is not only self-defeating, but also fucks over other people. Thus we realize the temptation and the danger of male dominated institutions.

And in "Cocksucking Is an Act of Revolution":

> Men tend to measure themselves by their power--not their ability to love. They order their lives by force--not by cohesion, togetherness or support. Their sexual politics takes its purest form in rape. In 'forceful' rape, men use their muscles, power or some weapon (knife, club or gun) to make another person submit to their will. We faggots too often tend to lust after such men: uniformed killers (soldiers, sailors, marines, etc.), construction workers, musclemen, sportsmen, etc. All become identified with their use of force; and this force is measured in our society by their ability to rape a woman.
>
> We faggots escape rape only by straight-fronting --that is, trying to pass as straight men--in other words, we try to disguise ourselves as rapists.

Other articles discuss demands of Gay Male Liberation as presented to the Eastern Psychological Association and the New England Regional Hearing of the Democratic National Platform Committee; "treatments" of homosexuality such as psychosurgery, aversive conditioning therapy, and drug therapy; "Out, Out, Damn Faggot," experiences of gay people on the 4th Venceremos Brigade to Cuba; "Gay Yoga: On Body, Mind and Politics"; and a professional drag queen. There are also more than two pages of gay poetry. (MM)

Feedback:

"We like the précis you sent...." "The first issue of Fag Rag appeared [in] June 1971; we were a continuation of Lavender Vision #1, which was half faggot, half lesbian, appearing [in] November 1970; Lavender Vision #2 appeared [in] May 1971 [and was] entirely lesbian."

## FAGGOTRY

"Approximately" quarterly; 50¢ an issue
Date: 1972
Circulation: 500

Format: 50 pages (offset)
Issue examined: undated "First issue"

The dedication of Faggotry says, in part: "Faggots who have been unable to hide and those who are no longer hiding have suffered severe penalties: forced into suicide, beaten, raped, imprisoned, and tortured. This is our history."

Although Faggotry does not call itself a "poetry magazine," this is the term used by The Double-F Journal to describe it. Poetry predominates in the first (and only) issue, but there are also three articles. One is a long essay by the editor ("God, Freud, Daddy, and Us Faggots") linking psychology and religion as perpetrators of the oppression of homosexuals. The author cites anthropological data to explain the rise of male supremacy and states that, contrary to belief, homosexuality is often an integral part of a dominating male brotherhood. The goal of homosexuals, he says, should be "to end sexism in all its forms and not only to confront one part of our oppression" (that being the inability "to have sex whenever, with whomever we please"). He criticizes the Gay Liberation movement for this "one-sided attack" and for not seeing that "male supremacy [is] the root from which all other oppressions branch." He concludes:

> We are what is feared most: effeminists. Men who are struggling to become unmanly, men who oppose the hierarchy and ideology of a masculine fascism that requires the domination of one person by another, of one sex, race, or class by another. We will become gentle but strong faggots who will fight their oppression in militant ways, faggots who are vulnerable to each other, able to cry, but not passive or paralyzed in our struggle to change....

The brief text of a leaflet circulated by the Flaming Faggots of New College (Sarasota, Fla.) explains the shift in terminology from gay to faggot:

> We felt [the word gay] trivialized us: we're not gay, we're angry.... We disliked the two-word phrase 'gay men.' It made clowns of us.... Then we learned that the word 'faggot' originated from our persecution in the middle ages: when a woman was

> to be burned as a witch, men accused of homosexuality were bound together in bundles, mixed in with bundles of kindling wood (faggots) at the feet of the witch, and set on fire 'to kindle a flame foul enough for a witch to burn in.' So the enemy has known all along the danger in strong women and gentle men, has known that both present the same threat to masculine domination. That is why we have decided to embrace the word faggot....

Besides an account of a homosexual's early life on a farm, the rest of the first issue consists of long poems about lovers, family relationships, society, and the personal struggles involved in growing up gay in America. (MM)

Feedback:

Steven Dansky said that he would like the concluding paragraph to read:

> The rest of the issue consists of long poems ... about family relationships, lovers, and about the political struggle of faggots to understand how male supremacy has destroyed their humanity. 'Words on Mother,' 'To an Image Long Ago Faded,' and the article 'Down Home' attempt to analyze a faggot's relationship to his mother. Faggotry represents the beginning attempt of men to become effeminists: anti-male-supremacists.

The address of Faggotry was: Steven Dansky, Ed., Templar Press, Box 98, F.D.R. Station, New York, N.Y. 10022.

FOCUS: A Journal for Gay Women

c/o Boston DOB
419 Boylston St. (Room 406)
Boston, Mass. 02116
Monthly; $5
Started: Dec. 1969
Circulation: 200
Format: 12-16 pages (5" x 7" or 8 1/2" x 11", originally mimeo.; usually offset, starting Feb. 1971)
Issues examined: May, Summer, and Sept. 1972
Microform version available from Bell & Howell, Drawer E, Wooster, Ohio 44691

Focus is the publication of the Boston chapter of Daughters of Bilitis. (DOB was the first Lesbian organization formed in this country.) Much of its emphasis is on the

Boston area and the East Coast, but some articles are of general interest.

In the May issue, the lead article (reprinted from The Furies) refutes much of the research that has been done on Emily Dickinson in the "crazy quest for Emily's male lover," the supposed object of her love poems:

> it is strange that while Emily was supposed to have been enamoured of the newspaperman, for example, she was carrying on a vastly more ardent and affectionate correspondence with his wife, Mary. In fact, the five to fifteen male candidates suggested as Emily's lover never received a fraction of the love-filled letters that went to ... [various] female friends. Strange that the heterosexual mind sees no discrepancies.

The author goes on to discuss Dickinson's life, some excerpts from her poetry and letters to women, and her concessions to social convention:

> She began to use masculine pronouns to disguise the poetry that was nearly always written about a woman. After she died, several of the rough drafts, in which she used feminine pronouns, were found. In later drafts she changed them, or her editors changed them, in order to make them 'suitable' for publication.

Another article ("Relating to the Abortion [Repeal] Movement") explains why the movement is important to gay women: "We are all potential victims [through rape, etc.] of backroom butcher abortionists." Other items report on cases of discrimination against gay people, including the refusal by the Boston Globe to accept paid advertising from Focus. An editorial reprinted from the Charlotte (N.C.) Observer opposes North Carolina's laws against homosexuality. A Focus editorial criticizes some participants in Boston's International Women's Day march for being "a bunch of hysterical, foul-mouthed, ugly bitches parading up and down the streets of Boston shouting obscenities and defacing property." An apparently regular column by gay activist Martha Shelley reveals "More Tales of Mid-America" gleaned from a cross-country trip. (MM)

The sample issues contain coverage of gay activities (such as a Gay Pride march) and news of the formation of gay groups: Boston Gay Speakers' Bureau (which sends people out to address church groups and college classes), a National Lesbian Information Service (which intends to publish an 8-page monthly newsletter), and High School Gays United. "MUL Intensifies Anti-Gay Crusade" criticizes William Loeb's Manchester [N.H.] Union Leader. "Hands Across the Dollar Gap" defends the motives of some so-called "welfare chiselers" and the untidy appearance ("breasts hanging at waist level") of some "Lower East Side dykes" criticized in the previous issue's editorial. "DOB Referrals" lists sources of legal, medical, and religious help. Regular features are letters to the editor and poetry. (A brief article praises Edna St. Vincent Millay's "Prayer to Persephone" as "a poem which Lesbians would forever hold dear.")

A back file of Focus is housed at Northwestern University Library. (TJS)

Feedback:

"The review is o.k...."

THE FURIES

Box 8843, S.E. Station
Washington, D.C. 20003
Monthly; $5 ($15 institutions)
Started: Jan. 1972

Format: tabloid
Issues examined: v. 1, nos. 1-3
Indexing: Alternative Press Index

The Furies takes its name from the Greek legend in which the "Angry Ones," the Furies, tormented Orestes for killing his mother (who killed Orestes' father)--their point being that matricide is not justifiable to avenge patricide.

> We call our paper The Furies because we are also angry. We are angry because we are oppressed by male supremacy. We have been fucked over all our lives by a system which is based on the domination of men over women, which defines male as good and female as only as good as the man you are with. It is a system in which heterosexuality is rigidly enforced and Lesbianism rigidly suppressed. It is a system which has further divided us by class, race, and nationality.
>
> ...
>
> The base of our ideological thought is: Sexism is

the root of all other oppressions, and Lesbian and woman oppression will not end by smashing capitalism, racism, and imperialism. Lesbianism is not a matter of personal preference, but rather one of political choice which every woman must make if she is to become woman-identified and thereby end male supremacy. Lesbians, as outcasts from every culture but their own, have the most to gain by ending race, class, and national supremacy within their own ranks. Lesbians must get out of the straight women's movement and form their own movement in order to be taken seriously, to stop straight women from oppressing us, and to force straight women to deal with their own Lesbianism. Lesbians cannot develop a common politics with women who do not accept Lesbianism as a political issue.

...

For the Chinese women whose feet were bound and crippled; for the Ibibos of Africa whose clitori were mutilated; for every woman who has ever been raped, physically, economically, psychologically, we take the name of the FURIES, Goddesses of Vengeance and protectors of women.

The Furies differs ideologically from some other gay papers, such as Ain't I A Woman, in its belief that "sexism is the root of all other oppression." In other words, the domination of men over women came first and served as a precedent for the domination of some men by other men (class), and the domination of white over black (race). For this reason, The Furies women are separatists, believing that gay women should work on their own and not in conjunction with other men or heterosexual women.

Theory and analysis of gay (and class and race) oppression dominate the paper, but other articles deal with self-defense and other survival measures; real or alleged lesbians in history (such as Queen Christina of Sweden and Emily Dickinson); and the arts (e.g., book reviews of gay feminist poetry). A series of articles (one of which is entitled, "Corporate Capitalism: Survival of the Richest") makes what amounts to a Marxist analysis (although it is not named as such) of the economic system in the United States. (MM)

GAY BOOK NEWS

Ian Young, Ed.
Catalyst Press

315 Blantyre Ave.
Scarborough, Ontario

MIN 2S6 Canada
Irregular; $2
Started: Aug. 1973
Circulation: 300

Format: 5 pages (offset, stapled)
Issues examined: Aug. 1973; and three undated issues of GayOkay

GayOkay was the newsletter of the University of Toronto Homophile Association. It contained a little news: on activities of the Association and on such topics as police harassment of homosexuals. The rest of the paper was usually given over to poetry, letters from readers, interviews, and--a large section--to book reviews. When the Association was superseded by the Gay Alliance Toward Equality, GayOkay ceased publication, but its book news section survived (under the same editor) as Gay Book News (Aug. 1973- ).

This new publication alerts readers to new books and periodicals related to homosexuality. (The editor says that all works received are reviewed.) A typical review consists of a brief notice of the new book, giving some information about its author, a brief statement of its subject, and (occasionally) news about its publication--if this has been controversial. New periodicals are described very briefly, and the necessary bibliographic information is given. There are advertisements for books and booksellers specializing in gay literature.

It is probable that few of the books described in GBN would be covered by better-known reviewing journals. The editor describes the situation: "In the past, collectors and those interested in gay literature have had to find information haphazardly, with the result that many of the items of interest could easily be overlooked. We hope GBN will make things easier by noting and reviewing as many new gay books as possible, including small press material, privately printed and more obscure titles, etc." One such work, privately published, is The Sexual Adventures of Sherlock Holmes. The reviewer's comment: "Seems Holmes, Watson, and just about everyone else ... [was] queer! What a shock for all those respectable English gentlemen who collect Sherlockiana."

(SA)

Feedback:

"It is excellent."

THE GAY CHRISTIAN

Metropolitan Community Church of New York
Box 1757, GPO
N.Y., N.Y. 10001
Irregular (every 2-3 months); $5

Started: Mar. 1972
Circulation: 1,200
Format: 12-16 pages (offset)
Issues examined: July 1973; Jan. & Mar./Apr. 1974
Back issues available from publisher

Published by a church whose ministry is primarily to the gay community, TGC tries to "publish articles of general significance and interest concerning Christianity from a gay point of view" and "gay life and liberation from a Christian point of view."

As the journal of the Northeast District, Universal Fellowship of Metropolitan Community Churches, TGC offers news of the activities of those churches. It shows pictures of a recent ordination, covers a conference, writes about a gay caucus at Union Theological Seminary (N.Y.), and publishes (on the back cover of each issue) a directory of affiliated churches and other gay religious groups in the Northeast.

TGC covers topics dealing with the union of homosexual and religious expressions of personality. Its editors do not feel that homosexuality and Christianity are mutually exclusive. To them, homosexuality is just one of the paths a person may choose in order to express himself as a sexual being. It is no less desirable than heterosexuality, except perhaps for the pressures that society may bring to bear. However, this does not mean that the editors are not concerned with morality; one of their major concerns is forging a homosexual ethic:

> Unfortunately, in its attempts to counteract the burden society and the institutional church place upon gays, the gay liberation movement has sometimes seemed to say that 'anything gay is good,' and anything going contrary to that claim is 'straight, sexist oppression....' Our community may not require the same moral guidelines that straights embrace, but we do need some sort of moral guidance and accepted practice in order that our lives may achieve greater meaning and fulfillment.

A reprint of a sermon argues that the world would be greatly improved if society would view homosexuality as an acceptable norm of human life. The author feels that sexual role-playing would decrease, the association of sex with power would disappear, and the world would open up when individuals no longer felt constrained to limit their affection to members of the opposite sex. "When one imagines and thinks of all the single men and women ... who never experienced passion and sexual tenderness with anyone because a society told them that those feelings were only legitimate with a certain percentage of the human race, one could weep."

An issue devoted to women in the church offers practical tips for reaching women who may be alienated because of lesbianism or because of their feeling that the churches are dominated by males. In order to point up some of the problems women encounter with religion, the editors have included a "Reading from the Queen Jane Authorized Version," pointing out how even the wording of the scriptures tends to offend women. Another article explains that the bias against women's equality in the Bible is a product of the culture in which the Bible was written and does not reflect a bias on God's part. On a more personal level, the problems of lesbian motherhood are discussed.

Articles deal not only with religious matters but also with the difficulties of a lifestyle not generally accepted by society. The anonymous author of "Come In and Out of the Closet" explores some of these problems, stating that homosexuals often do not admit their sexual orientation even to themselves because they believe they ought not to be "in love" with a member of the same sex. Even when they admit their real sexual needs, the author continues, problems arise as they attempt to hide this part of their lives for reasons of job or position, particularly if they are involved in work within one of the institutional churches.

> If everyone around you tells you that you ought to be something else, and you pretend most of the time, it is hard to remember that you are a person of worth just as you are. It even gets hard to remember that the secret love you share is indeed a beautiful creation of God.

An article of particular interest to gay Christians analyzes the Biblical passages dealing with Sodom and Gomorrah, and concludes that the sin of Sodom was not one of homosexuality; therefore, this passage so often cited to prove the sinfulness of homosexual activity does not actually do this. (It is obvious that TGC does not consider homosexuality to be sinful.)

The topics described above give an idea of the ground covered by TGC, and of how its editors attempt to carry out their ministry. They are preaching a kind of religion that is free, open, accepting of homosexuality, and liberal in its attitudes on other theological questions. (BK)

Reviewer's opinion:
A bright and attractive magazine with something to offer to those who are gay and Christian.

## GAY LIBERATOR

Box 631-A
Detroit, Mich. 48232
Monthly; $3
Started: 24 Apr. 1970

Format: 16- to 20-page tabloid (started with five mimeo. pages, stapled)
Issues examined: Mar.-May 1972

Although the Gay Liberator is not technically a male-only paper, there is only one woman on the staff, and coverage of lesbian concerns is minimal; most female contributions are on the poetry page.

Most issues cover local and regional gay conferences, activities of the Michigan Gay Confederation, and various news items. Reviews of books or films on homosexuality are common. "The Vice Report," a regular feature, covers recent arrests in bars and other public places. It is illustrated with a traffic sign that reads: "Cruise with Care."

Among the articles in the sample issues are "Musical Sexism," about sexism in rock music; "Fight, Kill, Be a Man," about gays in the armed forces; and "You're Damned Right We're Untreatable!," about gays and mental health. "Venceremos!" discusses Cubans' negative attitude toward homosexuality: "Cuba is not a socialist society; and the Castro regime's puritanical view on homosexuality is not a socialist view." However:

> The ideas of Revolutionary Socialism are relevant to gay liberationists not despite the practices of Cuba, but because Cuba and other 'socialist' countries (in reality ruled by a bureaucratic class) and the United States and other capitalist countries (ruled in the name of the people but for the sake of private profit) depend on repressive ideologies and systematically oppress gay people. Is it not logical that the process of striking off the fetters of economic and political slavery should also include the striking off of the fetters of silence and hate of homosexuals? Is it not logical that our fetters can only be struck off completely if, in our struggle for our own rights and liberation, we also forge a society in which all are free?

In "Three Boys I Know," the gay father of three children explains why he wants his sons to be gay:

> The gay man recognizes the oppression of women and strives to erase the prejudices which stand in the way of relating to them as equal beings. The gay appreciates the softness that should be a part of all men. The gay man gives up his privileged position of power and glories in his femininity. Gay women and men touch and trust. That's what I want for my boys!

(MM)

Feedback:

The respondent said that GL also contains "political analysis and occasional short fiction." He objected to the end of our first sentence, about the role of women on the periodical, and said: "Please re-assess, in view of recent issues. I think this is an inaccurate description." He enclosed the issues of July, September, and October 1972. We looked at them and found that there was still only one woman on the staff, and that most female contributions were still to the poetry page. The issues did, however, show more coverage of lesbian concerns.

## GAY PEOPLE AND MENTAL HEALTH

John Preston, Ed.
Box 3592, Upper Nicollet Station
Minneapolis, Minn. 55403
Monthly; $6 ($12 to institutions)

Started: Oct. 1972
Circulation: 3,000
Format: 4 pages (multilith)
Issues examined: Oct. & Dec. 1972; Jan. & Feb. 1973

The purpose of this newsletter is to facilitate and encourage communication among the men and women involved in mental health work who deal with gay people. The editorial viewpoint is stated clearly in the first issue:

> We are coming from a position that would be labeled as 'Gay Activism.' ... We cannot lose our biases, but we do hope to produce an open forum, not a propaganda sheet. This newsletter is not intended as another publication for the Gay community alone, it is also for those who work with Gay people and who are desperately looking for direction and resources.

An editorial begins each issue, but--with one exception (the Lesbian Issue)--it does not set the tone for the news content. Instead, it attempts to focus attention on a specific matter of concern to the readers, such as "Chemical Dependency and the Gay Community" and "Gay People and History."

While the format does not yet seem to be firmly defined, news items fall into the following loose categories: (1) Publications (announcements and brief critical reviews of new books, pamphlets, papers, films, bibliographies, and other resources); (2) Conferences (pertinent information about upcoming meetings, workshops, and conventions); (3) Organizations (news of people, agencies, and institutions active in the field); (4) Miscellaneous information on questions of political importance to the readers. Some of the topics discussed in the sample issues are: "Paper Presented on Sister Love," "Gay Man Hired by Sexuality Program," and "Psychosurgery." (BC)

Feedback:
Editor expressed no disapproval.

## GAY RAIDERS' NEWSLETTER

Box 15786
Philadelphia, Pa. 19103
Monthly; free

Started: Aug. 1972
Circulation: 10,000
Issues examined: none sent

"We explain to the reader what the activities of the Gay Raiders are. We also discuss what has happened in the country that relates to gay liberation.... We have worked in ... television and other ... media. The Gay Raiders ... disrupted the CBS Evening News with Walter Cronkite. We have been responsible for the change in the standards in programming of the subject 'homosexuality' by the three national networks."

## GAY TEACHERS' ASSOCIATION NEWSLETTER

452 W. Rosyln Pl.
Chicago, Ill. 60614
Bi-monthly; $5

Started: June 1972
Circulation: 210
Issues examined: none sent

"The organization's purpose is to educate the general public and the profession to recognize the inherent rights of ... [all] human being[s] to be productive, to make their contribution to the community at large and in so doing earn their livelihood. The organization will be composed of professional educators who realize that their first commitment is to the children they serve. Under no circumstances can, nor will, we condone acts of sexual aggression directed against children. The organization will further undertake the task of ... [showing] the community at large that in fact homosexuality and lesbianism are viable, healthy alternative lifestyles, which are in no way related to child molestation; that homosexuality and lesbianism are unrelated to classroom competence; and that gay women and gay men are as responsible for separation of their private and professional lives as are their heterosexual colleagues."

## HOMOSEXUAL COUNSELING JOURNAL

Ralph Blair, Ed.
Homosexual Community Counseling Center
45 E. 74th St.
N.Y., N.Y. 10021
Quarterly; $10 (institutions $15)
Started: Jan. 1974
Circulation: 700

Format: 50-60 pages (5 1/2" x 8 1/2", offset)
Issue examined: Jan. 1974
Indexing: Psychological Abstracts
Back issues available from publisher
Microform version available from Xerox University Microfilms

The editor sent this information by way of a pamphlet:

> The Homosexual Community Counseling Center was founded in May 1971 and fills the counseling needs of New York's homosexual men and women and their families. A service of homosexuals and heterosexuals, it includes both professionally trained and lay people. HCCC, Inc., is a private agency supported by the donations of friends. The men and women of the staff view homosexuality as a variety of sexual expression and not as a deviation which must be seen as sickness or sin. Services include individual and group counseling and psychotherapy, family therapy, parent education, marital and relationship counseling, sexual dysfunction consultation, vocational guidance, psychological testing, pastoral counseling, sociotherapy, and peer support. The consulting staff is composed of certified psychiatrists, psychologists, psychoanalysts, sex educators, clergy, social workers, and other professional counselors and psychotherapists as well as peer counselors.

The Center is a member of the International Association of Counseling Services and the American Association of Sex Educators and Counselors and is an institutional associate of SIECUS, the Sex Information and Education Council of the United States.

The sample issue contained a long article based on a dissertation: "Counselors', Psychologists', and Homosexuals' Philosophies of Human Nature and Attitudes Toward Homosexual Behavior." An editorial expressed approval that the Trustees of the American Psychiatric Association had dropped homosexuality from their listing of mental disorders in their *Statistical Manual of Mental Disorders*; and *disapproval* that the trustees had created a new category entitled "Sexual orientation disturbance" which might encourage homosexuals "to invest large amounts of time and money to try for psychiatric reversal of orientation."

The *Journal* says that training in the helping professions has not prepared counselors and therapists to deal realistically with homosexuals and their families, but the *Journal*

> is uniquely prepared to bring you forthright and responsible discussion and suggestions on meeting these needs realistically. Each issue of this new quarterly will inform and encourage with feature articles, book reviews, media and journal reviews, news, a free professional placement section, a cartoon essay, and editorial comment by the best-informed men and women working with homosexuality in the individual and in society today.

(JMS)

*Feedback:*
Editor expressed no disapproval.

INTERCHANGE

National Gay Student Center
2115 S Street, N.W.
Washington, D.C. 20008
Bi-monthly; $3
Started: 1970

Circulation: 600-1,000
Format: 4-8 pages (offset)
Issue examined: Mar. 1974
Back issues available from publisher

*Interchange* is published by NGSC, a project of the National Student Association. The center

> was established several years ago to provide information and services to the gay community and

> students and organizations on campus. The NGSC is and always has been run by gay people. It is composed of a small number of people and receives input in three major ways: correspondence, the Gay Caucus of the National Student Congress, and from visits to campuses and conferences by its staff.... We have embarked on certain projects which will be outlined in the rest of this newsletter.

The editor sent the following information:

> Our major focus is on the gay experience in higher education. We have interpreted this to mean printing information of value to gay student groups, gay students in general, and such additional subjects as gay studies and activities which may be of interest to groups. We also print brief statements from other groups which service the gay community.

Such items as "Gay Students Win Court Case," "ACLU to Represent Gay Students," and "Brigham Young Locks Closet" (on the flunking of male students at that university for wearing their hair too long) were covered in the sample issue. The "Bulletin Board" section contained announcements and information of interest to gays, and another section ("Resources") gave a list of other gay publications. (JMS)

IT'S TIME

| | |
|---|---|
| National Gay Task Force | Started: May 1974 |
| 80 5th Ave. (Rm. 903) | Circulation: 4,000 |
| N.Y., N.Y. 10011 | Format: 8 pages (offset) |
| Monthly; $15 membership | Issue examined: May 1974 |

The National Gay Task Force, founded by men and women prominent in gay organizations (including two of the largest in the country--the Gay Activists' Alliance of New York City and the Lesbian Feminist Liberation), is

> devoted to re-educating society, including its homosexual members, to esteem gay women and men at their full human worth and to accord them places in society which will allow them to attain and contribute according to their full human and social potential.... NGTF is broadly patterned after such other associations as the American Civil Liberties Union, the

Fortune Society, and various minority-group civil rights bodies.

It seeks to change public attitudes toward homosexuality and to inform and educate individuals and organizations in those fields--medicine, law, and religion--that have been the "chief fonts" of hostility toward homosexuality. The organization is working to end "legal discrimination against gays in areas ranging from immigration and naturalization to admission into drug programs, and in child visitation and custody suits by gay parents deprived of access to their children." NGTF, which is a major source of information about legislative reform, is also working with the American Bar Association for the repeal of sodomy laws in 42 states, and with the American Civil Liberties Union in a wide range of legal test cases. "In the area of religion ... a major effort is being made to work with both established religious institutions and with the rapidly-growing gay churches."

The newsletter intends to cover the activities of the organization and to carry articles and letters from members "in all areas of concern to gay people."

Barbara Gittings, a founder and "co-coordinator" of the Gay Task Force of the American Library Association, is a member of the Board of Directors of the NGTF.

## JOURNAL OF HOMOSEXUALITY

Haworth Press
130 W. 72nd St.
N.Y., N.Y. 10023
Quarterly; $12 (libraries $25)
Started: Spring 1974

Format: 128 pages (7" x 10", offset)
Issues examined: none sent
Indexing: contains subject & author index (bound in 4th issue each volume)

"Comprehensive journal from the professional community providing empirical research on homosexuality and gender identity from the fields of psychology, anthropology, sociology, medicine, and law. Articles demonstrate significance of recent research for helping professionals, psychotherapists, crimino-legal professionals, institutional and agency heads, educators, and others."

## LIS NEWSLETTER

Lesbian Information Service
Box 15368
San Francisco, Calif. 94115
Monthly; $12

Started: June 1971 (as Mother; became Proud Woman in Mar. 1972)
Circulation: varies (up to 5,000)
Format: 8 pages (offset)
Issues examined: none sent

When we wrote to the editors of Proud Woman (reviewed later in this chapter), we received a reply from the editors of LIS Newsletter, explaining that their collective had taken over activities from Mother Publications, publishers of Proud Woman.

> Lesbian Information Service acts as a national clearinghouse for lesbian news, information, resource materials, resource groups, as well as information for the concerned heterosexual parent or professional. ... [it] publishes the monthly LIS Newsletter on lesbian news in the political, legal, religious, community, and intercommunity levels, as well as regular features on questions such as 'What is lesbianism?,' 'What are the problems of coming out?,' and articles on community and counselling service projects for the lesbian community. Coverage is national. No advertising is accepted. LIS Newsletter is intended as a source of information which is reliable, objective, and accurate....

## LAVENDER WOMAN

Box 60206
1723 W. Devon
Chicago, Ill. 60660
Bi-monthly; $3 ("free to women in penal institutions --including mental hospitals")
Started: Nov. 1971
Format: 16-page tabloid (offset)
Issues examined: Nov. 1971; May 1972; Jan. & Mar. 1973
Copies of the paper, formerly on file at the Women's History Library in Berkeley, are now at Northwestern University Library

This newspaper of Lesbian Liberation in Chicago is a composite of local work by lesbians. Although personal viewpoints and experiences are expressed in poetry and short prose pieces, an over-all political tone is set by articles on Negro lesbians, the political implications of lesbianism, critical reviews of books on lesbians, the relation of abortion to the lesbian struggle, and the "coming out" process through which lesbians cease to hide. Regular features include "Lavender Handywoman," a column on making household repairs;

"Dear Mother," a series of real or would-be letters from lesbians to their mothers; and the "Lesbian Librarian," a book review.

In its first issue, LW describes its purpose:

> The Lavender Woman is a collective attempt to stop running, to stand still and firm in our places, so that we can stop depleting ourselves with evasion, manipulation and all those other defenses we've needed for our survival. We have to stop running in order to grow. We have to stop running from ourselves, from our sisters, to turn around and face one another, confront one another, love one another. We need to let it be, let ourselves be. We need to say loud and clear, who we are, and where we are going. A Lesbian relationship, we are beginning to discover, is not a hazard, or a liability, but a gift and a virtue--a strengthening, redeeming relationship in which we mutually confirm our identities as women, in which we are free to let ourselves be real, rather than meet a male-sexist stereotype which society is always holding up for us to clumsily imitate. Our awkwardness we discover is grace, our so-called ugliness is beauty--in this world, everything is upside down--we are through the looking glass. Straight society seems dull, unreal, several layers from the truth. Our failure to meet straight standards of behavior is our ultimate success as real women. In this sense, Lesbianism is a powerful, revolutionary force within the Women's Movement--a kind of avant garde, as Flo Kennedy points out--we are the first women who have elected to survive without men. We even find ourselves being exploited by straight sisters in Women's Liberation who see Lesbianism as a kind of revolutionary Bandwagon, they can jump on to get there quicker. We are attacked by supposedly non-sexist Gay men because we prefer to meet by ourselves, and recognize ourselves as a separate group in the Gay Liberation Movement. These and other challenges we are learning to face head-on. We found that running from them gets us nowhere. If we speak the truth, from where we see it, we can keep our heads and our souls together. We can keep others from foisting off their truths onto us--or speaking for us. Only then will we be able to honestly contribute to a revolutionary movement, in which groups working separately at their

own liberation from where they are at, converge toward a common goal--the reworking of this sexist and racist society closer to the heart's desire--a society based on real human need.

(MM)

A "Policy Statement" in the Jan. 1973 issue explains that LW was provincial when it started: it covered primarily the north side of Chicago. It is trying to expand its coverage to include "the South side, the suburbs, and other towns." The paper's policy: "We are diverse lesbians dedicated to diverse goals, all along the basic line of 'Truth, Beauty, and the Womanly Way.'"

There is news of events of interest to lesbians (e.g., "Chicago's Gay Pride Week"; or a concert by "The Family of Woman"); poetry; comments on religion (a lesbian writes about a mass celebrated at her home); and politics (reprint of a speech by the editor of Lesbian Tide at an anti-war convention).

Articles on problems facing lesbians warn lesbian mothers to be careful in the divorce courts, if they want custody of their children (even "liberal" judges look upon homosexuality as something on a level with "a drinking problem"); and homosexual teachers "are constantly threatened, fired, or humiliated into quitting," regardless of their skill at teaching.

Medicine.--An article ("Lesbian Shrinkdom") by a graduate student in counseling and psychology proclaims that "We as Lesbians are the ones who best know ourselves and each other. We know we are not a bunch of sickies or perverts."

Directory.--There is a listing of Chicago-area gay coffee houses, groups, workshops, and services. There are also announcements ("Little Informations") of the meetings of various groups: gay law students; gay social workers; the Chicago Women's Liberation Rock Band; the Rogers Park [War on] Rape Project; and others. There are also ratings (based on a survey of readers) of gay bars in Chicago.

Letters to the editor (variously entitled "Sisters Speak Out" or "We've Decided to Comment, After All").--In the Jan. 1973 issue, six letters condemn Richard Nixon for his bombing of the Vietnamese, and for his repeated lies about the Indochina war. (TJS)

LAZETTE

| | |
|---|---|
| Daughters of Bilitis in New Jersey | Box 62<br>Fanwood, N.J. 07023 |

Monthly; $3
Started: Sept. 1971
Circulation: 70

Format: 4-6 pages (mimeo., stapled)
Issues examined: Dec. 1973; Feb., June 1974

A Lesbian Counsellor of DOBNJ sent this information:

> We have no 'editorial policy.' Lazette [has] ... pertinent local information of local interest to members of Daughters of Bilitis in New Jersey. We discuss what's happened in New Jersey with DOB, with women's liberation groups, with gay groups. We have a calendar page. Jinx [editor] occasionally does a graphic (to change the pace). Lazette is put out by the 'J' commune, members of the Lesbian Core Group in New Jersey, for DOBNJ. I really doubt that Lazette is of interest to you, except for historical reasons. We do not sell to bookstores. We do not knowingly accept subscriptions from men, so aren't all that anxious to have publicity. DOBNJ and Lazette are totally political--not social. DOB is not a dating or introduction service of any kind; it is a political and social-service organization--at least here in New Jersey.

One issue was devoted to "A Day in the Life of a Lesbian Counsellor" and described the anxieties and problems of a divorced woman (with a child) who had recently discovered she was a lesbian. Another issue concerned itself with the emnity that has arisen between DOBNJ and NOW-NJ (National Organization for Women) which Lazette described as a "white middle-class straight" women's organization that no lesbians "need apply" to. A deeply resented (by DOBNJ) letter from the president of a NOW chapter is reprinted.

A third issue defined the goals and services of DOBNJ which include counseling and encouragement on coming out: supplying literature and bibliographies on Lesbianism, and supporting research projects; supplying women who will speak to groups or write articles; and working for political goals which include civil rights legislation and the ratification of the Equal Rights Amendment. (JMS)

Feedback:

"Enclosed I am returning the corrected review--you misunderstood (understandably--it's a complicated situation) some of the aspects of our fight with NOW. Mid-East Jersey NOW was a chapter formed to give minority women a platform--so DOB NJ's fight was not with Mid-East Jersey NOW, but with the State Organization--NOW-NJ. Also, the letter was from the President of one of the chapters of NOW --not the President of NOW (national). Otherwise it's o.k. -- if you really want to give us all that much space."

## THE LESBIAN TIDE

| | |
|---|---|
| 373 N. Western Ave. (#202) | Circulation: 2,000 |
| Los Angeles, Calif. 90005 | Format: 32-40 pages |
| Monthly; $7.50 | Issues examined: Feb.-Apr. |
| Started: Aug. 1971 | 1972 |

The Lesbian Tide is "a feminist lesbian publication, written by and for the rising tide of women today. It will speak of their numbers, their lives, their ideas and their pride." It is primarily a news magazine of the women's and lesbian movements, rather than an ideological journal.

Most news items, reports of conferences, and profiles of activists are centered around Los Angeles and California activities, but the editors "try to avoid provincialism, aiming to be of interest to gay feminists around the world." General articles have dealt with lesbian research, psychotherapy, lesbianism and revolution, and the language used against homosexuals. Poetry is included in every issue.

The organizations most often reported on are Daughters of Bilitis (DOB) and National Organization for Women (NOW). A continuing column called "Herstory" features the personal narratives of lesbian movement activists. (MM)

Feedback:

DOB and NOW are no longer the organizations most reported on. The "Herstory" column no longer appears.

## MATTACHINE MIDWEST NEWSLETTER

| | |
|---|---|
| Monthly; $3 (free to members) | Format: 16 pages (offset) |
| | Issue examined: Mar. 1973 |

"Mattachine Midwest is a non-profit organization.... Through an active program, it seeks to improve the legal, social, and economic status of homosexuals. Membership is open to anyone 18 years of age or older, regardless of sex or sexual orientation." The organization "maintains a 24-hour telephone-answering service, and can refer you to competent doctors, lawyers, psychologists, employment counselors, draft advisers, and clergymen at any hour of the day or night."

The Newsletter covers the organization's activities. The sample issue carried such features as "The Answer Corner" (social and psychiatric questions answered); a book review; an events calendar; letters to the editor; "Mother Tucker" (a gossip column); "The President's Column" (by the president of the organization); several short news items ("Teens Dig Gays"; "Gay New York Candidate"; and "Governor Walker Booed"--when the Illinois politician "refused a gay activist's request for an executive order to ban discrimination against homosexuals in hiring state employees"); and advertisements. (JMS)

Feedback:

The editor informed us that the last published issue was January 1974 and that he did not know when the publication would be resumed. The address had been: Box 924, Chicago, Ill. 60690.

MIDWEST THING

2728 N. Hampden Ct.
Chicago, Ill. 60614
Semi-monthly; $10
Started: Oct. 1972 (Detroit, Milwaukee, St. Louis editions)

Circulation: 20,000+
Format: 24-30 pages (8 1/2" x 5 1/2")
Issues examined: undated, unnumbered early issue; vol. 1, nos. 4-6

Midwest Thing is described by its publisher and editor-in-chief as the Midwest's "underground, avant-garde entertainment guide."

> MIDWEST THING covers all scenes, doing 'our thing,' whether it be politics, gay and women's lib, or just plain old voyeurism. A complete bar guide and recommended restaurant guide is the intent, without regard to sexual policy.

The issues examined have a gay male orientation. Most articles are "reviews" of restaurants, bars, and current entertainment appearing in the area, either Detroit-Toledo, Chicago, Milwaukee, or St. Louis, with a separate edition for each city. At least one article in each issue features an interview with a local or locally-appearing entertainer. The rest of a typical issue includes a "bar guide" and a "dining guide" (addresses of recommended bars and restaurants); a regular column on fashion for men; a calendar of film, theatre, and musical events; movie and theatre reviews; and an abundance of ads for restaurants, bars, and adult bookstores. Other items include short (one or two-page) essays--"No More Sex Roles," "Small Town Gay," "On Love," etc.; an advice column; and news "flashes" about gay liberation and gay civil rights activities. (MM)

ONE INSTITUTE QUARTERLY: Homophile Studies

2256 Venice Blvd.
Los Angeles, Calif. 90006
Occasional; sold by single issues
Started: 1958

Format: 14-34 pages (6 3/4" x 9 1/2")
Issues examined: Winter/Spring 1964; 1967; 1970

ONE Institute Quarterly does not cry for "gay liberation" as such but has for years advocated understanding of male and female homosexuality. Contributors to this scholarly, educational, nonpolitical journal approach homosexuality from the standpoints of anthropology, biology, history, law, philosophy, psychology, sociology, religion, etc., and usually consider this "deviation" neither a crime nor a disease but a social phenomenon.

In the latest issue examined appears the complete report of the National Institute of Mental Health Task Force on Homosexuality, chaired by Dr. Evelyn Hooker, a major researcher in the field. The report emphasizes the diverse characteristics of homosexuals and the various degrees of sexual adjustment among homosexuals. "Homosexuality is not a unitary phenomenon, but rather represents a variety of phenomena which take in a wide spectrum of overt behavior and psychological experiences." The report estimates the extent of homosexuality in the United States: "At least three or four million adults in the United States ... are predominantly homosexual and [there are] many more individuals in whose lives homosexual tendencies or behavior play a significant role." Recommendations of the report include the establishment of an NIMH Center for the Study of Sexual Behavior which would carry out programs in research, training, and education (of professionals, the public, law enforcement personnel, etc.), prevention, treatment (to "decrease discomfort" and "increase productive functioning"), and social policy (changes in the law and in employment policies and practices).

Another issue includes excerpts from the writings of the

late Dr. Blanche M. Baker, a psychiatrist who counseled male homosexuals for many years, partly through a column ("Toward Understanding") in ONE Magazine (now defunct). Dr. Baker did not believe that homosexuality is a disease. When questioned about the "manifestly disturbed behavior patterns of some homosexuals" she replies, "Any human being who suffers from pain, rejection by his fellows, overly strict authoritarian control, neglect, or over-indulgence, may develop neurotic or even psychotic conditions." She continues:

> Homosexuals are human beings too. They are interesting, real, unusual, creative, beauty-loving people, if one can get behind the mask of camping pretense and sham so many of them feel compelled to wear to protect their sensitive souls from condemnation and hate levelled at them by a hostile, prejudiced, and uncomprehending society.

ONE Institute Quarterly generally includes an editorial, book reviews or correspondence, and two or more long articles like the ones quoted above. (Others are "Music: the Hermaphroditic Art," "Some Recent Empirical and Non-Empirical Observations on Male Homosexuality," and a set of articles on "The Homophile of the Future.") (MM)

Feedback:

"Very good, with the slight exception: we do not at all consider ONE Magazine 'defunct.' Rather, for lack of funding it is not currently in publication and has many hopes for the future." In 1973 neither ONE Magazine nor ONE Institute Quarterly was published because of lack of funds.

PROUD WOMAN

Bi-monthly; $5 (offset)
Started: 1971 Issue examined: Mar./Apr.
Format: 12-page tabloid 1972

When Mother changed its name to Proud Woman (with the issue examined) it also changed its editorial scope to include the women's as well as the Lesbian movement. A paper concerned with professional journalism, its articles are mostly news stories or analyses of the news regarding the legal battles and civil and professional rights of women and Lesbians. Its scope is best described in this listing of coming articles in the issue examined: Women in Industry, the

Women's Movement in the U.S.S.R., Lesbian Mothers, History of the Women's Press, Women and Male MDs, and National Election Roundups.

Much of Proud Woman is similar to the politics and approach of the National Organization for Women. In the issue examined it reports on the restricted rights of married women, the failure of NOW to support a Lesbian in a custody case, lawsuits filed for equal pay or against sex discrimination, a group that works to eliminate sexism from elementary school readers, prominent women in politics, the wedding of two black women, the divorce laws in Italy, the opening of the Sisters' Liberation House in Los Angeles, and--to celebrate International Women's Day--some facts about Vietnamese women. The longest piece in this issue is an interview with "a lesbian prostitute who's also a junkie and a half-breed Indian." Book reviews discuss "Mother Jones" (a pamphlet from the Radical Education Project) and The Lonely Trip Back, the autobiography of a woman drug addict. The issue also includes a petition to the American Psychiatric Association to strike homosexuality from the Standard Diagnostic Manual as an illness or character disorder. Regular features include "Herb Lore," a column about plants by Lesbian poet Elsa Gidlow; and columns on "Self Defense" and "Legal Notes." Proud Woman is making a conscious attempt to locate and publish artwork by women artists. Two drawings appear in the issue examined. (MM)

Feedback:

Has ceased publication. See LIS Newsletter in this chapter. Address of PW was Mother Publications, Box 8507, Stanford, Calif. 94305.

SAPPHO

BCM/Petrel
London WCIV 6XX, United Kingdom
Monthly; £5.85 (incl. surface postage)

Started: Apr. 1972
Circulation: 1,500
Format: (5 3/4" x 8 1/4", offset)
Issues examined: Dec. 1973; Feb. & Mar. 1974

Sappho says it's "the only lesbian magazine in Europe in any language" and is concerned with "radical feminism in general and lesbian feminism in particular."

Some of the aims of the magazine are to disperse the isolation of gay ghettos by the interchange of information with heterosexual societies, to support all minority groups, and to encourage social groups to relieve the loneliness of the lesbian.

The articles, stories, and poems are not explicitly sexual. Feature articles include a wide range of topics, such as "A Day in the Life of the Probate Clerk," "Belgian Women's Election Campaign," "All Ireland Union for Sexual Freedoms," and "Lesbian Teach On." "The Gay and Women's Struggle" examines some of the root causes of the lack of cooperation between the gay movement and the women's rights movement.

Regular columns are also included. "Sapphoscene" presents notices of meetings, materials, and news items; "Heteraecetera" includes fairly long letters to the editor; "The Spike" prints addresses of national organizations, local groups, publications, and counselling and befriending services throughout the United Kingdom and Europe. "Happy Families" discusses gay couples who have children, and includes personal experiences with fostering, adoption, intercourse, or Artificial Insemination by Donor. Book reviews, poetry, and crossword puzzles are occasionally included. (NK)

Feedback:
The editor expressed no disapproval.

SISTERS: By and For Gay Women

DOB
1005 Market, #208
San Francisco, Calif. 94103
Monthly; $5
Started: 1970

Circulation: 500
Format: 32 pages (5 1/2" x 8 1/2", offset)
Issue examined: Nov. 1971

Sisters is the publication of the San Francisco chapter of Daughters of Bilitis (DOB), the organization formed in the 1950s "for the purpose of aiding the Lesbian to discover her place in society and of educating society to understand and accept her, without prejudice...."

Sisters places emphasis on local and organizational news and events but also publishes prose, poetry, and artwork. Three book reviews dominate the issue examined. "America and Women" heads a review of America the Violent by Ovid Demaris.

> In the book we must wade through 386 pages of wars, labor strikes, lynch mobs, religious strife, race

> riots, assassinations, organized crime, and political violence, including the youth rebellion of the 60's and sociopaths such as Richard Speck. In the modern times section the reader has a difficult time determining whether the Left or the Right is more dangerous. To me the most disgusting part of the book is the few items concerning groupies, the camp followers of our present-day revolutionaries; they are simply whores who are no better than their barbaric masters.

The rest of the review is an essay on the possibility that increasing violence will be directed at women. "Men love women as long as we are in our place, and men protect women as long as we are in our place, but what would happen if we stepped out of place?" The author goes on to discuss male backlash and the politics of rape and asks, "Can women depend on each other?" She concludes that

> it might ... be wise for us to quit begging our straight sisters to let us be their niggers in the movement and to stop taking all the insults and shit-work the pussycats and their toms can heap on us. If we can step forward, we should do so with the intention of working for our own cause. Either way, we Lesbians are going to get it right between the legs in a sex war unless we realize soon the folly of our pollyanna relations with straight sisters and gay brothers and especially Big Brother.

The other book reviews are of A Place for Us by Isabel Miller, later published at Patience and Sarah ("does more to delineate Lesbian love than a thousand ponderous technical works") and Kate Millett's Sexual Politics. Some poetry, a monthly calendar of events, an astrological column, a brief report on the class "Gay People and the Law" sponsored by the People's Law School, and news and progress of the publication complete the issue. (MM)

## SPECTRE

| | |
|---|---|
| Box 305<br>Ann Arbor, Mich. 48107<br>Bi-monthly; $2 ($6 to "established" institutions; "free to all prisoners") | Format: 16-page tabloid (offset)<br>Issue examined: Jan./Feb. 1972 |

"Spectre is published by the Spectre Collective of white revolutionary lesbians." Its finances are shaky and its editorial opinions are in a state of flux: a note warns that no more back issues will be sent out, because "they're so bad we just don't agree [anymore] with what we wrote."

Most of the content of Spectre is written by the Collective. There is an occasional letter to the editor.

The tone of Spectre is, as the editors realize, one of constant anger:

> We get asked a lot why we're so angry.
> ...
> THE QUESTION ISN'T 'WHY ARE WE SO ANGRY?' BUT 'WHY THE HELL ARE YOU NOT ANGRY?'

What makes Spectre so angry? The oppression of women by men, and of youth by age. "Ageism" (a word apparently coined on analogy with "sexism") is a constant target. "Ageism" is the repression of young people by older people, especially parents. (The family is called the "U.S. training camp," the home is a "concentration camp," and the words "mother," "father," "parent," and "family" are often placed in quotation marks, as a sign of contempt.) The sample issue contained a number of case histories of young lesbians abused by adults: gang-raped; harassed by police; beaten by males; sexually molested by "fathers."

A notice in Spectre says that the paper is on file at the International Women's History Archive (2325 Oak, Berkeley, Calif. 94708), and that microfilm versions can be obtained from (1) Bell & Howell (Wooster, Ohio) and (2) University Microfilms (Ann Arbor, Mich.). (The periodicals in the Women's History Archive have since been sent to Northwestern University Library.) (TJS)

Reviewer's comment:

Spectre's angry tone is reinforced by the continual use of obscene and excrementitious language.

UVA URSI

Aestherchild and Reuben, Owners
RFD
Robbinston, Me. 04671
3 issues a year; $1 an issue or $5 for 2 years
Started: July 1973
Circulation: 500
Format: looseleaf, unnumbered packet; various sized pages;

mimeograph and serigraphy Issue examined: July 1973

Uva Ursi, as the authors explain, is the official Latin name for the herb "bearberry." The name is particularly appropriate for a Lesbian publication, since its two parts--bear and berry--symbolize the masculine and feminine roles in a Lesbian relationship. Bearberry is an attempt to deal with "something that really is difficult in gay relationships--who is who, what is what. But every Lezzi knows that no one is pure bear or all berry."

The authors state that "Uva Ursi is a funky down home Lesbian journal dedicated to turning dykes on to a self sufficient rural lifestyle." The packet examined was a miscellany of essays dealing with the use of natural herbs as medicine, the personal habits of one of the authors ("I've always been a slob. Something feels satisfied in my soul when I see a clutter I've made or a big shit in the toilee."), and an article entitled, "Those Old Monogamy Blues or It Feels Good to be Two but We Used to be Three." In addition, poetry, drama, short stories, cartoons, and a poster formed a part of the packet. Illustrations play a major role in the journal, and these are often explicit depictions of Lesbian love-making.

The various parts of the issue--the drawings, poetry, stories, etc.--are an exploring and an attempting to come to terms with the Lesbian lifestyle. Problems arising from this type of relationship are discussed and also smiled at. There is a refreshing lack of defensiveness on the authors' parts; the overriding tone of the issue was one of good humor. Uva Ursi is principally the creation of two women who seem to have established for themselves a workable relationship, and who are interested in helping other Lesbians to do the same. (CH)

Feedback:

"My initial reading of your review of UU left me most displeased. But subsequent readings enabled me to reconcile myself to it. But in no way can I stomach the opening [para] graph, as it is an error of fact. 'Uva Ursi is a particularly appropriate name for a Lesbian publication because it is an extremely effective herbal remedy for female diseases, particularly those that afflict the vagina and uterus.' And not--as you state--because it symbolizes the masculine and feminine roles that exist in a Lesbian relationship.

"You see, Uva Ursi is a single plant which--when boiled--can be consumed as a tea or used as a douche.

"I also seem to recall only one graphically explicit illustration of Lesbian lovemaking--that being the poster. To insist that you correct this item would be bickering. If you imagine there were many such illustrations, then so be it."

## WICCE

| | |
|---|---|
| Box 15833 | Circulation: 2,000 |
| Philadelphia, Pa. 19103 | Format: 16-page tabloid (offset) |
| Bi-monthly; $3.50 (institutions $7) | Issues examined: Fall 1973; Early Spring 1974 |
| Started: Nov. 1973 | |

Wicce is a "lesbian/feminist publication carrying news, political analysis, poetry, fiction, interviews, and artwork." The title is "the old version of the word, which meant then 'wise-woman,' not witch (evil)."

In an article by one of the staff, radical lesbian feminism is interpreted as

> a total commitment to women.... We are committed to being fulfilled emotionally, politically, and sexually by other women.... We must recognize lesbianism as the key to an effective radical feminist strategy.... If we have in fact identified the male as the enemy, all non-lesbians are guilty of consorting with the enemy; classically, collaborators are as guilty as the enemy.

Other articles in the sample issues included: "Witches, Midwives, and Nurses," an analysis of a pamphlet showing the history of sexism in the medical profession; "Meeting the Amazons," an interview with two editors of a lesbian arts journal; and "Notes from a Third World Woman," on the twin-edged oppression of a black woman.

Regular features include book reviews; ads for other lesbian or feminist publications; and "Handywoman," articles "on all facets of self-reliance with tools and mechanical things."

Wicce is published in Philadelphia, and some of its features (such as a list of gay bars), articles, and services ("Lesbian Hotline" and "Open House") are local rather than national. (SLA)

## Chapter 15

## RACIAL & ETHNIC PRIDE

> We, the first people of this land, are tired of being third-rate citizens.
> ---The Nishnawbe News

> The Arabs have a case.... Zionism is not Judaism and to oppose Zionism or the policies of the State of Israel is neither to be anti-Semitic nor to wish to throw Jews into the sea. ---Middle East Perspective

> The ideas we talk about come from pain. The pain of oppression we have felt as women, men, workers, and Jews in America....
> ---Chutzpah

> We demand that all oppressed white people be exempt from military service. We demand an immediate end to police brutality and murder of oppressed white people....
> ---The Patriot

Periodicals in this chapter range from moderate to radical in their tone and outlook. New Dawn (Asian-American), emanating from a San Francisco collective, labels itself anti-imperialist, supports national liberation struggles, admires the People's Republic of China, and condemns Russia and the U.S. Palante (Young Lords Party), also anti-imperialist, stresses the need for self-determination for all Latinos and Third World peoples; Third World News (minority students at the University of California, Davis) expresses the same political outlook. The Patriot is published by a revolutionary party for poor and oppressed whites, mainly of southern origin: "We are the living reminder that when they threw out their white trash they didn't burn it."

## ARAB OR PRO-ARAB

In the past few years, a number of English-language Arab periodicals have been published in Britain, Canada, and the U.S., aimed not only at overseas Arab communities but at British, Canadian, and American opinion. (Similar periodicals are published in other countries as well.) These periodicals hope to create a new attitude toward Arab countries, and thus change American Middle Eastern policy, which they feel has been influenced or controlled by American Jews. This chapter reviews such periodicals from five nations:

Britain: Middle East International

Canada: Arab Canada; the non-political Arab Community Newsletter; and The Canadian Arab World Review

France: Israel & Palestine (anti-Zionist)

Lebanon: Journal of Palestine Studies and Middle East Newsletter (both anti-Zionist)

United States: ANERA Newsletter (concerned with Palestinian refugees); Action (dedicated to the establishment of a democratic and non-sectarian state in Palestine); Arab Tribune; The Palestinian Voice; Resistance in the Middle East.

An unusual Jewish periodical, the Report published by American Jewish Alternatives to Zionism, is pro-Arab, believing that Israel is at fault and should cease her expansionist policies and return Arab lands captured in the Middle East wars. Dr. Alfred M. Lilienthal's Middle East Perspective is also anti-Zionist, and asks that Palestinian Arab refugees be allowed to return--as full citizens--to their homeland. New Outlook is published by Israeli doves.

## JEWISH OR PRO-ISRAELI

The pro-Israeli viewpoint on the Middle East is represented by such periodicals as

Dawn (New York students)

The Israel Digest (news directly from that country)

Near East Report (a well-balanced analysis)

Outlook (Women's League for Conservative Judaism)

Ha Peh (American Students for Israel)

Pioneer Women (Women's Labor Zionist Organization of America).

Network is published by the North American Jewish Students Network, and Hayom by the Philadelphia Union of Jewish Students. Genesis 2, put out by academics in the Boston area, aims at "Jewish renewal." Chutzpah is edited by young persons working for a radical Jewish movement free from established organizations and synagogues. The students at Brandeis University who produce Response consider it to be the "leading dissenting Jewish publication in America" independent of major Jewish institutions. Hasidic Jews publish the Holy Beggars' Gazette.

INDIAN AND ESKIMO

A number of periodicals come from (what seem to us as) the far corners of Canada:

Alberta: Elbow Drums (considered non-political by its editor)

British Columbia: Nesika

Manitoba: Indian and Metis Brotherhood Organization Newsletter (prisoners) and The Scout

Northwest Territories: The Drum, Midnight Sun, and Native Press (the first two are Eskimo)

Nova Scotia: MicMac News (Maritime Indians)

Ontario: Tekawennake (Mohawk)

Saskatchewan: Saskatchewan Indian

Yukon: Skookum Jim News and Yukon Indian News.

Of the periodicals published in the United States, some speak for a tribe, some for an individual, some for an institution, and some for all Indians. The Blue Cloud Quarterly is an artistic literary periodical published at a Benedictine abbey in South Dakota. The Voice of Brotherhood speaks for the "native population of Alaska." The Raven Speaks is the one-woman effort of a Cherokee. Akwesasne Notes is Mohawk; The Tribal Tribune speaks for the Washington Colville tribes; and The Navajo Times and Diné Baa-Hané are both Navajo. The Nishnawbe News is put out by Indian students. Whispering Wind is devoted to American Indian customs, traditions, arts, and crafts. The militant Many Smokes speaks for Indians in general.

Indian Record is published occasionally by the Bureau of Indian Affairs. The American Indian Historical Society publishes The Indian Historian and Wassaja, while the Journal of American Indian Education is published at Arizona State University.

LATINO

The politically-conscious Ideal serves the Mexican-Americans of California's Coachella Valley. Aztlan is a "Chicano Journal of the Social Sciences and the Arts" published at the University of California (Los Angeles). The Rican (Chicago) dwells upon Puerto Rico's cultural heritage, and Que Ondee Sola (Puerto Rican students at Northeastern Illinois University) advocates independence for the island. Other periodicals represented in this chapter are El Chicano Community Newspaper (Southern California); Echo (Austin, Texas); El Gallo (Denver, Colorado); El Popo (California State University, Northridge); and El Hispano (Sacramento).

BLACK

The ideas of Marcus Garvey are expounded in African Opinion and Mazungumzo. Black Creation covers activity in what it refers to as the "black arts." African Agenda presents "Afro-American Opinion." The Black Community Newsletter serves an area in Alabama. Palo Alto's Black Times ("Voices of the National Community") publishes short stories and poetry. Grass Roots News ("The Opportunity Paper") stresses business and education. Impact wants radical social change.

The following periodicals come from Canada: Africa Speaks ("The Voice of the Colored Man in Canada"); The Black Action Party (Montreal); Contrast and Spear (both published in Toronto and aimed at the middle class); and Grasp (Black United Front of Nova Scotia).

Black African periodicals are reviewed in our Civil Rights and Marxist-Socialist Left chapters.

MISCELLANEOUS

Trait d'Union is a voice of the Melkite community in Canada. Europa Ethnica deals with the problems of linguistic and ethnic minorities in Europe.

--Janet & Theodore Spahn

ANERA NEWSLETTER

733 15th St., N.W., Rm. 900 Washington, D.C. 20005

Six times a year; $10 contribution to ANERA

Started: 1968
Circulation: 9,000
Format: 4 pages (offset)

Issues examined: five, from 1970, 1972, and 1973
Back issues available from ANERA

The ANERA Newsletter informs members of American Near East Refugee Aid of the activities of the organization and the situation of Palestinian refugees. With AMER (American Middle East Rehabilitation), a group formed in 1948 and joined to ANERA in 1971, and the United Nations Relief and Works Agency, ANERA provides pharmaceuticals, direct financial aid, and scholarships for vocational training to needy young refugee men and women. The Newsletter reports on many efforts to aid refugees, mainly schools and orphanages that have been established in camps and keep going against tremendous military and financial odds. Book reviews, poetry, and editorials from other newspapers dealing with the Arab/Israeli conflict are also included. The main focus is on the plight of the refugees left homeless by the creation of Israel after World War II; both Israel and the Arab nations are criticized for their present aggression and indifference. The general tone of the Newsletter is characterized by this statement by John P. Richardson, ANERA's Executive Vice-President:

> Israel expands and grows stronger, and the Palestinian refugees remain in the limbo which began when their return to their homes was blocked when the fighting stopped. Yet neither the passage of time, nor military superiority, nor an indifferent (and even antagonistic) world attitude will change the basic human factor in the Palestine issue. Until their future as a people is determined, the mass of refugees will remain in their sad status, producing the desperate bombers and gunmen whose acts bear less and less relationship to a political program. The Palestine refugees have no representatives in the halls of power; they have no presidents and ambassadors to negotiate for them. Thus they are ignored and despised by the power-brokers of the world. For all of the attention being given these days to resolving major 'contradictions' in international politics, it is puzzling indeed that after 25 years so much effort is still expended in focusing attention on every aspect of the Palestine issue but its most central one: the existence of the Palestine refugees and the continued gross denial of their rights in their own homeland.

(CP)

Feedback:

Editor expressed no disapproval.

ACTION

Action Committee on American-Arab Relations
4 E. 43rd St.
N.Y., N.Y. 10017
Weekly; $20
Started: May 1969
Circulation: 15,000

Format: 8-page tabloid (offset)
Issues examined: 29 Oct., 5 & 12 Nov. 1973
Back issues available from publisher

Action is "dedicated to the establishment of a democratic non-sectarian state in Palestine." Articles deal with activities of pro-Arab groups in the U.S., as well as with events in the Middle East. The paper frequently contains petitions and form letters encouraging readers to write to Congressmen, Senators, and the President and urge them to stop all aid to Israel. The editorial policy was summarized by the executive editor as follows:

> We are concerned with peace in the Middle East. Editorials are opposed to U.S. and U.S.S.R. arms shipment to Israel or Arab states. We call for suspension of military and economic aid to Israel, and the recognition of the right of the people of Palestine to their land, as a prerequisite for peace. Also, we are concerned with civil rights and freedom of speech, press, etc., in U.S. and Arab world.

(SMA)

Feedback:

The Secretary-General of the Action Committee, Dr. M. T. Mehdi, replied: "I believe that you are rendering a very significant service not only to the libraries which will use the Directory, but also to the whole field of freedom of press in the country." He proposed the following addition:

> Action is the organ of a movement to change the totality of American policy towards the Middle East. The movement, institutionalized in the Action Committee on American-Arab Relations, believes that American policy towards the Middle East has been to the detriment of America and the Arab people, and a threat to international peace and the long-range security of the Jewish people. Action is the instrument to bring the change.

AFRICA SPEAKS: The Voice of the Colored Man in Canada

41 Sanderstead Ave.
Toronto, Ont., Canada
Monthly

Format: 4-page tabloid (offset)
Issue examined: Feb. 1973

Much of the sample issue was devoted to "A Political Biography of Angela Davis." Illustrated with photographs, carries advertisements.

AFRICAN AGENDA: A Voice of Afro-American Opinion

Harold S. Rogers, Ed.
Box 1941
Chicago, Ill. 60690
Bi-monthly; $2 ($10 institutions)
Started: Mar. 1972

Format: 8 pages
Issues examined: Feb. & Apr. 1974
Back issues available from publisher

The purpose of African Agenda is "to propagate the ideas of the African-American Solidarity Committee, and to discuss the social, political, economic, and cultural issues that affect the Afro-American community."

Feedback:
"The African Agenda is a national and international publication that is read by important people in the country and in other countries."

AFRICAN OPINION: Journal of Independent Thought and Expression

African Picture and Information Service
244 Lenox Ave.
N.Y., N.Y. 10027

Bi-monthly; $2
Format: 16 pages (offset)
Issue examined: Oct. 1973

Devoted to expounding the ideas of Marcus Garvey. Illustrated with photographs.

AKWESASNE NOTES

Mohawk Nation via Rooseveltown, N.Y. 13683
7 issues a year; donation

Started: Jan. 1969
Circulation: 71,000
Format: 48-page tabloid (offset)

Issues examined: 22 issues from May 1970 through Winter 1975
Microform version available from Xerox University Microfilms; Microfilm Corp. of America; Bell & Howell; Kraus-Thomson

"Akwesasne," a Mohawk word meaning "place where the partridge drums," is the name for the area where the St. Regis Mohawk Reserve is located. Akwesasne Notes (winner of two journalism awards) is the official newspaper of the Mohawk Nation there, and also contains--from time to time--the Longhouse News (formerly a separate publication), official paper of the Mohawk Nation at Caughnawaga. AN "has few assets" and is put out by a collective of ever-changing membership. There is no paid advertising, so financial support comes from readers. To comply with postal regulations, the paper is said to be published by the Program in American Studies, State University of N.Y. (Buffalo).

Issues of importance to this activist paper are "the institutionalized racism in Western culture, the victimization of native people by powerful companies, governments, and agencies; and the suppression of native thought and religion and freedom." [Feedback: "as well as contemporary thought, religion, and dialogue about the natural way of life of native peoples."]

Using information and articles from other Indian newspapers, from the American Indian Press Association, and from the paper's readers, Akwesasne Notes brings together news of Indians throughout the hemisphere. The articles deal most often with the spoliation and theft of Indian lands, and with struggles to regain them; and they detail the injustices that have been and are being dealt out to Indians. For example, an article entitled "Destroy the Land, You Destroy the Animals; Destroy the Animals, You Destroy the Indians" charges that "Seven thousand Cree Indians might lose their age-old hunting grounds and their entire way of life to a Quebec hydroelectric project. This by definition is genocide." Another article, "Genocide in New Mexico," complains of disrespect for and exploitation of Indian culture and traditions, as well as of job discrimination and political, social, and economic oppression; and it points out that "blatant and total abuse of our civil and human rights" is a way of life for New Mexican Indians.

Some articles tell of Indians' fighting back. For example, in 1974 a group of Mohawks occupied an area in the Adirondacks, in order to establish a beach-head for a "reconstituted Mohawk nation." They wrote a manifesto and AN reprints part of it.

Akwesasne Notes is also interested in the struggles of other native peoples in various parts of the world: Lapps, Puerto Ricans, Micronesians, and Filipino tribesmen. For years the paper has been concerned about the plight of Latin American Indians, and has run articles (in a section, "Genocide in South America") exposing the intentional extermination of these Indians--especially in Brazil and Peru--by starvation, poisoning, contamination with disease germs, firearms, and bombs; and their exploitation through forced labor. Missionaries are blamed for their "pacification programs which preceded the advance of the 'pioneers' and armies."

In sections on "Adoption" and "Social Genocide" the paper protests the placing of Indian children in non-Indian homes. Indians should not allow outside agencies, however well-meaning, to take charge of Indian children and permit them to lose their cultural heritage. An Indian official is quoted as saying that such placements are "psychologically disastrous" and that the children "must overcome a language barrier, adjust to a new religion, learn new food, and are often faced with overt and covert racism."

The Summer 1974 issue carries several articles on an Indian meeting in South Dakota. Its purpose was to decide how to enforce the hundreds of treaties between Indians and the U.S. government, and to form an International Treaty Council that would ask for support from the world's nations and recognition from the U.N. The same issue contains articles on trials of Indians resulting from the occupation of Wounded Knee and the riots in Custer, S.D. (The riots started because a white gas-station attendant who slew an Indian youth was acquitted of manslaughter charges. This event "was one of the things which drew the American Indian Movement to South Dakota, paving the way to Wounded Knee.")

An occasional feature, "The Washington Scene," contains short articles on the federal government's actions. A section on "Racism" contains short items pointing out the ingrained and often unconscious racism and disrespect toward Indians manifested by American culture and institutions. (Example: Indian Trader magazine carried an advertisement offering skulls for sale.)

Other topics covered by the paper are the removal of Indian bones from burial sites by archaeologists; health programs and alcoholism among Indians; and the need for schools in which Indian children would learn of their heritage and not be discriminated against.

The paper also contains historical articles in a section entitled "Indian Affairs: From the Archives"; a calendar of events; a listing ("Tidbits") of grants, programs, scholarships, and jobs; an annotated bibliography ("Resources") of books and audio-visual materials of interest to Indians; several pages of letters to the editor; book reviews; poetry; and photographs and graphics. (JMS)

Reviewer's opinion:
The best Indian paper I've seen, it has a spirit of energy, enthusiasm, and independence.

Feedback:
The editor replied:

> Several features of AN which we feel should be added to the summary are the Poetry section, which consists of prose and poetry contributed by many native people; our pages dealing with the situation of our brothers and sisters in prison, and the many letters they write to us; and the graphics in our paper which reflect the talents of the different native people who support us.

American Jewish Alternatives to Zionism REPORT

133 E. 73rd St. (Suite 404)
N.Y., N.Y. 10021
3 or 4 times a year; free
Started: 1960
Circulation: 600

Format: 70-90 pages (offset)
Issues examined: Feb., June, Oct. 1973
Back issues available from publisher

> American Jewish Alternatives to Zionism is a District of Columbia Non-Profit Organization. Its educational program applies Judaism's values of justice and common humanity to the Arab/Zionist/Israeli conflict in the Middle East. In the United States we advocate a one-to-one human relationship between Jews and all Americans. In both areas of our concern we reject Zionism/Israel's 'Jewish people' nationality attachment of all Jews to the State of Israel. These political-nationality claims distort constructive humanitarian programs. They are inconsistent with American Constitutional concepts of individual citizenship and separation of church and state.

This publication is issued in the form of numbered reports which analyze the Middle East policies of the United

States from the organization's point of view. Each report contains long quotations from relevant books and periodicals.

A large part of Report #17, February 1973, consists of an examination of basic documents relating to Palestine's history during the last quarter century. In this and in other discussions, there is pointed criticism of both the U.S. and Israeli attitude toward the Palestinians. The reporter states that both countries

> refuse to concede that the more the Palestinians are ground to bits the more extreme are the pieces of the 'entity' which fly off the center.... Rejection and defamation of people with a cause admitted--on paper--by almost the entire world to be a just cause, make only for more radical and 'irrational' behavior.
>
> The issue--finally surfacing after decades of deceit and camouflage--was Zionism, a Zionist state and the alleged rights of the whole 'Jewish people' nationality which were to be granted precedence over the established rights of the non-'Jewish people,' legitimate citizens of Palestine.

The American press is also found wanting:

> If, as, and when the Middle East erupts again in violence at a level which may threaten world peace the culpability of the American press will be at least as great as that of the Washington decision-makers who have, for 25 years now, not only not told the truth but have mouthed untruths pre-fabricated for them in the Zionist/Israel propaganda machines.

Harry Truman's attitude toward Israel is discussed in Report #18, June 1973. He was not, according to the author, the pro-Zionist "which Zionist propaganda and ignorant American politicians have portrayed." He was persuaded to recognize Israel reluctantly after "excruciating political pressure--and the most cynical political advice based on domestic politics...." This issue also charges that it is the American Jews who are largely responsible for "the debacle of American interests and prestige in the Middle East." They have been "emotionalized, ignorant of the facts, privileged with tax deductibility for contributions. ... They have not only never met an Arab, but they slander and defame anyone who has."

Oil and energy needs are discussed in Report #19,

October 1973, and the U.S. is enjoined by AJAZ President, Elmer Berger, not to support Israeli aggression:

> If this racist/theocratic state persists in its posture of retaining 'territories acquired by war' it will continue to infect the entire Middle East with instability and growing radicalization.... It is American military, economic, political and moral support which feeds the Israeli Caesars.

Most of the commentary in these reports is by Berger. He reminds readers that Old Testament Prophets were against the establishment, as are dissident Jews today. (EC)

Feedback:

The President of AJAZ, Mr. Elmer Berger, replied: "The summary is excellent. I have only one (I hope) minor suggestion to offer. While it is perfectly true that we hold American Jews must share responsibility for 'the debacle of American interests and prestige in the Middle East,' I think I have never been satisfied that they are 'largely' responsible. The word, of course, is vague. But it would be more consistent with our published record if this particular sentence could be amended to read something like: '... American Jews must share a large part of the responsibility for the debacle,' etc."

ARAB CANADA

170 Laurier W., Suite 709
Ottawa, Ontario K1P 5V5
Canada
Monthly; free
Started: Apr. 1971

Circulation: 3,000
Format: 4 pages (offset)
Issues examined: Aug., Oct., Nov. 1973

Arab Canada is published by the Arab Information Centre in Ottawa, which represents the League of Arab States. Its main purpose is to promote better understanding between Canadian and Arab peoples by providing different political, economic and social topics on the Arab League's member-states (20 countries), and presenting the Arab point of view with regard to the Palestine question and all its related aspects.

One editorial in the issues examined expresses the

belief that the United States "supports the Zionist state, right or wrong, and makes only half-hearted efforts to end the stalemate" in the Middle East. The veto by the U.S. of a Security Council resolution on July 26, 1973, deploring the continued occupation by Israel of Arab land, is cited as an example of this support. Another gives the Arab position on the exporting of oil to the West. There is a reminder that in the past a fair price was not paid by the U.S. and now "any amount of oil produced by the Arab states beyond their needs for regional development will serve no Arab interest ... only the interests of the consumer countries." A third editorial reasserts the position that Israel "can only reach its goal by giving up Arab territories and recognizing the legitimate rights of the Palestinian people."

Among the subjects discussed in articles are the problems faced in Israel by immigrants from the Soviet Union, the completion of the first stage of the Euphrates Dam in Syria, the Israeli responsibility for the Fourth Arab-Israeli War, and the meeting of the Non-aligned Conference in Algiers in September, 1973.

Each issue contains a long book review. One commented on the Palestine Papers 1917-1922: Seeds of Conflict which contains the record of the British Cabinet, the Foreign Office and the Colonial Office during the most critical years of decision for the area. They "tell a story of intrigue and skullduggery which in its consequences makes the American Watergate seem little more than the petty excesses of an ambitious but intemperate adolescent."

Every issue is published separately in both French and English. (EC)

Feedback:

The editor supplied three minor corrections, and all of them have been incorporated into the review.

## ARAB COMMUNITY NEWSLETTER

175 St. Clair Ave. West
Toronto, Ontario, Canada
M4V 1P7
Quarterly; free
Started: Feb. 1973

Format: 8 pages (offset)
Issues examined: Feb., May, Aug. 1973; Jan. 1974
Back issues available from publisher

The Newsletter "is a non-political means of communication between the Arab Community Centre of Toronto (an agency concerned with immigrant aid, social services, and cultural activity) and the Arab community, as well as the interested public. It reports on the activities of the Centre and publishes news articles and literature of specific relevance to the Arab Community. It is bilingual and it is devoted to improving community relations with its surroundings."

ARAB TRIBUNE: Official Voice of the International Arab Federation

Joseph Hayeck, Ed. & Publ.
302 E. Central Ave.
Toledo, Ohio 43608

Bi-monthly; $10
Format: 26 pages (offset)
Issue examined: Jan. 1974

The Tribune is also published in Beirut, Lebanon.

AZTLAN: Chicano Journal of the Social Sciences and the Arts

Chicano Studies Center
University of California
405 Hilgard Ave.
Los Angeles, Calif. 90024
Twice yearly; $6
Started: 1970

Circulation: 1,500
Format: 180 pages (6" x 9")
Issues examined: Fall 1971; 2 issues in 1972
Back issues available from publisher

A scholarly journal which contains long, documented articles on such topics as Chicano art, periodicals, dialects, political parties, and farm workers.

THE BLACK ACTION PARTY

4180 De Courtrai St. (Suite 300)
Montreal, Quebec, Canada
Semi-monthly; $6.50

Format: issue examined was 16 pages; tabloid planned for future
Issue examined: 14 Aug. 1972

A black community-action paper which stresses community development through self-help programs. In the future the newspaper will be printed on a small offset press recently purchased by the B.A.P.

Feedback:
Draft, originally sent to Box 1831, was returned marked "Unknown."

## BLACK COMMUNITY NEWSLETTER

Mitchell Sullen, Ed.
Black Community of Tuscaloosa & The Afro-American Association
Box 996
University, Alabama 35486
Weekly; free
Started: 1969 or 1970

Circulation: 1,000
Format: 7 pages (legal size, mimeo., stapled)
Issues examined: 21 Nov. 1973; 21 Feb., 7 & 21 Mar. 1974
Some back issues available from publisher

## BLACK CREATION

Institute of Afro-American Affairs
New York University
10 Washington Pl. (Rm. 500)
N.Y., N.Y. 10003
Annual (was quarterly); $4
Started: 1970

Circulation: 20,000
Format: quarterly was 50 pages (offset); Annual not out yet
Issue examined: Fall 1973
Back issues available from publisher

The magazine sent this information:

> As you know, Black Creation is the only publication that regularly publishes material on all aspects of black arts, letters, and entertainment. In our four years of publication we have published more new young writers than any other nationally-circulated black magazine in the country. We have been the only black magazine that regularly published ... interviews and articles on both established and upcoming black artists, including such well-known artists as James Baldwin, Nikki Giovanni, Ralph Ellison, Ossie Davis, John O. Killens, Melvin Van Peebles, Ishmael Reed, Ed. Bullins; the list seems endless. Moreover, many of the unknown young artists, first published in the pages of Black Creation, have gone on to publish books, write movies, and record albums. For example, Linda Baron has published a volume of her poetry, Black is Beautiful; Alexis DeVeaux, first-place winner in our Literary Contest, has published a first-rate work, Spirits in the Street.... In short, Black Creation has made a major contribution to black arts and letters in the past four years and we are proud of Black Creation's role. It is not possible, however, to continue Black

> Creation as a quarterly magazine. As of Fall 1974, Black Creation will become an annual review of black arts and letters including a yearly overview covering the past year in film, dance, theater, art, music, and photography. We will continue to publish interviews, essays, and a collection of the best of short stories and poetry selected from several hundred entries received over the past 12 months.

Founded at New York University, the magazine was originally conceived "as a vehicle to provide exposure to student writers and journalists on the NYU campus," but now "the magazine regularly features professional, student, and community contributors."

The issue examined contained a short story; one page of poetry; a book review section; a section ("Film") which discussed black musicians and record companies "invading the movie industry and doing their own thing"; a section ("Theater") which discussed the political and philosophical ideas of Sonia Sanchez, a playwright; a section ("Art") on "Kay Brown: An Artist and Activist"; an article on "Stan Latham: The TV Director as an Artist"; and brief reviews of black films and records. A major part of the magazine was devoted to black music "with features profiling noted blacks as well as articles examining institutions and events related to black music."

(JMS)

BLACK TIMES: Voices of the National Community

Box 10246
Palo Alto, Calif. 94303
Monthly; $10
Started: Jan. 1971
Circulation: 31,000
Format: 24-page tabloid (offset)
Issues examined: Oct. & Nov. 1973
Indexing: Black Information Index, Herndon, Va.
Back issues available from publisher
Microform version available from publisher

"Black Times provides a celebration and news summary (including book reviews, short stories and poetry) of Black America for persons of all colors.... [It] is used variously as an incentive reader, Black Studies reference, and general interest news publication in libraries at all levels." According to a flyer sent by the paper, Black Times is subscribed to by hundreds of libraries.

## THE BLUE CLOUD QUARTERLY

Blue Cloud Abbey
Marvin, S.D. 57251
Quarterly; $1
Started: 1954
Circulation: 2,900

Format: 8-16 pages (6" x 9", offset)
Issues examined: v. 14, no. 3; v. 17, no. 1; v. 18, nos. 1, 3, 4; v. 19, nos. 1-4

This "publication of the Benedictine Missionaries" contains creative writings (stories, essays, poems, and translations of narrations and legends) by American Indians, as well as articles and stories by non-Indians, relating to the social, historical, and cultural aspects of Indian life.

Each issue generally carries one or two stories or articles by a single author. (Issues devoted to poetry contain the works of from one to six poets.) Issues have included a John Updike story ("The Indian"); songs by Buffy Sainte-Marie; and narrations by Wambdi Wicasa ("Two Legends of the Sioux").

Articles and poems are often beautifully illustrated with sketches by Indian artists, or with historical photographs from the National Archives. (KL)

Feedback:
"Very fine."

## THE CANADIAN ARAB WORLD REVIEW

Raymond Kneider, Ed.
Box 237, Youville Station
Montreal, Quebec, Canada
H2P 2V4
Monthly; $10

Started: Dec. 1969
Circulation: 8,500
Format: 16-page tabloid
Issues examined: Nov., Dec. 1973; Feb. 1974

The Canadian Arab World Review, written primarily for the Arabic-speaking community, serves the non-Arabic-speaking population as well. The tabloid is written in English, French, and Arabic, with different articles in each language.

Articles cover a variety of topics, including activities of local Arab organizations and recent events in the Middle East. One apparent objective is to promote cooperation and mutual understanding between the Arab community and their neighbors in Canada and the U.S. A concern expressed in many of the articles is to correct distorted and misinformed views of the situation in the Middle East. Despite the prevailing Arab point of view, however, the tone throughout is moderate, with an emphasis on Arab cultural heritage and achievements.

Representative titles are "Who Are the Palestinians?" giving a sympathetic view of the Palestinian refugees; "Arab American Friends for the Middle East," describing efforts to aid Arab war victims; and "First Multinational Arab Company," honoring the company's founder.

Regular features include "Professionals of the Community," in which local Arab business and professional men and women advertise their services; and "Choice Arabian Tales," which illustrate with gentle humor the widsom of ancient Arab sages. (WP)

Feedback:

"Description O.K."

EL CHICANO COMMUNITY NEWSPAPER

Box 827
Colton, Calif. 92324
Weekly; $10
Started: Apr. 1969
Circulation: 10,000

Format: 8- to 16-page tabloid (offset)
Issues examined: 13 Dec. 1973 & 10 Jan. 1974

Contains some articles in Spanish and serves "Southern California's Bilingual Population," according to the masthead.

CHUTZPAH

Box 60142, 1723 W. Devon
Chicago, Ill. 60660
2-4 issues a year; $1.25 (institutions $3) for 4 issues
Started: Feb. 1972
Circulation: 5,000

Format: 24-page tabloid (offset)
Issues examined: Feb./Mar. & Summer 1973; Winter 1974
Back issues available from publisher

Chutzpah is an independent journal created by nine young Jews who came from the new left, anti-war, woman's and gay liberation movements. The articles are largely subjective, first-person accounts.

> The ideas we talk about come from pain. The pain of oppression we have felt as women, men, workers, and Jews in America.... The articles in this paper come also from the increasing joy we feel in our

> Jewishness. The joy we feel in a culture, a music, a literature which is truly ours.

The editors work toward a radical Jewish movement, free from the established organizations and synagogues. Some of their basic principles are

1. JEWISH PEOPLEHOOD.... We want to know our history and identity ...
2. SECULAR JEWISHNESS.... identity based on music, language, political commitments....
3. RELIGIOUS SEARCH. We encourage exploration of Jewish spiritual expression....
4. LANGUAGE.... we are interested in Yiddish for historical insight, communication with present Yiddish speakers ... entrance into a wealth of literature and music....
5. We believe that there should be several strong centers of Jewish culture, especially in the United States, U.S.S.R., and Israel ...
6. SOVIET JEWRY. Soviet Jews should have full cultural and religious freedom....
7. ISRAEL. Israel has come into being because of Jewish peoplehood and because of vicious repeated anti-semitism. ... But if Israel is to survive it must become a part of the Middle East....
8. We are part of a radical movement in the United States ... opposing capitalism, and working towards a humane socialism....
9. We will work towards ending ... the second class citizenship of women in the United States and Jewish society....
10. We are against all class oppression....

Each issue examined contained articles about what it means to be a Jewish woman. The patriarchy in Jewish society is deplored. "All of us ... have five thousand years of history to overcome before women with the independence and strength of Ruth and Deborah are no longer the exception and become the rule." Similar alienation was expressed by those who are both homosexual and Jewish. The writer of "What's a Nice Jewish Boy ..." found that "an open faggot" has no place in the established Jewish community. Among the other subjects discussed are Judaism in Cuba, immigration to Israel, rape, and the joys of learning Yiddish.

The publication contains numerous poems, cartoons and photographs. There are often book reviews and letters from readers. Since the journal is not funded and carries no advertising, contributions are encouraged. One small item extends this invitation: "To all of you leading lives of quiet desperation: end your silence! Join us in noisy desperation!" (EC)

Feedback:

The editor suggested changing the second sentence of the review to read: "The articles include subjective, first-person accounts, historical and political analyses, and original poetry."

CONTRAST

Box 438, Station E
Toronto, Ont., Canada
M6H 4E3
$11 Canada; $13 outside

Canada
Format: 16-page tabloid
Issue examined: 23 Mar. 1973

"Serving the black community coast to coast" and aimed at the Negro middle class.

DAWN

Ayni Newman &
R. David Brown, Eds.
Long Island University,
Brooklyn Center
Brooklyn, N.Y. 11201

Started: Apr. 1970
Format: 8-page tabloid
Issue examined: Apr. 1970

The first issue of Dawn, a newspaper published by young Jews from New York area universities, contains a variety of articles and stories, all stressing Jewish nationalism. Theodore Bikel, Martin Luther King, Jr., and Lenny Bruce are among those quoted in strong pro-Israel statements. Several articles deal with Soviet Jews; the poem, "Babiy Yar," by Yetvushenko appears on the last page with a brief note commenting "How ironic it is that a gentile is the one to write with such anguish over this injustice done to the Jews while world Jewry itself has remained silent on this very subject." American Jewish philanthropists are castigated editorially for not assessing the real needs of the Jewish community, including the need of Jews to get out of Russia. An open letter to Fatah from the National Union of Israel Students invites the Palestinian group to discuss their goals and strategy in the pages of the newspaper, suggesting that both organizations of young people want peace and harmony and are united against a common enemy, the Arab government.

In a parody of the David and Goliath story, a "political commentator" sympathizes with Goliath for his great height and heavy armor, which made him vulnerable to David's attack; another story is about an Israeli terrorist kidnapping. Throughout the newspaper there are many references to the glories of living in the homeland; several ads for special trips to Israel contrast with a tongue-in-cheek cartoon entitled "Six Very Good Reasons for Not Settling in Israel." The credo of the editors is expressed in a brief article entitled "The Spirit": "Jewish nationalism is an all-encompassing feeling bathing one's entire body and mind in a culture, a heritage, a religion, a land.... We the Jewish students from coast to coast, from nation to nation, have caught this drive. We are Jewish. We are proud." (CP)

## DINÉ BAA-HANÉ

| | |
|---|---|
| Navajo Nation, Box 527 | Format: 16- to 24-page tabloid |
| Fort Defiance, Ariz. 86504 | Issues examined: Aug., Oct.-Dec. 1970; Jan., Feb. 1971; 17 Feb., 4 & 17 Mar., 5 Apr., 11 & 25 May, 3 & 22 June 1971 |
| Bi-weekly (formerly monthly); $4.75 | |
| Started: 1969 | |
| Circulation: 9,000 | |

Diné Baa-Hané sees its role as "A Navaho Newspaper published for the Navaho Nation," providing a community forum for "discussion of vital issues affecting Navaho welfare ... establishing the organizational and economic basis for social, economic and political development of the Navaho Nation; and ... furthering the cause of Navaho self-determination."

Combining a presentation of problems (poverty, dropouts, alcoholism); grievances (racism, police brutality, discrimination at schools, lack of doctors, lack of water, misuse of federal funds, misuse of tribal lands, inter-tribal conflicts); with news of community action (formation of Indian commission, legal action, tribal and school board elections); and community events (art shows, rodeo and sports events, tribal activities). A cartoon character, "Supernavajo," presents Indian values and attitudes toward Indian life and problems.

A community paper fostering Navajo pride and activism. (KL)

Feedback:

"Your review is quite complete.... The newspaper is fostering the development of a Navajo style of journalism which can communicate most effectively with all the Navajo people."

THE DRUM

Box 1069
Inuvik, Northwest Territories, Canada
Weekly; $15
Started: Jan. 1966
Circulation: 1,500

Format: 12-page tabloid (offset)
Issues examined: none sent
Some back issues available from publisher

Eskimo.

ECHO

Zeke Romo, Ed.
Box 6354, 2801 E. 5th
Austin, Tex. 78701
Bi-weekly; $3.50
Started: 3 Mar. 1970
Circulation: 2,000

Format: 12-page tabloid (offset)
Issues examined: none sent
Some back issues available from publisher

"Our sources are Chicano, and we believe Chicano sources before we believe 'official' sources. For example, on cases of police brutality, if upon investigation we find Chicano's facts are straight, we will believe them and publish them without waiting for the 'official' report from the police or city. We advocate the causes of the Chicano; we give the Chicano a voice. Our feeling is that an informed Chicano population is the most powerful and meaningful way to bring about changes. Whereas we have been known to initiate action, we try to first inform the people, and then let other Chicanos in the community pick up the action."

ELBOW DRUMS

M. Price, Ed. & Program Director
Calgary Indian Friendship Society

140 Second Ave. S.W.
Calgary, Alberta, Canada
Monthly; $3.50
Started: 1967

Circulation: 400
Format: 10 pages (offset)
Issues examined: none sent
Back issues available from publisher

The publication sent this information: "Non-political, non-denominational. Information on: activities, news stories of Calgary Indian Friendship Centre and other native organizations in Calgary."

EUROPA ETHNICA: A Quarterly Review for Problems of Nationality

Wilhelm Braumüller, Publ.
Universitäts-Verlagsbuchhandlung
Servitengasse 5
A-1092 Vienna, Austria
Quarterly; $9
Started: 1958
Circulation: 1,000
Format: 192 pages (6 3/4" x 9 1/2", offset)
Issues examined: No. 2 (1972); No. 2 (1973)

Brief articles on the problems of European linguistic or ethnic minorities. (The articles are often based on clippings from other periodicals.) Examples of the many problems adverted to in the sample issues: Spain.--Increased freedom, since 1967, for the nation's Protestants (1/10 of 1% of the population). Repression of a Catalan nationalist movement. Switzerland.--Problems faced by speakers of the nation's fourth language, Romansch. France.--Bi-lingualism in Alsace. Poland.--Ethnic Germans in the Oder-Neisse area annexed after World War II. USSR.--Jews wishing to emigrate to Israel. Ethnic Germans wishing to move to West Germany.

Articles in one language (e.g., English) are often followed by a summary in another (e.g., German).

Other features: obituaries; signed reviews of books; commemoration of scholars' birthdays (Jubiläen).

Former title: Nation und Staat. (TJS)

EL GALLO: La Voz de la Justicia

1564 Downing St.
Denver, Colo. 80218
Irregular; $2.50 for 12 issues
Started: 1967
Circulation: 2,000
Format: 12-page tabloid (offset)
Issue examined: May 1974
Back issues available from publisher

An editorial in El Gallo explains the purpose of the

newspaper: It was started by Rodolfo "Corky" Gonzales, who founded the Crusade for Justice, and is produced by "students from the high school and undergraduate program at Escuela Tlatelolco." Member, Chicano Press Association.

GENESIS 2

298 Harvard St.
Cambridge, Mass. 02138
Monthly; $3.50 ($3 to students)
Started: 1969

Circulation: 16,000
Format: 12- to 16-page tabloid
Issues examined: Mar.-May, Nov. 1972

Genesis 2, "an independent voice for Jewish renewal," is apparently read mostly by students. For an indication of what is meant by Jewish "renewal," an article on the Jewish student movement mentions a few areas of progress:

> the continuing evolution of new communal forms ... the partially successful efforts to reform and influence the philanthropies; the struggle to discover and assert authentic Jewish culture and art forms in America, while beginning to develop new ones; the redefinition of attitudes toward Israel and the Diaspora; the growing awareness of Jews in persecution situations, notably the Soviet Union; as well as certain overtures within Jewish education.

All of these interests and many others are represented in the paper's articles, which are generally well written and reflect thought and research on the part of the writers, many of whom are students of Judaic studies. The articles are, for the most part, written for an educated Jewish audience; many expressions and references would be lost on a reader without this background. (For example, several writers have discussed the controversial role of the North American Jew and his relationship to Israel in terms of "alijah" and "galut.") Israeli-Arab (and Israeli-American) relations and the plight of Soviet Jews figure prominently in many of the articles. Generally, "news" is not given; rather, interpretations of (and reactions to) news are voiced. During the Democratic primary campaigns for the 1972 presidential election, an analysis was made of the distribution of Jewish money and votes among various candidates. The paper often publishes interviews with well-known figures, focusing on Jewish issues; Sen. George McGovern was questioned, before the election, on his Middle East stance. An interview with a student activist brought to light some of the problems facing leftist groups in Israel. Other subjects treated in the paper have included tuition vouchers for Jewish education; interfaith marriages; and Jewish women and the liberation movement here and in Israel.

Every issue contains news of Jewish activities and conferences, usually local, either in the form of reports (often quite critical) or in a section called "Guide for the Perplexed." Usually there are a few long reviews of books or plays. A particularly interesting feature appeared in one issue: several old Yiddish songs (with translations) on work and struggle; they had been very popular around the turn of the century.

(SA)

Feedback:

"In general, we found your description and comments about our publication to be accurate and fair. There are a couple of things I did want to mention, however. The write-up states that we are 'mostly read by students.' More accurately, we are a publication by and for the academic community of Greater Boston. Most of our writers are graduate students and young professors. We also have a limited national circulation and seem to have particular appeal to rabbis and the lay leadership and professional workers within the Jewish community. In other words, the intellectual level of our publication has earned genesis 2 [the periodical's editors spell 'genesis' with a lower-case 'g'] a reputation that goes beyond the Boston student community only."

## GRASP

| | |
|---|---|
| Wayne Talbut, Ed. | Circulation: 1,200 |
| Black United Front of Nova Scotia | Format: 4- to 8-page tabloid (offset) |
| Trade Mart Bldg. (Suite 430) | Issues examined: May 1972; Jan., Aug., Nov. 1973 |
| Halifax, Nova Scotia, Canada | Back issues available from publisher |
| Monthly; $1 | |
| Started: Aug. 1970 | |

"This paper is primarily concerned with informing blacks in Nova Scotia of what we are all up to--a communication link. The content of the paper is exclusively black material and articles are sent in from various parts of the province. This is not meant to be a controversial paper, nor a militant printing, but rather its main aim is to break down the communication gap which exists between the blacks due to scattered geographical locations."

GRASS ROOTS NEWS: The Opportunity Paper

Jackson R. Champion, Ed. & Publ.
Box 24027
Washington, D. C. 20024
Monthly; $10

Started: Jan. 1970
Circulation: 50,000
Format: 24-page tabloid
Issues examined: Mar. & Apr. 1974

This paper covers Negro business, education, and community development. The publisher describes one issue:

> The first part of the paper offers the small businessman news and leads about buying and selling. Shorts on corporate activities in the community come before a new pictorial center page section on people and places in the news.
>
> The educational section gives lots of information on grants and scholarships for students, faculty, colleges, and universities. In future issues we plan to expand the personnel section featuring job openings and highly qualified candidates. The aids on page 22 will help today's consumer in the marketplace. All small businesses who subscribe to Grass Roots News will appear in our Small Business Directory each month.

HAYOM

Ilene Schneider, Ed.
Philadelphia Union of Jewish Students
401 S. Broad St.
Philadelphia, Pa. 19147
Monthly; $4 for 10 issues (distributed free on campus)
Started: Spring 1971

Format: 12-page tabloid (offset)
Issues examined: Sept.-Dec. 1973
Indexing: Jewish Student Press Service
Limited number of back issues available from publisher

Hayom deals with topics of interest to the Jewish student groups represented by the Philadelphia Union of Jewish Students. Though each issue of the paper usually covers a variety of subjects, often including news and events of the current month, a single topic is regularly selected for more extensive treatment. Often the topic to be featured is announced in the preceding issue, and readers are encouraged to contribute articles expressing their views on the subject. One issue, for example, was chiefly devoted to Jewish education. Another featured articles concerning Christian missionaries and their proselytizing activities among Jewish students, particularly in Philadelphia. A special Yom Kippur War Supplement was published in December 1973, upon the renewal of Arab-Israeli hostilities in the Middle East.

In addition to readers' contributions on selected topics, "The Open Shouk," a regular feature of Hayom, serves as an open forum for letters to the editor on any subject of the reader's choice. Thus the newspaper strives to fulfill one of its major goals as defined by the editor: "We try to give a balanced view on issues with articles by persons holding divergent opinions." (SMA)

Feedback:
"Approved."

EL HISPANO: Al Servicio de la Comunidad

| | |
|---|---|
| Box 2856 | (offset) |
| Sacramento, Calif. 95812 | Issues examined: 3 Sept., 22 & 29 Oct. 1974 |
| Weekly; $5 (out-of-state $7) | Back issues available from publisher |
| Started: 1966 | |
| Circulation: 6,076 | |
| Format: 8-page newspaper | |

This bi-lingual periodical carries news of community meetings, accomplishments of local citizens, marriages, and sports. There are advertisements for Latino businesses and political candidates.

The sample issues contained news of Puerto Rican nationalist bombings in New York City; of the conviction of a Latino woman who had (in California) killed the man who had (she said) raped her; of Bay Area organizers of the United Farm Workers arrested in an Oakland store as they tried to prevent shoppers from buying grapes (photographs show that the demonstrators included two clergymen and a nun); of César Chávez (head of the UFW); of illegal aliens from Mexico "working long hours for low wages throughout the United States despite increased federal efforts to ferret them out"; and of Border Patrol efforts to arrest these aliens. (TJS)

HOLY BEGGARS' GAZETTE: A Journal of Hasidic Judaism

House of Love and Prayer Publications
1456 Ninth Ave.
San Francisco, Calif. 94122

Quarterly; $5
Started: 1972
Circulation: 1,200
Format: 24 pages (5 1/2" x 8 1/2", offset)
Issues examined: Apr. & Aug. 1973; Jan. 1974
Back issues available from publisher

The Gazette began as "a publication containing transcriptions of the teachings of our rabbi, Shlomo Carlebach. Now we are a more extensive magazine of Hasidic teachings." One of the sample issues was a "wedding issue" with "Hasidic stories and teachings from weddings performed by Shlomo." Another contained Reb Nachman's (one of the greatest Hasidic Rebbes) teachings on joy, Hasidic teachings on anger, and "Shlomo's teachings on our father Abraham."

> We would like contributions for publication to include good things that people have found within Torah, original stories with words of Torah, original drawings of a Jewish nature. Women are especially requested to contribute as we are planning a special issue about women soon.

The publication includes original poetry and graphics. (JMS)

IDEAL

Ray Rodriguez
Box 21
Coachella, Calif. 92236
Monthly; $5
Started: Nov. 1969
Circulation: 7,000
Format: 8-page tabloid (offset)
Issues examined: 20 July, 5 Oct., 5 Nov., 5 & 20 Dec. 1973
Microform version available from Xerox University Microfilms

This informative bi-lingual newspaper reports national and local (Coachella Valley) concerns of the Chicano people. There are two lead stories on the front page with photos. Some topics covered in the issues examined were: report on recall elections in the city of Coachella, illegal hysterectomies performed on welfare recipients in Los Angeles county, activities of the Cabinet Committee on Opportunities for the Spanish Speaking in Washington, and reports on United Farm Workers actions. The 20 December 1973 issue headlined an interesting article concerning the 8% to 10% undercounting of Spanish surnamed Americans by the U.S. Census Bureau. Henry Ramirez, Chairman of the Cabinet Committee, feels a correct count is crucial because "public monies--such as revenue sharing funds--are allocated to communities on the basis of their minority population." The last census reported 10 million Spanish-speaking but Spanish-speaking groups estimate 16 million is a more accurate figure.

The remainder of the newspaper is filled with shorter articles dealing with events of interest taking place around the United States. These range from the establishment of a Mexican-American Curriculum Office in Toledo to the conviction of a police officer for the slaying of a Chicano youth in Dallas.

Regular features include letters, an editorial column entitled, "The Spectator: an objective point of view," local commercial advertisements, legends and stories of the Chicano heritage. The back page generally carries a political cartoon or announcement. Beginning with the 5 October 1973 issue, Ideal printed a series of articles of human interest covering successful business and professional people, students, and politicians from the Coachella Valley. These articles occupy about a page and are accompanied by photos.

The overall tone of the newspaper is reflected in these words of the editor concerning editorial policies. "Our policy regarding editorials is directly related to the Chicano people in regards to the various areas of concern. Most editorials deal in areas of politics; job-housing-educational prejudices. When an agency, organization or institution does something commendable, we praise it; racist actions, insensitive directives, etc., are criticized." (JA)

Feedback:

"We find the ... information very accurate."

IMPACT

1701 Martindale
Indianapolis, Ind. 46202
Bi-weekly; $5

Format: 8-page tabloid (offset)
Issue examined: 1 June 1974

Black activist Impact's Platform appears on the second page of the sample issue: liberation from racism and economic exploitation through "development of community control of economic, political, and governmental operations affecting black people"; an "end to monopoly capitalism in America" and a "redistribution of wealth, power, and privilege"; an adequate guaranteed income for everyone; health care for all, regardless of ability to pay; a massive effort to build adequate housing; a government program to eliminate addiction to hard drugs (amnesty and free treatment for addicts, with a job or income guaranteed during and after rehabilitation; life sentences for dealers); equal rights for women; and a realignment of U.S. foreign policy "with the liberation movements in South Africa, Rhodesia (Zimbabwe), Angola, Mozambique, Guinea-Bissau, and other Third World nations suffering colonial or neo-colonial oppression."

Articles covered police brutality; summer jobs for black teenagers; a new city-wide coalition to end neighborhood deterioration; the independence of Guinea-Bissau (formerly a Portuguese colony); formation of a united black political front; the rights of public-housing tenants; racism and discrimination in labor unions and jobs; and Malcolm X. (JMS)

## INDIAN AND METIS BROTHERHOOD ORGANIZATION NEWSLETTER

George A. Quantrill, Ed.
Box 101
Stony Mountain, Manitoba, Canada ROC 3AO
3-4 issues a year; free

Started: 1964
Circulation: 200
Format: 15 pages (mimeo.)
Issue examined: Dec. 1973

This free newsletter is published in limited quantity by members of the Indian and Metis Brotherhood Organization of the Stony Mountain Institute. The editor urges the recipients to pass it on to others.

The issue examined opens with a two-page report by one of the Institute members, Arthur E. Arnott, concerning a visit to OO-ZA-WE-KWUN Center in Rivers, Manitoba. This is a training center for Manitoba Indians to help them develop "life skills" for coping with a changing society.

The remainder of the newsletter is filled with signed informal essays, poetry, and brief thoughts by members of the Institute and others. Most contributions express personal reminiscence or introspective feelings on Indian life, freedom, and love. There is an Indian Version of the Twenty-Third Psalm from Navajo Missions, Farmington, New Mexico.

In an essay entitled My Treasures, Alfred Beauchamp, guidance counsellor of the Institute, expresses his appreciation of nature and asks readers to understand that "the Greatest Talent and Show is on our Mother, the Earth, which the Great Spirit has given to us." The piece closes with this thought: "If only we can learn and teach through Nature, We, the so-called human race, will be able to learn to stand side by side like the Black and the White Poplar Trees; even the small Red Willow was standing proud as his Big Brothers in Nature's own way."

In another essay Garvin Larocque destroys the myth that Indians introduced scalping to history. He protests the role of motion pictures in perpetuating this belief.

Several of the contributions from residents of the Institute express thanks for the understanding and guidance they have received. This theme is carried on by the editor who asks for community support in welcoming Institute members back to society. (JA)

Feedback:

Editor supplied a minor correction, which has been incorporated into the review.

THE INDIAN HISTORIAN

American Indian Historical Society
1451 Masonic Ave.
San Francisco, Calif. 94117
Quarterly; $5

Started: Aug. 1974
Circulation: 7,000
Format: 64 pages (linotype)
Issues examined: Fall 1969 & Winter 1970

The Indian Historian, official publication of the AIHS, is edited and published by Indian scholars, although it hopes to reach all Indians, laborers and farmers as well as scholars. Articles relevant to Indian history and contemporary society have included--to mention only a few--a feature on Alcatraz, from its discovery by native Americans to their seizure of it in 1969; a study of the Indian reservation system; archaeological investigations in the Monterey, California, area; and an ethnographic study of the Iroquois. Most of the articles include extensive bibliographies. In addition to these regular lengthy feature articles, there are reviews of books relevant to Indian culture, and letters, poems, and works of art (such as wood cuts, photographs, and paintings), all by Indians. An Indian artist's work illustrates the cover of each issue. The illustrations, the paper, and the printing in The Indian Historian are of excellent quality.

The emphasis of the writing and of the journal as a whole is to stimulate a deep awareness and appreciation for Indian history and culture and for the present situation of the Indian in society, rather than to expound revolutionary doctrines. From an editorial written in 1964 and reproduced in the Winter 1970 issue:

> This journal is for the Indians in tribe, community, and Indian organization. Their activities, problems, history and languages will be reported here. To answer their questions, to probe their past and report it honestly, to serve them intellectually in any way needed.... For the true Indian bears within him the pride of the race, the love for his people, the desire to serve them, the longing for truth and justice.... There is a great and rich store of information still locked in the hearts and minds of Indians all over the nation. Only The Indian Historian is so placed at the present time as to uncover this treasure. Friends of the Indian may join in our great work, helping but not leading, aiding but not pushing, taking part but not taking over.

(SA)

Feedback:
"Approved."

INDIAN RECORD

1951 Constitution Ave. N.W.
Washington, D.C. 20245
Irregular; free
Started: Oct. 1966

Circulation: 1,000
Format: 4 pages (multilith)
Issue examined: Apr. 1974

The publication sent the following information:

> We would prefer that this publication not be listed in your directory because it is now coming out very infrequently (when there is a special incentive) and because it is aimed toward an all-Indian audience. We fear that listing it in a general directory will engender requests from non-Indians and that whether Indian or non-Indian they would be disappointed at the present time in the infrequency of the publication.

The issue examined was a special one devoted to reproducing the words of the new Commissioner of Indian Affairs, Morris Thompson. The publication was evidently printed by the U.S. Government Printing Office, for it bears the inscription, "GPO 875-256." It was mailed to us in an envelope bearing the return address, "Department of the Interior, Bureau of Indian Affairs." Indian Record is not listed in the May 1974 edition of Superintendent of Documents Price List 36 ("Government Periodicals and Subscription Services"). (JMS)

## ISRAEL & PALESTINE

Box 130-10
75463 Paris Cedex 10, France
Monthly; $12 (airmail)
Started: May 1971
Circulation: 6,500

Format: 10 pages (9 3/4" x 12 1/2", letterpress)
Issues examined: Aug. & Sept. 1972; Oct. & Dec. 1973
Back issues available from publisher

This is a "free forum" for Jews and Arabs, Israelis and Palestinians--anyone who wants peace [Feedback: "and justice"] in the Middle East. It therefore prints contributions by persons whose beliefs differ (within limits) from those of the publisher (Louis Marton) and editor (Maxim Ghilan). An interesting feature ("Letters to Other Newspapers") contains letters that readers sent (vainly) to newspapers in various countries.

Editorial policy reprobates atrocities, whether carried out by Arabs or by Jews. It condemns Zionism, and what it sees as the expansionism of recent Israeli governments, and asks that Israel withdraw from occupied territories. (Israel has "expansionist dreams." A contributor refers to "the Israeli Zionist leadership" and says that "Zionism equals expropriation.") The editor looks upon Moshe Dayan and Golda Meir as hawks, and makes reference to "the relentless and gifted machine of Zionist propaganda" and "the smoothly-working American-Zionist propagandists." Arab members of the Black September organization who murdered Israeli athletes at the 1972 Munich Olympics were "embittered madmen" whose action obscured the "rightness" of the Palestinians' cause, but Israeli reprisals are condemned. An Arab terrorist hijacking at Lod (Israel) airport is called "a war crime against civilians," and Japanese leftists who murdered a number of foreign (Christian) civilians at the same airport are described as "frustrated sadists." In other instances the reader is told that Israel has also committed war crimes and massacres, and that the Israel Defense Force has committed atrocities against Arab soldiers.

Other articles by contributors have put forward these ideas: Israelis torture Arabs, and use terrorism more often than Arabs do (author has a Jewish surname); Israelis committed massacres in the Gaza Strip (author has a Jewish surname); and Israel is moving toward dictatorship (pseudonymous article by an Israeli journalist). In an interview, Dr. Nahum Goldman (president of the World Jewish Congress) complains of corruption, scandals, and intolerance as features of life in Israel.

A two-page feature ("Contacts") contains brief news reports on such topics as: Israeli war resisters; "discussion groups" in the Israeli armed forces; Black Panthers in Israel, fighting against the Jewish Defense League (a "neo-Fascist body"); and "organized repression" by Israel in the Gaza Strip.

As for oil, a pseudonymous article by an American-Jewish scientist puts forward the theory that the Organization of Petroleum-Exporting Countries undertook its oil boycott with the tacit approval of the U. S. and the oil companies--if not with their direct management. "This boycott accomplishes their mutual aims of maintaining profits while decreasing oil flow. The boycott is far more serious against our principal commercial rivals--Europe and Japan--and is primarily directed against weakening their economies rather than destroying or damaging Israel." (TJS; JMS)

Feedback:

"We do not get the impression that your choice of extracts is without biais [sic]. However, that is your privilege." Mr. Ghilan described I&P as "a free tribune of all views on the Middle East, between the pan-Arab and extremist Zionist camps." He said that it has

> published articles and features by Rabbis, Bishops, Trotskyites, Maoists, Communists, US scientists, liberals, Israelis, Palestinians, Arabs and Jews. I&P's editors believe in the need for two independent states on the territory of historical Palestine--a Jewish-Israeli one and an Arab-Palestinian one. They also believe in the right of Palestinian refugees to return to their homes and in the need for an Israeli withdrawal to the 1967 borders. However, many of the monthly's contributors' views differ from this position. Excluded from the paper are opinions which maintain the need for eliminating the existence of the State of Israel--and those which do not accept the Palestinians' right to an independent state of their own and to justice and compensation. The paper tries to give continuous and analytic information on repression in the Middle East, and particularly in the territories occupied by Israel.

THE ISRAEL DIGEST

Zvi Soifer, Ed.
World Zionist Organization, American Section
515 Park Ave.

N.Y., N.Y. 10022
Bi-weekly; $5
Started: 1948
Circulation: 8,000
Format: 16-page tabloid (offset)
Issues examined: 14 & 26 Sept. 1973

Established in 1948 as the Jewish Agency Digest, this publication offers "News of Israel--Direct From Israel," according to its masthead. It presents a polished, professional appearance. Most of the articles contain a byline. "Books from Israel" and "The Editor's Corner" appear to be regular features. The Digest also devotes some of its space to a review of the arts and music. Articles run from one or two paragraphs to a page in length, and are often accompanied by black-and-white photographs.

One front-page article, contributed by the treasurer and acting chairman of the World Zionist Organization, assesses the state of Jewry throughout the world and examines its ties with Israel. The article restates goals for the "absorption of immigrants" and stresses the "intensification of Jewish education." Another lengthy article examined Israel's interception of a Lebanese aircraft and chastises "one-sided condemnations" of Israel's actions by the U.N. Security Council. The comment is made: "Israel was asked to keep the law. But they did not tell her how to observe the letter of the law and stay alive." Reference is also made to Arab terrorist attacks. Many articles are devoted to a description of life in Israel or to commentary on the activities of the Israeli government. Some stories concern restrictions on, or the oppression of, Jews in other countries.

One unusual feature is a calendar of events. Contained within the last pages of the newspaper, it is a detailed, daily coverage of events which had occurred since the last publication of the paper. Its titles were "Israel's Month," or "Israel's Fortnight." (MN)

Feedback:
"O.K."

## JOURNAL OF AMERICAN INDIAN EDUCATION

Center for Indian Education
Farmer College of Education (Rm. 417)
Arizona State University
Tempe, Ariz. 85281
3 times a year; $3.50
Started: 1961
Circulation: 1,000
Format: 32 pages (6" x 9")
Issue examined: May 1967 (this old issue was received Aug. 1974)
Back issues available from publisher

Microform version available
from Xerox University Microfilms

"Articles must be relevant to the North American Indian and Indian affairs, in general. Views expressed ... are those of the authors and not necessarily those of ASU, the Center for Indian Education, or the Editorial Board."

JOURNAL OF PALESTINE STUDIES: A Quarterly on Palestinian Affairs and the Arab-Israeli Conflict

Hisham Sharabi, Ed.
Box 7164
Beirut, Lebanon
Distributed by I. P. S., Box 329, R. D. 1, Oxford, Pa. 19363; and by A. S. P. Distributors, 7 Bishopsthorpe Rd., London SE26 4NZ, U. K.
Quarterly; $12
Started: 1972

Format: around 150 pages (6 1/2" x 9 1/2", offset)
Issue examined: Summer 1974
Indexing: Historical Abstracts; Documentation Politique Internationale; Sociological Abstracts; Current Contents/Social and Behavioral Sciences; Social Sciences Citation Index
Back issues available from publisher

"The only English-language quarterly devoted exclusively to the Arab-Israeli conflict and to the Palestine problem" contains essays, book reviews, an index to periodical literature, and documents. Examples of the last are excerpts from the Report of the Israeli Commission of Inquiry into the October War and the Political Resolutions Adopted by the Central Committee of the Lebanese Communist Party (Beirut, 3 May 1974).

There is no editorial comment. The tone of the essays is restrained, expressing a steady current of anti-Zionism but no anti-Semitism. Typical of the opinions expressed are these: "There can be no real solution but a revolutionary one, which will enable the Arabs of Palestine to overcome imperialism and to reverse the effects of their expulsion and dispersion, and which will allow the Israelis to shed the oppressive and self-destructive mantle of Zionism, colonialism, and militarist expansion." "The most desirable option is ... the de-Zionization of Israel in favour of a state where there will be no discrimination and Jews, Christians, and Muslims will enjoy equal democratic rights." Many of the contributors live outside Arab countries; they have included Malcolm Kerr, Jean Genêt, and Joseph Ryan, S. J.

Some titles: "The Jewish National Fund" (analyzing

JNF land acquisitions, 1909-50); "The Biblical Bases of Zionist Colonialism"; and "Palestine's Arab Population: The Demography of the Palestinians," which compares population, education, and distribution statistics for the Christian, Muslim, and Jewish populations and concludes that the Palestine resistance movement should conceive of the Palestine population as a "major resource which requires considerable management and planning."

Three sections of the journal are devoted to excerpts from the press--Hebrew, Arab, and foreign--which tend to present the Palestine Liberation Front sympathetically and to highlight indications of Israelis' disenchantment with their government. The Journal is published jointly by Kuwait University and the Institute for Palestine Studies. (SN)

MANY SMOKES: Native American Magazine

Box 1961
Klamath Falls, Ore. 97601
Quarterly; $2
Started: 1961
Circulation: 6,000
Format: 22 pages (offset, stapled)

Issues examined: Spring, Summer, Winter 1974
Back issues available from publisher
Microform version available from Microfilming Corp. of America

"We are traditional in view," states Wabun of the Editorial Board. Each issue contains an editorial that is usually an expression of anger or bitterness at government policies. The Winter 1974 editorial ("For Lack of Love") condemns the U.S. role in Vietnam:

> In Asia this nation [the U.S.] recently murdered many of the inhabitants, destroyed their rice fields and rice supplies, and sprayed their lands with chemicals so no food can grow. America[ns] grew fat from their exploitation of people all over the world, just as, in their earlier days, they stole from the Indians and ignored and mocked their hunger. When they bombed hospitals and murdered people with contract killers, they said, 'God is dead, no one will see.' But the great Spirit saw all that happened both in this country and abroad.

An editorial in the Summer 1974 issue is especially bitter in its comments on an aspect of the Patricia Hearst kidnapping:

> I used to go to motion picture shows where they would show the bad guys setting fire to the house to force the good guys out. That way they could murder them and there would be no one to testify against them.... the Los Angeles police and FBI used these tactics to murder six Symbionese Liberation Army members.

The editorial goes on to describe the case of a black man killed by police when he emerged from a house to which they had set fire.

> Watching this I wonder if the Los Angeles and Albuquerque police still carry guns to plant on the people that they kill by mistake.... I wonder if the border patrolmen still procure women in Mexico for the 'entertainment' of their superiors? I wonder if they still give marijuana back to the informers who fink on the people that they've sold it to? I wonder if the Gallup, New Mexico, police still rape the passed-out Indian girls before they take them to the drunk tank? I wonder if the New York Police Department ever found the 90 million dollars' worth of heroin they lost?

The rest of the editorial describes the sins of Richard Nixon and Spiro Agnew and contrasts their non-punishments with the refusal of amnesty for the "50,000 young men who left their country rather than participate in the crimes of murdering innocent people trying to defend their country against foreign aggression and corrupt government."

This activist publication also reflects grave concern over the ecology and environment (stressing organic gardening) and encourages Indian culture and heritage. (A long article traces the origin and training of the Native American Theater Ensemble; Indian legends are retold; a special section of Indian poetry appears in each issue; and "Take It out in Trade" encourages Indians to go back to the old ways of barter.) A section called "Drumbeats," usually several pages long, reports on Indian affairs around the country: legal disputes and land claims; bills, laws and federal services and programs; Indian organizations, meetings, and leaders; education; adoption of Indian children by whites (opposed by most Indians); and health services (most "Indian Health Service hospitals are obsolete, and 22 need to be replaced completely.... There is little possibility of attracting more doctors through higher salaries since Nixon has impounded Indian Health

Service money for four of the last five years"). Much of the section's recent news has been devoted to coverage of the Wounded Knee trials in South Dakota. (The paper views the trials as biased.)

Other regular features are "Pow Wows" (a calendar of Indian activities and ceremonial events around the country) and a book review section. The Winter 1974 issue carried a long "News in Review" section, reviewing all notable activity affecting Indians in 1973. The publication carries ads for Indian businesses. (JMS)

Feedback:

"While we feel that the review is basically fair, we do feel that you spend an undue amount of space on the 'bitter' aspects of the editorials. While we do feel bitterness toward a system that seems so inhumane, we don't just complain. Most of Many Smokes is devoted to presenting positive alternatives. Being traditional in view we devote a lot of the publication to presenting the idea of retribalizing, and to publishing ideas that would make such retribalization practical. In almost every issue we have a 'doing it' article that explores the how-tos of such diverse things as gardening and bartering. We also have a germinator column in each issue that covers such things as 'Fire Safety,' 'Starting (your garden) Early,' 'Drying and Canning,' 'Food Storage.'"

MAZUNGUMZO: Journal of African Studies

Quarterly; $4 donation (institutions, $6 for 3 issues)
Format: 69-139 pages

Issues examined: v. 3, no. 1 (Fall 1972) & no. 2 (1972)

Mazungumzo is published "by the Afrikan Information Bureau, a non-profit educational organization. Members and associates of the Marcus Garvey Institute for the studies of African people assemble Mazungumzo and the journal is printed by the Garvey Institute press."

Each issue carries this information about the philosophical or heraldic implications of the design on the publication's cover (designed by a Nigerian):

> Africa, in the focal point of world attention today, is in the center of the circles. The circles, too, represent information and better knowledge of the continent to be radiated to the ignorant world through Mazungumzo.

> Just as the ceremonial sword is a symbol of authority in Benin Kinship tradition, Mazungumzo is a symbol of academic authority in all spheres of African study.
>
> Of the colors used, black stands for the people, red for their struggle for emancipation, and green for the people's main occupation--agriculture.

Individual subscribers are asked to send a donation because "The publishers of Mazungumzo are not profit-makers, neither are they rich." The organization cannot afford to distribute its periodical free of charge.

Mazungumzo's aims are: to expose myths about Africa; and to teach the world about the traditional greatness of Africa and her people, about their present position, and about their struggle and future. The same organization publishes a monthly, World Journal and Review.

Mail addressed to Mazungumzo was returned marked "Address unknown." The address had been: Chui Karega, Box 1554, East Lansing, Mich. 48823.

MICMAC NEWS

Roy Gould, Ed.
Union of Nova Scotia Indians
Box 961
Sydney, Nova Scotia, Canada
Monthly; $3
Started: Dec. 1969
Circulation: 5,000

Format: 16- to 24-page tabloid (offset)
Issues examined: Dec. 1972; Sept. & Oct. 1973
Back issues available from publisher

The MicMac News is the organ of the Union of Nova Scotia Indians. It carries Indian news of the Maritime Indians, its only restriction being to carry no articles on religion. Leading news articles appear on its front page; the issues of Sept. and Oct. 1973 have stories of actions of the Canadian Government in affairs affecting the Nova Scotia Indians and other groups of native people of Canada. Elsewhere, it has articles on Indian history and cultural events; the Dec. 1972 issue has a carefully researched article on the Gold River Reserve in Nova Scotia from the 1700s to the present, and a set of reports on a lecture series on the native people, held at the Nova Scotia Museum, Halifax. In the Sept. 1973 issue is an account of the Wounded Knee (S.D.) affair, an article on the Nova Scotia Native Women's Association, and a story on Chief Dan George, and, in the Oct. 1973 issue, an article on the Iroquois Confederacy of the Six Nations Reserve in Ontario and in Quebec and New York State, "the oldest government in North America," and a summary of Indians' rights ("Know Your Rights"). The pride of race and the concern for their people is evident throughout this paper.

Picture stories and photographic material are included in all issues, and a poetry section is a regular feature. Letters to the editor carry the ideas and opinions of readers, and a sports section tells of athletic exploits. (MEH)

Feedback:

"Your review is well prepared and concise. You may be interested to note that we carry religious articles as long as ... they don't tend to convert readers.... Our priority for news starts with ... Nova Scotia Indians, then to the remainder of the Maritime Provinces. Our national news coverage is limited and [we carry such news] only when it pertains to the Maritime Indians."

MIDDLE EAST INTERNATIONAL

Michael Adams, Ed.
105 Grand Buildings,
Trafalgar Square
London WC2N 5EP, U.K.
Monthly; $12 airmail
Started: Mar. 1971

Circulation: 6,500
Format: 32 pages (offset)
Issues examined: Nov. 1973-Jan. 1974
Some back issues available from publisher

"Middle East International is the only magazine exclusively devoted to the affairs of the Middle East. It aims to promote the objective discussion of issues of current political and economic interest, especially those issues generally neglected by the world's press, for example, the internal conflicts of Israel and the necessity for any settlement in the Middle East to take account of the rights of the Palestinian people."

In addition to its coverage of current affairs and articles on the international oil industry, the magazine devotes attention to the history and culture of the peoples of the Middle East. It condemns Israel's actions in Palestine and its treatment of the Palestinian Arabs, and articles frequently refer to the Arab-Israeli conflict. One lengthy feature suggested the Arabs should decide their future in a referendum under international control. Some stories referred to recent Arab unity in the oil embargo. One featured a discussion of the legal aspects of the Arab-Israeli conflict.

Contributors to the magazine are frequently prominent scholars, newsmen, and diplomats who are "specialists in the history and contemporary politics of the Middle East."

Regular features include an editorial; "News out of Israel" (translations from the Hebrew press); "For the Record" (reprints from other sources, texts of speeches, official letters and other documents); book reviews; and letters to the editor. (MN)

Feedback:

"The editorial attitude is internationalist" and "The magazine gives stray backing to the United Nations." The editor rewrote part of the review and most of his additions have been incorporated into our review.

MIDDLE EAST NEWSLETTER

Americans for Justice in the Middle East
Bi-monthly; $10 (students $5)
Dates: Sept. 1967 - Summer 1974
Circulation: 6,000
Format: 16 pages (8" x 11", offset)
Issues examined: Sept. & Nov. 1972; Jan., Mar., Spring (Special Issue), Summer/Fall 1973
Back issues available from publisher

The Newsletter, which concentrates on Lebanon and Palestine,

> was founded after the June War of 1967 by Americans living in Lebanon who were and continue to be concerned about the tragedy of the Middle East situation. AJME hopes to bring about a situation, particularly in the United States, which will allow the Arab case a fair hearing and Arab rights and aspirations the possibility of recognition.

The Newsletter is anti-Zionist but not anti-Jewish. Articles by Dr. Alfred Lilienthal (editor of Middle East Perspective, reviewed in this chapter), Rabbi Elmer Berger (editor of American Jewish Alternatives to Zionism Report, also reviewed in this chapter), and other Jews have appeared in its pages.

One article, "The Tragedy of Political Zionism," is reprinted from the Observer, organ of the United Church of Canada. Its original printing caused outrage in the Jewish community and a libel suit [withdrawn after an apology by the United Church] against the Observer by B'nai B'rith. Dr.

Lilienthal says, in his Middle East Perspective, that the pressure brought to bear against the United Church of Canada "was one further illustration of the inordinate power of Zionism and the near impossibility of bringing both sides of the Middle East conflict to Western peoples." Other articles: "Towards a Critique of U.S. Middle East Policy"; "Israeli Murder Squads Hit Beirut"; "The Jews of Lebanon" (well treated); "Who Has Been Sending the Letter Bombs?" (the author, Dr. Lilienthal, expresses doubt that it's Arab guerrillas); "Civil Rights in Israel: An Arab Voice"; and "David and Goliath Collaborate in Africa" (Israel plays a role in Africa as an agent of the U.S.). Articles are often reprints from other publications.

The Newsletter also carries descriptions of Israeli attacks on refugee camps and other Jewish terrorist activities. Illustrated with photographs. (JMS)

Feedback:

The organization informed us that it no longer publishes the Newsletter but for anyone interested in information on the Middle East there are complete back files dating from September 1967 until Summer 1974. "The Newsletter has always tried to present material on the Arab point of view and on the civil rights aspect of the problems which are not readily available to the U.S. Public." AJME is now distributing the Journal of Palestine Studies which is also reviewed in this chapter.

The address of AJME is Box 4841, Beirut, Lebanon.

MIDDLE EAST PERSPECTIVE: A Newsletter on Eastern Mediterranean and North African Affairs

Alfred M. Lilienthal, Ed.
850 7th Ave.
N.Y., N.Y. 10019
11 issues a year; $15 (students $6; overseas airmail $20)
Started: Apr. 1968

Circulation: 5,500
Format: 6-8 pages (offset)
Issues examined: June, Oct., Nov. 1973
Back issues available from publisher

Middle East Perspective is emphatically anti-Zionist and, as does American Jewish Alternatives to Zionism Report (reviewed in this chapter), supports the Arab position in the Middle East. The editor tells us that

U.S. policy toward the Middle East must be

drastically altered to become even-handed and to serve the national interest. The Arabs have a case, which Israeli supporters, the Congress, and the media refuse to recognize. Anti-Semitism has nothing whatever to do with the problem, despite the continued efforts of the cult of anti-anti-Semitism to link what happens in the Middle East with the spectre of Adolf Hitler. Judaism is a religion; Zionism is an international political movement. Zionism is not Judaism and to oppose Zionism or the policies of the State of Israel is neither to be anti-Semitic nor to wish to throw Jews into the sea.

The way to peace can come only through implementation of UN Resolution 242 and the de-Zionization of the State of Israel so that Palestinian Arab refugees can live as full citizens with Jews indigenous to the area, as they have done for centuries peacefully prior to the advent of the Zionist movement.

A further explanation of the publication's editorial policies is set forth in an "Outline of Political Philosophy of Middle East Perspective: Our Middle East Policy Has Brought Us an Energy Crisis and to the Very Brink!"

Once more [October 1973], without being consulted, Americans have become most seriously involved in war. U.S. military personnel were placed on a world-wide alert. As in 1967 and in 1970, the arms escalation threatened a Big Power confrontation and World War III. A new Vietnam has been in the making.

...

Thanks to the most powerful lobby in Washington and to a vote-conscious Congress, Israel has been accorded a unique special status, better than being a 51st state. We have become increasingly involved as the fountainhead of Israel's might, the chief provider of her military preponderance by every means possible: gifts, bonds, economic and military aid, loans, and even the forgiveness of reparations to enable Germany to pay Israel--all to the extent of the staggering figure of over eleven billion dollars or $3,500 per Israeli citizen.

...

NEW TACK NEEDED: Peace, justice, and oil depend on this: we must cease treating the Middle East conflict in terms of Israel's survival versus

> Arab vengefulness, but rather as Israel's presently-constituted Zionist expansionist character versus Arab grievances, including the Palestinian determination to realize their human and political rights.
>
> ...
>
> ... Israel must be persuaded ... to withdraw from Arab territories occupied in past wars in return for the Arab recognition of the sovereign existence of an Israel.
>
> ...
>
> ... The origin of the conflict stems from the denial by Zionists of Israel of the rights of the indigenous Arabs of Palestine. No lasting Middle East peace is possible until the Palestinian Arabs are given the right to return to their homeland and are permitted to join in the building of a secular democratic Palestinian-Israeli state in which Arabs and Jews would enjoy equal status.

The Outline goes on to say that the U.S. is to blame for the Russian presence in the Middle East and that the Arabs are justified in using their oil as a weapon.

Regular features of the newsletter are a column ('Dimensions in the News'') by the editor which contains short commentaries and news tidbits on politics and current events relating to the Middle East (as did I. F. Stone, Dr. Lilienthal draws our attention to little-noticed items buried in the inner pages of newspapers); and "Myth Information," which exposes inaccuracies, bias, and misinformation in books, radio, television, and news periodicals (e.g., a New York Times story of the Israeli downing of a Libyan plane, killing 110 people--the story played down the culpability of the Israelis).

The November 1973 issue prints extracts from Diary of a Citizen without a Country by the Palestinian poet, Mahmoud Darwish, which describes the difficult lives that Arabs lead in territory under Israeli military occupation. Little boxes in the newsletter's pages contain pertinent quotations from Jews (e.g. Elmer Berger, editor of American Jewish Alternatives to Zionism Report), prominent Arabs, and Americans.

Each issue usually contains an editorial and one or two articles, some by recognized authorities in the field. (JMS)

Feedback:

"I think you have done an excellent job of getting the spirit of our newsletter and particularly so inasmuch as you have done this on the basis of only a few issues of the publication." The editor added: "No other publication analyzes ... the cult of anti-anti-Semitism, the deliberate analogizing of day-to-day happenings to Jews, Israelis, and the state of Israel with the Hitlerian anti-Semitism, 'poisoning' the atmosphere in which public opinion is molded."

In another letter (24 February 1975), Dr. Lilienthal enclosed a reproduction of an ad rejected by the Wall Street Journal on the grounds that it was inflammatory. "We are now battling them over this. It is obvious that their action resulted from pressures exerted on them when we ran our ad in 1974, and also out of fear of antagonizing the people who are now attacking the Arabs as the sole blame for the inflation, depression, rising prices, etc." The ad shows a U.S. Air Force plane being loaded with American arms and troops. "U.S." and the American insignia are crossed out on the plane and replaced with "Israel" and the star of David. Caption reads: "Aren't we already at war? The Middle East: our new Vietnam."

## MIDNIGHT SUN

| | |
|---|---|
| Simona Arnatiaq, Ed. | Circulation: 150 |
| Igloolik, N.W.T. | Format: 20 pages (legal size, ditto, stapled) |
| (Via: Montreal, A.M.F.) Canada | Issue examined: 2 Nov. 1973 |
| Weekly; $5 | |
| Started: 1969 | |

Midnight Sun, the "Igloolik Newsletter," provides community information, territorial news items, and editorial comment for members of the Canadian Eskimo community. Two-thirds of the content are printed in the Inuit (Eskimo) language printed on single side sheets, with seven pages of English printed on four double sides.

Features short items of community interest (adult education; public library; community council); and daily short territorial news bulletins ("Coral Harbor": "One man dead ... in boating accident...."; "Pangnirtung": "... another oil spill in the North ... 3,000 gallons of oil spilled....").

Major concerns are education, alcoholism, ecology, and assimilation and the disappearance of the Inuit lifestyle and values ("Inuit Value in Danger: Honesty").

The back side of the English print pages contains a telepone directory of the Igloolik community (109 telephone numbers). (KL)

## NATIVE PRESS

Ted Blondin, Ed.
Box 2338
Yellowknife, N. W. T., Canada
Bi-monthly; $6
Started: 11 June 1971
Circulation: 4,600
Format: 16-page tabloid (offset)

Issues examined: 1 & 17 Nov. 1973
Back issues available from publisher
Microform version available from Sun Colorpress, Edmonton, Alberta

Native Press is published by the Indian Brotherhood of the North West Territories, and its stated purpose is "promoting the right to self-determination of the natives of the North West Territories." Its news articles cover issues and events important to the people of the area; for instance, the 1 November issue carries a story of a meeting of the Yellowknife Housing Association to decide on allocation of a fund for housing repairs, and an account of the meeting of the Territorial Council. It also treats affairs with a wider application; for example, the lead article of 17 November, captioned "Natives Win James Bay Fight," tells of the success of the Eskimos and Indians of the region east of James Bay against the Quebec government in saving a large tract of land from exploitation for a huge power development. In the same issue, a sympathetic view of the problems of other native peoples is exemplified by an article on Australian aboriginal rights and a report on the American Indian Movement and its occupation of Wounded Knee.

Serious concern is shown for the personal and communal needs of the people: the problem of alcoholism, educational opportunities and rights, welfare, the ever-present concern for the land and for preservation of the environment. News articles and editorials are frank and outspoken, as, for instance, in an editorial article, 'Education is Power":

> This emphasis that the Territorial Government places on vocational skill training will mean that native people will continue to qualify only for jobs that keep them away from being powerful enough to have a say in their own affairs.
>
> It seems that the way they think in Education is that there are all sorts of funds for vocational education, and they feel safe in doing this because it keeps natives busy and out of their hair. However, they do not view Basic Literacy (learning to read, write and speak English) as having any good results....

> It is surprising then in Canada in 1973, the same Canadian Government that gives this kind of foreign aid and good wishes to developing countries chooses in the case of the native people of the N. W. T. to abandon or disqualify illiterate peoples from participation in a mass drive to become literate....

The paper carries a number of features: letters to the editor; stories based on native legends; short poems and other original pieces; cartoons; recipes. The illustrations range from excellent photographs to illustrate news stories, to sketches and drawings of native life and legend. (MEH)

Feedback:
"Your summary of the Native Press is very good."

Reviewer's opinion:
The paper gives a very good cross-section of the life and concerns of the native people of the North West Territories and some excellent commentaries on problems and matters of general Canadian and international interest.

THE NAVAJO TIMES

Box 310
Window Rock, Ariz. 86515
Weekly; $5
Circulation: 17,800

Format: 36- to 40-page tabloid (offset)
Issues examined: 20 Jan., 16 & 23 Mar. 1972

The Navajo Times is the official newspaper of the Navajo Tribe. It consists mainly of news articles relating to members of the tribe and to programs of the Bureau of Indian Affairs. Navajo recipients of scholarships and awards are frequently cited; such articles are usually accompanied by photographs. Civic, educational, and sports events are covered.

An editorial and letters to the editor appear in each issue. Public notices, especially those issued by the tribal court, are also printed. Regular features include "Navajo Homemaker's World," which provides recipes and household hints. The comic strip "Rick O'Shay" appears weekly, and book reviews are printed occasionally. (SMA)

NEAR EAST REPORT: Washington Letter on American Policy in the Near East

Near East Research
I. L. Kenen, Ed.
1341 G Street, N. W.
Washington, D. C. 20005
Weekly; $10
Started: 1957
Circulation: 27,000

Format: 4 pages (linotype)
Issues examined: 10 & 24 Oct., 7 Nov. 1973
Indexing in annual bound volumes
Back issues available from publisher

This newsletter deals with events in the Near East insofar as they affect Israel. The articles also focus on American relations with Israel. For example, "Congress Considers Aid to Israel" quotes extensively from testimony by the chairman of the American Israel Public Affairs Committee--coincidentally, the editor of Near East Report--who urged assistance for Israel.

Although the Report is pro-Israel, its tone is measured and not strident. It avoids hostile diatribes against Israel's opponents. Its techniques are not defensive: it assumes an attitude of presenting the facts calmly and letting them speak for themselves. For example, it lists U. S. Senate and House members supporting a resolution of support for Israel and then lists some of the dissenters, quoting their objections to the proposal and leaving pro-Israeli voters to draw their own conclusions. (BK)

Reviewer's judgment:

The approach is effective, the writing and editing is well done, the format is attractive, it is a thoroughly professional job. This might be a good source for information on the Near East if the reader keeps in mind that despite its measured and rational tone, Near East Report is basically pro-Israel propaganda. (This paragraph was not included in the copy of the review sent to I. L. Kenen for comment.)

Feedback:

"I am pleased with your comment on the Near East Report. While I am the chairman of the American Israel Public Affairs Committee, I have tried, in the Near East Report, to be 'objectively' partisan. While most people are skeptical when I use this seemingly contradictory term, I feel that it is possible to advocate a cause and, at the same time, attempt to be accurate and fair.

"I began writing for newspapers, believe it or not, in 1920, some 54 years ago. I was for many years a political and editorial writer for a conservative newspaper while I was busily organizing the American Newspaper Guild.

"I don't think we need to add anything to your own comment. The Near East Report does reach many people on both sides of the Arab-Israel issue, and I think that it has broad acceptance because of its attempt to be accurate."

NESIKA: The Voice of B. C. Indians

2140 W. 12th Ave.
Vancouver, B. C., Canada
V6K 2N2
Monthly; free to registered B. C. Indians and $5 to others

Circulation: 7,500
Format: 12-page tabloid (offset)
Issue examined: Nov./Dec. 1973

Nesika (Chinook for "us") is published by the Union of British Columbia Indian Chiefs (UBCIC) and its goals are "To provide unbiased news reports of matters affecting Indian People," "To provide a vehicle for the exchange of ideas and opinions among Indian people," and "At all times to be just and fair-minded to Indian and non-Indian."

The newspaper is a straightforward, non-radical, business-like presentation of news about local political, social, and educational activities of B. C. Indians and their organizations. The main interest now of Nesika and the UBCIC is the negotiation of native land claims. At a recent conference the organization decided that because of the weakened political stance of the Trudeau government the climate was right to begin negotiations and it was decided to set up a Land Research Center to give Indian people technical assistance in compiling evidence on these claims--claims which include not only land but also special rights regarding hunting and commercial fishing, water use for irrigation, and money (for housing, education and economic development). A guest editorial ("Solid Approach to Settlement Lies in People's Movement") stresses the need for Indians to work together and choose well-informed dedicated leaders. Another guest editorial with a more bitter tone (unusual for this periodical) laments:

> I have seen our rivers teeming with thousands and thousands of salmon, our forests filled with wildlife. Who, may I ask, destroyed the environment and caused the most damage? These are the culprits whom we should seek retribution from.... If I had

a magic wand, I would take over all land holdings of the E & N railway. They sold millions and millions of dollars of our prime timber, destroyed our watersheds, from whence the rivers and streams were fed.... Their motto was and is still, 'let's exploit now and the hell with tomorrow.'

Nesika also supports the Quebec Indians in their fight against the James Bay hydroelectric power development which calls for the damming of six or seven rivers and the flooding of 6,000 square miles of land in a wilderness area of northern Quebec. A court decision on the project declared that the interest of the majority outweighs that of the minority. Angered by this, an editorial in Nesika asks: "If the law won't, who will protect minorities?" The editorial goes on to point out the grave ecological consequences of the project and the uneconomical way in which it is being handled.

The paper carries many articles of only local interest on grants, awards, workshops, native people who have made good, sports and entertainment, services, etc.; and has a section of letters to the editor as well as one on Indian children up for adoption. (JMS)

Feedback:

"O.K. with a note and a minor correction. Thanks!" (The suggested changes have been incorporated into the text of the review.)

NETWORK

North American Jewish Students Network
36 W. 37th St. (10th floor)
N.Y., N.Y. 10018
About every 3 weeks; $10 (students $5); overseas $12
Started: 1970
Circulation: 6,000

Format: 4-page tabloid (letterpress)
Issues examined: 23 Nov. 1972; 5 Feb., 9 Apr., 3 May 1973
Back issues available from publisher

Network is the newsletter of a national organization formed to "promote and co-ordinate Jewish student activity." The publication itself, which serves as an information service for Jewish students throughout the country, is a major part of the effort to coordinate activity. It reports on Jewish student groups in the U.S. and Canada, and conveys information on classes, events, organizations, and publications that might be of interest to its readers. Most of the articles are edited versions of items sent in by readers; some letters are also printed. Occasionally there are articles on major trends or events that the editors think to be of importance to Jewish students. The issues examined contained, for example, an article on EZRA (an organization founded to help the Jewish poor); a discussion of the future of Soviet Jewry; announcements of Jewish student conferences; a description of the Philadelphia Union of Jewish Students; and an article on a Jewish communal living project in Chapel Hill, N. C. Regular columns inform readers of available "Media and Resources" (films, books, pamphlets, newspapers, and buttons) and list current activities in New York City. (AS)

Feedback:
Several minor changes in wording were suggested, and one of them was incorporated into the review.

NEW DAWN

Cecilia Yoshida, Ed.
J-Town Collective
Box 26310
San Francisco, Calif. 94126
Monthly; $2.50
Started: Aug. 1971
Circulation: 3,000

Format: 12-page tabloid (offset)
Issues examined: Mar., Apr., Oct., Nov. 1973
Back issues available from publisher

New Dawn is dedicated to "news and analysis of the struggles and victories of the Japanese and Asian peoples here in the United States and the world." It is strongly anti-Israel, and firmly opposed to the "aggressive designs of the two superpowers--the U.S. and the U.S.S.R." It states that "their attempts to dominate, divide, and rule over the land, resources, and people of the world are clearly last-stand attempts that are certain to be defeated." The article, "CANE's Strategy To Win," states that the Redevelopment Agency in San Francisco is committed to the interests of big business and "its plan is to destroy the Japanese community."

The paper addresses itself frequently to stories and problems of Asian peoples abroad and actively supports the Arab revolution. Locally, one of its continuing causes is the redevelopment problems of Asians in major cities, particularly San Francisco.

Concerning the signing of the Vietnamese peace treaty, the J-Town Collective urges continued vigilance, because "the U.S. imperialists are treacherous and cannot be trusted."

The articles vary in length, ranging from a two-paragraph box item to several pages. They are liberally accompanied with photographs or cartoons. Occasionally, a letter from a reader is carried, if it is sympathetic to a cause promoted by New Dawn. One sample issue contained several pages in Japanese. Ads carried are from the New Dawn Bookstore. (MN)

Other opinions or themes noticed in the sample issues:

1. Admiration for the People's Republic of China.
2. Opposition to martial law in the Philippines.
3. Criticism of the Saigon regime's cruel treatment of its political prisoners.
4. Condemnation of the Chilean military coup that overthrew the elected Marxist government of Dr. Salvador Allende; and the suggestion that the U.S. Central Intelligence Agency had a hand in the affair.
5. Support for "national liberation struggles" throughout the world.
6. Criticism of the herding of Japanese-Americans into concentration camps, during World War II.
7. Support for Cesar Chavez' United Farm Workers' Union.
8. Support for American Indians, in their struggle against oppression.
9. Criticism of brutality and harassment by police; and of the wearing by some Cleveland police of swastikas on their uniforms!
10. Characterization of S. I. Hayakawa (semanticist, and former university president) as a "renowned enemy of all Third World communities." (TJS)

NEW OUTLOOK: Middle East Monthly

Jewish-Arab Institute at Givat Haviva
Karl Netter 8
Tel Aviv, Israel
9 times yearly; $12 surface mail ($16 airmail)
Started: 1957

Circulation: 5,000
Format: 64 pages or 80-page double issue (6 3/4" x 9 1/2")
Issues examined: Nov. 1972; June & Dec. 1973

This liberal voice of conciliation in Israel has, since its inception in 1957,

> emphasized the necessity for Israeli peace initiatives and efforts to break through the wall of enmity surrounding the Jewish State. Our motto has consistently been, 'the enemies of today will be the allies of tomorrow.' The fourth Israeli-Arab war has precipitated a situation whereby the whole world is pressing for an immediate solution to the conflict, the continuation of which has become too dangerous to the peace and welfare of the world at large. Rather than be pushed by external pressure to the Peace Conference, Israel should take the initiative by itself to present our Arab neighbors with peace proposals that ensure security and justice for all concerned and open the way to a cooperation beneficial to all peoples of the region.

The editors played an active part in bringing about the nationwide petition for a Peace Initiative--Now, the main points of which (presented in the Dec. 1973 issue) reflect the journal's political philosophy:

> The Yom Kippur War exposed the illusion and errors of the politics of stalemate and creeping annexation which did not lead to peace and did not prevent war. In the wake of the cease-fire, a historical opportunity for peace has arisen. In the absence of peace, further wars are to be expected, possibly even more difficult and cruel than the Yom Kippur War. Israel should take the initiative in immediately formulating a realistic peace plan. Israel's security will not be achieved by annexation ... or occupation of territories but through peace agreements, creation of demilitarized zones, and increasing the strength and vigilance of Israel's Defence Forces. Peace is more important to us than territories. Israel should recognize the existence of the Arab Palestine people and help promote their participation in the peace efforts.

The late Martin Buber, the philosopher, was one of the journal's sponsors. Members of the Editorial Council represent "a broad cross-section of trends and views, Jewish and Arab, in Israel." A Statement of Purpose appearing in each issue explains that New Outlook serves "as a medium for the clarification of problems concerning peace and cooperation among all peoples of the Middle East" and will

> be open to the expression of opinions, however

diverse, that have that general aim in view. New Outlook will strive to reflect those aspirations and accomplishments in the economic, social, and cultural fields that are common to all peoples and countries of the area and could, given the elimination of frictions and animosities, flourish and produce an ever greater abundance of well-being and happiness.

Reviewer's judgment:

We'll review this interesting and valuable publication at length in Volume IV.

THE NISHNAWBE NEWS

Organization of North American Indian Students
Michael J. Wright, Ed.
214 Kaye Hall
Marquette, Mich. 49855
Monthly; $5 donation (free to American Indians)

Started: July 1971
Circulation: 7,000
Format: 8-page tabloid (offset)
Issues examined: v. 1, nos. 5, 7-9

The Nishnawbe News is "published for Indians of the Great Lakes area" by The Organization of North American Indian Students. According to the editor, its purposes include opposing acculturation and furthering Indian education, unity, cultural awareness, and religion. The tone of the newspaper is one of serious concern for the plight of Indians and a determination to improve their situation through Indian power and unity. In No. 9, the editor writes:

> We, the first people of this land, are tired of being third-rate citizens. We are tired of hearing those who tell us that good things are coming if we only be patient and work with the system. We have seen how the system works.... We must be ready to accept even death in our fight for what truly belongs to us and our children: Freedom, Human Dignity, and Justice.... Change will come only when we make Indian power a reality.

Many of the articles deal with political issues (especially land and fishing rights) at the state and federal levels. Special sections cover Indian legends; articles from other Indian newspapers ("Other Voices"); brief profiles of living persons ("Indian Who's Who"); poetry by Indians; "Indian

Youth News"; and "Woman's News" (poetry, recipes). There are also letters to the editor. (CT)

OUTLOOK

48 E. 74th St.
N.Y., N.Y. 10021
Quarterly; $1 (overseas, $1.50)
Started: 1930

Circulation: 170,000
Format: 36 pages (6 1/2" x 10")
Issues examined: Winter 1972; Spring & Summer 1973

Outlook is the journal of the Women's League for Conservative Judaism (formerly National Women's League).

> Among the goals of the magazine and the League are the promotion of the observance of the tenets of the Conservative Movement, appreciation of and support for the State of Israel, strengthening Jewish family life, and open discussion of all issues that bear directly on the lives of Jewish women.

The Spring 1973 issue celebrates the 25th anniversary of Israel's statehood with articles on such subjects as Israel's economy, the "essential and unique quality" of Jerusalem, and the Conservative Movement in Israel. In "Ghetto, Shtetl --And Israel," the editor discusses whether Israel bears resemblance to the Jewish ghettos (formal restriction) and shtetls (self-restricted community) of the past.

> Does Israel the nation, enclave-like, all but surrounded by hostile Arab neighbors, possess boundaries comparable to the ghetto, locking the inhabitants within its borders?

She answers,

> The important, significant distinction lies in the actuality of Israel's being a 'sovereign nation.' With the rights and privileges which accrue to a nation among nations, Israel may devote itself to resource development and the unification, by a common ideology, of its people.... The problem of adherence to common goals, of conversion of European Jews, Moroccan Jews, Soviet Jews, Yemenites, etc., into Israeli Jews must be resolved.... Religiously, all spectrums from the Orthodox to the secularist Jews,

> must learn to live together (when war no longer threatens) as Israeli Jews, with adherence to national loyalties and symbols.

In another issue, devoted completely to the 1972 convention of the Women's League, one article summarizes a formal debate on the question, "Resolved, That the Woman in Judaism Should Have More Rights." One debater contended that

> Jewish feminists have had enough of apologetics; they now want change. They have not rejected Judaism; they are struggling with it in a way to fulfill themselves as Jews and as women.

Another "defended traditional practices, stating that male and female each has a distinct role to play--a role set by Divine order."

In the Summer 1973 issue, "Berlin's Other Walls" compares East and West Berlin on their attitudes toward Jews, finding that

> The climate under Communism is simply not congenial to Jewry. Communist governments tend to feel that any striving for cultural identity detracts from a citizen's attentiveness to the class struggle and, in leading to separatism, constitutes disloyalty to the totalitarian state.

In the same issue, "An Experiment in Jewish Communal Living" is the account of an attempt to create an ideal Jewish commune in New York City and the religious and interpersonal conflicts that have arisen among the 16 men and 14 women who live there.

Regular departments include book and music reviews, "Our President Speaks," "Idea Exchange," and recommended books for children. (MM)

Feedback:
Editor expressed no disapproval.

PALANTE

| | |
|---|---|
| Latin Revolutionary News Service | Richie Perez, Mng. Ed. |
| Young Lords Party, | 202 E. 117th St. |
| | N.Y., N.Y. 10035 |

Bi-monthly; $6.75 (offset)
Started: May 1969
Circulation: 16,000
Format: 24-page tabloid
Issues examined: Vol. 3, Nos. 4, 7 and 8

This bi-lingual paper supports the programs of the Young Lords Party, a "revolutionary political party fighting for the liberation of all oppressed people." Its platform proposes self-determination for Puerto Ricans, all Latinos, and all third world people; and equality for women. It opposes racism, capitalists, alliances with traitors, and the "amerikkkan" military.

Articles in Spanish and English support these party platforms. "Historia de Boriken" is a continuing article dealing mainly with the history of Puerto Rico in the light of its oppression by foreign powers.

Articles dealing with the problems of living in New York are "Have You Seen the Taxi Prices Lately?," "Why Pay So Much for Milk?," and "More Trash Pick-ups!"

Oppression of other people is detailed in such articles as: "U.S. Orders Asian Sisters Tortured," "Laos: People's Army Stops U.S.," and "People's War in Argentina."

Two of the issues examined contained a "Pig of the Week" column. The award is presented to a Puerto Rican who, in the estimation of the editors, has sold out the people of Puerto Rico.

Rules of Discipline of the Young Lords Party are included in two of the issues. (DB)

Addendum:

The history and aims of the YLP can be found in Michael Abramson's Palante: Young Lords Party (New York: McGraw-Hill, 1971). He reproduces the Party's "13-point program and platform" on pp. 150-51. Its final plank: "We want a socialist society."

## THE PALESTINIAN VOICE

Mustafa Siam, Ed. & Publ.
6513 Hollywood Blvd., #207
Los Angeles, Calif. 90028
Monthly; $5
Started: July 1971
Circulation: 5,000
Format: 8- to 16-page tabloid
Issues examined: June 1973-Jan. 1974

The Palestinian Voice is an independent publication with texts in English and Arabic. The primary platform is

"Palestine for All the Palestinians." Every issue is a combination of original editorials and of news articles gathered from other sources. The front page usually carries a lengthy article of news of interest to the Arab community in the U.S. Topics include religion, economics of the oil crisis, labor struggles, and the situation in the Middle East. Articles sometimes contain the complete text of a speech, interview, or letter which appeared in other news sources in an incomplete form. Emphasis is on presenting the Arab point of view to Americans, exemplified by the occasional feature in the form of "An Open Letter to the American People." Typically, there is an appeal to the people to support the Arab nations' "legitimate struggle in resisting Israeli expansionist policies and rectifying the injustices done to the Palestinian people."

Mottoes such as "Support the United Farm Workers' Union in its Struggle," "Join the United American-Arab Congress," and "Remember Palestine" are interspersed among the articles.

A regular feature is the editorial page, headed with the motto, "I may not agree with a word that you say, but I will defend to death your right to say it."

Although The Palestinian Voice is political, its tone is moderate. The purpose seems to be to educate and persuade rather than to denounce and inflame. (WP)

Feedback:

"Your review of the Palestinian Voice is accurate. This means that you are an honest writer and good reporter. The truth and the gathering of facts should be everybody's business, and you certainly achieved it."

## THE PATRIOT

Weekly; $7.50 Format: 16-page tabloid
Started: 1970 Issue examined: 21 Mar. 1970

The Patriot is published by the Patriot Party, a "revolutionary Party for poor and oppressed people." The Party was born of a division among members of the Young Patriot Organization, a white radical community group in Uptown Chicago working with poor whites of mainly Southern origin. Some members felt that it was not enough to concentrate on Uptown Chicago and broke with the Young Patriots to form the Patriot Party, found a national headquarters, and form chapters in five cities across the country.

The Patriot Party has a 10 Point People's Program based on "the day-to-day reality" of people's lives--a reality made up of "not enough to eat, lack of decent clothing, lack of decent housing, lack of good medical care, lack of justice, police brutality, taxation, being drafted into the pig army, being abused and forgotten, being purposely kept miseducated about the true nature of this country."

The demands of the Party, which were listed twice in the issue examined, are as follows:

1. We demand freedom. We demand power to determine the destiny of our oppressed white community.
2. We demand full employment for oppressed white people, and that the means of production should be placed in the hands of the people.
3. We demand an end to the robbery by the capitalists of our oppressed white community; we demand that they do not make a profit on things we need for survival.
4. We demand decent and adequate housing, fit for shelter of human beings, regardless of our income.
5. We demand education that exposes the true nature of this decadent American society; that teaches us our true history; that teaches us cooperation rather than competition.
6. We demand that all oppressed white people be exempt from military service.
7. We demand an immediate end to police brutality and murder of oppressed white people, and that the people of our community control the police.
8. We demand freedom for all oppressed white people held in federal, state, county and city prisons, and that all our people be tried by a jury of their peers or from their communities.
9. We demand the end of the rape of our land by the corporations and monopoly farmers, and the land be returned to the people to meet their basic needs.
10. We demand an end to racism, and the inequality of the sexes, as tools of capitalism to divide the people.

We demand these things in the interest of the people, and we the people will have them and defend them by any means necessary.

These demands and a variety of other slogans--"The South will rise again, only this time with the North, and all oppressed people throughout the world," "All Power to the

People," "Educate, Liberate," "Guns in the Hands of the Police Represent Capitalism and Racism. Guns in the Hands of the People Represent Socialism and Solidarity," "Law and Order: Fascist Tool"--appear throughout the paper. On the front page there is a statement by Party Chairman, "Preacherman": "We are the living reminder that when they threw out their white trash they didn't burn it."

Articles in the issue examined included: "John Howard," the story of a man "viciously stabbed to death by mad-dog Maddox's fly-by-night fascist-loving pigs because they convicted him of being a nigger lover"; "John Howard Memorial Free Breakfast for Children," about a new Party program in New Haven, Connecticut; "The Real Enemy," demonstrating why "the Wealthy" are to blame; "Patriot Party Supports Bobby Seale," explaining that "the struggle of poor black, white, and brown people in this country is one against a common oppressor"; "PeeWee Speaks To The People," opinions of a twelve-year-old child of Uptown; and "Interview with Turco," Party Chief of Staff. (JW)

Feedback:

Mail returned 1973, marked "Moved, not forwardable." Address had been: Ministry of Information, Patriot Party, 1742 Second Avenue, N.Y., N.Y. 10028.

HA PEH

American Students for Israel
Northeastern University
Boston, Mass. 02115

Format: 6 pages (mimeo., stapled)
Issue examined: Apr. 1970

The one issue of Ha Peh reviewed consists of three mimeographed sheets containing unsigned articles about the plight of Soviet Jews, French President Pompidou's snubbing of American Jews during his visit to the United States, and plans for the creation of a new cooperative community near Jerusalem. The Arab-Israeli conflict is referred to in a listing, without comment, of quotations from various media revealing the Arabs' aggression and their plans for the violent and total destruction of Israel, and in a consideration of how Arab terrorism has only made Israel stronger. Several ads for extended study or work experiences in Israel are interspersed with the articles. The articles were evidently printed as submitted; ideological differences between Pompidou and Nixon are described as "nihil," Pompidou was "visible upset," Nixon acted as a "seditive." No editors' or authors' names are given. (CP)

PIONEER WOMEN

315 Fifth Ave.
N. Y., N. Y. 10016
9 issues a year

Format: 32 pages (offset)
Issue examined: Nov. 1972

Mainly concerned with the role of women in Israel. Contains a six-page section in Hebrew. Published by "The Women's Labor Zionist Organization of America."

EL POPO

Chicano Studies Dept.
California State University
18111 Nordhoff Ave.
Northridge, Calif. 91324
Monthly; $3.50
Started: 1970
Circulation: 5,000
Format: 10-page tabloid
(offset)

Issues examined: 30 Mar. 1973; and undated Vol. 7, Nos. 1 & 2 (probably Nov. & Dec. 1973)
Back issues available from publisher

The editor gave us this information about El Popo's editorial policy: "To convey Chicano news (and movement-related information) to Chicano students and Chicano Communities." The paper is "published ... by the Chicano students at C. S. U. N." Illustrated with photographs, cartoons, and graphics.

QUE ONDEE SOLA

Union for Puerto Rican Students
Northeastern Illinois University
Bryn Mawr at St. Louis Aves.
Chicago, Ill. 60625

Semi-monthly
Format: 12 pages (offset)
Issue examined: 15 Mar. 1973

A bi-lingual community publication. The sample issue contained an interview with the secretary-general of the Partido Socialista Puertorriqueño; criticism of a Chicago school principal "insensitive" to the needs of Latino students; exhortations to free Puerto Rican "political" prisoners (including would-be assassins); the contention that Puerto Ricans, whose country is illegally occupied by the U. S., have the right to free themselves "by any means necessary"; and photographs of what is said to be "brutality" inflicted by the police on Latinos in Chicago. (TJS)

THE RAVEN SPEAKS

Raven Hail, Publ.
Box 35733
Dallas, Tex. 75235
Monthly; $3
Started: Apr. 1968

Format: 4 pages (5 1/2" x 8 1/2")
Issues examined: all issues from Apr. 1970 through Mar. 1971

The Raven Speaks is published by a Cherokee Indian for the purpose of presenting "Indian information from an Indian's point of view." The tone of the magazine is one of a good-humored but sincere appreciation of Indian culture.

Each issue begins with a couple of short articles containing information on tourist attractions, events, interesting individuals, and the Cherokee language. Book reviews cover books on Indian customs, songs, cooking, etc. Frequently used titles for these sections are "Adventures in Indianland," "Talking Leaves," "Instant Cherokee," and "People and Stuff."

Each issue also contains one longer article describing some aspect of Indian culture. Examples are "From Buck to Buckskin (How to Tan a Hide)," "The Seal of the Cherokee Nation," "Will Rogers (The Cherokee Kid)," "The Creation Legend," and "Cherokee Masks (or, Halloween--Indian style)." Occasionally more serious articles discuss bills or court decisions of concern to Indians. The back of each issue contains the English and Cherokii translations of a hymn, Bible verse, poem, or prayer. (CT)

RESISTANCE IN THE MIDDLE EAST

Box 134
West Newton, Mass. 02156
Quarterly; $2 (institutions $6)

Started: Winter 1972
Circulation: 200
Issues examined: none sent

Pro-Arab.

RESPONSE: A Contemporary Jewish Review

415 South St.
Waltham, Mass. 02145

Quarterly
Started: 1967

Circulation: 6,000
Format: 96-128 pages (6" x 9", offset)
Issues examined: Fall 1970; Winter 1970-71

"Response began as an attempt on the part of several serious Jewish undergraduates to confront American Jewry and Judaism. They had been disenchanted with the way American Jews had organized themselves, and at the same time were committed to some kind of progressive Judaism. More recently, Response has become the province of graduate students (who run the magazine) and dissenting Jews of all ages, who write for it.... More recently we have attempted to deal with a variety of religious and political issues, and have at the same time attempted to act as the literary forum for a new generation of Jews. We are recognized as the leading dissenting Jewish publication in America. We are independent, we have no political ideology, we are particularly hospitable to new, young, and controversial writers. At the same time we are respectable and serious...."

Response is edited by a group of young Jews centered at Brandeis University who, according to a New York Times article (25 April 1971, p. 54), are searching for a new religious style traditional in belief, but independent of major Jewish institutions. "Several of the essays expressed disillusionment ... with ... [among other things] a New Left that turned anti-Semitic." [See above, p. 712.]

In Volume IV we hope to review more recent issues of Response.

THE RICAN: A Journal of Contemporary Puerto Rican Thought

Box 11039
Chicago, Ill. 60611
Quarterly; $3.50
Started: Fall 1972
Circulation: 5,000
Format: 72 pages (6" x 9", offset)
Issues examined: Fall 1972; Spring 1973

The publication carries this description of its goals and content:

> The historical period in which we are living emphasizes the humiliation of identifying very little with our native brothers and less with our Latin compatriots who are products of distorted stereotypes. Being victims of the negation of our linguistic, cul-

tural, and patriotic heritage, we find ourselves disinherited in our land as well as in 'America.'

The Rican ... is a first step in the enhancement of our rich cultural heritage. We expect many young writers will be encouraged to submit their works for publication. This is an important step in a cultural and ideological campaign to generate the necessary Rican cultural revolution.

The Rican would like to remain an open forum for the expression of conflicting and opposing viewpoints. Although the editorial staff cannot support all of the articles submitted, it will reflect and expose the concerns and opinions of our people. We will examine Puerto Rican ideologies while debating and evaluating present issues. Articles which research, document, and analyze the Puerto Rican experience will be published as well as essays, drawings, poems, and short stories.

In the sample issues, two pertinent speeches were reprinted from the Congressional Record. One, by a former chancellor of the University of Puerto Rico, protested against the U.S. Navy's continued shelling (for target practice) of part of the tiny isle of Culebra. The other, by Democratic Congressman Hermán Badillo of the Bronx, suggested ways of improving the economic status of Puerto Ricans on the Island and on the mainland.

An editorial explained the difference between the terms "Rican" (one born or reared on the mainland) and "Puerto Rican" (an Islander). Ricans are subject to types of repression different from those on the Island; their "life experience" is different in other ways, too.

There were interviews with Piri Thomas (author of Down These Mean Streets) and with a former president of the New York City Board of Education. Other items: poems; a one-act play; book reviews; and a two-part article by The Rican's publisher (Samuel Betances) on race prejudice in Puerto Rico. A number of the contributors were professors; two were doctoral students. Most of the content is in English; the rest is in Spanish. (TJS)

SASKATCHEWAN INDIAN

1114 Central Ave.
Prince Albert,
Saskatchewan, Canada

Monthly; $3
Started: Summer 1971
Circulation: 12,000

Format: 20- to 32-page tabloid (offset)
Issues examined: none sent

According to the editor, the paper's goal is "The protection and continuation of rights guaranteed Indians in their treaties with Canada."

THE SCOUT

Indian-Metis Friendship Centre
836 Lorne Ave.
Brandon, Manitoba, Canada R7A 0T8
Monthly; free
Started: 1964
Circulation: 400
Format: 10 pages (mimeo.)
Issues examined: 30 Aug., 8 & 30 Nov. 1973

The Scout is devoted to announcements of activities taking place at the Centre: dances, bingo, games, parties, athletic events, educational programs, counseling services, etc. The magazine is also a source of information on recommended books, government actions and appointments, job openings, and Indian history. One of the major concerns of the Centre is the alcoholism problem among Indians. The Native Alcoholism Council offers counseling services and regular weekly meetings.

In addition to information, The Scout includes short anecdotes and a "Wit and Wisdom" section which consists of short quotations from famous people. Occasionally, poetry expresses the more serious aspects of the Indians' and Metis' plight. (CT)

Feedback:
Editor expressed no disapproval.

SKOOKUM JIM NEWS

3159 Third Ave.
Whitehorse, Yukon, Canada
Format: 10-12 pages (mimeo., stapled)
Issues examined: Jan. 1974 and one undated issue from late 1973

A local newsletter aimed at the Indian community. News and announcements of all sorts of events, activities, and programs. Concern over alcoholism among Indians. Implied criticism of the way in which the Royal Canadian Mounted Police treat Indians. (TJS)

SPEAR: Canadian Magazine of Truth & Soul

Spear Publications;
Sam Donkoh, Ed.
932 Bathurst St.
Toronto, Ontario, Canada
M5R 3G5
Monthly; $5
Started: July 1971

Circulation: 8,000
Format: 52 pages (offset)
Issues examined: Nov. 1973 through Feb. 1974
Back issues available from publisher

The editor sent this information:

> Spear is not anti-white but definitely pro-black. We are primarily concerned with issues relating to black people within the Canadian society. We also carry material on West Indians, Africans & Afro-Americans. Our editorial content ranges from law through religion to medicine. As a black publication, we seek out the best in blacks and highlight this. We criticize where there is a shortcoming and offer alternatives. We also like Spear to maintain its image of a family magazine. This means we avoid carrying stories on violence, crime, obscenity, and other items which we think will offend the moral standards of our broad public. An exception is when we carry these stories to illustrate a shortcoming, e.g., discrimination.

Each of the sample issues contained ten or more short articles on black entertainers, prominent members of the black community, and such topics as: "The Meaning of Apartheid"; independence for African nations ("Justification for Freedom" contains excerpts from an interview with the president of the new African country, Guinea Bissau); prejudice in Canada ("Down Home and Down South" notes similarities between blacks reared near Halifax, Nova Scotia, and southern blacks of the U.S.); "Feminine Liberation" ("black woman must not sacrifice her womanhood for the black man to achieve his manhood"); "Correlation Between the Pill and Sickle Cell" (pill may be dangerous for large numbers of black women); and "The Case for a Summer Camp for Black Children."

The magazine also has sections on black movies, music and records, book reviews, astrology, and beauty queens. "Your Right" is a regular feature which interprets the law for black people and explains their rights. "International Rap Up" is a column by Odimumba Kwamdela (formerly J. Ashton Brathwaite); written in a be-bop style, it covers everything from renaming rivers in Africa (from colonial to African names) to criticizing Sammy Davis, Jr., for his support of Richard M. Nixon. There are also articles on religion.

Spear is aimed at the black middle-class. (JMS)

TEKAWENNAKE

Six Nations-New Credit Reporter
Carolyn Beaver, Ed. & Publ.
R. R. No. 6
Hagersville, Ont., Canada
Bi-monthly; $8.80
Started: 1966
Circulation: 700

Format: 24 pages (mimeo., stapled)
Issues examined: 10 Oct. & 5 Dec. 1973
Back issues available from publisher
Microform version available from Microfilming Corp. of America

Tekawennake is published for the native people of the Six Nations Reserve. It carries current news of the area and news stories of particular interest to Indians. The issue of 10 October has stories of an Indian minister and writer, Enos Montour; of the sale of honey on a reserve in Manitoba; and of an album of Indian music published at Phoenix, Arizona. The issue of 5 December lists, with photographs, nominees for election to the council of the Six Nations Reserve, and carries stories of various matters of interest and concern to Canadian Indians, including the James Bay area Hydro development project in Quebec, against which the native people registered a strong protest. A section captioned "Did You Know" gives a story on Indian culture or history.

Sports news, original poetry, a crossword puzzle and other games, horoscope, advertisements, and short local news notes fill out the paper. (MEH)

Feedback:

"Kindly be advised that I have checked your summary of Tekawennake and it covers the newspaper quite fully.... As you requested, the title Tekawennake is a Mohawk word; when translated, means 'Two Voices,' which is significant because the newspaper covers two reserves, Six Nations and New Credit."

THIRD WORLD NEWS

Lower Freeborn (Room 12)
University of California
Davis, Calif. 95616
Weekly; $15

Started: Oct. 1970
Circulation: 5,000
Format: 8- to 12-page tabloid
Issues examined: 11 & 31 Oct., 7 Nov. 1973

This is published by and for minority students on the Davis campus: Negro, Chicano, and American Indian, as well as "Third World" (Arab, Asian). Its orientation is primarily Afro-American.

Aggressively New Left and anti-imperialist, opposing the U.S., Israel, and such "rightist regimes" as those of Chile and Greece. Provides an outlet for student grievances, as well as information on ethnic studies on campus.

Each issue presents articles on a particular theme: "Law Edition"; "Native American Edition"; or "Ethnic Studies: Asian, Black, Chicano." Regular columns include "New Blacks on Campus," "China Correspondent," and "Announcements" (course offerings, calendar). (KL)

TRAIT D'UNION: Review of the Melkites in Canada

Msgr. George Coriaty, Publ. & Dir.
329 Viger Ave.
Montreal, Quebec, Canada H2X IRG
4 issues a year plus supplements; $5
Started: Mar. 1964
Circulation: 4,000
Format: 20-28 pages (offset)
Issues examined: Oct. 1969; July & Oct. 1973; Jan. 1974

This newsletter is published by and for part of the Melkite Community in Canada. (Melkites are Near Eastern Catholics who recognize the authority of the Pope, but whose services are usually held in Arabic.) There is news of the Melkite communities in Montreal, Ottawa, and Toronto. Articles are in English and French.

THE TRIBAL TRIBUNE

Carleen M. Hall, Ed.
Box 150
Nespelem, Wash. 99155
Monthly; $5
Started: Jan. 1962
Circulation: 3,300
Format: 32-page tabloid
Issues examined: Oct. & Nov. 1973; Jan. 1974
Photocopies of back issues available from publisher

This newspaper is funded by members of the Colville tribes. Its principal purpose is to provide tribal members with information about legislation passed by the tribal governing body. It also informs them of various public services available on the reservation. A section entitled "Spokane Area Services" regularly gives a listing of such services as immunization, food stamps, vocational rehabilitation and legal services, along with brief instructions as to time and procedure for securing them. Numerous articles offer details on these and related topics. Representative titles are: "Public Defender Program Is Approved for Colville Indians," "Management Training Project Seeks Trainees," "GED Testing Program Is Offered Adults," "Tribal Members Eligible to Collect Coyote Bounty," and "Earning College Credits at Home Via Television." There is also a column in which questions about Social Security are answered. School news and reports on sports activities are included in some issues. A humorous feature, "The Coyote Made Me Do It," offers tribal gossip and quips concerning events on the reservation.

The following statement by the editor presents an important aspect of the newspaper's editorial policy:

> Controversial or political subjects are avoided because of the tribal funding--it is the feeling of the governing body and editor that such issues could not possibly present the views of all 5,000 plus tribal members.

(SMA)

## THE VOICE OF BROTHERHOOD

| | |
|---|---|
| 423 Seward St. | Format: 6-page tabloid |
| Juneau, Alaska 99801 | Issues Examined: July & |
| Monthly | Sept. 1974 |

"A monthly publication intended to be a VOICE concerning the native population of Alaska. We hope to create interest, concern, and action within the native culture."

## WASSAJA

| | |
|---|---|
| American Indian Historical Society | Started: 1973 |
| | Circulation: 80,000 |
| 1451 Masonic Ave. | Format: 24-page tabloid |
| San Francisco, Calif. 94117 | Issue examined: June 1973 |
| Monthly; $10 | |

Wassaja ("Let My People Know") views itself as a

"National Newspaper of Indian America," heralding the "Indian's Signal for Self-Determination." It presents coverage of various concerns of Native American groups on and off the reservations: political ("Watergate and Indians"; "McDowell Tribe Elects New Council"); legal ("Havasupai Seek To Regain Land"; "BIA [Bureau of Indian Affairs] Must Follow Law on Hiring"); economic ("Colville Shows Way in Tribal Enterprise"; "Housing Project Under Way"); and educational ("Coeur d'Alene Dictionary To Be Designed by Indians"; "Project Sun: Bilingual Education for a Quad-Culture").

Wassaja reports on problems involving Indian self-determination ("Indians Push Claims in Struggle for Survival, Native Rights"); discrimination ("Discrimination Charged in Rights Report"); relations with the U.S. government ("New Commissioner Explains Position on Indian Affairs"); and treaty, land, resource, and water problems ("Michigan Treaty Rights Demanded"; "Ft. McDowell Indians Face Loss of Land").

News of tribal and inter-tribal relations is reported, as well as cultural events in the Indian community. (KL)

Feedback:

"Entry approved."

WHISPERING WIND

8009 Wales St.
New Orleans, La. 70126
Monthly (except July & Aug.); $4.20
Started: Oct. 1967
Circulation: 600
Format: 16-20 pages (offset)
Issues examined: none sent
Back issues available from publisher
Microform version available from Microfilming Corp. of America

The editor said that the periodical's aim is "publication of the true customs, traditions, arts, and crafts of the American Indian, both past and present."

YUKON INDIAN NEWS

Frank Lacosse, Ed.
22 Nisutlin Dr.
Whitehorse, Yukon, Canada
Every month or two
Started: 1974
Format: 4- to 8-page tabloid (offset)
Issues examined: July, Sept.-Dec. 1974

Coverage is confined to the Yukon. Articles on Indian businesses; land claims; alcoholism; programs (in health, housing, recreation); meetings of groups, and reports on their elections. Brief profiles (with photographs) of men and women active in Indian affairs. Letters to the editor; poems; editorials. The paper is informative rather than militant. (TJS)

## Chapter 16

## PEACE

> We reject the concept of amnesty that implies 'forgive and forget.' Resistance to the war is not a crime to be forgiven or forgotten. The crime is the slaughter in Indochina, and this we must not forgive or forget. The issue of amnesty must be a constant reminder to the American people that the criminals are not those who refused to be part of the war machine, not those in U.S. jails and in Canada and abroad. Those truly responsible are and have been in the White House and in the Pentagon. ---*Peaceletter* (May 1973)

Since the end of active American participation in the Vietnam War, many peace-seeking organizations and their periodicals have folded. A small number will, however, surely endure. *Peaceletter* (Women Strike for Peace), published since the mid-1960s, has broadened its scope to cover --among other things--the problems of farm workers, multinational corporations, military installations, and military spending. *Business Executives Move for Vietnam Peace* (reviewed as *News Notes*) has changed its name and emphasis. It now keeps an eye on war-making at the Pentagon, while *Counterspy* and *Intelligence Report* watch the American intelligence community. *Across Frontiers*, published by the World Constitution and Parliament Association, speaks for an international organization emphasizing one-worldism. *World Peace News* also supports world government, while *Freedom & Union* hopes that the members of NATO can form a federation. *Disarmament News & Views* keeps track of military spending, and legislation on weapons programs. *Peace Gazette* covers a wide range of national and international problems. The anti-war *Indochina Bulletin*, *Indochina Chronicle*, and *Indochina Focal Point* give detailed information on what is happening in that part of the world, and *Understanding China Newsletter* wants to improve our relations with the mainland.

An unusual type of periodical is put out by young American deserters and draft evaders in various countries. Stockholm's American Exile Newsletter describes itself as "a means for keeping our identity, reaffirming our refusal to grease the war machine, and strengthen[ing] our ties with fellow resisters around the world."

For a fuller discussion of peace periodicals, see the appropriate chapters in our previous volumes. --Janet Spahn

## ACROSS FRONTIERS

Philip Isely, Ed.
1480 Hoyt St. (Suite 31)
Lakewood, Colo. 80215
Irregular; no price at present

Started: 1958
Circulation: 4,000
Format: 6 pages (8 3/4" x 11 1/4")
Issue examined: No. 9 (1972)

This is the newsletter of the World Constitution and Parliament Association, an international peace organization with headquarters in Colorado and regional offices in England, Denmark, India, Pakistan, Bangladesh, Ceylon, Ghana, Nigeria, Mexico, Australia, the Philippines, and South Vietnam. According to the sample issue, the organization had recently run full-page ads in The New York Review of Books, Ramparts, The Humanist, The Progressive, and The New Republic. The Association's goals include the forming of a world government, with a world university and world citizenship. It also supports international auxiliary languages such as Esperanto. It is opposed to the testing or installation of nuclear weapons, the super-sonic transport, off-shore drilling for oil, the use of DDT, military conscription, and other dangers to mankind.

The newsletter consists of letters to the editor (from various supportive organizations) and reports from the world office (and local chapters) on progress toward and plans for the goal: one world that allows for diversity (political, economic, cultural, religious, and philosophical). (JEH)

## AMERICAN EXILE NEWSLETTER

Bill Schiller, Co-Ed.
Schlytersvägen 61 post: 126 49
Stockholm, Sweden
Monthly; $3 (free to war resisters)

Started: Jan. 1972
Circulation: 300
Format: 20 pages (mimeo.)

Issues examined: Nov. 1973-Jan. 1974 | Back issues available from publisher

This newsletter is published by the Center for American Exiles in Sweden. The editors describe the publication as "a means for keeping our identity, reaffirming our refusal to grease the war machine and strengthen our ties with fellow war resisters around the world." The newsletter provides information on special activities open to American exiles in Sweden. Cultural activities, job training opportunities and availability of gym facilities for sports are among the services promulgated. Reports on the food collective and financial reports on community projects are also published in the newsletter. Names and addresses of persons and organizations dedicated to aiding American exiles in Sweden are listed in every issue. Included among these is a "counselor who can give information for those who are really dissatisfied with life in Sweden and are determined to change scenes."

News of war resistance efforts in other countries usually occupies a prominent part of the newsletter. Information on feminist causes is sometimes featured. Readers are invited to contribute "letters, suggestions and original comments" and to help with the various operations of publication. Editorial censorship of written contributions is not practiced, but, as explained by the co-editor, the definite editorial viewpoint results inevitably from the character of the contributing group: "The publication is, by the nature of the war resisters' very reason for existence, anti-war and anti-imperialistic." (SMA)

ANOTHER MOTHER FOR PEACE

407 N. Maple Dr.
Beverly Hills, Calif. 90210
Bi-monthly; $3
Started: Oct. 1967
Circulation: 250,000

Format: 4 pages
Issues examined: Dec. 1970; Feb., Apr., June, Oct., Dec. 1971

"Another Mother for Peace is a non-profit, non-partisan association whose goal is to eliminate war as a means of settling disputes between nations, peoples, and ideologies. To accomplish this we seek to educate women to take an active role in creating peace by re-establishing the dialogue between them and their elected representatives in Washington, thereby strengthening our Democracy." The organization's newsletter is usually made up of letters: from soldiers, from veterans, or from the distraught parents of sons whose lives were being (or had been) taken by the Vietnam War. Occasionally, nationally-recognized figures have contributed letters. (Daniel Berrigan wrote one at Christmastime, 1971.) Some of the letters are poignant, others are angry voices crying out for change; most are articulate and moving.

Each issue of the newsletter usually focuses on one topic: POWs; oil in Southeast Asia; or the Daniel Ellsberg case (with Pat Ellsberg writing a short letter of appreciation for the support given her husband). The newsletter serves not only as a forum for individual pleas for peace and cries of outrage: a regular feature ("Peace Homework") contains concrete suggestions for action: contributing money to various funds and peace organizations; writing letters to Congressmen and other public officials about specific bills and issues (all of which are carefully explained to the reader); boycotting certain products; or sealing mail with peace stickers. Occasionally the newsletter will contain pertinent excerpts from other sources (the Pentagon Papers and a speech by a lieutenant before the Senate Foreign Relations Committee, for example). None of the material in the newsletter is peripheral to the cause of peace in Vietnam: all of the articles and letters are directly focused on ending the war. (SA)

Business Executives Move for New National Priorities
NEWS NOTES

901 N. Howard St.
Baltimore, Md. 21201
5 or 6 issues a year; $5
Started: 1967
Circulation: 5,500

Format: 4 pages (offset)
Issues examined: 1 June, 5 July, 26 Nov. 1973
Some back issues available from publisher

When BEM was founded, its objective was to end our participation in the Vietnam war, and its name reflected this: Business Executives Move for Vietnam Peace. It has since broadened its activities and changed its name. BEM feels that it is unique and effective because its members represent an important segment of our society--a segment often accused of favoring military expenditures over civilian and domestic ones. Members try to influence legislation by lobbying: phone calls to Congressmen, and appearances before Congressional committees. In addition to business sponsors, BEM has military and diplomatic sponsors, including John Kenneth Galbraith (former ambassador to India), and Edwin Reischauer (former ambassador to Japan). "One indication of our effectiveness," boasts News Notes, "is that BEM was prominent in John Dean's list of President Nixon's Political Enemies." (Dean had been Counsel to the President.)

Besides keeping an eye on Vietnam, BEM watches government spending, and favors the meeting of urgent domestic needs rather than alleged military ones. In this, it works with other organizations in the Coalition To Stop Funding the War and the Coalition on National Priorities. It also keeps in contact with such research organizations as the Arms Control Association and the Center for Defense Information. Examples of things that BEM has recently opposed: a huge increase in funds sought by the Pentagon; the transfer of funds from one account to another in order to pay for U.S. bombing in Cambodia; and a foreign aid bill which included funds for Gen. Thieu's secret police and interrogation center in South Vietnam.

News Notes keeps track of Congressmen's votes on pertinent legislation; reprints portions of the Congressional Record; urges members to write to their representatives and express their opinions; discusses upcoming bills and BEM's plans for dealing with them; and occasionally recommends books or pamphlets. (JMS; TJS)

Feedback:

Editor proposed a minor correction, which has been incorporated into the review.

## CANADIAN PEACE RESEARCH INSTITUTE NEWS REPORT

119 Thomas St.
Oakville, Ont., Canada
L6J 3A7
Quarterly; free
Started: 1962
Circulation: 1,400

Format: 4 pages (7" x 8 1/2", offset)
Issues examined: Aug. 1972; May & Nov. 1973
Some back issues available from publisher

> Peace research is a new application of scientific discipline. It utilizes economics, history, psychology, sociology, political science, law, and the physical sciences. Its aim is to use the techniques of scientific research to re-examine the causes of war and to develop practical peace-keeping methods that could be applied through the United Nations or through governments.
>
> The ... Institute is one of many groups attempting to establish ground-rules for this new branch of

science--the science of peace. It is a non-profit non-partisan organization entirely supported by public donations and foundation grants.

The Report comments on studies, meetings, projects, publications, and public statements by members of CPRI, and draws attention to events and recent publications of interest to members. The August 1972 issue discusses the implications of The Limits to Growth and agrees with that book's theory that "To achieve a livable equilibrium, zero economic growth and zero population growth must be realized in the next two decades."

The May 1973 issue discusses one of CPRI's projects, a study of civil war. The November 1973 issue discusses the Middle East war and says: "We must reduce arms shipments to the Middle East, especially from the major powers; maintain a U.N. peace-keeping force in the Middle East now and through 1976; resolve the Palestinian refugee problem which is at the heart of the tension." The same issue discusses the concept of a World University in Canada; mentions some sizeable grants received by the Institute; and laments the demise (through Richard Nixon's budget cuts) of the U.S. Arms Control and Disarmament Agency's quarterly abstracts journal, Arms Control and Disarmament, which CPRI had considered a sister publication to its own Peace Research Abstracts Journal (750 abstracts a month). CPRI had had a friendly exchange agreement with the American publication, by means of which abstracts in one journal might be reprinted in the other. (JMS)

Feedback:

"Read with interest and happily o.k'd."

## COUNTERSPY and INTELLIGENCE REPORT

CARIC
Box 647, Ben Franklin Sta.
Washington, D.C. 20044
Counterspy: quarterly; IR: bi-weekly; $6 ($10 to organizations)
Started: Spring 1973
Circulation: 1,000

Format: C, 24 pages; IR, 4-12 pages. Both offset
Issues examined: C, Fall 1973; IR, Special Report #3
Back issues of Counterspy available from publisher

Counterspy and Intelligence Report are:

> the official publications of the Committee for Action/Research on the Intelligence Community (CARIC). Each issue presents information and analysis on different aspects of the U.S. intelligence effort. Written in non-hysterical lay terms, the publications of CARIC--prepared by former U.S. intelligence workers--promote a deeper public understanding of the tax-financed activities and structure of our government's security community in an age of increasing repression and secrecy. It is CARIC's aim not to raise the American public's level of paranoia, but its level of education as to our government's operations in the taxpayer's name.

The two publications complement each other: one is bi-weekly and the other is quarterly. Both present detailed reports on the work of the American Intelligence Community ("an amorphous grouping of U.S. personnel and agencies having input into secret government operations") in other countries and within the United States. For example, one issue concentrated on the history of the AIC's involvement with Cambodia; another focussed on Chile. In addition to describing the activities of the AIC, the articles identify and provide brief descriptions of people who are working as agents in those countries.

In a pamphlet accompanying one issue of Counterspy, CARIC's attitudes and goals are further defined:

> Although CARIC does believe that a massive government spy apparatus is at work in the world, we hope to dispel some of the paranoia citizens naturally feel when there is talk of spies and wiretaps. We know that the FBI does not have agents behind every tree, but there are agents in every major community in this country who have spied on innocent private and public citizens. Only a full and undisguised look into this hidden world can displace unwarranted fears, and guide the public effort to end this illegal and unjustified espionage. The secrecy with which the government surrounds itself must end.

(CT)

DISARMAMENT NEWS & VIEWS

Nathaniel F. Cullinan, Publ.
211 E. 43rd St.
N.Y., N.Y. 10017

Bi-weekly; $36
Started: Sept. 1970
Format: 4 pages (offset)

Issues examined: 7 & 21 Oct., 4 & 18 Nov. 1973

Microform version available from Xerox University Microfilms

Disarmament News & Views is an apt title for this compact collection of hard news relating to disarmament. Military growth is cited. House and Senate approval of weapons or missile programs is reported. Diverse topics such as chemical warfare and disarmament talks are noted.

Liberal use is made of reprinted material from such impeccable sources as The New York Times and the Wall Street Journal. Other well-known sources used were Newsweek and Business Week. An occasional comment is injected by the editor into what otherwise is almost a straight news treatment. Each item is numbered, and if a topic is treated again, earlier references to it are cited.

One regular feature itemizes military spending. Companies receiving current defense contracts are listed alphabetically. Amounts to be spent and services contracted are then quoted.

Editorial policy as indicated by the editor is: "Developing, I think would be the word. Am beginning to think civil disarmament may be necessary prelude to gaining support or understanding of need and practicality of national disarmament." (MN)

Feedback:

"Excellent."

FREEDOM & UNION: Magazine of the Democratic World

Clarence Streit, Ed.
Federal Union
1736 Columbia Rd. N.W.
(Suite 402)
Washington, D.C. 20009
Bi-monthly; $5
Started: 1946
Circulation: 8,000

Format: 24 pages (offset)
Issues examined: Aug./Sept. 1972; Jan./Feb. & Mar./June 1973
Indexing: PAIS Bulletin
Back issues available from publisher

Supports the concept of an Atlantic Union or Federation as the eventual goal of NATO--in other words, the transformation of the NATO military alliance into a federal union which would be a member of the United Nations. (Each nation would, however, continue to govern its national affairs in complete independence.)

## INDOCHINA BULLETIN

Asia Information Group in California
Box 4400
Berkeley, Calif. 94704
and Indochina News Project
852 W. Belmont Ave.
Chicago, Ill. 60657
Monthly; $3 (institutions $5)

Started: Apr. 1972
Circulation: 50,000
Format: 4-page tabloid (offset)
Issues examined: 22 Sept.-6 Oct. & 4-14 Dec. 1972 (under title War Bulletin); 23 Feb.-15 Mar. 1973

The publication changed its title from War Bulletin to Indochina Bulletin with the 23 February issue. The Bulletin provides "accurate up-to-date news" and "analysis about Indochina and U.S. involvement in the area" plus "anti-war activities in the U.S." The Bulletin uses a variety of news sources "not often seen in the U.S. press." Among the sources are "Vietnam News Agency (Hanoi), Giai Phong Press Agency (PRG, South Vietnam), Agence France Presse (France), Prensa Latina (Cuba), and Radio Hanoi's Voice of Vietnam Program, Far Eastern Economic Review (Hong Kong), Pacific News Service (San Francisco), eyewitness accounts from visitors to Indochina, and U.S. press sources."

## INDOCHINA CHRONICLE

Indochina Resource Center
Box 4,000 D
Berkeley, Calif. 94704
10 issues a year; $5
Started: July 1971
Circulation: 2,000

Format: 12-24 pages (offset)
Issues examined: 11 June, 31 Aug., 23 Nov. 1973
Back issues available from publisher

The Indochina Chronicle is published by the Indochina Resource Center. According to the Co-Director of the Center, it "provides reasonably specialized, [detailed] ... discussion of all facets of the continuing Indochina question--political, military, economic, social, and cultural. It is designed to be read by people who want more than the establishment press offers them. Most of the authors are Indochina area specialists, and this provides them with a means to get their relevant work to a largely non-academic audience."

Each issue examines a different aspect of the Indochina situation. A long feature article runs nearly the entire length of the journal, accompanied by one or two short related articles. The three sample issues are devoted to Laos, refugees in Vietnam, and Congress and Indochina. Articles detail the series of events and phases of the war leading up to the current situation being considered. The agreements, tactics, political maneuverings, and probable motives of the U.S., North and South Vietnamese governments are interpreted and criticized. The journal reviews Congressional legislation, Supreme Court decisions, and Executive orders, with regard to how effective they were, and how they were carried out. Emphasis is placed upon the negative effects that the war has had upon Indochina's own citizens (particularly refugees). Articles in the Chronicle quote from many outside sources, including newspapers, other journals, books, Congressional hearings, and governmental reports and statistics. Short bibliographies of additional materials of interest are included in some issues. The experiences and observations of American and European volunteers working in Indochina areas are sometimes related.

The writers and editors of Indochina Chronicle stress the idea that, throughout the entire war, the people of Indochina have been political pawns of foreigners, and innocent victims of policies that are designed to promote and support the military and political goals of the governments, rather than to fulfill the needs of the people living in Indochina. Articles expose their plight--the dehumanizing and dangerous conditions, and the suffering that the Vietnamese have experienced since the war began. The cruelties and miseries that have been inflicted upon them in prisons, rural camps, and urban slums are described, and emphasized with photographs. The journal attempts to point out the undesirable changes that the constant psychological warfare, bombing, and relocation have made on their traditional ways of life. It accuses the U.S. government of attempting to "cover up the scope and magnitude of bombing," and of deceiving the American people regarding the actual extent of U.S. involvement in the war. It also deplores the fact that so many Americans are unaware of, or apathetic toward the plight of Indochina refugees and orphans.

The Indochina Chronicle desires permanent peace for the people. It recommends total U.S. withdrawal from Indochina; an end to U.S. support of the Saigon government; and an end to the bombing. It desires an active reconstruction program that would actually aid the people of Indochina, and that would give them the freedom to live where they prefer to live, allowing them to return to their traditional ways of life. One article suggested that budgetary allotments should be used to encourage "diversification and innovation instead of single-minded attention to propping up puppet administrations." Readers are urged to act in behalf of the refugees.

(PMK)

Feedback:
Editor suggested several minor changes of wording, which have been incorporated into the review.

INDOCHINA FOCAL POINT

National Resource Center,
Indochina Peace Campaign
181 Pier Ave.
Santa Monica, Calif. 90405
Bi-weekly; $4
Started: Aug. 1973

Issues examined: 1 Sept. & 16 Dec. 1973; 15 Jan. & 1 Feb. 1974
Back issues available from publisher

The publication sent this information: IPC wants to stop all U.S. aggression in Indochina, so that "peace and self-determination" can be achieved there. The South Vietnam government of Nguyen Van Thieu is "the world's most massive police state"; its political prisoners should be freed, and "a government of national reconciliation" created in its stead. Americans who opposed the Indochina war should not be subject to legal persecution. The U.S. presidency should be deprived of its power to dictate this country's Indochina policy. Part of IFP's mission is to print "news and information 'blacked-out' by the mass media."

The organization also publishes Indochina Peace Campaign Report, an irregularly-produced leaflet.

International Registry of World Citizens INFORMATION BULLETIN

55 Rue Lacepède
75005 Paris, France
Semi-annual; 4 francs
Circulation: 5,000

Format: 4 pages (8" x 12")
Issues examined: Jan. & Nov. 1973

The goal of this organization is world government. An editorial in the Bulletin's November 1973 issue, after denouncing the coup in Chile (against the elected Marxist government of Dr. Salvador Allende) "perpetrated with the support of foreign political and financial forces," goes on to explain the political philosophy of the organization:

> The political and economic forces of world domination have not allowed the poor peoples to take their fate in their hands and find the way to development.
> ...

> The freedom of expression of peoples or men can only be respected by a World Law, whether it concerns the Chilean People or the Soviet scientist, Andrei Sakharov, father of the Russian atomic bomb, who is at present being troubled and watched.... We think that the present structure of the world divided into sovereign Nation States can only eternally continue the same fatal errors and lead to the same catastrophic situations.

The Bulletin reports on the activities of the organization throughout the world, and gives news of other organizations and events of interest to World Citizens. (JMS)

## THE PEACE GAZETTE

Rick Hind, Exec. Dir.
Clergy and Laity Concerned
535 Schenectady St.
Schenectady, N.Y. 12307
Monthly; donation
Started: Nov. 1971
Circulation: 400-600

Format: 4-12 pages (8" x 11" & 8" x 14", mimeo.)
Issues examined: Vol. 2, Nos. 10-12 (No. 12 is dated Oct. 1973)
Back issues available from publisher

The Peace Gazette is published by the Schenectady area Clergy and Laity Concerned to "provide accurate information and view-points concerning peace, justice, non-violence, [and] the military industrial complex." Although the United States is officially at peace, the position of the Gazette is that "a nation which budgets over one-half of its income for 'defense' is not at peace at home or abroad."

A calendar of meetings, vigils, leafletting, films, and TV programs begins each issue. Articles discuss the war related problems of amnesty, political prisoners in Saigon, Vietnamese orphans, war crimes, and defense budgets. Other subjects of continuing concern are the problems faced by the American Indian and the migrant farm worker. International problems are also covered: starvation in North Africa; the official position of the United States government in Rhodesia and Chile; etc.

Regular features are poems; recipes; letters; and a list of bills before Congress, with sponsors. Speeches and articles by Daniel Berrigan, William Sloane Coffin, Jr., and others active in the peace movement are reprinted. Readers are encouraged to write letters, to take part in vigils, boycotts and fund raising; in short, "to do all they can to oppose U.S. war policies and promote peace." (JS)

Feedback:
Editor expressed no disapproval.

PEACELETTER

Women Strike for Peace
799 Broadway
N.Y., N.Y. 10003
Monthly; $5
Started: Dec. 1966

Circulation: 2,000
Format: 8-14 pages (legal size)
Issues examined: Apr.-June 1973; Jan., Apr., June 1974

Women Strike for Peace is the name for many loosely-organized groups operating around the country. It was begun in 1961 when "in response to a call from a few Washington housewives, women across the country held public walks and meetings, and visited officials, appealing to all governments to End the Arms Race, not the Human Race." (There are dozens of local WSP newsletters and a National Memo.) The organization says it has

> caused endless discussion in local communities, by walks, vigils, forums, panels; by emblems, seals, car stickers, umbrellas; by tables in shopping centers, neighborhood meetings, letter-writing campaigns; and by distributing millions of pieces of literature ... about radiation, shelters, the spiralling arms race, and the war in Vietnam.

The "WSP Action Agenda" says that the organization will work to "stop American intervention in Indochina"; "use [our] national resources to eradicate poverty and inequality at home"; "ban ... production and use of chemical and biological weapons"; get "a total nuclear test ban treaty and an end to nuclear proliferation--No ABM--No MIRV! Let's start world disarmament!"; achieve a new U.S. foreign policy ("No more military intervention in the affairs of other countries!"); and "repeal ... the Selective Service System." WSP also supports universal amnesty, and believes that "no distinction should be made between draft resisters, military deserters, self-retired veterans, [and the] dishonorably discharged."

This activist publication covers WSP's activities and contains short articles on current legislation, congressional reports, anti-war conferences, demonstrations, military installations and spending, the problems of farm workers, the continuing war in Southeast Asia, and multi-national corporations. Other topics: "Arming the 3rd World" (biggest arms deal in history is the sale of U.S. planes, helicopters, and missiles to the Shah of Iran); a new poison gas developed by the Army; children in Vietnamese prisons; the torture of Spanish political prisoners; Green Berets in the Philippines ("quietly working in a manner that is identical to U.S. military activity in Indochina 10 years ago"); the possibility of American military intervention to seize Middle East oil fields; poverty and starvation in Latin America; the establishment of Junior ROTC units in New York; child labor on farms; U.S. plans to build a naval and air support base on an island in the Indian Ocean (condemned as an escalation of outside military presence in the area); toy guns for children manufactured by a subsidiary of Quaker Oats (readers urged to protest by letter); atrocities committed by the South Vietnamese army against Vietnamese villagers; and Haitian refugees who have escaped to the U.S. (jailed by U.S. authorities and deported back to Haiti to face death and torture by the Duvalier dictatorship--readers asked to protest). Information for articles comes from a wide range of sources such as the New York Times; Washington Post; London Times; Boston After Dark (weekly underground); Akwesasne Notes (American Indian tabloid); (London) Medical Aid Newsletter; and other WSP newsletters.

Although an editorial statement in the June 1974 issue condemns Arab terrorism and supports Israel's right to a secure existence, it also supports self-determination for the Palestinian Arabs and the return of Arab territories occupied by Israel since 1967.

Each issue contains a calendar of WSP and other events. Petitions are often included and members are urged to write to Congressmen and other (presumably) influential persons.

(JMS)

Feedback:

The editor felt that our original review did not "accurately reflect our program or our basis as an organization or movement." She sent more recent material, saying that she intended to prepare another review herself. Since she never did, we rewrote the review, taking cognizance of the new material she had supplied.

PEACEWORK: New England Tax Resistance, Anti-Draft, and Peace Movement Newsletter

American Friends Service Committee
48 Inman St.
Cambridge, Mass. 02139
Monthly; $3
Started: Jan. 1973 (with

present title and format)
Circulation: 2,000
Format: 8-12 pages (offset)
Issues examined: Sept. 1973-Jan. 1974
Some back issues available from publisher

The editor sent this background information: "Final Draft merged with a war tax resistance newsletter, Only for Life, in the Spring of 1972. As of January 1973, they became Peacework." The periodical describes itself as follows:

> Formerly an anti-draft and a war tax resistance newsletter, Peacework now attempts to reflect the spectrum of peace movement activities in New England.... [It is] primarily a communications tool, but carries some theoretical and background reporting. It carries letters and articles on upcoming events, speakers, issues, resources, etc.

QUAKER SERVICE BULLETIN

American Friends Service Committee
407 S. Dearborn
Chicago, Ill. 60605
Format: 8-page tabloid (offset)
Issue examined: Winter 1973 "Consolidated Edition"

Reports on national and international activities of AFSC. Includes a section of "Chicago Regional News."

THE RESISTANCE

Semi-monthly; $5
Format: 8- to 12-page tabloid (offset)
Issues examined: 15 May & 15 June 1968

This was published in both a regional and a national edition by the 500 men of the New England Resistance, a group devoted to "building a humane society through ending the draft, the war in Vietnam, and racism."

The articles reflected these concerns, and were strongly opposed to the war and the draft. The sample issues focused on the following events: the opening of the trial of Dr. Benjamin Spock and the "Boston Five," with an examination of the issues involved, and sketches of the principals; news of two resisters who received religious asylum but were nonetheless seized by FBI agents; the U.S. Supreme Court decision making the willful destruction of draft cards a crime; a Poor People's March on Washington, D.C.; and the burning of draft files by Fr. Philip Berrigan and the "Baltimore Nine." There was also news of what was happening with the movement nationally: induction refusals, suits filed, progress of trials, protests held, and signed advertisements placed in periodicals.

The Resistance not only reported news of the peace movement, but provided a network of support to sympathizers. (JW)

Feedback:

Mail returned in August 1973, marked "Moved, not forwardable." Address had been: 27 Stanhope St., Boston, Mass. 02116.

TAX TALK

War Tax Resistance
912 E. 31st St.
Kansas City, Mo. 64109
Bi-monthly; $3
Started: Dec. 1969
Circulation: 3,500

Format: 8- to 12-page tabloid
Issues examined: Aug., Sept., Dec. 1973
Back issues available from publisher

WTR is committed to changing U.S. "military and financial priorities. We advocate open, principled refusal to pay federal taxes, the majority of which support the military, and encourage resisters to join together with other resisters to pool their resisted taxes and use them to meet community needs."

Tax Talk contains articles on tax resisters, court cases, the U.S. military budget, U.S. arms sales to the Middle East (criticized), the principles of non-violence, the Roxbury War Tax Scholarship Fund (a proposed alternative for taxes), overthrow of the elected Marxist government of Dr. Salvador Allende in Chile, resistance to the telephone tax, and a tax protest in France. Regular features include letters to the editor; news from WTR centers around the country; and "To Live outside the Law You Have to Be Honest," which discusses points of law and tactics to use in tax resistance. The September 1973 issue contained a summary of arrests of WTR members since 1970. (JMS)

## UNDERSTANDING CHINA NEWSLETTER

Louise Bennett, Ed.
Understanding China Committee, American Friends Service Committee
Box 203
Ann Arbor, Mich. 48107
$3
Format: 8 pages (offset)
Issue examined: Sept. 1971

The Newsletter seeks "to make at least a small contribution toward improving U.S.-China relations by: seeking to report and interpret what is happening in China; evaluating developments in U.S. policy toward China, believing that changes in that policy hold the key to breaking the present stalemate; encouraging more communication in the hope that increased mutual understanding will lead both sides to seek an honorable settlement of their differences and take the road to peace and cooperation."

A form letter said that AFSC was hoping to re-establish (after 20 years) its Chinese programs and that AFSC representatives were visiting China. Also, a number of Concerned Asian Scholars (sponsored by that group and AFSC) had recently visited China, and their impressions were to appear in the Newsletter.

Feedback:

Mail returned March 1975 marked "Moved, left no address."

## WASHINGTON PEACE CENTER NEWSLETTER

Mary Bray Norton, Ed.
2111 Florida Ave. N.W.
Washington, D.C. 20008
Monthly; $5
Started: 1970
Circulation: 1,800
Format: 8-16 pages (offset)
Issues examined: Oct.-Dec. 1973
Back issues available from publisher

"Our policy is flexible, depending upon the situation. But basically the Newsletter is an educational and informational tool concerning groups, especially local, who espouse peace ... or justice through non-violent means; and ... we try to deal with [issues or events] in more depth than the media, or with other facts not brought out ... [by them]. Some of our issues emphasize one issue ... and others are just straight news of the Peace Center and other groups."

Some of the "other groups" covered were the United

Farm Workers, National Welfare Rights Organization, Washington Area Impeachment Coalition, Washington Area Committee Against Repressive Legislation, and Attica Legal Defense Fund.

The December 1973 issue concentrated on the "Energy Crisis," accusing the oil companies of making huge profits; the October issue was on the military coup that overthrew the elected Marxist government of Dr. Salvador Allende ("First Victim of Nixon-Kissinger 'Low Profile' Strategy"); and the November issue (on the Middle East) advised Israel to give up conquered territories and recognize the national aspirations of the Palestinians, and advised the Arabs to recognize Israel as a sovereign state.

The Center's Amnesty Project ("a co-operative effort, emphasizing an educational campaign, with a new organization, the National Campus Alliance for Amnesty") supports complete and unconditional amnesty for deserters and draft resisters.

Each issue includes a calendar listing activities of interest to Center members. (JMS)

## WORLD CITIZEN/FEDERALIST LETTER

Michael Shower, Ed.
World Federalists, USA
2029 K St., N.W. (5th fl.)
Washington, D.C. 20006
11 issues a year; $5
Started: (combining WC & FL) Oct. 1973
Circulation: 22,000

Format: 16- to 20-page tabloid
Issues examined: WC/FL Oct./Nov. & Dec. 1973; WC Sept. 1973
Some back issues available from publisher

This "is the joint publication of World Federalists, USA, and Action for World Community (World Federalist Youth), and succeeds the separate publications of The Federalist Letter and The World Citizen (formerly To Free Mankind)." It "is concerned with issues of global problems which can be solved through global cooperation," and covers "news of US and UN legislation, of activities within the general world order movement and our own organizations; and signed articles or reprints ... or speeches/documents which contribute to the provocation of public discussion of issues of global concern." (See our review of The Federalist on page 246, Volume I.)

## WORLD FEDERALIST

World Association of World Federalists
63 Sparks St.
Ottawa, Ont., Canada K1P 5A6
Quarterly; $3

Circulation: 4,000
Format: 20 pages (offset)
Issues examined: Jan.-Oct. 1973
Recent back issues available from publisher

See reviews of The Federalist and World Citizen/Federalist Letter.

## WORLD PEACE NEWS

American Movement for World Government
777 United Nations Plaza (11th floor)
N. Y., N. Y. 10017
10 issues a year; $5
Started: Nov. 1970

Circulation: 2,000
Format: 8-page tabloid (offset)
Issues examined: Oct.-Dec. 1973
Back issues available from publisher (complete file $20)

World Peace News, "while maintaining its editorial and publishing autonomy, recently became the publication of the American Movement for World Government." According to this periodical, the ills of today's world--poverty, war, pollution, over-population, etc.--will improve only when world law is enforced by democratic, federal world government. Tom Liggett, editor and publisher, states the viewpoint of the magazine as to how this can best be brought about: "Although we tend to believe that the surest and therefore the best way to develop federal world government is through the United Nations, we think the U. N. status quo is more a part of the problem than the solution."

Luther H. Evans, President of World Federalists, USA, is an editorial advisor of this independent publication which prints U. N. news, interviews with prominent people, and reports on various troubled countries. An article in the November 1973 issue asserts that "World Government is Backed by Irish, Indian Leaders at U.N. General Assembly" (Feedback: "and articles in the Oct. and Nov. 1974 issues report that the governments of Norway, Denmark, and West Germany contributed money to an independent group ... planning to set up an institute to research and write a ... constitution for [a] ... world government.").

The overriding concern of the contributors is the U. N. 's

ability to function strongly and effectively, and their general attitude is not hopeful. (Feedback: Replace "not hopeful" with "critical of the U. N. establishment and national governments for not acting on the insights of Albert Einstein and others.") "Fewer and fewer U. N. pronouncements these days spread optimism that the U. N. leadership will militate for the authority it needs to carry out its most basic purposes."

(GKS)

Feedback:

"We're in the middle--if anywhere--on this spectrum.... Looks as though you're doing a good and important job." Some of the editor's suggestions were incorporated into the text.

## Chapter 17

## SERVICEMEN'S PAPERS

> Join the Navy. Travel to exotic, distant lands. Meet exciting, unusual people--and kill them. ---Up From the Bottom

Because America is no longer deeply involved in the Vietnam War, and because our armed forces are now staffed with volunteers, these papers are fading out of existence.* (See our previous volumes for a fuller discussion of the genre.) Rage is a GI paper from North Carolina; Up From the Bottom is aimed more at sailors. Winter Soldier is published by Vietnam Veterans Against the War, who oppose American military and commercial presence in Southeast Asia, as well as in Africa and Latin America. The organization wants to change the social, political, and economic institutions that caused and perpetuated the war, and to end racism and sexism. Consequently, its periodical covers a wider range of topics than most such papers. --Janet Spahn

*"There were 10 underground GI newspapers in Germany a few years ago. Only two are left." Paul Kemezis, "GIs in Europe Are 'Cooler' Than Those of Vietnam Era, But Many Defy Old-Army Rules," The New York Times, 21 April 1975, p. 19.

### FORWARD

1 Berlin 45, Postfach 163, West Germany
Monthly; free (institutions $25)
Started: Jan. 1971

Circulation: 2,000
Format: 20 pages (offset)
Issues examined: none sent
Back issues available from publisher

"Forward is dedicated to the political principle of people's democracy.... Specifically, it aims to provide U.S. service people with the information not available ... [through]

Pentagon sifted channels (S[tars] & S[tripes], A[rmed] F[orces] N[etwork]); legal advice; and a progressive political perspective on current political affairs. It is also dedicated to the struggle for the emancipation of men and women. The Forward staff is a collective."

GRAPES OF WRATH

The Defense Committee (Tidewater)
Box 1492
Norfolk, Va. 23501
Monthly; $2
Started: Nov. 1972

Circulation: 8,000
Format: 12 pages (12" x 15")
Issues examined: none sent
Back issues available from publisher

This is published by "an organization of enlisted men and women, their families and friends, workers for the rights and betterment of enlisted people. The Committee is founded on a Statement of Principles that is class-conscious, anti-racist, anti-sexist, and anti-imperialist."

RAGE

Box 301
Jacksonville, N.C. 28540
Monthly; free
Started: Oct. 1971
Circulation: 2,000

Format: 8-12 pages (11 1/2" x 15 1/2", offset)
Issues examined: none sent
Back issues available from publisher

The publication sent this information: "The paper is put out by active duty GIs, vets, and civilian dependents. Articles and other contributions are viewed by everyone working on the paper, and in that way suggestions are made, and articles refined to their finished state. At the present time we feel there is no need for a permanent editor."

UP FROM THE BOTTOM--By and for San Diego Based Servicemen, Women, Family, and Friends

Box 2016
San Diego, Calif. 92102
Every 4-6 weeks; $6 (civilians), $10 (libraries)
Started: Spring 1971

Circulation: 6,000
Format: 12-page tabloid (offset)
Issues examined: Apr., 15 May, 15 Dec. 1973

Up From the Bottom is published chiefly for servicemen and their acquaintances. Its publication appears to be a co-operative enterprise involving the donated services of enlisted men, veterans, and sympathetic civilians. The paper consists mainly of letters and articles submitted by readers. Its purpose can be inferred from the very first line printed under the title on the front page of each issue: "D. O. D. DIRECTIVE 1325. 6: THIS IS YOUR PERSONAL PROPERTY AND CANNOT LEGALLY BE TAKEN FROM YOU." Most of the articles deal with grievances alleged by enlisted men (especially Navy personnel) against their officers, and with possible means of legal redress. The following clear statement of the publishers' goals has appeared in some issues, accompanying a plea for help in producing the paper:

> We know that there are a lot of things that need to be changed in the military. We believe that the only way that'll ever happen is if we make it happen. We believe that it's right for people to fight to better their lives, and that all of us--in the military and out--need to support each other if things really are going to get better.
>
> Because we believe this, we put out Up From the Bottom--to inform you of your rights under the UCMJ, to make you more aware of what's wrong with the military and why, to give you a way to express your opinion and air your gripes, and to let you know you are not alone in fighting back against the system.

The paper features many cartoons satirizing various aspects of military life. One large illustration bore the following caption, printed in capital letters spread over two pages: "Join the Navy. Travel to exotic, distant lands. Meet exciting, unusual people/and kill them." (SMA)

Feedback:

"We have no objection to this draft. Our feeling is that the poster is not representative of the paper or its line, and that it was much more of a one-time affair than other material you mention. The description would probably be more accurate without it."

## WINTER SOLDIER

827 W. Newport<br>Chicago, Ill. 60657

Monthly; $6 ($3 for GIs, $15 for institutions)

Started: Oct. 1971 (offset, color, web press)
Circulation: 25,000 Issues examined: Sept.-Nov.
Format: 16-page tabloid 1973

Winter Soldier (originally named The First Casualty) is the official publication of the Vietnam Veterans Against the War/Winter Soldier Organization. A history of the organization and a detailed description of its objectives appear in each issue. Members oppose U.S. presence--military and commercial--in Southeast Asia as well as in Africa and Latin America; they also oppose such evils as racism and sexism which promote war. "We understand [that] this war is imperialist in origin, and affirm that the membership of VVAW/WSO is not only concerned with ending this war, but with changing the domestic, social, political, and economic institutions that have caused and perpetuated" it. Membership is open to anyone agreeing with these objectives, as "all Americans are in fact Vietnam veterans." Activities of the organization range from those oriented toward the military (military counseling and efforts to secure unconditional amnesty for war resisters) to more local community projects to ease the oppression of "working and third world people at home and around the world." Winter Soldier serves as a news forum for these activities, and its contents represent the concerns and programs of the organization.

Coverage of important news stories continues from issue to issue. Some of these recurring topics in the autumn of 1973 were: the trial of the "Gainesville 8" (members of the organization charged with trying to commit acts of violence during the 1972 Republican national convention); the continuing state of war in Indochina after "peace" had been achieved; and the right-wing military coup that toppled Salvador Allende's Marxist government in Chile. (After the Chilean coup one article presented a fairly long background of the CIA's involvement in that country.)

Veterans' benefits (or the lack of such) and trials of war resisters or protesters also receive frequent coverage. Subjects not directly related to the war but of concern to VVAW are also treated: strikes by the United Farm Workers and the United Auto Workers; prison rebellions; and trials of "political prisoners." These articles often end with a plea for financial support--for defense funds, or for striking laborers. News reports are consistently written from the viewpoint of the organization. (SA)

Feedback:

"We have absolutely no problems with the review."

## Chapter 18

## CONSERVATIVE

> The influx of tens of thousands of left-wing draft dodgers on America's college campuses would constitute a very real and definite threat to our educational system.
> ---Young Americans for Freedom

> ... racial differences are rooted in complicated factors which the busing of school children to achieve 'racial balance' will not remove. ---The Alternative

> ... the present state of unpreparedness and the consequent likelihood of over 60% American fatalities in nuclear war invite aggressor consideration of war against the United States.... ---Survive

Conservative publications are against many things: aid to (and trade or treaties with) communist or socialist countries; foreign entanglements (except for the Korean and Vietnam Wars, and CIA activities abroad); the United Nations; concentration of power in Washington, and federal interference in many spheres of private life (forced integration, school busing, prohibition of compulsory school prayer); sex education; the Equal Rights Amendment; welfare; and reporters.

Conservatives think of themselves as strict constructionists and favor limited government; a "strong military posture" abroad; a tough "law-and-order" stance at home; free enterprise (except when it comes to bailing out failing companies such as Lockheed, or replacing the losses incurred by chicken farmers); God; patriotism; and conscription (although The Pitysmont Post is against "no-win wars and drafting men for service in them"). The Citizen-Observer strongly supported Lt. William Calley, the convicted war criminal, and led a petition drive aimed at freeing him.

The Borger News-Herald, which could have been placed

in the Anti-Communist chapter, warns that "there is a conspiracy to surrender our national sovereignty and the freedom of our people into the framework of a one-world, powerful, Soviet dictatorship." The Citizen-Observer and The National Educator (whose circulation figures may be inflated) may not have trusted us to write impartial reviews, so they sent their own, which we have printed.

Some conservative periodicals with a single cause are Morality in Media Newsletter; The Taxpayers' Committee to End Foreign Aid; The Pink Sheet on the Left, which keeps track of what communists and other radicals are up to; and No Amnesty, a Young Americans for Freedom periodical opposing clemency for draft evaders. (See our Index for other YAF publications.)

Discussion, Evangelical Methodist and The Exalter, and News and Notes of Interest to Christians have a strong religious underpinning and might equally well have been placed in the Metaphysical chapter--except that they engage in some politicking. Discussion, which advocates "racial purity and integrity," shows a racist tinge.

Some of our other chapters (Anti-Communist, Libertarian, and Race Supremacist) include periodicals with conservative traits. --Janet Spahn

## THE ALTERNATIVE

R. Emmett Tyrell, Jr., Ed.
R.R. 11, Box 360
Bloomington, Ind. 47401
9 issues a year; $6
Started: Sept. 1967
Circulation: 30,000
Format: 32 pages (9 1/2" x 13 1/4", offset)

Issues examined: Nov. & Dec. 1973; Mar. 1974
Back issues available from publisher
Microform version available from Xerox University Microfilms

The picture of the late Senator Robert Taft on the November 1973 cover of The Alternative as well as its title provide some clue as to the journal's views. Its managing editor calls it "moderate-to-conservative." Each issue includes a number of regular columns, a few longer articles, and three or four book reviews.

The columns vary in approach from a serious analysis of current politics and ideas to humor. Some of the regular columns are described below:

"The Continuing Crisis" offers brief, sometimes witty comments on current news items, while "Correspondence" presents the viewpoints of readers who praise or are hostile to The Alternative. "Current Wisdom, by Assorted Jackasses" quotes from the American press, prefacing each quotation with a brief, often sharp, comment on why the piece was chosen.

"Brudnoy's Film Index" (quickie film reviews) and his longer "Talkies" (also film criticism) are unusual for The Alternative, because their author rarely expresses an opinion on political, economic, or social problems.

C. Bascom Slump, in "Letter from a Whig," expresses a conservative point of view, and is critical of the Democrats as well as of the Nixon administration: "This is one Republican administration that knows how to alienate its most loyal supporters." In his column on the Spiro Agnew resignation, Slump writes:

> But what is the lesson? I guess it's that they just don't make things like they used to, including party machines. As Plunkett of Tammany Hall observed, good politics means loyalty, all the way to the prison gates.

If not a defense of Agnew, the column is at least a playing-down of his crime on the grounds that the Maryland political game is played that way and that Agnew was "hounded out of office by 'Nixonites.'"

"Public Policy" criticizes the National Welfare Rights organization and busing: the nation's "racial differences are rooted in complicated factors which the busing of school children to achieve 'racial balance' will not remove."

Following the school of humor which by exaggeration carries an idea to its outrageous conclusion, "The Bootblack Stand" offers tongue-in-cheek advice in response to "Dear Abby" letters purportedly written by the famous. Its author states that the IQ of Sen. Joseph Montoya "ranks in the 'vegetable' category."

In its articles, The Alternative presents a variety of subjects within its primarily political sphere of interest. Opinions differ widely, although the general drift is conservative.

In one issue, Thomas Molnar predicts the political form of the society of the future. Other articles deal with the Watergate affair, minimizing its importance, while nevertheless criticizing Richard Nixon. Another represents the European press as believing that American foreign policy would be irrevocably damaged by Nixon's departure from office.

"The California Welfare Reforms of 1971" praises Gov.

Ronald Reagan for cutting back on the welfare rolls, and blames the expanded rolls on overzealous social workers ("about to sell the glories of life on the dole") rather than the state of the economy or the employability of the recipients.

The author of "Everybody Above Average" states a truth unpalatable to many educators:

> The recent problems of higher education spring from educational inflation. An unprecedentedly high proportion of the college-age group--more than 40 percent--now attends college.... Since ... only 25 percent have the required IQ, a significant number cannot benefit unless the curriculum is adapted to their understanding, i.e., degraded.

Other articles present an analysis of Soviet goals in the Middle East, praise the state of Israel, and defend multinational corporations.

The books chosen for review reflect the interests of the editors, whether they are criticized for being contrary to the generally conservative viewpoint espoused or praised for being in agreement. Books written about include a biography of Taft, an attack on the futility of the social sciences, Harold Macmillan's memoirs, a work on the decline of American power, and a book arguing that IQ is largely inherited rather than the product of environment.

The Alternative cultivates a debunking, iconoclastic attitude; it is humorous, rarely taking itself too seriously and often being the first to make fun. It is decorated with the kind of silhouette cutout one might find in Godey's Lady's Book, in what is perhaps an intentional reminder that some of its attitudes--like its illustrations--are usually considered to belong in the last century. It quotes--with good humor rather than outrage--a Rolling Stone (a conservative journal quoting Rolling Stone?) article describing its Editor-in-Chief as a "wild man" and "crazy." In its "Great American Series," which features aphorisms by such patriots as George Washington and Ralph Waldo Emerson, it quotes Donald Segretti, LL.B.: "I really regret getting involved in this [Watergate] thing."

The Alternative can be savage, as well as funny:

> It appears that a new mode of thrill-seeking has claimed its first victim, rock star Steve Perron, who Rolling Stone reports 'died from inhaling vomit during his sleep.'

Contributors have included a former Spiro Agnew press secretary, a Wall Street Journal editor, university professors and graduate students, newspaper writers and other literary professionals, and a White House speech-writer. With few exceptions, they have excellent credentials, and are intelligent, articulate writers, staunchly conservative. Sometimes, however, The Alternative throws us a curve and includes an article by--for example--the National Chairman of the Young People's Socialist League. (BK)

Reviewer's judgment:
"Reading The Alternative is an experience which is thoroughly enjoyable and thoroughly infuriating."

Feedback:
The editor says that recently Alternative has been "publishing a lot more liberals and moderates.... My basic objection to what you say is that you imply that I, as an editor, orchestrate the magazine more carefully than I really do.... I am one of the few editors--I suppose--who really tries to avoid orchestrating a party line in our magazine. Naturally, there are some things that I do not want said in The Alternative, but I attempt to allow a great deal of latitude. I publish many things that I myself do not believe in."

BORGER NEWS-HERALD

J. C. Philips, Ed.
W. Glynn Morris, Publ.
Borger, Tex. 79007
Daily; $22.50
Started: 23 Nov. 1926

Format: daily 14 pages; Sunday 90 pages
Issues examined: 7 & 8 Oct. 1973

The Borger News-Herald is a general daily newspaper: it reports local, national, and international news, and includes such features as women's pages, society, sports, and cultural events. Its editorial policies are strongly conservative. The sample issues contain articles and editorials in support of patriotism, the draft, free enterprise, and a free press; and against communism, the United Nations, foreign entanglements and foreign aid, and the news media in the United States.

The article, "Nation's Hope in UN?" is preceded by the following "Editor's Note":

> Should the Kissinger-Nixon Administration involve us in a war against the Arabs ... are we to presume

> that it would be a holy war, such as the war to make the world safe for 'democracy,' with unconditional surrender of Arab lands ... enthusiastically supported by the controlled news media? Will the U.S. Congress even go so far as to declare war against Egypt and her Semitic Moslem allies?

In observance of "National Newspaper Week," an article by the editor emphasizes his newspaper's commitment to a free and honest press, upholding the principles of Christianity and self-government. The editor comments that the news media seem to focus on only one thing at a time (e.g., Watergate) and this confuses the American audience. In the meantime, he says, we tend to forget such events as our surrender in Korea and in Vietnam, our "accommodation of Moscow and Peking with aid and trade,... [and] the dictatorial busing of school children across town for the purpose of homogenizing the races." He goes on to say:

> Without ... informative and responsible news media, we, the people, are just too feeble to grasp it all; and, therefore, the [communist] conspiracy prospers and flourishes because poorly-informed people cannot believe that there is a conspiracy to surrender our national sovereignty and the freedom of our people into the framework of a one-world, powerful, Soviet dictatorship.... our federal government in the U.S.A. does not own the national news media, WHICH, HOWEVER,... [are] owned or controlled by that handful of ambitious, power-mad men who exercise practically absolute rule over the American people (who are too brainwashed by the news media to know what is going on).

One issue contains the proclamation of "United States Day" and "United States Week" in Hutchinson County, Texas, by a judge of that county. The observance of "United States Day" is intended "to offset a certain powerful influence at work among us," and to promote "a deeper appreciation of the benefits obtainable under our form of government with its powers limited by the Constitution and Bill of Rights." (MG)

Feedback:

"The descriptive matter set forth in your analysis ... seem[s] fairly presented. Thank you. I might mention that I have been editor and manager of the Borger News-Herald (formerly the Borger Daily Herald) since 27 July 1931. I have been connected with the paper since it was first published 23 November 1926."

THE CAMPUS

Box 1089,
Bishop's University
Lennoxville, Quebec, Canada
Weekly; $4
Started: 1944
Circulation: 4,000

Format: 12- to 16-page tabloid (offset)
Issues examined: 4 & 18 Oct. 1973; 24 Jan. 1974
Back issues available from publisher

The Campus, a student newspaper, covers "student activities, politics, and some film and theatre reviews. Editorial policies vary widely from editor to editor." According to an editorial in the paper, "The Campus is one of the tiny minority of university papers today which has a conservative (right-wing) editorial policy. To the best of my knowledge, only one other member paper of CUP (The Cord Weekly) has dared to differ from the general left slant of college papers today."

CHICAGO RAP

Martin Northway, Ed.
5655 S. University
Chicago, Ill. 60637
Weekly (irregular)

Started: Feb. 1971
Format: 8-page tabloid
Issues examined: 12 Feb. & 16 Apr. 1973

The paper (published by students and residents of the area, and serving the Hyde Park and University of Chicago community) carries this description of itself:

> Its purposes are literary and educational. An actual misunderstood underground newspaper in the vanguard of the counter-revolution (there is one?) ... a community ... newspaper dedicated to the dissemination of news and to the stimulation of free intellectual discussion, in the tradition of the Whig newspapers in eighteenth-century Great Britain. [The reviewer did not receive this impression of the paper.] The editors of the Rap welcome--indeed, thrive on--articles and letters (particularly hostile ones) from members of the community.

The February issue carried a description (by the editor) of the paper's founding. The Rap had survived (in "a society as complex and cynical as Hyde Park") against "overwhelming odds," these odds being: (1) competition with a second student-community newspaper, the Maroon, "a hulking, 80-year-old leviathan among student papers" which publishes a huge weekly ad section; (2) the paper's conservative stance; and (3) the survival rate (80% failure) of other papers in environments even more conducive to survival.

> Ever since the founding of Chicago Rap ... there have been those who have deprecated the achievements of the periodical. Because of our relatively conservative stance (compared with the radical and heavily political Maroon), we became the target of rumor and invective. One sensationalist crusading liberal lawyer actually believes that the Rap is secretly funded by the Minutemen.... A mimeographed handout which recently paraded as incarnate campus truth, and as the only truly 'independent' newspaper on campus, claimed that Rap was secretly funded by a certain 'conservative Indiana newspaper editor.'

The editor goes on to explain that the paper's survival is due solely to its advertising.

Unlike other community papers reviewed in the present work, Rap is not concerned with community problems, minorities, racism, and the like. It does not encourage the formation of clinics or self-help groups, nor does it criticize or run exposés of local bureaucrats or businessmen.

The paper covers social and educational activities: prints a "Campus and Community Bulletin Board," reviews movies and plays (usually one of each), and discusses talks given by visiting lecturers on campus. Examples of short articles: "POWs Steal Jane Fonda's Thunder"; "Decline and Fall of the Underground Press"; and "Are Urban Renewers Guilty of Fraud?" (reprint of an article by the conservative author, Russell Kirk).

The following quotation may serve to illustrate the paper's anti-Communist viewpoint:

> In a classical propaganda manoeuvre, Jane Fonda and her co-activists deliberately or stupidly misrepresented the Hanoi regime to the American people as a poor David defending itself from an aggressive Bully. The truth of the matter, as it has gradually emerged, is that the relative size of North Vietnam

> has no moderating effect on either the ferocity of its regime or its territorial voracity in the Indochinese theater. The massive deployment of Hanoi's forces not only in South Vietnam but also in Laos and Cambodia, and continued military operations in disregard of the cease-fire, should be a sufficient hint of what Hanoi's Politbureau has in mind for anyone not blinded by the nonsense of selfless proletarian internationalism.

In the paper itself, Rap is spelt with a lower-case "r." (JMS)

## THE CITIZEN-OBSERVER

| | |
|---|---|
| Richard Barrett, Ed. | Circulation: 2,000 |
| 3030 N. State St., Box 3333 | Format: 8-page tabloid (offset) |
| Jackson, Miss. 39207 | |
| Bi-monthly; $2 | Issues examined: none sent |
| Started: 1968 as Battlefront; changed title in 1970 | Some back issues available from publisher |

The editor sent us the following information on The Citizen-Observer's editorial policies:

> The Day's News 'In Depth': Insight into 'behind the headlines' topics of general interest.
> Accent on Youth: The Positive side of Tomorrow's Leaders.
> Americanism: Highlighting the vital role of the Southern Way of Life in the nation's future.
> Strong military posture abroad, and tough law-and-order stance at home.
> Working people and rural people: Their contributions and problems.
> Building Mississippi: The heritage and hopes of a unique and brave people.
> Industry, Education, and Agriculture: News and views to advance man and his environment.
> Led the recent nation-wide petition drive to free [convicted murderer] Lt. Calley (presented 20,000 petitions at the White House).
> Led a successful drive to establish a dental school in Mississippi.
> Non-political; leans toward the 'Populist' or 'grass roots' point of view.
> Critics have referred to paper as 'Voice of the Silent Majority.'

## DIALOGUE ON LIBERTY

Young Americans for Freedom
Woodland Rd.
Sterling, Va. 22170
Quarterly; free
Started: 1971

Circulation: 120,000
Format: 8-16 pages (offset)
Issues examined: Spring & Fall 1973
Back issues available from publisher

YAF was founded in 1960 by a group of young persons meeting on the family estate of William F. Buckley, Jr. (National Review). Its members are usually white, of high school and college age, and middle-class. It has opposed abortion, the legalization of marijuana, mandatory student fees, and amnesty for draft evaders; and it has supported a strong "national defense, the free market, and Soviet dissidents." Currently it is sponsoring a school "voucher" plan through which parents would have the choice of sending their children to public schools, or receiving tuition vouchers to send them to private schools.

Dialogue on Liberty covers YAF strategy and activities (especially conventions and conferences) and carries a few short articles (e.g., "YAF Lashes Soviet Tyranny" and "YAF Launches Campaign against Aid to Hanoi"). A section called "Spotlight On ..." presents short biographies of prominent members.

One of the sample issues carried a full-length ad (by the Citizens' Committee for the Right to Keep and Bear Arms) attacking the Young Women's Christian Association for supporting firearms control legislation. (JMS)

Feedback:

The editor suggested several textual additions which were incorporated into the review.

## DISCUSSION: A Forum in Which Readers Express Their Opinions

Robert C. Darnell, Ed.
Box 925
Millen, Ga. 30442
Monthly; donations; the magazine will be sent free to any university or college librarian who requests it
Started: 1952

Circulation: 1,000
Format: 12 or more pages (offset)
Issues examined: Sept.-Nov. 1973
Indexing: Theology & Religion
Some back issues available from publisher

This readers' forum is composed principally of articles advocating "fundamental, scriptural religion; conservative, constitutional government; high moral standards; and racial purity and integrity."

There is much discussion of the root meanings of Biblical words and the importance of correct translation. Many references are given to support the use of Yahweh as the name of the Creator and Yahshua as the name of the Son. (See our review of Kingdom Voice & Kingdom Newsletter in Volume I for more about "Yahweh.")

A frequent contributor writes: "How many churches today use the titles Lord or Baal, also God, and burn incense, and still think they are doing Yahweh's will? I thank Yahweh that I found his true name!" Dr. J. Franklin Snook in his article, "A Gentile Church," states the conviction, reiterated in other articles, that Yahweh's Kingdom will be restored on earth. There will be no separation of church and state when Yahshua, the Messiah, takes rule of this kingdom, and there should be none now.

> The fallacious doctrine of separation of church and state has created a vacuum which prevents effective measures of crime control. The preacher says he cannot do anything about murder, rape, robbery, pornography, etc., because he can't make laws; that is the politician's job. The politician says he can't legislate morals; morality is the preacher's problem. Both ignore the fact that Yahweh has already made the laws and the judgments, and that their jobs are teaching and administration, not legislation.

Dr. Snook also believes that in early America religious congregations operated schools where Yahweh's laws were taught and obeyed as the laws of the land. However, the religious congregation deteriorated and "abdicated its position as schoolmaster to the nation." Eventually a high government official will accept Yahweh's laws and administrators will be taught them. Then Yahweh's laws will be the laws of the United States.

Commenting on the mysterious UFOs, Leo Bartsch writes that, though religious leaders tell us that they are satanic, the Bible states that there shall be great sights and signs from heaven before the Savior returns (Luke 21:11). He gives other Biblical references to the Creator's flying objects, and it is He who controls the skies.

The periodical contains classified and display advertisements, mostly for religious literature. (EC)

Feedback:

"I think you have done a remarkably fine job in presenting information about Discussion."

THE EVANGELICAL METHODIST; THE EXALTER

Street, Md. 21154
Monthly; TEM $2, TE free
Started: TEM 1943
Circulation: TEM 1,200; TE about 22,000
Format: TEM 12 pages (offset); TE, 4 pages (offset)
Issues examined: TEM, Mar., May, Oct. 1973; TE, June 1964, Mar. 1972, Jan. 1973
Back issues available from publisher

The Evangelical Methodist is handsome in appearance. The paper is of good grade and there is a quietly tasteful cover each month. Occasional photographs are included to enhance the articles. The back page of each issue contains an advertisement for a theological school.

Regular features include a section on church news around the world. It is written by Dr. W. W. Breckbill, editor of the magazine. The "Evangelical Methodist Women's Page" offers brief inspirational poems, news of women's group activities and recipes. The "Children's Page" contains an original short story.

Articles are normally about a page in length. Among them are human interest stories about individuals presently contributing to the church. Other stories confined themselves to figures historically active in Methodism. The centerfold is a two page message of faith. In a brief text entitled "God and the Supreme Court" the court is chastised for some of its recent decisions which flout the Ten Commandments. In general the feeling presented by this church magazine is of strong conservatism.

Included in this mailing is The Exalter, a four page newsletter. The newsletter has the same publishing address. It contains short articles, usually with a strong biblical flavor. Advertisements suggest attendance at a particular church and church school. The church itself is designated as "Bible-centered" and "gospel-preaching." Again, the basic outlook can be described as conservative. Donald McKnight is editor of The Exalter, and managing editor of TEM. (MN)

Morality in Media NEWSLETTER

487 Park Ave.
N. Y., N. Y. 10022
8 times a year; $1
Started: 1962

Circulation: 40,000
Format: 4 pages (11" x 17", folded to 8 1/2" x 11", offset)

Issues examined: questionnaire and brochure only
Back issues available from publisher @ $1

The president of Morality in Media, Morton A. Hill, S. J., sent a brochure explaining that Morality in Media

> is people. It is the community. It is an interfaith organization (a membership corporation) working to stop the traffic in pornography effectively and constitutionally. Morality in Media is the concerned community expressing its concern in order to inhibit the flow of smut, and to bring about mass media based on the principles of LOVE, TRUTH and TASTE. Morality in Media was founded in 1962, as Operation Yorkville, by three clergymen, brought together by their mutual concern for children and youth. Policy, today, is formed by a Board of Directors of twenty-seven representing all faiths and professions. The National Planning Board is manned by top-level leaders of business, industry, labor, and the arts. The organization is non-sectarian, non-political, and anti-censorship.... The President of the organization was appointed in 1968, by Lyndon B. Johnson, to the Presidential Commission on Obscenity and Pornography. He co-authored the dissenting Hill-Link report of that commission.

The organization attempts to alert the community to the distribution of obscene material (nudie, homosexual, sado-masochistic and teenage sex magazines and paper-backs; underground newspapers pushing drugs and obscenities as "in" things; sexploitation films and commercial films; sadistic violence on TV; titillating ads in the mail, etc.) which it feels is inciting the nation's youth to "violence, perversion, promiscuity, drug experimentation, hatred, tastelessness."/ The organization works through radio and TV broadcasts and advertising spots, by addressing community groups and organizing chapters, by keeping in contact with police and district attorneys, and through "a monthly Newsletter circulated nationally. Each issue carries a Target of the Month--a person or persons to whom groups from all over the nation can write simultaneously to pinpoint action."

The organization began an intensive campaign in 1973 to see that the obscenity decisions of the 1973 U. S. Supreme Court are understood and implemented, and "to counteract a million-dollar scare campaign mounted to nullify the effects of the decisions." Another project of Morality in Media has been the creation of The National Legal Data Center on the Law of Obscenity. The library already has available all obscenity decisions in the U.S. from 1800 through 1970 and contains a medical-psychiatric section of reference material. "From this section will emanate research to provide even more ammunition for the nation's prosecutors and jurists."

## THE NATIONAL EDUCATOR

Jim Townsend, Ed. & Publ.
1110 S. Pomona Ave.
Fullerton, Calif. 92632
Monthly; $6
Started: June 1969
Circulation: 78,000

Format: 16-page tabloid (offset)
Issues examined: none sent
Back issues available from publisher

The following remarks concerning the editorial policies of The National Educator were received from its editor and publisher and are reprinted without correction:

> We are a critic of the government and inovative education. We believe in strengthing the concept of the Constitutional Republic ... rather than the move to bureaucratic socialism. We believe programs should be developed first before inovater are allowed to experiment with students. Our newspaper has been well received, and we have many congradulations from government officials, elected officials, school administrators, professors, teachers, etc. While the liberal press takes us to task, we have a surprisingly little critical mail. We have never been threaten with libel and have had only one minor retraction since the paper started in 1969. We have writers that are qualified in all fields, and our paper covers every state and nine foreign countries. We have not been branded anti-semites, anti-negro, anti-christian, anti-union, etc., and even though we have been branded republicans and democrats, depending on the one reading our newspaper, the facts are, we support neither of the two parties ... believing that politicians will never solve problems for the people ... that people must solve their own problems. We are recognized as a conservative publication, but the extreme right does not subscribe or contribute articles. We are our own voice.

## NEWS AND NOTES OF INTEREST TO CHRISTIANS

Bolton Davidheiser, Ed.
Box 22
La Mirada, Calif. 90637
Semi-monthly; free (contributions accepted)
Started: Jan. 1968
Circulation: 800
Format: 6 pages (offset, stapled)

Issues examined: vol. XI, no. 11 and no. 12; vol. XII, no. 1 (issues not dated but probably end of 1973 and beginning of 1974)
Back issues available from publisher

The purpose of News and Notes of Interest to Christians is "to uphold the Bible as the Word of God and to oppose all that leads to apostasy, such as liberalism, ecumenism, evolution, and the cults." The newsletter is Fundamentalist and hence anti-materialist. Communism and Darwinism are opposed primarily because of their materialism and their emphasis on the "concept that man is the master of his own destiny." The cults attacked in the newsletter include Freemasonry, Mormonism, Divination and Voodoo. Even evangelists like Billy Graham are not above criticism. In Graham's case, he is criticized for recruiting evangelicals toward ecumenism and for comparing Mao's eight precepts to the ten commandments.

The majority of the articles are concerned with various forms of cultism. Sample titles are "Mexican Death Cult" and "Voodoo in New York." Jews are preferred to Arabs and thus the Vatican is criticized for its failure to recognize Israel while it recognizes Arab countries. An article on missionary work among the Jews points out that Jews are less antagonistic to Fundamentalism than are the "liberal 'Christians.'"

News and Notes opposes communism, the United Nations and women's liberation. UNICEF is seen as sympathetic to communism because of its financial aid to the Castro regime and because some UNICEF cards have been designed by "communists and communist sympathizers." A short article on women's liberation suggests a relationship between the women's liberation movement and increased suicides among California women. Another article connects women's liberation and communism. Mrs. Jaquie Davis is quoted as saying, "I was told by the FBI in Los Angeles that in fighting women's lib, I am fighting communism."

The newsletter regularly features book reviews and articles on questions of biblical interpretation. One such article deals with the question "Was Phoebe a Deacon" by proposing that an appropriate interpretation might be that Phoebe was a church servant and that diakonos did not mean deacon.

(JMA)

Feedback:

> I realize it is difficult to appraise a publication from a few issues.... I realize I appear to be 'attacking' the cults, but really I am not, for I am not writing for people in the cults--I am warning Christians about getting involved in liberalism, ecumenism, the cults, etc. I was a liberal and evolutionist myself until 32 years old.
>
> Obviously you are Catholic. [No one connected with the review is Catholic. TJS.] You would consider my paper 'anti-Catholic.' But I am not writing to Catholics. I am writing to Bible-believing Protestants, telling them some things they may not know about Catholicism, so they may be more astute in avoiding ecumenical functions.
>
> The main problem I see in your publication is that the 'radical left' might use it to make trouble for publishers of conservative publications.
>
> Billy Graham not only is not above criticism--he is to be warned against since he is the chief leader of the ecumenical movement among evangelicals.
>
> Communism and Darwinism are opposed primarily because of their materialism and opposition to the spiritual values taught in the Bible.

NO AMNESTY!

| | |
|---|---|
| Young Americans for Freedom<br>1221 Massachusetts Ave., N.W.<br>Washington, D.C. 20005 | Format: 2 pages (legal size)<br>Issue examined: one undated one |

No Amnesty reports on the progress of a nationwide campaign against the granting of amnesty to those who evaded the draft or deserted the military as a protest against the war in Vietnam. It is sponsored by YAF, an organization of more than 60,000 members in more than 600 communities and colleges.

The newsletter strongly opposes the "War Resister's Exoneration Act of 1973," a bill introduced by Bella Abzug, which would grant total and unconditional amnesty. It deplores the campaign launched by those who favor amnesty and have called for lobbying, demonstrations and "sit-ins" to gain support for their cause. Readers are asked to contact their state legislators and ask that they sponsor or support No Amnesty legislation, and there is news of those states where such resolutions have been introduced. They are also urged to express their views in letters to newspapers, on "talk" shows, at local club meetings, and by giving support to the National No Amnesty Campaign.

Attention is called to a letter sponsored by YAF and sent to more than 500,000 Americans by Congressman O. C. Fisher of Texas, a member of the organization's National Advisory Board. This letter, which accompanied the newsletter, explains the congressman's opposition to the granting of amnesty and solicits help for the campaign against it.

> The influx of tens of thousands of left-wing draft dodgers on America's college campuses would constitute a very real and definite threat to our educational system. The possibility of violence which would threaten both property and the lives of law-abiding students would be a very real danger.

A reprint of a speech by Sen. John Tower and a statement by New Guard editor, Jerry Norton, also accompanied the newsletter. Both expressed their agreement with YAF's position. (EC)

Feedback:
Editor expressed no disapproval.

THE PINK SHEET ON THE LEFT: Your Biweekly Report from Prospect House

Phillip Abbott Luce, Ed.
7777 Leesburg Pike
Falls Church, Va. 22043
Bi-weekly; $25
Started: May 1971
Circulation: 6,000

Format: 4-6 pages (offset)
Issues examined: 20 Aug. through 15 Oct. 1973
Back issues available from publisher

This newsletter keeps its readers informed about "current activities of Communists and other groups and individuals on the radical left" in America. "It also covers political events and developments of interest to informed conservatives and anti-Communists." The news is reported briefly and factually, and is relatively free of sensationalism; occasionally statements considered especially noteworthy are underscored.

"Enemies" are usually identified by a tag such as "ultra-radical," "radical," or "liberal." Among those groups whose activities The Pink Sheet watches are The New York Times and Washington Post, the "ultra-radical" American Indian Movement, and the Black Liberation Army. Local elections in which former radical activists participate are reported, and the editors observe: "There is clearly a national trend developing for radicals to become actively involved in conventional politics.... The Pink Sheet will continue to keep you informed as radicals seek to use conventional politics to impose their goals on America."

Although most of the news items are only a few sentences long, special topics receive more extensive treatment. An article by the former director of the Office of Economic Opportunity focused on the amount of federal aid going to radical organizations and activities. The Soviet intellectuals Solzhenitsyn and Sakharov were mentioned in nearly every issue examined; in their plight The Pink Sheet recognizes an "historic opportunity to weaken the Soviet slave state.... No Westerner can truly comprehend the courage of these men.... Will we ignore their pleas, dazzled by the sight of Nixon and Brezhnev clicking glasses, slapping backs, and making jokes?" Indeed, the editors are keenly aware of the rare opportunity this complex situation offers of aligning liberal and conservative forces in America. (SA)

Feedback:

"O.K. Thank you for the very fair consideration. No complaints at all."

## PITYSMONT POST and THE AMERICAN EAGLET

3214 Wade Ave.
Raleigh, N.C. 27607
Monthly; PP $1; TAE $3
Started: PP: 30, 40, or 50 years ago; TAE, Jan. 1973
Circulation: PP 260; TAE 200

Format: PP: 4-6 pages (mimeo.); TAE: 4-6 pages (legal size, mimeo.)
Issues examined: PP, Aug.-Sept. 1973; TAE, Apr., Sept.-Nov. 1973
Back issues available from publisher

The Pitysmont Post and The American Eaglet of the North Carolina American Party are both the work of one man, Owens Hand Browne. [Feedback: "... hardly the work of one man. My wife proofs all of the material and also serves as Circulation Manager for the Eaglet, which involves the red tape of bulk mailing. Also, most of the copy for the Eaglet is supplied by other members of the party, while I confine my editorial opinion to the Post."] Through the former publication he communicates his ideas about the actions of the U.S. government. He describes the Pitysmont Post as

> strongly 'Conservative' but not violently so. It is for the restoration of the Constitutional Republic founded by our Forefathers and the restoration of the Constitution as the basic charter of the Nation. It is for return of political power to the people. It is in almost complete agreement with the newly-written Platform of the American Independent Party. The Pitysmont Post is opposed to Socialism, Communism and governments of that nature; concentration of political power in Washington; federal involvement in religion, education, welfare; federal income tax; the Federal Reserve; the Council on Foreign Relations, the United Nations and the many other Communist Fronts; forced integration; forced school busing; pornography and pornographic 'sex education' in the schools; no-win wars and drafting men for service in them; aid to and trade with socialist countries or any treaties with communist nations; etc.

Every issue of the Pitysmont Post opens with the words, "All necessary for the triumph of evil is that good men do nothing." The publication is essentially a letter from Mr. Browne to the people, describing and analyzing events from his point of view.

The American Eaglet of the North Carolina American Party is a local version of the national American Party's American Eagle covering events within the American Independent Party: meetings, election of officers, resolutions passed, etc. Letters to the editor from members of the party comment on political figures and events and recommend courses of action. Some of the articles (or texts of speeches) are an appeal to people to join the Party. One such article, "An Appeal to Black Fellow Americans," states:

> If you wish to live as free men, if you desire to share in an ever-rising standard of living, and if you sincerely wish for an unfettered opportunity to advance as fast and as far as your talents and motivation will permit, then it is in your interest to seek a return to limited government and American traditions.

(CT)

Feedback:

"I am quite pleased with the copy you have sent me." (Mr. Browne is, incidentally, opposed to the "Equal Rights" Amendment.)

SURVIVE: The American Journal of Civil Defense

Association for Community-Wide Protection from Nuclear Attack
Box 910
Starke, Fla. 32091
Bi-monthly; $5
Started: May 1968

Circulation: 3,000
Format: 8-12 pages (offset)
Issues examined: July, Sept., Nov. 1973
Back issues available from publisher

Civil Defense Forum, Oak Ridge Civil Defense Society, and Professional Society for Nuclear Defense also sponsor Survive. These organizations, recognizing that public indifference does not diminish the threat of nuclear war, work "to enlighten leadership and the public by holding special meetings, publishing papers, briefing community leaders and legislators, and sponsoring public conferences." Survive's primary objective is to ensure a lasting peace by encouraging the development of a strong civilian defense posture.

> ... the present state of unpreparedness and the consequent likelihood of over 60% American fatalities in nuclear war invite aggressor consideration of war against the United States.... A reasonably strong posture of civil preparedness ... and the consequent likelihood of less than 10% American fatalities in nuclear war sharply discourage aggressor consideration of war against the United States.

The point is made that the civil defense structure can be used in cases of natural disasters as well.

In the past the scope of the publication has been limited to classic civil defense, that is, "preparation for facing aggression. Articles were developed to inform Americans of the strength of potential enemies of our country, to explain how to react to nuclear attack, to educate builders in construction that would serve as shelter with little or no increase in cost, and to report on national and international events related to classic civil defense." In future issues, articles will also cover emergency response to natural disasters, improved warning and communication systems, local government services with civil defense implications, and the impact of patterns of land use upon civil defense. They will also encourage educational activities at elementary and secondary schools, to "provide the basis for loyal civic behavior in later years."

An issue usually contains four articles, an editorial; a section ("Spotlight") which singles out an individual or group for praise; "Soviet Civil Defense"; and two advertisements, one for special nuclear shielding, the other for survival food ("How can you sleep tonight, when tomorrow you may have nothing to eat?").

Examples of articles: "Under the Good Earth" (describes the extensive network of air raid shelters beneath the Peking streets); and "A Glass House" (three American scientists "expose the unprecedented position of weakness" of American civil defense). (JMS)

Feedback:

"I think it is a good and accurate description."

## THE TAXPAYERS' COMMITTEE TO END FOREIGN AID

Weekly while Congress is in session; free
Dates: 1959-Sept. 1969
Circulation: 10,000
Format: presentations (sometimes a single page) before appropriate Congressional committees
Issues examined: revised text of a presentation sent to President Nixon on 19 Feb. 1969; also, various tables and other related materials, and a covering letter to "our mailing list of 10,000"

Publications of the Committee carried no title other than the name of the organization. At the foot of the Committee's letterhead was the motto: "Balance the Budget--Embargo Our Gold--Strengthen the Dollar." Among the appendices to the main presentation was a list of nations receiving U.S. aid in the fiscal years 1946-69. (For each country, the dollar amount was given.) Another table showed the U.S. balance-of-payments surplus or (much more frequently) deficit for each fiscal year from 1950 through 1968. In an open letter addressed "to the American taxpayers" and dated 1 July 1969, Rep. Otto E. Passman (Dem., La.), a member of the Appropriations Committee of the House of Representatives, pointed out that the United States, while continuing to extend foreign aid, had itself borrowed money from other nations in recent years: e.g., from Thailand, $100,000,000 for 4 1/2 years at six percent interest. Besides foreign-aid expenditure, the presentation decried the trend toward "abandonment of representative government [of the United States] with increased concentration of power in the executive branch," as well as the decline of the nation's strategic bombing force.

The Committee became inactive in September 1969. Its address had been: Brig. Gen. Bonner Fellers, National Chairman, 3535 Springfield Lane, Washington, D. C. 20008 (WJS)

THE VOICE OF POWs AND MIAs

| | |
|---|---|
| Voices in Vital America | Format: 8-page tabloid |
| 10966 Le Conte | (offset) |
| Los Angeles, Calif. 90024 | Issues examined: Sept. & |
| Monthly; free | Oct. 1972; Jan. 1973 |

The paper carried this information about its purpose:

> In response to numerous requests we have initiated this national POW/MIA newspaper to further our common goal: the identification of MIAs and the safe return of all our men. The first issue includes some of the discrepancies which indicate that Hanoi has not yet given a complete list of prisoners.
>
> We hope this paper will be a step forward in coordinating all efforts and activities, learning from each other's experiences, and reviewing all successful efforts that may be used as guidelines by others.

The paper offers an editorial; news of VIVA and similar groups, and what they are doing ("POW/MIA Efforts around the World"; "Greta Anderson Will Swim from Catalina for POWs/MIAs"); news of the VIVA bracelet campaign which urges individuals to wear a bracelet bearing a POW/MIA's name ("This ... slender band that ties a nation to its heroes in foreign lands"); and pictures and histories of missing men. One issue contains a map of North Vietnam pinpointed with places where the missing aviators were downed while on bombing missions. (The paper never mentions the devastation inflicted by these bombings.) Editorials dwell on the inhumanity of the North Vietnamese: "we can easily say that anyone would know that a government that has shown such flagrant disregard for the basic laws of humanity as North Vietnam would not so easily live up to their agreements to give us an accurate list of our prisoners" and

> All of us who believe in the dignity of man and the preciousness of a human life--human life which has an immortal soul--cannot help but be shocked and horrified at the continuing inhumanity of a people that would deliberately trade upon the hopes, desires, and fears of human beings as pawns in their attempt at conquest.
>
> The bumper stickers, the buttons, yes, even the thin silver or copper bracelets, are only outward manifestations of the sadness and sorrow we feel because brave men, whose only fault is loving their country, and the families who are so patiently waiting for even the barest word, are forced to undergo a barbaric mental torture of uncertainty.

The paper emphasizes a certain type of patriotism: "With the pledge of allegiance, millions of Americans each day pay tribute to our flag, the symbol of free man, unity, and love of country. In the final line of our pledge, we reverently say with hand over heart, facing the colors, 'One nation under God with liberty and justice for all.'"

The January 1973 issue, under the headline, "Many POWs Are Finally Coming Home," printed a list of prisoners released by North Vietnam, and expressed anger that 1,400 men were not yet accounted for. The organization vowed to continue its efforts until all prisoners were identified. (JMS)

## YAF IN THE NEWS

Young Americans for Freedom
1221 Massachusetts Ave., N.W.
Washington, D.C. 20005
Monthly or bi-monthly; $6

Started: Apr. 1969
Circulation: 1,500
Format: 24 pages (offset)
Issues examined: Mar. & Oct./Nov. 1970; Jan./Feb. & Mar. 1971

A former executive director of YAF stated: "*YAF in the News* is ... about the activities of Young Americans for Freedom: its officers, its staff, its committees, its regional offices, its state organizations, its chapters (high school, college, and community), and its members. The compilations include news clippings, magazine articles, cartoons, [and] reprints of radio and television editorials. It is, quite simply, a 'cut and paste' job to let all YAF leaders and adult advisors know what YAF is doing." Articles and photographs are arranged in no perceptible order [Feedback: "in topical order."], and there is no table of contents.

YAF was founded in 1961 at Sharon, Conn., chiefly by the conservative author and publicist, William F. Buckley, Jr. Basically an association of conservative students (although membership is open to any person under 40), it is an avowed opponent of the Black Panther Party, Students for a Democratic Society, and other "New Left" organizations. [Feedback: "It also opposes concentration of power in government, business, or labor, in the view that such power represents a direct threat to individual liberties."] By 1970 it had grown to 500 chapters, and had enrolled more than 55,000 members. In the early 1970s, YAF advocated an all-volunteer army for the U.S. Spiro T. Agnew, Barry Goldwater, Strom Thurmond, Ronald Reagan, and James L. Buckley (brother of William) were the nationally-prominent politicians most frequently praised by YAF spokesmen in the sample issues. (WJS)

Feedback:
Editor expressed no disapproval.

## Chapter 19

## ANTI-COMMUNIST

Some periodicals in this chapter fear that a communist takeover of the United States is imminent. Alarming Cry warns that Russian spies are planning to overthrow our government in the next year or two, and the Alabama Independent asks its readers, "How many more Christmases will we be allowed to sing 'Away in a manger, no crib for a bed'?" The U.S. has been "betrayed and cowardly surrendered to the bondage and slavery and torture and slaughter of the most horrible, atheistic international monster that ever disgraced God's creation!" cries the fanatical Truth Crusader. (Don't miss this review!)

A number of periodicals, such as Alarming Cry, Biblical Missions, and The Voice of Liberty, are produced by Christian fundamentalists, and refer to or quote extensively from the Bible. The Voice of Liberty also has racist overtones, a quality not uncommon in anti-communist literature. (See the Race Supremacist chapters in this and our previous volumes.)

While The South African Observer sees "World Communism" as connected to "Political Zionism" backed by "International Finance," The Truth Crusader explains that communism is merely a front for the Council on Foreign Relations--alias the "Illuminati": "murderous, unprincipled, bloody, international bankers." The AAJ Docket, on the other hand, proclaims "liberals" and "do-gooders" to be even worse than communists.

Anti-communist periodicals tend to blame social changes and ills upon communist influences, and to condemn pointy-headed intellectuals, politicians (except George Wallace and a few others), institutions (United Nations; National Council of Churches), and movements (black militancy, pacifism, legal abortion, Equal Rights Amendment) as being communist-inspired or having communist supporters.

As for Watergate, The Voice of Liberty offers an interpretation: "Men who were indicted for the Watergate bugging indicated they believed the Democratic Party was involved in a conspiracy, and suspected that McGovern received financial support from Fidel Castro! If the whole truth were known, they might receive Medals of Honor!" --Janet Spahn

## AAJ DOCKET

American Association for Justice
201 Columbia Bldg.
Tulsa, Okla. 74114
4 to 6 issues a year; voluntary contributions

Started: Apr./May 1971
Circulation: 300-500
Format: 4 pages
Issues examined: Vol. 3, Nos. 1 & 3; Vol. 4, No. 1 (1973-1974?)

The following information regarding editorial policy was received from "George Washington, General Counsel": "To unswervenly [sic] support the first Ten Amendments to our Constititution [sic] and to strive for the establishment of justice."

The Docket frequently attacks the American Civil Liberties Union: "Everyone in our country who has an ounce of brains knows that the ACLU has always been a liberal, communist-front organization." An article entitled "Amendments? No!" expresses these sentiments.

> Decisions of the United States Supreme Court become more evil with each passing year, as witnessed by the 1972 edict declaring capital punishment illegal, and last year's declaration that abortion is legal. While these decisions have been praised by the moral degenerates (a sizable group), we still believe that a majority of Americans want their State laws to be reflective of God's moral law rather than the idiosyncratic attitudes of Supreme Court justices.... We also believe that a majority of the citizens in most states would prefer to send their children to racially-segregated schools, and would be in favor of state laws requiring such schools.

The article "We Need Help!" (viz., funds) describes the association as "a small group whose only function is to help patriots in trouble.... The staff consists of volunteers." One patriot in trouble is Robert Bolivar DePugh (founder of the Minutemen; jailed for violation of a federal gun-control act), who was represented by AAJ lawyers. The Docket reports his parole from prison. It supports the cause of two men convicted of bombing school busses in Texas, and reprints an appeal for funds from their attorneys.

Who are the Docket's enemies?

> Many of our best people have been led into a spirit of 'defeatism' by the unworkable projects of so-called conservatives who depict our enemies as either Russian or card-carrying American Communists. Of course we all know that these two groups ... [constitute] a part of our enemies, but the liberals (and do-gooders) who are either in or out of our government are our most deadly enemies. Certainly those ... [who] are a part of our government and who actively carry out unconstitutional and unamerican programs, should be the primary target for the actions of patriotic Americans. [The Justice Department and the federal judiciary are the targets.]

The Docket also reports on bills, amendments, and laws that it considers to be unconstitutional. (JMS)

ABN CORRESPONDENCE: Bulletin of the Antibolshevik Bloc of Nations

Slava Stetsko, Ed.-in-Chief
Press Bureau of the ABN
Zeppelinstr. 67
8000 Munich 80, West Germany
Bi-monthly; $6
Started: 1949

Circulation: 7,000
Format: 48 pages (6 3/4" x 9 1/2", linotype)
Issues examined: May-Sept. 1973
Back issues available from publisher

This publication reports on repression in Russia and other iron-curtain countries and supports "human rights and national independence." "The USSR is not a voluntary community of peoples, but a power scheme construed by Russian Communists.... The USSR is a vast impenetrable concentration camp of peoples...."

Some articles that have appeared in past issues: "Prominent Croatian Intellectuals Imprisoned in Zagreb"; "Behind Barbed Wire in Mordovia"; "Ingushets Driven Out of Their Native Land"; "Jehovah's Witnesses Imprisoned in Lithuania"; "Life Under Russian Tyranny"; "Genocide of the Ukrainian People"; "Religious Persecution in Albania Protested"; and "Long-Term Prisoners of Russian Concentration Camps."

ABN Correspondence also covers conferences and other activities of the organization and contains occasional book reviews. Two regular features are "From Behind the Iron Curtain" (news of arrests, imprisonments, torture, conditions of prison camps) and (worldwide) "News and Views." (JMS)

Reviewer's opinion:

An interesting periodical which contains news not often found in the American press.

Feedback:

"We have checked the summary ... and agree with the examples of the content you have selected."

ALABAMA INDEPENDENT

25 W. Oxmoor Rd., Suite 54
Birmingham, Ala. 35209
Semi-monthly; $5
Started: 1961

Format: 12-page tabloid (offset)
Issues examined: 1 July 1972; 1 July & 15 Oct. 1973

The feisty Alabama Independent, "The newspaper without a muzzle," presents itself as "a timely summary of the news" offering "expert views [and] factual news." In fact, very little current world news is reported. The newspaper consists primarily of conservative editorial commentary on timely social and political issues such as abortion ("Murder of Babies: Presbyterians Say It's O.K. If Women Want It"), equal rights for women ("The Fraud Called the Equal Rights Amendment"), internationalism and disarmament (Alien Troops to Police U.S.A."), bussing ("Courts Destroy Another School System"), and gun control ("Guns for Outlaws Only?").

The stated purpose of the paper is "To tell the truth for God and country, To expose Communism and the way it is taking over the U.S., [and] To awaken apathetic Americans to the Communist threat." Major targets of criticism, charged with promoting the Communist cause in the U.S., are the United Nations ("Get the U.N. out of the U.S. and the U.S. out of the U.N."), the National Council of Churches ("Compare the purposes and objectives of the Council [with those of the Communist Party] as they seek to aid the Reds in Worldwide Conquest"), and political actions which seek to increase the power of the federal government over the rights of the individual states ("The 'grande design' of gradualism in the takeover of America is becoming more and more apparent.... The machinery is in motion and the traitors elected to 'represent' you and me are running for the trough.") Social ills spawned by the spread of Communist influence include the breakdown of traditional morality, family life, and religion: "American young people are being lured away from their homes, parents, and all that they have been taught by the forces dedicated to the destruction of the American way of life"; "What Became of Principle?"; "How many more Christmases will we be allowed to sing, 'Away in a manger, no crib for a bed'?" Readers are strongly encouraged to write their legislators to protest these and other developments and actions of which they disapprove.

Regular features are "Views of the Week," a column which focuses on the anti-Christian aspect of Communism and its effect on our lives; several chatty reports such as "Straight Talk," "Marilyn Manion," and "Pecking Around," offering an untra-conservative viewpoint on a variety of topics; "Thumbs Up/Thumbs Down," which briefly applauds or decries recent federal actions; and "Grass Roots Talk," the letters-to-the-editor section. "The Birch Log" reprints material from publications of the John Birch Society.

Even the advertisements tend to reflect the paper's editorial policy: several ads include slogans such as, "We Believe in Conservatism for America," "Support your Local Police," and "Total Christian Radio." The only apolitical regular feature is a half-page section on gardening tips.

(BC)

ALARMING CRY

Bob LeRoy, Ed.
Box 262
Liberty, Mo. 64068
Quarterly; $2
Started: Dec. 1953
Circulation: 3,000
Format: 4-8 pages (letter or legal size; offset)
Issues examined: Winter, Summer, Autumn 1972; Winter 1973
Back issues available from publisher

Alarming Cry "promotes Christian Education, Gospel Preaching, 20th-Century Reformation, and Anti-Communism." The editor founded the Christian Sons of Liberty (CSL) in 1968, and was National Chaplain of the Minutemen, an anti-communist organization, from 1966 to 1968. The newsletter is closely connected with the CSL, whose beliefs are fundamentalist and include opposition to ecumenism, "Romanism," and evolution.

Communism and Negro militancy are topics frequently mentioned. The two are often inter-related, as in such articles as "New Red Front 'Black Egyptians' Grows in St. Louis Area." Another article describes a protest the CSL staged against Angela Davis, an American Negro Communist. The protest was led by LeRoy, who observed "Negroes saluting each other with the upheld arm and clenched fist which is the official communist salute." Communism is also believed to be related to pacifism and hippies. A cartoon, captioned "Peace with Communism, OR ELSE," shows a male hippie wearing the slogan, "Perversion Now"; a female hippie wearing the slogan, "Free Luv and Reefers"; and a professor with a book bearing the word, "Marxism."

The Summer issue is concerned with the combined threat of communism and Satan. "Satan Attempts to Destroy Rev. Bob LeRoy" suggests that only God's grace saved LeRoy's life in what is viewed as a Satanically-planned automobile accident. In "God Takes Some, Leaves Others," a chronology lists all the occasions on which Satan attempted to "destroy" LeRoy, beginning with his slipping on a throw-rug at the age of three. Another article describes a protest "Easter Parade" in front of the home of a "KGB agent." According to this article, "Russian Spies" plan to overthrow the American government with a "revolution in the next year or two."

Most issues contain news items about evangelists and their crusades or revival meetings. CSL meetings are also regularly publicized. Photos of LeRoy and his family often accompany articles, especially those on CSL activities. Anticommunist books, films, and tapes are advertised. Various appeals are addressed to Richard M. Nixon, including an open letter asking him to "'fire' all of the pro-communist traitors in our government offices." The freeing of Robert Bolivar DePugh, founder of the Minutemen (jailed for violating gun-control laws), was the subject of another petition to Nixon. (JMA)

Feedback:

"O.K. by Rev. B. L." LeRoy enclosed a mimeographed letter about a planned retreat for the All-American Bible Camp on the Fourth of July. It reads, in part:

> Some have suggested we have a 'TV BURNING' on the afternoon of July 4th, at 4 P.M. I am willing to go along with this idea, since I am the only preacher in America that has ever sponsored a 'City-Wide Book Burning': Liberty, Mo. (town square, July 4th, 1969). Then we burnt--in public--books promoting Communism, Evolution, and Sexual Immorality, etc. However, since we have never owned a TV since they were invented, you will have to bring yours along. Be sure it's dead by smashing it up first, then you may place it on our big trash pile to be creamated [sic] at our campsite.

## BIBLICAL MISSIONS

Independent Board for Presbyterian Foreign Missions
246 W. Walnut Lane
Philadelphia, Pa. 19144
10 issues a year; $2
Started: 1935
Circulation: 4,500

Format: 16 pages (5 1/2" x 8 1/2", offset)
Issues examined: Jan., June, Aug. 1973
Back issues available from publisher

This is the official organ of "a fundamental Christian mission board." In the sample issues, one editorial was a tribute to a man who had been a missionary in Korea for 31 years. An accompanying reprint of an article written by him in 1958 listed "great defeats in specific battles upon the Church of the Living God": "Islam and the territories it has wrested from the church; Roman Catholicism and its possession of vast territories; the whole Far East, which once had the Gospel and [now has] lost it." The author was confident, however, that there was still a remnant of faithful witnesses, and that Jesus Christ would "give victory to His Saints."

Dr. Carl McIntyre was once a minister in what is now the United Presbyterian Church. A dispute over the presence of "modernism" in this church's missionary board led to the creation of the Independent Board, of which McIntyre is a member. It is "committed to maintain a militant, fundamental, Bible-believing position" and carries on the "true foreign missionary work" once performed by his former denomination. Another organization to which McIntyre belongs--he has been its only president--is the International Council of Christian Churches, "raised up by the Lord in 1948 to be a banner to the truth, in opposition to the inclusiveness of the apostate World Council of Churches." Biblical Missions praises McIntyre as "The one person who has had the vision for the need of this banner of the truth, and who is committed to keep the banner flying high."

An editorial in one issue strongly attacked the World Council of Churches, asserting that it is wrong in its attitude toward and application of Holy Scripture. "Those who control the WCC have openly departed from the historic Christian teaching." They have rejected the authority of the Bible, and "their god is a god of social service, not divine power." There is criticism of the WCC's president, who had said that "liberation" means salvation. This definition of liberation "explains why the WCC sends thousands of dollars to support Communist-inspired 'liberation fronts.'"

A sermon printed in another issue asserted that attempts

to heal the troubles of the world with social justice and social welfare only "help the socialists do their devilish work." The

> Christian's task is not to seek to change this world as it lieth in the hands and embrace of the Wicked One, but to call upon men and women to prepare for the next world when by grace and mercy blood-washed sinners can rest their heads on their Savior's bosom.

In addition to editorials and sermons, BM contains news of missionaries and their work around the world; reports of meetings; poems; and lists of prayers requested or answered. Among the Ten Most Urgent Prayer Needs in one issue was one "for the removal of the Socialist government in Chile." This prayer was answered in September 1973, when a military coup overthrew Dr. Salvador Allende's government.

(EC; TJS)

Feedback:
Editor expressed no disapproval.

BOIAN NEWS SERVICE; PORUNCA VREMII; and FIII DACIEI

George F. Boian, Dir. & Publ.
300 E. 91st St.
N.Y., N.Y. 10028
BNS weekly; PV monthly; FD quarterly; $24 for all 3
Started: 1968

Format: BNS 2-5 pages (legal size, mimeo., stapled); PV 20-24 pages (mimeo., stapled); FD 17 pages (offset, stapled)
Issues examined: BNS, 8 issues from 1971, 1973, 1974; PV, 3 issues in 1973 & 1974; FD, Apr. 1972

According to the Director, these periodicals are concerned with "political science, anti-communism, Romanian history." Boian News Service (text mostly Romanian) deals with current events. Porunca Vremii (text mostly in Romanian; some in English) deals with political science. Fiii Daciei (text in Romanian and English) deals with Romanian history. (The sample issue contained "official documents"--in English--on ecclesiastical affairs.)

## CUBAN-AMERICAN SERTOMA CLUB OF CORAL GABLES NEWSLETTER

Pedro A. López, Jr., Ed.
1015 N. American Way
(Suite 113)
Miami, Fla. 33132

Format: 4 pages (offset)
Issues examined: 10 Oct. & Nov. 1974

Reflects the anti-communist, anti-Castro sentiments of the Cuban refugee community in Florida. In "Another Treason in the Making," Senators William Fulbright, Edward Kennedy, Jacob Javits, and Claiborne Pell are referred to as "the enemies of a free Cuba," and the foreign ministers of Costa Rica, Colombia, and Venezuela are called "Ambassadors of indignity who are remote-controlled by the forces of darkness" because of "their pressure on the Organization of American States to lift the embargo on Cuba.... The new Judas of the U.S. Department of State [H. Kissinger] seems to be behind this move."

See also our review of Florida Latin News, which has the same editor. (JMS)

## FLORIDA LATIN NEWS

Pedro A. López, Jr., Ed. & Publ.
1015 N. American Way
(Suite 113)
Miami, Fla. 33132
Monthly; free
Started: Aug. 1972

Circulation: 25,000
Format: 12-page tabloid (offset)
Issues examined: Apr., July, Dec. 1973
Some back issues available from publisher

"Our major editorial policies are to defend the philosophy and principles necessary to the existence of free, representative, democratic forms of government, and to combat one and all who in one way or another constitute a threat to these premises and to individual and collective freedoms." The anti-communist, anti-Castro Florida Latin News addresses the Cuban community in Florida. (See also our review of the Cuban-American Sertoma Club of Coral Gables Newsletter, immediately preceding this one. It, too, is edited by López.)

Before he was forced from office, Richard M. Nixon was supported "without reservations" by the paper, which thought that he was

> being subjected to a vicious attack by the liberal

> press, who have taken an incident and inflated it far beyond its importance. We refer to the 'Watergate affair.' Our definition of this incident is that it was an unsuccessful attempt at surveillance on the communists, the leftists, the draft dodgers, the hippies, and the yippies, that rallied around the opposition candidate [Sen. George McGovern], who--in the midst of a long and painful war--was campaigning on a program of surrender to the enemy.

Examples of articles: "Don't Let the Press Destroy America"; "No Peace in Americas While Red Cuba Exists"; and "Communist Cuba Had Armed and Organized the Communist Rabble of Chile." (JMS)

## THE GREEN BERET

Monthly paper)
Format: 28 pages (coated Issue examined: Mar. 1968

There's something special about a Special Forces Man. A full-page ad (the only ad in the sample issue) tells what it takes "to rate a beret." The magazine's articles, by men who have already won their berets, give uniformly optimistic, almost jovial accounts of the two major activities in Vietnam: successful maneuvers against the enemy ("Charlie," "Clyde Cong," "Creeping Cong," or "Charles") and rebuilding the villages destroyed in that process.

The thrust of these reports is that our men are brave ("CPT Joseph Z-----, who was with O'Neil, was killed. He was in Nha Trang to process through on his way home, but couldn't resist one last go at Charlie"), the enemy is game but not too smart ("They came gooned to the gills on opium"), the South Vietnamese Army is O.K. ("Each man had a job to do and, like a precision machine, no movement was wasted by these small, rugged men"), and the innocent civilians show promise ("These folk were not looking for a handout, nor had they given up in despair").

Many pictures of good quality accompany the articles, although the photographers are not credited. A chaplain's message ("Viet Customs, Taboos Are Your Business") and a listing of decorations received by members of the 5th Special Forces Group seem to be regular features of the magazine. (CP)

Addendum:

Mail addressed to The Green Beret was returned in

June 1971, marked "Unit deactivated." The address had been: 5th Special Forces Group (Airborne), 1st Special Forces, APO San Francisco, Calif. 96240.

ICR WORLD BULLETIN: The Cry for International Christian Relief

Rev. Ray Martin, Ed.
International Christian Relief, International Council of Christian Churches
801 Haddon Ave.
Collingswood, N. J. 08108

Quarterly
Format: 8- to 12-page tabloid (offset)
Issues examined: Vol. 4, Nos. 1/3 & 4/6 (1973)

Covers relief activities of the organization in many countries, with some expression of anti-Communist sentiment, as in this excerpt from an article on "Korea's Orphans and the IRC":

> The leftist-inclined press is interested in picking up some isolated story of an atrocity carried on by the American GI--and then letting the whole world hear about it. Moscow and Peking and the devils of hell gloat and are filled with glee. Then some pink-embroidered Senator or Congressman, at public expense, sets out to make a big investigation of the matter, and for days and weeks the papers are full of the red propaganda about the 'imperialist, murderous, aggressive Americans.'
>
> Our servicemen--our fighting men--in both Korea and South Vietnam have done remarkably well considering that they have always had to fight and die with one hand tied behind their backs by the political coalition of Washington, Peking, and Moscow. But we know that some of our boys--perhaps many more than we think--have found the true riches in the mud and sludge of Korea and Vietnam. Those boys who have so unselfishly helped the civilians of these nations, the orphans and the ill, have discovered these riches.

(JMS)

THE SOUTH AFRICAN OBSERVER: A Journal for Realists

S. E. D. Brown, Ed. & Publ.
Box 2401
Pretoria, South Africa

Monthly; $5
Format: 16 pages
Started: May 1955

Issue examined: Feb. 1974
Some back issues available from publisher

The Observer, dedicated to "racial and national integrity for all peoples," warns that the world is threatened by the twin evils of World Communism and Political Zionism:

> two forces which spring from a common root in Russia.... backed to the hilt by International Finance, they are only as different as the main branches of one tree. They aspire to securing eventual control of political, economic, and military power over the entire human race. Their purpose is to de-nationalize all races, nations, and governments, and to erect on the breakup of Western civilization a collectivist new world order. Their organization and political instrument today is the United Nations Organization.

An article on "Henry Kissinger--Deadly Threat to All Mankind" asserts that the American Secretary of State has "worked tirelessly and brilliantly to advance the Communist cause, the Zionist cause, and the global aspirations of International Finance."

The Observer supported Portugal's rule in its African colonies, and attacks members of Frelimo (Mozambique) as terrorists and as a "front for the communist world revolution in Africa." The white settlers' regime in Rhodesia is strongly supported. The South African government and Prime Minister Vorster are accused of "deviationism" and leftist leanings. The "Socialist government of Australia" is criticized for granting independence to Papua New Guinea, a "land of primitives," some of whose inhabitants smear themselves with mud while others worship a discarded flashbulb.

Other things opposed in the sample issue: abortion; loud pop music; the Grand Orient Lodge of Free Masonry in France; and the appointment of a liberal Jew as Chief Justice of Canada's Supreme Court.

Many of the articles in the Observer are reprints from other sources. (JMS)

Feedback:

Editor Brown suggested several changes in wording, and we have incorporated them into the review. He concluded:

> In the present climate of 'world opinion' my journal

> is invariably classified as 'extreme right,' but I would dispute this in that I believe that the maintenance of racial and national integrity, by all peoples, is commensurate with the natural order of things from a human point of view.

## THE TRUTH CRUSADER

Dr. & Mrs. Ernest L. Miller, Eds. & Publs.
Drawer 959
Harrisonburg, Va. 22801
Quarterly; $5
Started: 1953
Circulation: 8,000

Format: 48 pages (offset)
Issues examined: Winter 1970; Spring & No. 41 (1971?); Nos. 42 & 44-45 (1972?); Nos. 46 & 47 (1973?)
Back issues available from publisher

The Truth Crusader is an unusual blend of fundamentalist Christianity and Bible prophecy; health foods, vitamins, and herbal remedies; libertarianism; conservatism; and anti-communism. (The health food and back-to-nature movements have usually been the concern of left wing and hippie groups.) The Crusader is

> Dedicated to the harmonization and dissemination of Biblical and scientific truth; the conservation and utilization of the nutritive and medicinal values and delicious flavors of natural organic foods; the restoration of the inviolable and divinely instituted sanctity of marriage, home, and family; the universal recognition of the freedoms, distinct uniqueness, sovereignty, and autonomy of individuals, races, states, and nations.

Although the Crusader refers to itself as a "Health Publication," more than three-fourths of a typical issue consists of political articles: the "world's best documented, most factual, most fearless, most highly condensed national and international news reports interpreted in the light of Bible prophecy." The Millers warn Americans that their country is on the verge of a takeover.

> The United States has been deliberately and treasonably betrayed and cowardly surrendered to the bondage and slavery and torture and slaughter of the most horrible, atheistic international monster that ever disgraced God's creation! Unless a merciful Almighty

> God miraculously and supernaturally intervenes, the take-over, slaughter, and mopping up will take place within a year!
>
> ...
>
> WE HAVE JUST RECEIVED AUTHENTIC INTELLIGENCE REPORTS ... STATING THAT RUSSIAN SATELLITES OR SPACE PLATFORMS CARRYING HYDROGEN BOMBS CAPABLE OF REDUCING THIS ENTIRE CONTINENT TO ASHES ARE PASSING OVER OUR HEADS DAILY.
>
> ...
>
> In addition to all of this there is within the United States a highly trained, well-armed revolutionary or guerrilla army ready to plant explosives in all major industries, munition plants, oil refineries.... When Russia's powerful military might strikes from without, these Castro and Mao trained and equipped villains supported by wealthy, tax-exempt foundations and apostate, ecumenical National and World Harlot Churches [World Council of Churches] will create general chaos and demoralization from within.

The article goes on to explain that Communism is a "tool" or "front" of the Council on Foreign Relations. "Satan, the prince of this world disguised as an angel of light, has ... gained complete control of the United States government...."

The Winter 1970 issue gives further background on the "international conspiracy that is destroying America and Christian civilization, spoken of in the Bible as the Mystery of Iniquity and as the Synagogue of Satan. In our present time it is called the Illuminati, or Invisible Government, or CFR." The Council on Foreign Relations is

> a secret order of arrogant, self-conceited intellectuals founded ... in 1776. Their purpose is ... to ... destroy the sovereignty of all nations and the ... characteristics of all races by forced integration, homogenization and mongrelization; to do away with marriage, with the home, with the private ownership of property and business, and to eternally abolish Christianity from ... the earth....

The Illuminati, a den of "murderous, unprincipled, bloody, international bankers," caused the French Revolution, World Wars I and II, and the Korean and Vietnam wars in order to weaken and impoverish the earth's nations so as "to force them to surrender their sovereignty to a one-world, illuminati-controlled-government."

The Millers frequently address urgent appeals to the President and Congress:

> Why do you lead us straight into the Spider's Web? The CFR has brainwashed, blindfolded, and hypnotized you. Humble your proud, deluded heads, and repent and fast, and pray until you awake from your CFR-induced sleep. Do this before you lead this nation into bondage, slavery, torture, and slaughter and land your own souls into the lake which burneth with fire and brimstone.... I entreat you to read your Bibles, put your faith in Almighty God.... Be Christian Patriots instead of puppets ... manipulated by ... your Illuminati, CFR Communist masters.... You probably have been brainwashed ... to think there is no HELL. But unless you repent and lead this nation out of the Illuminati, CFR Communist, United Nations Death-Trap and lead it back to the God whom you have repeatedly ignored and insulted, you will land in the hell you don't believe in.

The *Crusader* often runs exposés on American culture and institutions. An exposé of rock music explains that Pavlov and other Russian scientists

> developed sound and music techniques for completely changing, debasing, demoralizing, corrupting and doing irreparable physical and mental injury to individuals and nations.... [They] contacted educational and entertainment leaders and record producers and persuaded them to promote and encourage the music and records designed to subtly accomplish their diabolical objective....
>
> ...
>
> Every detail, every move, every line of music of every appearance of the Beatles was scientifically designed and laboratory tested to demoralize and completely destroy the youth of America.... They [the Beatles] were trained and paid by the Communists for their Satanic role in the overthrow of the United States.

An exposé of sensitivity training ("the sister of communist-inspired sex education") explains that it

> was started by the Illuminati in 1789 to destroy Christianity, individualism, personal freedom,

> marriage, morality.... It was introduced into the United States by Alger Hiss. Sensitivity training destroys all religious and moral convictions of right and wrong, all loyalty to God and country, all respect for parental authority.... It is designed to so degrade and integrate and homogenize, and depersonalize and dechristianize, and demoralize all mankind as to make them the submissive puppets of a Communist, One-World Slave State.

A sensitivity session is described:

> They closed their eyes, joined hands and formed a circle. After a period of swaying and twisting and rubbing their bodies together ... they all fell to the floor, a sexually aroused pile of humiliated, condemned, degraded, homogenized victims of the international Communist sensitivity training conspiracy.

Other articles and exposés make the following accusations:

1. "At the close of World War II there were 4,000 Communists in the State Department. They have directed the foreign affairs of this nation ever since."

2. "The Communists now control the National Education Association, the UNESCO, and America's entire educational system. Practically every text book from kindergarten through the University including the Weekly Readers subtly little-by-little teach[es] one-worldism, socialism, evolution, and atheism. They are designed to demoralize, depersonalize, homogenize, and dechristianize this generation for a one-world Communist Soviet State."

3. "The bombing, burnings, police murdering, guerrilla warfare and Black Panther atrocities and bloody revolution were all planned by the CFR."

4. Foreign aid is "a Communist-planned ... method to bleed and impoverish America and spread Communism.... Nearly every dollar of foreign aid is used ... to encourage, promote, and establish Communist regimes. It has delivered 33 free countries and 950,145,000 people to bondage, slavery, brutality and ... made possible the slaughter of over 200,000,000 people."

5. The World Council of Churches is a frequent target: "We have irrefutable, documented evidence that the ... [WCC] have rejected the Gospel of Jesus Christ for a social, revolutionary, Communist ideology." They "are teaching and practicing the immorality and sexual perversion and atheism and pornography and drug addiction that the Communists always use to destroy nations, people, and Christianity."

Also condemned and exposed are "Welfarism"; day-care centers; mental health programs; civil rights; the theory of evolution; the UN (a frequent target); urban renewal; astrology; the Federal Reserve Act ("planned by the Luciferean Illuminati over a hundred years ago to be the Satanic tool to destroy Christianity"); practically all government agencies (e.g., the Business Advisory Council, a tentacle of the CFR, "planned ... the destruction of that great and noble American patriot, Senator Joe McCarthy"); income tax; and symbols such as the peace symbol (for 2000 years "universally recognized to be the symbol of the Devil and Satanism.... [It is the] cross of Jesus Christ broken and inverted ... [and an] antithesis of the true cross").

The Crusader reviews and recommends such books (sold by the Millers in their health food store and obtainable by mail order) as Satanism, Diabolical Religion of Darkness and The Conflict of the Ages. About the former, the Millers write that there are 600 Satanist churches in one American city and over half a million Satan worshippers in Great Britain and many more in the U.S. Among these worshippers are prominent lawyers and college professors. "Thousands of babies, children, and adults are being murdered to secure fresh human blood to serve in the masses in Satan Churches." The Conflict of the Ages "traces the diabolical Illuminati conspiracy which now threatens the entire world from its origin through its entire dirty, bloody, slimy trail to the present time. There is no book on earth, excepting the Bible, as indispensable to our national survival...." The Millers are offering a study course on the book.

Issue No. 44/45 contains an "Encyclopedia of Natural Drugless Therapies" (vitamins, plants, herbs, etc.) and a directory of health food stores and organic farms throughout the country. The Crusader also offers a course in nutritional therapy. Examples of health and nutritional articles that the Crusader has carried are: "Aluminum and Teflon Cooking Utensils Are Very Dangerous"; "Raw Virgin Olive Oil Is a Divinely Provided Natural Medicine"; and "Cholesterol and Vitamin C."

The publication carries ads for like-minded publications and occasional letters to the editor. (JMS)

UNDERGROUND EVANGELISM: A Ministry to the Suffering Church in the Communist World

L. Joe Bass, Ed.
Evangelism Center
Box 808
Los Angeles, Calif. 90053

Monthly (except Aug.)
Format: 16 pages (offset)

Issues examined: Jan. & Apr. 1973

Underground Evangelism contains news and articles on individuals and groups persecuted or martyred for their Christian beliefs in communist countries, and reports the activities of the UE organization which prints and distributes Christian literature "for the written-off and forgotten people of the Communist world." Readers are encouraged to contribute to the "Martyrs' Relief Fund":

> Safe, proven, and reliable channels have been opened by UE teams to provide emergency relief and support for the persecuted Church, its 'prison widows' and 'fatherless orphans' left bereft because of the Christian witness of husbands and fathers now imprisoned and suffering for their faith.

The UE also beams shortwave radio broadcasts into communist countries.

Examples of articles: "Pastor Imprisoned--Serving Six-Year Sentence while Family Suffers Alone" (a pastor of an underground church in the Ukraine); "A Russian 'Jesus Baby' Pays a Price" (fictional account of a "young Russian girl who chose to pay the consequences rather than wear the 'badge' of Godless Communism"--a red neckerchief, part of the uniform for the Pioneers, a Communist Party youth group); and "John: Russia's 20-Year-Old Martyr for Christ" (tortured to death for his beliefs while serving in the Soviet Army).

(JMS)

THE VOICE OF LIBERTY

692 Sunnybrook
Decatur, Ga. 30033
Quarterly; contributions
Started: Oct. 1959
Circulation: 2,500

Format: 10 pages (mimeo.)
Issues examined: Spring 1966; Summer 1968; Fall 1969; Spring 1971; Fall 1973

This is a "non-sectarian, non-profit, non-partisan" periodical, dedicated to anti-communism and Christian ideals. Its stated purpose is to "disseminate facts exposing enemies of God and Country, pointing to documented facts--not private opinion." (Both of these quotations appear on the front page of each issue.) These references come most often from the Bible, although there is occasional reference to individuals, newspapers, and periodicals.

Format varies, but each issue usually includes several short articles written as news items of current interest, followed by one or two essay-length articles. In the sample issues, shorter articles reflect concern with the influence of communism in American society, and especially on American youth; the danger to free enterprise from too strict an anti-pollution policy; the revolutionary views of the Chicago Seven; and the threat posed to the racial purity of Anglo-Saxons by the presence of "strangers" in their land.

Articles of greater length address such national issues as the 1968 presidential election, providing information on the political records of each of the three major candidates and an endorsement of George Wallace. A more recent issue is devoted almost entirely to Watergate and the parallels believed to exist between today's situation and the situation related in the Biblical Book of Nehemiah.

Almost all of the articles discuss Biblical prophecy and its fulfillment in today's world. Every line is punctuated with quotations from and references to the Bible, with the purpose of interpreting current happenings. Numbers and numerical patterns are often mentioned as proof of the links between the world of the Bible and the world of today.

"From the Mail Bag" (which seems to be intended as a regular feature, although it appears in only one of the sample issues) consists of letters to the editor. (Both supporters and critics are represented.) Another more-or-less regular feature is an annotated list of publications available at minimal cost through the Voice of Liberty Association. (WP)

Feedback:

"Your write-up of The Voice of Liberty is excellent and a very accurate summary of our periodical."

## THE VOICE OF THE MARTYRS

Pastor Richard Wurmbrand
Box 11
Glendale, Calif. 91209
Monthly; free
Started: June 1967
Circulation: 2,000,000 in 44 languages

Format: 4 pages
Issues examined: Sept., Oct., Dec. 1973; Jan.-June 1974
Back issues available from publisher

The Voice of the Martyrs is the newsletter of the organization, Jesus to the Communist World, Inc. It is a non-profit missionary organization represented in 53 countries.

Pastor Wurmbrand, who spent fourteen years in a Romanian Communist prison, is the General Director.

A major part of each issue consists of a lengthy article by Wurmbrand written in the form of a letter. Each issue also contains "Notes and Comments" (short articles of news from various countries) and several photographs: pictures of victims, prisoners, families, and atrocities committed against Christians.

The purposes of the mission are printed in each newsletter:

> (1) to give the persecuted Christians in Communist countries Bibles, Christian literature, and Evangelical broadcasts in their own language; (2) to give relief to families of Christian martyrs in these countries; (3) to bring to Christ leftists and Communists in the free world; (4) to warn Christians in the West of the dangers of Communism by informing them about the atrocities committed against our brethren in faith in the Communist countries.

All of the articles and pictures pertain to one of these four purposes. Headlines in various issues indicate some of the topics presented. "Bible Smugglers Alarm Soviet Press!" depicts the work of the mission. "Solzhenitsyn and Wurmbrand--Giants in Church History" says that both of these men have told of atrocities in Communist countries. "New Communist Attacks against Wurmbrand," "Wurmbrand--Main Deteriorator of Christian-Communist Relations," and "Soviet Press Attacks Wurmbrand" tell of Wurmbrand's personal influence in the fight against Communism. Other headlines: "Was Lenin Ever Converted?" and "20,000 Christians in Cuban Jails."

Additional topics covered: "USA Betrayed by Oilmen," "Christians Buried Alive," "Terror Against Christian Children," "100 Million Worship Secretly in Soviets," and "Vatican Praises Mao."

Topics mentioned often are the work of the mission through literature, broadcasts, speeches, and distribution of Bibles; atrocities committed by the Communists; and the Underground Church in Communist countries. Wurmbrand's opinion of various events appears regularly. Appeals are made for letters to prisoners and families and for prayers for various persons. Books, many of which were written by Wurmbrand, are advertised for sale. (NK)

Feedback:

Editor expressed no disapproval.

Chapter 20

## RACE SUPREMACIST

> The Beast referred to in the Bible is the same beast that is living among us today--the negro! ---Christian Vanguard

> ... race-mixing is genocide to all races, and ... the one-world planners cannot solve the race problem by integrating the races into one super-mongrelized UNESCO-brown man. ---Christ Is the Answer

> On any issue before you choose, check for influence of the Jews!
> ---Christian Vanguard

These periodicals on the far right of the political spectrum are characterized by a belief in the superiority of the non-Jewish white race. They see communism as Jewish; Negroes (and other non-whites) as sub-human; and the world as being in the grip of Satanic forces. (The High I. Q. Bulletin, reviewed in our 1972 volume, affords an extreme example of such Apocalyptic vision.) Many of these periodicals are pervaded by a sense of doom and impending world disaster. Christ Is the Answer fears that "economic depression and a total failure of the money system of America and the world" are imminent and that "we are living in the very end time." Population Report warns that hostile "non-European elements are flooding America" and seeking "the downfall of the European elements." Countdown believes that "a countdown is in progress for our civilization" and "There is not much time left in which to reverse the present trend toward socialism ... and the complete destruction of our traditional morality and way of life."

Most of the periodicals reviewed here are National Socialist. The WUNS Bulletin is one of several journals emanating from Arlington, Virginia, seat of the late George Lincoln Rockwell. Attack! stresses revolution, not reform. It is published by the National Youth Alliance, which describes itself as a "revolutionary organization of action-oriented young Americans determined to build a new order of health, sanity, and beauty in American life." (The editor, William Pierce, is connected with several other National Socialist periodicals published in Arlington.) Christian Vanguard (New Christian Crusade Church) is published by James K. Warner, an early disciple of Rockwell's. Christian Advocate (Anglo-Saxon Christian Crusade) is the product of Russell R. Veh, a young admirer of Rockwell's. Veh also edits NS Mobilizer, which appeals primarily to homosexuals. Straight Talk (Canada) is put out by the Western Guard Party, and Perseverance (Australia) is the organ of the Hungarist Movement. NRP Bulletin and Nordisk Kamp come from Sweden; Folk og Land is from Norway.

It may come as a surprise to some that individual planks in National Socialist platforms are not devoid of merit. Some of the points in the Western Guard Party's "Manifesto" might appeal to liberals, conservationists, feminists, or labor unionists: protection of the environment and natural resources; profit-sharing in industry; full employment; collective bargaining; safe and healthful working conditions; equal opportunity (and pay) for women; interest-free loans for home buyers; adequate health care for everyone; and the prevention of chemical adulteration and the over-refining of foods.

Race supremacist publications make fascinating reading. For a fuller discussion of the genre, see our previous volumes. --Janet Spahn

## ATTACK!

William Pierce, Ed.
National Youth Alliance
Box 3535
Washington, D. C. 20007
Monthly; $5
Started: Oct. 1970
Circulation: 16,000

Format: 12 page tabloid (offset)
Issues examined: June & Aug. and Special Issue 1973
Back issues available from publisher

Attack is the organ of the National Youth Alliance, a "revolutionary organization of action-oriented young Americans determined to build a new order of health, sanity and beauty in American life." The NYA is opposed to the present ruling "System" in America, regardless of whether it is liberal, moderate, or conservative. [Feedback: "The NYA is opposed to the present ruling 'System' in America primarily because it is racially destructive."] Revolution, not reform, is necessary to establish the "new society based on the values of race and personality." [Feedback: "These two values are complementary. The first implies that the individual has a meaningful existence only within the context of his racial community and fulfills himself through service to that community, while the second implies that the racial community acts and fulfills its destiny only through individual men and women who are a part of that community, rather than through the annonymous 'masses.'"] Although the new society will not be based on class or economic privilege, it will be based on a "recognition of the natural inequality of men." The new society brought about by the NYA would restore a sense of racial and national identity, and an appreciation for the achievements of Western civilization.

The NYA program opposes communism, "neo-liberalism," Zionism, integration, and "all race-defiling efforts of the System." Communists are considered to be "state" capitalists, and "revolutionary Marxism" is regarded as disguised "neo-liberalism." "International capitalist activities," such as trade with the Third World, must be abandoned, and "racial interests" must sometimes [Feedback: "Always"] be placed above economic interests. At the present, the NYA expects to reach only "an elite minority" with its message. [Feedback: The preceding sentence is "outdated."]

A common topic of articles in Attack! is Zionist control of the mass media. An editorial in the August 1973 issue explains how Zionists take over the media and use them "as instruments of Jewish policy and control elections with them." "Richest Man Sucks Americans' Blood" describes Michel Fribourg as "a capitalistic Zionist." Zionism is related to Marxism through a description of the symbol of the Jewish Defense League as the "Marxist clenched, upraised fist superimposed on a Magen David." [Feedback: The preceding sentence is a "trivial example."]

Other articles emphasize segregation and "White world solidarity." An editorial advises America against sharing its technology with Third World countries because they are "our natural enemies." Instead, the Zambians should be left "happily squatting in their own filth." The editorial rejects the "equalitarian mythology" of the United Nations, which places the votes of persons in the Third World on a par with the votes of a "Canadian or a German."

An "NYA-WGP in Action" article appears in every issue. One such article describes the fight that occurred when communists tried to break up a celebration of the anniversary of Mussolini's birth. Each issue also contains NYA's program, an editorial, and a list of books sold by NYA. (Titles range from Mein Kampf to Beowulf.) Another regular feature is "Sick Pic of the Month," one example of which is a photo of Richard M. Nixon saluting Golda Meir. (JMA)

Feedback:

As can be seen from the material in square brackets (above), the editor of Attack! made several comments and suggested several additions. Dr. Pierce edited three journals reviewed in our earlier volumes: The National Socialist Liberator, National Socialist World, and White Power.

CHRIST IS THE ANSWER: A Christian Journal with the End Time Message

Clyde Edminster, Ed.
Box 128
Rainier, Wash. 98576
Monthly; voluntary contribution
Started: Dec. 1967
Circulation: 5,000

Format: 28 pages (5 1/2" x 8 1/2", offset)
Issues examined: Oct.-Dec. 1973
Back issues available from publisher

Christ Is the Answer, official publication of the Woodbrook Chapel, is published with "the express purpose of spreading the Personal and National Message of the Gospel of Jesus Christ and furthering the Kingdom of God on earth, and to give the Bible answer to the perplexing prophetic, political, and spiritual problems of our day." The periodical appears to be a family operation with the editor being assisted by members of his family both in the writing of articles and in the production of the magazine.

This periodical is much concerned with America ("But there is a great and mighty nation, and one which has been a blessing to all other nations in more ways than one, and that is our own United States"), with the threat of communism ("We are entering into an era of one-worldism, designed and financed by Satan's brood to dominate the whole world under INTERNATIONAL WORLD-COMMUNISM"), and with race relations:

> If you disobey the Seventh Commandment, commit adultery [mongrelize with a non-white] and conception takes place, the child is a mongrel [bastard]. He is impure, imperfect and inferior physically [and] mentally, and is an abomination in the eyes of god.--Because the offspring is non-White, a mongrel.

In an article entitled "Ten Truths Your Pastor Should Be Telling," other concerns are set forth, including a warning that an "economic depression and a total failure of the money system of America and the world is eminent [sic]," a statement that "the people commonly called Jews by most Christians are, in reality, the very synagogue of Satan," and the belief that "we are living in the very end time and that the return of Jesus Christ is eminent [sic]." Most of the themes mentioned above recur in each issue, along with other articles devoted more exclusively to the study of the Bible. Quotations from the Bible are always used to support and reinforce the stated tenets of the magazine.

A regular feature, "News Flashes from Woodbrook," contains pictures of visitors to Woodbrook Chapel, or of the Edminster family. (CH)

Feedback:

Mr. Clyde Edminster, the editor, replied:

> Your draft was quite concise and to the point. However, one of the main issues you seemed to leave out is that we stress in all of our issues ... that the Anglo-Saxon Nordic white race of people are the real literal modern-day Children of Israel. We also stress that America is that great and mighty nation promised to Abraham, identifying Manasseh, while the British Commonwealth is the Company of Nations identif[y]ing Ephraim promised in Gen. 48:19. The Jews are not--as they contend--all Israel, but represent only a small remnant of the Kingdom of Judah in which the Kingdom of God was taken from in Matt. 21:43.
>
> We also stress [that] race-mixing is genocide to all races, and that the one-world planners cannot solve the race problem by integrating the races into one supermongrelized UNESCO-brown man.
>
> Perhaps you may want to incorporate these points into you[r] report, as they are some of our principal themes we stress--outside of a personal experience with Jesus Christ, and a deeper walk in his Spirit life.

## CHRISTIAN ADVOCATE

Russell R. Veh, Pastor-Director
6311 Yucca St. (No. 931)
Hollywood, Calif. 90028
Monthly; $5
Started: Nov. 1972

Circulation: 1,000
Format: 10-16 pages (5 1/2" x 8 1/2" or letter size, offset, stapled)
Issues examined: Mar. (publ. in Toledo, Ohio) & June 1973

This is the official publication of the Anglo-Saxon Christian Crusade, which has as its "pastor-director" the founder of the American White Nationalist Party. (Mr. Veh is also the editor of NS Mobilizer, reviewed later in this chapter.) Christian Advocate was first published in Toledo, with the title White Power--not to be confused with the White Power reviewed in our 1970 volume. Some Toledo issues bore the present title.

In one of the early issues of Christian Advocate the publication was self-described as "The Nation's Fastest Growing Anti-Communist Paper." However, most of the articles in the two copies examined dealt with racial questions, particularly those concerning the Jews, some referring incidentally to Communism as a Jewish movement. Appended to one issue were several pages of reproduced clippings from various newspapers describing Veh's political activities. The other edition contained reprints of two articles published in The Century Magazine in 1928. In these articles, the first of which was entitled "A Real Case Against the Jews--One of Them Points Out the Full Depth of Their Guilt," Marcus Eli Ravage alleged that Christianity itself had originated as a Jewish subversive movement against Roman domination, which eventually destroyed the Roman Empire and finally insinuated itself into every phase of Western civilization. Ravage's ironical approach is evident in questions such as the following:

> If you really are serious when you talk of Jewish plots, may I not direct your attention to one worth talking about? What use is it wasting words on the alleged control of your public opinion by Jewish financiers, newspaper owners and movie magnates, when you might as well justly accuse us of the proved control of your whole civilization by the Jewish Gospels?

And from the second article:

> Why bandy about unconvincing trifles when you might so easily indict us for serious and provable offenses? Why throw up to us a patent and clumsy forgery such as the Protocols of the Elders of Zion when you might as well confront us with the Revelation of St.

> John? Why talk about Marx and Trotski when you have Jesus of Nazareth and Paul of Tarsus to confound us with?

Although these two articles practically constituted one entire issue of Christian Advocate, they seem to be in contradiction to the general editorial policy of the paper. It is conceivable that Ravage's irony was not recognized by the editor. On the other hand, the inclusion of these articles might represent fair play and a willingness to give an opponent an opportunity to be heard. The editorial comments on the articles, however, did not seem to warrant the latter conclusion. (SMA)

Feedback:

"Why don't you give our 'editorial comments' too?"

## CHRISTIAN VANGUARD

New Christian Crusade Church
James K. Warner, Ed. & Publ.
Box 3247
Hollywood, Calif. 90028
Monthly; $6

Started: 1970
Circulation: 10,000
Format: 12 pages (offset)
Issues examined: Oct.-Dec. 1973
Most back issues available from publisher

The editorial viewpoint of Christian Vanguard is partly exemplified by two slogans which frequently appear in its pages: "White People of the World Unite!" and "On any issue before you choose, check for influence of the Jews!" The following quotation from an editorial entitled "Segregation of Prisons Needed" illustrates the religious orientation characteristic of the paper, in which references to the Bible are frequent:

> The Bible distinctly tells us about Beasts with hands, beasts that talk and beasts that wear clothes.
>
> The Beast referred to in the Bible is the same beast that is living among us today--the negro! He is the same as in Bible days. The only thing that has changed since then is the common sense of the White man and the current lack of love for his own RACE.

In addition to editorials, another regular feature of the paper is "News Notes," which includes brief accounts of events bearing on racial questions, interspersed with editorial comments. Representative of frequent articles concerning Jews were those entitled "Here's Proof--'Jews' Caused Food & Gas Crises!" and "Who Are the Israelites?" The latter was one of several rather lengthy essays devoted to the distinction between the Jewish people of modern times and the "Israel" denoted in the Bible as God's people. (For more information on James K. Warner's National Socialist theories, see the review of Action in our 1970 volume.) (SMA)

## COUNTDOWN

F. Paul Fromm, Ed.
Box 278, Station K
Toronto, Ont., Canada
M4P 2G5
10 issues a year; $5
Started: June 1972

Circulation: 1,075
Format: 20 pages (offset)
Issues examined: v. 1, no. 7 (Jan. 1973), no. 10; v. 2, no. 1

Countdown, in the words of its editor, "attempts to provide readers with an impartial account of the activities of all groups on the Canadian right." The magazine also provides the conservative interpretation of the news and tries to encourage Canadian writers.

In the latest issue examined, the editor makes the following comprehensive statement of position and purpose:

> We believe that a countdown is in progress for our Civilization. There is not much time left in which to reverse the present trend toward socialism, loss of personal freedom, and the complete destruction of our traditional morality and way of life.
>
> This magazine is founded on the belief that certain moral values have created our Western Civilization and that these values can be preserved and must be preserved!
>
> Proudly Canadian, we are committed to a healthy society and a strong Canada. We stand for economic justice for all, within a free enterprise system. We uphold the idea that because God has endowed man with a free will, man must be held responsible for his actions. We, therefore, reject Marxist materialism and economic determinism.
>
> We are a culturalist magazine. We respect the value and uniqueness of each human culture. Attempts at forced 'equality' of all peoples are both

> false and destructive of all concerned. As far as possible, we will strive for the cultural homogeneity of Canada as the best means of preventing destructive racial tensions and of promoting the healthy growth of our beloved country.

One of the major purposes of the periodical is to warn readers of the danger of communism, and to alert them to communist influence. Readers are warned to watch out for specific people suspected of being communists, and to be aware of slanted articles in the media. Articles in Countdown identify dangerous attitudes. For instance, the policy of peaceful coexistence is called a "sellout to the Communists," and the United Nations is described as a dangerous leftist organization:

> By the purposeful falsification of true facts, the objective of the UNITED NATIONS is to ensure the ultimate triumph of Left-wing forces, and to corrupt the minds of mankind until we are inextricably enmeshed in a ONE WORLD GOVERNMENT. Let us beware of this Godless organization.

Countdown defines the "Steps to Destruction" as "Liberalism, Socialism, Communism." Therefore, the magazine opposes Trudeau and the Liberal government. An article in the January 1973 issue ("Liberalism Bankrupt") describes the Canadian government as a "WEAK, ineffective government which cannot rule decisively." It is a "GOVERNMENT OF POLITICIANS WHO NEVER LEARN." Liberalism is summed up in the word "weakness." Among the complaints against the Trudeau government are "the coddling of the welfare parasites, the open door immigration policies, the abuse of the parole system, the downgrading of our army, [and] the increase of big brother welfarism." Readers are exhorted to "WORK ACTIVELY TO DEFEAT THEM NEXT TIME!"

Countdown does not believe that it is possible or desirable for people of different races to live together. Consequently, it is opposed to a lenient immigration policy. "Milksop leftist politicians" are accused of promoting racial crisis. Countdown's message is "CANADA FOR CANADIANS!" The magazine supports the Ku Klux Klan, agreeing with them that forced integration is a denial of freedom. Readers are warned about movies or books which present slanted viewpoints. A review of "Sounder" warns the reader that the "movie is filled with sly but effective propaganda devices aimed at making a White audience feel guilty." In conclusion, the reviewer states, "This subtle and sordid propaganda job could well do more harm in the demoralization of our people than two dozen putrid pornies with sex in every frame!"

In addition to informing readers, Countdown urges them to act. ("The time to act on the things we believe in is now!") The magazine itself is actively involved in pressuring the government and preventing the spread of communism. Countdown has participated in such activities as demonstrating to close down Rochdale College (a "major center of drug distribution and crime"); sending a letter to members of Parliament urging them to vote to stop immigration from India, Pakistan, and the West Indies; and joining other anti-communist organizations to protest the appearance of the Red Army Chorus at the Canadian National Exhibition. (CT)

Feedback:

The editor, Mr. F. Paul Fromm, replied:

> The only inaccuracy in your write-up is ... where you say: 'The magazine supports the Ku Klux Klan, agreeing with them that forced integration is a denial of freedom.' While we certainly hold the position that forced integration is a denial of freedom, so do many non-Klansmen in Canada and the U.S. COUNTDOWN DOES NOT SUPPORT THE KU KLUX KLAN. Any reference to the Klan in Countdown (and there has only been one) would be in the context of a report on the Klan as a Canadian right-wing group.
> ...
> While the description of Countdown as an anti-communist journal is correct, I might point out that our main interest is in the financing of communism and socialism. In other words, we are more concerned with the establishment people, who finance leftist groups (either directly or through government grants) than we are with some shaggy-haired demonstrator, who is spouting Karl Marx. We believe that there is extensive collusion between the revolutionary and anarchist rabble and international, monopoly capitalism. The victims of these two forces ... [are] the productive middle- and working-classes. I could go on--but you envision a descriptive write-up, not a book.

## FOLK OG LAND: Uavhengig Politisk Publikasjon

Odd Isachsen, Ed.
Box 3214 Sagene
Oslo 4, Norway
Fortnightly; 70 kr.
Started: 1950
Circulation: 5,000

Format: 8- to 16-page tabloid
Issues examined: June & July 1973; Feb. 1974
Back issues available from publisher

Editor Isachsen describes Folk og Land as an "independent nationalist newspaper." One of the contributors, Odd Melsom, was an admirer of Major Vidkun Quisling's during World War II. A section of the paper contains excerpts from other national socialist periodicals: Nation Europa, Nordisk Kamp, Spearhead, and White Power. The July 1973 issue carries an appeal for assistance to disabled war veterans--presumably those Norwegians who fought against the Soviets during World War II. Other items in the same issue:

1. The suggestion that "Anne Frank propaganda" made the Dutch unduly pro-Israel, thus causing the Arabs to cut off Holland's oil supply during the winter of 1973/74.
2. An objection to biassed anti-Nazi propaganda.
3. Excerpts from the memoirs of one of Adolf Hitler's aides, recalling the last days in the Fuehrer's bunker beneath the Chancellery in Berlin.
4. An article on the Rothschild dynasty, based on material published in The Cross and the Flag.
5. The statement that Anwar el Sadat (now the president of Egypt) was, during World War II, in touch with the German General Erwin Rommel, passed information to him, and hoped to bring the Egyptian armed forces into the war on the side of Germany.
6. The Column, "For Ungdommen" [For Young People], expresses sympathy for Hitler's deputy, Rudolf Hess, who "risked his life for peace" by flying to Britain in 1941. At the "death-festival" (war crimes trials) of Nuremberg, the Allies sentenced him to prison, and he is still there--the only remaining inmate of Spandau Prison, a four-power establishment maintained at considerable expense.
7. The paper's "book service" offers works on 20th-century military history; a biography of Hitler; and phonograph records (speeches by Hitler, songs of the SS, Wehrmacht, and Nazi youth movement).

The June 1973 issue comments on the Western Guard Party's opposition to colored immigration into Canada [see our review of Straight Talk in this chapter]; makes fun of NATO soldiers as pot-smoking, flower-bedecked hippies; and carries an article by Ralph Hewins (author of the only English-language biography of Quisling) on Norwegians who collaborated with the German army of occupation during World War II. (TJS)

NRP BULLETIN and NORDISK KAMP

Nordiska Rikspartiet
Box 162
152 00 Strängnäs, Sweden
Monthly; 50 kr.
Started: NK 23 Jan. 1956; Bulletin 1969

Circulation: 2,000-10,000
Format: NK 28-38 pages (8 1/4" x 11 3/4", mimeo., stapled); Bulletin (8 1/4" x 5 3/4")
Issues examined: Nos. 4-6 (1973) of NK

Although Nordisk Kamp is in Swedish, an English-language NRP brochure supplied the following information. Goran A. Oredsson founded the Nordiska Rikspartiet in Malmö, Sweden, in 1956 and started the official NRP newspaper, Nordisk Kamp.

> From 1956 to 1959 NK was published as a printed newspaper. This newspaper ... was ... so dreaded and hated by those in ... power that in 1960 they print-boycotted the newspaper (by directives from the Trade Union Federation of Sweden).
>
> After years of irregular publication and changing printing procedures the newspaper since 1966 has been printed by electro-stencil and is now the largest electro-stencil newspaper in Scandinavia. NK is often quoted by the Swedish newspapers. Even in countries outside Sweden NK is featured, as the object of the NRP is to achieve big articles. Subscriptions to the Newspaper from ... [libraries] are continually arriving....
>
> Much of the activity of the NRP is ... taken up with written explanations for students.

The NRP's flag is red with a black (in commemoration of the national-socialists who fell fighting against Communism during the Second World War) sunwheel ("an old symbol of our people"), and similar armbands are worn on the organization's grey uniform shirts.

What has divided NRP from most other national movements in Scandinavia is

> that the party-leader G. A. Oredsson, always open and clear, has declared: 'We are national-socialists! We believe in the ideas of national-socialism and we preserve tenderly the memory of A. Hitler and the German people who showed us the way.' This open and bold attitude has resulted in our enemies' demanding, several times,... Oredssons's head on a dish!

The brochure goes on to say that in spite of lies, slander, and terrorist methods employed against it, the party has become so well known in Scandinavia that newspapers carry news of its activities almost daily.

The NRP has a special action group, RAG, which spreads political propaganda throughout Scandinavia and Finland by distributing posters, stickers, buttons, and leaflets. Four slogans that the NRP pushes are: "Stop the immigration into Sweden," "Reject the help to the developing countries," "Stop the de-population from the countryside," and "Stop the asocial-bustling (coddling!)." Through such tactics as painting catch-words (on bridges, cliffs, and rocks) and sending telegrams (to the Soviet embassy in Stockholm), the NRP is demanding the release of Rudolf Hess (former deputy to Adolf Hitler) from Spandau Prison, in which he has been incarcerated since the Nuremberg trials.

The brochure also speaks of "young party-comrades" attacking Communists in the streets and of NRP establishing contacts with like-minded groups in England, Italy, the USA, and Germany. "NRP is a working-platform for National-Socialism in the whole North. NRP ... works to build upright National Socialist governments in all countries for a close alliance. NRP works for a united Europa."

The NRP-Bulletin "is smaller in size and form because the object of the Bulletin is to be the NRP voice on actual political problems for mass-distribution to the people."

Feedback:

"The draft is approved by us."

## NS MOBILIZER

Russell R. Veh, Ed.
Box 26496
Los Angeles, Calif. 90026
Bi-monthly; $6
Started: Mar. 1974
Circulation: 1,000

Format: 16 pages (offset)
Issues examined: Mar.-July 1974
Back issues available from publisher

NS Mobilizer (formerly NS Kampfruf) is the newspaper of the National Socialist League, "an international organization promoting the free association of proud White men, united by faith in their race and their determination to seek sexual and political freedom." The cover of the first issue shows Richard M. Nixon nailed to a cross, wearing a Star of David and a crown of thorns, and looking up to where a figure labelled "Ike" hovers in the clouds; the caption reads: "My God, My God, Why Hast Thou Forsaken Me?"

In subsequent issues the homosexual [Feedback: "sexual nonconformist"] orientation of the publication becomes more evident in photographs of sculptures of male nudes and in the classified advertisements. In response to criticism from the National Socialist White People's Party, an article in the July 1974 issue urges the compatibility between homosexuality and National Socialism, citing Hitler's admiration for Frederick the Great ("an unabashed homosexual"), Richard Wagner ("favorite of homosexuals"), and Friedrich Nietzsche ("no model hetero"). The writer asserts that the purge of Major Ernst Roehm and his followers from the Nazi Party was motivated by Roehm's insubordination rather than his homosexuality. [Feedback: "The piece concludes: 'It's tragic that White men of good will must squabble while our racial enemies advance on all sides.'"]

News briefs protest possible Vatican recognition of mainland China, the imprisonment of the former head of the Michigan Ku Klux Klan, "affirmative action" in employment practices, and the removal of gold and silver from circulation by the Federal Reserve System "and its Jewish stringpullers."

In the editor's words, "the paper is unabashedly pro-White and anti-Semitic in its editorial stance." He continued:

> A typical issue would contain two pages of world and national news, from a right-wing perspective; two pages of editorial statement on issues of topical interest; two pages of membership news for the NSL; two pages on the interaction of the sexual-freedom movement and the right wing; four pages of reprints and analyses of articles in other underground publications; one page for subscription blanks and membership applications; one page of letters; and two of classified advertising.

(SN)

Feedback:

"Excellent and highly objective! In particular, please note ... the distinction between 'homosexual' and 'sexual nonconformist'--believe it or not, we have a few real bisexuals and even a heterosexual among our members." The editor suggested textual changes, some of which we have incorporated into the review.

## PERSEVERANCE

Béla Kántor, Publ.
Box 125
Merredin, Western Australia
6415
Australia

Monthly; $4.25
Format: 20 pages (legal size, mimeo., stapled)
Issues examined: Feb.-Apr. 1974

Perseverance "is not published for the general public but is made only for those National Socialists who do not read Hungarian, as an information service." It is an organ of the Hungarist Movement, whose members are followers of the "Co-Nationalist" Ferenc Szálasi. Contributors come from several countries.

The April issue contains a speech entitled "What is Communism?"; a description of the circumstances surrounding the Fascist march on Rome in 1922; an extract from Mussolini's last speech; and an interview. "Who Are the Rulers of Russia?" ("by a man who lived 25 years under Communism") raises 31 questions; the first, "Why is it that every country where Communism has taken over, they first destroy the educated class along with their entire families, with the exception of the Jews?" and the last, "Why was Communism based on the Talmud?" are representative. The author of "Battle for the Liberation of Cuba" asserts that the Zionist conspiracy intends to rule the world through Communism, and that Communism took over Cuba "with the complicity and help of the American State Department and the Zionist-controlled press." He says that when the CIA has intervened to provide arms and aid to the Cuban resistance, resistance leaders have subsequently been seized, implying that the CIA lured them to reveal their identities and then betrayed them to Castro. In "Danger: A Big Collapse," from Great Britain, the writer wants to "Curb the exorbitant demands of the unskilled mass in industry, but reward the skilled industrial worker and craftsman, the scientist and the technician, and greatly raise standards in the under-paid services." Increased production, stabilized prices, a "viable continental system" to provide food and raw materials, and direct government action are proposed.

An article in the March issue favors a combination of

"old-style Capitalist private enterprise and old-style Socialist public control" in opposition to the "Marxist-socialist ideas" of the Labor Party. The writer distinguishes between "Private individual enterprise working within a Free Market economy, with its necessary concomitant free Trade Unions and free wage bargaining," and capitalism, which is "above all the money manufacturing Banking System dealing on an international plane...."

Despite the international character of the publication (it also appears in French and Spanish), it is intensely nationalistic in spirit. World government is viewed with hostility as a disguise for Jewish/Marxist ambitions. (SN)

POPULATION REPORT: To Restore Fair European Immigration
INSTAURATION: Viewpoint of the Majority Student

American Immigration Committee
Box 1221
Decatur, Georgia 30031
Occasional; $5 (on mailing list indefinitely)
Started: 1971

Format: PR, 6 pages (offset); I, 8-page tabloid (offset)
Issues examined: PR, Oct. 1971; I, Fall 1973
Back issues available from publisher

The Committee distributes various publications or newsletters supporting "Right-wing, Christian Conservatism, America First" positions and projects, according to the publisher and editor, Steven N. McKinney.

The sample issue of Population Report warns readers that "Non-European elements are flooding America," and that it is "under an invasion of hostile elements which seek the downfall of the European elements whose culture, labor, and scientific know-how made this nation great." These hostile elements are identified as Latin Americans (particularly Mexicans), Negroes from the West Indies, Filipinos, and Chinese. The last-named are also discussed in the article, "Communist Chinese Flooding America." Citizens are urged to "preserve White Civilization" by contributing to the Committee, and to write Congress demanding repeal of the Kennedy Immigration Act of 1965.

A special campus edition of Instauration declares that "Colleges Discriminate against Majority Students," and calls "For the liberation of America from liberal-minority racism and bigotry." There are articles supporting those who have found a relationship between heredity and learning capacity;

criticizing college admission policies in regard to minorities; and warning of campus crime, particularly rapes.

Majority students are urged to speak and work actively for their beliefs and rights--such as a fair representation of right-wing writers in college libraries. They are given advice on how to work for majority rights:

> All such agitation should be accomplished in an unassuming, low-key style that reeks of irreproachable erudition. By using this holier-than-thou technique you are 'outsnobbing' the opposition, a very profitable ploy in a pseudo-scholarly atmosphere. It is much more difficult for a newspaper or an academic committee to reject a well-written petition than a sloppily-composed set of allegations replete with fuzzy and ungrammatical Birch Society overtones. Your language should never contain the least hint of racial inferiority or superiority. Let the facts speak for themselves.

(GKS)

STRAIGHT TALK

| | |
|---|---|
| Box 544, Station A<br>Scarborough, Ont., Canada<br>M1K 5C4<br>and<br>Box 193, Station J<br>Toronto, Ont., Canada<br>M4J 4Y1<br>10 issues a year; $5 | Started: 1967<br>Circulation: 2,000<br>Format: 18 pages (legal size)<br>Issues examined: v. 5, nos. 8 & 10 (1973?); v. 6, no. 1 (1974?); also the first draft of the Toronto Manifesto of the Western Guard Party |

This is a "White Power" publication of the white-nationalist Western Guard Party, formerly the Edmund Burke Society. On the masthead is the declaration that "The Western Guard Party is dedicated to preserve and promote the basic social and spiritual values of the White People. Under the symbol of the Celtic Cross, we fight for our Christian moral values, our European heritage, and the spiritual and cultural rebirth of our people." Also on the cover page: "Articles which are signed do not necessarily represent the views of the Party." The Party is opposed to all use of non-medicinal narcotics. (See Point 35 in the Toronto Manifesto, below.)

Among the articles examined is "Mongrelization in Totonto" by Emilio de Bono, associate editor of ST. Mr. de Bono urges public denunciation, in Toronto and elsewhere, of sexual relations between whites and blacks. (There seems to be no suggestion that denunciation should give way to violent enforcement of sexual segregation.) He foresees the extinction of the white race unless race-mixing is prohibited. In Brazil and other Latin-American nations wherein racial intermarriage has been taken for granted, he perceives "a lack of moral fibre deep within the people [that] condones both personal dishonesty and government corruption of such widespread nature that an honest system is inconceivable." He attributes to the sexual assimilation of black Africans the disappearance of Portugal as a world power.

Elsewhere in the same issue, Mike Collins writes: "At this time the WGP is dedicated to the peaceful taking of power in Canada and therefore cannot endorse all of these actions [violence by white-supremacists] although personally many of us may hold sympathy for the thoughts behind them." Also in that issue is mention (under the heading, "Party Activities") of a "birthday party for Benito Mussolini." In "Who Are the Media Masters?" Dr. William Pierce with evident disrelish calls attention to the ownership of several leading U.S. newspapers by persons of Jewish ancestry. (Pierce is the editor of The National Socialist Liberator, reviewed on pp. 847-50; National Socialist World, pp. 850-54; and Attack!, reviewed in this chapter.)

One issue announces the organization of Defence Group Don Andrews (named for the head of the WGP) "for the further instilling of loyalty and discipline in the physically fit WGP members...." In another issue, Pierce refers to World War II as Franklin D. Roosevelt's "drowning in blood [of] the youthful renaissance of racial idealism which was manifesting itself in Europe...." (WJS)

Feedback:

"We sincerely hope you can include our Toronto Manifesto.... The ideology of the WGP has not varied since the first draft of the Manifesto, and has remained constant. The Toronto Manifesto is the only official policy document in the contemporary right-wing. However, we in the WGP object to being labelled as being 'right wing.' We are White Nationalists, concerned with the future of Canada's White population, while some consider us to be National Socialist."

The 44 points of the Western Guard Party Manifesto are herewith quoted in full:

1. A WGP government will stop all coloured immigration immediately, no matter under what pretext it is currently allowed, particularly from such places as

Africa, India, Pakistan, Bangladesh, the Caribbean, and the United States.

2. A WGP government will support a program of repatriation of non-White peoples to countries or areas where their own race is the majority.
3. In order to halt the mongrelization of our White race, the WGP will change marriage laws to guarantee only marriages of the same or similar racial stock.
4. Substantial financial aid will be given White families at the birth of each child.
5. The WGP will create self-administered Indian and Eskimo states.
6. The Bank of Canada, under firm WGP Government supervision, will have the sole right to create new credit for the economy.
7. The WGP advocates the cancellation of that part of the National Debt incurred through inflationary credit creation by international banking houses. This does not, of course, prejudice the nation's obligation towards the small saver, and will result in a substantial saving to the Canadian taxpayer.
8. A WGP government will initiate a direct international trade or barter system, thus eliminating the brokerage fees of foreign financiers, with a substantial saving to the Canadian taxpayer.
9. A WGP government will adknowledge no obligation on the part of the Canadian people to make economic sacrifices in order to subsidize the so-called "underdeveloped nations." This will result in a substantial saving to the Canadian taxpayer.
10. A WGP government will withdraw Canada from the United Nations on the grounds that that body has fallen much too heavily under Communist and Afro-Asian influence. This will result in a substantial saving to the Canadian taxpayer.
11. A WGP government will propose the creation of a Commonwealth of anti-Communist White Nations for the purposes of preferential trade and cultural exchange.
12. A WGP government will press for the liberation of the captive nations under Communist imperialism. Any dealings with the Communist bloc will be with the express purpose of achieving this goal.
13. A WGP government will maintain a strong Canadian defence force and will be prepared to aid and cooperate materially and financially with all anti-Communist countries throughout the free world.

14. The WGP supports the desire of the Palestinian Arabs to return to their homeland with full civil rights.
15. The WGP recognizes the need for racial amity throughout the world, based on the concept of well-defined racial spheres of influence.
16. A WGP government will create jobs for all able-bodied workers, including those who are trapped on welfare, with a substantial saving to the Canadian taxpayer.
17. The WGP supports the practice of profit-sharing in industry as the best incentive to all workers. It further supports workers' partnership schemes, and advocates consultation between workers and management on profits as well as wages.
18. The WGP supports the principle of Canadian control for Canadian industry and unions.
19. The WGP favors unions and collective bargaining, but also upholds as a principle the right of all to work.
20. The WGP will ensure that Canadian workers will have safe and healthy [sc. healthful] working conditions.
21. The WGP favors equal opportunity for women as well as men, with equal pay for equal work. However, this concept should not interfere with the preservation of a strong family unit, which is a basic building block of Western society.
22. The WGP will ensure a fair price for all farm products, and very low mortgage rates to any farmer who depends on farming for his livelihood.
23. A WGP government will prevent the chemical adulteration and over-refining of basic foods.
24. The WGP will control food prices by minimizing the influence and eliminating the profiteering of the non-productive middleman, with a substantial saving to the Canadian taxpayer.
25. In order to end profiteering on human misery, a WGP government will nationalize the entire drug industry (to include the manufacture, distribution, and retail levels), with a substantial saving to the Canadian taxpayer.
26. A WGP government will provide adequate hospital facilities and train more doctors by building more medical schools. The WGP will enforce a realistic schedule of doctors' fees.
27. The WGP is opposed to abortion, except for emergencies involving life or death.
28. A WGP government will provide adequate food, clothing,

housing, and health services to the elderly, the sick, the disabled, and the destitute.

29. A WGP government will give small, interest-free loans to Canadian families who wish to obtain their own homes.
30. The WGP will abolish succession duties.
31. The WGP will ensure that an essential part of all education should be the development of character, physical health, patriotism, and of the Racial and moral values necessary to the maintenance of a stable and vigorous society.
32. The WGP believes that in a civilized society, the arts and sciences should flourish. Hence, a WGP government will patronize true art and subsidize pure scientific research.
33. The WGP advocates the formation of a voluntary but strong citizens' militia.
34. A WGP government will guarantee the right of Canadian citizens to possess any firearms necessary for the protection of their homes and families.
35. The WGP will re-introduce capital punishment for murder and other capital crimes (to include trafficking in hard drugs on second conviction).
36. The WGP will attempt to ensure the rehabilitation of the criminal and the protection of society by introducing hard labour within the penal system.
37. The WGP will review bail laws in order to aid the police and protect the public from habitual criminals.
38. The WGP will institute a speedier and more efficient court system. Judges' appointments will come under review regularly. A WGP government will re-imburse those acquitted of charges for any expenses incurred.
39. The WGP stands for environmental health and the protection of Nature's gifts to Canada.
40. Recognizing that Canada is a maritime nation, a Western Guard Party government will build a large merchant shipping fleet.
41. In order to protect Canada's fishing resources, a WGP government will declare a 200-mile offshore limit, which a strong Canadian Navy will enforce.
42. A WGP government will make new laws that will restrict the growing pornographic trade and eliminate decadence in all fields of Canadian life.
43. A WGP government will break up monopolies of the news media in order to ensure truthful news reporting and the real freedom of the press.

44. The WGP supports the European system of Parliamentary representation of political parties, which is in ratio to the popular vote received. The WGP advocates a ceiling on election expenses.

## WUNS BULLETIN

2057 N. Franklin Rd.
Arlington, Va. 22201
Quarterly; $5 (available only to members)
Started: 1962

Format: 8-12 pages (offset, saddle-stapled)
Issues examined: July 1972 & Spring 1973

WUNS Bulletin is a publication of the World Union of National Socialists, founded by George Lincoln Rockwell (American Nazi Party) and some European Nazi leaders in England, in 1962 (Cotswold Agreement). Leadership was inherited from Rockwell by Matt Koehl who is known as Commander of WUNS. (In earlier volumes, see our reviews of Action, White Power, National Socialist Liberator, and National Socialist World [official organ of WUNS].)

WUNS, made up of National Socialist parties in 26 nations, "is a global organization ... [composed] of persons dedicated to the creation of an Aryan World order based on the immortal idea of our spiritual leader, Adolf Hitler."

The purpose of the Bulletin is to report briefly on the activities of the movement throughout the world, country by country. For example, in the Argentina section, Juan Peron's return to power is applauded. (There doesn't seem to be a National Socialist group there, however.) Australia: the National Socialist Party of Australia captures 0.5% of the vote and the alarmed Jewish community is pressing parliament to outlaw it. Italy:

> Neo-Fascists, wearing crash helmets and even the blackshirts which are proscribed by government decree, have effectively swept Italian streets of the militant Reds who but a year ago arrogantly boasted that the streets belonged to them. Over 20,000 men have joined the MSI's [Movimento Sociale Italiano] Public Defense Committee which, in co-operation with Prince Valerio Borghese's Italian National Front, has wrought fear into the hearts of once self-confident Marxist terrorists.

North America: both major political parties held their nominating conventions in Miami Beach.

> Grasping at this golden opportunity, Commander Koehl led a group of stormtroopers to this Jewish metropolis to protest for the forgotten White American. Activities started with a bang when the troopers, in civilian dress, entered the Marxist stronghold of Flamingo Park. In the midst of 2,000 Reds, the National Socialists stormed the main speaker platform and held it for two hours. Commander Koehl demanded that all Red Flags be removed before they would give up the platform. Naturally the Reds finally refused and a battle broke out in which one National Socialist and four Reds were hospitalized....

Spain: the Falangists held a mass rally to express opposition to Franco's intent of reinstalling the monarchy.

The first page of the Bulletin carries a quotation from Mein Kampf and an editorial on the nature and function of WUNS. George Lincoln Rockwell is held in esteem--second only to Hitler--and quotations from his White Power appear on the last page. The names and addresses of foreign National Socialist periodicals are listed, and their front pages are sometimes reproduced (in reduction), as are photographs from them. Other features: reproductions of National Socialist posters; and obituaries of members or sympathizers (e.g., Ezra Pound). (JMS)

## Chapter 21

## METAPHYSICAL

I am a Tel-thought channel between the Space Brothers and the Earth's people....
---Marianne Francis of Starcraft

Tired of that Old-Time Religion? The Odinist and The Sunwheel, Human Dimensions, Order of the Universe, The Church of Light Quarterly, Rays from the Rose Cross, and Green Egg will get you out of your rut. They offer religions based upon such elements as eastern mysticism, western Odinism, extra-sensory perception, astrology, fusion with nature, exercise and healthful diet, and paganism.

Garuda, Human Dimensions, and Sadvipra present religious philosophies based upon yoga and eastern mysticism. Sadvipra represents a service organization, founded in India, that sends its spiritually enlightened members to work in drug programs, prisons, and with the aged and mentally ill.

Aquarian Agent, Horoscope, and The Church of Light Quarterly are concerned primarily with astrology; WICA Newsletter and Witchcraft Digest with witchcraft; The Journal of Parapsychology and Breakthrough! with ESP; and Gnostica News with just about everything. (In its pages you will find information on the topics already named, as well as the occult, UFOs, monsters, and health foods.)

For the daring--those willing to risk prison sentences--there are the publications of the Neo-American Church (American Solipsist and Divine Toad Sweat), which advocate the use of drugs to achieve religious expreiences. And for those who wish to open channels with extraterrestrial beings, there is Starcraft.

The New Age Interpreter--hard to categorize--seems to be a blend of Christianity, mysticism, and astrology. Cornerstone, Hollywood Freepaper, and The Pearl are published by Jesus People. Up-Look and CBF Good News are Christian evangelistic periodicals which undoubtedly view with dismay many of the other publications in this chapter. --Janet Spahn

## THE AMERICAN SOLIPSIST

Jack Call, Ed.
RFD 2 Box 96-B
Vergennes, Vt. 05491
Monthly; $6
Started: Feb. 1974
Circulation: 50

Format: 5 pages (Xerox and offset)
Issues examined: Feb. & May 1974; one undated Special Fictional Supplement
Back issues available from publisher

The editor (and Primate of California) writes to us that

> The American Solipsist prints news stories about activities of the Neo-American Church, satires of our occultist rivals, and fiction written from a solipsistic point of view. The editorial position of The American Solipsist is that there is no 'objective truth' and no 'external world' except as concepts in my own consciousness. Everything I know and perceive is a product of my own consciousness, as in a dream. This is the realization attained at the peak of an LSD trip and by enlightened mystics throughout the ages. Time is an illusion. Space is an illusion. Life is a dream.

The publication is one of several put out by members of the Neo-American Church (see our Index). One of the founders of the religion (which uses drugs to achieve a religious experience) and writers of the Church's Boo Hoo Bible is Timothy Leary, but (according to the May 1974 issue) he has fallen into disfavor. "Head Quarters reports that letters responding to the Excommunication of Timothy Leary are running 10 to 1 in favor, with many expressions of enthusiastic agreement."

The first issue (entitled The Daily Nihilist) consisted of a short story; a description by the editor's wife of her first "trip" on mescaline; some drawings produced under drugs; and news of members. The second issue consisted of a philosophical description of a hike in the mountains by the editor and some friends; and short news tidbits of drug trials. The third issue was a special fictional supplement which reviewed the collected works of Geza Larouzy. The publication is illustrated with reprints of old prints and etchings. The editor writes us that he's

> happy to see that there are some librarians who are not only not afraid of, but actively interested in,

minority opinions. I mean let's face it: the masses have always been a bunch of blubber-headed role-players, right? Hurray for the creative minority! Victory over horseshit!

(JMS)

Feedback:

Editor expressed no disapproval and sent his new address (publication formerly came from Long Beach, California).

AMONG FRIENDS

Doris Peters, Ed.
Illinois Yearly Meeting (Quaker)
1217 Michigan Ave.
Rockford, Ill. 61102

3 times yearly
Circulation: 1,000
Format: 16 pages (offset)
Issue examined: Summer 1974

"Illinois Yearly Meeting is a group of people searching for Divine guidance. We meet for a brief time each year to share our spiritual gifts and to try to create a caring spiritual community. We are a diverse group which comes together to continue a mutual effort to strengthen Friendly ties and faith."

AQUARIAN AGENT

127 Madison Ave.
N.Y., N.Y. 10016
Bi-monthly; $11 for 12 issues
Started: Sept. 1969
Circulation: 1,800
Format: 40 pages (8 1/4" x 10 1/2"); new format is 48 pages (6" x 9")
Issues examined: July & Nov. 1973
Microform version available from Xerox University Microfilms

Aquarian Agent ("For the Contemporary Astrologer"), published by Astrology Services International, is written to "inspire an intelligent and penetrating interest in Astrology." Aimed at the serious astrologer and astrology student, it requires more than a superficial knowledge of the terminology and philosophy of the subject.

Four or five articles in each issue detail aspects of astrological knowledge and processes. Articles are generally in a "scientific" or rational mode ("Astrological Psychodynamics" or "To What Degree Should Astrology Influence Our Decisions in Daily Living?"). Occasional articles emphasize mystical and subjective aspects of astrological thought. Features of Indian Astrology are examined.

A column on the finer points of charting for the astrologer ("Astrology For the Person") appears in each issue. Relevant book reviews and lists of publications received are presented, as are notices of conventions of astrological groups. (KL)

Feedback:

"Fine."

## AQUARIAN ESP HERALD

Harmony Hills,
3859 Valley Creek Rd.
Newport, Minn. 55055
$10

Format: 12 pages (offset)
Issue examined: Vol. 1, No. 1 undated (1972-73?)

The maiden issue of this "first national non-profit, nonpartisan spiritual newspaper" (press run: 250,000) explained its spiritual and earthly aims: It is

> dedicated to 'throwing the light of knowledge' on totalitarianism in any form, whether in politics, religion, economics, or whatever! When certain citizens grow aware of the true cause of high prices, wars, pollution, crime, and violence, they will gather ... at local, state, regional, and national levels--to make the necessary changes. However, it will be a non-violent battle of ballots, not bullets!
>
> We believe that the Aquarian ESP Herald can act as a strong unifying organism between otherwise impotently divided spiritual individuals and groups in our nation....
>
> We are deliberately acting as the 'reader's digest' of the newspaper and magazine world. Therefore, we are now collecting, stockpiling, and publishing the best material we can get from all sources. We also need specialists and laymen to write new articles concerning the cause and prevention of pollution, wars, violence, crime, new discoveries in ESP, science, medicine, economy, politics, art, and whatever else you can add that will illuminate public consciousness (and conscience)! This is an action-

oriented newspaper! We need active crusaders--doers, not talkers--from all walks of life....

The maiden issue contained articles on tarot cards; the control of one's own blood circulation, and of pain; reincarnation; astrology; keeping a diary of one's dreams; dowsing; an herb that might be effective against cancer; transcendental meditation; and Kirlian photography (of objects acted upon by electricity).

The Herald is illustrated with photographs. Most of its articles are--in keeping with its role as a digest--reprinted from other periodicals. It hopes to have 25 million (!) readers by 1976. (JMS)

THE AQUARIAN LIGHT: Newsletter of the Psychic Research Foundation

192 N. Clark St. (Suite 711)
Chicago, Ill. 60601

Format: 10 pages (mimeo., stapled)
Issue examined: Fall 1972

Part of the sample issue was devoted to a schedule of the classes offered by the Foundation.

AQUARIAN MESSENGER

Noree Pope, Ed. & Publ.
2716 N. E. 30th Pl.
Sutton Place East, Apt. #1
Ft. Lauderdale, Fla. 33306
5 times yearly; $1
Started: Dec. 1971
Circulation: 250

Format: 9 pages (5 1/2" x 8 1/2", offset)
Issues examined: Apr. & June 1974
Some back issues available from publisher

"The magazinette is based on metaphysical studies and beliefs--its sole purpose is to bring light to would-be seekers of Truth--it hopes to make people think for themselves and to become aware that no one faction, school, ism, etc., has the complete answer, that in the final analysis man must find the answers for himself 'within'--where all truth and knowledge are stored from time immortal--an attempt is made to touch the three-fold bodies of man (the mental, physical, and spiritual) with some thought for each one."

The issues examined contained several short essays and some poetry.

THE AWAKENER: A Journal Devoted to Meher Baba

Filis Frederick, Founder & Ed.
Universal Spiritual League in America
Box 1081
Berkeley, Calif. 94701
Semi-annual; $4
Started: Summer 1953
Circulation: 1,000
Format: 80 pages (6" x 9", offset)
Issues examined: Vol. 14, Nos. 3/4 (1973?); a Special Photo Issue (1971?)
Back issues available from publisher

*The Awakener* is "devoted to the life and teachings of Avatar Meher Baba, a unique spiritual personality of our time. As we believe him to be the 'great world teacher,' Christ, Messiah, Avatar, Rasool, or Maitreya of the New Age--our publication may be, to some, 'radical' in the field of religion. We publish his teachings; photos, diaries and reminiscences of disciples and devotees; and other related material."

BEADS OF TRUTH

Sardarni Premka Kaur, Ed. & Admin. Director
3HO Foundation
1620 Preuss Rd.
Los Angeles, Calif. 90035
Quarterly (Summer and Winter Solstices & Spring and Autumn Equinoxes); $6
Started: 1971
Circulation: 5,000
Format: 48 pages (offset)
Issues examined: Mar., June, Sept. 1973

The editor sent this information on the publication's policies: "To present the teachings of Yogi Bhajan, Master of Kundalini Yoga and the Siri Singh Sahib of the Sikh Dharma; to provide our readers with the most pertinent and up-to-date information relating to our Healthy, Happy, Holy way of life. To give a history of our growth, of our work, and of the progress of our lifestyle within the United States and other western countries."

Each issue carries a list of centers and ashrams, and of family centers in the U.S. and other countries.

BREAKTHROUGH!

Institute of Psychic Science
2015 S. Broadway
Little Rock, Ark. 72206
Bi-monthly; $5

Started: Sept. 1971
Circulation: 1,200
Format: 20-24 pages (5 1/2" x 8 1/2", mimeo.)
Issues examined: Dec. 1972; Feb. & Apr. 1973

Published "for the purpose of instruction," this newsletter is concerned primarily with the Institute's activities: announcements of courses ("Astrology for Beginners"), seminars, information about teachers, and books for sale at the Institute's bookstore. It also provides information on the activities of other organizations involved in psychic phenomena and metaphysical instruction and research in Arkansas.

The focus is on one- to five-page how-to articles explaining how one acquires understanding of and the ability to use such gifts as clairvoyance, precognition, and astral projection. (Examples: "Develop Your Own Ability to Forecast the Future"; "How to Increase Your Healing Energy.")

Up-beat poems and maxims ("Whatever you vividly imagine, ardently desire, sincerely believe, enthusiastically act upon--must inevitably come to pass") are features of the periodical.

The items advertised include articles useful in inducing psychic phenomena, for example the Mystic Pentagram Fortune-Telling System. (KL)

Feedback:

"Thank you! Very well written."

CBF GOOD NEWS

Rev. Carl T. Abbott, Ed.
Campus Bible Fellowship
University Ministry of
Baptist Mid-Missions
Box 111
Camillus, N.Y. 13031
3 issues a year; free
Started: 1971
Circulation: 30,000
Format: 8- to 12-page tabloid (offset)
Issues examined: Spring & Fall 1972; Spring, Special ed. & Fall 1973
Back issues available from publisher

According to the editor, CBF Good News is "directed toward both evangelism on the campus as well as informing the local church as to the progress of our Bible study groups on campus. It acts as a printed liaison between the local church and the campus." The Spring 1972 issue describes the publication as

> a voice on campus in contrast to that of the 'mod'

> Jesus movement and the politically slanted left wing propaganda sheets. We seek to present Jesus Christ in a way that will bring honor and glory to Him. We seek to give solid 'meat' of the Word to those who are wandering on the vain and vacillating institutions of higher learning.... It should be stated that the purpose of CBF Good News is to assist our 'on campus' CBF groups in their outreach, to encourage the local churches to involve themselves with the campus in the area of evangelism, counselling, and teaching the Word in dorm studies, rap sessions, etc.

Although Good News bills itself as a campus newspaper, there appear to be few if any students on the staff. Articles usually come from ministers, theologians, and laymen within the Baptist organization. Examples of topics covered are: "Is Reincarnation a Christian Option?" (no, it cannot be reconciled with Christianity); "Sex Can Be Spiritual"; "What Is Mysticism?"; "The New Sound in Religious Music"; and "Who Is Jesus? A Good Man or God?" (the latter).

Good News also contains personal religious testimonials. In "Liberated From Astrology," a young man describes how he experimented with astrology, palmistry, numerology, Tarot cards, ESP, and Edgar Cayce's meditation, and became very disturbed, finally turning to alcohol. He was saved by a girl who brought the Bible and God into his life. CBF and Baptists [Feedback: "Bible believers" in place of Baptists] in general disapprove of Eastern mysticism, the occult, and astrology.

The paper also contains book reviews; poetry and hymns ("Take Christ to the Campus"); interviews with and profiles of students and other members of the organization; letters; and coverage of CBF's activities (with emphasis on the northeast--especially New York--colleges). Each issue carries a listing of the Baptist Bible study groups on various campuses in nine different states. (JMS)

Feedback:

Editor suggested two textual changes. In the third paragraph, the sentence "he was saved by a girl...." should read "through the witness of a girl...." "We do not feel that individuals can save one another." The other textual change is noted in the review.

## THE CHRISTIAN CYNOSURE

Rev. B. Essenburg, Managing Ed.
National Christian Association
850 W. Madison St.
Chicago, Ill. 60607

Monthly; $2
Started: 1869
Circulation: 2,000
Issues examined: none sent
Back issues available from publisher

According to the editor, the goals of the publication are to spread the Gospel and to give information about secret societies. An enclosed leaflet gave this information:

> The National Christian Association was organized by a company of Christian men and women in 1868 in Pittsburgh, Penn., and incorporated under the laws of Illinois in 1874.
>
> Its object is to point to Jesus Christ as the world's only Redeemer and to warn against the paganism of Secret Societies, which destroys the soul.
>
> This it attempts to do in various ways, one of which is by sending out literature to all places as funds permit.
>
> This Association is not affiliated with any church or denomination, and therefore it seeks financial help only from those who are in sympathy with its principles. A special responsibility thus rests upon all who are enlightened respecting the vast evils resulting from secret orders.

## THE CHURCH OF LIGHT QUARTERLY

659 1/2 S. St. Andrews Place
Box 76862, Sanford Station
Los Angeles, Calif. 90076
Quarterly; $1 donation
Started: 1925

Circulation: 1,500
Format: 24 to 32 pages (7" x 8 5/8")
Issues examined: Spring & Summer 1973

This is the official organ of the Church of Light, which follows the Religion of the Stars. In both sample issues, the belief is professed that to obtain freedom from want and fear, and freedom of expression and religion, a person must have knowledge of the facts of ESP, astrology, induced emotion, and directed thinking. He must not be greedy or excessively acquisitive, but should be happy to contribute his best to the welfare of all mankind. Astrology is of central importance in the faith. It is

> the science of finding and utilizing the natural potentialities as indicated in the planetary chart of birth. It becomes a religion when it shows the individual how these natural tendencies can and should be utilized for the benefit of all mankind and the furtherance of the purposes of deity.

Most articles are by members of the Church. They give news of it, explain its policies and research, and offer inspiration to the reader. Among the subjects covered in the sample issues were circus astrology; sacrifice for the sake of religion; and Lucille Ball, the entertainer (a five-page article, with horoscope).

The news items concern such things as deaths (one who dies is said to have "passed on to the inner planes"), ordinations, announcements of classes and services, a list of recent contributors (those who give $25 or more belong to the Stellarian Honor Guard), and a list of persons in various parts of the world who can be consulted for information on the Religion of the Stars. There are also advertisements for a complete set of Brotherhood of Light lessons (24 books plus Tarot cards: $171). (EC)

Feedback:

"Draft O.K."

CORNERSTONE

Jesus People USA
817 W. Grace St.
Chicago, Ill. 60613
Every six weeks; donation

Format: 12-page tabloid (offset)
Examined: one undated 1974 issue

The publishing organization, a non-profit Christian community, is a "Discipleship Training School" whose aim is

> to teach believers a mature and consistent walk with Jesus. We preach the gospel through personal witnessing on the streets and sharing our newspaper, Cornerstone. Resurrection, our band, presents salvation through music; and the Holy Ghost Players through drama. At the time of this printing, we have 76 full-time disciples under a council of deacons, deaconesses, and [two] elders....

The issue examined contained testimonials and case histories of those saved (often from drugs); an adult fairy tale with a moral Christian ending; an essay on "Situation Ethics" (as opposed to true Christian morality); news of the conversions of such persons as Alex Smith (former drug pusher, son of Ian Smith, Prime Minister of Rhodesia); an article disproving the theory of evolution; reviews of books, records, and plays with a biblical theme; two comic strips poking mild fun at the Amish and the Jews as being of inferior religions; and letters. An editorial warned that

> The Jesus Movement is at a crossroads. Some converts have journeyed on to 'perfection,' throwing away their deodorant (their glorified bodies no longer stink); walking in such a spiritual plane that they can no longer dirty themselves with the problems of sinners in this world.
>
> Many see visions, have great 'spiritual Dreams,' give beautiful prophecies, and embrace all manner of extraneous spiritual manifestations--but if you asked those same people to empty the garbage after the fellowship dinner, you might see some rather extraordinary manifestations of the flesh.
>
> On the other end of the spectrum, we have those who have matured beyond the need for the straightforward truth of the Bible. They have looked to the left and to the right to see the man-made solutions: psychology, education, socio-economic structures. [They are likely to say:] 'Certainly you must realize that the complex problems of our modern civilization cannot be solved by a primitive religious fanaticism. Life is a maze of different directions. One answer cannot be for all questions.'

The editorial goes on to say that the only answer is the gospel of Jesus Christ.

The paper informed us that its "main aim is to bring people to Jesus Christ through the stories of our changed lives and attitudes. We speak out on the issues of the day. We hold to no political party or organization. We simply speak out for what is right."

*Cornerstone* is colorfully and imaginatively illustrated.

(JMS)

DIVINE TOAD SWEAT

The Neo-American Church North Troy, Vt. 05859
East Hill Road Monthly; $12 (includes copy

of the Boo Hoo Bible)
Started: 1964
Circulation: 150

Format: 3-6 pages (mimeo., stapled)
Issues examined: Aug. 1972; Apr., May, July 1973

Divine Toad Sweat, bulletin of the Neo-American Church (a "psychedelic religionist" group), consists of "three or four mimeographed pages of instructions, castigations, [and] philosophy for the benefit of Church members written entirely by Art Kleps, Chief Boo Hoo of the Church." Although future plans call for the broadening of editorial policy to include letters and "philosophic essays" from other clergy and members, all of the sample issues followed the above format. The following quotation offers examples of the Chief Boo Hoo's concerns:

> In a dishonest maneuver typical of the rhetorical strategy which characterizes much of the theoretical thought in sociology and anthropology these days, we are now seeing a disguised return of supernaturalist and matter-mind dualist ideas dressed up in fancy pseudo-scientific terminology. Slightly stoned and narrowly-educated people such as Castaneda, Lilly, Laing, and Huston and Masters. Typically, the notions produced by these characters are never explained in philosophic terms ... but are offered in a very off-handed manner as something that ought to be quite obvious to anyone who has sampled the psychedelic drugs or the wondrous 'alternative reality.'... Well, I have experienced hours and hours of visionary productions and witnessed many events which were inexplicable in terms of ordinary physical theory, but I do not care to be associated with occultist theory in any way, and I resent the now common assumption ... that psychedelic drug use tends to support occultist theory.... There are no occultists at the peak of an acid trip: only mystics, nihilists, solipsists, radical empiricists, Madhyamika and Yogacara Buddhists, idealists, monists. All the occultism is on the other side, coming down, where the ignorant, stupid, cowardly, and dishonorable are gathered together to repress as best they can the knowledge of the Void and the illusory nature of the world (and themselves).

The Chief Boo Hoo employs Divine Toad Sweat to alert his fellow Neo-Americans to their responsibilities as Church members, and to remind them of the need for both philosophic and financial support:

> Now, just because the essence of Neo-Americanism is a profound joke rather than something superficial and 'serious' ... doesn't mean that we do not have certain practical objectives which require practical means of achievement--which require money.

A separate publication, the Boo Hoo Bible: The Neo-American Church Catechism, explains the purposes, basic principles, theology, and organization of the Church, "a loose band of drug-soaked mystics." The Church's tenets [see Feed back]:

1. Everyone has the right to expand his consciousness and stimulate visionary experience by whatever means he considers desirable and proper, without interference from anyone.
2. The psychedelic substances (such as LSD) are the True Host of the Church, not drugs. They are sacramental foods, manifestations of the grace of God, of the infinite Imagination of the Self, and therefore belong to everyone.
3. We do not encourage the ingestion of psychedelics by those who are unprepared.

The motto of the Neo-American Church is "Victory over Horseshit." (JYH)

Feedback:

"The philosophic statement is 'I Deny the Externality of Relations.' Immediate goal is to test the constitutionality of the laws which prohibit the use of LSD and the other psychedelics by church members. Long range goal is the bombardment and annihilation of the planet Saturn." The Church's tenets have been changed, and now read:

1. Everyone has the right to expand consciousness and stimulate visionary experience by whatever means he considers desirable and proper, without interference from anyone.
2. The psychedelic substances, such as marijuana and LSD, are sacraments, in that they encourage Enlightenment, which is the realization that life is a dream, and the externality of relations an illusion.

3. We do not encourage the ingestion of psychedelics by those who are unprepared, and we define 'preparedness' as familiarity with solipsist-nihilist epistemological reasoning on such models as David Hume and Nagarjuna.

Mr. Art Kleps went on to add that "the 'loose band' concept is out of date, since we are now frankly doctrinaire, elitist, and authoritarian--although local congregations remain autonomous as to property and organization. We are not a 'society of spiritual seekers,' but a group with a definite point of view."

EAST WEST JOURNAL

29 Farnsworth St.
Boston, Mass. 02210
Monthly; $9
Started: Jan. 1971
Circulation: 50,000

Format: 48-page tabloid (offset)
Issues examined: Apr., June, July 1973

A statement of purpose in each issue explains that the paper's aim

> is to help people gain control and direction over their lives. It is our hope that ... [it] will be a useful tool for the conduct of daily life in accord with the order and harmony of the universe. We hope to develop the worldwide and broadly-based readership necessary to realize our dream: the Kingdom of Heaven on earth.

Each issue is devoted to a particular theme. One carries informative stories on camping, clearly describing the equipment and its uses, and including a page of first aid techniques based on acupuncture. Another supplies information on seeds and natural agriculture. A third describes profitable "businesses of [the] counter-culture." (Suggestions include publishing books and selling health foods.) There are also many articles on spiritual practices and philosophies.

Regular features include an editorial section and "Natural Foods Cooking." [Feedback: "and alternative technology, healing, book reviews, record reviews, women, and community."] Readers express their opinions in "Letters." "East West Notes" are items of wide variety deemed of interest to readers. The sample issues included interviews with an author, an astronaut, an actress, and a former ambassador to Japan.

The Journal is enlivened with poetry and many photographs, and contains a good number of advertisements. (MN)

## ECK WORLD NEWS

Eckankar
17885 Skypark North (Suite E)
Irvine, Calif. 92707
Monthly; $6
Started: Feb. 1972
Circulation: 10,000

Format: 8-page tabloid
Issues examined: Oct. & Dec. 1973; Jan. 1974
Back issues available from publisher

This periodical comments on "life and world events from the viewpoint of Eckankar, an ancient secret science whereby the individual is able to move beyond the limits of the physical state of consciousness and gain personal knowledge of the ECK, the current of light and sound that supports and sustains all life." It reports on seminars held to acquaint people "with the teachings of Eckankar and the current Living ECK Master, Sri Darwin Gross, and also features profiles of some of the unique individuals who are the chelas, or students, of ECK."

## ESOTERIC COORDINATING NEWS: Metaphysical News and Events of the South

Donna M. France, Ed. & Publ.
Christialand Foundation
206 Pasadena Ave.
Metairie, La. 70001
Monthly; $3
Started: Aug. 1971

Circulation: 1,000
Format: 28-32 pages (5 1/2" x 8 1/2", offset)
Issues examined: Nov. 1973; Jan. & Feb. 1974
Back issues available from publisher

The editor describes her policies this way:

> To give information on local organizations and international get-togethers in the parapsychology, ESP, metaphysical, and occult realms. Articles pertaining to health, self-improvement, astrology, book reviews, film reviews, information on organizations, previews on speakers in these and related fields.

The publication includes "all religions and philosophies, yet endorses no single one, knowing that each person must find his own proper channel, accepting Truth to the degree that he is ready for" it.

These are some of the subjects dealt with in the sample issues: a form of yoga; diet ("Confessions of a Carbohydrate Addict"); spirit messages from Gandhi (on freedom) and Edgar Cayce (on the Second Coming); a message received from a comet that entered the solar system in late 1973; astrological predictions; and interpretations of the Bible. (JMS)

Feedback:

The editor expressed no disapproval.

## THE FATHER'S HOUSE

Brother Francis, Ed. & Publ.
2606 Newhall St., #42
Santa Clara, Calif. 95050
Quarterly; $5
Started: 1969

Format: 36 pages (8" x 11", offset)
Issues examined: 4 issues of 1973 bound into an annual

The publication carries this message: "The Father's House is a New Age Spiritual Activity, universal and world-wide in scope. It is not the mouthpiece of any church or philosophical organization though we recognize that all have their place in serving the spiritual needs of mankind. The material presented in these pages comes from the very cream of New Age authors and thinkers, both East and West."

The material presented in The Father's House seems to be a blend of Christianity, eastern mysticism, astrology, and spiritualism.

## GARUDA

1111 Pearl St.
Boulder, Colo. 80302
Roughly annual; variable $2 to $2.50
Started: Spring 1971

Circulation: 7,500-8,000
Format: 60-100 pages (offset)
Issues examined: none sent
Back issues available from publisher

The Vajradhatu agent for Garuda sent this information: "Garuda has consisted primarily of the work of Chogyam Trungpa, Rinpoche in lectures, essays, art work and translation. Also we have included articles by Shunryu Suzuki-roshi, late abbot-founder of Zen Center, San Francisco, and Tassahara Mountain Retreat Center; and various students of Trungpa, Rinpoche."

GNOSTICA NEWS

Ronald Wright, Ed.
Box 3383
St. Paul, Minn. 55165
Monthly; $5
Started: Sept. 1971
Circulation: 20,000
Format: 24- to 36-page tabloid

Issue examined: 21 June 1973
Back issues available from Llewellyn, Box 3383, St. Paul, Minn. 55165
Microform version available from Xerox University Microfilms

The editor states that

> Gnostica News is a serious commentary on the Occult: Astrology, Witchcraft, ESP, scientific aspects of occult phenomena, Magick. We take the subject seriously and attempt to teach, emphasizing methods and theories.

The periodical solicits "articles on everything from astrology to herbs, from Frankenstein to feminism, from magick to macramé." The lead article in the sample issue, "UFOs and Monsters," contained the observations of a number of persons on the Loch Ness phenomena. There was also a piece announcing "nightly meetings and programs for initiated witches only" held at the Gnostic-Aquarian Festival in Minneapolis; a section ("Lunation Forecast") with information on the zodiacal signs; one article in a series on "The Tarot"; and one about "Gemstones: Their Psychic Symbolism."

Also included in the sample issue were instructions on "How to Develop Psychic Ability," an article on "Wiccan Sects," and the second part of a series on "The What and Why of Magick," giving reasons for forming a Magickal Lodge.

Regular features: information on the use of herbs; reviews of books and records; and advertisements for pertinent books and periodicals, as well as for occult supplies ("Jinks removing, conquering, or blessing spray") and practitioners ("Gifted and psychic Reader: 3 questions $1.00"). (EC)

Feedback:
"O.K."

GREEN EGG

Church of All Worlds
Box 2953
St. Louis, Mo. 63130
8 issues per year; $6

Started: April 1968
Circulation: 1,000
Format: 48-56 pages (7" x 8 1/2", offset)
Issues examined: 1 May, 21 June, 1 Aug. 1973

Green Egg is a magazine representing the "Aquarian Age religious scene, especially that aspect known as Neo-Paganism." It is published by the Church of All Worlds, "a Neo-Pagan Earth Religion dedicated to the celebration of Life, the maximal actualization of Human potential, and the realization of ultimate individual freedom and personal responsibility in harmonious eco-psychic relationship with the total Biosphere of Holy Mother Earth." It serves as the official journal of the Council of Earth Religions, and includes articles about the various Neo-Pagan religious groups represented by the Council. Such articles may describe the philosophical basis of a religion, or its activities and rituals, or initiation rites into covens; or one religious sect may be compared with another. Some of the topics covered in this journal are witchcraft, American Indians, occultism, magic, sacramental psychedelics, wildlife, sexual ethics and ecstasy, science fiction, and organic gardening, to mention only a few of those reported by the editor. Many of the contributions, whether expository or creative, contrast neo-paganism with Christianity, or merely attack Christianity. [The editor of Green Egg suggested deleting the last four words.] In one issue the words to "Battle Hymn of the Republic" and "Amazing Grace" were cleverly changed to honor Pagan Deities. A feminist view is taken in an article "Christianity vs. Women" in which the Christian ideology and practice is found at the roots of the oppression of women in society.

An 18-page section "Forum" concludes each issue with letters from readers who request information or express reaction to Green Egg in general or to a particular article or letter in a previous issue. The letters are usually lengthy and quite lively. No editorial censorship is practiced in the "Forum," a policy which the editor claims provides for "VERY controversial" material. (SA)

Feedback:

"O.K." The editor suggested, and we have made, several minor changes in wording.

HARVEST NEWS LETTER: A Letter of Facts

E. T. Tennyson, Ed.
Box 33
Jefferson City, Mo. 65101
Bi-monthly; $2

Started: 1939
Circulation: 2,000
Format: 8 pages
Issues examined: Special Edition #149; Nov. 1973; Mar. 1974
Back issues available from publisher

Each issue of Harvest News Letter carries this information:

> Prophecies of the Bible are like news flashes written in advance, and the purpose of Harvest News Letter is to report these strange and often unknown words of the prophets. Edited by a layman (a plain businessman), it is not a religious magazine, but is a News letter Service and is therefore free of fanaticism, creedism, and denominationalism. Purposely brief and condensed for busy people, it is published for one purpose only: to restore lost truths and help its readers KNOW THEIR BIBLE!

In "Resurrected Millions Will Farm Fertile Ocean Bottoms when Seas Are Removed by Coming Whirlwind" the editor explains that

> the original words of the prophets ... reveal a startling message of good news for the world.... The whole purpose of this News Letter, therefore, is to point out this amazing discovery ... that the words of the prophets definitely and unequivocally reveal that the man Christ Jesus will return to the old city of Jerusalem where he will set up a literal and physical Kingdom or Government, and from the old 'throne of David' (Isaiah 9:6) he will actually and literally 'save the world' (John 3:16, 17, 18)! Far from a 'pie in the sky' dream, the prophets assure us that this is an actual event that will take place upon this earth, and that will bring about reforms and a 'society' such as men today have never dreamed!

The rest of the issue is devoted to describing this wonderful society: There will be

> ample room for all to return to earth from the dead, and ... the whole earth will be air-conditioned like the garden of Eden! For even ... 'the waste and desolate and ruined cities will become fenced and inhabited' (Ezekiel 36:35)! But more than that, the

> heartless and competitive commercialism we are compelled to endure today will be no more! For we are told that **EVERY ONE** will have his own small farm--that 'they shall build houses, and inhabit them, and they shall plant vineyards, and eat the fruit of them.'

The News Letter is a strange blend of modern science ("Biblical Study Leads to Food-Growing Idea and to Treatment by High Pressure Oxygen") and Biblical prophecy.

(JMS)

HOLLYWOOD FREEPAPER ["Upper Midwest Edition"]

Jesus People International
Box 533
Hopkins, Minn. 55343
Donation

Format: 8-page tabloid (offset)
Issues examined: two undated issues from 1972 & 1973

Illustrated with photographs and cartoons. The address of the group's main headquarters is Box 1949, Hollywood, Calif. 90028.

HOROSCOPE

Dell Publishing Co.
245 E. 47th St.
N.Y., N.Y. 10017
Monthly; $6
Started: 1935
Circulation: 300,000

Format: 130 pages (7" x 10", letterpress)
Issues examined: none sent
Back issues (past year only) available from publisher

The associate editor sent the following information: "We deal only with astrology--tropical (based on the zodiac, determined by the earth's passage around the sun) and not sidereal (based on the actual constellations). This is the system most commonly used in the western world. We accept articles on any topic by competent astrologers."

HUMAN DIMENSIONS

S. Thompson Viele, Ed.
4380 Main St.
Buffalo, N.Y. 14226
Quarterly; $5

Started: Winter 1972
Circulation: 3,000
Format: 20 pages
Issues examined: Spring &

Summer 1973 publisher
Back issues available from

Human Dimensions carries about five articles in each issue. Most of them are prefaced by an abstract and conclude with a list of references. There are profiles of the authors. Photographs in black-and-white or color accompany some of the articles.

The sample issues contained several conference papers with such titles as "Further Research into a Chromatographic Technique for Vitamin Analysis" and "The New Bio-Technology's Potential Applications to the Educational Environment." An article on "The Significance of Kirlian Photography" explains a method of high-voltage radiation field photography which produces pictures which suggest the aura surrounding the human body. The articles are written for the layman--despite such titles as "Acupuncture: Consider the Ion a Theoretical Electromagnetic Explanation."

Activities of the Human Dimensions Institute are also reported. In "Tuning In: The Natural Alternatives to Drugs," a pilot project sponsored by the Institute is summarized. (Young people in a high school were encouraged to experience their own potentials through field trips and lectures on Yoga, meditation, and the wisdom of the Seneca Indians.) A selection of course offerings printed on the back of one issue included Introduction to ESP, Beginning Astrology, and Continuing New Approaches to Healing.

The Special Meditation Issue of HD is available as a separate publication for $2. 50. Highlights of a past issue include the "Tibetan Book of the Dead" and verses by Lama Anagarika Govinda (accompanied by illustrations created from his meditational experiences). Book reviews and letters to the Institute appear in some issues of HD. (JA)

## THE JOURNAL OF PARAPSYCHOLOGY

Dorothy H. Pope, Ed.
Box 6847, College Station
Durham, N. C. 27708
Quarterly; $10 ($10. 50 foreign)
Started: 1937
Circulation: 1,500
Format: 100-120 pages (5 1/2" x 8 1/2", offset)

Issue examined: Dec. 1973
Indexing: Annual self-index
Some back issues available from publisher and Walter J. Johnson
Microform version available from Xerox University Microfilms

The Journal of Parapsychology, published by the Parapsychology Press (a subsidiary of the Foundation for Research on the Nature of Man), has the sub-title: A Scientific Quarterly Dealing with Extra-Sensory Perception, the Psychokinetic Effect, and Related Topics.

According to the editor, "Most of our articles are devoted to experimental reports of laboratory research. Survey articles, statistical notes, and theoretical articles, when they are accepted, are closely tied in with the research."

In the sample issue, "Introduction of an Activity-Wheel Testing Cage into the Rodent Precognition Work" discusses apparatus that helped researchers trying to determine whether rats in a laboratory cage made use of precognition in avoiding randomly-generated electrical shocks.

"ESP with Unbalanced Decks: A Study of the Process in an Exceptional Subject" describes an experiment with a deck of 25 cards with unequal frequencies of the five standard symbols (circle, square, cross, star, waves). The unbalanced deck was found to illuminate some aspects of ESP, and the study increased knowledge of how it works in an exceptional subject.

There are regular sections: Letters, Book Reviews, News and Comments, Books Received, and Parapsychological Abstracts. This last section has abstracts of books and reports (both foreign and domestic) from other journals, as well as of unpublished reports on file at the Institute for Parapsychology. (The sample issue contained five abstracts, including two from the Journal of the American Society for Psychical Research: "Radial and Tangential Forces in the Miami Poltergeist" and "The Measurements of Psi.") (GKS)

Feedback:

Editor expressed no disapproval. An enclosed flyer informed us that in addition to experimental reports "there are articles which attempt to interpret the findings and relate them to knowledge in various other fields. Historical reviews and discussions of some of the challenging questions that arise also appear occasionally." Some articles that have appeared in recent issues of the journal are: "Personality Characteristics of ESP Subjects"; "A PK Test with Electronic Equipment"; "Does Extrasensory Perception Affect Psychological Experiments?"; "Location of Hidden Objects by a Man-Dog Team."

MYRRH

Box 11
Saint John, New Brunswick,
Canada

Irregular; donation
Format: 8-page tabloid (offset)
Issue examined: Spring 1972

An evangelistic Christian publication.

NEW AGE INTERPRETER

George Perkins, Ed.
4636 Vineta Ave.
La Canada, Calif. 91011
Quarterly; $2
Started: 1949
Circulation: 800

Format: 32 pages (6" x 9", offset)
Issues examined: 2nd & 3rd quarters 1972; 4th quarter 1973
Back issues available from publisher

The New Age Interpreter has articles about Christ, the Sacred Scriptures, astrology, and the Law of Karma in relation to healing. The editor writes about the importance of altruistic love and states, "The star of Christ stands before the gates of Aquaria calling upon those who would be his disciples to carry its living waters to a thirsty world." Theodore Heline feels that our civilization focuses more on mental than on spiritual values and says that not reason but rather intuition "catches truths from a higher realm by contacting cosmic wisdom."

The New Age Press offers editions of the writings of Theodore and Corinne Heline, such as the latter's volumes describing music and color as healing and regenerative forces in healing temples of the future. The Press cooperates with the New Age Bible and Philosophy Center to offer correspondence courses in Esoteric Philosophy which use Max Heindel's The Rosicrucian Cosmo-Conception as a text.

Book reviews are a regular feature, and most of the books are available from the periodical. (They are all religious, philosophical, or mystical.) Another regular feature ("Cooperative Notes") says that

> In this transition period between the Piscean and Aquarian ages, many groups and individuals are to be found on the highways and the byways of life who sense the vision of the New Age and who steadfastly have aligned their efforts with the Great Ones to help to externalize the Divine Plan into the hearts

> and minds of men that It may manifest in physical reality.

The column is dedicated to bringing such efforts to the attention of readers. (GKS)

Feedback:
The editor expressed no disapproval and suggested a minor textual change which was incorporated into the review.

THE OCCULT DIGEST: A Periodical of Reprint and Research

Daliniated Press
Box 11074
Chicago, Ill. 60611
"every new moon"; $3.50

Format: 24 pages (offset)
Issue examined: Vol. 2, No. 5 (1972)

"The object of this publication is to voice the theories and practices of all occultists and metaphysicians and to give each one a chance to voice his or her views--something that is exceedingly difficult to do in a biased religious culture. The editors do not necessarily agree with every view stated in these pages, but offer space to all in an attempt to show the necessity of religious and spiritual freedom."

THE ODINIST and THE SUNWHEEL

Box 731, Adelaide Station
Toronto, Ont., Canada
M5C 2J8
Monthly (combined); combined subscription $2
Started: June 1971
Circulation: 500
Format: Odinist, 10 pages (offset); Sunwheel, number of pages variable (same dimensions; duplicated)

Issues examined: Odinist, Nov. 1971; Mar., June, Sept., Dec. 1972; Mar., June, Sept. 1973. Sunwheel, July 1972; Feb., Apr., May, July 1973
Back issues available from publisher

The Odinist and its supplement, The Sunwheel, are published by the Odinist Movement which is governed by the Odinist Council with members in the United States and Canada.

> There is no general membership and therefore no membership fee,--but we expect that every person who agrees with our ideas and the scope of our

undertaking will realize that sacrifice of time, effort and money will be necessary in order to further our purposes.

The purposes of the movement are

1. To bring to the many people who are rejecting the principal tenets of the Christian Church an alternative in keeping with the natural instincts and the basic philosophical characteristics of the people in the West.
2. To bring positive information about our cultural heritage which has been excluded from the regular teachings of Western churches and schools.
3. To instill in our people a pride in past achievements, a feeling of individual worth and confidence in the vitality of the Western folk soul.

Named after the greatest of the gods in Norse mythology, The Odinist expresses religious ideas of Indo-European origin in which there is a fusion of God and Nature. Adherents believe that the world is good. A basic conviction of The Odinist is that to achieve a meaningful life, man must accept and live in harmony with nature and its laws and not try to oppose them as he is taught to do by many other religions. The periodical contains numerous statements which contrast traditional Christian teachings with those of the Odinist movement. The following passage is from an article on "Morality":

> The greatest contribution Christianity has made to man is to burden him constantly with a sense of guilt and shame. I cannot understand why a supposedly omniscient god like Yaweh would allow his creation, man, to fall into such a state if his love was so great that he subsequently had to 'sacrifice His only begotten Son' in order to save him.... The spiritual attitude of the Odinist accepts the supremacy of human values as derived from human instincts. It also accepts that the purpose of every individual's life is the fulfillment of motives which are part of his human nature.... Odinism, as should now be clear, does not see man as needing salvation from anything, certainly not himself.

Many of the articles explain the Odinist's interpretation of various concepts, such as "Existence," "Creation," "Culture" and "Loyalty." The issues examined also contained a series on "Man and His God," giving the movement's reply to such questions as "What Is God?" and "Does Man Need God?" Other articles are largely historical: "The Beginning of Art," "The Viking Discovery of America," and "The Most Ancient Barbarians."

The supplement, The Sunwheel, contains mostly "speeches held at important Odinist Celebrations, the old Sages re-told and information concerning the Odinist religion." These celebrations include the summer and winter solstices, and the spring and fall equinoxes. (EC)

ONTOLOGICAL THOUGHT: Journal of the Ontological Society

Robert Moore, Ed.
Box 328
Loveland, Colo. 80537
Monthly; $4.50
Started: 1969

Circulation: 2,000
Format: 32 pages (5 1/2" x 8 1/4", offset)
Issues examined: Feb., Apr., June 1973

Ontologists envision man as mired in a destructive, chaotic environment instead of enjoying the positive, harmonious experiences and relationships that would characterize his "true state of being." Ontological Thought, published by the Eden Valley Press at Sunrise Ranch, Loveland, encourages readers to free their minds and emotions and bring order and creativity into their lives. The editor states that changes "in deeper and more basic levels of human endeavor than politics and economics" are required in order to bring about profound alterations in our environment.

Each issue has a theme--some area or aspect of our civilization,--and all readers (whether individuals or groups) are invited to contribute articles describing their experiences with the subject. Recent issues have considered our culture in relation to Business, World Consciousness, Science Fiction, and Criminology. The editors and staff writers contribute regularly, but readers' offerings are also published. (GKS)

ORDER OF THE UNIVERSE

Richard Baume, Ed.
62 Buckminster Rd.
Brookline, Mass. 02146
Every 1 1/2 months; $15 for 12 issues
Started: 1971

Circulation: 5,000
Format: 40 pages (6" x 9", offset)
Issues examined: none sent
Back issues available from publisher

The editor sent the following information:

> In ancient times man lived in order and harmony with the laws of the universe. He intuitively knew the principles that would bring him health, happiness, and long life. Modern man, through generations of bad eating, has lost this understanding and lives in darkness and ignorance. His health both mental and physical is impaired to such a point that he must construct an artificial environment around himself to survive. This publication offers practical studies showing ways to apply the principles known by the ancients to our modern context. These principles are eternal and universal and can bring man once more into harmony with the order of the universe.

PSI MAGAZINE

| | |
|---|---|
| Helen Reid, Ed. | Circulation: 2,000 |
| 495 Lyon St. North | Format: 16 pages (12" x 17", offset) |
| Ottawa, Ontario K1R 5X6, Canada | Issues examined: none sent |
| Bi-monthly; $2 | Back issues available from publisher |
| Started: 1971 | |

The editor sent this information: "PSI Magazine attempts to present metaphysics and related psi science subjects (psi=psyche or indwelling essence, spirit) in the most positive and progressive way possible. Editorial policy does not favor sensationalism, but strives to inspire and present positive and uplifting concepts for the readers' consideration, leading to possible growth in any sincere individual."

THE PEARL

| | |
|---|---|
| Calvary Evangelistic Center | Circulation: 5,000 |
| Jesus People | Format: 12-page tabloid (offset) |
| Box 1126, 120 Belmont St. | Issues examined: none sent |
| Worcester, Mass. 01605 | Back issues available from publisher |
| Quarterly; $3 | |
| Started: Apr. 1971 | |

The publication sent this information: "The main purpose of our paper is to proclaim the Gospel of Jesus Christ. We endeavor to maintain an evangelical position."

RAYS FROM THE ROSE CROSS: The Rosicrucian Fellowship Magazine

Perl Williams, Ed.
2222 Mission Ave. --Box 713
Oceanside, Calif. 92054
Monthly; $4.50
Started: June 1913
Circulation: 4,000
Format: 48 pages (6 3/4" x 9 3/4", offset)
Issues examined: May, July, Aug., Nov. 1973; Jan. 1974
Indexing: annual self-index
Back issues (from 1930) available from publisher

Established by Max Heindel, this journal regularly presents excerpts from his writings on religious philosophy. In accord with the founder's interests, Rays from the Rose Cross is concerned with the whole man: his spiritual, mental, and physical health, as well as the society in which he lives.

Each issue discusses the Bible, astrology, nutrition, health, and healing. Book reviews, answers to readers' questions, and a children's section are regular features.

Rosicrucians recommend a vegetarian diet without alcohol or such stimulants as tobacco. They believe that prayer and creative thought can heal, but that healing can also be helped by physical means. They believe that souls [Feedback: we, as spirits] have lived in other (human) bodies in the past [Feedback: and the goal of this evolution is self-conscious union with the Father]. Spirits that have developed special talents (such as musical ability) tend to seek to be reborn in bodies with suitable physical characteristics (such as long, slender fingers, and anatomically-perfect ears).

An editorial on vegetarianism discusses the four life-waves: mineral, plant, animal, and human. The writer quotes a law about assimilation: "No particle of good may be built into the body by the forces whose task that is until it has been overcome by the indwelling Spirit." "The consciousness of the plant is that of dreamless sleep, making it easy for the human Ego to overpower the vegetable cells and keep them in subjection for a long time." However, since animals "have individual desire bodies, they suffer much more when slaughtered than do the vegetables, which are permeated only by the planetary desire stuff." Because of this, "it requires greater effort on the part of human beings to overcome the individual cell life in animal tissue.... Also, such particles will not stay in subjection." (GKS)

Feedback:

Editor suggested some textual additions (indicated in the

review) and the deletion of the sentence beginning "Spirits that have...." (third paragraph). The publication has no connection with Rosicrucian Digest (San Jose, Cal.) which "is from another organization entirely."

The editor also included some literature which offered an explanation of Rosicrucian Christianity from which we quote in part.

> The Rosicrucian Fellowship is a movement for the dissemination of a definite, logical, and sequential teaching concerning the origin, evolution, and future development of the world and man showing both the spiritual and scientific aspects; a teaching which makes no statements that are not supported by reason and logic.... 'but'--Rosicrucian Christianity does not regard the intellectual understanding of God and the universe as an end in itself, far from it. The greater the intellect, the greater the danger of its misuse. Therefore the scientific teaching is only given in order that man may believe and start to live the religious life which alone can bring the true fellowship.
>
> The Rosicrucian Fellowship ... encourages people to remain with their churches as long as they can find spiritual comfort there, and gives them at the same time the explanations which creed may have obscured.

Anyone is eligible to enroll with the Rosicrucian Fellowship as a student as long as he or she is not a hypnotist, medium, palmist, or astrologer.

SADVIPRA: The Journal of Social and Spiritual Progress

| | |
|---|---|
| Barry Wallach, Ed. | Circulation: 5,000 |
| Ananda Marga | Format: 12- to 16-page tabloid |
| 1644 Park Road N.W. | Issues examined: Nov. 1973-Feb. 1974 |
| Washington, D.C. 20010 | Back issues available from publisher |
| Monthly; $2.50 | |
| Started: Oct. 1972 | |

The editor sent this information:

> Our major aim is to provide the information which is needed by those persons who are to provide service and leadership for society. Persons who are

> spiritually, mentally, and physically developed can best provide the inspiration which will elevate all of society. Despite the current crisis that the world is passing through, we are optimistic and believe that a new society can emerge in the coming years. This society will be global, it will make full and rational use of all physical, psychic, and spiritual potentialities that exist in the world, and it will make [provision for each individual to be] ... provided with an opportunity to progress on the physical, mental, and spiritual levels. With this worldview we approach current events, developments in the sciences, arts, economics, education, etc.

"Ananda Marga is a spiritual organization whose members practice meditation for individual development ... [and] engage in service for the welfare of the wider community." Founded in India in 1955 by Shrii Shrii Anandamurti, the organization has provided schools, medical services, and disaster relief. According to Sadvipra, critics within the Indian government have attempted since 1967 to curtail Ananda Marga's activities. In 1971, Anandamurti and some of his followers were arrested for abetting the murder of six former members of the group. His followers maintain he was arrested under false pretenses and has since been subjected to inhumane treatment including an attempt to kill him with poison. In the U.S., members of Ananda Marga are working in drug programs, in prisons, and with the aged and the mentally ill. Recently, Ananda Marga stepped up its social service programs, opening primary schools and group boarding homes for troubled adolescents. The article "ERAWS House: Center Combines Social, Spiritual Growth" describes the Education, Relief and Welfare Section (ERAWS) of Ananda Marga, which trains people in these projects in a program of physical, mental, and spiritual activity combined with field work with social agencies in the Washington area.

Examples of other articles that have appeared in Sadvipra are: "New Methane Generator Makes Homemade Fuel, Gas from Waste"; "Drought Threatens Nomadic Lifestyle" (West Africa); "Yogi Amazes Scientists, Stops Heartbeat for Seven Days"; "Can Good Diet Prevent Cancer?"; "Poverty and Malnutrition Plague Native American Reservations"; "Three Great Spiritualists Pass Away" (one of them Alan Watts, popular English-born American interpreter of Far Eastern thought); "Lessons of the Oil Crisis"; and "Recognizing and Restoring Women's Rights." The publication also has articles on cooking, gardening, ecology, and science, and a section ("Rawa Review: A Supplement of the Arts Prepared by the Renaissance Artists' and Writers' Association") which contains poetry, reviews (of books, films, and records), and philosophical essays by Shrii Shrii Anandamurti and others. (JMS)

Feedback:

"We think your reviewer did an excellent job in describing Sadvipra." The editor suggested a few minor textual corrections which have been added to the review.

STARCRAFT

| | |
|---|---|
| 7700 Avenue of the Sun | Format: 22 pages (6 3/4" x 8 1/2") |
| Central Point, Ore. 97501 | Issues examined: Summer/Fall 1967; Summer & Fall/Winter 1968 |
| Irregular; $3.25 | |
| Started: Mar. 1966 | |
| Circulation: 1,000 | |

A publication of the Solar Light Retreat (formerly Solar Light Center), Starcraft is edited by Marianne Francis. She is said to be a "channel" between the Space Brothers (perhaps inhabitants of other planets--their precise relationship to the human race is not made clear) and human initiates or adepts. In one issue, she reports a telethought transmission to her (on 27 July 1968) from one identifying himself as Sut-Ko of the Saturn Council, about geological and psychological changes occurring on earth. Sut-Ko said that he was speaking from a "craft stationed above this mountain locality" (i.e., above the Solar Light Retreat). Each issue also contains transmissions from a certain Orlon, evidently the chief spokesman or publicist of the Space Brothers. The predictions of events on earth lack specificity, except that an earthquake (or a series of earthquakes) will devastate a large part of North America. (WJS)

Feedback:

The Director and Channel of the Solar Light Retreat, Marianne Francis, Dr. Sp. Sc., replied that "There are many corrections needed on the draft you sent...." She continued:

> I have a religious degree of Doctor of Spiritual Science and have been trained in this field of par[a]psychology and allied subjects since childhood both here and in England my native land.

> On the basis of simply reading three issues ... your summary ... does not give a clear po[r]trayal of what we are doing. You also have to bear in mind that we do not expect to explain our principles aims etc in every issue as the magazine is by sub-[s]cription and our readers have a clear idea of what is going on from their original contact with us. At no time have I stated I was a channel between the Space Brothers and Human initiates and adepts. I am a Tel-thought channel between the Space Brothers and the Earth's people as are many other such channels.
>
> At no time does Orlon state he is the 'chief publicist of the Space Brothers.' He is merely one of my more constant contacts over the years I have been in contact.
>
> Predictions as such are not the purpose of the Brothers but information is given from time to time of impending events within a scale of CYCLIC time. The main data recieved [sic] here at headquarters ... [are] spiritual and philosophical; also data of a technical kind for our research Lab (which is in the building stage) ... [are] being channelled but ... [are] mainly classified at this time.

Director Francis said that the Internal Revenue Service considers the Retreat to be a non-profit, tax-exempt organization.

## THE SUN

Skip Whitson, Ed.
Box 4383
Albuquerque, N.M. 87106
Monthly; $5 for 8 issues
Started: as Astral Projection in 1968. (Title changed to Tribal Messenger in 1969 and to present title in Jan. 1974)

Circulation: 3,000-5,000
Format: 32-page tabloid (offset)
Issue examined: Apr. 1974
Back issues available from publisher
Microform version available from Xerox University Microfilms

Contains fanciful illustrations and cartoons in an underground format, and covers a wide variety of subjects--drugs, Zen, astrology, Meher Baba, astronomy ("Jupiter: Cold Star" and "Black Holes: Seeds of the Cosmic Age"), "The Underground Newspaper Collectors," health food, pollution, and the oil shortage (oil companies blamed). The paper has been carrying installments of Art Kleps's "Millbrook," a "story of the early days of LSD experimentation in the upper New York State estate where Kleps participated along with Timothy Leary, Dick Alpert, and others." [See our reviews of Neo-American Church publications in this volume.]

The paper also contains poetry, record album reviews, a half page of book reviews and annotations, an entertainment calendar, and a community directory for such things as abortion information, spiritual groups, medical aid clinics, and ecology centers. (JMS)

Feedback:
Editor expressed no disapproval.

UNITED FAITH MAGAZINE: Brother Al's Magazine of "Health and Happiness"

Box 707
Fresno, Calif. 93712
Format: 8 pages (offset)

Issues examined: two undated issues (1974?)

The cover of one issue announced that "Brother Al, famous minister, will help you with the problems you are facing through faith in God." The other cover reported that "Thousands upon thousands across the nation love this humble man, and God is doing some great things through this servant who carries such a burden for those who need prayer."

A coupon inside the magazine lists 20 human desires, such as "Better job," "More finances," "Someone to care for me," "I want to quit drinking," "I have Sickle Cell Anemia." The reader is instructed to mark with an X each prayer need ("If you mail it today we can be in prayer for you tomorrow or the next day") and if possible to include a small donation.

The sample issues contained testimonials from people helped by Brother Al's prayers; a personal account by Brother Al ("When Doctor Jesus Touched Me") of how he was healed; "snapshots from Brother Al's photo album" showing his ministerial activities; and a sermon ("Have You Mountains You Can't Seem to Climb? Rivers You Can't Cross? Troubled Home? Money Worries? Troubled Mind?"). (JMS)

UP-LOOK

George Ekeroth, Director of Publications

4665 Mercury Street
San Diego, Calif. 92111

Approximately 1 a year; 10¢ each
Started: 1971
Circulation: approximately 600,000
Format: approximately 26-page tabloid (web-offset)
Issue examined: Vol. 2, No. 3 (1972)

Up-Look is a publication of Morris Cerullo World Evangelism. As stated by the publisher, the chief purpose of the newspaper is "To inform youth of things that could harm them or could be a destructive force in their lives." Most of the articles consist of religiously oriented warnings against these possible dangers.

A special edition, half of which was devoted to the dangers of occultism, the other half to those of drug abuse, was published in 1972. Some titles from that edition are suggestive of the publication's general tone and editorial point of view: "Junkies Cry Out for Help of Jesus Christ," "Ex-Junkies Offer God as Answer to Drug Battle," "How to Be Delivered from Occult Bondage," "Origin, Characteristics and Activities of Demons," and "Sex Drives Many into Witchcraft Practices."

Many of the articles described the work with drug addicts carried on at the San Diego Youth Action Center founded by Morris Cerullo. There was also an illustrated article promoting the "Witchmobile," described as "the World's first traveling educational anti-occult mobil unit, produced by Morris Cerullo World Evangelism.... It contains a wide range of occult items including potions, voodoo oils, a Satanic altar, goat's hoof, Satanic Bible, Devil's pentagram, and a genuine human skull."

(SMA)

## WICA NEWSLETTER and WITCHCRAFT DIGEST

Leo Louis Martello
153 W. 80th St. (Suite 1B)
N.Y., N.Y. 10024
WICA, 10 issues a year; WD, annual; $5.20 for both publications
Started: Jan. 1970
Circulation: 3,000
Format: WICA, 4 pages; WD, 28-32 pages (both offset)
Issues examined: WICA, #19 & #20 (both 1972); WD, #1 (1971) & #2 (1972)

Dr. Martello writes:

> WICA and WD are organs of the Witches' Liberation Movement, journals of the Old Religion, part of the Witches International Craft Associates (WICA) and the Witches' Anti-Defamation League. We exist to fight

> religious discrimination [against] and distortion of true Witchcraft, to confront and challenge the Church-induced prejudices against Witches, to inform [the] public that Witches are a pre-Christian religious body having nothing to do with the Christian Satan or Devil Worship or Black Magic; ... that, unlike most male chauvinist religions, the supreme deity of Witches is a Goddess ...; that we will take legal action any time there is discrimination [against Witches]....

In addition to editing these periodicals, Dr. Martello, a professional graphologist, has written _Witchcraft: The Old Religion_, _Curses in Verses_, and other books. His (and others') writings published in the _Newsletter_ and the _Digest_ call favorable attention to the works of Charles Godfrey Leland (1824-1903), occultist born in the United States and resident in Italy; and attack Owen S. Rachleff, author of _The Occult Conceit_ (1971). (WJS)

## Chapter 22

## UFOs

> We know UFOs exist, that they are intelligently controlled, and that they emanate from somewhere other than this planet.
> ---Victorian UFO Research Society

Our UFO chapter has shrunk considerably, perhaps because not many new periodicals have been appearing or perhaps--if they're as afraid of ridicule as Inter-Galaxy News--because they're keeping their appearance a secret. UFOlogy, the science of studying unidentified flying objects, has been greatly advanced by the Victorian UFO Research Society, which laments the fact that Australia is--"UFO-wise"--a most frustrating country: sightings do not occur there, so the Society must content itself with analyzing and evaluating reports from overseas. For a fuller discussion of UFO periodicals, see our previous volumes. --Janet Spahn

### AUSTRALIAN FLYING SAUCER REVIEW and AUSTRALIAN UFO BULLETIN

Victorian UFO Research Society
Box 43
Moorabbin, Victoria
Australia 3189
Rev., quarterly, $1.25; Bull., monthly (?)
Started: Rev., Mar. 1970; Bull., 1959

Circulation: 1,000
Format: Rev., 20 pages (7" x 10"); Bull., 6 pages (8 1/2" x 14", mimeo.)
Issues examined: Rev., Mar. 1970; Bull., Oct. & Dec. 1969, Mar. 1970

These two periodicals are said to provide the only source of information on UFOs in Victoria. Although they emphasize Australian developments, they include news of overseas sightings and research. As expressed in one Bulletin:

> Australia may be a wonderful country in which to live,

> but it is a most frustrating country UFO-wise. We read about 'touch-downs' and near contacts overseas, but reports of this nature either do not take place here or else people are too afraid to report such an incident, for fear of ridicule. Perhaps the 'UFO-nauts' find us somewhat dull and give us only cursory glances in passing....

Much of the news is, indeed, from the United States.

The platform of the Society and its periodicals is that "We know UFOs exist, that they are intelligently controlled, and that they emanate from somewhere other than this planet. We prefer to keep away from the 'airy-fairy' and supposition and present thoroughly investigated material to the public and members."

UFOlogy, as the science of studying unidentified flying objects and UFOnauts is called by UFOlogists, involves more than is commonly understood by the public. One contributor informs us that the Society's investigation of sightings involves reports by and interviews of the observer. Evaluating the report is another long procedure involving computing mathematically the strength of various factors in the report, such as time of day of the sighting, quality of description of the object, and speed at which the object disappeared. The sightings reported in the periodicals are described in considerable detail, and occurred under surprisingly dissimilar circumstances.

UFOlogists must struggle against many skeptics--official and private--and much of their work lies in combating those who have deliberately deceived the public into discounting all "tales" of UFOs. One long article in the *Review* dissected one such deceptive project in Colorado, pointing out carefully its oversights and lies. The article was rather convincing, even to a skeptic. (SA)

## INTER-GALAXY NEWS

| | |
|---|---|
| 5224 Hub Street | Started: 1955 |
| Los Angeles, Calif. 90042 | Circulation: 1,700 |
| Quarterly, with "specials"; | Format: 60 pages (letterpress) |
| available to members only | Issues examined: none sent |

Jim Jordan, the Records Officer of the organization (APPORT) that publishes *Inter-Galaxy News*, declined to send us any samples of the periodical, and offered the following explanation:

Since the 'Ideals' of our organization are 'Fortean' in nature, we have received much ridicule from the news media. Our viewpoints have been slanted [i. e., misrepresented] to such a degree that the public in general are often misled. To make matters worse, the U. S. Government has on occasion, unwittingly, through well-meaning religious personal [i. e., personnel] in their employee [i. e., employ] aided in this ridicule. It is therefore the policy of our organization (APPORT) since 1958 to discontinue any and all publicity or reviews of the periodical <u>Inter-Galaxy News</u>. This publication is limited to members of APPORT only.

## Chapter 23

## MISCELLANEOUS

> ... after abortion we can expect positive euthanasia and all the rest.
> ---Illinois Right to Life Committee Newsletter

> ... it is becoming glaringly apparent that what this Continent needs is a new social order: a Technocracy.
> ---Technocratic Trendevents

> All cruelty inflicted upon animals, inside or outside the experimental laboratory, brutalizes the perpetrator. ---The A-V

Many of the periodicals in this chapter deal with a single problem or interest. In Street Drug Survival former drug users tell "how to survive in a world saturated with chemicals." (Scene is also opposed to the use of drugs.) The Dry Legion condemns alcohol and tobacco.

Through such organizations as the American Association for Retired Persons (AARP News Bulletin) the elderly are lobbying for increased Social Security and Medicare benefits, and better nursing homes.

A number of periodicals take sides on the issue of abortion. Those opposing it are the Illinois Right to Life Committee Newsletter, National Right to Life News, The New Human, and The Uncertified Human. On the other side are Illinois Citizens for the Medical Control of Abortion Newsletter, National Abortion Rights Action League, and Saskatoon Women for Abortion Law Repeal Newsletter.

The San Francisco Ball is after sexual freedom. The A-V opposes vivisection. The New Harbinger's interest is the cooperative movement ("unite or perish"). Technocracy Briefs and Technocratic Trendevents offer a political philosophy based upon technology, and International Humanism offers humanist philosophy.

The neutral Swasia, concerned with the Middle East, offers translations from Hebrew and Arabic newspapers. (Partisan pro-Arab or pro-Israeli periodicals are reviewed in our Racial & Ethnic Pride chapter.) Tapwe and Taiga Times '71 deal with the problems of northern areas of Canada, while The Goose and Duck tells of the fight waged against Progress by some inhabitants of Toronto. --Janet Spahn

## AARP NEWS BULLETIN

C. J. Dooley, Exec. Ed.
1909 K St., N.W.
Washington, D.C. 20006
11 issues a year; $2 membership includes subscription
Started: 1960

Circulation: 4 million
Format: 8-page tabloid (offset)
Issues examined: Nov. & Dec. 1973; Jan. 1974
Back issues available from publisher

This is published by the American Association for Retired Persons, and its articles deal with topics of interest to the elderly. Of major concern is an increase in Social Security benefits, and AARP lobbying efforts toward this end are described. Changes in the Medicare "deductible" are explained, as are changes in federal law affecting the quality of nursing home care. (The Bulletin fears that these changes will lower the standards of nursing homes.) The Association's lobbying efforts on various legislative fronts are frequent topics for news articles.

Other articles deal with non-legislative topics. One ("Is Your Accident Coverage Adequate?") describes new insurance recommended by AARP. [See Reviewer's opinion, No. 1.]

Of general interest to elderly persons are descriptions of the activities of foster grandparents (this type of volunteer work is encouraged by AARP), an illustrated article explaining the new road signs recently introduced throughout the nation, and a special report explaining how the consumer price index will be used to determine increases in Social Security benefits. News of activities of AARP chapters and members is included in the Bulletin, which is generously illustrated with pictures of smiling elderly people. Yet the plight of retired persons with little to smile about is not forgotten, as AARP's lobbying activities show. Nonetheless, the over-all picture presented is one of happy, active retirees pursuing hobbies, travelling, serving as volunteers, and in general leading the good life. [See Reviewer's opinion, No. 2.]

(BK)

Reviewer's opinion:

1. As this is a news bulletin published by an organization for its members, one of its functions is to inform them of its activities on their behalf, whether they be in the area of legislation or insurance. Even keeping this in mind, I was put off by the blatant hard-sell of the article, which was written by the insurance company offering the policy.

2. Perhaps the editorial motivation for this is to provide inspiration to older citizens for getting out of the house and finding new interests. But in a world where many retired persons cannot afford European trips, and often can't even afford public transportation downtown, I cannot help but feel that the editors of AARP News Bulletin are equipped with rose-colored glasses.

Nevertheless, the information offered by the periodical is useful, and the articles deal with exactly those topics that affect the lives of retired persons. For these reasons, the Bulletin cannot help but attract many readers among the retired. And perhaps the elderly would like to look at their world with rose-colored glasses for a while.

THE A-V

The American Anti-Vivisection Society
1903 Chestnut St.
Philadelphia, Pa. 19103
Monthly except Aug.; $2
Started: 1892

Format: 16 pages (7 1/4" x 10 1/2")
Issues examined: none sent
Back issues available from publisher

The Society is opposed to "all experiments on live, vertebrate animals, because vivisection is morally wrong--cruel, futile, and retards the progress of good medicine." Going further, it opposes all forms of cruelty to wild or domestic animals. "Kindness to animals inevitably leads to kindness to human beings. All cruelty inflicted upon animals, inside or outside the experimental laboratory, brutalizes the perpetrator. Pain ends with the death of the animal but the degrading effect lives on."

THE DRY LEGION

Church of the Pillar of Fire
1845 Champa St.
Denver, Colo. 80030

Monthly; $2.50
Started: Nov. 1934
Circulation: 1,200

Format: 16 pages (9" x 12", letterpress)
Issues examined: June, Nov., Dec. 1973
Back issues available from publisher

This is the official organ of the Dry Legion, an organization advocating nation-wide prohibition. In its pages, Christian prohibitionists attempt to dispell public apathy toward, and acceptance of, drinking and smoking. Sermons make clear the role of alcohol and tobacco in leading to ruin, damnation, and hell. Biblical stories are used to offer examples of successful resistance to evil, or of the ultimate judgment imposed on the unregenerate sinner ("Daniel Purposed in His Heart"; "Belshazzar's Night of Intoxication"). Vignettes ("I Preach to a Drunkard"), homilies ("The saddest, most remorseful, most heart-rending of the lost opportunities of the drinker and the drunkard is that of neglecting his soul's salvation"), and testimonies ("The Temperance Dog") give witness to the evil of strong drink, as well as to the unhealthfulness of smoking. Six cartoons in each issue illustrate vividly the connection between the liquor trade, the evils wrought by strong drink, and death. Parents are counseled on ways of providing a Christian example, and are given factual information on the effects of alcohol, as an aid in combatting its use. (KL)

Feedback:
"All o.k."

THE GOOSE AND DUCK: Toronto Island Community News

David & Elizabeth Amer, Eds.
11 Willow Ave.
Wards Island, Toronto, Ontario, Canada M55 1Y1
10 issues a year; $3
Started: Apr. 1970
Circulation: 1,000

Format: 4- to 8-page tabloid (offset)
Issues examined: May, June, Sept. 1973
Back issues available from publisher

The paper advocates "saving the Toronto island community of 700 people in 254 houses threatened since 1956 by pure park-expansion policy of Metropolitan Toronto Council. Tool for organizing and boosting morale of local residents threatened with eviction on an almost yearly basis."

## ILLINOIS CITIZENS FOR THE MEDICAL CONTROL OF ABORTION NEWSLETTER

700 East Ohio (Rm. 608)
Chicago, Ill. 60611

Format: 8 pages (mimeo., stapled)
Issue examined: Summer 1974

"The National Abortion Rights Action League is the only national organization whose sole purpose is to support and protect the U. S. Supreme Court ruling. Because ... [its] legal status is now very much in jeopardy, we believe it is crucial to have both a strong national organization and strong individual state groups. NARAL and ICMCA work very closely together, coordinating ... efforts and exchanging information. ICMCA took the initiative of collecting congressional questionnaires in the state, an effort which NARAL encouraged in other states. Besides its New York office, NARAL now has a full time office in Washington, with two fine lobbyists working full time 'on the Hill.'"

The Newsletter reports on legislation, congressional hearings, and political elections that affect the status of abortion; gives abortion statistics; and covers the activities and strategy of ICMCA and NARAL.

## Illinois Right to Life Committee NEWSLETTER

Suite 1264, 53 W. Jackson Blvd.
Chicago, Ill. 60604
Monthly; $5

Format: 4-8 pages (offset)
Issues examined: May-July 1974

Pro-lifers believe that "the unborn child is a person in the full sense of the term at every stage of biological development." They consequently oppose abortion, and want to reverse the U. S. Supreme Court decision that made it legal. This Newsletter covers IRLC meetings, conventions, speaking engagements, and fund-raising and benefit activities, and the related activities of such organizations as Illinois Nurses who Feel Abortion Is Not Tolerable (INFANT) and The World Federation of Physicians Who Respect Human Life. The publication urges members to boycott companies such as Upjohn that develop and market abortion drugs; to take part in picketing, parades (often of ethnic groups), and letter-writing campaigns; to sponsor Pro-Life advertisements; and to buy right-to-life T-shirts. The Newsletter calls attention to the latest materials available on abortion, and alerts members to radio and television programs, newspaper and magazine articles, and politicians' pronouncements on the subject, and urges them to respond with letters, telegrams, and telephone calls.

In June 1974 the organization set up a telephone newsline which carries a recorded news program, Pro-Life Hotline, presenting the latest local and national developments and directing callers "to watch certain TV programs and read and respond to newspaper and magazine articles on life issues. It also informs callers about abortion clinics being closed and important Pro-Life events which should be attended." Each issue has a section on the Hotline.

An editorial complains that Pro-Life forces do not get the publicity that the abortion side does:

> We must replace four-page Sunday supplements, reaching thousands, and 60-minute specials, reaching millions, with face-to-face talks to little groups gathered in church basements and dusty classrooms. We must accept invitations to drive 30 miles with slides and handouts.... We must accept insults and blame for speaking for the voiceless unborn in half-filled rooms with bad lighting.
>
> We have no choice. If we do not give these talks, abortion on demand will surely become fixed in the American way of life, and after abortion we can expect positive euthanasia and all the rest.

Much of the July 1974 issue is devoted to a condensed version of a report (by the U. S. Coalition for Life Educational Fund) purporting to prove that the UN's 3rd World Population Conference (August 1974) was bound to be biased against Pro-Life positions.

The Newsletter carries short news articles such as: "'Manslaughter' Charge Filed in Fetus Death" (against a doctor); "House Bans Live Fetus Study"; "'Crowded' Holland 'Best Place to Live'" (according to poll by European business magazine, Vision); "Pro-Lifers Protest Rockefeller Speech"; "Regrets Her Abortion, Becomes Active IRLC Member" (at YWCA meeting a woman confronts an abortion speaker who counseled her to have an abortion); "Doctors Testify Before Senate Subcommittee" (for and against abortion); and "Latest Gallup Poll Good News for Pro-Lifers." (JMS)

Feedback:

"It is quite thorough and captures the purpose of the publication." The editor suggested two textual changes which were incorporated into the review.

## INTERNATIONAL HUMANISM

Ernst van Brakel, Ed.
Oudegracht 152
Utrecht, Netherlands
Quarterly; DFL. 7
Started: Jan. 1962
Circulation: 1,300
Format: 16-20 pages (6 1/4" x 9 1/2", letterpress)
Issues examined: 1972 (No. 4); 1973 (Nos. 1 & 2)

International Humanism is published for the International Humanist and Ethical Union (IHEU). For an explanation of the organization's goals and beliefs, see reviews of The Humanist (American), AEU Reports, The Ethical Forum, and Humanist News in our first volume; and The Humanist (English) in our second volume. These organizations are members of IHEU.

The publication of the umbrella organization, IHEU, contains news of member organizations, of IHEU conferences, meetings, and congresses, and of other conferences or events that are of interest to humanists. International Humanism also mentions or reviews new humanist publications; carries several articles (often philosophical); and gives detailed outlines or reports of subjects discussed at conferences.

Some of the articles or philosophical essays that appeared in the issues examined are: "The Psychic and Mental Needs of the Residents of Old People's Homes"; "Killing Handicapped Babys [sic] as the Fundamental Problem of Philosophy" by Leszek Kolakowski, a Polish philosopher; "Humanism in Finland"; and "A Basis for Universal Morality."

(JMS)

## NATIONAL ABORTION RIGHTS ACTION LEAGUE

250 W. 57th St.
N. Y., N. Y. 10019
8 to 10 times yearly; $10 with membership
Started: 1968
Circulation: 3,000
Format: 6 pages (8 1/2" x 14" or standard size, offset)
Issues examined: 5 Apr. & June 1974
Back issues available from publisher

"We report on the abortion situation including action in Congress and the state capitals, availability of service, lawsuits, statistics, activity of the opposition, etc."

## NATIONAL RIGHT TO LIFE NEWS

Alice L. Hartle, Ed.
5516 Lyndale Ave. S.
Minneapolis, Minn. 55419
Monthly; $6

Started: Nov. 1973
Circulation: 20,000

Format: 16-page tabloid (offset)
Issues examined: July-Oct. 1974

According to the editor, the general goals of NRL News (the official publication of the National Right to Life Committee, Washington, D. C.) are to "unify, inform, and educate the growing pro-life movement." More specifically, the newspaper seeks:

> To encourage commitment to the task of giving constitutional protection for human life from conception until natural death, regardless of age, health, or condition of dependency. To bring political force to bear to enact and ratify a Human Life Amendment. To alert the electorate on voting records of members of Congress on life issues. To educate on issues such as abortion, euthanasia, and infanticide. To fill the gap left in the public media because of biased or incomplete coverage of issues. To alert readers to the growing dangers in the abortion mentality. To serve as a vital link between the National Right to Life Committee and grass roots organizations throughout the country.

Articles in the sample issues covered law suits and congressional activity touching on the pro-life movement; nation-wide activities of pro-life organizations; activities of what pro-lifers term "anti-life" organizations and individuals; and such topics as difficulties faced by pro-life physicians pursuing academic careers, abortion in western Europe, and pro-abortion bias in the media.

Regular features include an editorial section; "Washington Watchbird" (statements and positions of members of Congress, and elected and appointed federal personnel); letters from readers; and "Letters for Life" (listing individuals that pro-lifers should write to). The October 1974 issue contained a record of House and Senate votes on pro-life issues in the 93rd Congress. (JMS)

Feedback:

The editor sent us a slightly revised version, which we have used.

THE NEW HARBINGER: A Journal of the Cooperative Movement

North American Student Cooperative Organization
Box 1301
Ann Arbor, Mich. 48106
Quarterly; $6 for 6 issues
Started: Fall 1971
Circulation: about 600

Format: 24-40 pages (offset)
Issues examined: Mar., May, Sept. 1973
Indexing: <u>Alternative Press Index</u>
Back issues available from publisher

Each issue of this publication deals with a single topic defining some aspect of the cooperative movement. The choice of topics for key issues of the first volume indicates that the economic aspects of cooperatives are by no means the only concern of the editors. The very first issue dealt with the topic "Cooperatives: A Lifestyle" and the last issue of that volume was devoted to "Cooperation ... A Way of Life." Other editions discussed such themes as "Board and Management" and "Co-op Strategies." Readers' opinions are solicited regarding the choice of topics, and readers are also encouraged to submit articles. In addition, the "Correspondence" section regularly publishes comments which are not in the standard form of brief letters to the editor. Frequently a single reader's remarks run to several columns and amount to a full-length article. This is in accordance with the official policy of the publication.

> Its purpose is to provide a forum for the discussion of issues and problems pertinent to enterprises owned by consumers and operated according to the Co-op Principles. <u>The New Harbinger</u> publishes a cross-section of analyses and reports on pre-announced topics and welcomes contributions from its readers.

Some titles indicative of the range of subject matter treated in the articles are: "A Do-It-Yourself Pension Plan," "Toward a Blueprint for Student Housing," "Co-ops vs. Cooperation," "Measuring Director Performance," and "A New Selling Concept: Computer Food-Buying--By Phone." (SMA)

<u>Feedback:</u>
"The content summary of <u>TNH</u> is good."

THE NEW HUMAN

National Youth Pro-Life Coalition
10720 Adeline Rd.
Cleveland, Ohio 44111
Suggested donations: $2 high school; $5 college; $10 groups
Format: 4 pages (offset)
Issue examined: undated (Mar. 1973 postmark)

Anti-abortion. Covers activities of the organization; reports on abortion legislation; and gives some other news.

THE RIGHT OF AESTHETIC REALISM TO BE KNOWN: A Periodical of Hope and Information

141 Green St.
N. Y., N. Y. 10012
Weekly; $12
Started: 4 Apr. 1973
Circulation: 4,000
Format: broadsheet (offset)
Issues examined: 4 Apr., 22 Aug., 5 & 12 Dec. 1973
Back issues available from publisher

Eli Siegal, founder of Aesthetic Realism, explains that the first issues of TRO "try to make clearer, in a somewhat controversial way, why Aesthetic Realism should be known." He complains that "There is a block on the subject in journalistic and other circles."

According to his "Four Statements of Aesthetic Realism": (1) Every person is always trying to put together opposites in himself. (2) Every person in order to respect himself has to see the world as beautiful or good or acceptable. (3) There is a disposition in every person to think he will be for himself by making less of the outside world. (4) All beauty is a making-one of opposites, and the making-one of opposites is what we are going after in ourselves. (These statements appear on a card headed "The world, art, and self explain each other: each is the aesthetic oneness of opposites.")

Topics dealt with have included "Why Psychiatry Failed" and "We Have to Stir the Conscience of the Times" (the New York Times and Arthur Sulzberger are frequently chidden by the periodical).

Aesthetic Realism seems to be a method for attaining self-awareness and self-improvement. One issue reports, for example, that the philosophy had helped fifty persons "to say they had changed from homosexuality." (JMS)

Reviewer's opinion:

This reviewer found the periodical's prose almost impenetrable.

THE SAN FRANCISCO BALL

13234 Sherman Way
North Hollywood, Calif. 91605
Weekly; $32

Circulation: 110,000
Format: 32-page tabloid
Issues examined: none sent

The following remarks were received from the publisher:

> Our basic editorial thrust is to turn people on to the idea that sex is fun. We are concerned with sexual entertainment and information. While we do not tend to be a political publication, we do get very concerned when politics get into sex. We take a strong stand against censorship and basically follow a libertarian line on personal freedom. Humor is of great importance to us and much of our material is in the form of satire. We are concerned with turning our readership on to alternatives [sic] forms of sexual expression and getting them to understand there is something more to sex than just orgasm.

SASKATOON WOMEN FOR ABORTION LAW REPEAL NEWSLETTER

Sub P.O. 4
Saskatoon, Saskatchewan, Canada
Irregular; $3 Canada; $4 U.S.A.
Started: Nov. 1971
Circulation: 400

Format: varies 1-3 pages (8 1/2" x 14" or 8 1/2" x 11", mimeo., stapled)
Issues examined: Nov. 1971; Apr. 1972; Feb. & June 1973
Some back issues available from publisher

The Saskatoon organization is connected with the Canadian Women's Coalition to Repeal Abortion Laws--laws which make it impossible for a woman to legally obtain an abortion in Canada unless she is declared physically or mentally ill. The Saskatoon group takes the following stands: (1) Everyone should have ready access to birth control information and devices. (2) There should be early and honest sex education in the elementary and secondary schools. (3) Sterilization should not be forced on (or refused to) anyone, and the question of abortion should not be linked to that of population control. (4) The provincial minister of health should investigate the questionable ethics of doctors who charge an additional fee to abort patients. (5) The government should set up well-publicized counselling and referral services to acquaint women with current abortion procedures. (6) The age of medical consent should be lowered to 16 years. (7) Birth control research efforts should be intensified. (8) Medical students should receive more specialized training in the mechanics and psychology of contraception, sterilization, and abortion. (9) The Canadian government should repeal all sections of the Criminal Code dealing with abortion.

The purpose of the Newsletter is "To discuss issues related to repeal of the Canadian abortion laws and to birth control information dissemination." It mainly covers the activities (meetings, conferences, demonstrations, workshops, petition drives, etc.) of the organization and presents its strategy. (JMS)

SCENE: Youth Action Today, for a Better Tomorrow

Smart Set International
1680 N. Vine St. (Suite 1200)
Hollywood, Calif. 90028
9 issues a year; $2
Started: Dec. 1968
Circulation: 20,000

Format: 8- to 16-page tabloid (offset)
Issues examined: Nov. & Dec. 1973, and special "Drug Prevention" supplement of Aug. 1973; Jan. 1974

Smart Set describes itself as a world-wide program "to make it socially acceptable and desirable to work for A Better Tomorrow," and "To prevent rather than try to cure use of drugs and other anti-social acts."

> The SOS ('Stamp out Stupidity' and 'Speak out Sensibly') program is not just 'anti-drug'.... Smart Set is positive and pro-life. In thousands of schools throughout the United States as well as in many foreign countries.... students are organized into clubs, with those in elementary and junior high schools called Smarteens. In senior high the students are referred to as members of Smart Set or SOS. Ecology, politics, and public service are major areas of concern for SOS.... They sign a pledge which

> states that the individual will do his best to create a society free of drugs, pollution, hate, class prejudice, or other anti-social behavior.
>
> Students not only work to put down drugs as stupid, but also take part in recycling and anti-litter campaigns, walk many miles for the March of Dimes, visit hospitals and drug rehabilitation centers, collect food and clothing for needy families....

Examples of articles: "Why Drug Education Is a National Disaster"; "Saga of a Successful Smart Set Club"; "Drugs Will Pull You Down in a Big Hurry"; "New York Drug Law May Not Be Working"; and "Smoking's a Bummer."

Much of the paper is devoted to the nation-wide activities of the organization. (JMS)

STREET DRUG SURVIVAL

Vic Pawlak, Ed.
Box 5115
Phoenix, Ariz. 85010
Quarterly; $1
Started: 1970
Circulation: 30,000

Format: 8-12 pages (offset)
Issues examined: v. 2, no. 3; v. 3, nos. 1-2
One year's back issues available from publisher

Street Drug Survival (formerly Vibrations: Drug Survival News) is a publication of the Do It Now Foundation, a national non-profit drug survival organization that "disseminates factual information about street drugs." There is no attempt "to cover the broad sociological problems relating to street dope ... [but it concentrates on] medical facts, information on other problems, with a little good humor occasionally added." "Literally, this publication tries to tell readers how to survive in a world saturated in chemicals, both legal and illegal." The Foundation is directed by former drug users who understand the drug culture and have no connection with regulatory agencies.

Feature articles cover a range of topics from "Drugs in Europe" and "Tobacco Abuse" to a "Report on Quaaludes and Other Methaqualone Drugs." One issue presents a "Drug IQ Test" with advice to readers that they had better "find out all the answers before getting burned, ripped off, or having to handle an emergency situation." Another lengthy article connects the Drug Wipeout Syndrome with schizophrenia, and examines the efficacy of megavitamin therapy, particularly niacin and vitamin C.

A regular column, "Drug Analysis," consists of reports based on laboratory tests of street drugs. An example of the information provided is that mescaline samples, when tested, contained other drugs; virtually no mescaline is available in the U. S. Such reports indicate that there is a "gross misrepresentation of drugs sold on the street." Comic strips and cartoons are regular features in the publication, and "Keep on Truckin'" has information on the services of the Foundation.

In addition to Street Drug Survival, the Foundation offers printed materials on street drugs, educational sound recordings, a news service for other publications, radio public service spots and programs, and special advisory help programs (in the U. S., Canada, and Europe). The Foundation also sponsors a program of non-cash grants of materials on drug education. (JM)

Feedback:
Editor expressed no disapproval.

SWASIA

Middle East and Europe Working Group
Division of Overseas Ministries
National Council of Churches
Rm. 612, 475 Riverside Dr.
N. Y., N. Y. 10027

Weekly; $20
Started: Feb. 1974
Format: 8 pages (offset)
Issues examined: Feb., June, July 1974
Back issues available from publisher

The first issue of Swasia carried this description:

> Swasia is a weekly digest of Southwest Asian and North African news, including translations of complete articles from Hebrew and Arabic newspapers. It is designed to meet the needs of a broad group of readers who are concerned to keep up with events in this critical part of the world, and who want a wider perspective than is reflected in the American press alone. It is our aim to present as comprehensive and accurate a picture as possible of events and opinion in the region. We will introduce in Swasia no interpretive material of our own. While we will give prominent play to our coverage of the Israel-Palestine conflict, the key Persian Gulf area, and Great Power policies throughout the region, we intend

to report on important developments from Iran to Morocco, Turkey to Sudan. The area ... of Southwest Asia and North Africa is more commonly--and more ambiguously--called the Middle East. By using the geographical names, and by calling the publication Swasia (swā'-zee-a), we hope not only to be more accurate, but to convey with a new name something of the new importance the area has acquired for the world, and something of the new independence its people are presently asserting. Swasia is a combination of the Middle East News Review, published by the National Council of Churches, and Know, edited and published by Norton Mezvinsky.

The first four pages of the publication contain summaries and excerpts from the world press. Among the sources covered are Christian Science Monitor; Jerusalem Post; Le Monde; London Times; New York Times; Washington Post; BBC Summary of World Broadcasts; and Wall St. Journal.

The second section of Swasia is devoted to translated articles from Arab and Israeli newspapers. (JMS)

Reviewer's judgment:

This appears to be a valuable publication for both public and academic libraries.

Feedback:

The editor said "The entry was fine."

TAIGA TIMES '71: Serving Churchill, Manitoba, and the Keewatin, N. W. T.

Joe Cloutier, Ed.
Hudson Square
Churchill, Manitoba, Canada R0B 0E0
Weekly; $12 (to U. S. subscribers)
Started: 11 Nov. 1971
Circulation: 1, 100

Format: 12 pages (11" x 17", offset)
Issues examined: 25 Oct., 1 & 15 Nov. 1973
Microform version available from Microfilming Corp. of America

The publisher (Doug Beiers) and the editor present a miscellany of news and feature articles, and a considerable number of paid advertisements. Emphasis is on regional development, community government, and the outdoors: hunting, a winter carnival, extreme weather. Political issues of particular relevance to northern Manitoba and the Northwest Territories are discussed; the editorials thereon are forceful but not tendentious. The date [19]71 is retained in the title to commemorate the year in which the newspaper was first published. Beiers indicates that the major editorial policies are: (1) northern input into northern development; (2) northern self-government; (3) government purchasing from local businesses rather than centralized bulk purchasing; (4) accelerated development and increased use of the port of Churchill; (5) improved communication among Indians, Eskimos, and whites, and between the north and south sections of the Prairie Provinces and the Northwest Territories. (WJS)

Feedback:

"This sounds very nice, not sure if you are referring to us or not! Sounds so good."

TAPWE

Don Taylor, Ed.
Boreal Press
Box 130
Hay River, N. W. T., Canada
Weekly; $5 in Canada;
$6 foreign

Started: 9 Apr. 1963
Circulation: 1, 400
Format: 20-24 pages (offset)
Issues examined: none sent
Back issues available from publisher

The editor sent this information: "Politically independent; advocating freer enterprise, less government meddling in social and economic matters; political autonomy for Northwest Territories; elimination of existing discrimination by government in matters of education, justice, commerce, etc."

TECHNOCRACY BRIEFS

Technocracy, Inc.
5509 University Way N. E.
Seattle, Wash. 98105
Periodically; 1¢ each

Format: broadsheet (offset)
Issues examined: #22 through #64
Back issues available from publisher

The publication sent this information: "Technocracy is concerned with the social impact of technology. It is the position of Technocracy that our social system is obsolescent due to technology. Technocracy proposes a new social system consonant with our advanced technology." The organization, Technocracy, puts out four other publications: Technocratic Trendevents (reviewed in this volume); The Northwest Technocrat; The Technocrat; and Technocracy Digest. For an explanation of Technocracy and its goals see the reviews of these last three magazines in Volume II.

The Briefs discuss various goals and aspects of the political philosophy of Technocracy.

TECHNOCRATIC TRENDEVENTS: Research Bulletin

433 E. Market St.
Long Beach, Calif. 90805
Monthly; $1.50

Format: 8 pages (offset)
Issue examined: Oct. 1973

This is a "technocratic analysis of trends and events in the news compiled by the research staff of the Technocrat." (The Technocrat is one of a trilogy that includes The Northwest Technocrat and Technocracy Digest. For an explanation of Technocracy, see our reviews of these three periodicals in Volume Two.)

The bulletin consists of short news stories (often reprinted from other periodicals) demonstrating the bad shape the economy is in, or telling of some new technological discovery or agricultural method that may help society. Considerable attention is paid to pollution and ecology.

Examples of articles: "U.S. Faces More Shortages"; "Seattle Tries Free Transit"; "Indians Reap Grain from Sea"; "Sorghum Rich in Protein"; and "Era of Cheap Fuels Coming to an End."

> The job of providing comfort and security for the people of this Continent is not being handled very well at present, and the Price System offers no visible hope for the future. Again it is becoming glaringly apparent that what this Continent needs is a new social order: a Technocracy.

(JMS)

Feedback:
Editor expressed no disapproval.

THE UNCERTIFIED HUMAN: The Voice of Pro Life

1295 Gerrard St. E.
Toronto, Ont., Canada

M4I 1Y8
$2.50

Format: 8-page tabloid (offset)

Issue examined: Oct. 1973

Anti-abortion.

## ERRATA IN VOLUME II

Page 561: In first line of Feedback, for "Address" read "Addressee."

Pages 618-20: Running head should be "Rock Culture."

Page 705: In last line, underline "Gay."

Page 746: First paragraph, first line: for "cricitism" read "criticism."

Page 756: In third paragraph, eleventh line, for "purchsed" read "purchased."

Page 771: Supply quotation marks at end of Feedback.

Page 810: In third-to-last line of final indented quotation, for "Communits" read "Communists."

Page 851: In running head, for "Race-Supermacist" read "Race Supremacist."

Page 957: In entry for "Americans for Democratic Action," capitalize "party."

Page 958: In entry for Avant-Garde, underline the title.

Page 964: In entry for "Conservative publications," for "Chapter" read "Chapters."

Page 968: In entry for "Ft Holabird," for "Gi" read "GI."

Page 969: In entry for "German Democratic Republic," square bracket should replace parenthesis after "Germany."

Page 975: In entry for "Kelly AFB," for "Gi" read "GI."

Page 977: In entry for "Lodge," for "Diplomat" read "diplomat."

## GEOGRAPHICAL INDEX*



*The United States are listed first; after Wisconsin begin foreign countries.

OHIO (cont.)

Oberlin: *Coming Out*
Toledo: *Arab Tribune*

OKLAHOMA

Oklahoma City: *The Oklahoma Observer*
Tulsa: *AAJ Docket*

OREGON

Central Point: *Starcraft*
Eugene: *Edcentric*; *The Eugene Augur*
Klamath Falls: *Many Smokes*
Portland: *Portland Scribe*

PENNSYLVANIA

Grove City: *The Torch*
Media: *The Friendly Agitator*
Philadelphia: *The A-V*; *Biblical Missions*; *Communiqué*; *Gay Raiders' Newsletter*; *Hayom*; *A Single Spark*; *Solidarity Newsletter*; *Wicce*
Pittsburgh: *KNOW News Service*

RHODE ISLAND

Providence: *Literature & Ideology*

SOUTH CAROLINA

Columbia: *The New Banner*

SOUTH DAKOTA

Marvin: *The Blue Cloud Quarterly*

TENNESSEE

Memphis: Southern Committee to Free All Political Prisoners *Newsletter*

TEXAS

Austin: *Echo*; *The Gar*; *The Rag*; *The Texan Woman*
Borger: *Borger News-Herald*
Dallas: *The Raven Speaks*
Houston: *The Southern Voice*
San Antonio: *Honky Times*
San Marcos: *Weather Report*

VERMONT

North Troy: *Divine Toad Sweat*
Starksboro: *Vermont Freeman*
Vergennes: *The American Solipsist*

VIRGINIA
Arlington: Outdoor America; WUNS Bulletin
Charlottesville: The Virginia Weekly
Falls Church: The Pink Sheet on the Left; The Woman Activist
Harrisonburg: The Truth Crusader
Louisa: Communities
Norfolk: Grapes of Wrath
Richmond: Richmond Mercury
Sterling: Dialogue on Liberty

WASHINGTON
Bellingham: Northwest Passage
Nespelem: The Tribal Tribune
Rainier: Christ Is the Answer
Seattle: Pandora; Prison Law Reporter; Technocracy Briefs

WISCONSIN
Madison: Free for All; Take Over; Whole Woman; Wisconsin Patriot
Milwaukee: Amazon; Bugle American; Mom's Home-made Comics; Snarf
Winneconne: Women in Struggle

AUSTRALIA
Victoria - Moorabbin: Australian Flying Saucer Review; Australian UFO Bulletin
Western Australia - Merredin: Perseverance

AUSTRIA
Vienna: Europa Ethnica; Internationales Freies Wort

BELGIUM
Brussels: Agenor

CANADA
Alberta
Calgary: Elbow Drums
Edmonton: On Our Way
British Columbia
Nanaimo: The BC Voice
Vancouver: The British Columbia Access Catalogue; Nesika
Victoria: Fulcrum

## TITLE INDEX

This is an index of the titles of periodicals reviewed or listed in all three volumes of the present edition. It thus covers 1,324 reviews of periodicals, as well as 55 titles and addresses listed in the introductions of some chapters in Volume Two. In addition, the index contains the titles and addresses of more than 300 other periodicals with which we have corresponded--with varying degrees of success. Finally, it includes the titles of several periodicals referred to in reviews (examples: The New York Times, Reader's Digest, The Wall Street Journal).

As we pointed out in the Preface (p. vii) to Volume One, the periodicals that we cover frequently die, or change their titles, or move without leaving a forwarding address. Consequently, we made an attempt, in this index, to report on the fate or present status of periodicals reviewed in our two earlier volumes. (See, for example, the entries for AIR and AMEX.)

Throughout the index, we make use of certain abbreviations. Here is what they mean:

| | |
|---|---|
| API | Alternative Press Index, Box 256, College Park, Md. 20740. |
| B & H | Underground Newspaper Microfilm Collection. Micro Photo Div., Bell & Howell, Old Mansfield Rd., Wooster, Ohio 44691. |
| DC | Directorio Chicano. Hayward, Calif.: Southwest Network, 1974. |
| Fabbro | Fabbro, Anne. "Canadian Periodicals of Dissent," Ontario Library Review, 56 (September 1972): 171-73. |
| MR | Mail returned. Our letter to a periodical was returned unopened by the Post Office with some such explanation as "Moved, left no address." |
| NR | No response. We wrote to the periodical, but it never replied, and our letter was not returned by the Post Office. |
| N. U. | Special Collections Dep't., Northwestern Univ. Library, Evanston, Ill. 60201. This department subscribes to hundreds of current feminist periodicals, and has also acquired many serials from the former Women's History Research Center (p. 699, above), founded by Laura X. We are grateful for the help given us by the Curator, R. Russell Maylone, and by Bonnie Jo Sedlack. The Bibliographer of the library's Africana collection, Daniel Britz, kindly called our attention to a number of periodicals dealing with Africa. |

RR — Reply received.

SCG — Spiritual Community Guide. Rev. ed. San Rafael, Calif.: Spiritual Community, 1973.

TNWSC — The New Woman's Survival Catalog. New York: Coward, McCann & Geoghegan, 1973. Brief annotations of some feminist periodicals.

TS — Benedict, Russell G. Top Secret: Collector's Newsletter. Special Collections Dep't., Univ. of Nevada Library, Reno, Nev. 89507. This newsletter, referred to in the Preface of our 1972 volume, has now reached a total of more than 900 pages. Benedict often describes the slant of the periodicals that come to his attention.*

Ulrich's — Ulrich's International Periodicals Directory, various editions. New York: R. R. Bowker.

Woodsworth — Woodsworth, Anne. The "Alternative" Press in Canada: A Checklist of Underground, Revolutionary, Radical, and Other Alternative Serials from 1960. Toronto: Univ. of Toronto Press, 1972. In addition to her alphabetical listing of more than 400 periodicals, Woodsworth provides a Subject Index with such headings as "Comics," "Gay Liberation," and "Peace." In her alphabetical listing, she often provides a publication's starting date (and closing date, if it has ceased).

As for libraries' holdings, some of the periodicals we review are listed in James P. Danky's Undergrounds: A Union List of Alternative Periodicals in Libraries of the United States and Canada (Madison: The State Historical Society of Wisconsin, 1974).

This volume contains two other indexes: a Geographical Index, arranged by place of publication; and an index of Editors, Publishers, and Opinions.

*The collectors' network organized by Benedict is described in Richard Akeroyd and Russell Benedict, eds., "A Directory of Ephemera Collections in a National Underground Network," Wilson Library Bulletin 48 (November 1973): 236-54.

## Title Index

Australian UFO Bulletin 1649
Avant-Garde 148, 941. See Ulrich's 1975-76 for new address.
Avatar: see American Avatar
Awake! 418
The Awakener 1619
Ayn Rand Letter 1199. Supersedes The Objectivist
Azania Combat 1270; mentioned 1268
Azania News 1270; mentioned 1268
Aztlán 1464; mentioned 1454

BC Newsletter 539. Woodsworth implies that it has ceased.
BC Voice 1325; mentioned 1317
Back to Godhead 872. Ulrich's 1975-76 gives address in Los Angeles.
Baltimore Peace & Freedom News 650. N. U.: defunct.
La Barba 1154
The Barking Rabbit: see Buddhist Third Class Junk Mail Oracle
Basta Ya! 717. See Ulrich's 1975-76 for new address.
Battlefront: see The Citizen-Observer
The Baumholder Gig Sheet 778; mentioned 271. Probably defunct. N. U.: only issue received was from 1970.
Bay Area Socialist, Young People's Socialist League, Socialist Party U. S. A., Box 9284, Berkeley, Calif. 94709. In socialist tradition of Norman Thomas & Michael Harrington. "Anti-communist, highly critical of the New Left." Aim is to "build a coalition of labor, minority groups, and liberals within the Democratic Party." Pub'n started 1967.
The Bay Area Worker 1046; violent tactics 1103
The Beads of Truth 1619
The Bell, Foreign Friends of NTS, Possev-Verlag, D 6230, Frankfurt am Main 80, Flurscheideweg 15, Federal Republic of Germany. NR 1973. TS, pp. 6, 192, 330: revolutionary anti-communist underground operating in the U. S. S. R. TS gives addresses of representatives in other countries.
Bellyful, Women's Liberation, 380 Victoria St., Toronto, Ont., Canada. NR 1973.
Berkeley Barb 89; mentioned 1154. See Ulrich's 1975-76 for new address.
Berkeley Men's Center Newsletter 1326; mentioned 1321
The Berkeley Monitor 513. See Ulrich's 1975-76 for new address.
Berkeley Tribe 89. API list (June 1973): ceased May 1972.
Between the Lines 150. New address: Box 570. $4 a year.
Biblical Missions 1577; mentioned 1571
Big Fat Magazine 617
Big Mama Rag, 1635 Downing, Denver, Colo. 80218. NR 1974. TNWSC, p. 28.
The Big US: see Burning River.
Bijou Funnies 1186; mentioned 1183
Bill of Rights Journal: title of each year's 6th issue of Rights
Birthright: see US
The Black Action Party 1464; mentioned 1454
Black and Red 1
Black Bart Brigade 1206; mentioned 1205
Black Community Newsletter 1465; mentioned 1454
Black Creation 1465; mentioned 1454
Black Cross Bulletin: see Anarchist Black Cross Bulletin
Black Flag: see Bulletin of the Anarchist Black Cross
Black Light (INA Corp.), company underground 1154
Black Maria 1327; mentioned 1319
Black Mask 121. N. U.: probably defunct; last issue received was April/May 1968.
Black Mesa Fact Sheet: see Rainbow People
Black News 718
The Black Panther 204. Superseded by Black Panther Intercommunal News Service. See Ulrich's 1975-76 for new address.
Black Politics 3. Not found in Ulrich's after 1973-74 edition.
Black Rap 720
The Black Scholar 721. Ulrich's 1975-76: new address in Sausalito.
The Black Silent Majority Committee Newsletter, Box 7610, Washington, D. C. 20044. NR 1973. TS, p. 227: Republican.
Black Times 1466; mentioned 1454
Black World: see Negro Digest

Magazine to become Straight Creek Journal.
Christ Is the Answer 1594; mentioned 1591
Christian Advocate 1595; mentioned 1592
Christian Anti-Communism Crusade 350
Christian Battle Cry, Box 257, Englewood, Colo. 80110. Kenneth Goff, Ed. Anti-communist, anti-Jewish, anti-U.N. TS, p. 201: Goff & his wife claim to have belonged to the communist party in the 1930's in order to act as informants for the FBI. NR 1968, 1969, 1970. Also published Pilgrim Torch, defunct since 1967.
Christian Beacon 351
Christian Crusade 353; superseded by Christian Crusade Weekly 826
Christian Cynosure 1622
Christian Economics 296. New address: 7960 Crescent Ave., Buena Park, Calif. 90620. New title: Applied Christianity. Ulrich's 1975-76: "Suspended."
Christian Exercise, Box 90091, Nashville, Tenn. 37209. RR 1973 from Lee Galvani, Dir.: "The British Are Coming--Again." Anti-British, anti-communist, anti-Israel: "masonry and communism are British." TS, p. 338.
Christian News 298
The Christian Patriot 299. See Ulrich's 1975-76 for new address.
Christian Register: see UUA Now
Christian Statesman 300. See Ulrich's 1975-76 for new address.
Christian Vanguard 1597; mentioned 1592
Church and Society: see Social Progress
Church & State 446. New address: 8120 Fenton St., Silver Spring, Md. 20910.
The Church of Light Quarterly 1622; mentioned 1614
Chutzpah 1468; mentioned 1453
Cinéaste 1051; mentioned 1041
Cinema: Marxist journal 1051
Cinema Educational Guild News-Bulletin 827; mentioned 823
The Citizen 382
The Citizen-Observer 1555; mentioned 1547, 1548
City Hall, 554 Spadina Crescent, Toronto, Ont., Canada M55 2J9. RR 1973: "We have just stopped publishing City Hall with the Sept. 1973 issue." Fabbro: Community Action.
City Star: see New York City Star
The Civic Forum 800. See Ulrich's 1975-76 for new address.
Civil Liberties 193. New address in Ulrich's 1975-76.
Civil Liberties Bulletin 194. Ulrich's: defunct. N.U.: last issue received was May 1968.
Civil Liberties Newsletter 195
Civil Rights 1273; mentioned 1267. Former titles: Newsbulletin of NICRA and Fortnightly Journal of Northern Ireland Civil Rights Association.
Claridad 1052
Class Struggle 1053; mentioned 1040, 1041
The Cleveland Feminist 1333; mentioned 1316
Collage 1158; mentioned 1154. See Other Scenes.
The College Paper 625
College Press Service 1159; mentioned 1002, 1153
The Colonist, Black Students' Union, Stanford Univ., Stanford, Calif. 94305. NR 1974. TS, p. 120.
Combat [N.Y.] 801. Ulrich's: defunct.
Coming Out 1334; mentioned 1316
Comment 1055; mentioned 1041
Commentary on Liberty 125
Comments 654
Committee Against Government Secrecy, Forum for Contemporary History Newsletter, Box 4995, Washington, D.C. 20008. NR 1974. TS, p. 586: militant liberal.
Committee to Support Middle East Liberation Newsletter 513. Probably defunct. N.U.: Oct. 1971 last issue.
Common Sense [Alton] 593
Common Sense [Bloomington] 1007
Common Sense [Union] 829; mentioned 824. TS, p. 348: ceased publication on 15 May 1972.
Common Sense [Washington, D.C.] 1008; mentioned 1002
Communication 1210; mentioned 1205
Communiqué 1243; mentioned 1236
Communiqué for New Politics 7; see

also The Berkeley Monitor
The Communist; mentioned 1058, 1063
Communist Viewpoint 37. Supersedes Horizons, The Marxist Quarterly.
Communitarian, Walden Three, Box 969, Providence, R.I. 02901. TS, p. 336: communes, alternatives, betterment of the world. See Communities & Communitas.
Communitas, 121 W. Center College St., Yellow Springs, Ohio 45387. RR 1973: "Communitas has merged into Communities (along with Communitarian, Alternatives Newsmagazine, and the Modern Utopian)." TS, p. 377: arose from a New Community Project there (near Antioch College).
Communities 1211. Communitas, Communitarian, Alternatives Newsmagazine and Modern Utopian have merged into Communities.
Community 1009
Community of Women Newsletter: see Cowrie
Community Schools 1244; mentioned 1236
Compass 210
Concerned Officers' Movement Newsletter, Box 21073, Kalorama Sta., Washington, D.C. 20009. NR 1974. TS, p. 213: Vietnam; servicemen's rights.
Congress Bi-Weekly 211. Now: American Jewish Congress. Congress Monthly, same address.
Congressional Record Digest & Tally of Roll Call Votes 301. See Ulrich's 1975-76 for new address.
Connecticut Women, Box 800, Bristol, Conn. 06010. Helen Steele, Ed. NR 1974.
Connections 92. Ulrich's: defunct.
Conservation News 1222; mentioned 1217
Conservative Viewpoint: see Richard Cotten's Conservative Viewpoint
Contac (or Contact), Afro-American Cultural Center, Univ. of Connecticut, 7 Gilbert Rd., Storrs, Conn. 06268; mentioned 1179. NR 1974. TS, p. 344.
Continental Magazine: see The Adult Reporter
Contrast 1470; mentioned 1454
El Coquí, 3700 W. Grand Ave., Chicago, Ill. 60651. NR 1973. Issue examined: Mar. 1973. Advocates liberation of Puerto Rico. Entirely in Spanish.
The Cord Weekly: conservative college paper, mentioned 1553
Cornerstone 1623; mentioned 1614
El Corno Emplumado 8
Cos-Mos 887. Last listing in Ulrich's 1973-74 at new address.
The Councilor 384
Count Down [Wichita] 354
Countdown [Toronto] 1598; mentioned 1591
Counter-Spy 1528; mentioned 1523. In late Dec. 1975, after the assassination of the U.S. Central Intelligence Agency's chief agent in Greece, Counter-Spy and other periodicals incurred criticism because they had "blown the cover" of that agent and others.
Counterattack 302
Counterdraft 242
Counterpoint [Seattle] 277
Counterpoint [Stevens Point] 595. Last listing: Ulrich's 1973-74.
Country Senses 1212
Country Women 1334; mentioned 1317
Cowrie 1413; mentioned 1407
Crawdaddy 617. See Ulrich's 1975-76 for new address.
Creation: The Arts in Prison, Box 89, Iowa City, Iowa 52240. NR 1973. TS, p. 406.
The Creationist 447
Creative Californian 304; MR 1970: "Moved, not forwardable."
Creem Magazine 618. See Ulrich's 1975-76 for new address in Birmingham.
Cries from Cassandra, c/o Amazon Nation, 2916 N. Burling, Chicago, Ill. 60659. NR 1974. TNWSC, p. 29. Formerly Amazon Nation Newsletter.
The Crisis 212
The Cross and the Flag 841; mentioned 840
The Crucible 405
The Crusader Newsletter 9, 941. The former publisher's legal difficulties are discussed in "Black Revolutionary to Return to Face North Carolina Charge," The New York Times, 2 December 1975, p. 33.
Cuban-American Sertoma Club of

Coral Gables Newsletter 1579
Current 906. See Ulrich's 1975-76 for new address in Washington, D.C.
Czechoslovak Life 547. See Ulrich's 1975-76 for new address.

DC Eye: see The Capitol East Gazette
DC Gazette: see The Capitol East Gazette
DSS Free Press 1161; mentioned 1153
The Daily Nihilist: see The American Solipsist
The Daily Planet, Student Lobby, Rm. 220, Eshleman Hall, Univ. of Calif., Berkeley, Calif. 94720. NR 1974. TS, p. 488.
Daily Planet [Chicago]: former title of The Chicago Express
The Daily Planet (Detroit-area high school underground): mentioned 1027
Daily Planet [Miami] 595. Probably defunct. Last listed in Ulrich's 1973-74. N.U.: last issue received was May 1972.
The Daily Rag 1163; mentioned 1153
Daily Worker: predecessor of Daily World
Daily World 39; disagreements with 1082. See Ulrich's 1975-76 for new address.
Dallas News: see Dallas Notes
Dallas Notes 597. N.U.: defunct; continued by Hooka Notes & Outlaw Times (Ft. Worth). Ulrich's says, however, that Dallas News & Dallas Notes merged to form Iconoclast, a weekly underground Dallas newspaper. Original title of Dallas Notes was Notes from the Underground.
The Dan Smoot Report 305. Ulrich's: defunct, March 1971.
Dandelion, Newsletter of the Movement for a New Society, 4722 Baltimore Ave., Philadelphia, Pa. 19143. NR 1974. TS, p. 532: collective of collectives; Quaker influence.
Dare to Struggle: see Duck Power
The Dart Bulletin 357. Last listing in Ulrich's 1971-72.
Dateline: Ithaca 153
David 1415
Dawn 1470; mentioned 713, 1452
Defender, Defenders of the Christian Faith, 914-930 Linwood Blvd., Kansas City, Mo. 64109. Hart Armstrong, Ed. Founded in 1925 by Dr. Gerald B. Winrod (d. 1957). A militant religious organization opposing "religious modernism, godless evolution and humanism, Communism and Socialism, and many of the other evil forces threatening our homes, our churches, our schools, and our nation." Considered Vietnam war unwinnable and impracticable. Against unemployment compensation, guaranteed income, welfare, and international missionary program.
The Defender [Los Angeles] 1009; mentioned 1001. MR 1975: "Moved, left no address."
Defiance 1200
Democratic Change, Youth Project on Democratic Change, League for Industrial Democracy, 112 E. 19th St. (Room 1104), N.Y., N.Y. 10003. RR 1974: "publication of the newsletter has been discontinued." TS, p. 138: Socialist-reformist.
Democratic People's Republic of Korea 549
Demokratia 683
Despite Everything 40. Probably defunct. N.U.: last issue received was Spring 1971.
Detroit Newsletter - UFWOC: former title of Huelga
Detroit Scope Magazine 448. Defunct.
Dialogue on Liberty 1556
Dig This Now, The Young Adult Newspaper, 1900 N. Broad St., Philadelphia, Pa. NR 1974. TS, p. 90: put out by Philadelphia gang members.
Dignity 1416
Diné Baa-Hané 1471; mentioned 711, 1453
The Diode 126
Direct Action for a Nonviolent World 243. See Ulrich's 1975-76 for new address.
Direct from Cuba 552. See Ulrich's 1975-76 for new address.
Disarmament News and Views 1529; mentioned 1523
Discussion 1556; mentioned 1548

The Dispatcher 449. See Ulrich's 1975-76 for new address.
Dissent [Cape Town] 1274; mentioned 1268
Dissent [N. Y.] 41
Distaff 1335; mentioned 1316
Distant Drummer 598. Title changed to Thursday's Drummer [TS, p. 249] and finally to The Drummer. The Free Drummer was a thinner free edition of The Drummer, and both are defunct.
Diva (high school underground): mentioned 1027
Divine Toad Sweat 1624; mentioned 1614
The Dixon Line 154
Door and Door to Liberation: see San Diego Free Door
Doreinu 713
The Double-F Journal [new title: Double F: A Magazine of Effeminism] 1417; mentioned 1407. New address: Templar Press, Box 98, FDR Station, N. Y., N. Y. 10022.
Downsview Free Press: see DSS Free Press
Drag Magazine 1419
Dragonfire, YIP, c/o SAC Office, Kent State Univ., Kent, Ohio 44240. NR 1974. TS, p. 442.
Druid Free Press 599
The Drum [Inuvik] 1472; mentioned 1453
Drum [Philadelphia] 229. Probably defunct. N. U.: Dec. 1968 was last issue received.
The Drummer: later title of Distant Drummer. Drummer is a former title of Focus [Memphis].
The Dry Legion 1654; mentioned 1652
Duck Power 784; harassment of 774
Dull Brass 278. Probably defunct. N. U.: last issue received was May 1970.
Dykes and Gorgons, Box 840, Berkeley, Calif. 94704. NR 1974. TNWSC, p. 30.

EMK 656. See Ulrich's 1975-76 for new address.
The Eagle Eye ("America's Greatest Newspaper Bombarding Discrimination & Segregation"), Box 9189, Chicago, Ill. 60690. Arrington W. High, ed. NR 1973.
The Eagle Eye, National Democratic Party of Alabama, Box 2114, Huntsville, Ala. 35804. NR 1973. TS, p. 481: liberal, integrationist party.
The Eagle's Eye [Noblesville] 156
Early American [Modesto] 724
The Early American [Oxford] 138. Probably defunct.
Earth Times, 625 3rd St., San Francisco, Calif. 94107. NR 1973. TS, p. 135: environmental.
The East Village Other 94. Defunct, according to Chicago Rap.
East-West Journal 1627
Echo 1472; mentioned 1454
Echo of Sappho 1419
Eck World News 1628
The Ecologist 1222; mentioned 1217
Economic Council Letter 306. Last listing in Ulrich's 1973-74; new address.
Economic Notes 1136; mentioned 1133
Ecstasy, Gay Revolution Party, Box 410, Old Chelsea Station, N. Y., N. Y. 10011. NR 1973. TS, p. 378: praises Cuba, but apparently not Marxist.
Edcentric 1112; mentioned 1109
Edge 42. MR 1973: "Unknown" and "No longer in this box."
The Educator: see The National Educator
Edward M. Kennedy Quarterly: see EMK
Efficacy 625 (successor to Innovator). According to TS, p. 118, address has changed to Box 34718, Los Angeles 90034. Ulrich's: defunct.
The Egyptian Gazette 907
8-20 Voice of the City 658
Elbow Drums 1472; mentioned 1453
Elevator (high school underground): mentioned 1027
Elysium Journal of the Senses 1113
Emergency News Bulletin: predecessor of A Single Spark
Employee Press 1137; mentioned 1133
Environment 450. See Ulrich's 1975-76 for subscription address.
Environmental Action 1223; mentioned 1217
Environmental Education 1224; mentioned 1217
Environmental Quality 1225; mentioned 1217

Feminist Revolution, Box 694, Stuyvesant Sta., N. Y., N. Y. 10009. RR from Woman's World: "Feminist Revolution was a journal put out by our newspaper."
Feminist Studies 1339; mentioned 1319
The Feminist Voice, Box 11144, 227 E. Ontario, Chicago, Ill. 60611. RR 1973: defunct.
Fences, The Experimental College and The Inner College, University of Connecticut, Storrs, Conn. 06268. NR 1973. TS, p. 369.
Fibre, Box 1210, Tahoe City, Calif. 95730. RR 1973, from Rita Joan (Mrs. Stephen W.) Thomasberg, former co-editor: "Our last issue was published in March of 1972." TS, p. 317, calls it leftist, alternative-minded.
The Fiery Cross 385
The Fifth Estate 95; mentioned 1154. See Ulrich's 1975-76 for new address.
The Fifth Wheel 1138; mentioned 1133
Fiii Daciei 1578
Final Draft, New England Antidraft Newsletter, c/o American Friends Service Committee, 48 Inman St., Cambridge, Mass. 02139. See Peacework. TS, p. 442. NR 1973.
Final Flight 271; probably defunct 774
Fire and Police Research Association News Notes, 3354 Glendale Blvd., Los Angeles, Calif. 90039. NR 1973. TS, p. 106: right-wing, anti-communist.
Firing Line: see The American Legion Firing Line
The First Casualty: original title of Winter Soldier
The First Issue 515. Last listed in Ulrich's 1973-74 at new address. N. U.: last issue received was Fall/Winter 1974.
Fishcheer 1168; mentioned 1153
Flag-in-Action 271; probably defunct 774
The Flame 713
Flashes from the Trade Unions: see Trade Union Press
Le Fléau Social (The Social Plague), Sections Française et Belge de L'Internationale Homosexuelle Revolutionaire, BP 252-16, 757-66 Paris Cedex 16, France. NR 1973. TS, p. 619.
Florida Latin News 1579
Flourishes, Bulletin of the Univ. of Virginia Gay Student Union, Box 3610, Univ. Station, Charlottesville, Va. 22903. NR 1973. TS, p. 606.
Flying Saucer Digest 888
Flying Saucers 889; mentioned 886. See Ulrich's 1975-76 for new address.
Flying Saucers International 430. Last listing in Ulrich's 1971-72.
Focus [Boston] 1423
Focus, Box 11463, Memphis, Tenn. 38111. Was formerly called Drummer, and concentrated on draft resistance.
FOCUS/Midwest 157
Folk og Land 1601; mentioned 1592
Forsite, Entitas Foundation, Al Formisano, 16020 S. Virginia, RR# 1, Reno, Nev. 89502. NR 1973. TS, p. 102: organization for straightening out addicts, dropouts.
Fortnightly Journal of Northern Ireland Civil Rights Association: former title of Civil Rights
Fortune News 1300
Forum 911
Forward 1543
Forward March 271
Forward Motion; mentioned 1179
Fountain of Light 639
Four Lights 248; now entitled Peace and Freedom. See Ulrich's 1975-76 for new address.
A Four-Year Bummer 279, 481. Last listing in Ulrich's 1973-74.
The 4th Estate 1245; mentioned 1236
Fragments 128. Probably defunct. N. U.: last issue received was Sept. 1967.
Free China Weekly 358. See Ulrich's 1975-76 for new address.
Free Choice 451
Free Door, 6389 Imperial Ave., San Diego, Calif. 92114. NR 1970. See San Diego Free Door.
The Free Drummer: see Distant Drummer
Free Enterprise 308
Free for All 1168; mentioned 1153
Free Particle, Dunbar Aitkens, Ed., 2398 Bancroft Way, Berkeley, Calif. 94704. NR 1973. TS, p. 101: gay liberation.
The Free Press, Bob Ging, Ed.,

305 Student Union, Univ. of Pittsburgh, Pittsburgh, Pa. NR 1973. Liberal.
The Free You 515. Probably defunct. Last issue received by N. U.: Winter 1970.
Free Zanzibar Voice 1276; mentioned 1268
Freedom [Los Angeles] 310. This periodical, published by Willis B. Stone, supports the Liberty Amendment. Do not confuse with the Scientology Freedom reviewed in the present volume.
Freedom [Los Angeles] 1246; mentioned 1237. Scientology.
Freedom-Anarchist Weekly, Anarchist Federation of Britain, Freedom Press, 84B Whitechapel High St., London E. 1, United Kingdom, NR 1973. TS, p. 73.
Freedom & Union 1530; mentioned 1523
Freedom at Issue 1276; mentioned 1268
Freedom in Education, Citizens for Educational Freedom, 544 Washington Bldg., Washington, D.C. 20005. NR 1973. TS, p. 585: government aid for parochial schools.
Freedom News 659
Freedom Reader 1169; mentioned 1153
Freedom Talks: see Life Lines
Freedom to Read Foundation News 1277; mentioned 1268
Freedom's Facts 359. Ulrich's: defunct.
Freedomways 213
The Freeman 129
Freethinker 408. See Ulrich's 1975-76 for new address.
Freeworld Times 1301; mentioned 1299
Freeze - Wait - Reanimate 452
The Friendly Agitator 1249
Friends of Animals Report 1226
Friends of Rhodesian Independence Newsletter, 132 Third St., Washington, D.C. 20003. NR 1973. TS, p. 154: Benedict found it inserted in a copy of Liberty Lobby's Liberty Letter.
Friendship House Notes 1009
The Front ("People's Revolutionary News Service"), Ministry of Information, Malcolm X Liberation Front, 511 N. Macomb, Tallahassee, Fla. 32301. NR 1973. TS, p. 337: on pattern of Black Panthers.
Front Page, Feminist Library, The Women's Center, 414 North Park, Bloomington, Ind. NR 1974.
Fulcrum 1060; mentioned 1040, 1063, 1090, 1093, 1094
Full Moon, 200 Main St., Northampton, Mass. NR 1974. TNWSC, p. 31.
Fun, Travel, and Adventure 281; financial difficulties 941
Furies 1425; mentioned 1406
The Further Fattening Adventures of Pudge, Girl Blimp, Mike Friedrich, Owner, Starreach Productions, Box 385, Hayward, Calif. 94543. Approximately annual; $1.25 an issue. Started: 1974. Circulation: 10,000. Format: 52 pages (7" x 10", offset). The owner told us: "We believe the graphic story ('comic book') to be a unique, valid artistic medium for adults. In Pudge, author/artist Ms. Lee Marrs portrays the gradual rise of consciousness of the lead character in the communal San Francisco milieu, doing so in a grand humorous manner, with a keen eye for satire and social commentary."
The Futurist 453. See Ulrich's 1975-76 for new address.

GE Resistor (General Electric Co.), company underground 1154
The GI Organizer 271; probably defunct 774
GI Press Service 281; new street address: 15 E. 17th St. Probably defunct. N.U.: last issue received was Oct. 1971.
GI Voice 272
El Gallo 1473; mentioned 1454
The Gar 1171
Garuda 1629; mentioned 1614
Gay 703; column by its editors 762. See Ulrich's 1975-76 for new address.
Gay Activist, Box 2, Village Station, N.Y., N.Y. 10014. NR 1974. Newsletter of Gay Activists' Alliance.
Gay Book News 1426
The Gay Christian 1427

Gay Dealer, Box 13023, Philadelphia, Pa. 19101. NR 1973. TS, p. 363: pretty radical.
Gay Forum, Box 385, Ben Franklin Station, Washington, D. C. 20044. NR 1974.
Gay Liberator 1430
Gay People and Mental Health 1431
Gay Power 705. N. U.: probably defunct.
Gay Raiders' Newsletter 1432
Gay Scene 705
Gay Teachers' Association Newsletter 1432
Gay Ways 706
Gayokay: see Gay Book News
Genesis 2 1474; mentioned 713, 1453
Georgia Straight 601; pop supplement 619; mentioned 1154
Getting Together 1061; mentioned 1041
Gidra 726. New address according to several sources: Box 18649, Los Angeles, Calif. 90018.
Gigline 282. Probably defunct. N. U.: last issue was received in 1972.
Girl Fight Comics 1188
Gnostica News 1630; mentioned 1614
Good Times 95. API June 1973 list: ceased July 1972.
The Goose and Duck 1655; mentioned 1653
The Gospel Truth 311
Gothic Blimp Works 1189
The Graffitti 787; mentioned 272. See Ulrich's 1975-76 for new address.
Granma 43. See Ulrich's 1975-76 for new address.
Grapes of Wrath 1544
Grasp 1475; mentioned 1454
Grass Roots 387
Grass Roots Forum 159. See Ulrich's 1975-76 for new address.
Grass Roots News 1476; mentioned 1454
The Great Speckled Bird 13. Address on Feb. 1975 issue: Box 7847, Atlanta, Ga. 30309.
Great Swamp Erie Da Da Boom, Angry City Press, 2300 Payne Ave., Suite 600, Cleveland, Ohio 44144. Nelson B. Moore, Jr. NR 1973. TS, p. 362: "typical underground ... some text well composed." Alternative address given. API 1973 list: defunct.
Green Beret 1580
Green Egg 1630; mentioned 1614
The Green Revolution [Freeland] 139. Ulrich's 1975-76 gives same address without box number.
Green Revolution, Perspectives on Major Problems of Living. Richard Fairfield, Ed., School of Living - West, 442 1/2 Landfair Ave., Los Angeles, Calif. 90024. Bi-monthly; $6. Circ.: 4,000. Format: 48 pages (offset). TS, p. 414. See Alternatives Newsmagazine.
The Greenleaf 249. N. U.: defunct; 13 Aug. 1967 was last issue.
Grit City News: see Fishcheer
El Grito 214
El Grito del Norte 217, feedback 942. DC: ceased in Oct. 1973.
Group Research Report 159
Guardian 44, 481. National Guardian former title. See Ulrich's 1975-76 for new address.
Guerilla [Toronto] 1171
Guerrilheiro 1277; mentioned 1268
Guerrilla [Hanover] 14
The Guide 1139; mentioned 1133
The Guild Practitioner 160
The Gunman's Gazette: one-time title of The Lunatic Fringe

H du B Reports 831
HID Service, High School Independent Press Service, 160 Claremont Ave., N. Y., N. Y. 10027. RR 1973 from Liberation News Service: HSIPS ceased in 1970. TS, p. 42.
Hammer & Steel Newsletter 45
Harass the Brass: now A Four-Year Bummer
Harbinger 96. Fabbro: "Ceased."
The Hard Times, 80 Hampshire St., Cambridge, Mass. NR 1973. TS, p. 369: tenants; working-class problems.
Hard Times [Washington, D. C.] 661. API 1969 list: 2920 28th St. N.W. Last issue received by N. U.: Sept. 1970. Probably defunct.
Hartford's Other Voice 516, now entitled Wild Raspberry, new address in Ulrich's 1975-76.
Harvest News Letter 1631
Hash 603. Former title: Warren Free Press. Probably defunct. Last issue received by N. U.:

Semitic.
Iconoclast, Box 7013, Dallas, Tex. 75209. Doug Baker, Jr., Ed. NR 1973. TS, p. 367: formerly Dallas News, Dallas Notes (reviewed on our p. 597), and Notes from Underground.
Iconoclast: For Militant Atheism & Rationalism, 139 Elm Rd. New Malden, England. Supports scientific materialism & internationalism. Opposes Vietnam war, communism, censorship, and growing use by states of police as instrument for control of masses.
Ideal 1478; mentioned 1454
Ideas 803. See Ulrich's 1975-76 for new address.
Identity, Ministry of Christ Church, Box 423, Glendale, Calif. 91209. NR 1973. TS, p. 366: rightist, anti-Semitic.
Ikon 15
Illinois Citizens for the Medical Control of Abortion Newsletter 1656; mentioned 1652
Illinois Right to Life Committee Newsletter 1656; mentioned 1652
The Illuminated Way Monthly Letter, Box 5325, Las Vegas, Nev. 89102. Defunct. Editor had been Paul Twitchell, spiritual leader and healer. The Letter explained "soul travel" and "total consciousness" to those interested in the path of Eck and Eckankar. See Eck World News, which has been carried on by Twitchell's followers and his widow, who is married to the current living Eck master, Sri Darwin Gross.
Illuminations 1190; mentioned 1183
Ilotan 729
Imani, Black Allied Student Association, 566 La Guardia Place, Box 27, N.Y., N.Y. 10012. Formerly The Faith. NR 1973. TS, p. 230.
Impact [Indianapolis] 1479; mentioned 1454
Impact [Reno] 1227; mentioned 1217
Imua Spotlight: see The Fact Finder [Honolulu] and Spotlight
In, "A Magazine About Prisons," Box 368, Iowa City, Iowa 52240, Wesley Noble Graham, Ed. & Publ. NR 1973. TS, p. 585: art and writings of prisoners. Also described in On Ice, v. 3, no. 2, p. 16.
In a Nutshell 806. Last listing in Ulrich's 1973-74.
In Struggle, Box 609, San Jose, Calif. 95106. NR 1973. Asian-American.
The Independent 166. Last listed in Ulrich's 1969-70.
The Independent American 361. See also: Tax Fax Pamphlets.
The Independent Observer 454
Independent Socialist 47: see Workers' Power
Indian & Metis Brotherhood Organization Newsletter 1480; mentioned 1453
Indian Historian 1481; mentioned 1453
The Indian Leader, Haskell Institute, Lawrence, Kansas. NR 1974.
Indian Record 1482; mentioned 1453
Indian Truth 730
Indian Voices, Robert K. Thuma, Ed., Univ. of Chicago, 1126 E. 59th St., Chicago, Ill. 60637. NR 1974.
The Individualist [London] 313
The Individualist [Silver Spring] 625, 942. See Ulrich's 1975-76 for new address.
Individuals for a Rational Society, 330 Dartmouth St., Boston, Mass. 02116. NR 1973. TS, p. 584: libertarian.
Indochina Bulletin 1531; mentioned 1523
Indochina Chronicle 1531; mentioned 1523
Indochina Focal Point 1533; mentioned 1523
Indochina Peace Campaign Report: see Indochina Focal Point
The Industrial Unionist 1141; mentioned 1133
Industrial Worker 122. See Ulrich's 1975-76 for new address. Another I.W.W. publication we review is The Industrial Unionist.
Inform - National Reports 314
Information: former title of Communiqué
Information Bulletin (World Marxist Review) 556
Informations Correspondance Ouvrières, P. Bleckier, 13 bis, rue Lebois-Rouillon, Paris 19e, France. NR 1973. TS, p. 148.
Inner City Voice 519
Innovator 130; changed title (1970)

to Efficacy. Ulrich's: defunct.
Inside Eastside 732
Inside-Outside, "A Newsletter on Library Service to Youth and Adults in Prisons, Jails, and Detention Centers." Joan Ariel Stout, Ed., Box 9083, Berkeley, Calif. 94709. Quarterly; $2.50 ($3 if billed). Started: Oct. 1974. Circulation: 500. Format: 12 pages (legal size, offset).
The Inside Story 807
Insight 605
Insight and Outlook 315. Last listing in Ulrich's 1971-72; new address.
Instauration 1606
The Insurgent Sociologist 520. See Ulrich's 1975-76 for new address.
Integrated Education: Race and Schools 911. See Ulrich's 1975-76 for new address.
Intelligence Report 1528; mentioned 1523
Interchange 1434
The Intercollegiate Review 315
Intercontinental Press 48. New address according to API list 1973: Box 116, Village Station, N.Y., N.Y. 10014.
Intercourse: see Sexual Freedom
Inter-Galaxy News 1650; mentioned 1649
International 49
International Digest of the Trade Union and Working Class Press, World Federation of Trade Unions, Nam. Curieovych 1, Prague 1, Czechoslovakia. NR 1973. TS, p. 76.
International Humanism 1658; mentioned 1652
International Registry of World Citizens Information Bulletin 1533
International Socialist: see Workers' Power
International Socialist Review 50. New address according to API list 1973: 14 Charles Lane, N.Y., N.Y. 10014.
International Times: see I.T.
Internationale, International Club, Univ. of Kansas, Lawrence, Kan. 66044. NR 1973. TS, p. 500: Marxist.
Internationales Freies Wort 1062; mentioned 1041, 1090
The Internationalist: former title of New Internationalist
The Internationalist Perspective 766
Interplanetary News 891, 942. Ulrich's: defunct.
Interracial Books for Children 733. See Ulrich's 1975-76 for new address.
Invictu$ 627. Ceased publication, according to Ulrich's 1975-76.
Irgun: former title of Hashomer
The Irish Communist 1063; mentioned 1058
Irish Freedom News, National Ass'n. for Irish Freedom, 799 Broadway (Rm. 422), N.Y., N.Y. 10003. NR 1973. TS, p. 474: seems to favor "the main, Marxist-leaning body of the IRA."
The Irish People 1063; mentioned 1041
The Irish Worker, National Socialist Irish Workers' Party, 6 Brendan's Cotts, Irishtown, Dublin 4, Ireland. Leader: Terence Byrne. NR 1973. TS, p. 513.
Israel & Palestine 1483; mentioned 1452
Israel Digest 1484; mentioned 1452
Issues and Actions 250; superseded by weekly American Report, 235 E. 49th St., N.Y., N.Y. 10017. N.U.: AR is defunct (Oct. 1970-Nov. 1974).
Issues in Radical Therapy 1117; mentioned 1110
It Ain't Me Babe [Albany] 695. Defunct. April 1971 was last issue.
It Ain't Me Babe, Last Gasp Ecofunnies, Box 212, Berkeley, Calif. 94701. NR. 1974.
It's Time 1435

JLC News 734
JTTCW: see Voice of the Martyrs
Jackson Women's Coalition Newsletter, Box 3234, Jackson, Miss. 39207. NR 1974.
Jag 316
Jesus People Free Paper: see The Pearl
Jewish Agency Digest: former title of The Israel Digest
Jewish Currents 167
Jewish Liberation Journal 713
The Jewish Radical 736
The John Birch Society Bulletin 363
"Joint" Conference, Kathryn E. King, Ed. & Publ., Box 19332, Washington, D.C. 20036. Quarterly;

Lavender Vision: predecessor of Fag Rag
Lavender Woman 1437
Il Lavoratore 1068; mentioned 1041
Lazette 1439
Leader: see Unitarian Universalist World
The Leaflet 1250; mentioned 1236
League of Non-Voters Newsletter, Box 1406, Santa Ana, Calif. 92702. RR 1973: Refused to supply any information. TS, p. 366: condemns everybody.
The Learning Net: former title of The Madison Whole Earth Learning Community Network
Left Face 788; mentioned 272. Probably defunct. N. U.: only May 1971 issue received.
Left-Out News merged with Communiqué for New Politics 7
Left (Speak) Out 608. N. U.: received only Feb. 1969 issue.
La Legione, Via Andrea Verga 5, 20144 Milano, Italy. NR 1974. TS, p. 154: Called a veterans' monthly, it recalls the glories of Italian arms--but mainly those of Mussolini and Fascism.
The Lesbian Feminist, Box 243, Village Station, N. Y., N. Y. 10014. NR 1974. A newsletter of politics and the arts.
Lesbian Mothers' Union News, Council on Religion and the Homosexual, 330 Ellis, San Francisco, Calif. 94102. NR 1973.
The Lesbian Tide 1441
Letter from China 52. Anna Louise Strong is dead, so Letter is undoubtedly defunct.
Letters to Contacts: see Tactics
Leviathan 522. Supersedes Paper Tiger. N. U.: defunct.
Liaison: former title of Journal du FRAP
Libera 1343; mentioned 1319
The Liberal 415
Liberal Innovator: see Innovator
Liberated Barracks, Service News for Occupied Hawaii, 12 N. School St., Honolulu, Hawaii 96817. NR 1973. TS, p. 536: leftist.
Liberated Guardian 1012
Liberated Space [for women of the Haight], c/o Haight Switchboard, 1797 Haight, San Francisco, Calif. 94117. NR 1974.
Liberation, Ascria, Panafrican Secretariat, 30 Third St., Georgetown, Guyana. NR 1974. TS, p. 326: praise for African freedom-fighters.
Liberation [London] 169
Libération [Montréal] 1280; mentioned 1267
Liberation [N. Y.] 250. New address: 339 Lafayette St., N. Y., N. Y. 10012. $10 (libraries $20).
Liberation News Service 1014; mentioned 1002, 1153. One of the founders of LNS, Raymond Mungo, has written a book of chatty reminiscences, Famous Long Ago: My Life and Hard Times with Liberation News Service (Boston: Beacon Press, 1970).
The Liberator [Claremont] 625
The Liberator [Iowa City] 625
The Liberator [N. Y.] 220. Last listed in Ulrich's 1971-72.
Le Libertaire, Organe de l'Union Fédérale Anarchiste, Boîte Postale No. 1, 41 Chailles, France. NR 1973. TS, p. 148.
Libertarian Broadsheet 625
The Libertarian Connection 630. See Ulrich's 1975-76 for new address.
The Libertarian Forum 133
Libertarian Iconoclast 625
Libertarian Option 1201
Libertarian Review: see Books for Libertarians
Libertas 625, 943
Liberty [N. Y.] 170. Last listing in Ulrich's 1973-74.
Liberty [Washington] 912
Liberty Letter 319
Librarians for Social Change 1120; mentioned 1110
Life Lines 365
Lifestyle! 1213; mentioned 1205
Liga Arabe, Liga Estados Arabes, Libertad 1161, Buenos Aires, Argentina. NR 1973. TS, p. 284: Arab propaganda in Spanish; approach differs greatly from that used in this country.
Lightning, Box 326, Storrs, Conn. 06268. NR 1973. TS, p. 314: left.
Listen 459. See Ulrich's 1975-76 for new address.
Literature & Ideology 1069; mentioned 536, 1041

Logos [Montreal] 102. Fabbro & Woodsworth: ceased.

London Bulletin, Bertrand Russell Peace Foundation, International HQ, 3 and 4 Shavers Place, Haymarket, London SW 1, United Kingdom. NR 1973. TS, p. 36. Publication address: 45 Gamble St., Forest Rd. West, Nottingham, NG1 5LT, United Kingdom. Incorporated in The Spokesman.

Long Beach Free Press 524. Ulrich's 1973-74: title changed to Long Beach Sunset Press. Not in 1975-76 edition. N.U. says title changed to Pacific Coast Highway Press [or X-press]. Address on 10 Jan. 1972 issue [last one received by N.U.]: 3832 Long Beach Blvd., Long Beach, Calif. 90807.

Long Time Coming, Station E, Box 161, Montreal, Quebec, Canada H2T 3A7. NR 1973. TNWSC, p. 34: lesbian.

Longhouse News [Caughnawaga] 748. Woodsworth: c/o Louis Hall, Box 1, Caughnawaga; NR 1973.

Longhouse News [Rooseveltown]: part of Akwesasne Notes

The Los Angeles Advocate 231; now entitled The Advocate

Los Angeles Free Press 104; mentioned 1154. See Ulrich's 1975-76 for new address.

Louisiana Freedom Review, Box 5491, Alexandria, La. 71301. NR 1973. TS, p. 13.

Love: see Sexual Freedom

La Luchadora 1345; mentioned 1315, 1317, 1318

The Lunatic Fringe 1305; mentioned 1300

MERIP Reports 1070; mentioned 1042, 1077

Ms. 1346; mentioned 1315, 1317

The Madison Whole Earth Learning Community Network, 817 E. Johnson St., Madison, Wis. 53703. (Formerly The Learning Net.) NR 1973. TS, p. 612: "organic farming; food preparation; alternatives in jobs and education; health, community projects, etc." Publishers operate Whole Earth Store in Madison.

Maine Women's Herald, Sandy Lucas, Box 488, Brunswick, Me. 04401. NR 1974.

Mainely NOW, Box 534, Kennebunkport, Me. 04046. RR 1974: "When I couldn't get support for Mainely NOW--which was my idea and format and execution, basically--I resigned. It has since fallen by the wayside."

Majority Report 1349; mentioned 1318

El Malcriado 221. See Ulrich's 1975-76 for new address.

Man and Society 232

Manas 914

Manchester [N.H.] Union Leader: criticized 1425

Manhunt 1190

Manion Forum 321

Many Smokes 1487; mentioned 1453

Marijuana Monthly, Rick Sanders, Publ., Box 44428, Panorama City, Calif. 91402. Monthly; $12. Started: 1 Apr. 1975. Circulation: 250,000. Format: 64 pages (trim size 8 1/4" x 10 7/8", glossy, offset). The publisher told us that "Marijuana decriminalization is the main rationale of the monthly. We also deal with the facts and fiction, the humor, and the lifestyle of its smokers."

Marijuana Review 915; mentioned 897. Last listing in Ulrich's 1973-74.

Marine Blues 272; probably defunct 774

Marine Corps Gazette 460; mentioned 897

Maroon: radical newspaper at Univ. of Chicago, criticized 1554

Marx Memorial Library Quarterly Bulletin 54

Masada 713

The Match! 632. See Ulrich's 1975-76 for new address.

Mattachine Midwest Newsletter 1441

Mayday: see Hard Times [Washington, D.C.]

Mayibuye 1281; mentioned 1268

Mazungumzo 1489; mentioned 1454

Media Ecology Review 1228

Media Mix 1251; mentioned 1236

Memo 251. N.U.: probably defunct.

Men's Center Newsletter: see Berkeley Men's Center Newsletter

The Men's Section, Box 211, Ann

from Dian Terry, Director, National Public Information Office, NOW, 641 Lexington Ave., N.Y., N.Y. 10022: "At present, NOW Acts is not being published regularly: only for post-national-conference reports. We have no firm plans for revival as yet. We will be happy to advise you if this status changes."

NOW News: former title of NOW! [Los Angeles]

NOW Newsletter 1354; mentioned 688, 1318

NRP Bulletin 1602; mentioned 1592

NS Mobilizer (formerly NS Kampfruf) 1603; mentioned 1592, 1596

NUC Newsletter 17. In Ulrich's 1973-74 as New University Conference Papers (incorporating NUC Newsletter) at new address. Not in 1975-76 edition. N.U.: last issue of NUC N was received in 1972.

NWPC Newsletter, National Women's Political Caucus, 1302 18th St. N.W. (# 703), Washington, D.C. 20036. NR 1973.

N.Y. WSP Peaceletter: see Peaceletter

Nameless Newsprint, 2840 S. East St. (C-6), Indianapolis, Ind. 46225. MR 1973: "Moved, not forwardable." TS, p. 168: "sensitive to views in the youth rebellion." Former title: The Newspaper without Name. TS, p. 132: Sponsor: Liberal Religious Youth, Inc., 25 Beacon St., Boston 02108. NR 1974. Associated with Unitarian-Universalist Assn.

Namibia News 1283; mentioned 1268

Namibia Today 1284; mentioned 1268

The Nation 174

Nation Europa; mentioned 1601

Nation und Staat: former title of Europa Ethnica

National Abortion Rights Action League 1658; mentioned 1652

The National Anti-Vivisection Society Bulletin 464

National Ass'n. of Professional Educators Newsletter, 16024 Ventura Blvd. (Suite 201), Encino, Calif. 91316. TS, p. 383: likes Ronald Reagan. TS, p. 495: anti-NEA, anti-union. Or: 223 Thousand Oaks Blvd. (Suite 425), Thousand Oaks, Calif. 91360. NR 1974.

The National Catholic Reporter 175, 943

National Christian News 388

National Chronicle 389. See Ulrich's 1975-76 for new address.

National Decency Reporter 465. See Ulrich's 1975-76 for new address in Cleveland.

The National Educator 1560; mentioned 1548

National Fluoridation News 1228; mentioned 1217

National Guardian: former title of Guardian

National Law Women's Newsletter: see Pro Se

National Lawyer's Guild Practitioner: see The Guild Practitioner

National Lesbian Information Service Newsletter, Box 15368, San Francisco, Calif. 94115. NR 1973.

The National Newsletter of Politics 323

National Organization for Non-Parents Newsletter, Box 10495, Baltimore, Md. 21209. NR 1973. TS, p. 579: for a "childfree" life.

National Organization for Women (Southwestern Pennsylvania chapters) Newsletter, Box 86024, Pittsburgh, Pa. 15221. NR 1974. For a list of NOW periodicals reviewed in this volume, see p. 1318.

National Parks and Conservation Magazine 1229; mentioned 1217

The National Program Letter 324

National Renaissance Bulletin 391

National Review and National Review Bulletin 325

National Right to Life News 1658; mentioned 1652

The National Socialist Liberator 847; mentioned 1594, 1608, 1612. May be defunct. Same publisher as National Socialist World.

National Socialist World 850; mentioned 1594, 1608, 1612. Ulrich's: defunct.

National Socialisten, Danmarks National-Socialistiske Ungdom, Postboks 449, DK-8100, Aarhus C, Denmark. Paul H. Riis-Knudsen, leader. NR 1974. TS, p. 513.

Native Nevadan 744. See Ulrich's

1975-76 for new address.
Native Press 1497; mentioned 1453
The Native Sisterhood, Box 515, Kingston, Ont., Canada. NR 1973.
Natural: see Spokane Natural
Natural Food News [Atlanta] 917; mentioned 897
Natural Food News, 2021 N St., Sacramento, Calif. 95814. RR 1974: "We have ceased publication permanently in March 1973 and we have no back issues available. Our publication lasted for one year. The first four issues were an 8-page newspaper. Our last eight issues were a two-sided 8 1/2" x 14" newsletter. Our material was just about 100 per cent original and took a lot of time to produce. We enjoyed it while it lasted, receiving many favorable reviews, and didn't mind too much about losing some money. No, we aren't related to the Texas Natural Food News."
Natural Life Styles 1213
Navajo Times 1498; mentioned 712, 1453
Navy 918; mentioned 897
Near East Report 1499; mentioned 1452
Negro Digest 222. Now: Black World; same address.
Nesika 1500; mentioned 1453
Network 1501; mentioned 1453
The Network News, Connecticut Citizens' Action Group, 57 Farmington Ave., Hartford, Conn. 06105. NR 1973. TS, p. 315: a Ralph Nader thing that grew out of Earth Action Group. Citizen action.
The New Age Intellectual Newsletter 466. Ulrich's 1975-76 says superseded by Witches' Newsletter. We have reviewed two more publications of Dr. Martello's in Vol. III: WICA Newsletter [does this supersede Witches' Newsletter?] & Witchcraft Digest.
New Age Interpreter 1636; mentioned 1614
New America 58. See Ulrich's 1975-76 for new address.
The New Banner 1202
The New Broadside 687
The New Broom 688, 1355; mentioned 1320
New Canada 1016
New Catholic World: see The Catholic World
The New Crusader, Jefferson-Leavell Publg. Co., 6429 Martin Luther King Dr., Chicago, Ill. NR 1973. TS, p. 371: black community paper; doesn't admire Richard J. Daley, Mayor of Chicago.
New Dawn 1502; mentioned 1451
New Directions for Women in New Jersey 1356; mentioned 1316
New England Jewish Free Press 713
New England Military News, Legal In-Service Project, 355 Boylston St., Boston, Mass. 02126. RR 1973: "No longer being published." TS, p. 540: GI paper.
New England Tax Resistance Newsletter: see Only for Life
The New Feminist 1357; mentioned 1315, 1318
The New Guard 327
New Hampshire Sisters, 6 Rumford St., Concord, N.H. RR 1974: "Sorry, we are no longer publishing."
The New Harbinger 1660; mentioned 1652
The New Human 1661; mentioned 1652
New Humanist: see Humanist [London]
New Improved Tide 1174; mentioned 1153
New Internationalist 1252
The New Leader 662
New Left Notes 19. In June 1969 NLN split into two publications with the same name. The Chicago faction ceased publication 21 Oct. 1969 and the Boston faction ceased Nov. 1972. Information from N.U.
New Left Review 61, 481. Distributor: B. DeBoer, 188 High St., Nutley, N.J. 07110.
New Living: see Elysium Journal of the Senses
New Mobilizer 252. Probably defunct. N.U.: Feb. 1970 last issue received.
New Outlook 1503; mentioned 1452
The New Patriot (Incorporating The American Reporter) and Race, Box 16079, McWillie Station, Jackson, Miss. 39206. Stephen Langton, Ed. White Nordic race

championed; anti-communist; anti-Jewish (Jews associated with Russian communism). RR 1968: "Both publications have been discontinued." (This is probably the publication which merged with The Thunderbolt 395.)
The New Perspective 862
New Politics 559
The New Prairie Primer 1016; mentioned 1001
The New Republic 177
New Salute: merged with Open Ranks
New Schools Exchange Newsletter 919. See Ulrich's 1975-76 for new address. TS, p. 554 gives: Box 820, St. Paris, Ohio 43072.
New Solidarity, National Caucus of Labor Committees, Box 295, Cathedral Park Station, N.Y., N.Y. 10025. NR 1973. TS, p. 501.
New South 195. Superseded by Southern Voices. See Ulrich's 1975-76 for new address.
The New South Student 197. MR 1970: "Moved, left no address." Last issue received by N.U.: Jan. 1969.
New Statesman 664. See Ulrich's 1975-76 for new address.
New Times 253; mentioned 1236
New Unity 1144; mentioned 1133
New University Conference Papers: see NUC Newsletter
New University Thought 467. New title: Journal of University Studies.
The New Voice 1071; mentioned 1042
New Woman 1357; mentioned 688, 1317
New World Review 62
New York City Star 1017; supersedes Liberated Guardian
The New York Element 920. Last listing in Ulrich's 1973-74.
The New York Express 807
New York Mattachine Newsletter: see Gay Ways
New York News Service 1019; mentioned 1002, 1153
The New York Review of Sex & Politics 233
The New York Times: leftist 1564
News & Letters 64. See Ulrich's 1975-76 for new address.
News and Notes of Interest to Christians 1561; mentioned 1548
News-Facts: former title of Northern Neighbors
News from South Africa 921; mentioned 897. Ulrich's: defunct.
News from Vietnam, Ass'n. of Vietnamese Patriots in Canada, Box 324, Station N, Montreal 129, Quebec, Canada. NR 1974. TS, pp. 449, 483: pro-Viet Cong.
News Notes: for any periodical whose title starts with these words, look instead under the name of the issuing organization, e.g., Business Executives Move for New National Priorities News Notes, or Central Committee for Conscientious Objectors News Notes.
News of Greece 684; mentioned 943
Newsbulletin of NICRA: former title of Civil Rights
Newsletter: for any periodical whose title starts with this word, look instead under the name of the issuing organization, e.g., Society for Humane Abortion Newsletter.
The Newspaper without Name: see Nameless Newsprint
Nickel Review 526
Nishnawbe News 1505; mentioned 1453. The periodical is also the subject of "Michigan Indians Run a Newspaper," The New York Times, 26 March 1972, sec. 1, p. 63.
Nitzotz, Radical Zionist Alliance, Box 384, N.Y., N.Y. 10011. NR 1974. TS, p. 575: Marxist.
No Amnesty! 1562; mentioned 1548. Former title: No Amnesty Campaign Newsletter.
No More Fun and Games 482. New address: Cell 16, 2 Brewer St., Cambridge, Mass. 02138.
No More Teacher's Dirty Looks 1121; mentioned 1110
Nö Pintcha 1284; mentioned 1268
Nommo, Univ. of California, Los Angeles, Calif. 90024. Sonji Walker, Ed. NR 1972. Mentioned in Thomas A. Johnson, "Campus Racial Tensions Rise As Black Enrollment Increases," The New York Times, 4 April 1972, p. 57.
Nordisk Kamp 1602; mentioned 1592, 1601
North Carolina Anvil 610; mentioned 1154

North County Anvil 1214; mentioned 1205
North Star 1254
Northeast Dialog 665
The Northeaster, Unschool Corp., c/o U.E.S.C., Box 1126, New Haven, Conn. 06505. NR 1974. TS, p. 362: alternative schools.
Northern Neighbors 1072; mentioned 1041
Northwest Passage 1175
Northwest Safe Water Newsletter, 311 Cookson St., Shelton, Wash. 98584. NR 1974. TS, p. 310: opposes fluoridation of drinking water.
The Northwest Technocrat 923; mentioned 1668. See Ulrich's 1975-76 for new address in Savannah, Ohio.
Not Man Apart 1230; mentioned 1217
Notes 1359; mentioned 1319
Notes from the Third Year: see Notes
Notes from the Underground: see Dallas Notes
Notes on Health Politics 1123; mentioned 1110
Nueva Accion Femenina 1363. Feedback: editor expressed no disapproval.

OAS Weekly Newsletter 1254
OB People's Rag, Box 7750, Ocean Beach, Calif. 92107. NR 1973. TS, p. 350 says underground: "the standard everybody's-mean-to-us."
The Oak 272; probably defunct 774
The Objectivist (formerly The Objectivist Newsletter) 634; superseded by Ayn Rand Letter
The Obligore 272
El Obrero, La Raza Unida Party, 749 S. Chicago, Los Angeles, Calif. 90023. NR 1973. TS, p. 446: Chicanos cannot support Democrats, must have their own party.
Observer (United Church of Canada): sued by B'nai B'rith 1492
Occult Digest 1637
Octopus or Octopus Free Press 107. Woodsworth: ceased in Dec. 1970.
The Odinist 1637; mentioned 1614
Off Our Backs 1364; mentioned 688, 1319
Off the Pedestal 688
Oklahoma Limited 666; published by John D. Woodie, Jr.
The Oklahoma Observer 1255; mentioned 1236
The Old Mole [Cambridge] 19. N.U.: TOM (last issue received: Apr. 1971) superseded by The Mole (last issue received: Nov. 1974).
Old Mole [Toronto] 1073; mentioned 1041
Om 284. MR 1970: "Moved, left no address."
Omphalos 612. Fabbro & Woodsworth: ceased.
On Campus with Women 1366; mentioned 1315, 1317
On Ice 1307
On Our Way 1366; mentioned 1316
On Target 367
On the Way, Anchorage Women's Liberation Newsletter, 7801 Peck Ave., Anchorage, Alaska 99504. NR 1973.
ONE Institute Quarterly: Homophile Studies 1443. Ulrich's: defunct.
ONE Magazine 233; mentioned 1444. May be defunct.
One World 667. Ulrich's: defunct; last issue 1973.
ONEletter: see ONE Magazine
Only for Life, New England Tax Resistance Newsletter: merged with Final Draft to become Peacework.
Ontario Newsletter: see Voice of Women Ontario Newsletter
Ontological Thought 1639
Open Forum 198. See Ulrich's 1975-76 for new address.
Open Ranks 789. Probably defunct. N.U.: July 1970 last issue received.
Open Sights 272
Operation Yorkville: former title of Morality in Media Newsletter
Option: former title of Libertarian Option
Options 808
Ha-Orah - The Light 714
The Order of the Universe 1639; mentioned 1614
The Oregon Gay Liberator, or The Oregon Liberator, 4226 N. Montana Ave., Portland, Ore. 97217. NR 1974. Publication of Portland Gay Liberation Communications Committee.
Organizing Bulletin of Williamsport Committee for a Six Hour Day

With Eight Hours' Pay 65
Orion Magazine 424
Orpheus 107. Ulrich's 1971-72: ceased.
Other Scenes 108; mentioned 1154. Address on Late Fall 1974 issue: Dawes Press, 81a Dawes Rd., London, SW6, UK. John Wilcox is no longer with this publication; the above was his last issue. Publication will continue. Collage, now defunct, also published by Wilcox.
Other Stand 714
The Other Woman 1368; mentioned 1316
Our American Heritage Committee News Bulletin 328. See Ulrich's 1975-76 for new address.
Our Generation 20, 1074; mentioned 1042. Reviewed as radical in Vol. I, OG now refers to itself as libertarian socialist.
Outdoor America 1231; mentioned 1217
Outlaw Times: see Dallas Notes
Outlook 1506; mentioned 1452
Outmates 1308; mentioned 1299
Outside the Net 1019; mentioned 1001
L'Ouvrier: see Il Laboratore
Overload, New People Media Project, Box 4356, Sather Gate Station, Berkeley, Calif. 94704. NR 1973. TS, p. 101: critical of magazines, television, radio.
Oz 109, 944. Last listing in Ulrich's 1973-74. Last issue received by N.U.: Jan. 1973.
Ozark Access Catalogue 1214; mentioned 1205

PAIGC Actualités 1284; mentioned 1268
PAK Newsletter 1285; mentioned 1267
The PAR Journal 22. N.U.: probably defunct. Last issue received: Oct./Dec. 1969.
The PCCA Organizer, Pike County Citizens' Association, Box 10, Hellier, N.Y. 41534. NR 1973. TS, p. 209: against strip-mining.
PL: see Progressive Labor
PM, c/o Bill McCauslin, 472 W. Jefferson (#210), Tallahassee, Fla. 32301. NR 1973. TS, p. 212: an irregular "Movement" periodical.
PSI Magazine 1640
PWR, Pennsylvanians for Women's Rights Newsletter, 230 Chestnut St., Lancaster, Pa. 17603. NR 1974.
Pacific Coast Highway X-press: see Long Beach Free Press
Pacific Research & World Empire Telegram 668
Pack Rat, Berkeley High School Student Union, 2214 Grove St., Berkeley, Calif. 94709. NR 1973. TS, p. 63.
Pac-o-Lies 560. Probably defunct. N.U.: July 1970 was last issue received.
El Paisano 223
Pakistan Forum 1075; mentioned 1041; merged with MERIP Reports 1071
Palante, Calle 23 numero 358, Esquina a J, Vedado, Havana 4, Cuba. NR 1973. TS, p. 440: anti-U.S., humorous cartoons.
Palante [N.Y.] 1507; mentioned 1451
Palestine Resistance Bulletin, Palestine Solidarity Committee, Box 63, Norton Union, State University of New York, Buffalo, N.Y. 14124. NR 1973. TS, p. 291, says: a support group for the Democratic Popular Front for the Liberation of Palestine.
The Palestinian Voice 1508; mentioned 1452
Pandora 1369; mentioned 1316
Pandora's Box 1193; mentioned 1183
Panorama: replaced by ILO Information in Feb. 1971.
Papago Indian News, Sells, Ariz. 85634. NR 1974.
El Papel, Box 7167, Albuquerque, N.M. 87104. NR 1974. Chicano.
The Paper, Box 11076, Chicago, Ill. 60611. NR 1973. TS, p. 520: oddball theater, gay liberation.
The Paper, James Ebert, Ed., Box 367, East Lansing, Mich. 48823. "Student oriented." Member, Underground Press Syndicate & Liberation News Service. "Not, however, a 'hippie' publication." Defunct.
The Paper, 311 Chestnut St., Santa Cruz, Calif. 95060. "For constructive alternatives." NR 1973. TS, p. 124.
Paper Tiger [Boston] 23. Superseded by Leviathan.
Paper Tiger, New Jersey Student

Union, 687 Larch Ave., Teaneck, N.J. 07666. NR 1974.
Papers of the New University Conference: see NUC Newsletter
Parapluie, 105 Blvd. Malesherbes, Paris 8, France. NR 1973. TS, p. 367: considers it to be a spectacular underground.
Patriot [Kalamazoo] 1176; mentioned 1153
The Patriot [New York] 1509; mentioned 1451
The Patriot News, Box 8697, San Francisco, Calif. 94128. William Drexler, Ed. NR 1973. TS, p. 621: opposed to the income tax.
The Pawn 792
Pax Bulletin 254. According to TS, p. 310 (March 1972), the British Catholic peace groups, Pax and Pax Christi, merged; PB joined with and was called Pax Christi Bulletin. Same address as PB. According to Ulrich's 1975-76, PB (PCB title not used) superseded by Just Peace; new address.
Pax et Libertas (formerly Pax International) 767
Peace 254
Peace and Freedom: see Four Lights
Peace & Freedom News: see Baltimore Peace & Freedom News
The Peace Gazette 1534; mentioned 1523
Peace News 255
Peace Plans 256. Last listing in Ulrich's 1971-72.
Peace Research Abstracts Journal: see Canadian Peace Research Institute News Report
Peaceletter 1535; mentioned 1523
The Peacemaker 257. See Ulrich's 1975-76 for new address.
Peacework 1536
The Pearl 1640; mentioned 1614. Jesus People Free Paper is former title.
Ha Peh 1511; mentioned 714, 1452
Peking Review 66. Ulrich's 1975-76 gives new Peking address.
The Penal Digest International. TS, p. 261: "contents mostly on the penal press"; highly recommended. Inquiry answered by Prisoners' Digest International.
Peninsula Observer: see The Midpeninsula Observer
Penn House Newsletter 1256; mentioned 1236
Pensacola Fishcheer: see Fishcheer
The Pentagon Paper, 125 W. 4th St., Los Angeles, Calif. 90013. NR 1974. TS, pp. 446-447: the inner 4 pages of the sample examined were War Bulletin. Several other addresses given.
People Get Ready: predecessor of The Bay Area Worker
People's Appalachia, Rte. 3, Box 355B, Morgantown, W. Va. 26505. NR 1974.
People's Canada Daily News 1077; mentioned 1040
People's News Service, John Brown Party, 412 N. 4th Ave., Tucson, Ariz. 85705. Formerly Resurrection, which TS, p. 151 describes as revolutionary, aimed at Chicanos, blacks, and poor whites: "the usual imitation of Black Panther publications." TS, p. 444, refers to PNS as radical revolutionary. NR 1973.
People's Will, International League of Unity, 29 Cross St., Nutley, N.J. 07110. NR 1973. TS, p. 274: revolutionary, but not Marxist; attacks Jewish Defense League; talks of "racial democracy."
People's World 67; disagreements with 1082. See Ulrich's 1975-76 for new address.
Perjuangan 1145; mentioned 1134
Perpetual Motion Journal 468. Defunct: Ulrich's.
Perseverance 1605; mentioned 1592
The Petal Paper 670; mentioned 945. Ulrich's: defunct.
Philadelphia Health News, 3601 Locust St., Philadelphia, Pa. 19104. NR 1974. TS, p. 301: published by Health Information Project; about health and the poor.
The Phoenix, 230 Clarendon St., Boston, Mass. "Boston's Weekly Journal of News, Opinion, and the Arts." NR 1974. TS, p. 363: undergroundish-community paper.
The Phoenix [Kansas City] 234. MR 1970: "Box [?] closed, no order."
Picket Line, Student Worker Action Committee, L. A. Rank & File Labor News, Box 144--308 Westwood Pl., Los Angeles, Calif. 90024. NR 1974. TS, p. 447: a bit radical.

Prophetic Herald 876
Prophetic News Letter 427. See Ulrich's 1975-76 for new address.
The Protean/Radish 561. Has resumed publication; same address.
Protos 637
Proud Woman (formerly Mother), superseded by LIS Newsletter 1444; mentioned 1437
The Provoker 1233
Psychic 879
Psychic News 880
Pudge, Last Gasp Ecofunnies, Box 212, Berkeley, Calif. NR 1974. Comics.
Punch: see The Worcester Punch
Punji Stick, Liberation Support Movement, Box 338, Richmond, B.C. Canada. RR 1973: "We are no longer publishing this paper." TS, p. 233: "Supports MPLA in Angola, Tupamaros in Uruguay, etc. Talks a thundering good revolution."
The Pyongyang Times 563

Quaker Service 258
Quaker Service Bulletin 1537
Que Ondee Sola 1512; mentioned 1454
Québecoises deboutte, 3908 Mentana, Montreal, Quebec, Canada. NR 1973, 1974. TNWSC, p. 39, has annotation and gives this street address: 4319 St. Denis.
Quest News Service, Freepost, London SW1H DYY [or OYY], U.K. RR 1974: "Sorry, Quest ceased publication in April 1973." TS, p. 617: social change in Britain.
Quest - UFO Report 893
The Questers 142. N.U. has entry for The Quester Newsletter, The Questers Project, Cathedral City, Calif.; final issue was Aug. 1972.
Quicksilver Times 527. Defunct according to Chicago Rap.

RAW Truth, Reservists Against the War, 65A Winthrop St., Cambridge, Mass. 02138. NR 1973. TS, p. 322.
RITA Notes: a sub-series of 778
RT: Journal of Radical Therapy: see The Radical Therapist
Race: see The New Patriot
The Racialist, White Youth Alliance, Box 17006, Baton Rouge, La. 70803. NR 1973. TS, p. 247.
Radical America 26, 1081; mentioned 1041. Originally "An SDS Journal" (Vol. I), it is now Marxist. Address on Nov./Dec. 1975 issue: 60 Union Square, Somerville, Mass. 02140.
Radical Humanist: see Alternative to Alienation
The Radical Therapist 528, 945; mentioned 1110. Superseded by Rough Times which was superseded by RT: Journal of Radical Therapy. Address on Summer 1975 issue: Box 89, W. Somerville, Maine 02144.
Radical's Digest 26. MR 1970: "Moved, left no address."
Radicals in the Professions Newsletter (now entitled Something Else) 27. See new address in Ulrich's 1975-76.
The Rag [Austin] 110, 1177; mentioned 1153
The Rag, Reserve and National Guard Organizing Committee, 2801 N. Sheffield, Chicago, Ill. 60614. NR 1973. TS, p. 618: organization helps with grievances, legal needs; no radicalism.
Rage 1544; mentioned 1543
Rainbow People 745. API 1973 list: defunct as of 1970(?).
Rama Pipien 1178; mentioned 1153
Rampart College Newsletter (formerly Rampart Journal of Individualist Thought) 1202. See also the College's Pine Tree.
Ramparts 27. Address as of 1975: 2749 Hyde St., San Francisco 94109.
Rank and File Currents, New York Committee for Trade Union Action and Democracy, 799 Broadway, Room 628, N.Y., N.Y. 10003. NR 1973. TS, p. 534: not revolutionary.
Rank & File Voice, Rank & File Defense Committee, Box 3013, Barnum Station, Bridgeport, Conn. 06605. NR 1973. TS, p. 479: attacks corporations.
Rantings, c/o Nancy Wood, 11205 Euclid Ave., Cleveland, Ohio 44106. Questionnaire was returned (1974) filled out by What She Wants, with the explanation that Rantings merged, after 4 or

San Diego Free Door 614. Aug. 1974 may have been last issue. Other titles used were San Diego Free Press, San Diego Free Door to Liberation, Free Door, Door to Liberation and Door (last title). San Diego Free Press & San Diego Free Door to Liberation had the same address, 6389 Imperial Ave., and may have preceded SDFD. NR 1970 from above address. Teaspoon Door may be another earlier title resulting from a merger.

San Diego Street Journal, 360 Fifth Ave., San Diego, Calif. 92101. RR 1973: "Street Journal is no longer publishing."

The San Francisco Ball 1662; mentioned 1652

The San Francisco Bay Guardian 180. New address: 1070 Bryant St., San Francisco, Calif. 94103. Difficulties encountered by the paper are discussed in Martin Arnold, "'Alternative' Paper, the Target of a Unionizing Drive, Fears It Will Have No Choice but to Close," The New York Times, 2 December 1975, p. 27.

San Francisco Comic Book 1194

San Francisco Express Times: see Good Times

San Joaquin NOW Newsletter 1373; mentioned 1318

Sane World 261. See Ulrich's 1975-76 for new address.

Sanity Now, Box 261, La Puente, Calif. 91747. NR 1974. TS, p. 300: radical left-activist, education center, uses communist clichés.

Santa Fe Women's Community Magazine, 520 Jose St. (#5), Santa Fe, N.M. 87501. NR 1974. TNWSC, p. 39.

Sapphire, 310 Irving St., San Francisco, Calif. 94122. NR 1974. Lesbian. May never have progressed beyond planning stage.

Sappho 1445

Sash 1292; mentioned 1268

Saskatchewan Indian 1515; mentioned 1453

Saskatoon Women for Abortion Repeal Newsletter 1662; mentioned 1652

Saskatoon Women's Liberation Newsletter 1374; mentioned 1319

Satyagraha 263. Address on Aug./Sept. 1975 issue: Chicago Clergy and Laity Concerned, Room 510, 542 South Dearborn St., Chicago, Ill. 60605.

Saucer Magazine 432

Saucer News 894. Ulrich's: defunct.

Saucers, Space & Science 433. Last listing in Ulrich's 1971-72.

Sauti, 179 Cortland, Highland Park, Mich. 48203. NR 1970. Successor to Inner City Voice. (Title has apparently reverted to Inner City Voice.)

Scar'd Times 1311

Scene 1663; mentioned 1652

Schism 928

The Schoolpaper, 290 Vaughan St. (Suite 203), Winnipeg 2, Man., Canada. NR 1974. TS, p. 411: distributed at Winnipeg universities & high schools.

Schuylkill River Express, Box 8372, Philadelphia, Pa. 19104. NR 1973. TS, p. 240: community; opposition to Bicentennial celebration in or around the city.

Science & Society 571. See Ulrich's 1975-76 for new address.

Science for the People 1125; mentioned 1109

Science for Vietnam Newsletter, 1103 E. 57th St., Chicago, Ill. 60637. NR 1973. TS, pp. 439, 462: pro-Viet Cong; "must be condemned upon moral grounds."

Scientist and Citizen: see Environment

Scope: see Detroit Scope Magazine

The Scout 1516; mentioned 1453

Screw [N.Y.] 760; mentioned 756, 945. See Ulrich's 1975-76 for new address.

Search Magazine 427

Seattle Group Bulletin 123

Sechaba 530, 1293; mentioned 1268

Second City 112; mentioned 1154. N.U.: defunct; last issue was April 1975.

Second Coming Newspaper, Austin Women's Liberation, Box 8011, U.T. Station, Austin, Tex. 78712. RR 1974: "Defunct."

The Second Front [Boulogne] 272; probably defunct 774

Second Front, American Deserters' Committee, Drottninggatan 13, Stockholm, Sweden. RR 1970: No longer published.

The Second Page 1087; mentioned 1042

Second Wave 1376; mentioned 1315, 1319
Secret Storm 1377; mentioned 1316
Secular Subjects 417
Seed: see Chicago Seed
The Seeker 881. Ulrich's: defunct.
Self-Knowledge 882
Sentinel 434
Service d'Intelligence Canadien: see The Canadian Intelligence Service
Sexual Freedom 235. Probably defunct. N.U.: last issue received was from 1970.
Shakedown 272; probably defunct 774
Shasta County Chronicle: see National Chronicle
Sherwood Forest 531
Short Times 272; probably defunct 774
Si Se Puede! Salinas Citizens' Committee in Defense of Farmworkers, Box 1364 Salinas, Calif. 93901. NR 1973. TS, p. 575; bilingual; pro-United Farm Workers.
Sierra Review 1262
Silayan 1293; mentioned 1268
Sing Out! 675. See Ulrich's 1975-76 for new address.
A Single Spark 1025; mentioned 1001
Sipapu, "a newsletter for librarians, editors, collectors, and others interested in Third World studies, the counter-culture, the alternative (formerly called underground), and independent (also called small) presses." Noel Peattie, Ed. & Publ., Route 1, Box 216, Winters, Calif. 95694. Semi-annual; $2. 24 pages. Started: Jan. 1970. Issues examined: Nos. 11-12 (Jan. & July 1975). Indexing: Nos. 1-10 in No. 10. The copies examined contained news of conferences (of librarians, writers, small-press editors & publishers); brief review-notices of other periodicals; interviews (with an editor of The Mother Earth News; and an underground comic artist); and illustrations (line drawings; reproductions of old woodcuts).
Siren, 713 W. Armitage Ave., Chicago, Ill. 60614. NR 1974. TNWSC, p. 40: "anarchism as the logically consistent political expression of feminism."
Sister, New Haven Women's Liberation, Women's Center, 3438 Yale Station, New Haven, Conn. 06520. NR 1974.
Sister News, Women's Center, U-B, University of Conn., Storrs, Conn. 06268. NR 1973. TS, p. 542.
Sisters 1446
Skirting the Capital, Box 4569, Sacramento, Calif. 95825. NR 1974. Feminist legislative newsletter. TNWSC p. 201.
Skookum Jim News 1516; mentioned 1453
Skylook 435. See Ulrich's 1975-76 for new address.
Smoke Signals, Colorado River Indian Tribes, Route 1, Box 23-B, Parker, Ariz. 85344. NR 1973. TS, p. 304.
Snarf 1194
Social Progress 676. Superseded by Church and Society. See new address in Ulrich's 1975-76.
Social Questions Bulletin 182. See Ulrich's 1975-76 for new address.
Socialist Education Bulletin 1089; mentioned 1041, 1063, 1090
Socialist Forum 572
Socialist Press Bulletin 1089; mentioned 1040
Socialist Review 1090; mentioned 1060, 1063, 1093, 1094
Socialist Revolution 1090; mentioned 1041
Socialist Standard 1092; mentioned 1060, 1063, 1090, 1094
Socialist Tribune 574
Socialist Viewpoint 1093; mentioned 1041, 1060, 1063, 1090, 1093
Socialist Woman: former title of Women Now!
Society for Humane Abortion Newsletter 922
Society of Separationists Newsletter 866
Sojourner, Women's Interart Center, 549 W. 52nd St., N.Y., N.Y. 10019. NR 1973.
Solidarity, c/o N. Roy, 138 Walker Road, Torry, Aberdeen, Scotland. NR 1971.
Solidarity [Bromley] 576
Solidarity ["South London"], c/o J. Shreeve, 44 Sturgeon Rd., London S.E. 17, England. RR 1971: "No longer produced."
Solidarity ["West London"], c/o M. Duncan, 15 Taylor's Green, East Acton, London W. 3, England.

NR 1971.

Solidarity, Labor Committee for New York S. D. S., 212 E. 97th St., N. Y., N. Y. 10029. NR 1970. TS, p. 94: Box 49, Washington Bridge Station 10033.

Solidarity ["North West"], c/o Janet Harris, 96 Doveleys Rd., Salford M68QW, England. NR 1971.

Solidarity Newsletter 1094; mentioned 1042

Something Else. TS, p. 374. Succeeds Radicals in the Professions Newsletter (q. v.). Ulrich's 1975-76: new address.

Something Else for Teachers 1127; mentioned 1110

So's Your Old Lady, 710 W. 22nd St., Minneapolis, Minn. 55405. Lesbian. NR 1974. TNWSC, p. 41.

The Source 714

South 334

The South African Observer 1581; mentioned 1571

South African Scope 930; mentioned 897

South Louisiana Citizens' Council Newsletter, Jackson G. Ricou, Pres., Box 9048, Metairie, La. NR 1973. TS, p. 170: segregationist?

South Place Magazine: see The Ethical Record

South Vietnam in Struggle 578. See Ulrich's 1975-76 for new address.

Southeast Asian Perspectives: new title of Vietnam Perspectives

Southern Africa 1294; mentioned 1268

Southern Committee to Free All Political Prisoners Newsletter 1312

The Southern Courier 200

Southern International Times (high school underground): mentioned 1027

The Southern Patriot 183

The Southern Ute Drum, Southern Ute Tribal H. Q., Ignacio, Colo. 81137. NR 1973. TS, p. 369.

The Southern Voice 1179

Southern Voices: see New South

Space City! 1217 Wichita, Houston, Tex. 77004. Underground. B & H: ceased in Feb. 1972.

Spark, 6729 N. Ashland, Chicago, Ill. 60626. NR 1973. TS, p. 240: supports Black Panthers; considers Jimmy Hoffa a political prisoner.

Spark [N. Y.] 1128; mentioned 1109

Spark Monthly Newspaper ("Western Voice for Revolution"), Progressive Labor Party, Box 808, G. P. O., Brooklyn, N. Y. 11201. RR 1970: No longer published.

Spartacist 579; mentioned 1085, 1103, 1106. TS, p. 279 says S has been replaced by Workers' Vanguard. But Ulrich's describes it as a "supplement" to WV.

Spartacist-West 73; mentioned 1085, 1103, 1106. Probably defunct. N. U.: last issue received was March 1970.

Spartacus 272; probably defunct 774

Speak Out [Peoria]: see Left (Speak) Out

Speakout [Albany] 1378; mentioned 1319

Spear 1517; mentioned 1454

Spearhead: mentioned 1601

Spectre 1447; mentioned 1407

Spectrum 236

Spokane Natural 113. Title changed to Spokane Falls Provincial Press. According to Ulrich's 1975-76, ceased publication 1972.

Spokesman 1096

Spokeswoman 1379; mentioned 689, 1319

Sporting Dog Journal: see "Dog-fighting periodicals"

The Sportswoman 1380; mentioned 1320

Spotlight 369; succeeded by The Fact Finder [Honolulu]

Spotlight On South Africa, African National Congress of South Africa, Box 2239, Dar es Salaam, Tanzania. Ulrich's: ceased. Was an 11-page mimeographed magazine. Anti-colonialist; anti-imperialist; exposed evils of apartheid. "Revolutionary people's war against our White oppressors in South Africa."

The Staff, 6472 Santa Monica Blvd., Hollywood, Calif. 90038. NR 1973. TS, p. 301: underground weekly.

Stance 1262; mentioned 1237

Standard Oiler (Standard Oil Co. of Calif.), company underground 1154

Starcraft 1644; mentioned 1614

Statecraft 334; new address: Box 312, Alexandria, Va. 22313. Ulrich's 1975-76 says that it

ceased, but does not know when.
The StethOtruth 1148; mentioned 1133
Storrs Street Fish Gazette: mentioned 1179
Storrs Weekly 1179; mentioned 1154. Former title: Storrs Weekly Reader
Straight Creek Journal 1234. Created through merger with Boulder Magazine and Chinook.
Straight Talk 1607; mentioned 1592, 1602
Strawberry Network 677. N. U.: probably defunct.
Street Drug Survival 1664; mentioned 1652
Street Paper, Church of Man, Box 1222, Salt Lake City, Utah 84110. NR 1973. TS, p. 451: opposition to Mormon Church.
Struggle, Box 211, Grove Hall, Boston, Mass. 02021. NR 1973. TS, p. 610: militant revolutionary; mostly Negroes.
Student Federalist [TS, p. 80]: see The World Citizen
The Student Mobilizer 263. Probably defunct.
Student Mobilizer Wall Poster 769. Probably defunct.
The Summerhill Society Bulletin 470, feedback 483. Last issue received by N. U.: Aug. 1971.
The Summit Sun 815; mentioned 798
The Sun [Albuquerque] 1645
Sun [Ann Arbor]: see Ann Arbor Sun
Sun [Detroit] 1026; mentioned 1002
The Sun-Reporter 750
Sunburst, North American Libertarian Alliance, Box 3684, Tucson, Ariz. 85720. NR 1973. TS, p. 250.
Sundance 1027; mentioned 1002
The Sunwheel 1637; mentioned 1614
Survive 1566
Swasia 1665; mentioned 1653
Synergy 1129; mentioned 1110

TAP 1029; mentioned 1001
Tactics 371. See Ulrich's 1975-76 for new address.
The Tag-Rag, Tenants' Action Group, 310 Haight St., San Francisco, Calif. 94117. NR 1973. TS, p. 482.
Taiga Times '71 1666; mentioned 1653
Take Over 1180
Tales from the Ozone 1195
Tales of Toad 1195
Tangents 237
Tapwe 1667; mentioned 1653
Task Force [Ormond Beach] 817. See Ulrich's 1975-76 for new address in Annandale, Va. Same publisher for Alert.
Task Force [San Francisco] 286. MR 1970: "Moved, left no address."
Tax Fax Pamphlets 833
Tax Strike News, Box 175, Rosemead, Calif. 91770. Anita Kerns, Ed. MR 1973: "Moved, not forwardable." TS, p. 353.
Tax Talk 1538
The Taxpayers' Committee to End Foreign Aid 1567; mentioned 1548
Teacher Paper, 2221 N. E. 23rd, Portland, Ore. 97212. "...views, knowledge, experience of the working classroom teacher.... some exposés.... prose pruned of the jargon of education." Radical professional.
Teachers' Committee for Peace in Vietnam Newsletter 770
Teaspoon Door, 6411 Imperial Ave., San Diego, Calif. 92114. NR 1970. May be an earlier title of San Diego Free Door.
Technocracy Briefs 1667; mentioned 1652
Technocracy Digest 931; mentioned 1668
The Technocrat 933; mentioned 1668
Technocratic Trendevents 1668; mentioned 1652
Tekawennake 1518; mentioned 1453
Tell-A-Woman, Women's Liberation Center, 4634 Chester Ave., Philadelphia, Pa. 19143. NR 1974.
Telos 1130
Tempo 183. Ulrich's: defunct.
Tenant 1149; mentioned 1133
Tenants' Newsletter 1030; mentioned 1001
The Texan Woman 1380; mentioned 1316
The Texas Observer 678. See Ulrich's 1975-76 for new address.
Third World 1096; mentioned 1041
Third World News 1518; mentioned 1451
This Magazine Is About Schools 471. New address according to TS, p.

253: 56 Esplanade St. East, 4th floor, Toronto 215, Ont. Canada. Now entitled This Magazine.
Thoi-Bao Ga 1295; mentioned 1268
Thomas Jefferson Hogg Legal Gazette, Union of University Students, University of Virginia, Charlottesville, Va. 22901. NR 1974. TS, p. 542: liberal activist.
Thomas Jefferson Research Center Newsletter 472
Thunder 581. See Ulrich's 1975-76 for new address.
Thunder and Lightning, National White American Party, Box 1271, Olympia, Wash. 98501. MR 1973: "Unclaimed" and "address unknown." TS, p. 206: race supremacist.
The Thunderbolt 394. Last listing in Ulrich's 1973-74, at new address.
Thursday's Drummer: see Distant Drummer
Tightwire, Box 515, Kingston, Ont., Canada. Women's penitentiary paper. NR 1973.
Times of the Americas, 830 Woodward Bldg., Washington, D.C. 20005. Formerly The Times of Havana (anti-Castro).
Tits & Clits Comix 1196; mentioned 1183
To Free Mankind: former title of The World Citizen, which is now called World Citizen/Federalist Letter. TS, p. 431.
Today in France 473. See Ulrich's 1975-76 for new address.
Toiyabe Trails 1234; formerly Toiyabe Tattler
Tompkins Chemung Bulletin 647
Tooth and Nail 689. MR 1971 from 1800 Prince St., Berkeley: "Moved, left no address."
The Top of the News with Fulton Lewis III 335. Ulrich's: defunct.
Top Secret 272; probably defunct 774
The Torch 1203
Toronto Citizen 1263; mentioned 1236
Toward Freedom 474
Town Crier 1262
Trade Union Press, World Federation of Trade Unions, Nem. Curieových 1, Prague 1, Czechoslovakia. NR 1973. TS, p. 404: party line press service; founded during World War II by Stalin. Title now Flashes from the Trade Unions.
Trait d'Union 1519; mentioned 1454
Très Femmes, c/o Gay Center for Social Services, 2250 "B" St., San Diego, Calif. 92102. NR 1974. TNWSC, p. 42.
Tribal Messenger: former title of The Sun [Albuquerque]
The Tribal Tribune 1519; mentioned 1453
Tribune 583
Tribune Ouvrière: successor to Journal du FRAP 1143
Triple Jeopardy 1381; mentioned 1318
Triton College News 1263; mentioned 1236
Trud! 854
The Trumpet 185. Probably defunct. N.U.: last issue received was Dec. 1971.
The Truth (high school underground): mentioned 1027
The Truth About Communism 372. Ulrich's: defunct.
Truth and Liberty, Box 144, Wentworthville, N.S.W., Australia 2145. NR 1974. TS, p. 491: anti-Jewish.
Truth and Liberty Magazine 337
Truth Crusader 1583; mentioned 1571
Truth Seeker 395
Twin Circle 339. See Ulrich's 1975-76 for new address in Los Angeles.
Twin Cities Female Liberation Newsletter 689
Two...Three...Many 1031; mentioned 1002

UAW Solidarity 475
UE News 936
UFO Chronicle 894
UFO International: former title of Flying Saucers International
UFO Magazine 435
UFO Report: see Quest
UFOLOG Information Sheet 895
The UFORC Clipping Service 896
URPE Newsletter 532, 1130. Address on Aug. 1975 issue: Stew Long, Jim Dietz, Drew Barden, c/o Dept. of Economics, Calif. State Univ., Fullerton, Calif. 92634.
US 1382; mentioned 1316
USA 341
USAF 272; probably defunct 774
USLA Reporter 201. Last listed in

366, Station N, Montreal 129, Québec, Canada. NR 1973. TS, p. 579: "might as well be openly an organ of the Viet Cong."
Vietnam Perspectives 373. Ulrich's: defunct. TS, pp. 391-92: now called Southeast Asian Perspectives.
View from the Bottom 533. Ulrich's: ceased publication Feb. 1971.
Viewpoint 1151; mentioned 1133
Views and Ideas on Mankind 937. See Ulrich's 1975-76 for new address.
Village Voice 114; gutter level 763; mentioned 946, 1154. See Ulrich's 1975-76 for new address.
Virginia Weekly 1099; mentioned 1042
Vision 645. See also Modern Utopian (same publisher), recently merged with Communities. N. U.: Jan. 1970 was last issue received.
Vista 478. See Ulrich's 1975-76 for new address.
The Vocal Majority 1385; mentioned 1318
Vocations for Social Change 681. Superseded by Workforce. Communities Mar./Apr. 1974: 4911 Telegraph, Oakland, Calif. 94609. TS, p. 372, & Ulrich's 1975-76: Box 13 Canyon, Calif. 94516.
The Voice of Brotherhood 1520; mentioned 1453
The Voice of Liberty 1588; mentioned 1571
The Voice of POWs and MIAs 1568
The Voice of South Phoenix: see 8-20 Voice of the City
Voice of the City: see 8-20 Voice of the City
Voice of the Federation 343; mentioned 840
The Voice of the Martyrs 1589
Voice of Women Bulletin National Newsletter 1386; mentioned 1317
Voice of Women Ontario Newsletter 1386; mentioned 1317
Vortex: see The AWOL Press
La Voz del Pueblo, Frente de Liberacion del Pueblo, Centro Colitlan, Box 737, Hayward, Calif. 94543. NR 1973. TS, p. 460.

WDL News 189, 1278; mentioned 1268
WIA 1387; mentioned 1320
WICA, The Ames Feminist Newspaper, Women's Coalition, Room 6-S, Memorial Union, University of Iowa, Ames, Iowa 50010. RR 1974: "Unfortunately, due to a few political problems, we are no longer publishing. We hope to again in the future...."
WICA Newsletter 1647; mentioned 1614. See The New Age Intellectual Newsletter, a predecessor.
WIN 268. New address: Box 547, Rifton, N.Y. 12471. 44 issues a year; $11.
WIRE Magazine 835; mentioned 823. Last listing in Ulrich's 1973-74.
WONAAC Newsletter 1387; mentioned 1321
WRL News 264
WROs in Action: see The Welfare Fighter
WUNS Bulletin 1612; mentioned 1591
The Wall Street Journal: exalts cheating 1192; rejects anti-Israel ad 1496
The Wanderer 345
War Bulletin (Berkeley; Chicago): see Indochina Bulletin 1531
War/Peace Report 265. See Ulrich's 1975-76 for new address.
War Resistance 266. See Ulrich's for new address. Also issued in French and German. Former title: War Resister.
The Warpath 753
Warren-Forest Sun: alternative title of Sun [Detroit]
Warren Free Press: see Hash
The Warrior, American Indian Center, 4605 N. Paulina St., Chicago, Ill. 60640. NR 1974.
Washington Area Spark, Box 4256, Takoma Park, Md. 20012. NR 1973. TS, p. 576: building a socialist revolution in the U.S.
Washington Bulletin 268
Washington Free Press 115. Last listing in Ulrich's 1971-72.
Washington Observer Newsletter: see American Mercury
Washington Peace Center Newsletter 1539
Washington Post: leftist 1564
Washington Watch 1264; mentioned 1236
The Washingtonian 479
Wassaja 1520; mentioned 1453
A Way Out: see Modern Utopian
We Got the BrASS 794; mentioned 272
We the People, Box 252, Madison,

Young Communist [Toronto] superseded by Young Worker [Toronto] 1108

El Young Lord, Young Lords Organization, Box 5024, Milwaukee, Wis. 53204. MR 1973: "Box closed, no order." DC: defunct. TS, p. 398: very militant.

Young Socialist [N. Y.; Labor Publications] 1103; mentioned 1041

Young Socialist [N. Y.; Young Socialist Alliance] 83; "phony" 1104. From 1970 to 1972, the YSA published Young Socialist Organizer in place of Young Socialist, but publication of YS was resumed in Oct. 1972 and YSO ceased.

Young Socialist [Toronto] 1105; mentioned 1040, 1041

Young Socialist Forum 85. MR 1970: "Moved, address unknown." No listing in Ulrich's after 1973-74 edition. Superseded by Young Socialist [Toronto] 1105

Young Socialist Organizer: see Young Socialist [New York; Young Socialist Alliance]

Young Spartacus 1106; mentioned 1041

Young Worker [N. Y.] 1106; mentioned 1041

Young Worker [Toronto] 1107; mentioned 1041

Your Friend and Mine: see "Dogfighting periodicals"

Your Military Left 797; mentioned 272

Youth Action, Box 603, Hyattsville, Md. 20782. NR 1973. TS, p. 362: right-wing.

Youth International Party Line: see TAP

Yukon Indian News 1521; mentioned 1453

Zap: mentioned 1188

Zimbabwe News 1297; mentioned 1268

Zimbabwe Review 1297; mentioned 1268

Zion's Restorer, Church of Jesus Christ of Schell City, Destiny of America Foundation, Schell City, Mo. 64783. NR 1973. TS, p. 108: anti-Semitic, pro-white race.

## EDITORS, PUBLISHERS, OPINIONS

This is an index of the editors and publishers of the journals reviewed in the body of this book, and of the opinions expressed in our samples of those journals. The opinions--especially those about persons and organizations--are often uncomplimentary, and it should be clear that, although we quote them, we do not endorse them.

This volume contains two other indexes: a Geographical Index, arranged by place of publication; and a Title Index.